SPACE *frame* NARRATIVE

Edited by

THOMAS ELSAESSER

with

ADAM BARKER

BFI Publishing

First published in 1990 by the
British Film Institute
21 Stephen Street, London W1P 1PL

Reprinted 1992, 1994, 1997, 2006

British Library Cataloguing in Publication Data

Early cinema: space – frame – narrative.
1. Cinema films, history
I. Elsaesser, Thomas II. Barker, Adam
791.4309

ISBN 0-85170-244-9
ISBN 0-85170-245-7 pbk

Front cover still: *An Unseen Enemy* (D. W. Griffith, 1912)
Back cover still: *The Mender of Nets* (D. W. Griffith, 1912)

Set in Berkeley Oldstyle Book by
Fakenham Photosetting Limited
Fakenham, Norfolk
and printed in the UK by
Antony Rowe Limited,
Chippenham, Wiltshire

CONTENTS

NOTES ON CONTRIBUTORS

Jacques Aumont is Director of the Département pour l'enseignement et la recherche du cinéma et l'audiovisuel (DERCAV) at the Université de Paris III. He is author of *Montage Eisenstein* (1988) and *L'Oeil interminable* (1989).

Adam Barker is series producer on Channel Four's *The Media Show* and has written about the economics and aesthetics of cinema for *Screen Finance*, *Sight and Sound* and other journals.

Raymond Bellour is Research member of the Centre National de Recherche Scientifique (CNRS) in Paris. He is the author of many books, including *Le Livre des autres* (1971), and *L'Analyse du Film* (1980).

Stephen Bottomore is a film editor, writer and researcher, who has written regularly for *Sight and Sound*, notably about early cinema.

Kevin Brownlow is a film-maker, producer and writer. He is author of *The Parade's Gone By* and is probably best known for his *Hollywood* series on Thames Television and his restoration of silent films, including *Napoleon*.

Ben Brewster is Senior Lecturer in Film at the University of Kent. He was editor of *Screen* and has translated Christian Metz and Noël Burch.

Noël Burch is a film-maker, historian and writer. He directed *Correction, Please or How We Got Into Pictures* and *What Do These Old Films Mean?* and his most recent book is *Life to Those Shadows* (1990).

Michael Chanan is a film-maker and author of *The Dream That Kicks* (1980) and *The Cuban Image* (1985).

Richard de Cordova teaches film and television at De Paul University, Chicago. He is the author of *Picture Personalities: The Emergence of the Star System in America* (1990).

John Fullerton is Senior Lecturer in Film and Media Studies at the Derbyshire College of Higher Education and has published on early Swedish cinema.

Anne Friedberg teaches in the Film Studies Program, University of California, Irvine. She has written about the journal *Close-Up* and about avant-garde film.

André Gaudreault is Head of the Group de Recherche de l'Audio-visuel et du Film (GRAF) at the Université Laval, Quebec, Canada. He is the author of *Du littéraire au filmique* (1988) and has edited *Ce que je vois de mon ciné* (1988).

Tom Gunning teaches film history and film theory at the State University of New York-Purchase and is author of *D. W. Griffith and the Origins of American Narrative Film*.

Miriam Hansen is Professor of Film at the University of Chicago and author of *Babel and Babylon: Spectatorship in the American Silent Film*.

Leon Hunt is a teacher and freelance writer in Birmingham.

Patrick G. Loughney is Curator at the Library of Congress, Washington D.C.

Charles Musser teaches film studies at Columbia University and New York University. He wrote and directed *Before the Nickelodeon* and is author of *The Emergence of Cinema: The American Screen to 1907* (1990).

BARRY SALT teaches at the London International Film School and is the author of *Film Style and Technology: History and Analysis* (1983).

JANET STAIGER is Associate Professor of Critical and Cultural Studies at the University of Texas, Austin. She is co-author with David Bordwell and Kristin Thompson of *The Classical Hollywood Cinema* (London: Routledge and Kegan Paul, New York: Columbia University Press, 1985).

YURI TSIVIAN is a film historian, semiotician and researcher in Riga. He is co-editor of *Silent Witnesses: Russian Films 1908–1919* (1989).

DAI VAUGHAN is a film and television editor and author of *Portrait of an Invisible Man* (1983).

The Editor:

THOMAS ELSAESSER teaches Film and English at the University of East Anglia. He is the author of *New German Cinema: A History* (1989).

General Introduction
Early Cinema : From Linear History to Mass Media Archaeology

Cinema: the Script of Life

As the centenary approaches of the first public exhibitions of projected moving images, it has become commonplace to discuss the cinema in terms that acknowledge its cultural function: of having introduced a radically new, universally comprehensible and yet deeply contradictory logic of the visible. The quantum leap taken by the audio-visual media not just as entertainment, but in public life, politics, education and science also alerts us to the historical role of cinema in the more general transformation of the ways knowledge is stored and disseminated, social experience is recorded and subjectivity constructed. Some of this was already recognised by proselytising film-makers like D.W. Griffith[1] or early theorists like Hugo Munsterberg.[2] Inspired perhaps by Lenin's famous dictum, Walter Benjamin was convinced that the very existence of the cinema necessitated a new archeology of the art work, because of the fundamental changes film had brought to the notion of time, space and material culture.[3]

The cinematographe, bioscope or vitascope, despite their many antecedents and an almost total dependence on technologies typical of the 19th century, were right from the start recognised to convey a wholly modern experience. By involving the spectator with an uncanny directness and immediacy, by investing the world with presence, and the technological apparatus with a taboo-breaking power over life and death, a metaphysical wager seemed to have been entered that was reflected in the very name given to the invention. A direct line can be drawn from Prometheus, Faust, and Dr Frankenstein to Thomas A. Edison – all obsessed with the integral (re)production of life, which in turn needs to be juxtaposed to the desire for a new script, a mode of writing with images, associated with a scientific urge to analyse movement and break it down into constituent parts.[4]

A Historical Conjuncture

This Reader wants to be an introduction to some of the work laying the ground, both historically and theoretically, for a systematic account of early cinema: a precondition also for a cultural archeology of the new medium. Apart from Noël Burch and Michael Chanan (both influenced by Benjamin), there is perhaps not much evidence that interest in early cinema was prompted by reflections such as those above. Yet the renewed attention paid to its first manifestations and complex developments unquestionably springs from very diverse sources. Local initiatives, practical needs, individual enthusiasm have intersected with several critical debates. Some can be listed fairly briefly, others may only emerge as research is becoming surveyable in book form.

As far as a more popular interest in early cinema goes, one influence was, paradoxically, television. Kevin Brownlow and David Gill's restoration of Abel Gance's *Napoleon* for Thames Television brought seemingly esoteric issues such as print quality, preservation techniques and proper aspect ratios to the attention of a general public. Their previous series *Hollywood*[5] had already proven that a televisual history of the cinema could make for lively viewing. David Robinson was surely right, when he wrote

> Through these snatched extracts of films and fragments of old men's memories, the makers [of *Hollywood*] have nevertheless succeeded triumphantly in their broader aim, which was to capture and convey the mood, the atmosphere, the excitement, the essence of the era. It is indeed the first time since the actual demise of the silent film that so large a public has been brought so close to the actual experience of the silent cinema as our fathers and grandfathers knew it.[6]

No loving recreation or nostalgic celebration of a bygone age was in the minds of Jean Louis Comolli, Jean Louis Baudry and others when they set out to challenge André Bazin's influential realist ontology, in the name of a new epistemological, anti-teleological and 'materialist' history of the cinema. This critical agenda is most evident in Burch's essays devoted to early cinema. 'Porter or Ambivalence' marked for many in film studies their first encounter with a decisively different way of conceptualising the origins and early forms of cinema.[7]

Burch's paper, as it happens, was written for an event that will remain a key date for locating the beginning of a new era of research, the 1978 FIAF conference held in Brighton which brought together for the first time archivists and film scholars around a common purpose.[8] The spirit of cooperation, even of a crusade has continued, not least thanks to the annual Pordenone 'Giornate del cinema muto'. The Brighton meeting was itself symptomatic of a new urgency felt by film archives about the preservation and accessibility of materials from the early period. The urgency was partly in response to specific crises (the Langlois affair in 1968, various disastrous fires, the lifespan of nitrate film coming to an end), and also reflected the increased call made on all kinds of audio-visual records by television, with its appetite for authentic archive footage in political, documentary, biographical, educational programming.

The demand for preservation and access put a strain on the resources of all but the largest archives. Filmic and non-filmic material had to be processed, new ways of reliably identifying films had to be found, and thus methods of dating, attributing, periodising films and especially film-fragments. Hence the need for an internationalisation of research, and collaboration between archivists and scholars. For the latter it implied a change of focus: not aesthetic excellence and artistic value were at issue, but normative and comparative criteria had to be found. Here the work of Barry Salt, who for some time prior to the FIAF congress had worked on the possibilities of statistical and comparative style analysis, proved ground-breaking.

A New Historicism

One major effort in re-writing this history has been directed at establishing verifiable data, deciding not only what is verifiable, but what is pertinent. Are we to rely on the films alone, given how each surviving print has its own problematic history; are we to treat as fact what contemporary sources say about particular films and the often anecdotal histories of their production? The tendency in recent years has been to distrust received wisdom and widely held assumptions, to 'suspect every biography and check every monograph', as Robert Allen put it.[9]

A new generation of film historians mainly in the United States took up this task, and began a thorough re-examination of those accounts which told the history of the cinema as the story of fearless pioneers, of 'firsts', of adventure and discovery, of great masters and masterpieces. Gomery, Allen, Janet Staiger, Kristin Thompson, Charles Musser and Russell Merritt among others queried the textbooks in the name of different determinants (mainly demographic, economic, industrial, technological). They also proved how intimately the cinema in America fed on and was implicated in the history of above all vaudeville, but also other popular entertainments, such as penny arcades, medicine tent shows and Hale's tours: a history that runs counter to traditional 'theoretical' speculations about the cinema's relation to the novel and the theatre.

The media-intertext of early cinema, the industrialisation of entertainment and leisure turned out to be a rich source of insight, as well as opening up entirely new areas of research. It showed, for instance, that the study of the exhibition context could be the key to answering questions about production, as well as the development of film form. In the process, it suggested a quite different argument regarding the crucial transformations between early cinema and 'Hollywood' from those given by, say, Terry Ramsaye or Lewis Jacobs. The result was a revision of what counts as evidence in film history (local records, city planning ordinances, business files, law-suits and patent infringements) and a demotion of intrinsic filmic evidence. Gomery and Allen were not afraid of being blunt: 'For certain investigations, film viewing is really an inappropriate research method.'[10] In the case of early cinema, the combination of these new kinds of evidence with new conceptual models of cultural history have fundamentally changed our view of the period, especially that between 1905 to 1917. As so often in historiography, new criteria of pertinence necessarily affect the hypotheses historians forge, consciously or unconsciously, about the data in question.[11]

If much of the new film history has focussed on early cinema because here the claim was strongest that the models for understanding the cinema as a whole were inadequate, contradictory or based on unsound scholarship, there was a similarly strong sense that traditionally film scholars had misconstrued the meaning of the films themselves. Burch had indicated one possible direction by positing the so-called 'primitive cinema' as a distinct 'mode of representation' (the PMR), based on a different logic of the relation between viewer and film, on a different thinking about images and their presentation, on a different conception of space and narrative, when compared to the 'institutional mode' (the IMR). As the Reader makes clear, Burch's distinction has also led to some very productive reformulations, most notably perhaps those of Tom Gunning and André Gaudreault. Gunning's 'cinema of attractions' and 'cinema of narrative integration' pinpoint the dissatisfaction felt with traditional premises:

> These terms are an attempt to overcome the two primary approaches of the previous generation to understanding the change which occurs in film-making prior to the introduction of feature films. One (the most discredited now) has been the simple progress explanation which sees a movement, basically due to trial and error and the intervention of certain men of genius, from 'primitive' film-making to the foundation of the later narrative style. The other (somewhat more sophisticated, but we feel equally misleading) explanation has described this change as a movement from a reliance on theatrical models to a more cinematic approach to narrative.[12]

The Sense of and Ending of (Classical) Cinema?

There is also another more diffuse, but nonetheless important conjuncture. When Burch championed Edwin Porter over D.W. Griffith, it was clear that he also spoke on behalf of an avant garde who had recourse to early cinema in order to displace, at least conceptually, the hegemony of Hollywood.[13] The rediscovery of the 'primitives' seemed like a vindication of the avant garde's fifty-year struggle to rethink the foundations of 'film language', and dispel the idea that the cinema's turn to fictional narrative or adoption of illusionist representational forms was its inevitable destiny.

These polemics seemed the more timely, since the 1970s began to speculate on the demise of the classical cinema's hegemony from a quite different perspective. The transformation of film viewing, the re-privatisation of consumption of audiovisual material through television, videotape and other recent technologies of storage and reproduction were obliging historians to try and integrate the history of the cinema into the wider cultural and economic context of the entertainment and consciousness industries. In other words, important developments in the contemporary cinema itself appeared to have significant analogies with early cinema. Looking at the increasing predominance of technology and special effects in providing the primary audience attraction, and considering the resurgence (through television and popular music) of performative and spectacle modes, as against purely narrative modes, classical cinema may yet come to be seen as itself a 'transitional' stage in the overall history of the audio-visual media and the technologies of mechanical recording and reproduction.

As one would expect, such diverse motives do not make for unanimity. There is a perceptible tension between scholars with an interest in early cinema as part of a 'cultural' or ideological-theoretical history, and scholars who are simply concerned with 'facts' and micro-analyses, some of whom would not be offended at being called 'revisionists' or 'neo-empiricists'. It is nonetheless remarkable – and a sign of the vigour in this field of research – that the diverse contributions do actually form part of recognisable debates, perhaps even of a project. One of the premises of this Reader is that a perceptible coherence exists, which the diversity of approaches only helps to underline. Whether the collection manages to represent these debates in both their diversity and cogency is of course another matter.

Brighton and After

In this last respect the present volume differs from the publications that followed the 1978 FIAF meeting in Brighton, *Cinema 1900–1906: An Analytical Study* and John Fell's *Film before Griffith*, both of which this Reader tries to complement rather than duplicate. *Ce que je vois de mon ciné* (edited by André Gaudreault) and the American Federation of Arts' *Before Hollywood* are two other recent collections of essays, accompanying exhibitions and programmes of screenings, to which must be added the impressive catalogues edited by the organisers of the Pordenone festival.[14] By foregrounding the need to retrace the intellectual repercussions of the FIAF conference, the Reader wants to bring together some of the crucial contributions since Brighton, respecting the arguments in their complexity, as befits primary research, but also focussing on a range of circumscribed issues. The aim is to encourage the current generation of film scholars to study and teach more early cinema. With this in mind, it has seemed a risk worth taking, to weave, via the introductions, a kind of story, in the hope that the debates around early cinema will seem to recast film history, and also help reformulate a number of problems in traditional film theory. This story has two salient strands, which to a greater or lesser degree act as explanatory foils for each other: the first is the cinema's turn to narrative as its main form of textual and ideological support, and the second is the industrialisation and commodification of its standard product, the feature film. In one sense, this might seem an inadmissibly restrictive focus, running the danger of reproducing all the teleological and deterministic moves which the new history is trying to deconstruct. In another sense, it is the very intertwining of mode (narrative) and material support (commodity) that makes the cinema such a complex cultural force, and the history of early cinema in particular a site of shifts and struggles, of roads not taken and paths unexpectedly crossing.

For, finally, the double historical moment – that of the cinema between 1896 and 1917, and of its rediscovery in the late 1970s – does situate early cinema in a particular context, the one opened up by the revitalisation of film theory during the late 1960s and early 1970s, and its subsequent (post-Saussurean, post-Lacanian, post-modern) crises in the 1980s. Hence, several sets of questions have influenced the selection. Firstly, how did the diverse technical processes and economic pressures feeding into early film production undergo the kind of integration that was necessary before film-making became an industry? Secondly, how did this industrial logic impose itself to the point of becoming inextricably bound up with the narrative logic of the cinema we call 'classical'? Thirdly, and perhaps most intriguingly, given that the cinema manifests a unique combination of the drives towards pleasure and towards intelligibility, what is its psychic dimension, its cognitive role, its connection with the desire to picture the world in images and to experience it as doubled and mirrored, offering spectators idealised images of themselves, and therefore also letting us see other audiences' self images?

The Reader is organised into three parts: 'Early Film Form – Articulations of Space and Time', 'The Institution of Cinema: Industry, Commodity, Audiences', and 'The Continuity System: Griffith and Beyond'. The first part addresses the question whether early cinema in its manifest otherness demonstrates a coherence of its own, or whether its contradictory logic demands a wider analytic framework. The second part asks whether such a framework can be derived from its specific historical, economic and technological development. The last part is concerned with the emergence of continuity cinema and cinematic subjectivity, and the role played by Griffith's work, representative but also a-typical, amenable to so many different interpretations and applications, and thus prototype of alternative or nationally distinct variants to continuity cinema and its imaginary. Several themes, however, run through the collection as a whole, of which the most important one is how the cinema came to develop a particular kind of narrational logic. The research presented here into the formal articulation of cinematic space, into the questions of narration, into the material determinants shaping the cinema seem to me to provide new answers by pointing to hitherto neglected connections. One conclusion might be that the issue of the primitiveness or otherness of early cinema needs to be recast: not in a binary opposition to the classical, but as a signpost on the way to the increasing detachment of images from their material referents, 'freeing' them for narrative, for becoming bearers of cultural and social identities, which in turn support an industry. If only for this reason the history of early cinema has implications for a general history of the cinema, and of any medium dependent on a mass public and subject to technological change as well as institutional transformations.

As with any Reader, the choice of what to include was easy, what to finally exclude a painful one, since so much that is both pertinent and excellent is not present. Some essays were unfortunately not available for republication; in one or two instances the originals were slightly shortened. Even at a relatively late stage in the selection process, almost a quarter of the material had to be cut out for reasons of space. The rather lengthy introductions to the individual sections cannot hope to make up for the gaps, but they are an attempt, however inadequate, to synthesise issues and provide contexts. They also want to point in the directions where more relevant material can be found, as does the bibliography which lays no claim to being complete or exhaustive.

The idea and title for this Reader were first conceived in 1982, when Film Studies at the University of East Anglia organised its own post-Brighton conference on early cinema. Although the papers presented there still await publication, I want to thank all the participants for their contributions, as well as my colleagues Charles Barr and Don Ranvaud, who, together with Andrew

Higson and Helen McNeil, have over the years made teaching Early Cinema such exciting journeys of discovery. To their enthusiasm, and that of our students, both undergraduate and postgraduate, both past and future, this volume is dedicated. As editor, however, my thanks go to the authors, including those from whose work and cooperation I have benefited without being finally able to represent them here. Adam Barker, during the time he was associated with the project, contributed generously with ideas and practical assistance. His first draft of the introduction to the Griffith section has been very helpful, and I trust he recognises his formulations without objecting too much to the direction in which I have taken them. Barry Salt has always found time to answer queries and has given invaluable help by producing framestills for Leon Hunt's article as well as for his own. Geoffrey Nowell-Smith at the BFI proved to be a steady source of sound advice, patience and encouragement, especially in the belief that the subtle and self-evident pleasures of early films can be celebrated in many ways, of which scholarly debate and academic argument are certainly not the only, though neither the least passionate ones.

Acknowledgments

I should like to thank the editors and publishers of the following journals for kindly consenting to the reprinting of previously published material:

Australian Journal of Film Theory
Cinema Journal
Cinetracts
Framework
Iris
New German Critique
Quarterly Review of Film Studies
Screen
Sight and Sound

Thanks are also due to:

BFI Publishing
Editions Klincksieck
Fédération Internationale des Archives Filmiques (FIAF)
Institut Jean Vigo

for permission to reprint materials previously published in book form.

Details of previous publication are given in the Notes at the end of each chapter.

London, April 1990 *Thomas Elsaesser*

Notes

1. See D.W. Griffith, 'Some Prophecies', in Harry M. Geduld (ed.), *Focus on D.W. Griffith* (Engiewood Cliffs, NJ: Prentice-Hall, 1971), pp. 34–7, and Anne Friedberg, '"A Properly Adjusted Window": Vision and Sanity', below, pp. 326–35.
2. Hugo Munsterberg, *The Film: A Psychological Study* (New York: Dover 1969; first published 1916).
3. 'The social significance (of film), particularly in its most positive form, is inconceivable without its destructive, cathartic aspect, that is the liquidation of the traditional value of the cultural heritage.' Walter Benjamin, 'The Work of Art in the Age of Mechanical Reproduction', *Illuminations* (London: Collins/Fontana Books, 1973), p. 223.
4. This genealogy is drawn up by Noël Burch in at least two essays: 'A Parenthesis on Film History' in *To the Distant Observer* (London: Scolar Press, 1980), chapter 5, and 'Charles Baudelaire vs. Dr. Frankenstein', *Afterimage* no. 8/9, Winter 1980/81, esp. pp. 5–13.
5. The impact was greatly increased by Brownlow's books *The Parade's Gone By* (London: Paladin, 1968) and *Hollywood the Pioneers* (London: Collins, 1979). See also *Making Better Movies* vol. 3, no. 7, July 1987, pp. 327–9; *Film Comment* vol. 23, no. 4, July-August 1987, pp. 66–9, and my 'Innocence Restored', *Monthly Film Bulletin*, December 1984, p. 366.
6. David Robinson, 'Hollywood', *Sight and Sound* vol. 49, no. 3, Summer 1980, p. 159.
7. 'Porter or Ambivalence' (*Screen* vol. 19, no. 4, Winter 1978/9, pp. 91–105) also allowed one to read Burch's *Theory of Film Practice* differently. For a critique of Comolli's and Burch's critique, see David Bordwell and Kristin Thompson, 'Linearity, materialism and the Study of the Early American Cinema', *Wide Angle* vol. 5, no. 3, 1983, pp. 4–15.
8. Jon Gartenberg, in 'The Brighton Project: The Archives and Research', *Iris* vol. 2, no. 1, 1984, p. 6 has detailed the background to this collaboration.
9. Robert C. Allen, 'Film History Study File', *AFI Newsletter*, January/February 1980.
10. See their chapter 'Reading as Questioning' in Douglas Gomery, Robert C. Allen, *Film History: Theory and Practice* (New York: Alfred A. Knopf, 1987), p. 38.
11. See, for instance, Pierre Sorlin, 'Promenade de Rome', *Iris* vol. 2, no. 2, 1984, pp. 4–8.
12. Tom Gunning, 'The Cinema of Narrative Integration', in Paolo Cherchi Usai (ed.), *Vitagraph Co of America* (here quoted from the author's typescript, p. 4).
13. The case for connecting early cinema with avant garde cinema is most forcefully made in Rod Stoneman, 'Perspective Correction', *Afterimage* no. 8/9, Winter 80/81, pp. 50–63, and by Werner Nekes in *Film before Film: What Really Happened Between the Images*. But see also entries under Burch, Gunning, Wyborny in the bibliography.
14. See entries under Paolo Cherchi Usai in bibliography for details of volumes that have appeared to date.

I

EARLY FILM FORM

Articulations of Space and Time

Introduction

Film Form

This section of the Reader focuses on how the cinema developed its codes of intelligibility, and why it became a predominantly narrative medium. The essays are organised by formal categories but they also concentrate on film-makers whose work is likely to be best known and most accessible (Lumière, Méliès, Porter); what follows is intended to stake out the common ground uniting the various contributors in dialogue. In addressing the core issues, a term is revived familiar from film theory rather than film history: that of film form.[1] It was Barry Salt, in two articles published in 1976 and 1978 who gave the concept a new currency and helped to create a serviceable terminology for discussing early cinema.[2] More overtly than in the film form debates of Eisenstein and the Russian avant garde (largely based on linguistic models and on the compositional properties of the image and the shot),[3] Salt argues from what at first appear to be technical parameters. He begins pragmatically with a film-maker's problems: questions about staging, methods of lighting, of figure positioning in space, use of reverse-angle shots, analytical editing and scene-dissection. These aspects have always been part of the criteria for discussing film style, and Salt does, in a sense, no more than ask of early cinema some of the traditional questions of *mise en scène* criticism.[4]

Editing in particular has often been seen as the motor of change and the criterion of differentiation. Ever since Frank Woods' articles in the *New York Dramatic Mirror* boasted of the superiority of the American cinema over its European rivals thanks to faster cutting, and held up the work of Griffith as exemplary in this respect, shot length and editing speed have been the hallmarks of cinematic sophistication and modernity.[5] Nowhere more so than when Soviet directors immersed themselves in the productions of Griffith and other Americans, partly in order to learn from them, and to improve on their models, by devising ever more complex editing patterns.

For Salt, the crucial markers for the emergence of successive styles are cutting rate and shot length. But he sees these as functional values, not as ends in themselves, bound together by a non-specific, non-intrinsic priority, such as optimal efficiency in putting across a story.[6] Thus, it is match-cutting and diegetic unity which are the consequences of 'the pressures on evolution and development', as in the codification of screen direction (the plotting of scene entrances and exits), itself a consequence of the move from single-shot films to multi-scene filming.[7] Consistency in screen direction, however, also indicates increasing reliance on studio work as opposed to location shooting.[8] While both multi-scene films and studio work were determined by *external* factors, the coherent plotting of adjacent spaces laid the basis for continuity editing, a crucial element in the *internal* development of film form.[9] One of its features, the cut on action, became the commonest form of shot transition via the early cinema's most typical genre, the chase film, the pressure on form emanating in this case also from the subject matter. The pro-filmic, the internal and the contextual all emerge as determinants without aligning themselves in a causal hierarchy.

Salt's pragmatism allows him to break with one of the most persistent fallacies of the 'film grammar' school of theory, by showing that certain technical devices or shot transitions do not have stable, one-to-one meanings, but must be understood as relative: dissolves in Méliès for instance do not signify inner character states such as dreams, nor do they connote time lapses (as was the case from the 1920s onwards), but may simply indicate a change of location. By defining film language as use, Salt shares ground with more explicitly formalist theories, although he does not attach ideological significance to these emerging conventions and specific codes governing the articulation of filmic time and space.[10]

The significance of Salt's concept of film form, though biased towards aspects of early cinema that were to prove decisive in the transition from 'primitive' to 'classical' cinema,[11] is that it is sensitive to the construction of a space – through staging, lighting and shot scales and shot transitions – which is typical of the cinema and irreducible to any theatrical or even music hall antecedents. Secondly, Salt brings an historically informed knowledge of film technology to bear on his evolution of formal criteria. What is perhaps needed is a clearer idea whether these style parameters change separately and thus function in isolation from each other, or whether convention and use constitute a historical paradigm only when seen as interdependent variables together making up a style. Subsequent research has treated film forms more as systems of self-regulation or functional equivalence: this is true for Ben Brewster,[12] and also for David Bordwell and Kristin Thompson.[13] Their work implies a more sophisticated and explicit theory of narrative space, narrative structure and narration.

The Organisation of Space and Time: Theatricality and Deep Staging

Different film forms would seem to be determined by a film-maker's ability to construct space and time – the two dimensions simultaneously present in filmic representation – in a comprehensible manner. Such a logic of the visible depends on (an idea of) continuity: rendering spatio-temporal and causal relations coherently and consistently. The impression of intelligibility of an action is not so much a question of how real that which is being filmed actually is (i.e. the documentary value of what is before the camera), but whether the system that governs its representation is intelligible to the viewer. An often-quoted case is G. A. Smith and James A. Williamson's 1899 *Henley Regatta*, where shots of boats taken from the river bank are intercut with shots of crowds waving, obviously filmed from mid-river.[14] The decision to alternate these shots creates a causal relation – a diegetic space – (the crowds are cheering the boats visible in the preceding and subsequent frames) which exists independent of the reality of the event.[15]

Several questions are raised by such an example, beyond drawing attention to the difference between single-shot films and multi-shot films. Smith and Williamson did not merely join individual shots, but brought them together by virtue of a specific causal logic which implies definite temporal and spatial relations. Does this mean they had an idea not only of what we would now call 'editing', but of continuity editing? Basing the causal logic on the alternation of seeing/seen/seeing would suggest it.[16] But as John Fell pointed out, there are instances from other British and American films where a single shot setup allows for several 'simultaneous playing areas' (either by a cross-sectional view or by a division of the frame into foreground and background)[17] thus maintaining continuity and spatial coherence, without necessarily creating new causal relationships.[18]

'Simultaneous playing areas' and 'editing within the frame' are features of early cinema that have increasingly become the object of attention. First, because they refer to and reformulate the oldest (and usually pejorative) distinction made between primitive and classical cinema: the charge that early films were 'theatrical'.[19] But as Fell's examples above already show, the formal features of early cinema cannot be equated with its presumed debts to the theatre. Second, tableau scenes and other forms of elaborate staging are not necessarily the sign of 'primitive' or 'retarded' practice. Rather, they are specific choices or strategies, available as alternatives to editing. In particular, staging in depth – along with frontal staging the most obviously 'theatrical' trait – has come to be regarded as a crucial formal parameter for distinguishing both within American films and European from American productions.

The debate about theatricality, prominent in Jean Mitry and revived by Noël Burch,[20] has been taken up most vigorously by André Gaudreault[21] and Tom Gunning.[22] Gaudreault wants to extend the notions of narrative and narration, in order to subsume what to Mitry and countless other historians appeared to be practices borrowed from the stage. Gunning puts forward a distinction (possibly inspired by Burch's presentational vs. representational arts)[23] which overcomes the a-historicity of calling everything in early cinema that does not fit the later ideal of narrative continuity 'theatrical'. He posits a 'cinema of attractions' as distinct from a 'cinema of narrative integration'. Early cinema displays events and actions rather than narrates them; it addresses spectators directly, and as a physical collectivity; it has different kinds of closure, not all of which are textual; its unit is the autonomous shot or scene, where actions and events are continuous by virtue of some conceptual or narrational category, to which the autonomy of the shot becomes subordinated. These oppositions seem particularly fertile in a number of ways: they throw into relief the fact that one of the attractions of early cinema was the cinematic apparatus itself, quite apart from what it showed; secondly, that pleasure both for film-makers and audiences resided in all the objects, views, events the cinema could show, which need not necessarily have been in story form; thirdly, a 'cinema of attractions' underlines the fact that film producers were often show-men (and -women); fourthly, that interaction between characters on screen and audiences was frequently based on the performers' self-conscious, pleasurable exhibitionism, rather than, as in 'classical' cinema, determined by the spectators' unacknowledged voyeurism. Finally, it reminds us that in contemporary cinema and television, the performative mode (the 'show') exists as distinct but not separate from the pervasive narrativisation of all information.

Ben Brewster's article also takes up the case of 'theatricality'. His contention is not only that the cinema is fundamentally distinguished from the theatre by the construction of a single point-of-view for all spectators, irrespective of their position in the auditorium.[24] By examining Pathé, Vitagraph and some Scandinavian productions, he is able to isolate a consistent practice in staging which constitutes a historically and perhaps even nationally distinct alternative to a mode based on editing and scene dissection. Deep space cinematography emerges as a very complex, varied and heterogeneous phenomenon in early cinema, ranging from relatively direct reproduction of theatrical tableaux in some of the French *films d'art*, to very sophisticated dramatic manipulation of camera position, as in Perret's *Le roman d'un mousse* (1913). Even more exciting, though also more speculative, is his suggestion of a typology of staging, which together with other variables (camera position, lighting, shot scales and editing speeds) could form style paradigms distinct in period, production company or national provenance: in short, a much more sophisticated version of Salt's statistical style analysis based on 'average shot length'. The basic alternatives would then be between deep staging and slow cutting (European), and shallow staging and fast cutting (American). If among the films giving priority to staging in depth, French *films d'art* (deep space/slow cutting) and Scandinavian films (deep space, cued by lighting) find themselves on the same side of the divide with certain Vitagraph films (deep space, lower camera, emphasis on foreground as a distinct action space), then this introduces a further variable, namely prestige and quality productions, which in the United States at least, points to the desire to attract a better class of (or better-paying) patrons.

Gunning and Brewster implicitly argue against using the term film form other than in the context of the Soviet experiments. Despite an interest in staging, Salt for instance pays little attention to films as performative acts, based on spectacle-attraction; on the other hand, his instinctive preference for a narrative cinema (of editing, causal relations, diegetic unity and narrative economy) has not extended to any interest in or theoretical awareness of narration.[25] As a result, he has concentrated much more on multi-shot films, neglecting the internal dynamics of the individual shot or scene. By contrast, Brewster, Burch, Gaudreault and Musser have found the single-shot film very rewarding for the study of early cinema. Brewster's point about the interrelation of deep staging and production values throws into relief that Salt's style history is wholly producer- and product-oriented (the director, the cameraman and the set designer are the agents of change),[26] missing out the economic and ideological determinations emanating from audiences or exhibitors, so crucial to Burch or Musser.[27] Narrative efficiency and intelligibility are themselves not fixed and stable categories. As Yuri Tsivian shows in his essay on the Kuleshov effect and early cinema audiences, intelligibility may involve cultural variables such as class, ethnicity, gender and education.[28] It may also vary from one spectator to the next, because film is a constant negotiation of the flow of information and the uneven distribution of knowledge, which the spectator has to 'motivate', make sense of and integrate: all of which are processes generally subsumed under the term 'narration'.

Film Form and 'Patterning': Reconsidering the Lumières' Films

As a test-case for the interpenetration and inseparability of staging, editing and narration one might conveniently take the example of the single-scene film, excluded from consideration at the Brighton conference and which in Salt's early account is 'of no interest as far as film construction is concerned'.[29] Yet so-called 'non-edited' film has been discussed extensively in recent years, especially when trying to clarify one of the most basic aspects of cinema: the relation of the pro-filmic to the filmic, often discussed under the heading of realism. It has, not surprisingly, led to a thorough re-examination of the work of the Lumières, both for their films' formal organisation, and in terms of the underlying ideological and social contexts.

In 'Structural Patterning in the Lumière Films' Marshall Deutelbaum argues that *Sortie d'usine*, *Arrivée d'un train*, *Demolition d'un mur*, *Barque sortant du port* and other well-known single-scene films are not, as traditional film history has it, 'plotless' or 'the recording of unadjusted, unarranged, untampered reality', but highly structured wholes 'reflecting a number of carefully chosen decisions about sequential narrative'.[30] By attending especially to the beginning and the ending, Deutelbaum is able to show that most Lumière films record actions and events in which the end either rejoins or inversely mirrors the beginning (opening and closing the factory gates in *Sortie d'usine*) thus providing a very effective narrative closure. Alternatively, their films enact what Deutelbaum calls 'operational processes' such as the breaking up of a slab of coke, the firing of a canon, the demolition of a wall: in each case, the film's temporal and spatial organisation foregrounds the causal or functional logic of the event, making the beginning of the action coincide with and mirror the beginning of the film. Furthermore, Deutelbaum argues that scope and duration of the actions are signalled in the films themselves, providing a form of narrative suspense and anticipation which generates active spectatatorial involvement. In films like *Course en sac*, *Scieurs de Bois* and others, Deutelbaum finds evidence of a very complex 'structural use of space', doubling of protagonists, repetition of action, movement within the frame, and 'arrangement in depth' which indicates a sophisticated formal sense inflecting the apparently artless presentation of 'simple content'. Framing and camera-placing are chosen to heighten closure, balance, symmetry and thus, according to Deutelbaum 'impart a shape to the action depicted'. In Gunning's terms, the Lumière films' 'patterning' of events represent particularly sophisticated examples of the 'cinema of attractions'.

Dai Vaughan, in 'Let There Be Lumière' also wants to account for the fascination still emanating from a film like *Barque sortant du port*, but in order to speculate on the minimal conditions of fiction in a non-edited film. Seemingly inclined to locate it in the intrusion of the fortuitous and accidental (the rustling leaves behind the baby in *Repas de Bébé*, or the sudden wave in *Barque sortant du port*) and the unresolved conflict between the spontaneous and the staged, Vaughan makes two points in passing that have important implications. Firstly, unlike other early films, such as Edison's, whose mode was presentational ('perceived as performance, as simply a new mode of self-presentation'), the unpredictable in the Lumière films integrates performance with narrative. Secondly, Vaughan raises, although only to reject it, the notion of motivation as crucial to the perception of fictionality. While apparently unaware of the complex formal organisation which Deutelbaum points out, Vaughan, like Deutelbaum, shifts the argument from the pro-filmic ('realism') to the filmic (the staging and framing), but goes beyond Deutelbaum's 'patterning' in regarding the frame as part of the act of showing, thus anticipating Gaudreault's notion of 'monstration' (see below) as a form of narration.

Deutelbaum and Vaughan implicitly operate with a more traditionally literary or art-historical concept of form. Form in this sense not only posits a relation between parts and whole, but considerations of 'patterning' and of formal structure inevitably raise the question of chance and intentionality, reality and artifice. For Salt, as indeed for Eisenstein or Kuleshov, film form is always the result of a construction and an intervention (if only of the filmic apparatus). This explains why Salt insists that only when one deals with a multi-shot film and the possibilities of editing can one begin to discuss film form. Deutelbaum and Vaughan's approach, on the other hand, has the advantage of addressing the single-shot film (the norm until at least 1900) and thereby focusing on the tensions between the random and the patterned as a condition of perceptible meaning, drawing attention to the active participation of the spectator in the creation of intelligibility. They are also aware of the complex status of staging, involving as it does performative-presentational as well as narrative-narrational modes. Richard de Cordova's 'From Lumière to Pathé: The Break-up of Perspectival Space' specifically addresses this latter point, namely how, already in the Lumière films, the spectator is bound into the film by the complex function played by the frame, and therefore by the awareness of off-frame space.[31]

Views, Topicals and Actualities: From Editing to Narrating

Does event determine form or does form create event? The question can also be studied through another aspect of the pro-filmic and the filmic that has come under scrutiny: the topicals or actualities as a key genre of early cinema. Here, too, the issues centre on the imbrication of staging, editing and narration. The Brighton project had selected only fictional subjects and multi-shot films. And although these criteria seem to give the minimal conditions for investigating temporal and spatial construction, it is in practice often difficult to separate documentary from fiction, a difficulty largely arising from a conceptual impasse and a false dichotomy.

In a Brighton FIAF paper, 'Re-constructed Newsreels, Reenactments', David Levy discusses the confusion prevailing until 1907 in the area of newsreel-type actuality and of restaged or faked events. Although even then articles appeared describing the formal features that distinguished re-enactments from actual footage, the more interesting questions lie perhaps elsewhere. Levy cites research to the effect that 'a range of camera techniques including panning, tracking and dolly movements, tilts, long, medium and close shots of the same subject, reverse angles and continuity editing emerged accidentally from the efforts of early newsreel cameramen, working with unwieldy equipment in conditions over which they had limited control, to capture an actual event as it unfolded around them'.[32] It is on the basis of these marks of authenticity and of a participating observer's presence that many of the faked Edison war films, notably of the Boer War, arrived at very sophisticated effects of staging. They exploited depth of field as well as extreme close shots for dramatic impact, especially in scenes involving horses and cavalry charges.[33] By staging spectacular action scenes within an overall chase format, films such as *Capture of the Boer Battery* are more obviously precursors of the fiction film than of cinéma-vérité documentary. For Levy, early newsreel illustrates the peculiar leapfrog logic of film history: devices and techniques which may have owed their existence to the contingencies of filming a real event became in turn, after being adopted by film-makers intent on exploiting the topical value of the subject matter, the very conventions of the fiction film.

The relation between pro-filmic coherence and narrative coherence is fundamental to Stephen Bottomore's 'Shots in the Dark'. Discussing the origins of editing, he re-examines what the intervention, accidental or deliberate, of the shaping and 'directing' power of the cut (either in the camera or of the film strip) means for film form. Bottomore's argument is that the first instances of editing can be found in actuality films. Shooting scenes or events which occur outdoors must have encouraged the use of action in depth, with movement towards and away from the camera. Such movement becomes a significant factor in introducing temporal ellipsis or spatial discontinuity. Actualities obliged the film-maker to create, even as he records an event, a specific sequential or spatial logic, which becomes in some sense the event's (intensified) abstracted representation, as opposed to reproducing its (extensive) duration. The discontinuity resulting from the constraints imposed on the film-maker when filming a live event (the fact that he cannot be everywhere at once, that the action is non-repeatable, that his magazine loads only a limited amount of film stock) thus introduces a kind of negative, involuntary choice, of which 'editing' could be seen as the positive, intentional form.

What, however, also needs to be taken into account are certain aspects not so much of the pro-filmic (as is usually argued in the context of realism) but of the subject matter and its articulation in time, which 'naturalise' or 'motivate' peculiarities of staging and editing. For it seems what determines the filmic in actualities is not only the concern with the logic of the visible as the unfolding of an event, but also the logic of spectacle, as the deployment of a space (and point of view) in order to create a certain effect on the spectator. The difference would then be less between edited and non-edited films (between non-continuity and continuity), and instead attention would shift to analytical editing (discontinuity), as the moment of specifically filmic narration. Analytical editing, or scene dissection, not only dramatises time and space differently, but breaks with the possibility of cinematic images being seen as records of (actual) objects or events. Instead, they become motivated views (implying an act of showing) and semiotic acts (elements of a discourse): evidence that the cinema's representational space is not given but constructed, existing in an imaginary as well as a perceptual dimension.

In thinking about early film form, a move seems necessary from the discussion of film form as a question of signification and intelligibility to one where both time and space are understood as 'organised' in view of certain effects for a viewer. Signification when discussed by itself remains a-historical: what is needed is both a dynamic conception of how a film made sense and gave pleasure to this or that audience in this or that place,[34] and a concept which sees the generation of meaning in the film-text itself as a continuous process: one located in the tension between presentation and narration, rather than of formal patterning or a fixed semiotic system.

This point is forcefully taken up by André Gaudreault, in 'Film, Narrative, Narration – The cinema of the Lumière Brothers'. Rejecting Deutelbaum's approach as too concerned with the unity off the pro-filmic and the coherence of the event, Gaudreault tries to identify different levels of narrativity in films like *L'Arrivée d'un train en gare*. Distinguishing between the mobility of the represented subjects, which regulates the succession of images, and the mobility of spatio-temporal segments, which governs the succession of shots, Gaudreault sees the two levels of narrativity (the one inherent in any moving image and the other initiated by any kind of shot-change) as dialectically intertwined. Although he insists that one can talk about filmic narration only if both levels are present, since every shot-change implies the intervention of a narrator, the single-shot film constitutes a mode which is already narrative, even if it is one without a narrator. This leads him to posit a narrating instance which he calls 'monstrator', and to 'monstration' as the mode of narration typical of early cinema.

For Gaudreault, too, the issue of actualities and their staging does not lead to a reiteration of the difference between documentary and fictional forms (the Lumière/Méliès divide) but centres on the question of narration. In order to comprehend film as a system, one has to see the articulation of space and time not in isolation from, but in conjunction with the question of narrativity, preferably by distinguishing the story or event level from the act and process of narration. Continuity at the story level is one of the most powerful ways of disguising discontinuity at the level of the filmic articulation, a discontinuity which introduces the marks of narration. Narration in this sense is the sum total of the devices by which discontinuity is motivated, since it is the force that pulls the spectator into the action, even where the staging remains frontal and the space non-illusionist.

But Gaudreault's distinction has further ramifications. While Levy had already established a very sophisticated case for the emergence of the multi-shot film out of a combination of legal and industrial factors,[35] Gaudreault – using the same court material as Levy – in 'The Infringement of Copyright 1900–06' makes the case that the legal arguments around copyrighting as protecting either individual frames, or individual shots, or the entire film actually amount to a very instructive 'proto-theoretical' definition of the relation between the reality to be filmed and its filmic (he calls it 'filmographic') form in early cinema.[36] The difference that matters is thus neither between documentary and fiction, nor between edited and non-edited film, but between two kinds of discontinuity: one that emphasises the individual shot and its convergence with the scene, and one that starts with the logical or perceived unity of the scene, while ignoring the discontinuity of the individual shots.

Basic Paradigms: Non-Continuity, Discontinuity, Continuity

The most ambitious attempt to synthesise these problems and at the same time ground them historically is Gunning's 'Non-Continuity, Continuity, Discontinuity: A Theory of Genres in Early Films'. His objective, too, is to arrive via empirical evidence at a greater degree of theoretical rigour in defining early cinema, but also the classical paradigm, and even the avant garde, within a single conceptual model. For Gunning the prerequisites of a genuinely formal history which is also materialist history, are a uniform set of criteria, combined with a notion of narrative that is not functional, but dialectical:[37] an outlook and a term which brings his work close to that of Burch, for whom narrative, too, is not a given, but instead itself a historical variable.

Gunning distinguishes four cine-genres, the advantage of the term being that the marks of difference are not in the content or the iconography, but in the film forms, that is, in the treatment of time and space through the parameters of non-continuity, continuity and discontinuity. This model recasts significantly many of the preoccupations so far mentioned, notably the relation between the pro-filmic and filmic, but also the 'pressures' of content on form via the codification of time and space, which in turn can be rephrased as a question of how continuity, non-continuity and discontinuity can be motivated either diegetically or narratively, or both. With this, Gunning seems to have systematised and integrated the kinds of finding of Deutelbaum with regard to single-shot films, but also Gaudreault's arguments about narration, monstration, the narrator and the viewer's position of intelligibility.

Gunning's 'Primitive Cinema: A Frame-up or The Trick is on Us' can be regarded as a specific application of this theory of genres to the films of Méliès. Interestingly, he takes up a similar issue as Bottomore, but he differs in his assessment of the importance of splicing in early Méliès films, as opposed to camera stoppage. While for Bottomore the splicing of the film strip can still be considered as an extension of the theatre and the magic trick or stunt, for

Gunning the evidence of splicing indicates that even in the films where Méliès' transformations, displacements and disappearances are achieved by means of camera stoppage, his work already belongs to the genre of narrational discontinuity. What is crucial in Méliès is the relation (the 'trick') between spatial continuity and perceptual discontinuity, which is a deceiving of the eye in its own way as 'narrational' as invisible editing is in classical cinema.

Multi-Shot Films, Non-Continuity and Continuous Action

From Gunning's argument it is clear that the question of actualities cannot be discussed in isolation from, first, a closer consideration of the development of multi-shot films, and thus of the question of discontinuity, and second, from that of genre in early cinema, as both an issue of what constitutes original film subjects and as a question of the determinations exerted by a given subject on film form.

Charles Musser, in 'The Travel Genre in 1903–1904: Moving Towards Fictional Narrative' convincingly shows that Porter's *Great Train Robbery*, which historians like Kenneth McGowan or William Everson see as the prototypical Western, must in fact be placed within a different context in respect of both genre and subject: not only did Porter adapt a stage melodrama of the same title and imitate such highly successful British Films as *Daring Daylight Burglary* or *Desperate Poaching Affair*, he also responded to the topical interest in newspaper reports of hold-ups and the growing vogue for railway travel. Thus, if the logic of an event or process determined 'form' in the Lumière films, and the conditions of filming affected actualities and their stylisations into genre; if social customs and increased mobility can be read off the railway films, then the travel genre affords a useful opportunity to summarise the pressures exerted by the profilmic generally, and by subject matter, genre and social context in particular, on film form and the articulation of spatial relations. For what makes the travel genre and especially the railway films important for the history of the cinema is the experience of separation. As Musser notes, referring to Wolfgang Schivelbusch's *The Railway Journey: Trains and Travel in the 19th Century*, 'The traveler's world is mediated by the railroad, not only by the compartment window with its frame but by telegraph wires which intercede between the passenger and the landscape. The sensation of separation which the traveler feels on viewing the rapidly passing landscape has much in common with the theatrical experience of the spectator.[38] Separation joins discontinuity as one of the fundamental conditions of the new mode of perception which the cinema was to introduce into modern society and help to institutionalise as 'natural'.[39]

Similarly, a re-examination of the chase film might be said to have done the same for the experience of temporality, naturalising the conflation of logical relations with chronology, as in the famous 'post hoc, ergo propter hoc' principle. Burch, in 'Passion, Pursuite', has used the chase film as one of the models for understanding the development of coherent narratives of longer duration, which retain the spatio-temporal unity of the tableau shot while exploring the tableau's narrative potential.[40] This leads Burch to link the chase film with filmed versions of the Passion, on the basis of their set pieces and tableaux, as the dialectically intertwined genres crucial for the development of narrative forms prior to analytical editing, cross-cutting and other linking effects typical of classical cinema. Because the narrative of the Passion was 'universally known', the order of successive tableaux and the logic of their 'concatenation' did not require the individual images to encode any kind of linear trajectory in the representation of staging of events, nor clarify the spatial (continguous/distant) or temporal (successive/simultaneous) relations from one scene to the next. Filmed passions could dispense with centering the action, or hierarchising the characters via lighting or spatial depth typical of the classical mode, while nonetheless disturbing neither intelligibility nor causality, except to the modern viewer. From this, Burch concludes that early cinema is characterised by what he calls a 'topological complexity' that demands a scanning of the image for salient information, requiring from the spectator a special kind of attention. Such a practice has nothing to do with lack of technical expertise, but points to early cinema encoding a mode of perception dating back to the middle ages and coexisting alongside post-Renaissance perspectival vision in the popular arts well into the 20th century.

Central to 'Passion, Pursuite' is the attempt to explain what was involved in the shift from non-continuous film to continuity editing. Burch's preferred term for this change, which he sees as a gradual but contradictory one, is 'linearisation', the need to construct (and for the audience to read) successive shots within unambiguous spatio-temporal coordinates. Burch distinguishes two kinds of linearisation, because of the historical discrepancy between their introduction and codification. One is narrative linearisation, relatively quickly acquired, as in the case of the Passion films, because supported by knowledge already in the spectators' possession. The other he calls the 'linearisation of the iconographic signifier' which took 'twenty years to find its stable articulation'. These two kinds of linearisation can be discussed under several headings, each of fundamental importance for film form.

Narrative linearisation can be studied above all in the chase films, such as *Stop Thief!* (Williamson, 1901) where the spatio-temporal relations are organised unambiguously on the level of narrative without there being an equally unambiguous filmic articulation, either in terms of screen direction or match cutting.[41] The most telling sign for Burch that early chase films manifest the coexistence of two filmic systems is the fact that even in pursuits involving a large number of characters, the scene is held until the very last character exits the frame, thus creating a tension between the narrative trajectory demanding the next shot, and the tableau-like scene, having its own narrative-dramatic momentum. Although the chase thus motivates the action moving through different setups, while also ensuring narrative closure (in *Stop Thief!*, the retrieval of the sausages by the butcher), the cinema's ability to generate narrative momentum out of simple succession seems better solved for Burch in films using animals to dramatise at one and the same time an open topology and the narrative concatenation which leads to closure: for Burch *Rescued by Rover* (Fitzhamon/Hepworth, 1905) is the classic example of a film's subject matter motivating and at the same time demonstrating the filmic process itself.

Two devices above all are indicative of the linearisation of the iconic signifier: the history of the close up, and the development of cross-cutting. Burch argues that early examples of close-up, as in *The Little Doctor* (Smith, 1900), *The Gay Shoe Clerk* (Porter, 1903) or *Mary Jane's Mishap* (Smith, 1903) must not be mistaken for point-of-view shots, but 'serve exclusively in order to privilege a significant detail'.[42] The insert close-up thus has little to do with the scopic drive, but belongs more properly to a narrational logic developed independently from the codes of visual continuity.[43] As an example of a film relying on the primacy of spatial coherence and topological complexity, in preference to using an inserted close-up, Burch cites Griffith's *Musketeers of Pig Alley* (1912), where a particularly abrupt change in the action is motivated by the villain spiking the heroine's drink: the action is staged in a way that makes it barely visible within the overall composition of the scene.

Burch here raises several general issues: firstly, he wants to define the mode of perception which would correspond to the early cinema's respect for the autonomy of the scene, where all information contained in the shot is potentially relevant for intelligibility and narrative developments. Secondly, Burch wants to assign a specific function to spectatorial foreknowledge and familiarity with the subject matter, because of their importance for generating continuity within non-continuous films. But these two crucial features of early cinema may have to be examined separately. For instance, Musser in 'The Nickelodeon Era Begins' (see below) has taken up the question of foreknowledge as part of a complementary argument about the dependence of the film-text on the context (cultural, local, ethnic) of its reception, arguing that much of early cinema is rooted in the fact that the films, as it were, come into the life-world of the spectators, rather than taking them out of it, which is why the travel genre and the separation it inaugurates constitute for Musser something of an epistemic break in the history of early film and its turn to narrative.

Similarly, while scanning and the non-centred image are perhaps typical for the crammed frame of the tableau shot, they are not altogether satisfactory descriptions of the mode of perception required for films such as the Lumières'. As Burch himself has pointed out, the Lumière output modelled itself on the genre of the photographic or stereoscopic view, which quite self-consciously worked with composition and perspective, and if one follows Deutelbaum, the 'operational processes' depicted in say, *Firing a Canon* also direct the eye and focus attention by building on, but also complicating the contemplation of a pictorial view. In addition, the peculiar fascination that Vaughan notes and tries to account for, suggests not the scanning of the frame in more or less random order, but the kind of spectatorial involvement we usually call suspense and associate with feature films. Richard de Cordova's article very persuasively argues that due to a permanent movement into off-frame, the spectator implied in the Lumière films becomes the spectator par excellence of the cinema, distinct from the 'materially unrestricted time of contemplation' available to the spectator of a painting or still photography. Equally important are his observations about the frame itself, and the function of camera movement in centering the eye and at the same time containing movement, initiating a play of masking and doubling which makes the Lumière cinematographe as much a machine of 'magic and illusionism' as it is in the Méliès films, rather than supporting 'any notion of . . . referential transparency'. By discussing the relation of frame to movement in early film, de Cordova is able to show how the spectator is 'constituted in a movement of sense' and thus drawn into the representation in a way that is both different from traditional perspectival space, but also different from the 'suturing' effect of classical point-of-view structure. The spectator-positioning of *Demolition d'un mur* or the Pathé chase film *Policeman's Little Run* thus has to be understood as already part of the narrational process of the film.

What one might want to add is that the kind of involvement solicited by the Lumière films needs to be conceived in several dimensions as it were: not only the specular seduction exerted by the framing, or the use of staging, with its symmetries, repetitions and alternations within the frame, but also the spectatorial anticipation of and participation in the logic of the action portrayed, the involvement, in other words, which comes from typically narrational processes such as cueing and inferring, perceptual patterning, disequilibrium and closure. In this respect, the single shot film and the multi-shot film are not a crucial division, but part of a continuum insofar as certain forms of discontinuity and opposition within the individual frame and the single scene can be seen to extend to the multi-shot film. One way of describing these processes might be to discuss both staging and editing in terms of what could be called the question of motivation: narrative and spectator involvement are dependent on the degree to which the elements of a scene or of a sequence of scenes are either visually or cognitively linked, which is to say, perceived as motivated, whether on the basis of perceptual patterning and symmetry, conflict or suspense, or logical or chronological anticipation (and thus involving a more abstract, narrational coherence). This point has been debated much more fully – by Brewster and Gunning, among others – in relation to Griffith, and his use (or non-use) of point-of-view structures (see below).

What Burch has rightly emphasised is that only after parallel editing, cross-cutting, and what Metz called alternating syntagms were in place was it possible to use the close-up as an internally motivated, diegetically integrated element of a scene.[44] This alternation was itself a consequence of the kind of succession typical of the chase film, except that a succession of two shots had to be read not only as signifying temporal successiveness and relative spatial proximity, but as potentially also signifying an inverse relation: that of temporal simultaneity and spatial distance. In the classical cinema, it is the latter which eventually absorbs the former, to the point where analytical editing itself generally articulates shots according to a principle of alternation.[45] It confirms Gunning's point, namely that with parallel editing the function of continuity, non-continuity and discontinuity changes fundamentally, putting the burden on the viewer to construct different kinds of discontinuity as motivated from within the film itself, rather than in relation to a pro-filmic logic, be it spatial coherence, autonomy of the event, or audience foreknowledge of the subject matter. Thus, it becomes clear that the question of signification immediately raises the question of narrative, which in turn means that 'realism', as we saw in the case of the Lumière films is, right from the start, a matter of monstration/narration: evidence that the division montage vs. realism, semiotic vs. mimetic is an untenable one (see also Afterword, below, p. 407).

Edwin S. Porter

The formal characteristics of Burch's 'primitive mode of representation' in their most abstract manifestations can now be briefly summarised: single shot scene, tableau composition, frontal staging; no scene dissection, and instead, emblematic shot or insert, which does not function as a close up, but a (re)focusing of spectatorial interest; action overlap motivated by the autonomy of event; camera movement motivated by reframing and centering (external agency), rather than by character look or character knowledge (internal agency); the performer makes eye contact with spectator; narrative coherence supplied by spectatorial foreknowledge. Most aspects of the PMR thus seem to be in the service of one overriding necessity: to preserve the autonomy of the shot/scene and thus the coherence of space over that of time or causality. The principle has been most forcefully put by Gaudreault:

> Early film-makers were more or less consciously considering each shot as an autonomus self-reliant unit; the shot's objective was to present, not a small temporal segment of action but rather, the totality of an action unfolding in a homogeneous space. Between unity of pov and unity of temporal continuity, the former took precedent. Before releasing the camera to a subsequent space, everything occuring in the first location is necessarily shown. Spatial anchorage prevails over temporal logic. Stability, persistence and uniqueness of point of view remain so important that they supersede anachronism.[46]

This spatial coherence is eventually taken in charge by narrative logic, which is a differential logic (the logic of signification, abstraction from the signified) but also a logic of the subject and the spectator. The special interest for scholars of chase films, of the travel genre, of keyhole films, of the penetration of space as exemplified by Hale's Tours, of action overlaps, of the crowded frame, of left-right patterns in early Griffith and other formal features derives from their ambiguous articulation within early and transitional modes.

As Burch has shown, no other director embodies these contradictions and conceptual ambiguities as consistently as Edwin S. Porter. He is the key figure around which one can discuss not only the absolute difference or the mutual coexistence of the primitive, the transitional and the classical mode: his films have also required scholars to declare their hand, and show whether they read them as 'still' primitive or 'already' classical. Certain formal features, such as linearity and temporal articulation, the use of dual-focus space, parallel editing and a clear narrative logic seems to make a film like *The Great Train Robbery* almost the epitome of the classical system. On the other hand, the action overlap in *Life of an American Fireman* or the extremely opaque temporal articulation of *Life of an American Cowboy* make Porter one of the most sophisticated practitioners of the PMR, because the latter films have virtues (derived from their non-linearity and extreme non-continuity) which the former lacks.

Several possibilities offer themselves in order to deal with the Porter paradoxes. Gaudreault, by comparing different versions of *Life of an American Fireman* (one of which he regards as inauthentic) raises fundamental issues about temporality in early cinema, and the logic that might have determined cinematic thinking around 1904. 'Porter' for Gaudreault becomes in some sense the convenient name for asking whether a film-maker is interested in articulating time or not, whether he thinks in terms of succession, simultaneity, implications, causality, relative hierarchy in the importance of actions, or whether, rather like a sports commentator today, he gives the spectator 'action replays' because what we are witnessing is a demonstration, not an internally generated narration. Elsewhere Gaudreault discusses Porter in relation to non-continuity generally, once again making it revolve around the status of the individual shot as autonomous, and the consequences this has for staging, especially of chase films,[47] where the difference is that in one mode (the presentational) the characters exit the frame before we move to another scene, whereas in another mode (notably that made popular by Griffith) pursuer and pursued are separated into different shots and the action can cut to another space at any point.[48] A further ramification of Porter's film practice, for instance, in *Life of an American Cowboy*, is that the question of screen direction (screen exits and entrances) does not resolve itself by a definition of what is correct and what is not, but has to be seen in the context of the narrational mode one decides the film belongs to.

Does this mean that whether one reads Porter 'backwards' or 'forwards' is entirely in the eye of the beholder? In the case of the Lumière films, what to some appears to be pure flux and process, is to others multiple patterning; since patterning depends on perceptible separation, discontinuity, difference, it could be argued that it is the result of what any spectator can make of it, a kind of Rorschach test for early cinema. In the case of *Life of an American Cowboy*, precisely because its temporal logic is ambiguous, many kinds of patterns can be discerned: there are enough referents in play, as it were, to support several binary systems of relevant oppositions: good (reservation) Indian/good White; bad (wild) Indian/bad (drunk) Mexican; bad Mexican/bad White; bad Indian/good Mexican. The Whites are furthermore divided between East and West, townfolks/cowboys, and the horses between those belonging to the Indians, and those belonging to the Whites. Finally, the male/female division leads to the formation of a couple: all the elements of classical narrative and of the Western as genre are already assembled. The narrative progresses from tableau scenes to action narrative. Rich though such a reading might turn out to be, it strikes one as a-historical. Just as our knowledge that the Lumière films derive from the photographic view and are single shot films puts constraints on our reading, so the knowledge we have about the theatre intertext, or the Wild West shows, or the actuality genre in Porter's films makes us want to relate *Life of an American Cowboy* as much to lantern slides (with which the film share both the moralising theme – temperance – and the documentary/educational pretensions) as to classical narrative, without it detracting from what is so original and exciting about the film, namely its dramatisation of open spaces and the final chase.

Another way of approaching the Porter phenomenon is via the multi-shot film generally, and the issues it raises for a history of film form. Porter's work has become the touchstone and test-case for the more general significance of a cinema of non-continuity and its relation to narrative, for in his work, one finds the first systematic application of the practical distinction between the shot and the scene, giving rise to the theoretically so momentous realisation that a scene can be composed of several shots, intensifying rather than disrupting the coherence of an action. With this, the basic unit of filmic construction, the building block of classical narrative, so to speak, becomes the sequence, and the relation between shot and scene.

With the introduction of multiple action spaces comes the importance of rules, guidelines, conventions, expository techniques, but also unambiguous screen directions, the use of off-screen, which in turn formalises character movement. We are at the point of analytical editing, which means that space, even where there is frontal staging, is neither a theatrical space, nor the space of early cinema, but a narrational space. The 'cutting' into an action in progress affects the meaning of what is shown in every respect and introduces a specifically spatial logic (spatial cues, eyeline match, point-of-view structure) but it also introduces a different temporal logic (ellipsis of time) which together make up the typically narrative logic of the cinema (establishing shot, long shot, reverse angle), which allows one to talk about 'narrative integration' and the omnipresent, but invisible narrator. If we call early cinema a cinema of spatial coherence, and contrast it to a transitional cinema of articulated temporality, we could then distinguish them from classical cinema as a cinema of narrational logic superseding both.

The Janus-faced character of Porter is ultimately not in the director, but in the possibilities we have of understanding his work: whether from the 'autonomy' of the primitive mode towards what was to follow, or retrospectively, looking back at the primitive mode from the vantage point and the agenda of the classical mode. If we do the latter, we would actually start not with space or time, but with narrative (and assume narrative to be the terminal point). We would look at the development of diegetic unity which Porter's films establish across non-continuous shots and spaces, whether this be via repetition and juxtaposition of autonomous shots, or via match cutting and scene dissection.

Yet finally, there may be another, more historically precise way of looking at this momentous move, the severing of spatial coherence in favour of making both space and time the function of another logic – that of narrative causality and 'continuous action'. This would be to see the move as reactive: the response to very diverse (economic, cultural, ideological) pressures and the result of contending forces. Such is the approach adopted by Musser, for whom monstration and narration are neither formal opposites nor historical phases, but moments in a struggle for authority and control that join the textual and the extratextual in a kind of dialectic. If the (economic) use of individual scenes as single shots (as exemplified by the outlaw firing his gun in *The Great Train Robbery*) allowed the exhibitor to put together his own film, narrative authority was not with the producer/director/cameraman, but with the distributor/exhibitor/showman/lecturer. Non-continuity thus becomes an important historical marker of a stage in the development not just of film form, but of the cinematic institution, where 'editorial control' (Musser's term) must have been, for a time, floating between two aspects of what is to become a radical division: the production and the exhibition side of cinema. This development will be the subject of the second section.

Thomas Elsaesser

Notes

1. André Gaudreault has identified three areas which revitalised the study of early cinema towards the end of the 1970s: genesis of cinematic language, problems of narratology, evolution of editing. In the same paper he sees the 'evolution of film form' as a typically 'Anglo-Saxon' preoccupation. ('Le cinéma des premier temps: l'histoire et la théorie en question', pp. 1–2.)
2. 'The Early Development of Film Form' in *Film Form* no. 1, 1976 and 'Film Form 1900–1906' in *Sight and Sound*, Summer 1978.
3. But see Jacques Aumont, *Montage Eisenstein* (London: British Film Institute, 1987) for a thorough reinvestigation of Eisenstein's notion of film form.
4. Thus, there is a good deal more similarity between Salt's criteria and those of Andrew Sarris or even Raymond Bellour than he might be prepared to admit.
5. See the extracts from *The New York Dramatic Mirror* in George C. Pratt (ed.), *Spellbound in Darkness, A History of the Silent Film* (Greenwich, Conn: New York Graphic Society, 1973). Woods, of course, was not only the *Dramatic Mirror*'s first film critic; he also wrote scripts for Griffith at Biograph. See Blair Ratsoy, *Frank E. Woods* (unpublished MA thesis, University of East Anglia, 1989).
6. See Barry Salt, 'Fresh Eyes', *BFI News*, July 1976, where one of the chief virtues of the Vitagraph company is 'smoothness' and 'matching' in their films.
7. The determinants of the shift from single-shot to multi-scene film are themselves, however, quite complex. See John Fell, *Film and the Narrative Tradition*, or Stephen Bottomore, 'Shots in the Dark: The Real Origins of Film Editing', below, pp. 104–113.
8. '... It was made slightly easier for Méliès to come to grips with this problem, because he was working in one place, his studio stage, whereas everyone else making multi-scene films was working in a number of different real locations in the one film, and these locations tended to put some pressures on the way the action in each shot should be staged.' (Barry Salt, 'Film Form 1900–1906', below p. 35).
9. See Salt's remarks about the importance of the Western: 'The capital innovation in the outdoor action film (was) the use of off-eye-line angle-reverse angle combinations of shots.' Barry Salt, 'The Early Development of Film Form', in J. Fell (ed.), *Film Before Griffith*, pp. 290–91.
10. See David Bordwell and Kristin Thompson, 'Toward a Scientific Film History?', *Quarterly Review of Film Studies*, Summer 1985, pp. 224–37.
11. Notably his predilection for 'smooth continuity', match-cutting and cut on action, reverse angles and what he calls 'filmic angles' (see also Mitry, quoted in Barry Salt, 'Fresh Eyes', *BFI News*, July 1976).
12. See 'Deep Staging in French Films', below, pp. 45–55 and 'A Scene at the "Movies"' below, pp. 318–25.

13. Notably in the introduction and first part of D. Bordwell, J. Staiger, K. Thompson, *Classical Hollywood Cinema* (London: Routledge and Kegan Paul, 1985) and D. Bordwell and K. Thompson, *Film Art*, 2nd ed. (New York: Knopf, 1986).
14. See for instance, John Fell, *A History of Film* (New York, 1979), p. 34. 'Such an editing decision suggests early stirrings of film's capacity to create and to impose independent organising principles upon a world in which photography has required fidelity in the recording of experience'.
15. But see Bottomore (below, pp. 104–13, footnote 30).
16. The British pioneers (Williamson, Hepworth) occupy a special place in the discussion of early examples of continuity, since they seem to have been the first to organise consistently shots separate in time and space into 'coherent narrative patterns' (Fell). The importance of *Daring Daylight Robbery, Fire!*, and *Rescued by Rover* lies in the 'shot to shot movement' (Salt), the switching from place to place in response to a logic of question and answer, and the beginnings of parallel editing via a juxtaposition of scenes. In *Rescued by Rover* motion is used to bridge discontinuity in space in order to reinforce the illusion of continuity of action in time, as in the succession of locations (suburban avenue, river banks, narrow street in slum quarter) which Rover traverses in pursuit of the baby. *Rescued by Rover* also manifests the principle of repetition and repetition/variation which is to become one of the hallmarks of the classical cinema's concern with maintaining diegetic unity across different action spaces and temporal instances.
17. Fell, *A History of Film*, pp. 33–4.
18. See Fell's discussion of *Charge of the Boer Cavalry* (Edison, 1900) and *Blackmail* (American Mutoscope and Biograph, 1905) where framing and staging allow for clear divisions of the action into different phases. The issue becomes more complicated when individual views are either cut together to make up a longer film, or are projected together by an exhibitor, to give the impression of an event recorded in continuity, as in Robert Paul's 1898 *Colonial Troops Passing Westminster*, or the American Mutoscope and Biograph's 1904 *The Battle of Yalu*. According to Fell 'separate shots alternate camera angles, so that Japanese and Russian troops switch foreground-background relationships as if one shot were the reverse angle of its precedent'. Ibid., p. 34.
19. Thus, Jean Mitry talks about 'filmmakers, hypnotized by the obvious analogy between filmic spectacle and theatrical representation'. *Histoire du cinéma*, vol. I (Paris, Editions universitaires, 1967), p. 400.
20. Noël Burch, 'Porter or ambivalence', *Screen*, vol. 19, no. 4 (Winter 1978/79), p. 95.
21. André Gaudreault, 'Theatricality, Narrativity, and 'Trickality': Reevaluating the Cinema of Georges Méliès', *Journal of Popular Film and TV*, vol. 15, no. 3, 1987, pp. 110–19.
22. Tom Gunning, 'Primitive cinema – a Frame-up?', below, pp. 95–103.
23. Burch, 'Porter or Ambivalence', p. 97 (fn. 6).
24. Brewster sees this itself as subject to a historical shift in perception: '... two quotations from the trade press, in reply to queries from cinema owners as to the correct size of the screen. The first, from 1908, says the screen and lenses should be such as to ensure that the characters are life size on the screen; the second, from 1915, says that the size of the screen should vary in proportion to the size of the auditorium. Thus the earlier position has a literal, theatrical conception of the represented space, where the screen is a window immediately behind which the principal characters stand a measurable distance away from the spectators; while for the later one, the film image is treated as scalarly relative, so the distance of spectators from characters is entirely imaginary' (letter to the editor, April 6, 1988).
25. See the opening chapters of Barry Salt, *Film Style and Technology, History and Analysis* (London: Starword, 1983), pp. 5–39.
26. See, for instance, Salt's interest in finding 'the missing link' like Reginald Barker (in 'Early Development of Film Form', Fell, *Film Before Griffith*, p. 293).
27. Charles Musser, 'The Eden Musée: Exhibitor as Creator', *Film and History* vol. 11, no. 4, December 1981, pp. 73–83, and 'Towards a History of Screen Practice', *Quarterly Review of Film Studies*, vol. 3, no. 1, Winter 1984, pp. 59–69.
28. Yuri Tsivian, 'Notes historiques en marge de l'expérience de Koulechov' (first published in *Iris* vol. 4, no. 1, 1986, pp. 49–59), below, pp. 247–55.

29. See Barry Salt, 'Film Form 1900–1906', on pp. 31–44 below.
30. Marshall Deutelbaum, 'Structural Patterning in the Lumière Films', *Wide Angle* vol. 3, no. 1, 1979, p. 30.
31. One of the earliest descriptions of the film reflects this interest in spatial detail and concern with positionality and distance: 'A new picture was shown which represented the noon hour at the factory of the Messrs. Lumière in Lyons, France. As the whistle blew, the factory doors were thrown open and men, women and children came trooping out. Several employees had bicycles, which they mounted outside the gate, and rode off. A carryall, which the Lumières keep to transport those who live at a distance from the factory, came dashing out in the most natural manner imaginable. A lecturer was employed to explain the pictures as they were shown, but he was hardly necessary, as the views speak for themselves, eloquently.' *The New York Dramatic Mirror* (vol. 36, no. 915, July 11, 1896).
32. David Levy, 'Re-constructed Newsreels, Re-enactments', in Roger Holman (ed.), *Cinema 1900–1906, an analytical study* (Bruxelles: FIAF, 1982), p. 250.
33. Ben Brewster has drawn attention to the actuality effects achieved by staging in depth in Méliès' *Dreyfus*, but also warned against a conflation of deep staging with deep focus (see 'Deep staging in French Films' below, pp. 45–55).
34. See also Introduction to Part II, 'The Institution Cinema', below, pp. 153–75.
35. David Levy, 'Edison Sales Policy and the Continuous Action Film 1904–1906', in John Fell (ed.), *Film Before Griffith*, pp. 207–22.
36. André Gaudreault, 'The Infringement of Copyright Laws and its Effects (1900–1906)', below, pp. 114–22.
37. 'The importance of the elements I discussed is not primarily that they sketch an alternate approach to narrative than that of the classical style, but rather that they reveal how complex and dialectical the development of the classical style is. Rather than serving as markers on a deviant route in film history, the elements of non-continuity in early film punctuate the body of film history, becoming a series of blind spots.' Tom Gunning, 'Non-Continuity, Continuity, Discontinuity – A Theory of Genres in Early Films', below, pp. 86–94.
38. Charles Musser, 'The Travel Genre: Moving Towards Narrative', below, p. 127.
39. In recent film theory, and especially feminist film theory, the issue of separation has become crucial to definitions of subjectivity and gendered spectatorship through the concept of fetishism. See Laura Mulvey, 'Visual Pleasure and Narrative Cinema', *Screen* vol. 16, no. 3, 1975, and Mary Anne Doane, *The Desire to Desire* (Bloomington: Indiana University Press, 1987), pp. 11–13. Stephen Heath, in 'Lessons from Brecht', *Screen* vol. 15, no. 2, 1974 had already pointed out the difference between (Brechtian) distanciation and (fetishistic) separation.
40. Noël Burch, 'Passion, poursuite: la linéarisation', *Communications* no. 38, 1983, pp. 30–50. See also Introduction to Part III, 'The Continuity System: Griffith and Beyond', below, pp. 293–317, where other aspects of Burch's essay are discussed.
41. Burch also sees a connection between the French chase film and the travel genre (e.g. Feuillade's 1906 *Un coup de vent*), where a chase becomes the diegetic motivation for a succession of autonomous views of Paris and the suburbs.
42. Burch, 'Passion, poursuite: la linéarisation', p. 40. Barry Salt would probably argue that two other famous examples of close-ups, *Grandma's Reading Glasses* (G.A. Smith, 1898) and *As seen through a Telescope* (1900) are clearly point-of-view shots, but he, too, makes a distinction between insert shots and close-ups (see 'Film Form 1900–1906', on pp. 31–44 below).
43. See Ben Brewster, 'A Scene at the "Movies"', below, pp. 318–25, for a fuller discussion of the difference between optical and narrational point of view.
44. But see André Gaudreault (ed.), *Ce que je vois de mon ciné* (Paris: Meridiens Klincksieck, 1988), where the key-hole films, 'primitive' point-of-view structure and its motivation via reading-glasses, telescopes, etc. receive extensive treatment in essays by Elena Dagrada, François Jost, Tom Gunning, Dana Polan, Yves Bédard, Thierry Lefèbvre, Michel Marie, Paolo Cherchi Usai, Richard Abel and Gaudreault himself.
45. See Raymond Bellour, 'To Alternate/To Narrate', below, pp. 360–74, and the Introduction to Part III, 'The Continuity System: Griffith and Beyond'.

46. André Gaudreault, 'Temporality and Narrativity in Early Cinema: 1895–1908' in John L. Fell, *Film Before Griffith*, p. 210.
47. André Gaudreault, 'Le cinéma des premiers temps: l'histoire et la théorie en question' (unpublished paper), pp. 5–6.
48. See also Jacques Aumont, 'Griffith – the Frame, the Figure', below, pp. 348–59.

Film Form 1900–1906

BARRY SALT

The 1978 annual conference of the International Federation of Film Archives, held at Brighton in May, has been the occasion for the first complete survey ever made of the surviving fiction films from one period of world production. Even from so remote a period as 1900–6, about 1,500 films are preserved thanks to the efforts of the world's film archives, although several times that many are lost for ever. So although films tended in those years to be very short, about four minutes in length on average, it was necessary to reduce the bulk of the material by selection for presentation at the conference by experts from several countries working on a collaborative basis. I have myself viewed what I believe to be a representative sample of about 700 titles, ignoring in particular the many hundreds of one-scene 'knockabouts' in the Library of Congress Paper Print Collection, though not the more interesting dramatic films in that same place. On this basis, I have arrived at a picture of the development in the forms of films during this period which substantially revises the inadequate accounts given in existing film histories.

My overview of the rapid developments in the formal aspects of film in these early years sees some analogies with biological evolution, in the way that novel features which suddenly appear like mutations are sometimes rapidly taken up in other films, forming a line of descent, while on other occasions original devices die out because they have some unsuitability of a technical, commercial or artistic nature. This approach tends to put the emphasis on what most films come to be like, providing a descriptive norm. There are certainly other ways of looking at films from this and other periods, some of which will have been presented at the Brighton conference. For instance, other historians may take a quite different view of what I might loosely call 'evolutionary dead-ends'.

I should remark that although the subject and location of the conference acknowledged that at the beginning of the century the work of British film-makers was important in a way that was not to be the case again for thirty years, it would be futile to try to consider their work in isolation, since film production was already truly international, with complex interconnections between films made in the only significant producing countries: Britain, France and the United States.

Before the nickelodeon boom and subsequent world-wide increase in film production from 1906 onwards, the pressures on the evolution and development of the forms of film were low. The only absolute demand from audiences was that films be photographed (and printed) sharply in focus and with the correct exposure. Even after 1900, there were still audiences somewhere for just about anything that moved on a screen. Around 1903 there began a definite trend towards longer, multi-scene films, although the number of titles produced did not increase that much. Despite the relative lack of competitive pressure, some cinematic devices were taken up gradually by many film-makers, while others were never repeated after their invention; one instance is a unique handling of parallel action with an inset image within part of the main scene in G. A. Smith's *Santa Claus* of 1898. Another instance that had some influence for only a short while derives from Georges Méliès' way of making shot transitions in *Cendrillon* (1899) and a number of subsequent films.

Shot Transitions

When there was no appropriate intertitle to separate successive scenes, Méliès used dissolves rather than cuts from one shot to the next in his early films – examples occur in *Barbe-Bleue* (1901), for instance, and *Le Voyage dans la lune* (1902). And despite examples of what was to become the standard approach available in the work of contemporary English film-makers, E. S. Porter and others took up this type of shot transition. The shots in Porter's *Life of an American Fireman* (1902) are all joined by dissolves, even though the film is basically an imitation of James Williamson's *Fire!* (1901), in which all the transitions are made with cuts. And in *Life Rescue at Long Branch*, presumably made by Porter or under his supervision at Edison in 1901, the transition from a very long shot of a beach resuscitation to a closer shot of the same is made with a dissolve.

In *Alice in Wonderland* (Hepworth, 1903) there are a number of transitions of this kind, with dissolves in to a closer shot, and also dissolves when the actress walks out of one shot into the next. This is despite the fact that the position matching from one shot to another is what would come to be considered fairly good many years later. (It must be emphasised that Méliès was *not* using the dissolve to indicate a time lapse between shots: many of the instances occur when there is no time lapse between characters walking out of one shot into a spatially adjoining one. In fact, the use of a dissolve to indicate a time lapse was not established as a convention until the later 1920s.)

The use of fades is extremely rare in the early years of the century; those that occur in *Alice in Wonderland* are probably unsuccessful attempts at making a dissolve in the camera by fading out, then winding back and fading in on the next shot. The earliest cameras did not have accurate footage counters, and a miscounting of the number of turns back with the crank handle could easily replace a dissolve with a fade-out and in. For this and other obvious reasons, the use of dissolves made in the camera between every shot was not an efficient procedure; neither was making dissolves in the printer by an equivalent process for every separate print of the film produced. So it is no great surprise that the usage disappeared after 1903.

And it was displaced by J. H. Williamson's creation of action moving from shot to shot cut directly together in *Stop Thief!* and *Fire!* of 1901. The first of these is the source of the subsequent developments in 'chase' films, and has the characters moving out of the first shot into the second set in a different place and joined to the first with a straight cut, moving across that scene towards the camera, and then into the third and final shot. *Fire!* introduces this feature into a more complex construction. In this film an actor moves from a scene outside a burning building by exiting from a side of the frame and into a shot outside a fire station, then the fire cart moves out of this shot into the distant background of a shot of a street, advancing forward and out of the frame past the camera, and then into the original scene outside the burning house, all shots being joined by straight cuts, as are all the subsequent shots of the film. The next shot is of the interior of an upper room of the house, from which an occupant is rescued by a fireman who comes through the window. The next cut to the outside view is on the movement of rescuer and rescued through the window, though the continuity is imperfect, there being half a second of movement missing between the two shots. As with some of G. A. Smith's films, it seems that *Fire!* was modelled on narrative lantern slide sequences previously made by Bamforth on the same subject,* though obviously action continuity of the kind we have in the film was impossible in these.

Another contemporary example of 'outside to inside' cuts with time continuity occurs in *The Kiss in the Tunnel*, probably made for the Bamforth Company about 1900. This film shows a railway train going into a tunnel in extreme long shot, then the next shot shows the interior of a railway carriage compartment and then finally the train is seen coming out of the tunnel in very long shot.

So far no films repeating the continuous shot-to-shot movement of Williamson's films are known before 1903 and the appearance of *Daring Daylight Robbery*, made by the Sheffield Photographic Company. This film again has an onlooker moving from the first high-angle shot of a burglar breaking into the back of a house into a shot of a street elsewhere in which he alerts the police, and there is then a straight cut back to the original scene. The innovation in this film is that a chase then develops through a series of shots, so combining features of both *Fire!* and *Stop Thief!* into a whole that was one of the most commercially successful of all films made up to that date. *Daring Daylight Robbery* was made available for sale in America by the Edison Company under the title *Daylight Burglary*, and it seems fairly certain that Edwin S. Porter had seen it before making his *The Great Train Robbery* several months later.

In some respects *The Great Train Robbery* does represent an elaboration of its model. The most important of these was the addition of what might be called an 'emblematic' shot, which in this case shows a medium close-up of a cowboy bandit pointing a gun straight at the camera. This shot, which could be placed at either the beginning or end of the film by the exhibitor, does not represent any action that occurs in the film, but can be considered to indicate its general nature. At any rate, when the device was copied subsequently in many

---

* For the work of Bamforth and other Yorkshire film-makers, see Allan Sutherland's article in *Sight and Sound*, Winter 1976–7.

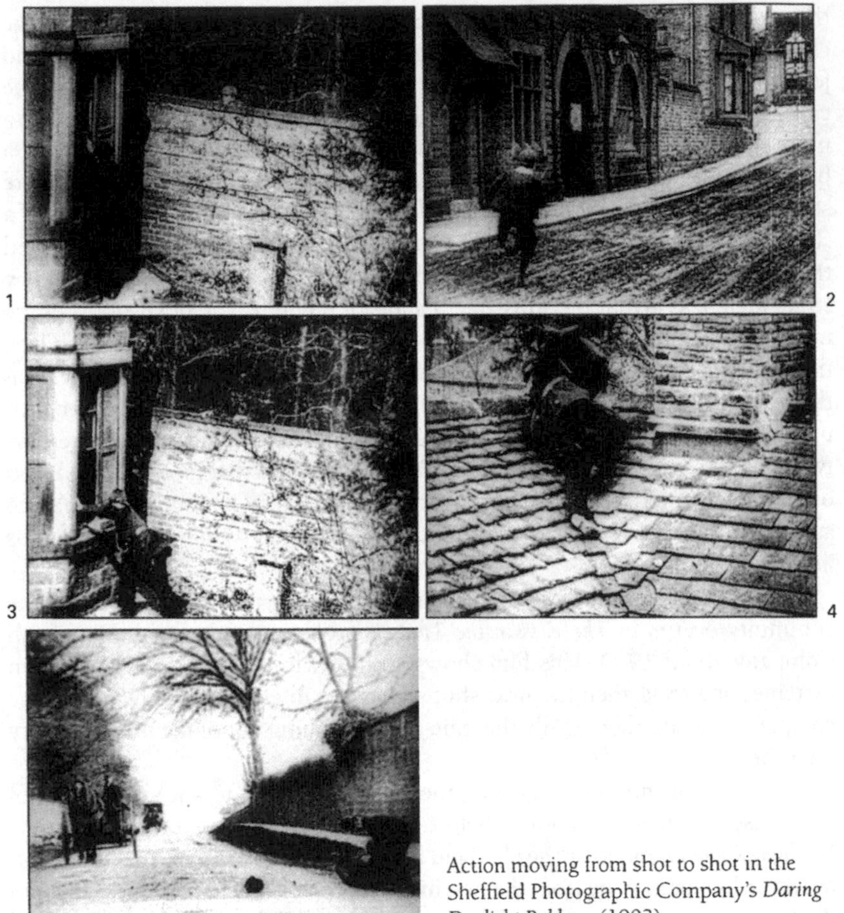

Action moving from shot to shot in the Sheffield Photographic Company's *Daring Daylight Robbery* (1903).

films, this is clearly the way it was used, as in *Raid on a Coiners' Den* (Alfred Collins, 1904), where the first shot shows a close-up insert of three hands coming into the frame from different directions; one holding a pistol, another with clenched fist, and the third holding a pair of handcuffs. A similar instance occurs in the famous *Rescued by Rover* (Hepworth, 1905), and various other films of these years, and the device continued to occur up to at least 1908, being used in some of Griffith's first films, among others. In a small number of cases the shot comes at the end of the film instead of the beginning. Since the emblematic shot may include characters present in the first true scene of the film narrative, it may not be immediately recognised as such, since it is always a close shot before the inevitable long shot framing of the first true scene, but the matter is clinched if there is wild positional mismatching between characters in the two shots and the rest of the film has fair continuity for the period.

The method of overall construction stemming from *Fire!* continued to be applied over and over again in the years after 1903; applied to new versions of the subjects already broached, and without much variation – though one later example has the chase in the middle rather than at the end (*Stolen by Gipsies*, Edwin S. Porter, 1905).

The genre of comedy chase films descending from *Stop Thief!* are invariably simpler in construction than the dramatic films incorporating chases, having a plainer linear movement of the action through shots set in a succession of different places, without cutbacks to an established scene. They too only emerge as a steady stream from 1903 onwards, with such titles as *The Pickpocket – A Chase through London* (Alf Collins, 1903), and most famously and influentially, Biograph's *Personal* of 1904. The descendants of the last named include a total plagiarism made at Pathé in 1905, *Dix femmes pour un mari*.

Films using the chase construction were all original film subjects, with the possible exception of *The Great Train Robbery*, which may have been based on a stage melodrama of the same name, and they are nearly all without intertitles between the shots. But there was also a category of film adapted from stage or literary works, or even actual events, in which a more complex narrative was handled within several minutes' running time by using a narrative or descriptive title before all (or most of) the scenes. This form was established before 1900 in some of Méliès' longer films such as *L'Affaire Dreyfus*, and in the period under consideration it was occasionally combined with the chase after 1904, as in Ferdinand Zecca's *Scenes of Convict Life* (1905), where the shots of the chase are cut straight together. This sort of construction obviously leads on to the flexible form that became usual in subsequent years.

It should be mentioned that around half the films surviving from before 1906 consist of just one scene done in one shot, and these are of no interest as far as film construction is concerned.

Directions

Méliès seems fairly quickly to have realised the importance of 'correct' directions of entrances and exits for the smoothness of film continuity, even though he was using dissolves between every shot. Certainly by *Le Voyage dans la lune* (1902) he was consistently using an exit frame right followed by an entrance frame left, and vice versa, when the characters moved out of one shot into the next set in a different, but neighbouring, location. This was not the case for most other film-makers at this period, though obviously anyone who makes the directions of entrances and exits purely at random without having thought about the matter is going to get them 'right' some of the time, just by chance. Of course it was made slightly easier for Méliès to come to grips with this problem, because he was working in the one place, his studio stage, whereas everyone else making multi-scene films was working in a number of different real locations in the one film, and these locations tended to put some pressures on the way the action in each shot should be staged.

In multi-scene films shot on real locations the transition to the next shot was often cued by movement forwards out past the camera, or conversely, as already established in Williamson's *Fire!*, and in the next shot the actors would be discovered already within the frame in a new location. For this type of transition it is almost immaterial which side of the camera the exit (or entrance)

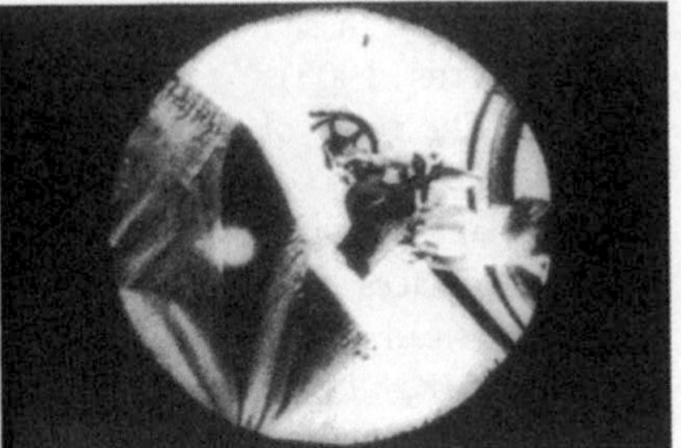

Left: Parallel action with inset in G. A. Smith's *Santa Claus* (1898).
Right: Telescope viewpoint in Smith's *As Seen Through a Telescope* (1900).

is made. However, if the actors are discovered moving strongly in one direction not too far from the camera in the next shot, it gives smoother continuity (according to subsequent ideas), if they exit in the same direction.

In general in this period one either has a series of shots with axial movement towards the camera from the far distance, or a series of shots with movement into the frame past the camera moving away into the far distance; but the subtler mixed combination of movement out of frame past the camera followed by a shot in the opposite direction with movement into the frame past the camera, as in Haggar's *Desperate Poaching Affray* (1903), is extremely rare.

Scene Dissection

Up to 1900, the only instance of a scene being divided up into a number of shots occurs in G. A. Smith's *Grandma's Reading Glass* (1900), in which the various objects a child looks at with the magnifying glass are shown inside a circular mask as point-of-view (POV) big close-ups. This device was repeated by Smith in *Scenes on Every Floor* (1902) and *As Seen through a Telescope* (1900), with masked vignettes representing the actor's POV through a keyhole and a telescope respectively. This device was applied to a slightly more extended narrative in *A Search for Evidence* (Biograph, 1903), in which the series of keyhole-peepings and associated POV shots lead the wife and detective to a confrontation with her unfaithful husband inside one of the rooms spied on, through a cut on action and change of camera direction of 90 degrees. By the definition of 'scene' being used here, which corresponds to the modern 'script scene' or 'master scene', this last cut described is a transition from one scene to the next.

An interesting example of the evolution of filmic devices through modified plagiarism is provided by Edwin S. Porter's *Gay Shoe Clerk* (1903), which combines, as so often with Porter, features from two or more previous films made by others to give something novel. This film, which shows a shoe salesman taking the opportunity to fondle a female customer's foot in a big close-up insert cut into the main scene, derives from *The Little Doctors* for its general construction, and from a French film of 1901 for its subject. This latter film shows a man with a telescope spying on another man who is taking advantage of helping a woman on to a bicycle to fondle her foot, but in this case an identical big close-up is seen inside a circular mask and cut in as a POV telescope insert.

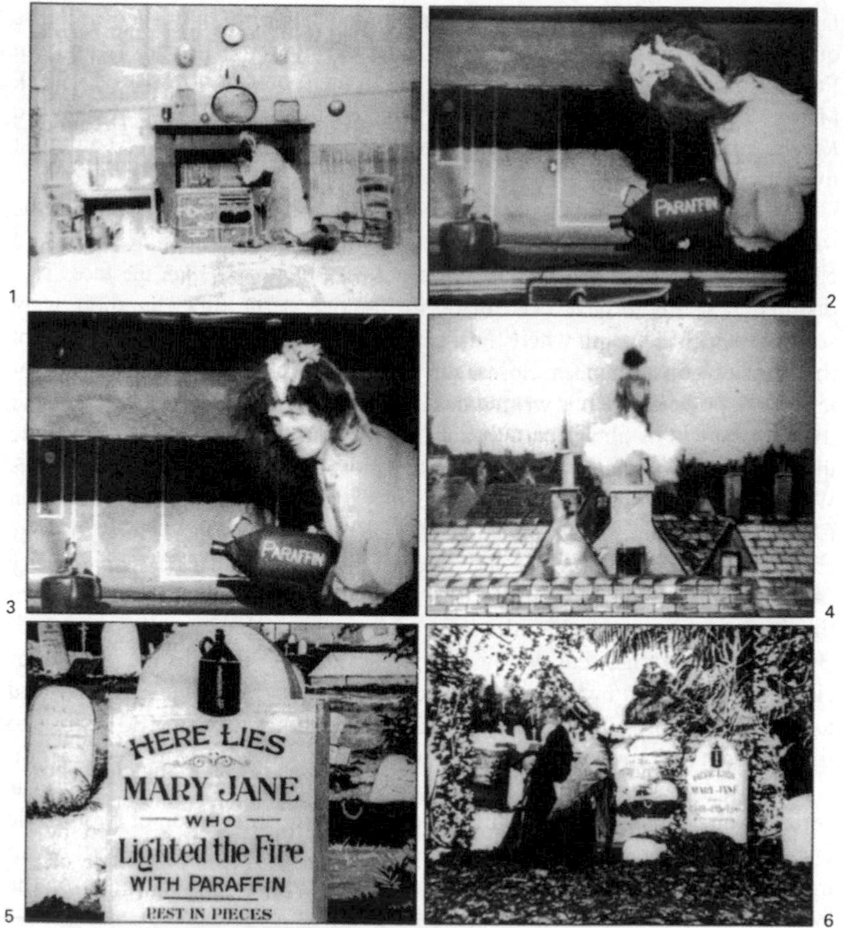

Mary Jane's Mishap (G. A. Smith, 1903).

For the development of cutting to another camera position within the course of a scene, we have to turn back to G. A. Smith's *The Little Doctors* (1901), which was reissued in shortened form as *The Sick Kitten* (1903). In this film there is a cut straight in from a long shot of two children administering a spoonful of medicine to a kitten to a big close-up insert of the kitten with the spoon in its mouth. The position matching across the cut is not exact, but it could be worse for what is the first ever use of this device.

As with other devices, 1903 saw the real beginning of the continuous development of closer shots cut into a scene, and the most remarkable instance occurs in that little-known master-work *Mary Jane's Mishap* again from G. A. Smith. Here there are repeated three times in the course of the first scene cuts in, and then out again, from a long shot of Mary Jane lighting the fire to a medium close shot of her, admittedly with poor position matching. The use of the device begins to proliferate in 1904 with medium shots cut into scenes in *The Strenuous*

Life (Edison) and *The Widow and the Only Man* (Biograph), and then becomes quite common from 1905 onwards in films too numerous to catalogue from France, Britain and the USA, though we might mention *La Calza* (Pathé, 1905), *Modern Brigandage* (Pathé, 1906), *The Firebug* (Biograph, 1905), *Dream of a Rarebit Fiend* (Edison, 1906), *Eine Fliegenjagd* (Skladanowsky, 1905) amongst many.

It really becomes necessary to distinguish at this point between the true close-up and the insert, which I define, following later nomenclature, as a close shot of some object or part of an actor's body *other than the face*. This distinction seems to have been made in practice at the time, for there were studios such as Vitagraph where the insert was used from 1905 onwards, but not the true close-up or medium close shot. The use of a close shot of a letter or other text at the point where it is written or read obviously makes a vast difference to the possibilities of film narrative, and early examples include the tombstone inscription in *Mary Jane's Mishap*, a cut to a close-up of a notice on a gate in *The Watch Dogs* (Pathé, 1904) and insert shots of documents in *Buy Your Own Cherries* (R. W. Paul, 1904) and *Honest Peggy* (Pathé, *c*. 1905). Inserts to show clearly details important to the story are used repeatedly in *The Missing Legacy* (Alf Collins, 1906) and *Falsely Accused* (probably Hepworth, 1905), and from this point on we can consider the usage well established.

The earliest cut within a scene *without* any real change of scale or closeness of shot, and with strict time continuity, occurs in *Ladies' Skirts Nailed to a Fence* (Bamforth, 1900), in which the second shot is taken at 180 degrees to the first from the other side of the fence, with time continuity, to make the action clear. This could be called in a vague general way a reverse angle cut, but is certainly not of the interesting kind that involves the interaction of two people facing each other. In any case, this particular instance is achieved by an ingenious cheat which depends on moving actors to the other side of the symmetrical fence without moving the camera for the second shot.

In 1901 someone at the Edison Company applied the Méliès dissolve to join together the shots that form the single continuous scene of *Life Rescue at Long Branch*, although Méliès himself had only used the dissolve between separate scenes in different locations. The Biograph Company imitation of this film, *Caught in the Undertow* (1902), has the shots joined together with straight cuts, and the last moves straight in down the camera axis to medium long shot of the resuscitation. Also in 1902, a British film, *The Interfering Lovers*, features a transition by a cut from very long shot with a simultaneous change of camera direction of 60 degrees, so covering any minor discrepancies of act position between the shots and ensuring a smooth transition (as seen in subsequent terms). However, this principle was not consciously realised by the film-maker or his contemporaries, and for the next decade cuts to a closer shot continued to be made straight in down the camera axis.

There was in fact no consolidated development in the use of cutting to different angles within a scene before 1906, unlike the case of cutting in to a closer shot, but for the sake of completeness I should also mention a true pair of reverse angles from pursuing car to pursued, and vice versa, in *The Runaway*

Match, made by Alf Collins in 1903. There are also a number of cuts to the other side of a wall in comedy chases, for instance the French film *Prenez garde à la peinture* (*Wet Paint*) of about 1905.

Other Forms of Transition

The already mentioned *Mary Jane's Mishap* includes a remarkable and quite unique pair of vertical wipes to effect the transition into and out of a closer shot of the inscription on her tombstone. And there are a few occasions when fades were used intentionally in the years between 1900 and 1906, one fairly trivial instance being their use to begin and end each of the one-shot scenes in *La Vie du Christ*, made by Jasset and Hatot for Gaumont in 1906. In this case every scene is preceded by a narrative title put in between the fades. Much more interestingly, in *The Old Chorister* (1905), scenes are joined directly by a fade-out and a fade-in, and in another case by an iris-out and a fade-in.

Another unique occurrence in these years is the use of a focus-pull to give an out-of-focus blur on a medium shot of a man kissing a beautiful woman, then a cut to another out-of-focus blur which pulls in to a medium shot of the same man in bed kissing his ugly wife, from whom he recoils when he realises that he has been dreaming. The film is *Let Me Dream Again* (1900) by G. A. Smith, but there were to be no other examples of this device for a couple of decades, transitions in and out of dreams being done with dissolves from Zecca's Pathé remake of this film as *Rêve et réalité* (1902) onwards to *And the Villain Still Pursued Her* (Vitagraph, 1906).

Cross-Cutting Between Parallel Actions

As has already been described, the practice of cutting away for one shot from the enclosing scene was quite well established by the end of these years, but the idea of doing this repeatedly was not. A preliminary stage of this latter development may be visible in a few films in which the shots alternate repeatedly between aerial events and happenings on the ground. One example occurs in *Rescued in Mid-Air* (Arthur Melbourne-Cooper, *c.* 1906).

But, most remarkably, fully developed cross-cutting appears in a race against time situation in *The Hundred-to-One Shot* (Vitagraph, 1906), with repeated cuts between a speeding car and events at its destination. This seems to be the beginning of a development that continued through 1907 into 1908, and for which D. W. Griffith incorrectly claimed credit.

Dreams, Memories, Visions

The first way that dream memories were treated was as a separate scene inset within the frame containing the scene showing the person dreaming. The famous example here is Zecca's *Histoire d'un crime* (1901). This film used the stage device of showing the sleeping man's memories by having part of the backcloth vanish and reveal a smaller set behind, on which was enacted the past scene, or in this case, series of scenes. This device is repeated using photographic means in the first scene of Porter's *Life of an American Fireman*, the inset being another scene placed in a dark part of the frame by superimposition. There must surely be other examples in the next several years, but I have not found them so far. The related representation of spirits, angels and so on by a simple superimposition had already appeared before 1900, and was continued through this period in films such as *Uncle Tom's Cabin* (Edwin S. Porter, 1903), *The Old Chorister* (1905) and *Drink and Repentance* (1905).

An alternative approach particularly convenient for representing multi-scene dreams must surely have appeared before the instance of *And the Villain Still Pursued Her* (Vitagraph, 1906), which has already been mentioned as using dissolves into and out of the dream section.

Dialogue Titles

Towards the end of this period there are isolated instances of dialogue titles being cut in before a scene in place of the usual narrative title, but the films being produced at this time are still not long enough to contain a continuously developed, complex narrative in which the usefulness of such a feature would be obvious. The earliest example I have noticed occurs in Porter's *The Ex-Convict* of 1904, and there are others in *La Vie du Christ* (Jasset and Hatot, 1906), *Ali Baba et les quarante voleurs* (Pathé, 1905) and an English film of unknown title produced by the Urban Company in 1906. (This last film is catalogued as *Father, Mother Wants You*, which is actually the first dialogue it contains, well into the body of the story.) In the case of the two French films, the dialogue titles they incorporate are the best-known lines their respective stories contain.

Trick Effects

It is my view that excessive attention has been devoted to early trick films, and particularly those of Méliès, in view of the fact that they proved a dead-end as far as the development of the cinema is concerned. Nevertheless, such films still formed a fair part of production in the early years of the century, though the decline in their commercial importance was already evident by 1906. This is not to say that they have no other interesting qualities, just that enough is enough. The basic techniques that Méliès and everyone else used had already been established as standard before 1900, with one exception which will be noted below. There is no necessity to describe these techniques, which involve stopping the camera and adding or subtracting elements of the scene, superimpositions of various kinds made in the camera, including those made on a dark field within the background shot, and reverse motion, or to comment on the films in which they appear. Their occurrence and manner of execution are always quite obvious, partly because no cameras of the period had perfect registration and hence the two parts of a superimposition always move with respect to each other. There was no development in what Méliès did with them either, with the possible exception of his science-fiction fantasies.

The transference of Méliès' techniques to scenes shot in real surroundings (rather than on a stage set) by English film-makers also has its place in the history books already, but since it largely happened after 1900 some discussion is in order. The earliest examples were made by the Hepworth Company in that very year, and consist of *Explosion of a Motor Car* and *The*

Bathers. The effects in the first are achieved in the standard way by stopping the camera, substituting an imitation motor car for a real one, then starting the camera again and exploding the imitation car, and so on. Similar later films show a man being literally flattened by a steamroller and other events effected in the same way. *The Bathers* simply shows two bathers undressing and diving into the water, then the action apparently reverses in time and runs its course backwards. The reversed second half of the film was produced by printing each frame of the original negative in reverse order, and the laborious manipulation this involved to make each separate print ensured that after one or two similar productions the idea was abandoned.

The British motor car trick films can be related to the extra-filmic tradition of British nonsense, and lead me to mention *How It Feels to Be Run Over*, also made by Hepworth in 1900. In this film a car drives straight at the camera and when it is right up to it and out of focus there is a cut to a black frame decorated with stars and dashes and exclamation marks, and then a cut to the title 'Oh, Mother will be pleased.' The climax of this sort of thing was *The Big Swallow*, made by Williamson in 1901. In this, a shot of a photographer about to take a picture of a reluctant pedestrian is succeeded by a photographer's point-of-view shot of the man approaching till his head fills the screen, at which point he opens his mouth to almost full-screen size. There is a cut to a shot of the photographer and his camera falling around in a black void, and then a final long shot of the pedestrian walking away munching. An interesting technical point is that the focus is adjusted as the actor approaches the camera to keep the image sharp. Such adjustment of the focus during the course of a shot is extremely rare before World War I; the only early example occurs in *W. Gibson – Excentricité américaine*.

The most important development in trick effects during the period first appears in a film made around 1900 by Arthur Melbourne-Cooper. This involves model animation done by shooting one single frame at a time, with minute adjustment of the models' position between exposures, so producing the effect of movement when the film is projected, and the subject is a match appeal for the Boer War. A stick figure made of matches is animated by this process, and it appears to write the text of the appeal on a blackboard. (The Méliès films that involve animated objects are done by pulling them about with invisible wires.) The technique of frame by frame animation requires a camera with gearing modified so that one turn of the crank handle exposes exactly one frame of film. It is possible that this technique was more widely known at the turn of the century than is now apparent, for there exists a 1902 Biograph film of the demolition of the Star theatre made by time lapse photography using the same type of camera adaptation. In any case, frame by frame animation became standard procedure from 1904 onwards, with films such as *The Whole Dam Family and the Dam Dog* (Edwin S. Porter, 1904), *El Hotel Electrico* (Segundo de Chomon, 1905), *Humorous Phases of Funny Faces* (J. Stuart Blackton, 1906) and many others.

A new development in Méliès work may be connected with single-frame animation. It is difficult to be certain if his *Le Roi du maquillage* (1904), which shows what would now be thought of as a 'Wolfman' type facial transformation, has been executed by single-frame filming or by a series of closely spaced and even dissolves from one stage of the addition of more hair, etc. to the next.

Photography and Lighting

Most film production in this period continued to be done under direct sunlight, either on natural exteriors, on open-air stages with built sets representing interiors, or in the case of some major companies on glass-roofed stages. In 1904, however, this natural light began to be helped out on occasion with artificial lighting. This was provided either by simple arc floodlights on floor stands of the type already in use in the theatre or still photography, or by racks of mercury vapour tube lamps. The latter were usually referred to by the name of their principal manufacturer, Cooper-Hewitt, and the light they gave, similar to that from a very large modern 'spot-light', is very difficult to distinguish from diffuse natural light coming into a studio through the glass ceiling. In the early years light from Cooper-Hewitt lamps was used only to supplement natural light, but arc floodlights were used straight away to create special lighting effects, possibly modelled on existing theatrical usage, though no definite records exist of such theatrical practice before 1906. In any case, the scene of 'Old Age' in Edwin S. Porter's *The Seven Ages* has a fire effect done with an arc floodlight in a fireplace before which an old couple sit, illuminated solely by its light.

Partial uses of arc lighting also occur in *Rescued by Rover* (Hepworth, 1905), in which the scenes in the gypsy's attic room are illuminated by a pair of arc lights to simulate the light from the window, though as an addition to the general diffuse natural light; and in *The Firebug* (Biograph, 1905) arc floodlighting is used to heighten the effect of the fire-raising, though without any attempt at a flickering effect. (In this context, it is worth mentioning that Williamson's *Fire!* seems to have a flash of arc light put in from a corner of the room interior which is on fire, though it is just possible that it is a photographic flash powder doing the job.) Another very early attempt at a lighting effect is the use of the sun reflected in a small mirror to produce a patch of bright light simulating a lantern beam in *Man Meets Ragged Boy*, a British film of 1902. An entirely different approach to the simulation of a beam of light occurs in a Pathé film of *circa* 1905, *Rescue from a Shipwreck*, in which a scene lit by the beam from a lighthouse is revealed within the confines of a diagonal band delineated by a soft-edged mask in front of the lens, which is meant to represent the outline of the beam.

Returning to the eruption of effect lighting in 1905, there is another extremely interesting example in *Falsely Accused*, probably from the Hepworth studio. Here a man searching a totally dark room by lantern light is photographed doing just that, the sole illumination coming from a tiny arc concealed in his lantern! It seems to have been several years before this technique turned up again in films. There would seem to have been someone at Hepworth aware of the possibilities of available light photography, because in the same year *Stolen Guy* has a bonfire scene lit solely by the light from the bonfire.

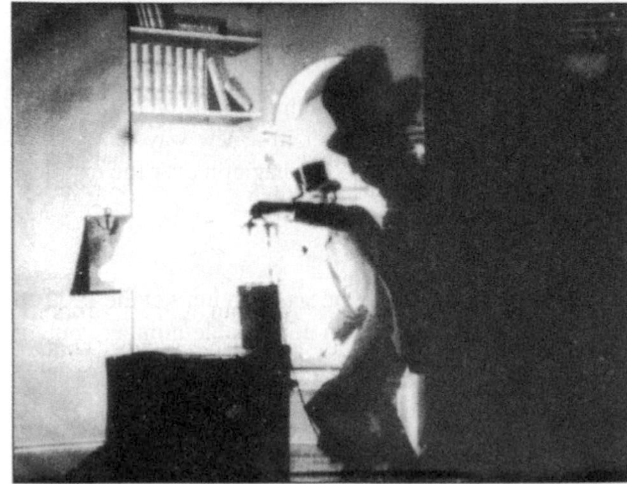

Lighting effect in *Falsely Accused* (1905).

Simulation of a lighthouse beam in *Rescue from a Shipwreck* (c. 1905).

The gypsy's attic room in *Rescued by Rover* (1905), lit by arc lights.

Finally, and more importantly, what might be considered the beginning of figure lighting, as something separate from general scene lighting, can be seen in *La Vie du Christ*. In a few scenes, extra arc lighting was applied to the figures alone, on top of general diffused daylight falling equally on both set and figures, so sharpening the modelling of the latter in a new way that was to become standard not only at Gaumont but also at Vitagraph over the next few years.

Acting

There are no general trends to be discerned in the acting in films of the 1900–6 period, though it should be pointed out that an appreciable number contain very naturalistic playing, from professional actors and non-professionals alike. To choose some examples at random, the acting in Williamson's *Soldiers Return* (1902), Porter's *The Kleptomaniac* (1905) and Biograph's *The Course of True Love* (1905) is very restrained. On the other hand, many films have extremely crude acting, one example being Porter's *The Great Train Robbery*. It is very difficult to see any patterns emerging, either taken by studio or by director.

Conclusion

It should be emphasised that the films made before 1906 which still exist are only a fraction of the production of that period, and so if a particular feature is found in several of them, it probably also appeared in many more which are now lost. For instance, if about thirty surviving films have closer shots cut into the middle of a scene, as indeed they do, it is likely that there were more than 100 films actually made with this feature. On the other hand, if there is only a unique occurrence of a particular feature in surviving films, then it may very well have been unique at the time.

With this in mind, we can say that the major trends in the development of film form which emerge quite clearly through this period are the practice of cutting in to a closer shot of one kind or another within a scene, the elaboration of 'chase' construction and the use of point-of-view shots. In 1904–6 we can also see the beginning of what was probably the continuous development of cross-cutting between parallel actions, and also the use of arc lighting for effect and figure lighting. Among the films that are still to be gathered in to the archives there may be some that will fill such obvious gaps as that in the development of dream sequences before 1906, or of chase films in 1902. I hope so.

First published in *Sight and Sound*, Summer 1978.

Deep Staging in French Films 1900–1914

BEN BREWSTER

This chapter[1] is about the design of sets or choice of locations for films to reveal or emphasise a wide range of distance from the camera, and about the organisation of the action in films in depth rather than along a line more or less perpendicular to the axis of the lens. The two things are not the same – it is possible to have sets with considerable real (let alone illusory) depth which is emphasised (e.g. by the placing of extras) while the action simply takes place in a shallow arena in front, and, given the preponderance of the long shot in all cinematography during this period, even with the flattest backdrop there is always a fairly large distance between the camera and the rear wall of the set which may be encroached on by the actors to give a form of staging in depth. It is this latter form of depth that is most commonly found in French (and other) films in the first five years of the century, and earlier. Two subjects from Méliès' 'Dreyfus' series (1899) – *L'Attentat contre Maître Labori* and *Bagarre entre journalistes* – despite having Méliès' standard flat perpendicular painted backdrops (though in the latter the backdrop has a painted deep, low-angle perspective based on contemporary magazine photographs),[2] allow characters either to enter or to exit relatively close to the camera, so they come forward from long shot to medium long shot or even close-up framing. (This gives me an opportunity to open a parenthesis and point out what this chapter is *not* about – it is not concerned with deep focus or depth of field. Given the standard 50 mm lenses of the period, standard film stocks and lighting levels, and the normal f11 to f16 apertures, it was perfectly easy to maintain sharp focus over a range of depths from medium long shot to very long shot, and on the rare occasions when something, almost always a person entering or leaving shot, got too close, it was simply allowed to go out of focus (as in these Méliès examples), or, much more rarely, focus was adjusted in shot (e.g. Williamson's *The Big Swallow* (1901), at the beginning of our period, Griffith's *The Musketeers of Pig Alley* (1912), near the end).[3] In the 'Dreyfus' examples, Méliès seems to be deliberately imitating effects obtained accidentally and reluctantly in actuality films, but this form of staging, in less extreme ways, persists in his fantastic subjects for a number of years, e.g. in the Wedding Feast tableau (no. 3) of *Barbe-Bleue* (1901) and the Firing of the Gun (Tableau no. 7) in *Voyage dans la lune* (1902).

In location-shot films, a more systematic use of this encroachment on the camera is found in the chase film. The earliest chase films (e.g. Williamson's *Stop Thief!* (1901)) and most of the chases in studio-shot films always (e.g. the pursuit of the astronauts by the Selenites in *Voyage dans la lune*) are staged more or less laterally, but most chases in exteriors stage the scene in depth, with pursuers and pursued running from the background to exit foreground left or right, or vice versa, in each shot of the chase. This makes it possible for the shots to be longer and the action within them – the various humiliations heaped on the participants – more varied, and obviates any need that may be felt for direction matching (such as the careful preservation of screen direction in *Voyage dans la lune*), and it remained the standard way of staging chases and last-minute dashes to the rescue until joined by the device of tracking shots at the end of our period (e.g. Griffith's *A Beast at Bay* (1912)).[4]

The organisation of studio sets to provide depth is largely independent of this development. Apart from the illusory painted depths frequent in Méliès' backdrops (e.g. the vast banqueting hall behind the 'high table' of live wedding guests in the tableau from *Barbe-Bleue* already mentioned), he does occasionally provide a deep stage, usually for the presentation of a ballet (e.g. *La Damnation du Docteur Faust*, Tableau no. 16 (1904)). The principal aim is thus a spectacular rather than a dramatic one, and in other companies' films the impulse to deeper settings seems to appear first in biblical subjects, often drawing more or less explicitly on traditions of Bible illustration in painting and prints. Gaumont's *La Vie du Christ* (1906), based on a series of water-colours and subsequently engravings by James Tissot, has very deep-staged exteriors (e.g. the scene of Christ and the Woman of Samaria), but also strongly three-dimensional sets with exteriors visible through arcades and doorways in the rear. This tendency spreads to other costume subjects, especially those produced by Pathé, where it was facilitated by the building of a studio tank at Montreuil in 1904, used for the Venetian canals in *Un Drame à Venise* (1906), for example. But there seems also to have been a slightly different motivation at Pathé, an interest in the revelation of space as such, which is more obviously marked by the panning across sets in *Au pays noir* (1905) and *Aladin* (1906), where the camera follows a character past a long backdrop. The same kind of effect is produced in depth in a modern (but costume) subject – one of the three films made at Pathé in 1905 about the Russian revolution of that year (perhaps *Les Troubles de Saint Pétersbourg*).[5] Here, in two street scenes large crowds of extras run across the sets at different depths and backwards and forwards in depth, pursued by mounted cossacks, and the flats representing rows of houses are distributed to give a strong division between background and foreground. This is very unlike the static depth in the biblical films, but it is also very difficult to make sense of what is being represented (Bloody Sunday? a pogrom?). The kind of rushing about in depth and on different planes found in this film is unique, as far as I know, though a more moderate version occurs within the more biblical restraint of a historical costume picture proper in the battle scenes of *Die Jungfrau von Orleans* (Pathé, *c.* 1908).[6]

A more significant push towards deep staging was given by the emergence of the Film d'Art, and *La Mort du duc de Guise* (1908) in particular.[7] In this film not only is there a greater attempt than in previous costume pictures to provide convincing three-dimensional sets, but, much more important, the camera height is lowered to waist level. This immediately means that a head-to-

L'Attentat contre Maître Labori (1899).

Les Troubles de Saint Pétersbourg (?) (1905).

The Scourging from *La Vie du Christ* (1906).

foot framing of a character gives in fact a larger, closer image of that character, as the full height of the frame can be used, whereas with the eye-level camera hitherto dominant the upper half of the frame is more or less empty most of the time; and, more important still, there is a much more striking scalar difference between characters closer to and further away from the camera, as head height drops the further away the character is, giving a much greater effect of depth if the action is staged in depth.[8] The aim may have been to produce a theatrical effect, a view from the stalls, or perhaps even simply to create an illusion of the principal character's height; whatever it was, it stuck, and the low camera position is used in later Film d'Art subjects (e.g. *La Tosca* (1909)) and in other 'art' series, notably those of SCAGL. By 1910, Pathé is using a low camera in all genres, not only costume pictures (e.g. *Cléopatra*) but also comics (e.g. *Les Débuts de Max au cinéma*, which is not only filmed from about waist height throughout, but shows Pathé Studio Cameras filming at the same height in a comic subject). But the technique is not used in Gaumont's earlier Série d'Art subjects (e.g. *Le Huguenot* (1911)). Finally, the key action of *La Mort du duc de Guise*, the murder, is (as Barry Salt discusses[9]) distributed across a number of different sets, i.e. through a continuous series of rooms, developing a Pathé tradition of cutting around doors. But whereas in most of the Pathé films these doors are to the side of the set, and if the doors when opened reveal a space and a setting beyond, that setting tends not to be matched with the corresponding scene in the next room (e.g. *Die schöne Kontoristin* (*c.* 1908)), in *La Mort du duc de Guise* the doors are at the back of the sets and show carefully matched glimpses of the space beyond. The 'door-at-the-back-of-the-set' device was taken up for spectacular effect in *Die schwarze Sklavin* (a film probably made in 1910 by Gaumont), for example, where otherwise laterally composed scenes in a Foreign Legion camp are played in front of windows outside which troops can be seen exercising. A variant of this where a closed rear window or an empty space is subsequently opened or filled respectively to dramatic effect, a *mise en scène* with a solid pedigree in nineteenth-century theatre (both romantic-historical and naturalist), became almost an obsession in Feuillade's films for Gaumont. In *Le Huguenot*, a window opens to reveal the St Bartholomew's Day massacre to the horrified hero, and the religious rivals are eventually reconciled when Coligny's chaplain draws aside a curtain to reveal a crucifix. In most later Feuillade films, certainly up to *Les Vampires* (1915), every set has a space or a door at the back which will be occupied or opened by the end of the scene (or very rarely in the first return to the same scene and set-up) – there are many examples in *Le Mort qui tue* (*Fantômas*, episode III, 1913). But Pathé and SCAGL use this style primarily for their costume pictures. In *Cléopatra* (1910), there are scenes using the studio tank mid-ground for the arrival and departure of Cleopatra's barge, her palace or Antony's tent occupying the foreground, while, beyond the tank, a garden or the Roman camp is populated by moving extras – slaves or soldiers. And *Le Siège de Calais* (Pathé, 1911) creates a perspective of soldiers and a mediæval gateway to frame its principals in one shot. And in the last scenes of *Le Courrier de Lyon* (Pathé, 1911), the guillotine on which the hero is to be executed is visible through the window of the house in which the real murderer is hiding.

These same impulses, deriving largely from *La Mort du duc de Guise*, led to slightly different results outside France, in the USA and Denmark. In the USA, Vitagraph adopted the low camera position, but combined it with a much closer forward camera position in the main action of the shots ('American foreground' or '*plan américain*') and the possibility of the principals in the foreground turning their backs to the camera. In North Europe, on the other hand, staging in depth in exteriors and division of the sets into interconnected spaces at various depths was taken much further, and the division of the action into different planes was emphasised by divisions of light and darkness, filming from a dark interior into a lit exterior, for example, with foreground characters reduced to silhouettes (a practice also notable in some earlier American films, e.g. Biograph's *Tunnel Workers* of 1906, and in slightly later films from Vitagraph, e.g. *A Friendly Marriage* of 1911). These types of staging also tend to move further away from their theatrical models than their French counterparts, in so far as they exploit the way projection on a screen can give many spectators a single viewpoint, whereas deep theatrical compositions are restricted by the need to keep the action visible from a relatively wide range of angles in front of the stage. But in another respect a certain staginess is emphasised: far from the Vitagraph practice of actors turning their backs to camera, the early films of Asta Nielsen show a staging where the main actress tends to gaze towards camera, or rather towards a point somewhere over the spectators' heads, and this characteristic was picked up and exaggerated in the Italian cinema with the development of the *diva*, so that in films like *Assunta Spina* (1915), Francesca Bertini spends a lot of her time looking at us while the male characters gaze at her in adoration and at each other in jealousy.

I would like to conclude with some rather speculative remarks comparing the development of deep staging and that of faster cutting. In a sense they can be seen as alternatives – once a simple shallow staging of action in long tableaux began to be felt (by audiences and/or film-makers) as tedious, variety could be introduced either by increasing the rate at which tableaux are replaced, or by creating more complicated settings and more complicated staging of the action in those settings. And, broadly speaking, the American cinema took the first road, and has consistently faster (and accelerating) cutting rates than those characteristic of Europe during the 1910s, whereas the tendency to emphasise depth is European. Moreover, in the USA itself, the characteristically shallow-staged films made by Griffith for Biograph[10] are faster cut than the deep-staged films made at Vitagraph at the same time. On the other hand, the difference between Europe and America might just be taken as a sign of the backwardness of the European cinema, which was at this time being rapidly displaced from its own screens by the American product. The two points are not incompatible. In so far as they discussed these matters at all, commentators on the cinema before the First World War on both sides of the Atlantic favoured the slower, more ornate 'European' style, precisely because it was more easily assimilable to discussion in the familiar and prestigious terms of the legitimate theatre; that these discourses were more effective in Europe might have a number of explanations, but it is at least clear that the attempt to produce an artistic, 'quality' product has been one of the most persistent strategies of European cinemas in response to American competition.

There is, however, another way of looking at the matter, in terms of fixity of viewpoint. Deep staging tends to encourage a fixed viewpoint on a setting, in so far as a deep composition changes much more rapidly with changes of camera angle and position in front of it than a shallow composition does. (I am not here talking about camera movement within a shot, but about different camera positions in different shots.) The framing with the star in the foreground gazing off towards camera also encourages fixity, in that, in a certain sense, such a shot cannot have a reverse shot, for that would give something mundane for the heroine to be looking at. The tendency to fixity can be seen clearly in Viktor Sjöström's *Ingeborg Holm* of 1913, where it has clearly become (or always has been) a convention rather than a simple convenience. Each set or location has one camera placement, however often it is returned to; at one point in the film, many years pass, and we return after an explanatory title to a familiar space filmed from exactly the same point as in earlier scenes, but with a slightly different set of furnishings to mark the passage of time.

There is, on the other hand, no necessary correlation of shallow staging and variety of camera set-ups. Griffith's Biograph films are a case in point. They are eminently shallow-staged – even if a figure does appear in the background behind a foreground group, as soon as there is any real action in the scene, he or she will come forward to join that group for that action. But despite the high cutting rate, Griffith almost never varies the viewpoint on a single interior set – cutting is *between* rooms, not within them (cf. *Three Sisters* (1911)), except for the occasional insert, usually shot from the same angle, or, later, cut to closer shot, also from the same angle. Vitagraph, on the other hand, despite the slower cutting rate of its films, also used shot-reverse-shot and point-of-view cutting, and with Ralph Ince's films from 1913 to 1915, fully developed a style with constant variation of angles and set-ups for each space of action.

French film-makers in general adopt the tendency to fixity of viewpoint along with that to deep staging. I do not know of any French film that takes it as far as *Ingeborg Holm*,[11] but for the most part Feuillade conforms to it. In the *Fantômas* films, he has one main set-up per space, with occasional cut-ins at the same angle for details. The epistemophilia which motivates these (they are usually clues or quasi-documentary items like how fingerprints are taken) does, however, on rare occasions lead to a shift in viewpoint. In *Le Mort qui tue*, the fourth scene takes place in Jacques Dollon's studio and is shot frontally to the back wall of a deep set with Dollon seated at a desk in the foreground facing the camera. Fantômas then erupts into the space at the back and comes forward to chloroform Dollon. The next scene is of the same space from the same side and distance, but with the camera shifted to the right and turned some 20 degrees to the left to include a chair right foreground containing the corpse of the Baronesse de Vibraye. . . .

Léonce Perret, however, goes much further. In *Le Roman d'un mousse* (Gaumont, 1913), he uses deep space in a much more 'Danish' manner than Feuillade, with spectacular silhouette shots and contre-jour lighting in exteriors,

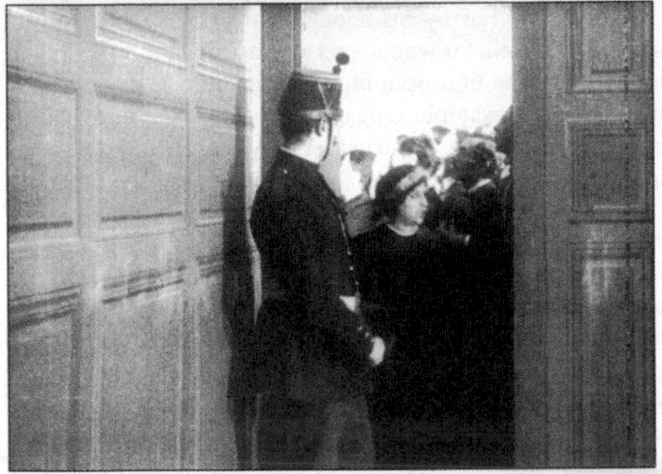

Three set-ups from *Le Roman d'un mousse* (1913).

and interiors with interconnecting spaces and action at several planes of depth (the cinematographer was Specht and the set designer Jean Perrier). But this does not go with any fixity of viewpoint – quite the reverse. Perret generally chooses less axial viewpoints on his sets than Feuillade; thus, the scene in the office of the *juge d'instruction* in *Le Roman d'un mousse* has basically the same furnishings as the equivalent setting in *Le Mort qui tue*, but chooses an oblique angle. Perret also varies the angle of view in intimate interiors, e.g. in the scene of the poison attempt against the Comtesse de Ker-Armor. Most spectacularly, in one long sequence, the trial scene at the end of the film, he uses sixteen different set-ups for a single, admittedly large, interior space. What is particularly interesting, paradoxically, is that some of these differ by only a few degrees or feet in camera position – they are so close that only by putting frame stills side by side can they be distinguished. This shows that, rather than having a viewpoint determined by the space he is going to photograph, Perret chooses where best to put his camera for the precise function of the shot in the sequence. His set-ups are determined not by his spaces but by his shots – unlike Sjöström and also Feuillade, but also unlike Griffith, for whom a set or space dictates a viewpoint. Perret soon left for America, and European film-making did not develop along these lines in general, but the example suggests that deep space and 'cutting around', the dominant style of scene construction in American and eventually European cinema, are not necessarily incompatible; and so does the American example of Biograph and Vitagraph.

Postscript November 1984

Given that I saw at the Perpignan conference (September 1984) many films that I had been unable to see before this chapter was written, I should like to add some clarifications and modifications to my theses. In the main, I am reasonably pleased that these films confirmed those theses, but there is one point, at least, on which I think I need to make a correction. The chapter implies too strongly that *La Mort du duc de Guise* was the *fons et origo* of the low camera. In fact, given the technical versatility of the primitive cinema, it would be surprising were there not, before 1905, some films revealing the use of such a low camera. And indeed, in *A Chess Dispute* (R. W. Paul, 1903), the camera is at the level of the chess board between the two protagonists and slightly tilted up, emphasising the space off below the screen in which most of the action occurs. Even in multi-shot narrative films it is clear that there were film-makers and production companies who used a below-eye-level position before 1908, and, in particular, that in Pathé films between 1905 and 1908 there are more and more shots taken from lower and lower positions. To trace this evolution in detail would demand the precise chronology of Pathé production in these years that we still lack (although Emmanuelle Toulet's contribution to the conference indicates we can hope to have it soon[12]). Nevertheless, the films I have seen suggest the following milestones. First, in location shots, Pathé film-makers began to demonstrate a certain flexibility as to the level of the camera and to tilting. (In locations, especially rural ones, which have few vertical lines, the problem of the convergence of verticals is much smaller than in a three-wall set.) For example, in *Les*

Chiens contrebandiers (1906), there are several slightly tilted-down shots, in one case without the dogs appearing in the shot as a motivation. Second, shots of seated characters with the camera at their eye level give rise to fairly frequent moments with the camera at chest height, given that in such shots it is very common for the characters to be standing for some part of the time. Finally, there are at least two films which appear in the 1907 catalogue in which there are shots taken from a really low position: *Un Drame à Venise* and *Le Tour du monde d'un policier*. In most of the studio shots representing exteriors in these films, the camera is very slightly below eye level, but in the first shot of *Un Drame à Venise* it is at a seated character's waist level, and in *Le Tour du monde d'un policier*, there is one location shot (at the entrance to the Gare de Lyon) in which the camera is at waist level, and a studio-shot interior (the last scene of the story, before the apotheosis) in which the camera is at waist level despite the fact that the characters are standing for most of the scene. Thus, like many other features of *La Mort du duc de Guise* which impressed and influenced contemporary film-makers (e.g. the distribution of an action across a variety of rooms and a corresponding variety of shots), the low camera seems to be the systematic and emphatic development of a trend in current Pathé practice.

I should also like to stress something I mentioned in passing, the fact that, although at Pathé and at the companies within its orbit (Film d'Art, SCAGL), the low camera became the norm around 1910 and got even lower around 1914, Gaumont films, while sharing most of the other tendencies deriving from *La Mort du duc de Guise*, retain a high camera, often at eye level or only a little below. Deeper sets are handled in two ways. Where the scene presents a large number of characters, as in biblical or historical subjects (e.g. *Le Huguenot* (1909) and *Le Festin de Balthasar* (1910)), but also in the ball scenes in the 'Fantômas' series, the camera remains further back from the scene, and a confusion of heads centre screen is avoided by the use of sets with stairs, ramps and various levels (almost all the big sets in *Le Roman d'un mousse* are split-level ones of this kind). In the more intimate sets of modern domestic subjects with fewer characters (notably the 'Scènes de la vie telle qu'elle est' such as *Les Vipères* (1911), and *Le Roi Lear du village* (1911), but also most of the interiors in the 'Fantômas' series), the camera is closer but slightly tilted down, so that the foreground figures are shown head to foot, all the heads are in the top quarter of the screen, and there is a lot of floor visible. It is the position of the feet rather than that of the heads that indicates the depth of placing of the characters.

Where Gaumont production in the 1910s is concerned, I now feel that the very axiometric style with one set-up per space I attributed to Feuillade may perhaps be rather the effect of a difference in genres. In Feuillade's own films, this very rigid style is found in crime subjects (e.g. *L'Oubliette* (1912), *L'Intruse* (1913), and the 'Fantômas' series), whereas the 'Scènes de la vie telle qu'elle est' reveal much more flexibility, *Le Destin des mères*, for example, using four oblique camera set-ups for a single space. But Feuillade is far from taking this tendency to the point attained by his colleague Perret in *Le Roman d'un mousse*.

One last point about camera position. *Les Victimes de l'alcoölisme*, directed by Gérard Bourgeois for Pathé in 1911, uses the typical low Pathé position, but combines it with a slight tilt *up*. This is perhaps why its deep staging so impressed Georges Sadoul, for the result is that the floor is almost never visible (except in location exteriors and in the very last shots of the film), and characters in medium long shot hang in the air between the spectator and the backdrop. It should, however, be said that the print screened at the conference (deriving from a 28 mm Pathé-Kok version) looked cropped, resulting in closer framings than there would have been in an original 35 mm release print.

Notes

1. This article was first presented as a paper at a conference on early French cinema organised by the Institut Jean Vigo and held at Perpignan in September 1984. It was modified as here for the publication of the proceedings of the conference as Pierre Guibbert (ed.), *Les Premiers Ans du cinéma français* (Perpignan: Institut Jean Vigo, 1985).
2. Cf. Stephen Bottomore, 'Dreyfus and documentary', *Sight and Sound*, vol. 53 no. 4, Autumn 1984, pp. 290–3.
3. When I mention a non-French example without further comment, it is because I do not know or cannot recall a French equivalent, but have no reason to suspect it might not exist.
4. Now, since the conference, I can add the example of *Erreur tragique*, directed for Gaumont by Louis Feuillade and released in 1913.
5. It consists of the first five shots in the print held by the National Film Archive, London, bearing the title *Revolution in Russia*. The next eight shots correspond to the description in the 1907 Pathé catalogue of the subject *La Révolution en Russie*, and the length of all thirteen shots (402 ft) is greater than that given for *La Révolution en Russie* (262 ft), but is close to that length plus that of *Les Troubles de Saint Pétersbourg* (130 ft) or that of *La Révolution russe* (148 ft). The catalogue gives no description of the last; for *Les Troubles de Saint Pétersbourg* it has (literally translated): 'Disturbances in St. Petersburg. Fanaticism and Superstition. The demonstrators set out. Legal Crime.' Cf. *Cinéma 1900–1906* (Brussels: FIAF, 1982), vol. 2, catalogue no. F317, and Alain Lacasse and Andrée Michaud, 'Ambitions et limites d'une filmographie' and 'Fiche signalétique/ Découpage technique: *La Révolution en Russie* (1905)', in Guibbert, *Les Premiers Ans*, pp. 248–66.
6. When the titles of French films are given in a language other than French in this article, it is because the original French title is unknown; the non-French title is that under which it is catalogued in the archive holding a copy.
7. I use this form, found in the main title of all prints of the film that I have seen, rather than the more familiar *L'Assassinat du duc de Guise*, although it seems that the latter was being used even before the film was premièred. Richard Abel tells me that a wartime re-release used the title *La Mort* . . ., and it may be that extant prints derive from material prepared for this re-release.
8. See the frame-stills reproduced in 'L'Assassinat du duc de Guise', *L'Avant-Scène Cinéma*, no. 334, November 1984, pp. 57–72.
9. Barry Salt, 'L'espace d'à côté', in Guibbert, *Les Premiers Ans*, pp. 198–203.
10. Shallow-staged in interiors, I should say. In exteriors, Griffith liked broad prospects with the characters silhouetted against a distant background of mountains or sea, often populated with extras. But the action itself still tends to be shallow-staged. In *The Coming of Angelo* (1913), for example, when Gudio sees his fiancée kissing Angelo on the beach, although the kiss is shot from a high cliff in very long shot, Gudio as witness to this kiss is shot in separate medium long shots looking laterally offscreen left, and he, too, is down on the beach. It is not hard to imagine the deep staging Feuillade would

have used for such an incident (cf. *Le Destin des mères* (1911), where the mother sees her fiancé kissing her daughter, the scene being shot with the mother in the foreground and the kissing couple outside the window in the rear).

11. Except perhaps *La Mort de Mozart* (directed by Feuillade for Gaumont, 1909). This film has only one set and one set-up on it, the sole variation consisting of the matting in over part of the frame of scenes imagined or remembered by the dying Mozart, each scene corresponding to a famous piece of his music.
12. Emmanuelle Toulet, 'Une année de l'édition cinématographique: 1909', in Guibbert, *Les Premiers Ans*, pp. 133–42.

The Cinema of Attractions
Early Film, Its Spectator and the Avant-Garde

TOM GUNNING

Writing in 1922, flushed with the excitement of seeing Abel Gance's *La Roue*, Fernand Léger tried to define something of the radical possibilities of the cinema. The potential of the new art did not lie in 'imitating the movements of nature' or in 'the mistaken path' of its resemblance to theatre. Its unique power was a 'matter of *making images seen*'.[1] It is precisely this harnessing of visibility, this act of showing and exhibition, which I feel cinema before 1906 displays most intensely. Its inspiration for the avant-garde of the early decades of this century needs to be re-explored.

Writings by the early modernists (Futurists, Dadaists and Surrealists) on the cinema follow a pattern similar to Léger: enthusiasm for this new medium and its possibilities; and disappointment at the way it has already developed, its enslavement to traditional art forms, particularly theatre and literature. This fascination with the *potential* of a medium (and the accompanying fantasy of rescuing the cinema from its enslavement to alien and passé forms) can be understood from a number of viewpoints. I want to use it to illuminate a topic I have also approached before, the strangely heterogeneous relation that film before 1906 (or so) bears to the films that follow, and the way a taking account of this heterogeneity signals a new conception of film history and film form. My work in this area has been pursued in collaboration with André Gaudreault.[2]

The history of early cinema, like the history of cinema generally, has been written and theorized under the hegemony of narrative films. Early filmmakers like Smith, Méliès and Porter have been studied primarily from the viewpoint of their contribution to film as a storytelling medium, particularly the evolution of narrative editing. Although such approaches are not totally misguided, they are one-sided and potentially distort both the work of these filmmakers and the actual forces shaping cinema before 1906. A few observations will indicate the way that early cinema was not dominated by the narrative impulse that later asserted its sway over the medium. First there is the extremely important role that actuality film plays in early film production. Investigation of the films copyrighted in the US shows that actuality films outnumbered fictional films until 1906.[3] The Lumière tradition of 'placing the world within one's reach' through travel films and topicals did not disappear with the exit of the Cinématographe from film production. But even within non-actuality filming – what has sometimes been referred to as the 'Méliès tradition' – the role narrative plays is quite different from in traditional narrative film. Méliès himself declared in discussing his working method:

> As for the scenario, the 'fable,' or 'tale,' I only consider it at the end. I can state that the scenario constructed in this manner has *no importance*, since I use it merely as a pretext for the 'stage effects,' the 'tricks,' or for a nicely arranged tableau.[4]

Whatever differences one might find between Lumière and Méliès, they should not represent the opposition between narrative and non-narrative film-making, at least as it is understood today. Rather, one can unite them in a conception that sees cinema less as a way of telling stories than as a way of presenting a series of views to an audience, fascinating because of their illusory power (whether the realistic illusion of motion offered to the first audiences by Lumière, or the magical illusion concocted by Méliès), and exoticism. In other words, I believe that the relation to the spectator set up by the films of both Lumière and Méliès (and many other film-makers before 1906) had a common basis, and one that differs from the primary spectator relations set up by narrative film after 1906. I will call this earlier conception of cinema, 'the cinema of attractions'. I believe that this conception dominates cinema until about 1906–7. Although different from the fascination in storytelling exploited by the cinema from the time of Griffith, it is not necessarily opposed to it. In fact the cinema of attractions does not disappear with the dominance of narrative, but rather goes underground, both into certain avant-garde practices and as a component of narrative films, more evident in some genres (e.g. the musical) than in others.

What precisely is the cinema of attractions? First, it is a cinema that bases itself on the quality that Léger celebrated: its ability to *show* something. Contrasted to the voyeuristic aspect of narrative cinema analysed by Christian Metz,[5] this is an exhibitionist cinema. An aspect of early cinema which I have written about in other articles is emblematic of this different relationship the cinema of attractions constructs with its spectator: the recurring look at the camera by actors. This action, which is later perceived as spoiling the realistic illusion of the cinema, is here undertaken with brio, establishing contact with the audience. From comedians smirking at the camera, to the constant bowing and gesturing of the conjurors in magic films, this is a cinema that displays its visibility, willing to rupture a self-enclosed fictional world for a chance to solicit the attention of the spectator.

Exhibitionism becomes literal in the series of erotic films which play an important role in early film production (the same Pathé catalogue would advertise the Passion Play along with 'scènes grivoises d'un caractère piquant', erotic films often including full nudity), also driven underground in later years. As Noël Burch has shown in his film *Correction Please: How We Got into Pictures* (1979). a film like *The Bride Retires* (France, 1902) reveals a fundamental conflict between this exhibitionistic tendency of early film and the creation of a fictional diegesis. A woman undresses for bed while her new husband peers at her from behind a screen. However, it is to the camera and the audience that the bride addresses her erotic striptease, winking at us as she faces us, smiling in erotic display.

As the quote from Méliès points out, the trick film, perhaps the dominant non-actuality film genre before 1906, is itself a series of displays, of magical attractions, rather than a primitive sketch of narrative continuity. Many trick films are, in effect, plotless, a series of transformations strung together with little connection and certainly no characterization. But to approach even the plotted trick films, such as *Voyage dans la lune* (1902), simply as precursors of later narrative structures is to miss the point. The story simply provides a frame upon which to string a demonstration of the magical possibilities of the cinema.

Modes of exhibition in early cinema also reflect this lack of concern with creating a self-sufficient narrative world upon the screen. As Charles Musser has sown,[6] the early showmen exhibitors exerted a great deal of control over the shows they presented, actually re-editing the films they had purchased and supplying a series of offscreen supplements, such as sound effects and spoken commentary. Perhaps most extreme is the Hale's Tours, the largest chain of theatres exclusively showing films before 1906. Not only did the films consist of non-narrative sequences taken from moving vehicles (usually trains), but the theatre itself was arranged as a train car with a conductor who took tickets, and sound effects simulating the click-clack of wheels and hiss of air brakes.[7] Such viewing experiences relate more to the attractions of the fairground than to the traditions of the legitimate theatre. The relation between films and the emergence of the great amusement parks, such as Coney Island, at the turn of the century provides rich ground for rethinking the roots of early cinema.

Nor should we ever forget that in the earliest years of exhibition the cinema itself was an attraction. Early audiences went to exhibitions to see machines demonstrated (the newest technological wonder, following in the wake of such widely exhibited machines and marvels as X-rays or, earlier, the phonograph), rather than to view films. It was the Cinématographe, the Biograph or the Vitascope that were advertised on the variety bills in which they premièred, not *Le Déjeuner de bébé* or *The Black Diamond Express*. After the initial novelty period, this display of the possibilities of cinema continues, and not only in magic films. Many of the close-ups in early film differ from later uses of the technique precisely because they do not use enlargement for narrative punctuation, but as an attraction in its own right. The close-up cut into Porter's *The Gay Shoe Clerk* (1903) may anticipate later continuity techniques, but its principal motive is again pure exhibitionism, as the lady lifts her skirt hem, exposing her ankle for all to see. Biograph films such as *Photographing a Female Crook* (1904) and *Hooligan in Jail* (1903) consist of a single shot in which the camera is brought close to the main character, until they are in mid-shot. The enlargement is not a device expressive of narrative tension; it is in itself an attraction and the point of the film.[8]

To summarise, the cinema of attractions directly solicits spectator attention, inciting visual curiosity, and supplying pleasure through an exciting spectacle – a unique event, whether fictional or documentary, that is of interest in itself. The attraction to be displayed may also be of a cinematic nature, such as the early close-ups just described, or trick films in which a cinematic manipulation (slow motion, reverse motion, substitution, multiple exposure) provides the film's novelty. Fictional situations tend to be restricted to gags, vaudeville numbers or recreations of shocking or curious incidents (executions, current events). It is the direct address of the audience, in which an attraction is offered to the spectator by a cinema showman, that defines this approach to film making. Theatrical display dominates over narrative absorption, emphasizing the direct stimulation of shock or surprise at the expense of unfolding a story or creating a diegetic universe. The cinema of attractions expends little energy creating characters with psychological motivations or individual personality. Making use of both fictional and non-fictional attractions, its energy moves outward towards an acknowledged spectator rather than inward towards the character-based situations essential to classical narrative.

The term 'attractions' comes, of course, from the young Sergei Mikhailovich Eisenstein and his attempt to find a new model and mode of analysis for the theatre. In his search for the 'unit of impression' of theatrical art, the foundation of an analysis which would undermine realistic representational theatre, Eisenstein hit upon the term 'attraction'.[9] An attraction aggressively subjected the spectator to 'sensual or psychological impact'. According to Eisenstein, theatre should consist of a montage of such attractions, creating a relation to the spectator entirely different from his absorption in 'illusory depictions'.[10] I pick up this term partly to underscore the relation to the spectator that this later avant-garde practice shares with early cinema: that of exhibitionist confrontation rather than diegetic absorption. Of course the 'experimentally regulated and mathematically calculated' montage of attractions demanded by Eisenstein differs enormously from these early films (as any conscious and oppositional mode of practice will from a popular one).[11] However, it is important to realize the context from which Eisenstein selected the term. Then, as now, the 'attraction' was a term of the fairground, and for Eisenstein and his friend Yutkevich it primarily represented their favourite fairground attraction, the roller coaster, or as it was known then in Russia, the American Mountains.[12]

The source is significant. The enthusiasm of the early avant-garde for film was at least partly an enthusiasm for a mass culture that was emerging at the beginning of the century, offering a new sort of stimulus for an audience not acculturated to the traditional arts. It is important to take this enthusiasm for popular art as something more than a simple gesture to *épater les bourgeois*. The enormous development of the entertainment industry since the 1910s and its growing acceptance by middle-class culture (and the accommodation that made this acceptance possible) have made it difficult to understand the liberation popular entertainment offered at the beginning of the century. I believe that it was precisely the exhibitionist quality of turn-of-the-century popular art that made it attractive to the avant-garde – its freedom from the creation of a diegesis, its accent on direct stimulation.

Writing of the variety theatre, Marinetti not only praised its aesthetics of astonishment and stimulation, but particularly its creation of a new spectator who contrasts with the 'static', 'stupid voyeur' of traditional theatre. The spectator at the variety theatre feels directly addressed by the spectacle and joins in, singing along, heckling the comedians.[13] Dealing with early cinema within the context of archive and academy, we risk missing its vital relation to vaudeville, its primary place of exhibition until around 1905. Film appeared as one attraction on the vaudeville programme, surrounded by a mass of unrelated acts in a non-narrative and even nearly illogical succession of performances. Even when presented in the nickelodeons that were emerging at the end of this period, these short films always appeared in a variety format, trick films sandwiched in with farces, actualities, 'illustrated songs', and, quite frequently, cheap vaudeville acts. It was precisely this non-narrative variety that placed this form of entertainment under attack by reform groups in the early 1910s. The Russell Sage Survey of popular entertainments found vaudeville 'depends upon an artificial rather than a natural human and developing interest, these acts having no necessary and as a rule, no actual connection'.[14] In other words, no narrative. A night at the variety theatre was like a ride on a streetcar or an active day in a crowded city, according to this middle-class reform group, stimulating an unhealthy nervousness. It was precisely such artificial stimulus that Marinetti and Eisenstein wished to borrow from the popular arts and inject into the theatre, organizing popular energy for radical purpose.

What happened to the cinema of attractions? The period from 1907 to about 1913 represents the true *narrativization* of the cinema, culminating in the appearance of feature films which radically revised the variety format. Film clearly took the legitimate theatre as its model, producing famous players in famous plays. The transformation of filmic discourse that D. W. Griffith typifies bound cinematic signifiers to the narration of stories and the creation of a self-enclosed diegetic universe. The look at the camera becomes taboo and the devices of cinema are transformed from playful 'tricks' – cinematic attractions (Méliès gesturing at us to watch the lady vanish) – to elements of dramatic expression, entries into the psychology of character and the world of fiction.

However, it would be too easy to see this as a Cain and Abel story, with narrative strangling the nascent possibilities of a young iconoclastic form of entertainment. Just as the variety format in some sense survived in the movie palaces of the 20s (with newsreel, cartoon, sing-along, orchestra performance and sometimes vaudeville acts subordinated to, but still coexisting with, the narrative *feature* of the evening), the system of attraction remains an essential part of popular film-making.

The chase film shows how, towards the end of this period (basically from 1903 to 1906), a synthesis of attractions and narrative was already underway. The chase had been the original truly narrative genre of the cinema, providing a model for causality and linearity as well as a basic editing continuity. A film like Biograph's *Personal* (1904, the model for the chase film in many ways) shows the creation of a narrative linearity, as the French nobleman runs for his life from the fiancées his personal column ad has unleashed. However, at the same time, as the group of young women pursue their prey towards the camera in each shot, they encounter some slight obstacle (a fence, a steep slope, a stream) that slows them down for the spectator, providing a mini-spectacle pause in the unfolding of narrative. The Edison Company seemed particularly aware of this, since they offered their plagiarized version of this Biograph film

(*How a French Nobleman Got a Wife Through the New York Herald 'Personal' Columns*) in two forms, as a complete film or as separate shots, so that any one image of the ladies chasing the man could be bought without the inciting incident or narrative closure.[15]

As Laura Mulvey has shown in a very different context, the dialectic between spectacle and narrative has fuelled much of the classical cinema.[16] Donald Crafton in his study of slapstick comedy, 'The pie and the chase', has shown the way slapstick did a balancing act between the pure spectacle of gag and the development of narrative.[17] Likewise, the traditional spectacle film proved true to its name by highlighting moments of pure visual stimulation along with narrative. The 1924 version of *Ben Hur* was in fact shown at a Boston theatre with a timetable announcing the moment of its prime attractions:

8.35 *The Star of Bethlehem*
8.40 *Jerusalem Restored*
8.59 *Fall of the House of Hur*
10.29 *The Last Supper*
10.50 *Reunion*[18]

The Hollywood advertising policy of enumerating the features of a film, each emblazoned with the command, 'See!' shows this primal power of the attraction running beneath the armature of narrative regulation.

We seem far from the avant-garde premises with which this discussion of early cinema began. But it is important for the radical heterogeneity which I find in early cinema not to be conceived as a truly oppositional programme, one irreconcilable with the growth of narrative cinema. This view is too sentimental and too ahistorical. A film like *The Great Train Robbery* (1903) does point in both directions, towards a direct assault on the spectator (the spectacularly enlarged outlaw unloading his pistol in our faces), and towards a linear narrative continuity. This is early film's ambiguous heritage. Clearly in some sense recent spectacle cinema has reaffirmed its roots in stimulus and carnival rides, in what might be called the Spielberg-Lucas-Coppola cinema of effects.

But effects are tamed attractions. Marinetti and Eisenstein understood that they were tapping into a source of energy that would need focusing and intensification to fulfil its revolutionary possibilities. Both Eisenstein and Marinetti planned to exaggerate the impact on the spectators, Marinetti proposing to literally glue them to their seats (ruined garments paid for after the performance) and Eisenstein setting firecrackers off beneath them. Every change in film history implies a change in its address to the spectator, and each period constructs its spectator in a new way. Now in a period of American avant-garde cinema in which the tradition of contemplative subjectivity has perhaps run its (often glorious) course, it is possible that this earlier carnival of the cinema, and the methods of popular entertainment, still provide an unexhausted resource – a Coney Island of the avant-garde, whose never dominant but always sensed current can be traced from Méliès through Keaton, through *Un Chien andalou* (1928), and Jack Smith.

Notes

First published in *Wide Angle* vol. 8 no. 3/4, Fall 1986.

1. Fernand Léger, 'A critical essay on the plastic qualities of Abel Gance's film *The Wheel*', in Edward Fry (ed.), *Functions of Painting*, trans. Alexandra Anderson (New York: Viking Press, 1973), p. 21.
2. See my articles 'The non-continuous style of early film', in Roger Holman (ed.), *Cinema 1900–1906* (Brussels: FIAF, 1982), and 'An unseen energy swallows space: the space in early film and its relation to American avant garde film' in John L. Fell (ed.), *Film Before Griffith* (Berkeley: University of California Press, 1983), pp. 355–66, and our collaborative paper delivered by A. Gaudreault at the conference at Cerisy on Film History (August 1985) 'Le cinéma des premiers temps: un défi à l'histoire du cinéma?'. I would also like to note the importance of my discussions with Adam Simon and our hope to investigate further the history and archaeology of the film spectator.
3. Robert C. Allen, *Vaudeville and Film: 1895–1915, A Study in Media Interaction* (New York: Arno Press, 1980), pp. 159, 212–13.
4. Méliès, 'Importance du scénario', in Georges Sadoul, *Georges Méliès* (Paris: Seghers, 1961), p. 118 (my translation).
5. Metz, *The Imaginary Signifier: Psychoanalysis and the Cinema*, trans. Celia Britton, Annwyl Williams, Ben Brewster and Alfred Guzzetti (Bloomington: Indiana University Press, 1982), particularly pp. 58–80, 91–7.
6. Musser, 'American Vitagraph 1897–1901', *Cinema Journal*, vol. 22 no. 3, Spring 1983, p. 10.
7. Raymond Fielding, 'Hale's tours: Ultrarealism in the pre-1910 motion picture', in Fell, *Film Before Griffith*, pp. 116–30.
8. I wish to thank Ben Brewster for his comments after the original delivery of this paper which pointed out the importance of including this aspect of the cinema of attractions here.
9. Eisenstein, 'How I became a film director', in *Notes of a Film Director* (Moscow: Foreign Language Publishing House, n.d.), p. 16.
10. 'The montage of attractions', in S. M. Eisenstein, *Writings 1922–1934*, edited by Richard Taylor (London: BFI, 1988), p. 35.
11. Ibid.
12. Yon Barna, *Eisenstein* (Bloomington: Indiana University Press, 1973), p. 59.
13. 'The variety theater 1913' in Umbro Apollonio (ed.), *Futurist Manifestos* (New York: Viking Press, 1973), p. 127.
14. Michael Davis, *The Exploitation of Pleasure* (New York: Russell Sage Foundation, Dept. of Child Hygiene, Pamphlet, 1911).
15. David Levy, 'Edison sales policy and the continuous action film 1904–1906', in Fell, *Film Before Griffith*, pp. 207–22.
16. 'Visual pleasure and narrative cinema', in Laura Mulvey, *Visual and Other Pleasures* (London: Macmillan, 1989).
17. Paper delivered at the FIAF Conference on Slapstick, May 1985, New York City.
18. Nicholas Vardac, *From Stage to Screen: Theatrical Method from Garrick to Griffith* (New York: Benjamin Blom, 1968), p. 232.

Let There Be Lumière

DAI VAUGHAN

To look critically and sympathetically at the beginnings of cinema – at those programmes of one-minute scenes first publicly exhibited in Paris in December 1895, and in London the following February – is like pondering what happened to the universe in the first few microseconds after the big bang.

We need not doubt that, so far as the genesis of film art is concerned, these shows mounted by the Lumière brothers represent the nearest we will find to a singularity. Before then, notwithstanding such precedents as the photographic analysis of animal movement by Marey and Muybridge, the public projection of animated drawings in Reynaud's Théâtre Optique or anticipations of film narrative methods in comic strip and lantern slide sequence, cinema did not exist. A story so frequently repeated as to have assumed the status of folklore tells how members of the first audiences dodged aside as a train steamed towards them into a station. We cannot seriously imagine that these educated people in Paris and London expected the train to emerge from the screen and run them down. It must have been a reaction similar to that which prevents us from stepping with unconcern on to a static escalator, no matter how firmly we may assure ourselves that all it requires is a simple stride on to an immobile flat surface. What this legend means is that the particular combination of visual signals present in that film had had no previous existence *other* than as signifying a real train pulling into a real station.

Yet already, in this primitive world, we find structures tantalisingly prophetic of some we know today. Compare the *Workers Leaving the Lumière Factory*, few of whom return our gaze with even a glance from the screen, with the members disembarking from a river-boat for the *Congress of Photographic Societies at Neuville-sur-Saône*, who greet the camera with much waving and doffing of headgear. Do we not see here that distinction, much a part of our television experience, between those who wield the power of communication and those who do not; between those granted subjectivity and those held in objectivity by the media?

Perhaps we should examine more closely the recorded responses of the earliest viewers. A curious example is offered in Stanley Reed's commentary to the BFI's sound version of the first British Lumière programme. This ended with *A Boat Leaving Harbour*; and we are told that visitors came forward after the performance to poke at the screen with their walking sticks, convinced that it must be made of glass and conceal a tank of water. While we may allow this to pass as a measure of the wonderment caused by the first cinematographic projections, it becomes on consideration rather puzzling. How could people have supposed that the screen concealed a tank when it would also, by the same supposition, have had to conceal a garden, a railway station, a factory and various other edifices? Yet I believe that this story, like the one about the train, is telling us something important.

A Boat Leaving Harbour does, even today, stand out among the early Lumière subjects. (Indeed, an ulterior motive behind this article is my desire to pay tribute to a film I have loved since first encountering it some thirty years ago.) The action is simple. A rowing boat, with two men at the oars and one at the tiller, is entering boldly from the right foreground; and it proceeds, for fifty-odd seconds, towards the left background. On the tip of the jetty, which juts awkwardly into frame on the right, stand a child or two in frilly white and two women in black. Light shimmers on the water, though the sky seems leaden. The swell is not heavy; but as the boat passes beyond the jetty, leaving the protection of the harbour mouth, it is slewed around and caught broadside-on by the waves. The men are in difficulties; and one woman turns her attention from the children to look at them. There it ends. Yet every time I have seen this film I have been overwhelmed by a sense of the *potentiality* of the medium: as if it had just been invented and lay waiting still to be explored.

I do not think it is just the Tennysonian resonances – crossing the bar, and so forth – which invest this episode with nostalgia for cinema's lost beginnings: a nostalgia which one would expect to be prompted equally, if at all, by the other items in the programme. One thing which will be obvious even from this brief description is that the subject could not possibly have been simulated in an indoor tank. So why *were* those early visitors poking at the screen with their sticks? A superficially similar reaction, this time to Edison's 'kinetoscope', is quoted in the first volume of Georges Sadoul's *Histoire générale du cinéma*. The kinetoscope was an individual viewing-box which ran continuous bands of film, the subjects being photographed by daylight in a blackened studio which could be revolved to face the sun; and in 1894 Henri de Parville wrote of it in *Les Annales politiques et littéraires*: 'Tous les acteurs sont en mouvement. Leurs moindres actes sont si naturellement reproduits qu'on se demande s'il y a illusion.' What he presumably meant by 'illusion' was some system by which the images of live actors might have been brought by mirrors under the eyepiece of the machine. But it is clear that the relevance of this lies not in similarity but in contrast; for there was no way that the image of a French harbour could have been reflected by mirrors into the auditorium of the Regent Street Polytechnic. The gentlemen with the walking sticks were not trying to discover how the trick worked. Their concern was not that they might have been victims of an illusion, but that they had experienced something which transcended the cosy world of illusionism altogether.

We need look no further than Sadoul's standard *Histoire générale* for evidence of the fact that what most impressed the early audiences was what would now be considered the incidentals of scenes: smoke from a forge, steam from a locomotive, brick-dust from a demolished wall. Georges Méliès, a guest at the first Paris performance (who was soon to become a pioneer of trick filming), made particular mention of the rustling of leaves in the background of *Le Déjeuner de bébé* – a detail which, as Sadoul observes, would scarcely be remarked today. It is worth asking why this should be so – and why, by implication, we consider Lumière cinema and Edison not: for surely, it might be argued, what mattered was the photographic rendering of movement, regardless of what moved. Sadoul entitles his chapter on Lumière 'La nature même prise sur le fait'; and Stanley Reed points out that audiences had hitherto been familiar only with the painted backdrops of the theatre. But to put it this way round is to understate the most revealing aspect: that people were startled not so much by the phenomenon of the moving photograph, which its inventors had struggled long to achieve, as by its ability to portray spontaneities of which the theatre was not capable. The movements of photographed people were accepted without demur because they were perceived as performance, as simply a new mode of self-projection; but that the inanimate should participate in self-projection was astonishing.

Most of the people in the Lumière show are either performing for the camera – whether knocking down walls or feeding babies – or engaged in such neutral activities as leaving the factory or alighting from a train. What is different about *A Boat Leaving Harbour* is that, when the boat is threatened by the waves, the men must apply their efforts to controlling it; and, by responding to the challenge of the spontaneous moment, they become integrated into its spontaneity. The unpredictable has not only emerged from the background to occupy the greater portion of the frame; it has also taken sway over the principals. Man, no longer the mountebank self-presenter, has become equal with the leaves and the brick-dust – and as miraculous.

But such an invasion of the spontaneous into the human arts, being unprecedented, must have assumed the character of a threat not only to the 'performers' but to the whole idea of controlled, willed, obedient communication. And conversely, since the idea of communication had in the past been inseparable from the assumption of willed control, this invasion must have seemed a veritable doubling-back of the world into its own imagery, a denial of the order of a coded system: an escape of the represented from the representational act. Thus what the early audiences suspected was not the presence of a water-tank but the presence, in some metaphysical sense, of the sea itself: a sea liberated from the laboriousness of painted highlights and the drudgeries of metaphor. And their prodding of the screen was comparable with our own compulsion to reach out and 'touch' a hologram.

If this helps to explain why, in 1896, a representation of the sea should have caused greater bemusement than those of a factory or railway station, it does not explain why *A Boat Leaving Harbour* should have retained its fascination for almost a hundred years. To understand this, we must turn the other way: not towards a notional first moment but towards the future already latent in Lumière. The earliest programme contained an episode, *L'Arroseur arrosé*, which is generally considered to mark the initiation of screen narrative. A man is watering a garden; a boy puts his foot on the hose and stops the jet; the gardener peers into the nozzle; and the boy removes his foot so that the gardener is squirted in the face. But is this a fiction film or simply a filmed fiction?

One answer would be that the fiction film comes into being only when the articulations of camera movement and editing form an inalienable component of the narration. Another, slightly more sophisticated, would be that the distinction is meaningless at this primitive level of organisation, and that *L'Arroseur arrosé* may be said to be filmed fiction and fiction film at once. But let us consider the question from the point of view of what seemed at the time the essential triumph of Lumière: the harnessing of spontaneity. It is clear how this applies to the men rowing the boat; but it is far from clear how it applies in the *Arroseur* episode.

At first it may seem that there are two simple alternatives: either this was an event observed in passing, perhaps with a concealed camera; or it was a scene staged by the film-maker with the complicity of both parties. Furthermore, the gaucheness of the performances suffices to resolve any doubt in favour of the latter, thus perhaps leading us – our definition swallowing its tail – to say that what we see is an *attempt* at a fiction film which, in so far as it is *perceived* only as an attempt, reverts to the spontaneous. But it is not so easy. Suppose, for example, that the camera had been set up only to record the garden-watering, and that the boy had played his trick unprompted; or that the boy and the cameraman had been in collusion to trick the gardener; or the boy and the gardener in collusion to surprise the cameraman.... Spontaneity begins to seem, in human affairs, a matter less of behaviour than of motivations – and of transactions in which the part of the mountebank *behind* the camera cannot long be excluded from question. 'Spontaneity', that is to say, comes down to what is not predictable by – and not under the control of – the film-maker. As for the gaucherie, it is arguable that flawless performances would have given us not true fiction but mendacious actuality.

Fiction film arises at precisely the point where people tire of these riddles. As audiences settle for appearances, according the film's images the status of dream or fantasy whose links with a prior world are assumed to have been severed if they ever existed, film falls into place as a signifying system whose articulations may grow ever more complex. True, the movement of leaves remains unpredictable; but we know that, with the endless possibility of retakes open to the film-maker, what was unplanned is nevertheless what has been chosen. Even in documentary, which seeks to respect the provenance of its images, they are bent inexorably to foreign purpose. The 'big bang' leaves only a murmur of background radiation, detectable whenever someone decides that a film will gain in realism by being shot on 'real' locations or where the verisimilitude of a Western is enhanced, momentarily, by the unscripted whinny of a horse.

A Boat Leaving Harbour begins without purpose and ends without conclusion, its actors drawn into the contingency of events. Successive viewings serve only to stress its pathetic brevity as a fragment of human experience. It survives as a reminder of that moment when the question of spontaneity was posed and not yet found to be insoluble: when cinema seemed free, not only of its proper connotations, but of the threat of its absorption into meanings beyond it. Here is the secret of its beauty. The promise of this film remains untarnished because it is a promise which can never be kept; its every fulfilment is also its betrayal.

First published in *Sight and Sound*, Spring 1981.

Film, Narrative, Narration
The Cinema of the Lumière Brothers
ANDRÉ GAUDREAULT

There is an expression which comes up frequently in debates and commentaries on film. I would like to discuss it here, with particular reference to films made when the cinema was at its very beginning. The expression is 'filmic narrative'. So obvious does it seem, so much to be taken for granted, that its appropriateness is hardly ever questioned. Of course narratives are what the cinema presents. In any case, the privileged relationship between cinema and narrativity has often been observed.

But there are certain, very widespread, ways of using words which cause endless trouble to the narratologist of the cinema. An example is the usage whereby film-makers produce either narrative or non-narrative films. Surely films – all films – are always narrative, contrary to what is implied by this dichotomy? Surely films are all basically narrative, whatever else they are? What exactly are the 'frontiers' of the filmic 'narrative'?[1]

These are some of the crucial questions which we face as we attempt to grasp the real properties and parameters of the filmic narrative. These properties and parameters deserve the narratologist's attention, if only because it is due to them that an art of 'representation' has effortlessly acquired an unchallenged narrative status which is sometimes systematically denied to the theatre, a 'representative' art *par excellence*, although the two have many characteristics in common. It seems more natural to group the cinema with the theatre than the novel, for example. But conventional wisdom credits the cinema and the novel with a capability which it often denies to the theatre: narrativity.[2]

What exactly should be required of a text (in the broad sense) for it to be granted the status of narrative? While narratologists do not all agree on the subject, certain basic principles have been identified. In my view Claude Brémond gives a good definition of them in *Logique du récit*,[3] when he tries to set out the minimal conditions in which a message can be said to convey a narrative: 'The message should place a subject (either animate or inanimate) at a time t, then a time $t + n$, and what becomes of the subject at the moment $t + n$ should follow from the predicates characterising it at the moment t.'

This definition is clearly not very stringent and will not meet with unanimous approval, but in my view, by virtue of its very generality, it makes possible an objective approach to the question (both on the thorny issue of the anthropomorphism of any *actants*, which some regard as essential, and on the problem of defining events suitable for narration[4]). In any case, this is the definition which I intend to work from here.

When considering very early cinematographic works, one of the first questions that narratologists may legitimately raise is whether or not they are narratives. Are the Lumière brothers' works narratives? A crucial question, which must be attempted if any progress is to be made in the study of the relationship between cinema and narrativity.

Before this apparently simple question can be answered, some distinctions must be established. Even if *La Sortie des usines Lumière* (1895) and *L'Arrivée d'un train en gare de la Ciotat* (1895) are narratives, their level of narrativity bears no comparison with that of *L'Arroseur arrosé* (1895). The action of the first of the three is easily summarised: the gates of a factory open to let the workers out, and then close again (length: about fifty seconds). The action is simple and contains no great surprises. Still, a searching analysis reveals some structuring, as Marshall Deutelbaum has shown:

> Less obvious, though even more intriguing is the way in which the film nearly returns the scene before the camera to the state at which it was when the film began. Both at the beginning and the close, the cinematic image offers only the exterior of the factory seen from the same point of view. So similar in appearance are these opening and closing images to one another, in fact, that if one were to loop the film into a continuous band, the action would appear to be a single periodic event.[5]

From this the author deduces that 'far from being a naive record of motion for its own sake, the film reflects a number of carefully chosen decisions about sequential narrative.'[6] Thus what he focuses on is the quality of the 'narrative content': the film opens, presents one action through to its conclusion, and then ends. Seeing them in this way, Deutelbaum regards the Lumière films as real little narrative 'gems', and wholly different from an Edison production for example: 'nothing akin to the presentational strategies discernible in the Lumière films lay behind the Edison productions.'[7] However useful this approach may be in Deutelbaum's framework of analysis, it will not help in the task of drawing a distinction between what is a cinematic narrative and what is not. Even when it is not normative, a qualitative analysis of narrative content can only constitute a second stage for those trying to define the minimal conditions of narrativity.[8] Otherwise there is a danger of merely differentiating between the various *kinds* of narratives.

A study of the two other Lumière films shows that each is an extreme case, to be placed one on either side of *La Sortie des usines*. On one side is *L'Arrivée d'un train*, which probably does not constitute a 'minimal complete plot', this requiring 'passage from one equilibrium to another', according to Tzvetan Todorov.[9] On the other side is *L'Arroseur arrosé*, one of the very first films to present a minimal complete plot – and perhaps this is why it has attracted so much notice. It may be summarised as follows: a young rogue steps on a hose which is being used by a gardener who, surprised to find that the flow of water has stopped, unwisely looks into the mouth of the pipe to see whether something has blocked it; at the same moment, the boy lifts his foot and the waterer is watered! The gardener runs after the boy who goes just out of frame, drags him back to centre screen and spanks him.[10] There can be no doubt that this is a minimal complete plot. It moves from an initial state of equilibrium (the gardener quietly getting on with his work) to one of disequilibrium (the young rogue disrupting the gardener's peace), then back to a final state of equilibrium (the gardener taking his revenge, after which he will be able to go back to work).

L'Arrivée d'un train, however, does not seem to present a complete plot (if only on account of its sudden ending: the train does not start off again). But is it a narrative? 'No' would seem to be the only answer to such a bald question about such a simple film (of a station where, after a few moments, a train arrives from the distance, stops and lets out a flood of passengers). What is told in it? Not much, admittedly. But in my view, some form of narrative, even if a muted one, is apparent in it: the action presented in the film fulfils all the conditions listed in Brémond's definition. There is a moment t, then a moment $t + n$, etc. There is a development: travellers become new arrivals and passersby become travellers. Sequence and transformation are certainly present. Although the 'plot' may not seem really complete and Todorov's state of disequilibrium may seem to predominate, I see it as a clear example of a narrative. Of course it does not move from one equilibrium to another, as *L'Arroseur arrosé* does, 'but a narrative may present only a portion of this trajectory.'[11] It is in fact a 'simple narrative', in the sense used by Greimas and Courtès:

> In view of the diversity of narrative forms, we wondered whether it was possible to define the *simple narrative*. Ultimately, this can be reduced to a sentence like 'Adam ate an apple'. This may be analysed as a transition from a former state (before the consumption) to a further state (following the consumption) effected by an action (or a process).[12]

'Adam ate an apple' is an apt example. Its narrative content must be wholly isomorphous to that of another Lumière film (apart from certain 'historical' connotations, of course!): *Déjeuner de bébé* (1895) must surely be the visual expression of the simple narrative (in Greimas and Courtès' sense), 'Lucie[13] (Lumière) eats her porridge.' (Incidentally, an essential difference is that I used the present tense in my verbal description of the simple narrative contained in the Lumière film, whereas Greimas and Courtès used the past in their example.) However laconic, it is a narrative none the less. The strict 'chronicity' of a narrative is precisely what characterises it as such. Once again, Brémond leaves no doubt: 'A report describing a sequence of events taking place in a certain period of time is surely, in the very literalness of its details, a complete and fully signifying narrative.'[14]

All the films mentioned so far have a characteristic in common: they are made up of only one shot. As I have been trying to show, all these shots are narratives. But does this mean that every shot must always, of necessity, be a narrative? From the point of view being developed here, I think this is the case. But the obvious problem is how to explain the essential difference which is bound to exist between a film like *L'Arroseur arrosé* and, for example, *Birth of a Nation* (D. W.

Griffith, 1915). Might the latter simply constitute an expansion of a structure which is technically present in the former? Is there merely a difference of quantity between the former, with its one-minute time-span, and the latter which lasts several hours? Are they both narratives in the same meaning of the word? Is it conceivable that as early as 1895, *L'Arroseur arrosé* should have achieved the narrative essence specific to the cinema? Not quite, I think. In my view, the narrative of, for example, *Birth of a Nation* is of a quite different order from that of *L'Arroseur arrosé* and the relationship between these two orders of narrative is far from being merely quantitative.

It seems, then, that any film comprising one shot is a narrative, whatever its level of narrative development. In fact, 'if a statement relates an event, a real or fictitious action (and its intensity and quality are of little importance), then it falls within the category of narrative.'[15] A corollary of this would be that each shot of a film, taken in isolation, constitutes a narrative.[16] Does this mean that a film of 700 shots comprises 700 narratives? If so, what becomes of the filmic narrative as a whole? My hypothesis is the following. There are two types of narrative in the cinema: the micro-narrative (the shot), a first level on which is generated the second narrative level; this second level more properly constitutes a filmic narrative in the generally accepted sense. There are two types of narrative, therefore; also two levels. The first level, which is not always easy to identify, probably corresponds to what Metz is referring to when he says, 'One can always "tell a story" merely by means of iconic analogy.' But it may be superfluous to add, as Metz does, 'and indeed that is what the earliest film-makers did (when, for example, they photographed a music-hall sketch) in the period when a specific cinematographic language did not exist (1895–1900 and even, in part, the period of 1900–15).'[17]

For even now, every shot tells a story merely by means of iconic analogy (and will continue to do so for as long as the cinema exists). This is the first level, or first layer of narrativity, produced by a machine which is doomed to tell stories 'for ever'. This special feature of the cinema, that of having always been narrative right from the beginning, explains why this art, which 'has narrativity built into it',[18] so quickly found its vocation of storyteller. For each segment of a film always recounts something. 'That the cinema could evolve into a machine for telling stories had never really been considered':[19] maybe, but the development was, to say the least, predictable.[20]

Thus, when cinema is said to have taken 'the narrative road'[21] at a certain moment in its history, this is not the 'innate' kind of narrativity just described, but the second level of narrativity, which has only been briefly mentioned so far. This narrative layer needs more than 'mere perceptive analogy' which, as Metz observes, 'allows one if necessary to economize on any language-like codification'.[22] A further comment by Metz may now be understood within this perspective on the duality of film's narrative capabilities:

> *Now, from the moment that the cinema encountered narrativity* [what I call the second level of narrativity] . . . it appears that it has superimposed over the analogical message a second complex of codified constructions,

> something 'beyond' the image, something that has only gradually been mastered (thanks to Griffith mainly).[23]

Roger Odin had an insight into these two levels of narrativity in his study of *La Jetée* (Chris Marker, 1963). He was determined to understand how narrative operates in a film made up of 'shots' in which nothing moves: he found that the film which consists entirely of photographic snapshots (or frozen images) has a 'slide effect'. The film, which in this respect is part of an unusual cinematic experiment, has no first layer of narrativity. Odin is well aware of this, since he writes: 'The absence of reproduction of movement . . . tends to block narrativity: since the lack of movement means that there is no Before/After opposition within each shot, the narrative can only be derived from the sequence of shots, that is from montage.'[24]

These two levels of narrativity correspond to the two 'articulations' of the double mobility which is cinema's characteristic: the mobility of the subjects represented (made possible by the sequence of photographs) and the mobility of the spatio–temporal segments (made possible by the sequence of shots). This double mobility constitutes the essence of the various kinetic possibilities of the cinematic art. The basic apparatus, the cinematograph, only produces the first type in any immediate sense: Roman Gubern[25] calls this the articulation between one photograph and another. Processes complementary to the mere recording of profilmic reality are needed to create the other narrative level: the articulation between one shot and another (Gubern).

Cinema theorists have hardly ever identified these two types of narrative clearly, or drawn a distinction between them. Jurij Lotman, although he did not go very deeply into this vein of ideas, showed that he was well aware of it:

> Joining chains of varied shots into a meaningful sequence forms a story. The second type of narration involves the transformation of one and the same shot. The chain of alterations is, of course, a narration. At the same time it is not the joining of a number of signs into chains, but the transformation of one and the same sign. Recall one of the first steps of the cinema, a film strip from Demeny's photophone: twenty images of an actor pronouncing the words 'Je vous aime' . . . The iconic sign can be transformed into a narrative text because it contains several mobile elements.[26]

Thus the image's essentially mobile nature creates the conditions for the 'innate' and 'spontaneous' narrativity of this articulation of photographs which constitutes the shot. For '. . . the moving image is one in perpetual transformation, showing a transition from one state of representation to another, this movement requiring time.'[27]

But although these two levels of narrative are concomitant, they tend inevitably to cancel each other out. Or more precisely, the second level can only operate by tending to cover up the first: spectators are not aware of watching a huge number of micro-narratives being linked together and accumulating piece by piece to create a macro-narrative. In other words, the macro-narrative is formed not by the micro-narratives being added together but by their being systematically disregarded as such.[28] This is the case, at least, in a certain type of narrativity (which has in fact always been dominant in cinematic practice and still is).

Another good question is whether the production of each of these two levels of narrative presupposes the same type of semio-narrative operation and depends on the same process. Could they simply be attributed to the cinematographic 'narrator', who is often mentioned in film theory but whose precise roles and functions have never been defined?

In conclusion, my thesis is that each of these narrative levels is produced by a different (sub-)process. In my view, the filmic narrative is the product of a dialectical combination of the two basic modes of narrative communication: narration and monstration.[29] According to this view, a film like *L'Arroseur arrosé* (and any other film made in one shot) comprises a single narrative layer; despite the symmetry of its action, it does not have a second level of narrativity. The narrative presented in it may be attributed solely to the discourse of the monstration, this resulting entirely from the articulation between one photograph and the next. The film shows no sign of any intervention by the narrator (whose discourse, or narration, comes from the articulation between shots). 'In so far as they act effectively',[30] it is the characters in the action who tell the story through the intermediary of the 'monstrator', to use the term I have coined. In a narrative of this kind, the narrating instance (*instance racontante*) would be none other than the monstrator, who is finally responsible for the concept of the characters. The very early filmic narrative is therefore bound solely and indissolubly to *mimesis*, in Plato's sense of the term. Filmic narrative cannot change register or acquire the status of narration unless there is an articulation between the various segments produced by the monstrator. Thus as well as the monstrator, who came into being at the same time as the ciné-camera, a truly cinematic narrator appears in parallel with the emergence of a kind of narrative communication which had been trying to find its way throughout the 'silent' period. There was no filmic narrator at the beginning of cinema. The narrator started to become apparent just before the turn of the century at the same time as the concept of juxtaposing a series of shots. But it can be argued, as it is by Tom Gunning, that 'the narrator in the early films is sporadic; an occasional spectre rather than a unified presence.'[31]

Notes

This article is republished here in its original version, which first appeared in *Iris*, vol. 2. no. 4, 1984. Since then I have considerably modified it in the course of turning it into a chapter of my book *Du littéraire au filmique: Système du récit* (Paris: Meridiens Klincksieck, 1988), and have reached substantially different conclusions, to which readers are referred.

1. See Gérard Genette's famous article, 'Frontières du récit', *Communications*, 8, 1966.
2. This denial may be challenged, as it is in my unpublished doctoral thesis, 'Récit scriptural, récit théâtral, récit filmique: prolégomènes à une théorie de la narratologie du cinéma', University of Paris III, Sorbonne Nouvelle, 1983.

3. *Logique du récit* (Paris: Seuil, 1973), pp. 99–100.
4. See A.-J. Greimas and J. Courtès, *Sémiotique. Dictionnaire raisonné de la théorie du langage* (Paris: Hachette, 1979), p. 137.
5. 'Structural patterning in the Lumière films', *Wide Angle*, vol. 3 no. 1, 1979, p. 30.
6. Ibid.
7. Ibid.
8. Deutelbaum 's area of study was quite other. In his opinion, the Lumière brothers' films should not be regarded as simple, naive recordings of scenes taken from life: 'Even the slightest of the slight events discussed here reveals an attempt to impart a shape to the action depicted' (ibid., p. 36). For my purposes, second place should be given to the kind of analysis which attempts to define the parameters of the actantial structuring of the action filmed, the conventions of its presentation and, ultimately, the intentions behind the narrative. The point which I want to discuss here is whether simple, naive recordings of scenes taken from life can be counted as narratives.
9. *The Poetics of Prose*, trans. Richard Howard (Ithaca, NY: Cornell University Press, 1977), p. 111.
10. Another version of the film, which sometimes has the title *Arroseur et arrosé*, has a different ending, in which the gardener does not spank the boy but gets hold of the hose and waters him in his turn. This closes the loop and the watered waterer of the title could be either character.
11. Todorov, *Poetics of Prose*, p. 118.
12. Greimas and Courtès, *Sémiotique*, p. 307.
13. This first name is fictitious and is modelled on the surname (*lux* meaning light – *lumière* in French).
14. Brémond, *Logique du récit*, p. 89.
15. Jacques Aumont, Alain Bergala, Michel Marie and Marc Vernet, *L'Esthétique du film* (Paris: Fernand Nathan, 1983), p. 77.
16. This means that every shot, taken out of its context and projected on to the screen as a single object, should be regarded as a narrative in itself. Whether or not the narrative is complete is not important (this belongs to problems of closure); nor does it matter – at this level of analysis – whether the shots were devised to articulate with others and form part of a series. Imagine a collection of old films whose splices have come apart and which wear and tear have reduced to a random heap of disconnected shots. Any subsequent projection shot by shot would be of a lot of little narratives.
17. Christian Metz, *Film Language: A Semiotics of the Cinema*, trans. Michael Taylor (New York: Oxford University Press, 1974), p. 118.
18. Ibid.
19. Ibid., p. 93.
20. Some7people apparently did predict it. Jurij Lotman cites William Paul and H. G. Wells' thesis of 1894: 'Telling stories by means of moving pictures'. See Jurij Lotman, *Semiotics of Cinema*, trans. Mark E. Suino (Ann Arbor: University of Michigan, 1976), p. 36.
21. Metz, *Film Language*, p. 44.
22. Ibid., p. 226.
23. Ibid.
24. Roger Odin, 'Le film de fiction menacé par la photographie et sauvé par la bande-son (à propos de *La Jetée* de Chris Marker)', *Cinémas de la modernité: films, théories* (Paris: Klincksieck, 1981), p. 150.
25. Roman Gubern, 'David Wark Griffith et l'articulation cinématographique', *Les Cahiers de la Cinémathèque*, no. 17, December 1975, p. 8.
26. Lotman, *Semiotics of Cinema*, p. 63.
27. Aumont *et al.*, *L'Esthéthique du film*, p. 64.
28. This idea was put forward by Marie-Claire Ropars-Wuilleumier. An interesting parallel can be made with Metz's statement in *Language and Cinema*, trans. Donna Jean Umiker-Sebeok (The Hague: Mouton, 1974), p. 191: '. . . that one may rightly assert that the cinema is not a machine for the purpose of combining photograms, but rather for suppressing them and making them imperceptible.' Also 'The sequence does not string the individual shots; it suppresses them (Metz, *Film Language* p. 45).
29. See Gaudreault, 'Récit scriptural'; also Gaudreault, 'Showing and Telling', pp. 274–81

of this volume; Gaudreault, 'Histoire/discours au cinéma', *Actes du premier colloque de l'Association québécoise des études cinématographiques* (Montreal: Cinémathèque québécoise, 1984).

30. Aristotle, *Poetics* 1448 a 23.
31. Tom Gunning, 'D. W. Griffith and the Narrator-System: Narrative Structure and Industry Organization in Biograph Films, 1908–1909', Doctoral Thesis, New York University 1986.

Translated by Rosamund Howe.

From Lumière to Pathé
The Break-Up of Perspectival Space

RICHARD DECORDOVA

The workers appear, exiting from the Lumière factory at Lyon – some from a small door screen left, which masks in shadows the space behind it, the majority from a gate expanding fully across the right side of the screen. A depth is visible here, a depth through which the workers walk into view and divide, exiting to either side of the 'place' marked by the absence of the camera. At one point a man trots out of the crowd calling a dog behind him. When the dog appears, however, we see it at the side of another man, who is pushing a bicycle. The first man disappears into the foreground, screen right, while the bicycle skids to a halt in the centre of the frame. Suddenly, an unidentifiable person, perhaps a child, dashes across the screen from left to right, in the foreground. Then the cyclist resumes his movement, followed by the dog, both disappearing 'into' the foreground screen left. Three more cyclists appear, each in movement towards the spectator, the first disappearing left, the second right and the third left.

As the film ends the dog re-enters the foreground of the image from the left, and a man runs into view from the right to help another man who has just closed the left half of the gate. Understandably, our attention has been drawn from the door on the left side of the screen. The people who exited from there also exited from our view in the most direct way possible. But after their exit, in the final seconds of the film, we can see two figures in the shadow of the doorway staring out as if they too were witness to some new sort of spectacle.

But what are they looking at? The camera, the projector, the spectator or the workers who have already exited from our view? One can see the play of absences that put this machine, the cinematograph, in place, and which in turn implicated the spectator in its play. Two figures look at the camera, which is absent. The spectator's view is that of this absence, but is not identical to it – split between the real time of filming and that of projection. The projector reconstructs the camera's view, but only by projecting it elsewhere, absenting itself from the lure of vision. Despite this, there were still perhaps those spectators who, easily distracted, followed these figures' gazes back to the flickering presence, the Lumière Cinématographe.

Another possibility remains – the figures are looking at a real offscreen event, the workers' movements after they exited the image. In terms of what Souriau has called the profilmic event, this can be argued.[1] However, this is not to say that this 'reality' entered into the representational system of the Lumière films as a possibility of meaning – that is, as offscreen space. It entered

La Sortie des usines Lumière.

precisely as an absence, a consequence of the material aspect of the apparatus itself – the presence of the frame. Thus, the workers move off-frame, not offscreen.[2] To assign a realistic space to this absence, at its origin, is to argue that such a space was guaranteed by the scientific nature of the apparatus alone. Rather, it was the result of a particular work, a work to be examined here, in the films of Lumière and Pathé.

Still another absence has been in movement in *La Sortie des usines Lumière*, one that constituted the most radical aspect of the cinematographic machine. The spectator was in fact put to a movement by the cinematograph, 'machinated'. Thierry Kuntzel has called the effect of this machination ttthe 'défilement'.

> Défilement ... means, in the vocabulary of cinema, 'progression, the sliding of the film-strip through the gate of a projector' and, in military art, the use of the terrain's accidents or of artificial constructions to conceal one's movements from the enemy. In the unrolling of the film, the photograms which concern us 'pass through', hidden from sight: what the spectator retains is only the movement within which they insert themselves.[3]

The spectator 'effected' by this défilement, produced as its effect, was unquestionably different from the spectator of photographed images before it. This was no doubt the novelty of the cinematograph (although this novelty was soon displaced on to its capacity to reproduce the real). The play of vision in painting, and later photography, had been fully contingent upon a materially unrestricted time of contemplation. The Lumière films, however, appear and disappear, and, at the base of this movement, each 'photogram' appears and disappears, imperceptibly. Left out in this movement, the spectator is at the same time taken up by it, subjected to its force.

Already this force is imbricated with what Barthes called the proairetic code.[4] This is of course not surprising in a work destined to equate the camera with the scientific representation of the real. The workers 'défilent'. The truth of *their* movement is to be the truth of the machine. But not yet – a term is in excess. The workers leave the factory and then our view, disappearing off-frame. These two actions hardly have the same status although the temptation in retrospect is to collapse their difference on to the spatio-temporal verisimilitude of the *workers'* défilement. This, however, is to ignore the historical specificity of the machine and the problems of representation it instituted.

The workers do not just move: they move *in perspective*. This must be seen as a violent discomposition of the perspectival system that had been dominant since the 16th century in painting (the system upon which photography itself had been modelled). Prior to the cinematograph, this system had placed the elements of the representation in a stable (though certainly not static) set of relationships.[5] The Lumière films fall solidly within the rules of perspectival representation, but the elements are in constant flux – in a mechanical movement.

The cyclists, for example, having been masked by the crowd, appear. Such an appearance had been impossible in both painting and photography. Masking was the predominant means of the representation of depth in pre-Renaissance painting and an element the system of Renaissance perspective engaged. However, an object masked was, *at the same time*, an object represented. The movement of the cinematograph posed problems for the elements of perspectival representation in that these elements were submitted to the exigencies of a radically different syntagma.

The cyclists appear near the centre of the frame and move towards the (absent) camera, exiting to its left or right side. It is evident that masking was only one of the elements of perspective discomposed in the movement of the machine. The centred vision of Renaissance perspective regularized, into a mathematical system, the physical proportion of similar objects relative to their placement on different planes of the composition – from foreground to background. It also necessitated a certain distortion of objects away from this centre towards the edge of the composition. Thus, the cyclists become larger and larger as they advance. For a moment, they reach the place where they are most recognizable (the first cyclist, in fact, stops 'here'). But then, as they continue, they become more and more distorted, and at the moment of their greatest abstraction they disappear.

Here, we return to the problem of off-frame, the 'place' of this disappearance. It is principally through the problems of representing movement in perspective that the frame becomes an active problem of representation in these films. The figuration of this larger problematic was in fact effected through a work upon the existence of the frame itself. This is not surprising since the frame marks the very possibility of both Renaissance perspective and movement within it. Stephen Heath has traced this historical development of the frame in the Renaissance.

> Before the fifteenth century frames hardly exist, other than as the specific architectural setting that is to be decorated (wall, altarpiece or whatever); it is during that century that frames begin to have an independent reality, this concomitant with the notion itself of a 'painting' . . . The new frame is symmetrical (the centred rectangle, clearly 'composable') and inevitable (the Quattrocento system cannot be realised without it, it becomes a reflex of a 'natural' composition).[6]

In the same article Heath quotes Merleau Ponty's description of the relation between fixity and movement in film: 'the spectator is not just responsive to what is moving but also to what stays in pale, and the perception of movement supposes fixed frames.'[7]

Thus, the frame is a 'reflex' of the centred, composed space of Renaissance perspective. The filmic representation of movement worked both within this centred space (necessitated by the photographic base of the apparatus) and against it, discomposing the fixed composition of objects within the fixity of the frame.

This was the structural contradiction the cinematograph introduced – an aspect of its historical specificity as a representational form. This contradiction above all presented itself as a problem of representation. In the Lumière films this problem was approached in two distinct ways.

In the first, the effect of movement was minimized and a centred space maintained. This is certainly the case in *Querelle enfantine*. Although movement is present it is held firmly within the conventions of nineteenth-century portrait photography. This solution is also employed in the *Barque sortant d'un port*. There is movement in perspective, but the boat's slow movement out into the infinite distance does not disrupt the more heavily stressed aspects of the composition, which are present from the very first image of the film. The position these films take in relation to the afore-mentioned contradiction is obvious. They work at masking this contradiction by containing movement within the centred space specific to earlier forms of perspectival representation.

In the second solution movement is emphasized as a movement of discomposition. As we have seen, the frame is the nexus of the contradiction through which this discomposition proceeds, permitting both a centred space and the possibility of movement 'against' that space. This contradiction is to be worked out very largely through another contradiction in these films, however, one which it in many ways implies. The problems of composition and discomposition are shifted on to the problem of the frame as both possibility *and* limit of representation.

It is in this way that the syntagmatic 'unrolling' of the film is subsumed into a play of appearance and disappearance, a play doubling the appearance and disappearance of the film on the screen. The cinematograph entered much more into the discourse of magic and illusionism than into some ready-made institution, 'the cinema'. The films of Méliès demonstrate this with the most insistence. The Lumière films cannot be excluded from this discourse by favouring any notion of their referential transparency.

One only has to examine this play of appearance and disappearance in the films to see the extent to which this purely *discursive* aspect was emphasized. In *Partie d'écarté* three men are sitting at a table in the centre of the frame playing cards. A waiter suddenly enters screen right. One of the men motions to him, and he exits screen right. Seconds later he comes back in with drinks, and, after setting them on the table, he watches the men's game, hysterically pointing to their cards and laughing as if in a fit. How does one account for the waiter's seemingly unmotivated hysteria? Were it not for the excess of his movement the composition of the shot would focus the spectator's attention on to the game of cards itself. It is precisely his movement that disrupts this composition, and it is his movement, from presence to absence and back, that is the subject of the film.

However, the waiter is watching the game of cards in the centre of the composition, a game which, as we have seen, is of only secondary interest to the spectator. It is this split between the spectator's 'interest' and the waiter's that disallows the possibility of seeing the waiter simply as a surrogate for the spectator. The mechanism at work here is more complex. There is definitely a complicity established between the spectator and the waiter. Diegetically, his hysteria is completely unmotivated through any aspect of the card game itself, but it is through this hysteria that the spectator is addressed. The complicity between the spectator and the waiter stems from the identification of the spectator with the enunciation. The waiter is to a large extent the symbolic bearer of the enunciation, and the play of appearance and disappearance is, accordingly, figured through him. However, the enunciation of the film is not to be assigned solely to him but to the relationship between his movement and the centred space within which the card game takes place. The waiter is perhaps hysterical because he 'finds himself' in a contradictory position in relation to the centred space of the perspectival system. It can be argued that the spectator in 1895 was in exactly the same position.

In *Partie d'écarté* the terms of a centred space are at least co-present. In *L'Arroseur arrosé* (1895) they virtually disappear. It is perhaps not surprising that the function of the frame is so overdetermined in the film. As the film opens we see a man positioned on the left side of the screen facing the left frame (already the rules of 'good' composition have been abandoned). He is holding a water hose and pointing it off-frame in such a way that only a small segment of the stream of water is visible. The rest disappears off-frame. A prankster appears from the right side of the frame and steps on the hose, making the flow of water 'disappear'. The man holds the hose up to his face. The prankster then takes his foot off the hose and the water squirts the man in the face.

The gag is more complicated than it may appear to be. The entrance of the prankster represents on one level the possibility of a composed space (the man could turn around and recognize the other, thus producing a balanced space), but at the same time, his action complicates the play – already present – around the man's discomposition. The water has already disappeared from the hose, off-frame. The prankster, by stepping on the hose, doubles this disappearance, assuring its diegetic motivation. He controls the appearance and disappearance of the water and makes the man the victim of its play. Here, one can note yet another instance in which a character is figured as enunciator in these films.

A chase ensues after the man recognizes the 'reason' for the disappearance and reappearance of the water. Both characters disappear off-frame, left. Then, a moment later, the man reappears, pulling the prankster by the ear to the centre of the frame. The man spanks him and then quickly returns to his watering as the prankster disappears off-frame right. Thus, the film ends as it began – thoroughly discomposed. This is its symmetry, and it is one that directly addresses the problem of the frame as limit of representation.

Démolition d'un mur is perhaps the most exemplary in this respect. Three figures are standing in front of two perpendicular walls that were perhaps, at one time, walls of a house. One of the walls extends from the foreground left into the background. The other wall connects with it in the background and extends from there well into the right side of the screen. A foreman sends the two other men off-frame, one to the left and one to the right. He remains in the centre of the frame while the others disappear. Soon, one of the men reappears in the small space between the wall and the left edge of the frame. Then, seconds later, the left wall collapses and the two men rush to the pile of rocks remaining near the centre of the frame. As the dust begins to settle we can begin to see, in perspective, the space the wall had masked.

Once again the figuration of an enunciative presence is evident, one that in turn articulates the play of appearance and disappearance in the film. The foreman is the 'central' figure that sends the other two men off-frame to demolish the wall. Two points should be stressed concerning this demolition. First, it is a spectacle entirely dependent upon the effect movement had on the system of Renaissance perspective. It could be argued, in fact, that this is its subject. Second, the two walls are 'composed' in such a way that they create a cubic space within the frame, typical of that of Renaissance perspective. In this respect, one can see the left wall as a double of the frame itself. The man who reappears, from off-frame, just behind the wall functions to demonstrate the similarity *between* these two aspects (frame and wall) since both subject him to the same play of appearance and disappearance. It is in fact along this play that masking and the frame will be linked, and the frame will come to be seen as an ever-present mask over a coherent space.

Of course, in *Démolition d'un mur*, it is the mask itself that disappears, revealing the depth hidden 'naturally' behind it. In this film, we can already see a work tentative to a coherent logic, preferential contiguity connecting spaces of appearance and disappearance.[8] The production of an offscreen space depends upon this logic, and thus the movement of shots within the classical sequence.

The films of Charles Pathé are still very far removed from what will be considered the classical model. However, the possibility of a movement from shot to shot is very much a part of their system. An examination of one of these films, *Policeman's Little Run*, will demonstrate that the movement from shot to shot in these films was figured precisely upon the same problematic posited in the Lumière films: the discomposition of perspective and the syntagmatic play of appearance and disappearance.

First, it should be noted that *Policeman's Little Run* must be situated well within the conventions of the chase film, a genre well established by 1907. That is, it is in no way formally or technically advanced for its time. The film's interest lies in its systematic and conventional aspects, the terms which rendered its coherence possible.

The film opens with a shot of the front of a butcher's shop. A dog appears from the left side of the frame. It jumps up on to the butcher's counter (centred in the composition), steals a bone, and then disappears off-frame right. Two policemen then enter left. They jump around hysterically for a moment and then 'follow' the dog's disappearance to the right.

This bone is the ostensible lack that motivates the narrative. However, it is much more an element of a centred space that the dog has 'stolen'. The chase is one of a discomposition, and its resolution will be a return to a composed space.

A short description of the next shots will facilitate the analysis that follows.

2. A policeman is standing on a corner screen left. The dog appears around the corner and exits right, slightly towards the camera. The other policemen appear from around the corner. The lone policeman joins these, and, after some hysteria, they follow the dog off-frame right.
3. The dog appears around a corner in the background, followed by the police. The chase proceeds from the background directly into the foreground, stressing the perspectival depth through which the actants move. The dog exits off-frame right from the immediate foreground. The police follow.
4. The dog appears from the left at the top of a stairway and begins running down the stairs. The police appear and follow. The dog reaches the bottom of the stairs (the level of the camera) and exits off-frame right. The policemen run about indecisively before exiting in the same direction.

The repetitive structure that will dominate the film is already evident. Two variations of this structure can be distinguished:

(A) The shot appears
Figure A appears
Figure B appears
Figure A disappears
Figure B disappears
The shot disappears

B) The shot appears
Figure A appears
Figure A disappears
Figure B appears
Figure B disappears
The shot disappears

In each, the appearance and disappearance of the characters doubles the appearance and disappearance of the shot on the screen. The diegetic logic of this doubling is simple. The shot becomes supportable only as a narrative unity – after the entrance and the exit of the characters it must disappear. However, the syntagmatic unity of the shot and the 'unity' of the narrative action are not coextensive in this film. Although they double each other in a play of appearance and disappearance, they do not *exactly* overlap. It is in the difference between the two that another logic is inscribed.

This logic is that of the enunciation, and, as in the Lumière films, it concerns itself with the effect movement had on Renaissance perspective. The appearance of each shot is the appearance of a composed space, well within the strictures of pictorial perspectival representation. The characters' movement from appearance to disappearance discomposes this space. Their disappearance marks the return to the composed space originally posited.

The frame is thus the limit of the narrative representation in the film. However, outside this limit, on either side of the characters' entries and exits, the frame is an index of the very possibility of a composed space. It is only from composed space to composed space that the movement from shot to shot can progress in *Policeman's Little Run*. Each shot contains the terms of its discomposition *within* it. The disappearance of a shot and its replacement by another renews and repeats in the spectator a predictable structure of expectation: the discomposition and the return to a centred, stable space.

The only shot devoid of significant movement is the last, a close-up of the dog with the bone in its mouth, wearing a police hat. This shot, which relies (like *Querelle enfantine*) on the conventions of portrait photography, arrests the movement the film had engaged in and resolves the conflict of movement, returning the spectator, finally, to a composed space. It is not incidental that this is the only close-up in the film. This was a conventional means of ending the Pathé films (*The Diabolical Itching* and *The Yawner*, for example). The point to be made here is that the close-up is not merely a means of narrative emphasis in these films; it functions much more crucially across the contradiction that movement introduced into the perspectival system.

In *Policeman's Little Run* the movement from shot to shot is founded upon a play on this same contradiction. There is no active production of offscreen space, and thus no logic of referential contiguity from shot to shot. There is a cut, for example, from the chase proceeding through a bedroom to its appearance on a street. One could argue that time had passed between the two shots, but this is an assumption in retrospect.

Contiguity in the classical model would be both spatial and temporal; it would depend upon a linearity represented along the linearity of the discursive chain. The reversal of the chase (the dog begins to chase the policeman) introduces an element of linearity, but it is effected through a mere reversal of the structure of repetition already in the movement (rather than A appears, B appears, etc., B appears and then A appears).

This repetition signals a difficulty in coming to terms with linearity and its metonymical figuration through referential contiguity. One series of shots in *Policeman's Little Run* ruptures this strict structure of repetition and does indeed proceed from shot to shot through a 'coherent' space.

9. The exterior of a building. The dog appears and begins to run *up* the wall of a building, defying all laws of gravity. The dog is still in the top part of the frame when there is a cut.
10. The dog is running further up the side of the building. It disappears at the top of the frame.
11. A repeat of 9 (the exterior of the building). The police appear and begin climbing up the building after the dog. They are still in frame when there is a cut.
12. A repeat of 10 but with the policemen climbing.
13. The policemen arrive on the roof. One falls down and disappears at the

bottom of the frame while, at the same time, the rest of the police disappear at the top of the roof on its other side. As they disappear the dog appears from the top of the roof and runs down. The policemen follow.
14. A continuous tracking shot of the policemen as they descend. They are about to leave the frame when there is a cut to the next shot.

A number of points are important concerning these shots. First, throughout the rest of the film, the narrative proceeds at the level of the shot (through the repeated action in each shot). Here, it is operative at the level of the sequence. It is only the production of a referential contiguity that permits this expansion: the building is posited as a coherent space. The tracking shot is a veritable confirmation of this space, although its formal novelty cannot be denied.

It is equally important that the representation of a temporal contiguity links the shots. In shots 9–12 the dog and the policemen are kept completely separate, but the 'time' of the chase is maintained through the repetition of 9 and 11, and 10 and 12. In the rest of the film the elements of the chase must appear and disappear in the same shot. This sequence marks the possibility of segmenting the elements of the narrative, all the while retaining their spatio-temporal relationship.

However, this sequence must be seen as a true rupture in the system within which the film otherwise remains. It is not incidental that the sequence, which is the most advanced in terms of the evolution of film, presents itself as a radical experiment in space. The fact that the dog and policemen run up the side of a building is only one aspect of this experiment – the editing and camera movement are the other. One could say that the sequence verges upon nonsense, but it is more accurate to see it as a definite work upon sense, one which will produce the conditions to render possible the conventional use of offscreen space.

This production, however, is continually that of a spectator constituted in a movement of sense. One could very well point to the theoretical problematic of the suture in this respect.[9] This chapter has attempted to demonstrate some of the historical problems of 'suturing' the spectator into early film discourse. This involved placing the spectator in a radically different position in relation to earlier perspectival representation. Movement, of course, was the major term of this difference – movement within the frame and movement off-frame. The play of appearance and disappearance that resulted in these films was an imaginary play, one made possible by the most novel characteristics of the cinematograph itself. The work we can see in them was one destined to represent a symbolic coherence upon this imaginary play.

Notes

First published in *Cinetracts* no. 15, Fall 1981.

1. Etienne Souriau, 'La structure de l'univers filmique et le vocabulaire de la filmologie', *L'Univers Filmique* (Paris: Flammarion, 1940).

2. See Pascal Bonitzer, 'Hors-champ: un éspace en défaut', *Cahiers du Cinéma*, nos 234–5. Bonitzer makes the distinction between off-frame and offscreen. The former is material and the latter is imaginary, fictional.
3. Thierry Kuntzel, 'The défilement: a view in close-up', trans. Bertrand Augst, *Camera Obscura*, 2, Fall 1977, p. 56.
4. The code of narrative action. See Roland Barthes, *S/Z* (New York: Hill & Wang, and London: Cape, 1974).
5. That is, the spatial relationship between objects is fixed. Within this fixity, however, there is a potentially infinite play, one limited only by the viewer's time of contemplation. Foucault shows this remarkably in his analysis, 'Les suivants' in *The Order of Things* (New York, Pantheon, 1970 and London: Tavistock, 1974). It should be noted that the play of the two figures' 'vision' described earlier would not be radically different except for the fact that its reflexivity invokes the existence of a completely different representational machine, one which effectively subjects this vision (more precisely, subjects the spectator's vision) to a *défilement*.
6. Stephen Heath, 'Narrative space', *Screen*, vol. 17 no. 3, Autumn 1976, p. 81.
7. Ibid., p. 74.
8. For Metz, metonymy. He provides the following chart:

	similarity	*contiguity*
Within the discourse	paradigm	syntagma
Within the referent	metaphor	metonymy

See Christian Metz, *The Imaginary Signifier* (Bloomington: Indiana University Press, 1982), p. 187.

9. See *Screen*, Winter 1977/78, for articles by Miller, Oudart and Heath on the suture.

Non-Continuity, Continuity, Discontinuity
A Theory of Genres in Early Films
TOM GUNNING

In my essay entitled 'The non-continuous style of early film',[1] I surveyed a group of what could be called anomalies in early film – elements which, from the viewpoint of the later dominant style of film-making (which we could all – with caution and reservation – the classical style of continuity) seemed deviant. Inspired partly by the work of Noël Burch and partly by my own interest in later 'deviant' styles of film-making in the avant-garde, I felt it was important not to see these anomalies as primitive mistakes groping towards the later established ideal of match cutting and diegetic unity but as indications of another direction in film narrative than that of later dominant cinema, a road not taken by the major film industries.

My essay was announced as preliminary, and in it I indicated my uncertainty as to whether the group of anomalies I surveyed could actually be thought of as forming an organic and unified style in early film. It now seems to me that the importance of the elements I discussed is not primarily that they sketch an alternative approach to narrative than that of the classical style, but rather that they reveal how complex and dialectical the development of the classical style is. Rather than servicing as markers on a deviant route in film history, the elements of non-continuity in early film punctuate the body of film history, becoming a series of blind spots. For traditional historians who see film as moving towards an ideal of continuity, the anomalies can only be seen as errors or failed attempts. For recent theorists such anomalies are significant as deconstructive deviations. But in fact these critical points in film discourse reveal precisely that film history cannot be conceived according to static models of coherence or non-coherence to an (often unspecified) ideal of classical continuity (which, after its establishment would seem to have no history, other than that of a static definition, while other films can only be conceived through the relation of deviance from the norm).

Early cinema, then, need not be viewed as either a moment in the natural development of the later modes of classical continuity, or as a prelapsarian era before the betrayal of cinema to the monopolistic representatives of bourgeois culture and morality. The challenge that early cinema offers to film history is a search for a method of understanding the transformations in narrative form in cinema's first decades; a method that maintains an awareness of early film's difference from later practices, without defining it simply as a relation of divergence from a model of continuity (that, in fact, has not yet appeared). It is precisely the *history* involved in these changes that must be understood.

There is no question that the understanding of this history ultimately must include not only a close and comparative viewing of all existing films with the tools of analysis that structuralism and semiology have provided to film study, but also an understanding of these films as economic products. The means of production and consumption (in a broad understanding of these terms) of early film are only now being described and investigated. It is only from a full description of the means of financing, the actual methods of production of films, the processes of their distribution, the practices of exhibition, and finally the way films were received by audiences, that a truly historical view of cinema will be possible. If the methods of analysis of films as signifying systems and as economic commodities are different, they are by no means mutually exclusive, or ultimately fully independent. I must single out the recent work of Charles Musser for his attempt to understand the signifying process in early films in relation to the strategies involved in their presentation and production.

If the history of film as a commodity is necessary for a full understanding of film form in history, it is not the only means of approaching the film historically. We must develop methods of analysis of the films themselves which include a historical dimension. The investigation of film texts as systems had encouraged an approach that is rigorously synchronic. Certainly this synchronic investigation of films was necessarily the founding task of a structural approach to film. However, the time has now come for a diachronic comparison of filmic systems within history. One particularly fruitful method in a diachronic approach to early film is the investigation of ciné-genres.

Two limitations on the recent study of genre in film are immediately evident. The first is its almost exclusive attention to the aspect of content in films rather than expression (of signifieds rather than signifiers). This limitation I will discuss somewhat later. The other limitation is that, like so much of recent serious film study, it is cut off from history. This is perhaps not surprising since the description of genre synchronically should precede its diachronic investigation. There have, of course, been genre studies that traced the modification of particular genres, supplying something of a specialized history of the gangster film, or Western. But the relation of such genres to film history in general has not been broached. This is surprising because there exists a conception of genre in which genre itself is a vehicle of historical change: the theory of genre of the Russian Formalists.

Although often criticized for removing the literary text from historical contexts, it is in fact in the theory of genres that the Russian Formalists introduced the historical dimension to the analysis of texts. The Formalist understanding of art as a process of defamiliarization gave to the history of art forms a necessity for constant change and renewal. As Tynyanov put it, 'any literary sucession is first of all a struggle, a destruction of old values and a reconstruction of new elements'.[2] In this view literary genres become dynamic, competing with rival genres for dominance as they move through a cycle of origin, canonization and eventual decay. As a genre gains popularity it loses its defamiliarizing role and moves inevitably into decadence, giving way to new forms.[3]

Certainly this dynamic view of genres as part of the 'dialectical self-creation of new forms'[4] has limitations as a model for film history. While it provides for a dynamic view of the succession of forms, its concept of 'self-creation' limits our access to other historical factors which influence the growth and decay of genres, factors which are essential to our understanding of film as a commodity. The Formalists themselves were aware of the limitations of the approach, however, and Eichenbaum described it as 'only a general outline of evolution surrounded by a whole series of complicated conditions'.[5] But, if in need of completion by a consideration of these 'complicated conditions' (which for me involves film as a commodity, primarily), none the less this concept allows us to grasp film genres as truly historical events. From this the conception of a historical series of film genres arises in which, to quote Hans Robert Jauss, 'the next work can solve formal and moral problems left behind by the last work, and present new problems in turn'.[6]

We can now turn from the limitation of the concept of genres in recent film analysis to aspects of content. Although there are reasons why this has been useful in the approach to later cinema (in which the concept of genre is basically one taken over from policy of production and distribution within the industry: hence the categories of musical, gangster film, horror film, etc.), it also has limited our approach to genre as an aspect of the actual form of films. The Russian Formalists come to our aid again in their (admittedly preliminary) works on film, with the concept of 'ciné-genres'.[7] Writing in the 20s, the Formalists were primarily concerned to establish what genres were uniquely cinematic as opposed to those 'parasitically' taken over from literature and drama. For our purposes, however, the most important aspect of the concept of ciné-genres is that it does not define genres simply in terms of content ('Story' for the Formalists), but also in terms of its actualization as expression through the specific stylistic devices of film ('Plot' for the Formalists). As A. Piotrovskij puts it:

> We shall define a *cine-genre* as a complex of compositional, stylistic, and narrative devices, connected with specific semantic material and emotional emphasis but residing totally within a specific 'native' art system – the system of cinema. Therefore, in order to establish the 'cine-genres', it is necessary to draw specific conclusions from the basic stylistic laws of cine-art, the laws of 'photogeny' and 'montage'. We will observe how the use of 'space', 'time', 'people', and 'objects' varies from the point of view of montage and photogeny, depending on the genre. We will also observe how the narrative sequences are arranged, and what the interrelations among all these elements are within a given ciné–genre.[8]

This approach to genres is particularly useful in dealing with early cinema. This is partly because such 'genres' as have already been discussed in early cinema – such as the chase film or the trick film – can partly be differentiated through their approaches to filmic space and time. Equally important is the way the genres of early cinema can be placed in a historical series in which each succeeds the former in dominating the output of film manufacturers. Of course this pattern of succession is not absolute. As Shklovsky put it, 'The vanquished line is not obliterated, it does not cease to exist. It is only knocked from the crest; it lies dormant and may again rise as a perennial pretender to the throne'.[9] Certainly competing ciné-genres occur during this period. But there are clear patterns of dominance of production by different genres, which indicate the cycles of origin of a new genre, dominance and then decay within the film industry. (The description of these cycles is only at a preliminary stage in this essay. Detailed research into production records and catalogues, information on distribution and exhibition are necessary to establish them with certainty. The difference in the cycle of genres from country to country also needs to be investigated, although during this early period film has an international distribution that is unparalleled in later history.)

I will offer a description of four ciné-genres during this early period (approximately 1895–1910) as a preliminary sketch for a theory of genres in early film. Certainly my discussion of these genres does not exhaust all existing genres during this period. But it does provide a framework into which other genres may be integrated (or which may be modified as other genres are defined and examined, or the patterns of succession changed by further research). My definition of genres depends primarily on their relation to the articulation between shots in terms of space and time. The first genre consists of narratives completed within a single shot. The second genre, which I term the genre of non-continuity, consists of a narrative in at least two shots, in which the disruption caused by the cut(s) between shots is used to express a disruption on the story level of the film. The third genre, which I refer to as the genre of continuity, consists of multi-shot narratives in which the discontinuity caused by cuts is de-emphasized by being bridged through a continuity of action on the story level. The fourth genre I call the genre of discontinuity, in which a multi-shot narrative conveys action which is continuous on the story level through a disruption caused by editing on the plot level.

The genre of single-shot narrative can be said to be inaugurated by the earliest fiction films of Edison and Lumière, such as *L'Arroseur arrosé* (1895) or *Eloping by Horseback* (1898), and would include any film in which some narrative action is developed within a single shot. Most often the action of these films is comic, a gag pulled on an unsuspecting victim, for instance. Incidents of erotic display are also frequent in these single-shot films, and a host of other sorts of action occur. It is somewhat surprising how long this genre lasted (in the US the medium of penny arcade exhibition via mutoscopes may be a partial explanation of its longevity). As late as 1905 both Pathé and Biograph are still making films in this genre (e.g. Biograph's *A Rube in the Subway** and Pathé's *Le Bain du charbonnier**).[10] The genre appears to have been dominant (at least in number of films released) until about 1903.

The next genre, the narrative of non-continuity, is more complicated to describe. It does not simply indicate films which contain the elements of non-continuity that I described in my earlier article, since many of those devices appear in a number of genres. Rather, this genre indicates a particular approach to the joining of shots. The disruption caused by the move from one shot to another, rather than being minimized through the rules of continuity editing, is actually emphasized (and explained) by a discontinuity or disruption on the level of story. A clear example of this genre would be Smith's *Let Me Dream Again** (Great Britain, 1900) or its near copy, Zecca's *Rêve et réalité** (Pathé, 1901). In both these films the first shot shows a man drinking and flirting with a young girl. The second shot (linked in Smith's film by a blurring effect, and in Zecca's by a dissolve) shows the same man waking in bed next to his quite unattractive wife. In both films the transition between shots is used quite visibly to express a contrast in the film's story: the discontinuity between dreams and life.

There are many other narrative lines within this genre, with the many dream films which cut from reality to fantasy being perhaps the most numerous. The dynamics of this genre may explain why the dream is such a popular subject in early cinema, since the discontinuity it represents could both be conveyed by a cut between two shots and at the same time could naturalize the disruption of editing on the story level. But a number of other situations allowed similar strategies. The radical ellipses that express explosions and deaths in such films as Porter's *Another Job for the Undertaker** and *The Finish of Bridget McKeen** (both from 1901) deal similarly with the cut that bridges the two shots of each film. Porter's *What Happened in the Tunnel* (1903) also acknowledges the transition between two shots with a disruption on the story line. A fade-out to black leader covers a kiss made in the darkness of a tunnel, but in the second shot the man discovers the women in the compartment have changed places and he is now kissing the wrong girl. Again this was a widely imitated gag in early cinema, finding its prototype in two 1899 British films by Smith and Bamforth, both entitled *A Kiss in the Tunnel*, and a later French version, *Flirt en chemin de fer** (Pathé, 1903?).

There are numerous other films which seem strongly related to this genre and should perhaps be included within it. Most important would be the magic or trick film, and not simply because many trick films are presented as dreams. In most magic films the rupture utilized is not primarily that between separate shots, but a rupture created within shots, between frames or photograms. The effect of magical transformation achieved through stop motion is certainly that of a disruption which calls attention to itself and expresses a disruption on the story level – the magical ability of the sorcerer to transcend the laws of nature. Given the fuzzy differentiation between montage between shots and stop motion transformation (particularly with the revelation in the work of Jacques Malthête, John Frazer and André Gaudreault that in many cases such transformations were accomplished by splices as well as camera stoppage),[11] it would seem that the magic film should be included in this genre. Certain other forms, such as films which consist of a series of thematically linked tableaux without narrative links, such as Biograph's *The Four Seasons** (1904), relate strongly to this genre.

Apart from the trick film, it might be questioned how pervasive this genre is, and if it ever is truly dominant. It appears quite early but seems to fade away by 1904. Later trick films relate to it, of course, but after 1904 such films of transformation are most often multi-shot narratives that deal with the actual cuts between shots without expressing a disruption within the story. In many ways this genre of non-continuity blurs into a number of transitional or mixed genres which would include narratives (such as the many versions of the Passion Play) in which a series of tableaux function semi-independently. Each shot in these films is a sort of micro-narrative, showing a single location and a complete action. However, continuity of characters and, frequently, the audience's fore-knowledge of the story[12] maintains a sort of sluggish continuity, rather than emphasizing the disruptions between shots. This tableau style functions, then, as a sort of transition between the narrative of non-continuity and the next genre, the narrative of continuity.

The narrative of continuity is unquestionably later than the previous genres. It is exemplified by a form often noted as a 'genre' in early film – the chase film. In this genre the disruption of the cut is naturalized by a continuity within the story. Specifically this continuity is the actual movement of a character(s) that bridges the cuts. The end of one shot is signalled by characters leaving the frame, while the next shot is inaugurated by their reappearance. The disruption of the cut is, as it were, smoothed over by the continuity of the character's movement and the brief ellipsis of his action between shots is minimized rather than emphasized. We find prototypes of this sort of continuity in early multi-shot narratives, such as Méliès' *A Trip to the Moon** (1902), in which the tableau form is modified by the departure from one location at the end of the shot and their arrival in the next locale in the following shots (not to mention the fully developed continuity of the sequence of the rocket's return to earth in Méliès' film).[13] But this form of continuity finds its complete expression in the chase film, in which the action of dashing from one locale to the next provides the narrative armature of the film.

Although there are prototypes of the chase form from as early as 1901 (Williamson's *Stop Thief!**), it becomes an important form about 1904 with such films as Biograph's *The Maniac Chase** and *Personal**. These films form a sort of template from which an enormous series of imitations and variations are produced over the next four years. The pattern is consistent: a character is chased by a group of characters from one location to the next, with each shot showing the character being chased at some distance from the pursuing mob, the shot held until first the pursued and then the pursuers exit from the frame. The next shot begins this movement through the frame over again. This continues until at some fairly arbitrary point the fleeing figure is captured. This form of narrative was extremely popular and appears in a large number of films. Its dominance is undoubtedly overdetermined, but its mastery of the problem of the disruption of the cut through a narrative continuity shows the way a genre responds to a formal issue raised by preceding genres.

This approach to continuity established by the chase film also allows a series of variations in which continuity of action over a series of cuts establishes a coherent synthetic geography. Films such as *Rescued by Rover** (Hepworth,

Great Britain, 1905) are examples of this, as a sort of sub-genre of the narrative of continuity in which the gags of the single-shot narratives are concatenated along the trajectory of a single character. These films present a series of linked vignettes as a character sets off a series of comic disasters along his route, as in Hepworth's *That Fatal Sneeze* (Great Britain, 1907), in which a man doused with pepper by a mischievous child causes disorder as he sneezes explosively in a succession of locales. Films of this sort appear particularly frequently in 1907 and may signal a recognized need for variation from the chase format and the decline of the genre of continuity.

The fourth genre, the narrative of discontinuity, refers to the reintroduction of the disruption of the cut into situations similar to the chase form. The disruption on the level of plot rather than story comes with the introduction of parallel editing, and its *locus classicus* is the last-minute rescues found in the Biograph films of D. W. Griffith. The appearance of parallel editing represents a particularly important juncture in the history of early film for a number of reasons, not the least of which is its specification of temporal and spatial relations between shots. But in the context of the succession of genres it can be seen as a dialectical response to the genre of continuity represented by the chase film. The earliest clear examples of parallel editing appear around 1907 in such films as *The Runaway Horse* (Pathé,1907) and *The Hundred to One Shot* (Vitagraph, 1906). Although there may be earlier examples, they remain too infrequent to signal anything other than the prototypes of a genre. It is only in 1908 and 1909 that a large number of films appear that make use of this editing pattern.

While the genre of continuity is based on the immediate continuation of an action interrupted in the previous shot, parallel editing interrupts this immediate continuity by interpolating another line of action. Griffith's first extended sequence of parallel editing in *The Fatal Hour* (1908) can exemplify this form. A woman detective has been tied up in front of a gun-clock contraption rigged to fire a bullet into her heart at twelve o'clock. Learning of this, the police rush off to rescue her before the gun goes off. The climactic shots proceed as follows:

Shot 10: Along a country road, a carriage filled with police rushes towards the camera, exiting from the frame (a trajectory familiar from chase films).
Shot 11: The woman detective bound and gagged in the crook's hideout. The clock hands move to 11.52.
Shot 12: A different location on the same country road. The carriage again enters the frame and rushes past the camera.
Shot 13: Return to the woman detective as the clock hands move to 11.57.

Parallel editing represents a discontinuity on the level of plot (the actual assembly of shots) that disrupts the continuity of action on the level of story (the carriage rushing down the road, the movement of the clock hands). By intertwining two lines of action, it literally suspends the outcome of each one, creating that device of narrative delay which is known as *suspense*.

By 1909 parallel editing had become dominant in such rush-to-the-rescue situations and has almost entirely displaced the older chase format. More than any other element it represents the transformation of film syntax that takes place during this period. With its specification of temporal/spatial relations, its effect of an omniscient point of view on action, it is exemplary of the techniques that begin to allow films to formulate works that aspire to the genres of the novel and drama. At this point the factors determining the ciné-genres become quite complex, and the sort of series I have been describing would have to deal with a number of other factors, such as the influence of literary and dramatic genres, the move towards longer films, and the appearance of forms that use a variety of syntagmas in dealing with relations between shots. Undoubtedly the next major syntagma to be introduced would be that of the scene. The scene in this context would be defined as a series of shots which, rather than presenting a succession of locales, analyse and establish a single locale and the action within it. The key articulation in the scene would be the cut-in (or cut-out) in which successive shots overlap spatially. This would find its beginnings in the cut-ins to medium shots in such films as *Mary Jane's Mishap* (Smith, 1903), but becomes a dominant practice around 1912 (in such films as Griffith's *The Lady and the Mouse* or *A Girl and Her Trust*). However, it does not simply displace parallel editing, but seems to perform a different narrative role, so we can see that genre at this historical point needs to be retheorized.

This sketch of a succession of genres needs further investigation in terms of the recognition of such genres by film-makers and audiences. If by genre we mean patterns that determine expectations aroused in audience and patterns followed by film-makers, more evidence of the way films were conceived by producers and understood by audiences is needed. The discussion during the lawsuit between Edison and Biograph over the film *Personal* shows a clear consciousness by the film-makers involved (Edwin S. Porter and Wallace McCutcheon and the companies Biograph and Edison) not only of the chase form but also of the genre of continuity as opposed to the single-shot film.[14] It is in this context that it is particularly clear that a theory of the succession of genres cannot rely on a treatment of the films exclusively.

Certainly other concerns within the corpus of films can supplement the foregoing sketch as well. The four genres I investigated derive from their approach to the articulation between shots. Although I think this is the most important aspect of cinematic plot during this period, there may be room for the consideration of genres based on other aspects of filmic discourse. Likewise consideration of genres outside fictional narrative is needed. It is evident that at least in the early period of this era the dominant genre is, in fact, that of actualities. The sort of cinematic form given to these early actualities needs to be examined more closely in relation to the fictional genres I have discussed.[15]

The discovery that early films were formulated in a different manner than later styles of film-making was an important insight. It allowed us to discover early film as a field of investigation in its own right, rather than as the infancy of an art form. The fact that this difference has been an inspiration to a number of recent avant-garde films is a part of the history of that difference.[16]

And, paradoxically, the fact that these same early films are also the ancestors of later dominant practice is another part of the history of that difference. It is a difference that must haunt us and impel us to discover a method of historical investigation that can do it justice.

Notes

First published in *Iris* vol. 2 no. 1, 1984.

1. This paper has since been published in French: 'Le style non-continu du cinéma des premiers temps', in *Les Cahiers de la Cinémathèque* (Perpignan, hiver 1979) and in English in Roger Holman (ed.), *Cinema 1900/1906: An Analytical Study* (Brussels: FIAF, 1982), Vol. 1, which anthologises all of the papers delivered at the Brighton Conference.
2. Tynyanov quoted by Boris Eichenbaum in 'The theory of the "formal method"' in Lemon and Reis (eds), *Russian Formalist Criticism* (Lincoln, Nebraska, 1965), p. 134.
3. The Formalist approach to genre is discussed in the Eichenbaum essay cited above and is usefully summarized in 'Literary history as a challenge to literary theory' in Hans Robert Jauss, *Towards an Aesthetic of Reception* (Minneapolis, 1982). pp. 16–18.
4. Eichenbaum, 'Theory of "formal method"', p. 135.
5. Ibid., p. 136.
6. Jauss, *Towards an Aesthetic of Reception*, p. 32.
7. Russian Formalist writings on the cinema are found in Herbert Eagle (ed.), *Russian Formalist Film Theory* (Ann Arbor, 1981). On genre, see particularly Tynjanov (Tynyanov) 'On the foundation of cinema', p. 100 and A. Piotrovskij, 'Towards a Theory of cine-genres', pp. 131–46.
8. Piotrovskij, 'Towards a theory of cine-genres', pp. 131–2.
9. Shklovsky, quoted in Eichenbaum, 'Theory of "formal method"', p. 135.
10. Films which are starred appear in the descriptive filmography in Holman, *Cinema 1900/1906*, Vol. 11.
11. See Malthête, 'Méliès technicien du collage', and Gaudreault, '"Théâtralité" et "narrativé" dans l'œuvre de Georges Méliès', both in Madeleine Malthête-Méliès (ed.), *Méliès et la naissance du spectacle cinématographique* (Paris: Klincksieck, 1984), and John Frazer, *Artificially Arranged Scenes* (Boston: G. K. Hall and Co., 1979).
12. See Charles Musser, 'The nickleodeon era begins', pp. 256–73 of this volume.
13. See Gaudreault, '"Théâtralité" et "narrativité"'.
14. See David Levy, 'Edison sales policy and the continuous action film', in John Fell (ed.), *Film Before Griffith* (Berkeley and Los Angeles: University of California Press, 1983), and Gaudreault 'Récit scriptural, récit théâtral, recit filmique: prolégomènes à une théorie narratologique du cinéma' (unpublished doctoral thesis. Université de Paris III), pp. 244–8.
15. David Levy's admirable 'Re-constituted news reels, re-enactments and the American narrative film' in Holman, *Cinema 1900–1906*, is an important beginning in this direction. This article appeared in French: '"The Fake Train Robbery": les reportages simulés, les reconstitutions et le film narratif américain' in *Les Cahiers de la Cinémathèque*, no. 29.
16. One can cite such films as Ken Jacobs' *Tom Tom the Piper's Son*, Ernie Gehr's *Eureka* and Hollis Frampton's *Gloria* as obvious examples. But without direct reference to early cinema, many other films of the American avant-garde can be related to the anomalies of early cinema. See my article 'An unseen energy swallows space: early film and the avant garde' in John Fell, *Film Before Griffith*, pp. 355–66.

'Primitive' Cinema
A Frame-up? Or The Trick's on Us
TOM GUNNING

'People will come back to that, you get sick of everything except sleeping and daydreaming. *The Trip to the Moon* will be back again ...' (Louis-Ferdinand Céline, *Death on the Instalment Plan*).

Frank Norris' 1899 novel *McTeague: A Story of San Francisco*, contains a sequence absent from the novel's definitive film version, Erich von Stroheim's *Greed* (1925). Stroheim updated *McTeague* to the contemporary 1920s and therefore omitted Norris' topical reference to 'the crowning scientific achievement of the nineteenth century, the kinetoscope'.[1] The kinetoscope occupies the next to last place on the bill of the vaudeville programme which Mac and Trina (along with Trina's mother, Mrs Sieppe, and her brother, little Owgooste) attend to celebrate their engagement. Norris describes the effect of this featured attraction:

> The kinetoscope fairly took their breaths away. 'What will they do next?' observed Trina in amazement. 'Ain't that wonderful, Mac?' McTeague was awestruck.
>
> 'Look at that horse move his head,' he cried excitedly, quite carried away. 'Look at the cable car coming – and the man going across the street. See here comes a truck. Well, I never in all my life. What would Marcus say to this?'
>
> 'It's all a drick' exclaimed Mrs Sieppe with sudden conviction. 'I ain't no fool; dot's nothun but a drick.'
>
> 'Well, of course Mamma,' exclaimed Trina; 'it's – '
>
> But Mrs Sieppe put her head in the air. 'I'm too old to be fooled,' she persisted. 'It's a drick.' Nothing more could be got out of her than this.[2]

Although a piece of fiction, this nearly contemporaneous account of the reception of the cinematic image contains rich material for understanding the horizon of expectations in which films originally appeared. Mrs Sieppe's reaction is presented as the pig-headed response of a recent, barely assimilated immigrant (the act on this vaudeville bill that she responds to most favourably is a group of yodellers: 'Joost like der old country'[3]), which exasperates her more informed, modern and American daughter. But what Norris presents as a naive response to the projected moving image directly opposes our now dominant conception of the naive viewings of the first movies. According to current myths of early projections, the first audiences for Lumière's *Arrivée d'un train* rushed from the auditorium for fear of being demolished by the oncoming engine. Far from confusing the film image with reality, Mrs Sieppe dismisses it as mere trickery.

The conflict in Norris' clash in cultural and generational responses does not lie in whether the kinetoscope is a trick: Trina takes this as a matter of course. Trina and Mac accept the trick as a scientific wonder ('Wasn't – wasn't that magic lantern wonderful, where the figures moved? Wonderful – ah wonderful' McTeague intones after the show[4]). Both the suspicious and the enthralled viewers immediately place the phenomenon within the context of visual illusions, the transforming tricks and magic lanterns which vaudeville at the turn of the century exhibited with increasing frequency.[5]

That even pure actuality footage such as Norris describes could summon up such associations calls into question another myth of early film history: the Manichaean division between the films of Lumière (documentary realism) and the films of Méliès (fiction, fantasy, stylization). Clearly the fascination and even the realism of early films related more strongly to the traditions of magic theatre (with its presentation of popular science as spectacle) than to later conceptions of documentary realism. Méliès himself recognized this at his first viewing of Lumière films, proclaiming the projection, 'an extraordinary trick' ('un truc extraordinaire').[6]

Placing the first projections of moving film images within the context of the tradition of visual illusions allows us to overcome the distorting view of the reception of early actuality films as simply achievements in cinematic realism. Likewise, a close examination of the genre of film-making which explicitly continued the tradition of visual illusions, the 'trick film', allows us to call into question the very terms of our discussion of this early period, particularly the rubric 'primitive' cinema and its connotations.

The notion of the first decade of film history as a 'primitive' period has been hard to shake. Recent scholars have expressed reservations about the term and emphasized that they employ it in a non-pejorative sense.[7] The term 'primitive' persists, I believe, partly out of inertia, but also because it cradles a number of connotations which stand in need of further examination and critique. The most regrettable connotations are those of an elementary or even childish mastery of form in contrast to a later complexity (and need we add that this viewpoint often shelters its apparent reversal in the image of a cinema of a lost purity and innocence?). But the limitations of this view seem fairly obvious and I believe it is disappearing.

However, a less pejorative variation of these connotations still persists, if only from a lack of an alternate way to view this early period of development. These connotations see the earliest period of cinema as a period of lack in relation to later evolution. This lack has most often been specified as a relative absence of editing, a nearly monolithic concept of the shot unsubordinated to any editing schema. Even those who maintain the uniqueness and value of early film within a non-linear view of film history have a hard time avoiding a description of early cinema as a sort of degree zero in the evolution of montage.

It is not my purpose to deny the subordinate role of editing in early film. In fact it is precisely the role played by the single viewpoint embodied in the monolithic shot that I wish to define with more precision. There is no doubt that one of the defining aspects of early cinema (and an element of what has been called the 'non–continuous style of early film'[8]) is the relative autonomy of the single shot. However, the meaning of this phenomenon is deceptively simple, and only apparently elementary. As I shall show, this regime of the single uninterrupted shot, independent and unsubordinated to the demands of montage, is often an appearance rather than a reality, a mask for a complex but easily ignored labour, a distraction from the traces of a historically neglected practice. Or, as Mrs Sieppe would put it, a trick. In fact, we could say that the single monolithic shot functions as a trick which film audiences and historians have not seen through for decades.

The understanding of editing in early film as primitive intertwines with the myth of early film as a simple reproduction of the pre-existing art of theatre (minus the voice). According to this view, the single shot functions as a reproduction of the theatrical proscenium (the long-shot framing) and the theatrical scene (the lengthy uninterrupted shot). This understanding oversimplifies the traditions from which early cinema derives. As a variety of researchers have recently shown, early film drew on traditions as various as the forms of popular entertainments appearing at the turn of the century, and not at all restricted to the legitimate theatre. The initial reception of film projections as one in a series of visual illusions alerts us to the particular importance of what Charles Musser has called the 'tradition of screen entertainments' (the magic lantern and related projected illusions), and the magical (rather than the dramatic) theatre to a new understanding of early film.

Anyone who has seen more than a handful of early films recognizes the many violations of the stage tableau and proscenium arch framing that are found in films before 1907. The 'facial expression' genre in which characters mug at the camera in close-up or medium shot forms one dramatic example. But my point goes beyond simply establishing the varied sorts of framing found in early film. I assert that early film's tendency to rely upon the space within the frame rather than the possibilities of juxtaposition between shots involves a particular attitude towards the filmic illusion and one which is far from a Bazinian aesthetic of non-manipulation. In fact the single shot contained (seemingly) by a single framing was manufactured by certain early film-makers precisely as an illusion. And the maintenance of a single point of view relates more to a particular mode of audience address than to a passive or primitive approach to film-making.

The most commonly recognized technique of early trick films, what is frequently referred to as 'stop motion substitution', provides a proving ground. This trick lies behind the magical transformations which find their *locus classicus* in the films of Georges Méliès, but which exist, of course, in trick films of all nations and producers, and which frequently can be found in non-trick films as well. Based partly on Méliès' oversimplified and (intentionally, I believe) misleading description of his technique, this process has been explained as a stopping of the camera at a predetermined point, a profilmic rearrangement of actors or props, and then a resumption of the turning of the camera. This was certainly part of the process.

However, as John Frazer has pointed out,[9] and as Jacques Malthête has systematically demonstrated, the trick only began here.[10] Examination of the actual prints of Méliès films reveal that in every case, this stop motion technique was in fact revised through splicing. Variation in hand-cranked camera speed when stopping and starting, as well as refinements possible only at this stage, called for the actual cutting of the film at the beginning and ending of the interrupted action and the subsequent splicing of it together. Examination of positive prints of Méliès films led Jacques Malthête to declare that in Méliès there is never any trick of substitution which does not make use of splicing. For Malthête, Méliès is not simply a master of 'trucage' but also an unacknowledged master of 'collage',[11] the altering of filmic reality through the act of cutting and splicing which we normally associate with the act of editing. This for a film-maker so often criticized for under-utilizing the possibilities of editing because of his attachment to the theatrical practice.[12]

This discovery of a previously unperceived process of film cutting raises enormous problems of definitions for the film historian. Does a film like *The Terrible Turkish Executioner*, which previously seemed to contain only a single shot with numerous substitution tricks due to stop motion, now demand description as a film made up of multiple shots? Is Méliès not only a master of collage, but in fact the father of montage? Although this could be subject to debate, I believe it would be equally distorting to see Méliès' trick splice as the equivalent of cuts which perform basic spatial and temporal articulations. As André Gaudreault has said in an essay which revises our view of Méliès:

> The point is not to turn Méliès into the predecessor of Griffith or Eisenstein or to turn him into the father of montage. Rather the point is to recognise that in his work and in many of the other films of the era there exists a type of editing which is all too often occulted by the privileged status that film historians regularly grant to the later form of narrative editing.[13]

What should astonish film historians here is the process of production, the painstaking technical labour this 'splice of substitution' involves, one which includes careful attention to the minutiae of 'matching' continuity and creates a particular mode of address to the spectator.

Such care taken with the problems of creating a seamless illusion of transformation should finally dispel any conception of early film-makers as primitive in relation to their technology (if anyone who has read Méliès' even incomplete description of the technical concerns surrounding the production of trick films is not already convinced).[14] But, further, it shows early film-makers were concerned with issues that traditionally they are thought to have ignored, those of precise continuity of action over a splice. The splices in Méliès' films are managed in order to maintain the flow and rhythm of acting which a mere stopping of the camera could not provide. While later classical editing can be referred to as 'invisible editing' only metaphorically, such 'substitution splices' are nearly literally invisible, having passed for the last eight decades for the most part without notice.

Does this mean that the concept of early film editing as 'non-continuous' needs to be abandoned? Although I feel the term still indicates something of the early film's alterity from later practice, it does need modification. Even if this early form of continuity editing (or splicing) does show a striking prefiguration of later ideals of matching action, it none the less serves a very different purpose and the alterity of early cinema remains evident within it. As is often the case, the insights of Noël Burch provide importance guidance. Burch refers to the lack of editing in early film in terms of 'the *autarky* and *unicity* of each frame'.[15] The clarification here is the use of the term *frame* rather than shot. Burch does not refer, of course, to the frame as a unit of celluloid, but to the framing of the shot. A consideration of Méliès' use of the 'substitution splice' shows that what is maintained is both a continuity of action *and* (in contrast to later continuity editing) a continuity of framing. It is the absolute duplication of framing over the splice which, along with the continuity of action, allows the interruption to be all but imperceptible to the viewer.

Burch has not elaborated his understanding of the unicity of the frame in exactly this way. However, his discussion of the 1902 Pathé trick film *The Ingenious Soubrette* clearly regards the continuity of framing as more important than the singleness of a shot in early cinema. This film consists of three shots which seem to frame identically the same set of a bourgeois parlour in which a maid hangs paintings on the wall. However, the second shot, which appears to reproduce faithfully the framing of the first, is in fact an overhead view of a set constructed so that the maid (ingeniously, indeed) seems simply to slide up the wall as she hangs the pictures. The film's third and final shot returns to the initial camera placement. The apparently identical framing of all three shots masks the switches in camera placement, so the film appears to be one continuous uninterrupted shot, and thus creates the illusion of the maid's seeming conquest of the laws of gravity. Burch observes that 'the overwhelming dominance of frontality and unicity of viewpoint in the Primitive Era must have made such tricks totally effective illusions . . . .'[16]

The continuity that is preserved and fostered in early cinema, then, is one of viewpoint, of framing, to make explicit a point Burch leaves implicit. This concern for a unified viewpoint of the action (an act of enframing which does not vary even as the action within it is synthetically constructed by a series of concealed splices) differs sharply from the classical continuity system based on dramatic and psychological analysis and fragmentation. In the classical system a variety of viewing angles and distances are related to a larger spatial whole and these relations are regulated by the rules of continuity editing. While the continuity system maintains a consistent spatial orientation for the viewer, the variations between shots allow a dramatic and spatial articulation of the action. In contrast, the approach of early film privileges the single viewpoint and its posture of displaying something to the audience. The substitution splice is based on maintaining the apparent continuity of this single viewpoint, rather than a dramatic articulation of a story through varied shots.

In contrast to this dramatic analysis, early film's unity of framing and viewpoint defines the primary act of film-making as one of display, of showing, of showmanship. To borrow a term from André Gaudreault's narratological treatment of cinema (and to revise its meaning a bit),[17] the film-maker of early cinema appears as a *monstrator*, one who shows, a showman. But this act of showmanship within a unity of framing differs considerably from the theatricality with which it has been identified, first by Georges Sadoul, subsequently by Jean Mitry,[18] and even by Burch. Pierre Jenn in his recent work on Méliès has launched a particularly strong attack against this conception of Méliès' 'theatricality', developing points first raised by André Gaudreault. Jenn points out that rather than passive theatricality, this unity of viewpoint plays an essential role in concealing the process of the trick. Unity of point of view gives the illusion of a theatrical unity of time, when, in fact, the substitution splice creates a specifically cinematic synthesis of time. The framing of Méliès' composition, taken by historians as a sign of his 'primitive' theatricality, reveals itself as consciously constructed illusion designed to distract attention from the actual cinematic process at work.[19] And, at least for some film historians, it has succeeded.

The importance of framing and unity of viewpoint in early cinema need not be identified with the proscenium arch. Although the frontality of the theatrical tableau may have presented one model of framing for early film-makers, there were several other sources from which they drew both inspiration and subject matter. The screen itself as the unchanging site of projected images in the magic lantern tradition is an important one, as David Francis among others has pointed out.[20] The variety of processes used in trick slides and dissolving views, in which one element of a slide might change while the setting remained the same, offers a clear parallel to the effect of the substitution splice. Similarly the role of the frame in stereoscope cards, comic strips and postcards may have exerted as much influence as the proscenium arch on early film-makers. Further, although certainly the staging and framing in a Méliès film often (although not always, as Jenn points out[21]) recall theatrical practice, a similar concern for unity of viewpoint can be found in patently non-theatrical films as well, from the 'facial expression' films to the radically non-theatrical framings of the English Brighton School film-makers.

One of the most astounding of these early British films, *How It Feels to Be Run Over* (Cecil Hepworth, 1900), shows the essential role a single viewpoint played in the structure of certain early British films, through humorously invoking the direct address it offers the spectator. This single-shot film shows a buggy passing the camera, followed by an automobile. The auto's driver seems suddenly blinded by the buggy's dust and veers directly at the camera threatening a collision with this fixed viewpoint of camera/spectator. This collision apparently occurs, as the front of the car engulfs the field of vision and the film cuts to a section of black leader to represent this total disaster. Words then appear scratched on the leader, reading: 'Oh Dear Mother Will Be Pleased'.

Such framing and motion contrast sharply with the frontality and distance that typify the theatrical tableau. However, in spite of its non-theatrical movement, the film employs a fixed framing for its trick effect, a viewpoint that is maintained until it is literally untenable, pushing the unity of point of view in early film to a *reductio ad absurdum* which bares the device. Many other films of early cinema (e.g. Williamson's *The Big Swallow* or the many railway films of the 'phantom rides' or Hale's Tours sort) play in similar ways with unity of point of view within a non-theatrical framing. It is the framing itself, its marking of the act of display, that remains primary. The spectator is directly addressed, even confronted, by these plays with framing. In the same way the trick film maintains its unchanging frame in order to display its magical transformations directly to the audience.

We are dealing, then, with an approach to cinema which stresses film's ability to present a view, a tendency André Gaudreault and I have referred to as the 'cinema of attractions'.[22] This cinema differs from later narrative cinema through its fascination in the thrill of display rather than the construction of a story. Burch, I believe, obscures the evolution of film style when he defines the 'linchpin' of the later institutional mode of representation (his term which basically corresponds to what I have been calling the classical system of continuity) as 'spectatorial identification with a ubiquitous camera'.[23] Spectatorial identification with the viewpoint of the camera is a linchpin of early cinema as well, as *How It Feels* dramatically demonstrates. For Burch this film and others like it 'act out' the process of centring a spectator within a diegesis through camera identification, thereby establishing the central strategies of the institutional mode of representation, strategies that Burch finds more central than the development of narrative.[24]

But without an understanding of the way the classical mode of film-making subordinates cinematic techniques to the task of narration, we lose our grasp on the fundamentally integrating role the narrative plays. Coherence of story and storytelling allows the classical mode to fashion a unity from a proliferation of viewpoints and shots, through identification of the camera with an act of narration. The classical film can absorb sudden ubiquitous switches in viewpoint into an act of storytelling, creating a cinema whose role is less display than articulating a story. The continuity of classical cinema is based on the coherence of story, and the spectator's identification with the camera is mediated through her engagement with the unfolding of the story.[25]

In early film spectator relations are direct and relatively unmediated by concern with the story. As Jean Mitry has said, speaking of Méliès, 'it is not the spectator who was introduced into the space of the film, but rather the space which comes forward to present itself to him within a uniformity of theatrical framing.'[26] However, as we have seen, this unity of framing should not be identified with theatricality. Rather a more primal fascination with the act of display grounds the theatrical tableau, the medium shot of such facial expression films as Edison's *May Irwin Kiss*, the mobile vantage-point of the 'phantom railway rides', and the magical transformations contained within a single framing but created by substitution splices.

If the enunciator of early film is less a narrator than a monstrator, we must recognize the monstrator's mark in the act of framing. The frame presents the action displayed to the spectator. It is the unity of this framed viewpoint which addresses her specifically and directly, and this is the continuity the film-makers wished to preserve. However, such framing is a far from passive act, and not all due to either a primitive lack of expertise or a purist's desire to avoid manipulation. Early films are enframed rather than emplotted, and what is contained by their framing is often a result of a complex and detailed labour, one which, in the tradition of nineteenth-century illusionism, labours to efface its traces just as surely as did the later classical style.

Here again we encounter the strange intertwining of the traditions of realistic illusionism and the magic theatre. In maintaining a single point of view through his concealed substitution splices, Méliès (and other early film-makers) were drawing undoubtedly on the tradition and methods of behind-the-scenes manipulation found in the late nineteenth-century magic theatre. The detailed description that Méliès produced of the mechanisms and methods for producing visual illusions at his Théâtre Robert-Houdin (which have recently been reprinted in both the Malthête-Méliès anthology and Jenn's book) show how much these stage illusions were based on controlling the audience's view of the action either through lighting or mechanical devices. The magic theatre of the turn of the century was a technically sophisticated laboratory for the production of visual effects using recent technology to control spectators' perceptions.[27] It is this aspect of Méliès' theatrical inheritance that demands more attention from film historians, rather than a simple reference to the primitive use of proscenium framing.

For Méliès, this theatre was a theatre of illusions rather than a theatre of illusionism. But in the evolution of late nineteenth-century theatre there is a subterranean connection between these two apparently different approaches. David Belasco, for instance, could begin his career as a master of the Pepper's Ghost Illusion, yet reach his height of fame as the man who managed the perfect recreation of Child's Restaurant on stage, complete with the smell of real pancakes cooking on the griddle.[28] We might wonder with Mrs Sieppe whether managing the illusion of reality does not fundamentally correspond with the trick that produces an apparently supernatural event.

We confront here the essential paradox of the history of early film and to which Buurch consistently calls our attention. It is simultaneously different from later practices – an alternate cinema – and yet profoundly related to the cinema that followed it. This relation must be approached avoiding the bioloigical or progress-laden metaphors which a term like 'primitive' supplies. The substitution splice reveals a film-making praxis which is strongly concerned with continuity, but conceives of this continuity in a radically different manner from the cinema which follows. Such a move from a cinema of attractions to one of storytelling involves a change in basic spectator address which must be recognized if the logic of film history is to be traced in all its complexity.

Notes

1. Frank Norris, *McTeague: A Story of San Francisco* (New York: Signet, 1964), p. 79. The kinetoscope, of course, was the original name for Edison's peep-show device. However, since Norris' reference is to projected images, he is undoubtedly referring to Edison's Projecting Kinetoscope which was placed on the market in February 1897 (see Charles Musser, *Thomas Edison Papers: A Guide to Motion Picture Catalogues by American Producers and Distributors 1894–1908* (Frederick, Maryland: University Publications of America, 1985), p. 8.

2. Norris, *McTeague*, pp. 85–6.
3. Ibid., p. 85.
4. Ibid., p. 87.
5. See Robert C. Allen, *Vaudeville and Film 1895–1915: A Study in Media Interaction* (New York: Arno Press, 1980), pp. 57–64, 311.
6. Anne-Marie Quévrain and Marie-George Charconnet-Méliès, 'Méliès et Freud: un avenir pour les marchands d'illusions?', in Madeleine Malthête-Méliès (ed.), *Méliès et la naissance du spectacle cinématographique* (Paris: Klincksieck, 1984), p. 235.
7. See Kristin Thompson, in David Bordwell, Janet Staiger and Kristin Thompson, *The Classical Hollywood Cinema: Film Style and Mode of Production to 1960* (New York: Columbia University Press, 1985), p. 158.
8. Tom Gunning, 'The noncontinuous style of early film', in Roger Holman (ed.), *Cinema 1900/1906: An Analytical Study* (Brussels: FIAF, 1982).
9. See John Frazer, *Artificially Arranged Scenes: The Films of George Méliès* (Boston: G. K. Hall & Co., 1979), pp. 74–5.
10. Jacques Malthête, 'Méliès, technicien du collage', in Malthête-Méliès, *Méliès*.
11. Ibid., p. 171.
12. See, for instance, Georges Sadoul, *Histoire générale du cinéma, Vol. II: Les pionniers du cinéma* (Paris: Denoël, 1948), p. 270.
13. André Gaudreault, 'Theatricality, narrativity and "trickality": reevaluating the cinema of Georges Méliès', *Journal of Popular Film and Television*, vol. 15 no. 3, Fall 1987, p. 118. (This is an abridged and revised translation by Paul Attalah, Vivian Sobchak and Tom Gunning of Gaudreault's '"Théâtralité" et "narrativité" dans l'oeuvre de George Méliès', in Malthête-Méliès, *Méliès*.)
14. See 'Les vues cinématographiques' in Georges Sadoul (ed.), *Georges Méliès* (Paris: Seghers, 1961).
15. Noël Burch, 'Primitivism and the avant-gardes: a dialectical approach', in Phil Rosen (ed.), *Narrative – Apparatus – Ideology* (New York: Columbia University Press, 1986), p. 486.
16. Ibid., p. 500.
17. André Gaudreault, 'Récit scriptural, récit théâtral, récit filmique: prolégomènes à une théorie narratologique du cinéma' (unpublished doctoral thesis, Université de Paris III, 1983).
18. See, for instance, Jean Mitry, 'Le montage dans les films de Méliès', in Malthête-Méliès, *Méliès*.
19 Pierre Jenn, *Georges Méliès cinéaste* (Paris: Albatros, 1984), pp. 26–9.
20. David Francis, 'Films à trucs (1896–1901)', in Pierre Guibbert (ed.), *Les Premiers Ans du cinéma français* (Perpignan: Institut Jean Vigo, 1985), p. 144.
21. Jenn, *Méliès*, passim. However, the strong influence of theatrical technique on Méliès should not be entirely discounted, as Jacques Malthête reminds us in 'Organisation de l'éspace scénique méliésien', in Guibbert, *Les Premiers Ans*.
22. In 'The Cinema of Attractions: Early Film, Its Spectator and the Avant-Garde', pp. 56–62, of this volume. Also Gunning and Gaudreault, 'Early film as a challenge to film history', paper delivered at Conference in Cerisy on Film History, 1985.
23. Burch, 'Primitivism', p. 491.
24. See Noël Burch, 'How we got into pictures: notes accompanying *Correction Please*', *Afterimage*, 8/9, Spring 1981; and 'Narrative diegesis – thresholds, limits', *Screen*, vol. 23 no. 2, July–August 1982.
25. I therefore state my agreement with Ben Brewster's article 'A Scene at the "Movies"', pp. 318–25 of this volume, which Burch's article in the same issue argues with. Brewster asserts the importance of narrative point of view over simple camera identification in forming the classical style.
26. Jean Mitry, 'Le montage', p. 151 (my translation).
27. See particularly Georges Méliès, 'Un grand succès du Théâtre Robert-Houdin', in Jenn, *Georges Méliès*, pp. 161–8.
28. Sée Lise-Lotte Marker, *David Belasco: Naturalism in the American Theater* (Princeton: Princeton University Press, 1975), pp. 24–5, 61–2.

Shots in the Dark
The Real Origins of Film Editing
STEPHEN BOTTOMORE

'In any study of the development of film technique, the lesson to be learned, I think, is not to neglect the actuality film in favour of the fiction film.' John Barnes, *The Rise of the Cinema in Great Britain*

From the earliest days, both film-makers and theorists have recognised the central role of editing in the art of the film. But how exactly did the editing process originate? And when? Over the years, there have been many attempts to answer these questions. It has been said that one or other film pioneer, such as James Williamson or Edwin Porter, 'invented' editing, some time between 1900 and 1903. I would argue, however, that much of the work had already been done in the first five years of the cinema's existence, before Williamson and Porter made their famous films. Like many early innovations both in film technique and equipment design, editing, the joining together of sections of film to recreate space and time, originated less with drama than with the actuality films of real events.[1]

The first films to be shown in 1895 were single shots, rarely longer than a minute, recording scenes of everyday life. It has been said that the Lumières set up their cameras and 'went on shooting until the stock ran out' (Karel Reisz).[2] But more care was involved than this would imply. Marshall Deutelbaum has observed that the Lumière single-shot actualities were not simply 'unadjusted, unarranged, untampered reality' but that 'each presents a process ... in such a way that the beginning of the film coincides with the beginning of the process.'[3] As early as 1897, Cecil Hepworth had an assistant to act as time-keeper, keeping an eye on the events before the camera to see 'that they finish before all the film is used up'.[4] Such standards were considered important, so that from the very first films there was often a kind of 'editing' implicit in the process of shooting.

In the earliest period, projector design did not allow for films to be joined together without the risk of tearing (this had to wait until autumn 1896, when apparatus with a small loop of film between the intermittent and the heavy reels was introduced by several manufacturers).[5] In the Lumière shows, films were shown singly, and there was a considerable wait while each was laced up. 'A picture lasting 45 seconds, succeeded by a wait of about two minutes, robs shows of this kind of much of the pleasure they would otherwise afford', noted the *Optical Magic Lantern Journal* (June 1897).

Some showmen projected lantern slides to fill the gaps, and shows combining films with slides soon became longer and more complex.[6] Indeed, cinema was often seen as an extension of the lantern, and 'cinematographic slides' was a common term for films. Hepworth suggested using slides and film, and 'stringing the pictures together into little sets or episodes', using an 'argument' or 'plot' in the commentary to make it hang together. (As in the lantern era proper, a running commentary read by the showman was the norm.) From 1897, at the Eden Musée in New York, long series of images were put together by the exhibitor, including a 'Panorama' during the Spanish American War of twenty or more films together with lantern slides. And an even more ambitious show was assembled in Australia in 1900. *Soldiers of the Cross* has been quoted as the first feature film ever made – at the stupendous length of two and a quarter hours. In fact, it only had thirteen short films: the bulk was made up of 200 slides shown with music and commentary.

Long before this, however, the new projection equipment had allowed exhibitors to join the minute-long films together, splicing twelve or more on to a single large reel.[7] Often they were not joined directly: a small length of blank film of 6 to 18 inches was inserted between each view, giving about a second of black between shots.[8] The main reason for this was that cutting directly from one shot to another was thought to be visually disruptive. Indeed, Hepworth continued to include blank film between shots in every film he made up to the First World War, and even in his 1951 autobiography still maintained that it 'avoided the harsh, unpleasant "jerk" usually associated with change of scene'. As late as 1918, in *How Motion Pictures Are Made*, Homer Croy observed that shot transitions 'without warning and without intermediate change' meant that 'the eye suffered a shock.'[9]

Despite this, there were early efforts at making multi-shot films. By 1897, complete boxing match films were being exhibited, lasting over an hour, as well as a thirteen-scene version of the *Vie et Passion de Jésus Christ* (Lumière).[10] A year later, two- and three-shot films were coming from Georges Méliès' studio, and in 1899 the twenty-shot *Cendrillon*.

So was Méliès a pioneer of film editing, as some historians have recently claimed? He certainly helped to establish the acceptability of longer films, and the idea that shots could be joined together. Ultimately, however, the technique of the magician/film-maker derives from the theatre: his multi-scene films are merely multi-scene theatre that has been filmed. Almost every shot is taken from the front, reproducing the viewpoint of someone in the theatre audience, and one shot is normally one scene.[11] Méliès' films, indeed, were often sold as separate shots (which gave purchasers the option of buying only some scenes), and he and others frequently used the lantern technique of dissolving rather than cutting, partly to reduce the possible disruption between shots.[12] In these early multi-shot drama films there seems to be what Tom Gunning has called a 'non-continuous style', a desire to emphasise the junctions between rather than the action across cuts.

The first genuine steps towards 'continuity editing', it seems to me, came from quite another direction. Most film historians maintain that there is no true editing before 1900, since in all multi-shot films made before that date each shot represents a different scene taking place at a different time or in a different place. But while this is true for dramas of the Méliès type, it is not true for non-fiction. Here, series of disparate shots were soon giving way to series of shots of one event, such as a procession or a horserace. At first, shots were listed in the company catalogues with no suggestions about combining them. But by 1897 hints were being given to purchasers that they should buy several views of one event. The Warwick Trading Company's 1897–8 catalogue says of three views of a Madrid procession that they 'should be joined in the above order'. Or, about eleven views of a bullfight: 'When joined and shown consecutively as here arranged, [they] constitute a thrilling exhibition of 10 minutes duration.'[13] Note that this is not just a case of separate films being shown together, as in the 'programmes' of films and slides. Here, rather, we have several shots covering one time period and adjacent spaces.

After the 1897 Jubilee of Queen Victoria, several firms offered films of the procession passing through London, taken from different points along the route. Such films were offered for sale with the recommendation that they be joined 'in the above order and shown consecutively'.[14] And in terms of editing, these combinations are a significant development, predating similar techniques in the drama. *Stop Thief!*, for instance, was made in late 1901 by James Williamson – the story of a tramp stealing some meat and being chased by the butcher. In three shots we see the protagonists come towards and then past the camera before cutting to the next shot. This style of editing was to become characteristic of the chase films, of which *Stop Thief!* was the first. Yet a very similar kind of cutting is seen in views of processions, with the procession coming towards and past the camera – just the direction of movement that chase films always employed – followed by a cut. The chase film cut from shot to shot to follow characters running; with real events, shots covering happenings over an extended space could be joined to follow the procession's progress.[15] So this kind of editing was already under way by the time the chase film came along and needed a similar treatment some four years later.

Another key example comes from a genre that had been popular since the lantern days: the fire brigade rescue. At the Grand Café in Paris, a series of four Lumière films was shown from January 1896 (*Departure of Fire Engine*, *Getting Ready*, *Playing on a Fire*, *Life Saving*).[16] The films showed Lyon firemen at work, and the fire was apparently set up. Despite being sold separately, the films clearly made up an edited sequence, as did a similar sequence of four films advertised in 1897 by the Warwick Trading Company in Britain (*The Big Fire*: 'The Alarm', 'The Run to the Fire', 'Arriving at the Scene of the Action', 'The Rescue from a Burning Building').[17] It is interesting that, unlike the Lumière films, these do not have consecutive catalogue numbers and clearly represent an effort by the company to create a sequence out of existing shots. Thus the distributor/manufacturer is starting to take over the exhibitor's creative role.

Again, these sequences make an interesting comparison with Williamson's work. His *Fire!*, made in late 1901, is considered a landmark of editing. It consists of five shots: 1. A policeman finds a building on fire. 2. He comes to the fire station and the engine races out. 3. In a street the engine speeds past the camera. 4. A fireman enters a burning building and carries out a fainting man. 5. Outside, the man is brought down a ladder and other rescues follow.

In editing terms, there is an obvious parallel with what the actualities were starting to do, as action is followed logically from one shot to another. The real advance was that *Fire!* used these techniques in a *acted* film (and included an interior scene), with the actor going from shot to shot providing an additional element of continuity.

Barry Salt believes that Williamson's films were the originators of 'action continuity through shots cut directly together' and that 'so far no other films repeating the continuous shot-to-shot movement of Williamson's films are known before early 1903.' But there are the beginnings of a similar kind of shot-to-shot continuity in the procession and fire films I have described, when we see, for instance, a fire engine coming towards and past the camera and cut to the next shot of the arrival at the fire.

Our reason that these films have been ignored by historians, no doubt, is that the shots were not sold ready joined. It was only *suggested* that they be shown as a sequence, though by May 1901 the *Showman* listed a twenty-two-shot documentary with the proviso, 'These pictures are not sold separately'.[18] Yet there were multi-shot actualities sold as single films in the earliest period, and the innovators here seem to have been not the distributors or the exhibitors, but the cameramen.

In his 1897 book, *The ABC of the Cinematograph*, Cecil Hepworth makes a useful distinction between filming 'the known and the unknown'. The former meant events specifically set up for the camera – men building a wall, a game of cards – which the film-maker could control. With 'the unknown' – public occasions, sporting events – one didn't know what would happen, and it was this factor that dictated some form of editing. One could simply show the whole event, and this was sometimes done. It was unusual, however, and as a rule such long films were sold in minute-long sections. A better way was needed to summarise the events on film.

Hepworth suggested this method to news cameramen:

> However promising the beginning may be, long before the end all interesting incident may have given out. In which case, perhaps the best thing to do is to at once leave off turning, without moving the instrument, and resume turning when suitable incidents recur.[19]

This would lead to what is called a jump-cut.

It was a remarkably common technique, and one can see such cuts in many surviving actualities. There is sometimes a slightly overexposed frame between the two 'shots' where the camera was stopped (which distinguishes a stoppage from an original splice, or later print damage). *Train Coming into a Station* (Smith, 1896)[20] shows a train coming towards us and going straight past. There is a camera stoppage, then another train is seen going away. The stoppage is clearly to get rid of the otherwise empty time between the two trains. The same effect was sometimes improved by an actual splice; the event was filmed and part was later excised. Such jump-cutting was also used by Méliès, to create his magical changes and disappearances. But where he used the technique to reproduce theatrical tricks, for actuality cameramen it was a first step towards better representing the real world on screen.[21]

Once this editing of real time was achieved, the division of real space into shots followed as cameramen moved about to get the best view of the action. Warwick's coverage of the Sheffield-Derby football match of 1899, for instance, consisted of five shots: entering field; midfield play; Sheffield gets a corner; Derby's only goal; players leaving field.[22] Here the cameraman has left off turning at moments of little interest and has also moved and/or panned his camera between sections to achieve multi-shot coverage of the space. A similar techniqe was used in *Salvaging a Steamroller* (GB, *c*, 1900)[23] in which the cameraman stops his camera (about ten times) to move to a better position to continue filming. And in *Admiral Dewey at State House, Boston* (Edison, 1899), a combination of jump-cuts and four changes of camera position were needed.[24] Such camera mobility through necessity was there from the earliest days: Birt Acres in 1896 had a horserace series with up to five shots, showing different aspects of one race.

It was the same inflexibility of real events that led to another innovation in actuality filming. The first use of a reverse angle – the camera changing its view of a scene by at least 90 degrees – is usually said to have been in *Ladies' Skirts Nailed to a Fence* (GB, 1900). Yet the cut here is not a genuine reverse angle but a Méliès-style cheat: the camera hasn't moved, but the fence is turned around to show the actors on the other side nailing the skirts. We must wait another three years to see the genuine article in drama, yet in actualities primitive reverse angles were in use before the turn of the century.

In *Arrest in Chinatown, San Francisco* (Edison, 1897),[25] there are two shots showing a Chinese being brought towards camera and then we cut to see him driven away in the paddy wagon. Clearly, the cameraman has filmed the first part of the action and then swivelled his camera as it moved away. But there were more sophisticated examples. *The Early Morning Attack* (Edison, 1899) was in four shots, showing a company of US troops advancing up a hill against an enemy. Here we have a reverse angle on the action in shot 2. Interestingly, this film was not an actuality but a reconstruction, which nevertheless borrowed the more sophisticated techniques that were being used on real events.

The history books say that the first film to divide a scene up into separate shots was G. A. Smith's *Grandma's Reading Glass* (September 1900), in which various objects a little boy examines with a magnifying glass in an establishing shot are cut in as point-of-view close-ups. This idea, using the cut-ins as a kind of 'stunt', seems to have been taken from a lantern original. Lantern shows could be surprisingly innovative in editing: as well as cutting in to close-ups and from exteriors to interiors, there were reverse angles ('here we have another view – only looking in the opposite direction': Mason, 1889) and point-of-view cutting, as a slide of a traveller is intercut with views of the countryside. Alexander Black even used a form of cross-cutting. The first genuine cutting within a scene had to wait until 1901 or 1902.[26]

Yet in actualities, even before this date, we find some use of intra-scene cutting. *Shoot the Chutes* (Edison, 1899), for instance, consisted of three shots of an amusement park ride: 1. looking across the bottom of the slide; 2. from the top, watching people sliding down; 3. point of view sliding into the water. Here the cameraman has obviously filmed the most interesting views to give us a better idea of the ride than we could get from a single shot. The difficulties of filming the real world dictated some kind of editing. When Warwick filmed an inaccessible waterfall in 1901, it was 'an impossibility to portray the entire falls in one picture',[27] so they used four shots, including a cut into a close-up. And even where one shot could have encompassed the whole action, actuality film-makers soon started using several. Only months after *Grandma's Reading Glass*, a Warwick film of a factory chimney being razed[28] started with a 'close view' of the props ablaze, cutting out to a distance shot of the whole chimney and then to another view to see it collapse.

It is apparent that by this time the makers of actualities were learning some key lessons about film-making. One of the most basic was that you don't need to show everything that has been filmed. Hepworth's advertisement in the *Showman* in February 1901 announced: 'Kindly note there is no "padding" to these pictures. We only publish 500 ft, though over 2,000 ft of film are exposed, for all the least interesting portions have been removed.' And there were other lessons. For example, in Hepworth's film of Queen Victoria's funeral (1901), shots of the procession at Cowes and at Victoria Station were separated by a short shot, 'Crossing Solent'. The *Showman* advertisement said that this 'was not of sufficient interest to form a subject by itself but . . . forms the completing link in the chain.'[29] This idea of a shot being used merely as a link would be crucial to later film-makers. And there was the cutaway. In *Taking President McKinley's Body from Train at Canton, Ohio* (Edison, 1901), a shot looking away from the main action is inserted to avoid a jump in linking separate views of the coffin being carried. (There is also a cut into a closer shot and a reverse angle in this remarkable film.)

By 1901, therefore, actualities were employing a range of new practices, all it seems to me pointing towards the idea of sequences using interdependent shots and away from the original view of shots as individual items. How does this relate to the early film-makers in drama, who are claimed as the inventors of editing? In fact, the link was a close one, and the early development of editing in factual and fiction films may be seen as part of the same process.

Many of the drama film-makers started off by filming actuality. Hepworth, an early user of dramatic editing with *Rescued by Rover* (1905), was also a producer of factual films. James Williamson began by making actuality films, of which some (including the 1899 *Bank Holiday at the Dyke*)[30] were multi-shot. G. A. Smith also made actualities, and was probably the first to combine drama and actuality (*The Kiss in the Tunnel*, 1899). In America, Edwin Porter, famous for *The Great Train Robbery*, began by 'editing' actuality and drama films together for the Eden Musée shows.

And the actuality continued to exert a powerful influence on drama films. Many historians have observed the liberating effect of exterior filming: the early films shot on location are usually more advanced in editing and use of camera angles than films made in studio sets. It has been claimed that this was due to the negative impact on studio films of the theatricality of Méliès and others. But I would argue that the positive influence of actualities may be just as important. Film-makers were used to moving their camera about to get the best views of events; and it was only a simple step to using this technique in films involving actors.

Refining the actuality's editing techniques and extending them to drama was in itself a major creative leap, allowing all kinds of new connections between shots. For example, in Williamson's *Attack on a Chinese Mission Station* (late 1900), there is a shot of the missionary's wife waving for help and an immediate cut to a distant group of soldiers starting to the rescue. Here we have editing between simultaneous actions, a prototype of cross-cutting undreamt of in actualities.

The fact remains, however, that because early cinema studies have concentrated so largely on post-1900 fiction films, the true contribution of the actuality has never been properly assessed. The often anonymous makers of these first films of real life were innovators in their own right. The 'creative treatment of actuality', as Grierson defined documentary, would seem to be almost as old as the cinema itself.

Notes

This article was first published, without footnotes but fully illustrated, in *Sight & Sound*, Summer 1988.

1. Part of the reason historians have ignored the actuality (which probably accounted for 80 per cent of films in the cinema's first five years) is that they've mainly studied surviving film *prints* rather than examining, through documents and similar sources, how films were *exhibited* at the time (as Charles Musser has pointed out (*Film and History*, December 1981)), and so have missed the 'editing' sophistication that was being brought to the actuality. And the date chosen by most scholars to start their examination of 'early cinema' is 1900 rather than the date of the first projections, 1896, exactly because fictional film-making only took off at the later date.

   Yet it has been increasingly noted by historians recently (see for example P. Guibbert (ed), *Les Premiers Ans du cinéma français*, 1985) that early drama films staged outdoors had a far greater freedom of movement and staging in depth than interior-shot films. Cecil Hepworth wrote of the advantages of filming outdoors in 1900: 'Needless to say, a woodland scene, if carefully selected, is very much better for photographic purposes than any painted representation of the same view could possibly be, and an open field or hill-side can be far better rendered by going direct to nature than by calling in the aid of the scene-painter's brush.' (*British Journal of Photography* (BJP), 6 July 1900)

   Such exterior filming originated in actualities, yet led to many technical developments taken up by the drama. For example, tracking shots were first used in actualities, often to show views from trains, and high-angle shots to show the expanse of a moving crowd. Both of these innovations were employed from 1896 or 1897, years before being seen in dramas. The need to follow real events as they happened led to various advances in equipment design: viewfinders were introduced by R. W. Paul in 1896 and by Wray and Hughes the following year; Paul and Edison had pan heads by 1897, and at the same time the film capacities of camera were being greatly increased –

up to 1,500 ft or half an hour of film in Warwick's 1898 camera which could be developed in one length in an automatic machine invented by Hepworth – to enable filming of lengthy real events in progress.

And film stock was available in extended lengths from a surprisingly early date. By 1896 Blair supplied up to 120 ft, Acres up to 300 ft, The Celluloid Co., NY, up to 500 ft. In addition these lengths could be joined to form much longer camera loads (*Popular Science Monthly*, 1897–8, p. 185). These long loads would not have been needed for controlled drama shooting.

2. Karel Reisz, 'The technique of film editing', p. 16.
3. Marshall Deutelbaum, *Wide Angle*, vol. 3 no. 1. See also articles by R. Cosandey and A.Gaudreault in *Iris*, vol. 2 no. 1, 1984. Henri Langlois wrote: 'When you look at a Lumière film it seems spontaneous. You think that it's taken by chance. Not at all. The cameraman has looked around and observed for a while what passed by; then he chose the best angle for filming. . . . It isn't luck, it's science.' (Chardere/Borge, *Les Lumière*, p. 210; my translation)
4. Cecil Hepworth, *Animated Photography: the ABC of the Cinematograph*, 1897, p. 128. The *British Journal of Photography*, February 1898, criticised a film for 'carelessness about the starting of a subject, so as to get the most interest out of it.' There was in fact a whole aesthetic for producing pleasing single-shot actualities. The attraction of the first films was movement pure and simple: trees swaying in the wind, smoke rising, and other such effects were the subject of wonder and comment. In the catalogues that advertised the first companies' films the main criterion of a good film seems to have been that it was 'full of animation', and the Warwick Trading Company in 1901 even said: 'The object of an animated picture camera is to take animation and plenty of it – the more action there is in the picture the more successful will be the subject' (WTC Catalogue, 1901, p. 18).

The anonymous writer went on to enunciate other rules for making films: 'the best results are to be obtained by refraining from placing the camera closer than about ten yards from the nearest object that you wish to include in your view.' This injunction was later – about 1911 – to become highly controversial as film-makers tried closer shots of actors, but in this era it was partly to avoid loss of focus, as there was a general desire for an image that was 'sharp and clear' (WTC Catalogue, 1897–8, p. 20). Two of the earliest books on cinema practice, *Animated Photography* by Cecil Hepworth (p. 97) and *Picture Ribbons* by Francis Jenkins (1898, p. 47) both suggest stationing assistants to direct pedestrians away from the camera when filming street scenes to avoid blurred and 'ill-defined forms' blocking the shot and ruining its clarity. Henry Hopwood (*Living Pictures*, 1899, p. 195) called them 'foreground intruders'.

Similarly, the *British Journal of Photography* wrote (4 September 1896): 'a grotesque and unnatural effect is produced when, in taking a street scene, for instance, vehicles and pedestrians approach to within a few feet of the camera, and jerk themselves out of the picture, so to say. The relatively vast dimensions the figures then assume cause laughter, it is true, but the effect is certainly better without them.'

See also BJP, November 1896; *Optical Magic Lantern*, April 1899, p. 52; *Photogram*, April 1899, p. 127. This desire for a clear image also meant that hand-held filming was not recommended (Warwick supplement, 1899, p. 10). These 'classical' rules for clear pictures derive mainly from still photography. Blurred moving images in films were attacked as 'photographic monstrosities' (BJP, 6 November 1896) just as were violations of the 'natural' and 'normal' in still photography, such as extreme wide-angle views of people. And Hepworth, *Animated Photography*, p. 97 remarked that 'the use of wide-angle lens, nearly always reprehensible, is generally most abominable in connection with the production of a living photography.'
5. By the autumn of 1896 loops had been introduced by Acres, Paul, Blair, Joly, Armat and probably others. Before they were generally introduced there were various ideas for allowing long loads of film, including a patent for a lighter reel (BJP, 2 October 1896) that could accommodate more film without an unacceptable increase in the feed reel's inertia; as well as various ideas for projectors using a continuous rather than an intermittent film movement. Incidentally, the first practical loop was described in the much-maligned Friese Greene's patent of 1889.

6. It came to be seen as an advantage not to have the films all joined together, as this enabled them to be used interchangeably with the slides, allowing 'the selection and arrangement of certain films for any desired lecture' (Hopwood, *Living Pictures*, p. 212). On this question of the exhibitor as the creative 'editor', see Charles Musser's article in *Film and History*, December 1981. Machines combining film and lantern projection were common from 1896, such as Ottway's projector made in Britain. These often used a swivel attachment in front of the lantern light source which could be swung back and forth by the operator to show either films or slides. Henry Hopwood (*Living Pictures*, p. 188) wrote that 'a film for projecting a living picture is nothing more, after all, than a multiple lantern slide'. C. Francis Jenkins (*Picture Ribbons*, p. 100) stated: 'The fact is, the moving picture machine is simply a modified stereopticon or lantern.'
7. The BJP, 2 April 1897, described one of these reels: 'and so large does it look when coiled that, at first, one's mind runs to a coil of a fireman's hose as a simile.'
8. Testimony varies on the exact length: see WTC Catalogue, 1901; BJP, 2 April 1897; *The Showman*, June 1901; Hepworth, *Animated Photography*; OMLJ, August 1897. Joining films in this way meant that showmen gained early familiarity with splicing. In May 1897 the *Scientific American* (p. 327) described making a splice by scraping the emulsion off the two ends of the film to be joined and then welding them with acetone, a system virtually unchanged to the present day (see also the *Photogram*, 1897, p. 149).
9. Homer Croy, *How Motion Pictures Are Made*, 1918, p. 184. René Clair in his book *Cinéma* noted: 'Editing is an extraordinary convention to which our eye is so well accustomed that we no longer see what is unusual about it. But for a new eye, one image replacing another in a flash does in fact give the impression of a magical substitution, a lightning-like metamorphosis.'

   The 'disruptive' effect of cuts was again noted when Cinemascope was introduced: Charles G. Clarke suggested that cutting in the wide screen format was too disturbing to the eye, and should be avoided (*American Cinematographer*, June 1955, pp. 336–7, 362–4).
10. The Corbett Fitzsimmons boxing match film of 1897 was 1,000 ft long. Hollaman's *Passion Play* of 1898 probably consisted of twenty-four scenes and lasted an hour. The first English fiction film sold as more than one scene was *Come Along Do* (Paul, 1898), with two linked scenes.
11. Georges Sadoul said of Méliès: 'The scenes follow one another like the tableaux of the theater. . . . In none of his scenes did Méliès change his angle. In his mind, theater and screen were two aspects of the same thing. Each of his scenes is viewed by his camera as it would be by a spectator seated in the middle of the orchestra of the Theatre Robert-Houdin.' (*Hollywood Quarterly* 1945). The only real exception, where Méliès uses movement towards camera, is significantly in a reconstructed *actuality* film: *L'Affaire Dreyfus* (1899).

    French theorist Pierre Jenn in M. Malthête-Méliès (ed.), *Méliès et la naissance du spectacle cinématographique* (Paris: Klincksieck, 1984); and 'Georges Méliès Cinéaste' (1984) has argued that Méliès' films do contain pioneering montage, of a type 'particular to his era', partly on the basis of certain isolated examples of shots which seem to form 'edited' sequences. For example, in *Voyage dans la lune* (1902) four shots show the space capsule falling from the moon, through space and into the sea. But his argument is doubtful, firstly because this and other examples cited are all post-1900–1 by which time editing of sequences had already been adopted by others. Secondly, the shots in the 'sequences' are all frontal, they do not dissect space: Méliès retained this theatrical style of film-making throughout his career, and well after many of the elements of the modern 'continuity' style had been evolved.
12. From *Cendrillon* in 1899, Méliès joined every tableau in his films with a dissolve (often spliced in), and other film-makers like Porter, and Blackton and Smith copied him for a time. Another reason why films continued to be sold as separate shots was to maximise sales – see David Levy in J. Fell (ed.), *Film before Griffith* (Berkeley and Los Angeles: University of California Press, 1983).
13. WTC Catalogue, 1897–8, pp. 52, 54. (This catalogue, though marked 1897–8 in the National Film Archive, is, John Barnes reveals, actually from 1898.)

14. WTC Catalogue, 1897–8, p. 52.
15. There were isolated uses of multi-camera shooting in this period, to follow events of this kind, e.g. of the Grand National horserace in 1898. The BJP (8 April) wondered of the separate shots, 'how they are to be joined up finally' – a question which was never answered.
16. McGuire and Baucus catalogue, September 1897, quoted in John Barnes, *The Rise of the Cinema in Great Britain*. p. 212. The films are numbered 1076 to 1079. See also Georges Sadoul, *Histoire générale du cinéma*, vol. 1 (Paris: Denoel, 1948), pp. 300–4. In the McGuire and Baucus American catalogue of January 1897 four similar fire films are listed.
17. The WTC Catalogue, 1897–8, p. 51, lists them as nos 1723, 1711, 1710, 1780, and says: 'the following four films should be joined in the order mentioned, and when so projected reproduce one of the most exciting scenes ever presented'. On p.46 yet another four fire films are listed.
18. It was called *Toilers of the Deep*. Multi-shot films were listed as one single film from at least two years earlier. In the WTC Catalogue of 1899, p. 19, for example, film number 5344 is three views of the Prince of Wales' visit to Edinburgh. Incidentally it is only in the 1901 Warwick supplement, p. 249, that we first are told that in joining actuality shots: 'no black divisional spacing between sections is necessary'.
19. Hepworth, *Animated Photography*, p. 127. As late as 1915 this method was still advocated by Bernard Jones in *The Cinematograph Book* (p. 34): 'When a long procession or pageant is filmed, it is seldom that the whole of it is taken. . . . It is more usual to expose only on the principal features or most striking portions, stopping the handle when one of these has passed and starting it again when the next appears. The sections of the film should not, however, be made too short and abrupt.'
20. In the NFA collection.
21. Despite recent claims of Méliès' technical precocity, the jump-cut to achieve magical transformation was widely used by other companies like Edison, and it is even explained to an enquirer in the *Optical Magic Lantern Journal* in June 1900. Jenn and others have recently claimed that it was an early editing achievement of Méliès, but I prefer to follow Sadoul in thinking it was a 'stunt' in Méliès' hands – a version of the stage transformation scene. Its use in the actuality seems to me to be more innately 'cinematic'.
22. WTC Catalogue, 1899, p. 29.
23. NFA collection.
24. Richard Arlo Sanderson has written, 'Most of these angles were dictated by the necessity of photographing the group as they proceeded on their way towards their coaches' (*A Historical Study of the Development of American Motion Picture Content and Techniques Prior to 1904* (London: Arno Press, 1977), p. 153). Sanderson is the only historian to date who had studied (if briefly) the importance of the actuality over the drama in the development of editing. He writes: 'News and sports films showed the greatest use and development of film techniques. . . . Since the action could not be manipulated, control was established by moving the camera and taking shots at various angles and various distances from the subject.'
25. These and the following Edison films are held in the Paper Print Collection, viewed through the courtesy of the Library of Congress, Washington, DC.
26. *The Interfering Lovers* (GB, 1902) is one of the first examples.
27. WTC Catalogue, 1901, p. 169.
28. WTC Catalogue, 1901, p. 160.
29. *The Showman* (London), 15 February 1901.
30. *Bank Holiday at the Dyke* consisted of four shots of different rides. See Rachael Low, *History of the British Film*, vol. 1, p. 51. Sadoul, *Histoire générale*, vol. 2, p. 135, describes Williamson's 1899 film of the Henley races which may have been a pioneering multi-shot film. The details are not clear, however, and since Low's and Sadoul's researches, the vital Williamson catalogues of 1899 and 1902 have disappeared from the NFA.

The Infringement of Copyright Laws and Its Effects (1900–1906)

ANDRÉ GAUDREAULT

The practice of copyrighting film material is nowadays a well-established part of the film production process.[1] This, however, has not always been the case. Despite the fact that film copyrighting began very early, at least in the United States, numerous companies and/or individuals tried from the very start to take advantage of the legal loopholes that existed in a body of law that had never been intended to cover phenomena such as the 'aggregation of photographs' that was the film strip. Their infringements, furthermore, were a natural extension of aggressive commercial policies whose hegemonic goals were openly stated. Such was the case of Thomas Edison who, at the turn of the century, tried, and succeeded for a short while, in dictating terms to the entire industry.

The transgressions which I want to study here are not related directly to either the form or the content of the films. This is because at a time when the cinema had not yet become an institution, questions of form or content could not yet pose any intrinsic normative difficulties. In the absence of any strictly cinematic norms or rules concerning form and content, there was no possibility of breaking them. . . . The only rules which could be 'broken' at that time were situated at the periphery of film or concerned matters which were at first totally extraneous to film (such as public morality). Indeed, as I have stated elsewhere, the early cinema was truly a cinema which knew 'neither law nor religion'.[2] It is only progressively, with the unyielding institutionalisation of the cinema beginning around 1908, that questions of law and morality came to locate themselves between the pictures.

I intend, therefore, to deal with a practice that was extremely common in the film world between 1900 and 1906, and one in which all the major production companies partook in England, France and the United States: film piracy. I shall look at two relatively famous cases of film piracy. The first is based upon the simple procedure of duping a print whereas the second is based upon the duplication of a film's narrative unfolding (a remake). I shall concentrate upon the legal proceedings which resulted from these piracy cases in order to draw out the effects of these illegal activities upon later film production and copyright registration. I shall also show how the arguments advanced by the litigants in each can be seen, somewhat paradoxically, as the first attempts to theorise the new narrative form that cinema was in the process of becoming.

When faced with the film strip, a new object which articulated syntagmatically a series of frames, which in turn represented a given scene, the first reaction of the various parties was to copyright the entire film as though it were a single photograph. Prior to 1900, films, which usually consisted of a single shot, were therefore registered for copyright as a single photograph (even though their composite nature was obviously recognised): a company wishing to protect its film would therefore send two paper prints of the film to the Library of Congress in Washington plus the 50 cents fee required to register a single photograph. This procedure was widely accepted and one can barely imagine that a producer would demand on the contrary that 50 cents be paid for each individual frame in order to protect all of them against copyright infringement. And yet that is almost exactly what happened! But before going into the details of this story, it is important for us to have a clear idea of the context for film piracy at the beginning of the century.

One of the first facts that must be remembered is that all producers at the time enthusiastically pirated (by duping a print) the films of competitors who had not taken the precaution of copyrighting them with the Library of Congress. As proof, one need only glance at an unequivocal statement made by Frank L. Dyer, an Edison Company lawyer, to the production manager, William Gilmore, in a letter dated 22 January 1904: 'The Pathé films are not copyrighted, and therefore you can make and sell as many copies thereof as you desire without molestation from him, just as copies of uncopyrighted books can be made in this country without infringement.'[3]

In this manner numerous hits were duped without compunction and fortunes amassed from the work of competitors. Méliès' *Voyage dans la lune* (1902) provides one famous example: the film was widely distributed in the United States where it was a smash hit without Méliès ever being able to collect a single cent. As a result of the series of incidents related to this film, Méliès sent his brother to the United States to take care of copyrighting his films.

The first court case which I would like to touch upon occurred shortly before Méliès' film was illegally distributed in the United States. Beginning in May 1902, the Edison Company undertook legal proceedings against the Lubin Company in order to prevent the latter from duping and selling parts of the film *Christening and Launching Kaiser Wilhelm's Yacht 'Meteor'* (shot in February 1902).[4] Edison only managed to obtain an injunction against Lubin in April of the following year.

The minutes of the court proceedings are particularly interesting because they afford us a detailed view of the everyday circumstances of film production at that time. In this sense, the main argument of the defendant (Lubin) is particularly interesting. He effectively forced the parties concerned to take a decision on certain fundamental issues, as will also be the case, and in a much more obvious way, with the second court case (in which the parties will have to present a battery of arguments concerning editing and shooting, and the narrative continuity and discontinuity of multi-shot films). In the present case, however, a decision will have to be made concerning the nature of the succession of frames of which a film is composed and concerning the artistic work involved in simply shooting the *natural* appearance of people taking part in the *actual* launching of a ship. Indeed, as says John J. Frawley, superintendent of film production for Lubin, one could maintain that:

There is no peculiar skill or intellectual conception or original effect embodied in the photographs representing the launching of the 'Meteor'. These photographs are purely the results of the functions of cameras, and a dozen different photographs with a dozen different cameras from the same general location would necessarily have obtained the same results. The same cameras were placed in a convenient and obvious position and represents [sic] the objects as they subsequently arranged themselves.[5]

Simply put, the Lubin position was to deny the artistic nature of the documentary. It hardly matters whether Lubin and his principals actually believed the argument. The important thing is whether or not the judicial institution would accept it, thereby establishing a precedent which would weigh heavily upon film's recognition as an art and, obviously, upon its economic development. One can easily imagine the effects of any ruling which stated that documentary films, unlike staged films (fiction films), were not protected by copyright laws. . . . But the court was not swayed by Frawley's arguments (at least not by that one). The proceedings followed a rather different path, as we shall soon see. Let us examine, however, the deposition of James H. White, Edison's manager of the film department, made a few days before Frawley's:

In taking moving pictures photographically, great artistic skill may be used. As a rule the nature of the subject taken prevents the artist from grouping or draping the objects photographed. But on the other hand, artistic skill is required in placing the camera in such a position that the lights and shades of the picture, when taken, shall have proper values, and the grouping of the figures and the background shall constitute a harmonious whole and have a graceful composition.[6]

On the basis of propositions I have defined elsewhere,[7] and to which I shall shortly return, it is clear that in this 1902 court case, the emphasis is laid squarely on monstration (to the detriment of narration). Since the cameraman, who is (in a sense) the monstrator, does not intervene in the actual unfolding of events (according to Frawley he 'represents the objects as they subsequently arranged themselves'), he cannot really claim to have acceded to the 'realm of Art'. . . . On the contrary, their opponents maintained that artistic skill is required even though the operator only intervenes by means of the camera.

Here, editing, for example, seems to play no significant part at this early stage of reflection on the artistic aspect of cinema (even though the film in question appears to be composed of two shots). The parties concerned are interested only in the relationship of the camera with the profilmic events and it is on that basis alone that the film's quality is to be judged. Editing, the filmographic[8] activity *par excellence*, is not yet called upon to testify at the witness stand.

The defendant's arguments were also based on the following considerations: since we are accused of having infringed the copyright of an object made up of dozens and even of hundreds of photographs (the frames), let us attempt to show that the object under litigation was registered as a single photograph and can therefore not be protected by the copyright laws. This is the argument that John J. Frawley, a Lubin employee, will attempt to establish: by no usual understanding of photographs could such a film or a section of it containing a number of pictures be considered a photograph, for a photograph is always understood to be the result of a single exposure. . . .[9]

And this largely explains Lubin's own allegations:

> But respondent denies that such photographic representations constitute one photograph and that the same can be copyrighted as one photograph or protected by a single copyright, and avers that such photographic films are the result of joining together distinct and independent photographs resulting from distinct and independent photographic exposures, each requiring a separate copyright for securing an exclusive right to such original intellectual conceptions as it may contain.[10]

The inevitable result followed. The judge was persuaded by these arguments and agreed that in order:

> to acquire the monopoly it confers, it is requisite that every photograph, no matter how or for what purpose it may be conjoined with others, shall be separately registered, and that the prescribed notice of copyrights shall be inscribed upon each of them.[11]

The ruling in favour of Lubin was never applied, however (and one can hardly imagine how it could have been . . . or at what expense – 50 cents per frame!), since the Court of Appeals overturned it. The original ruling held that since the film *Christening and Launching* . . . had not been copyrighted frame by frame, its copyright was invalid and Lubin could not have infringed it. But the reasons for which the Court of Appeals overturned the lower court rulings are much more interesting. The Court of Appeals ruled on the basis of the unity/identity/continuity of a series of frames:

i) since the series had been taken from one camera at one operation;
ii) since there was no distinguishable difference detectable by the naked eye between the separate pictures; and
iii) since the economic or commodity value of the footage was dependent on its status as a single entity, the series was practically one picture.[12]

These three principles became the precedent for our second court case involving a very successful 1904 Biograph multi-shot film entitled *Personal*. Indeed, it was so successful that competitors wasted no time in pirating it. The difference this time was that the pirates copied it not by duping a print but by systematically duplicating its narrative unfolding – in short, they made remakes. The Edison Company was the first to remake *Personal* when it got Edwin S. Porter to shoot *How a French Nobleman Got a Wife through the New York Herald 'Personal' Columns*, whose original title had been *Personal*![13] Shot in 1904, only a few months after the original, it was followed in 1905 by another American remake: *Meet Me at the Fountain* (Lubin) and, finally (?) by a French remake: *Dix femmes pour un mari* (Pathé).

Biograph launched proceedings against Edison. Whereas our first court case settled the matter of a succession of frames (articulation between frames), this case dealt specifically with the succession of shots (articulation between shots), since the film under examination was a multi-shot one.

The entire problem revolved once again around the proper procedure for copyrighting films. Edison, accused of having allegedly infringed the copyright laws, launched two distinct arguments:

1. Biograph's copyright pertains only to the film's photographic nature. Porter, however, did not dupe the film, only reproduce, in its own way, a story which had been told;
2. Biograph's copyright is at any rate invalid since there is only one copyright to cover seven or eight 'photographs' (i.e. shots).

The second argument was in fact a double-edged sword: if the judge concurred, then all of Edison's own multi-shot films (indeed, *every* multi-shot film ever made) fell into the public domain. . . . It is around this time that the Edison Company began, as a precautionary measure, to copyright its own films shot by shot.

The main legal arguments, however, involved a question which I find most interesting because it forced the litigants to define in a quasi-theoretical (or at least proto-theoretical!) manner, the nature of the two essential filmic activities: shooting and editing, activities which I have related to the two fundamental modes of narrative communication which are monstration and narration and which, in turn, can be seen to derive from two separate instances or agents responsible for communicating filmic narrative: the monstrator and the narrator.

The problem with *Personal* is, once again, a problem of unity/identity/continuity. The Court of Appeals' ruling that the film *Christening and Launching* . . . was 'in substance a single photograph', was dependent upon the fact that 'the copyrighted photograph represented one act or event'.[14] In the case of a multi-shot film, on the other hand, the temptation was great to point out the discontinuity, the disparity and the difference between shots. And this is precisely what the Edison lawyers did.

The entire proceeding, therefore, boiled down to an endless debate between the plaintiffs, on the one hand, who maintained that the film, despite its many shots, was in fact a single entity which could be legally copyrighted as one single photograph, and the defendants, on the other hand, led by Edwin S. Porter himself who, oddly enough, has been praised by a certain generation of film historians as *the* inventor of continuity in early cinema, struggling to prove by all means that a film like *Personal*, despite its apparent linearity, was in fact nothing more than an aggregation of discontinuous scenes![15]

Indeed, the Edison lawyers argued, in the case of this film composed of eight shots, that 'the full protection of complainant's production could only be secured by filing eight distinct titles, making eight distinct deposits of copies, the paying of eight distinct fees', etc.[16] The problem according to the Edison lawyers, was the film's pluripunctuality.[17] *Personal* cannot be considered a single photograph because it is, in reality, '*an aggregation of photographs* and as such cannot, in our opinion, be covered by a single copyright'.[18] Unlike *Christening and Launching* ..., *Personal* is not a 'connected series of "undistinguishable pictures"'.[19] Rather, it is made up of 'eight distinct acts or events' which were not filmed by means of a camera 'operated from a single point'.[20] The essential distinction between a unipunctual and a pluripunctual film and, in the final analysis, between filmic monstration and narration, is rendered in an astoundingly precocious manner by the following statement:

> Another fact noted ... in the Lubin case was that the negative simply photographically reproduced 'in continuous form the view which would be represented to the eye of an onlooker on the spot occupied by the camera'. Complainant's so-called negative reproduces in discontinuous form several views ... which could not possibly be presented to the eye of an onlooker, unless he travelled with the photographer and his pantomimic troupe from Grant's tomb through and around the surrounding country.[21]

What is being stated here, and as early as 1905, is that: a) the unipunctual film (the view) is based fundamentally on continuity; b) frame articulation, the production of the monstrator, is of the order of the *continuous*; and c) the monstrator resembles an observer (onlooker) who is an integral part of the here and now (*on the spot*) of the filmed event. It is also stated that: a) the pluripunctual film (*several* views) should not be considered a single object: it does not consist of one strip but of several strips (so-called negative); and b) the work of the narrator is rather of the order of the *discontinuous* and could not be the product of a single monstrator (could not possibly be presented to the eye of an onlooker). The pluripunctual film is consequently the product of a narrator who, in the gap[22] between two shots which is produced by their juxtaposition, makes us travel through the time and space of the monstrator's punctual views ('travelled with the photographer ... through and around the surrounding[s]').

As we can see, the arguments raised throughout the trials can justifiably be considered as the first efforts to theorise the cinema as a narrative art form. In this way, however, the prize, in our opinion, goes to Judge Lanning and to American Mutoscope and Biograph lawyers who, much better than Edison and company, recognised the contemporary and future importance of film editing. Indeed, Edison and his supporters seemed to side with a discontinuous cinema, in tableau-like form, a cinema of monstration (more than narration) which favoured the shooting, the shot and the articulation between frames. A cinema much closer to that of the Lumière brothers than that of Griffith, yet to come. As late as December 1904, Edison's people maintained that 'the negative alone requires the work of authorship',[23] bringing to the forefront what we have called the monstrator and literally relegating to oblivion what we have called the narrator (the agent responsible for implementing syntagmas at the editing stage, among others). On the contrary, Biograph's people commented on the degree of advancement of filmic art and accorded editing (and, therefore, the narrator also) an important role:

> The photographic art has advanced beyond the point of a single view of a single object . . . in showing not only single scenes of objects and persons in motion, but also the continuous action of objects and persons in the portrayal of episodes, public functions and events. . . . The composite photographs, showing continuous and progressive action of objects and persons, practically constitute books written in the primitive characters of the race, as illustrated in the picture-writing of the Indians and other early peoples, and in the picture-written books for children of today.[24]

All this is, of course, pure rhetoric: they wanted to win their case and were looking for every means to demonstrate that the film *Personal*, like the other pluripunctual films, was a single photographic entity ('a single photograph of the whole').[25] But what really counts is when such statements are made by a judge and are used to formulate jurisprudence. It was in this manner that, on 6 May 1905, Judge Lanning stated that even though they were taken from different points of view, 'a series of pictures that may be thrown in rapid succession upon a screen telling a single connected story'[26] could be copyrighted as a single and unique entity (photograph). This, from our perspective, directly legitimises the existence (it is a matter of theoretical existence, of course) of the agent whom we have called the narrator who is, as Judge Lanning explained so well, the solution to continuity between the monstrator's (uni)-punctual productions:

> I am unable to see why, if a series of pictures of a moving object taken by a pivoted camera may be copyrighted as a photograph, a series of pictures telling a single story like that of the complainant in this case, even though the camera be placed at different points, may not also be copyrighted as a photograph. . . . In that story, it is true, there are different scenes. But no one has ever suggested that a story told in written words may not be copyrighted merely because, in unfolding its incidents, the reader is carried from one scene to another.[27]

The theory of cinema was born much earlier than we generally believe. . . .

Notes

1. This chapter was first published as an article in *Framework* 29, 1985, and is the result of work undertaken over a number of years on the films of Edwin S. Porter (in collaboration with David Levy of Montreal) and on the evolution of film editing (in collaboration with Tom Gunning of New York). Of the numerous cinémathèques that have supported these research projects, I have worked most closely with the Cinémathèque québécoise. These projects have been funded by grants from the Social Sciences and Humanities Research Council of Canada, the Institut québécois du cinéma and the Société générale du cinéma.

2. 'Un cinéma sans foi ni loi', introductory article to *Archives, Document, Fiction: Cinema before 1907/Le Cinéma avant 1907*, *Iris* vol. 2 no. 1 1984, pp. 2–4.
3. Archives of Edison National Historic Site (ENHS), West Orange, New Jersey.
4. *Thomas A. Edison vs. Sigmund Lubin*. Legal documents deposited at ENHS.
5. Affidavit of John J. Frawley, 24 June 1902.
6. Affidavit of James H. White, 9 June 1902.
7. See my doctoral dissertation, 'Récit scriptural, récit théâtral, récit filmique: prolégomènes à une théorie narratologique du cinéma' (Paris: Université de la Sorbonne Nouvelle, 1983). See also 'Showing and Telling', pp. 274–81 of this volume; and 'Film, Narrative, Narration' in this volume, pp. 68–75.
8. The 'filmographic' and the 'profilmic' are concepts developed by Etienne Souriau. Though the concept of the profilmic has been maintained by successive generations, that of filmographic rapidly fell into disuse. I have tried to revive it and give it more precise meaning than Souriau's. I call 'filmographic' any effect or element, whatever it may be, resulting from manipulation of the cinematic apparatus and which, without affecting in a concrete manner the profilmic during the shooting, shapes the way the spectator will perceive it during projection. It applies, therefore, to editing, camera movements, certain special effects performed in the camera or in the laboratory, etc., but not to lighting for example (since it affects the profilmic during filming). Briefly, let us recall Souriau's definition of the profilmic: 'everything that was in front of the camera and that became imprinted on the film' (*L'Univers filmique*, Paris: Flammarion, 1953, p. 8).
9. Affidavit of John J. Frawley, 24 June 1902.
10. *The Answer of Sigmund Lubin, Respondent, to the Bill of Complaint of Thomas A. Edison, Complainant*, 1902.
11. Quoted in the Lubin case (119 Fed. 993) in *Defendant's Brief on Demurrer to Bill, American Mutoscope and Biograph Co. vs. Edison Mfg Co.*, 18 April 1905, pp. 5–6 (ENHS).
12. David Levy, 'Edison sales policy and the continuous action film, 1904–1906', in John Fell (ed.), *Film Before Griffith* (Berkeley and Los Angeles: University of California Press, 1983), pp. 212–13.
13. The descriptive file of the film preserved at ENHS and apparently handwritten by Porter himself indicates that the film was entitled *Personal*. They obviously changed their minds as the title was crossed out and replaced by another, much longer one. . . .
14. *Defendant's Brief on Demurrer to Bill*, p. 6.
15. By way of example, here is a series of Porter's statements from his affidavit of 3 December 1904 in the same case: 'Such a series of scenes, however, is really an aggregation of several series of negative impressions, each series constituting one photograph [he had not forgotten the *Meteor* case!] and each scene is generally sold separately . . . complainant's film was in no sense a single photograph, since the viewpoints are not the same in all the views. It is an aggregation of several views of scenes. . . . Furthermore, as it takes considerable time to arrange such pantomimes, some of the views were probably taken on different days and on different films from others of the views.'
16. *Defendant's Rejoinder to Complainant's Brief in Reply*, 24 December 1904, p. 2.
17. I have formed this noun from two terms put forward by Eisenstein: 'In the unipunctual cinema (single point of view with fixed camera), we are dealing with pictural composition. In the pluripunctual cinema (with changes in point of view), we are dealing with composition through montage.' Quoted by Jury Lotman, *Esthétique et sémiotique du cinéma* (Paris: Editions Sociales, 1977), pp. 83–4.
18. *Defendant's Brief on Demurrer to Bill*, p. 3.
19. Ibid., p. 5.
20. Ibid., p. 6.
21. Ibid.
22. A gap of which the text itself is not unaware when it states further on (p. 6): 'There are seven points in the film where there is a rupture, a wide and total difference in character, light, position, background, etc., between one picture and that immediately following it.'

23. *Defendant's Rejoinder to Complainant's Brief in Reply*, p. 3.
24. *Complainant's Brief in Reply*, 22 December 1904, p. 15.
25. Ibid., p. 14.
26. Quoted by D,. Levy, 'Edison sales policy', p. 218, from *137 Federal Reporter*.
27. *American Biograph and Mutoscope Co. vs. Edison Manufacturing Co.*, untitled document, ENHS, p. 9.

The Travel Genre in 1903–1904

Moving Towards Fictional Narrative

CHARLES MUSSER

The travel genre was one of the most popular and developed forms of film practice in the pre-nickelodeon era. Here the exhibitors maintained a central creative role as they selected short films from a wide range of subject matter being sold by different producers. These were arranged into a desired order and usually accompanied by a narration. Surviving documentation indicates that such programmes continued to be popular in 1902–3 among the various production and exhibition companies in the United States.[1] Approximately half of the 'features' listed in Vitagraph's 1903 catalogue of headline attractions are travel subjects.[2] For his seventeenth semi-annual tour (Fall 1903), Lyman Howe showed 'Seven Great Series of Moving Pictures' on India, Japan, Arabia, Africa, Switzerland, England and America.[3] In 1903 the Edison Company shared this general interest in travel subjects. After *Life of an American Fireman*, 61 of the next 62 films copyrighted by Thomas Edison were travel films. James White shot twelve of these on his honeymoon in the West Indies (December 1902). Another fifteen were taken by James (Jacob) Smith and Edwin Porter during April–May 1903: their films of New York City emphasized local colour rather than news events. Thirty-four were photographed by A. C. Abadie in Europe and the Near East during March, April and May 1903.

Histories of early cinema have tended to ignore the travel genre for a number of interrelated reasons. Generally, they have focused on the film as an object, not cinema as a practice. Because they have dismissed or downplayed the exhibitor's creative role, historians have evaluated the cultural significance of the genre from its isolated one-shot images. Surviving lectures indicate that these images could be made to carry rich and often disturbing meanings – assumptions about imperialism, racial and cultural superiority, sexism and Social Darwinism. Just as importantly historians have judged the parameters of the travel genre by later, much narrower standards. In the early 1900s the travelogue could deal with a much wider range of issues: the world traveller could present himself as an expert in history, literature, sports (covering the Summer Olympics), global conflicts (having visited both Russia and Japan, Burton Holmes gave programmes on the Russo-Japanese War), ecological policy (a visit to Yellowstone and other wilderness areas), etc. The travel genre as a practice also included fictional films like *European Rest Cure*, *Romance of the Rail* or *Hold-up of the Rocky Mountain Express*. It is this last aspect of the neglected travel genre which I would like to examine by looking at a number of films made by Edwin S. Porter during the 1903–4 period.

Edison film production early in 1903 ignored the advances Porter had made during the previous year and a half – his increasing control over the editing and the production of ambitious story films (from *Appointment by Telephone* to *Life of an American Fireman*). Nevertheless, by mid-1903, these trends were becoming more pronounced within the moving picture world as a whole. Biograph, which had resolutely continued to show actuality subjects in a variety format, lost its exhibition outlets on the Keith circuit to Vitagraph in March 1903. Vitagraph exhibitions emphasized unified programmes in general and story films in particular. Commercial expediency forced Biograph to shift to making multi-shot story films in June 1903, the same month Méliès, the leading producer of story films in the world, opened a New York City office. After the legal disruptions experienced by the Edison Company in the first months of 1903 were resolved and the intensified competitive pressures were recognized, Porter resumed production of longer films. Many of these pictures are marked by the transition from actuality to acted, fictional stories in their combination of elements from both categories. It is these transitional films which must be perceived within the framework of the travel genre if they are to be properly understood.

In August 1903, Edison cameramen took several films of Coney Island including *Shooting the Rapids at Luna Park* and *Rattan Slide and General View of Luna Park*. These were traditional travel scenes. They not only served as a substitute for those who could not visit the amusement park, they advertised the latest rides and sights. During this same month, Porter also made *Rube and Mandy at Coney Island* (© 13 August 1903) which followed two vaudeville comedians on their tour of Luna Park. The Edison catalogue claimed this film was 'interesting not only for its humorous features, but also for its excellent views of Coney Island and Luna Park'.[4]

Rube and Mandy can be compared to other travel programmes, constructed by exhibitors in the 1903 period, which combined travel views or scenics with short comedies. William Selig, Edison's Chicago-based competitor, urged exhibitors to interlace a programme of his Colorado travel films with a selection of comedies. He assured them that 'with an appropriate number of comics to keep up the laughter, a whole evening spent in showing Colorado pictures will pay big money'.[5] Working within this framework of synthetic juxtaposition, Porter integrated comedy and scenery, maintaining a consistent tone from one shot to the next, even as he perpetuated a dichotomy between these two genres within the individual shots. While the vaudeville actors did their bits in stage costume with exaggerated gesture, Porter treated Coney Island for its scenic value with a highly mobile camera (five shots contain significant camera movement) still associated with actuality material. In several scenes the performers' improvisations forced Porter to accommodate the unexpected by adjusting his camera. In another scene the actors moved about the amusement park in a way which allowed the camera to photograph a traditional panorama. The actors are often subservient to a scenic impulse, not only with the panorama but at Professor Wormwood's Monkey Theatre where the film viewer looks over the actors' shoulders to see the animals perform. The couple often mediate the audience's experience of the amusement park and tie together a series of potentially discrete views as they move from one ride to the next. At other moments, Coney Island provides the comedians with a setting for their business as they arrive in an absurd contraption in the opening shot, struggle across a rope ladder in the fourth, fall off a camel in the sixth and make fools of themselves at the punching bag in the twelfth.

The use of narrative in *Rube and Mandy* stands somewhere between a possible programme which interweaves views of Coney Island with studio comedies and a film like *Boarding School Girls* (© 1 September 1905) which Porter made two years later. This later film follows a group of attractive young women through Coney Island. The scenery serves as a background which is subservient to the narrative. The girls' appearance, activities and relationship to their surroundings come much closer to obeying basic rules of classic cinema, particularly the need for a seamless mimetic consistency. This dichotomy between comedy and scenics in *Rube and Mandy* continued the fluctuations between actuality and story material in *Life of an American Fireman*.[6] In this somewhat earlier film, the Edison Company offered two different descriptions of the film – one treating the film like a re-enactment documentary and another as a story film. The exhibitor, if he offered a lecture, could emphasize one way of looking at the film or another. It also makes clear the problems involved in the simple classification of early films into categories like 'new films', 'dramas', 'comedies', and 'travel films'.

Acknowledging the role of the exhibitor is crucial to a proper understanding of early cinema, particularly when the travel genre is considered. Porter had begun his career in cinema as a moving picture operator and exhibitor. Although he was manager of the Edison studio and a successful film-maker by 1903–4, he continued to project films at Edison charities and on other special occasions. Likewise he continued to use residual editorial strategies, central to early forms of the exhibitor-dominated travel genre, in many of his films. This legacy is pertinent to an appreciation of *European Rest Cure* which Porter began to film early in July 1904 but did not complete and copyright until 1 September. This spoof on the travelogue follows an American tourist across Europe and the Middle East on a 'rest cure' in which one physically or emotionally wrenching disaster follows another. Foreign scenes were all photographed against pasteboard sets of pyramids, Roman ruins or a French café, while others were shot outside – at the docks as the tourist leaves and returns. Porter combined this original material with footage from previously photographed travel films: *S.S. 'Coptic' Running Against a Storm* (© 21 April 1898) taken by James White on his trip across the Pacific Ocean in 1898, *Pilot Leaving 'Prinzessen Victoria' at Sandy Hook* (© 8 April 1903) also taken by White, this time on his honeymoon, and an excerpt from *Sky Scrapers of New York City from the North River* which James Smith had filmed on 20 May 1903. The short films incorporated into this longer feature could still be purchased individually: one or two were used by Lyman Howe for a programme he put together:

DETAILED SCENES OF A TRANS-ATLANTIC VOYAGE FROM NEW YORK TO SOUTHAMPTON

(a) The Good Ship in Dock.
(b) A Passenger Interviewing the Chief Engineer.
(c) Repainting the gigantic Smoke Stacks. (Their enormous size is well noted by contrasts with the men on the scaffolding.)
(d) Sorting the soiled linen for the Laundry.
(e)Coaling. Showing myriads of navvies tying up a coal barge alongside the ship when the boats are lowered filled, and contents shot into coal bunkers.
(f) Fire Drill on Board Ship. The crew is seen manning the apparatus and throwing 36 jets of water from the various decks and portholes.
(g) Life Boat Drill. This picture shows the whole operation from various points of vantage, from which can also be had a good idea of the tremendous size and height of the ship.
(h) Crowds on Deck Cheering their Departing Friends.
(i) Dropping the Pilot off Sandy Hook.
(j) Going 24 knots an hour. A beautiful view of the churned waters seen from stern of ship.
(k) The Ship's Band playing a Fanfare.
(l) Games of Shuffleboard and Deck Quoits.
(m) Life on the Promenade Deck on a Fine Day.
(n) Passengers Enjoying a Blow.
(o) Third Class Passengers Crowding the Forward Decks During good Weather.
(p) Running Into a Gale. Magnificent view of mountainous waves, the steamer laboring in heavy seas.
(q) The Storm Increases. Showing the prow shipping waves mountain high as viewed from the bridge.
(r) The Heavy Seas Subside.
(s) A Sunset After the Storm. A masterpiece of photography, clothed in the native tints of a gorgeous sunset.
(t) Moonlight on the Sea. Reflecting the enchanting blue sheen of the pale moon.
(u) Transferring the Mails and Gold and Silver bullion to the Decks of a Tender.
(v) Arrival at the Southampton Docks.[7]

European Rest Cure evolved out of the exhibitor-dominated travel genre and participated in the shift to dramatic material which was taking place within the cinematic institution during this period. Once again, Porter took a 'documentary' genre and reworked it as a comedy feature with a character other than the narrator/tour director to act as a unifying element. Porter probably saw the film as a comedy within the travelogue tradition rather than a spoof directed at the genre and its stylization. None the less, the film parodies the format of many travel lectures from the 19th century which used materials from different sources and combined scenes taken on location with others photographed in the comfort and artifice of the studio. It burlesques the romantic aura of travel perpetuated by exhibitors often beholden to railroad and shipping companies. As usual, Porter was working effectively within a well-established genre. In this case, however, the continuing popularity of the traditional form may have created audience resistance to the spoof and resulted in modest sales.

One of the major sub-genres of the travelogue involved the railroad. The railroad and the screen have had a special relationship which can be symbolized by Lumière's famous *Train Entering a Station* (1895) or half a dozen other films. Both have affected our perception of space and time in somewhat analogous ways. Wolfgang Schivelbusch described the shift from animal-powered transportation to the railroad in *The Railway Journey*:

> As the natural irregularities of the terrain that were perceptible on the old roads are replaced by the sharp linearity of the railroad, the traveler feels that he has lost contact with the landscape, experiencing this most directly when going through a tunnel. Early descriptions of journeys on the railroad note that the railroad and the landscape through which it runs are in two separate worlds.[8]

The traveller's world is mediated by the railroad, not only by the compartment window with its frame but by telegraph wires which intercede between the passenger and the landscape. The sensation of separation which the traveller feels on viewing the rapidly passing landscape has much in common with the theatrical experience of the spectator. The allusion of train window with the screen's rectangle was frequent within this travel sub-genre; it found its ultimate expression with Hale's Tours.

In the 1890s travel lecturers using stereopticon slides often featured railroads as the best way to reach and view American scenery. Their programs frequently created a spatially coherent world with views of the train passing through the countryside, of the traveller/lecturer in the train, of scenery which could be seen out of the window or from the front of the train, and finally of small incidents which took place on sidings or at the railway stations.[9] The railroad which projected its passengers through the countryside was ideally suited to move the narrative forward through time and space. John Stoddard and other lecturers presented these journeys as alternatives to travel for those who lacked the time, money or fortitude for such undertakings. Offering personal accounts of their adventures, these world travellers were the figures with whom audiences could identify and derive vicarious experience and pleasure. Audience identification with a showman like Burton Holmes took place on three levels – with the traveller shown by the camera to be in the narrative as a profilmic element, with the showman as the cameraman (Holmes took the stills and his assistant Oscar Depue the films, so Holmes could appear in the films but the stills were always his point of view), and finally as he spoke from the podium.[10] The point-of-view shot out of the window or from the front of the train was privileged in such a system because it elided camera, character and narration.

The introduction of moving pictures to this form of screen practice reinforced the parallels between travel and projected image. Schivelbusch observed that

> according to Newton, 'size, shape, quantity and motion' are the only qualities that can be objectively perceived in the physical world. Indeed,

those become the only qualities that the railroad traveler is now able to observe in the landscape he travels through. Smells, sounds, not to mention the synesthetic perceptions that were part of travel in Goethe's time, simply disappear.[11]

This new mode of perception which was initially disorienting, then pleasurable, was recreated as the moving pictures, taken by a camera from a moving train, were projected on to the screen. As early as June 1896, the Vitascope was showing the views of Niagara Rapids taken from a moving train.[12] Within a year, Biograph placed one of its cameras on the front of a swiftly moving train. A contemporaneous review begins by contrasting this new effect to an earlier moving picture novelty that also had antecedents in pre-cinema lantern shows, the onrushing express:

> The spectator was not an outsider watching from safety the rush of the cars. He was a passenger on a phantom train ride that whirled him through space at nearly a mile a minute. There was no smoke, no glimpse of shuddering frame or crushing wheels. There was nothing to indicate motion save that shining vista of tracks that was eaten up irresistibly, rapidly and the disappearing panorama of banks and fences.
>
> The train was invisible and yet the landscape swept by remorselessly and far away. The bright day became a spot of darkness. That was the mouth of the tunnel and toward it the spectator was hurled as if a fate was behind him. The spot of blackness became a canopy of gloom. The darkness closed around and the spectator being flung through that cavern with the demoniac energy behind him. The shadows, the rush of invisible force and the uncertainty of the issues made one instinctively hold his breath as when on the edge of a crisis that might become a catastrophe.[13]

As this novelty wore off, phantom rides became incorporated into the travel narrative, enabling the showman to literalize the traveller's movement through time and space. Railroads were also anxious to co-operate with film companies, perceiving motion pictures as a useful form of publicity. (The Edison catalogues of 1901 and 1902 are filled with references thanking specific railroads for their help.) As this genre of travel films became routine, the need for comic relief was felt. G. A. Smith made a one-shot film of a couple kissing in a railway carriage – a gag which had comic-strip antecedents. He suggested that showmen insert *Kiss in the Tunnel* into the middle of a phantom ride, after the train had entered the tunnel. Unlike the structuring strategies suggested by Selig, comedy and scenery were contained within the same fictional world, even though they remained in separate shots. Zecca's *Flirt en Chemin de Fer* (1901) was intended for the same use, but rather than require the entrance of the train into a dark tunnel, Zecca matted in a window view of passing countryside – integrating comedy and scenery in the same shot. Porter combined Smith and Zecca's variation in his own *What Happened in the Tunnel*, starring G. M. Anderson as a forward young lover.[14] Anderson tries to kiss the woman sitting in front of him when the train goes into the tunnel but ends up kissing her black-faced maid instead, giving a new twist to a familiar 'joke'. *What Happened in the Tunnel* was the last film Porter made before *The Great Train Robbery*: its matte shot served as an experiment for the matte shots appearing in the first and third scenes of the headliner.

Romance of the Rail, which Porter filmed in August but was not copyrighted until 3 October 1903, elaborated on the comic interlude. To counter its image as a coal carrier, the Lackawanna Railroad, known as 'The Road of Anthracite', developed an advertising campaign in which passenger Phoebe Snow, dressed in white, rode the rails and praised the line's cleanliness. As with *Rube and Mandy*, *Romance of the Rail* had a dual purpose: to present scenery and provide comic relief. Within the film itself the narrative is clearly paramount as Phoebe Snow meets her male counterpart, they fall in love and marry during the course of a brief train ride. Scenery is pushed into the background except in the fourth scene where the camera frames the shot to give equal emphasis to the scenery and the couple who are, like the spectator, watching the scenery. Although *Romance of the Rail* has a beginning, middle and end, it lacks strict closure since exhibitors often inserted the film into a programme of railway panoramas. The ratio and relative importance of scenery or story were left to their discretion.

Audiences for these films and the railway sub-genre continued to assume the vicarious role of passengers. One moment they would be looking out of the window, in another they would be looking at the antics of fellow passengers. Hale's Tours made this convention explicit by using a simulated railway carriage as a movie theatre with the audience sitting in the passenger seats and the screen replacing the view out of the front or rear window. This theatre/carriage came complete with train clatter and the appropriate swaying. The super-realism of the exhibition strategy[15] was adumbrated by bits of action along the sidings and in trains which contradicted the suggestion of a fixed point of view. Coherence was sacrificed for variety and a good show. Whether *What Happened in the Tunnel* or *Romance of the Rail* was used in the first Hale's Tour Car at Kansas City Amusement Park in 1905 is not known;[16] however, when Hale's Tours became a popular craze in 1906, these films were advertised again in the trades as 'Humorous Railway Scenes' with this purpose specifically in mind.[17]

The Great Train Robbery pushed the railway sub-genre to a new extreme. During the first eight scenes, the train is kept in almost constant view: seen through the window, as a fight unfolds on the tender, from the inside of the mail car, by the water tower or along the tracks as the cab is disconnected and the passengers relieved of their money. While this film was typically shown as a headliner in vaudeville theatres with its integrity intact, it was sometimes introduced by railway panoramas in a Hale's Tours-type situation. The spectators start out as railway passengers watching the passing countryside when they are abruptly assaulted by the close-up of the outlaw Barnes firing his six-shooter directly into their midst. (This shot could be shown either at the beginning or end of the film. In a Hale's Tours situation it would seem more effective at the beginning, in a vaudeville situation billed as a story film of violence its placement at the end would seem more appropriate.) The viewers, having assumed the roles of passengers, are held up. The close-up of the outlaw Barnes reiterates the spectators' point of view, brings them into the narrative which follows, and intensifies their identification with the bandits' victims. Since this shot is abstracted from the narrative and the 'realistic' exteriors of the earlier scenes, the title assigned to this shot – 'Realism' – might at first appear singularly inappropriate.[18] Yet the heightening of realism in twentieth-century cinema has not only been associated with a move towards greater verisimilitude but with a process of identification and emotional involvement with the drama. It is this second aspect of realism which the close-up intensifies.

The process of viewer identification with the passengers in a Hale's Tour presentation of *The Great Train Robbery* was overdetermined: introductory railway panoramas, reinforced by the simulated railway carriage and the close-up of Barnes turned viewers into passengers. These strategies of viewer identification, which were not incorporated into classic cinema, coincided with the viewers' social predisposition to side with those responsible members of society being victimized by lawless elements. The second portion of the film, however, breaks with the railway genre and this overdetermination and becomes a chase. The presence of the passengers is forgotten. Music (or simulated gunshots) much more than railway clatter would be the appropriate sound effects (the exhibitor may have stopped his effects machine at various points in the film when his patrons were not looking at images from the perspective of passengers). The breakdown of this viewer-as-passenger strategy, always just below the surface of this sub-genre, was completed by the end of *The Great Train Robbery*. This breakdown occurred on an entirely different level as well. Adolph Zukor, who would work with Porter ten years later, began his motion picture career as a Hale's Tours exhibitor in Herald Square. After the theatre's initial success, he began to lose money until the phantom rides were followed by *The Great Train Robbery*. While this combination revived his customers' interest and his own profits, Zukor eventually replaced the simulated carriage with a more conventional store-front theatre.

The Great Train Robbery's importance has been attributed principally to its commercial success and the stimulus it gave the American industry. Kenneth MacGowan attributed this success, in turn, to the fact that the film was 'the first important western'.[19] William Everson and George Fenin find it important because it is 'the blueprint for all westerns'.[20] These, however, are retrospective readings. One reason for *The Great Train Robbery*'s popularity was its ability to incorporate so many trends, genres and strategies fundamental to the institution of cinema at that time. The film includes elements of both re-enactment of contemporary news events (the train hold-up was modelled after recently reported crimes) and refers to a well-known stage melodrama by its title. Perhaps most importantly *The Great Train Robbery* was part of the violent crime genre which had been imported from England a few months earlier. Porter was consciously working (and cinema patrons viewing) within a framework established by Sheffield Photo's *Daring Daylight Burglary*, British Gaumont, Walter Haggar's *Desperate Poaching Affair* and R. W. Paul's *Trailed by*

Bloodhounds. He chose a particularly American subject which was part of the still limited Western genre which had not yet been established effectively in the cinema. When initially released, *The Great Train Robbery* was not primarily perceived in the context of the Western. Its success did not encourage other Westerns but other films of crime – Lubin's *The Bold Bank Robbery*, Paley and Steiner's *Burned at the Stake*, and Porter's own *Capture of the Yegg Bank Burglars*. Porter's first real Western was *Life of a Cowboy* (1906). It was only when the Western genre emerged as a vital force in the nickelodeon era that *The Great Train Robbery* was interpreted from this new perspective. At first the nature of the exhibition site and the showman's programming gave the exhibitor the opportunity to emphasize the film's ties to either the travel genre or the genre of crime.

The ambivalence of Porter's film[21] can be compared to a similar motion picture subject: Biograph's *Hold-up of the Rocky Mountain Express* (photographed in the Catskills by the Biograph Company in April 1906). The Biograph subject combines strategies of the railway sub-genre with fictional elements. While the camera alternates between two positions – one from the front of the train and another from inside a passenger car, it is able gradually to turn a travel programme of views into a railway hold-up. Such artificial (yet amazingly effective!) restraints on the *mise en scène* helped to reproduce a rigorous and univalent reading. While *The Great Train Robbery* intersects with many genres which maintain a variable relationship one to another (a relationship which can be altered by the exhibition format and the spectator's internalized expectations), *Hold-up of the Rocky Mountain Express* has a clearly defined hierarchy of genres which results in a much more consistent appreciation of the film across exhibition sites and to some extent over time.

Historians have begun to look at *The Great Train Robbery* and other early films with the purpose of trying to understand how they were seen and understood during the pre-Griffith period.[22] We can still push ourselves further in this direction. To do this successfully, we must re-examine the methodology associated with it. Here Raymond Williams offers some valuable advice in respect to genre:

> We have to break from the common practice of isolating the object and then discovering its components. On the contrary we have to discover the nature of a practice and then its conditions . . . .
>
> The recognition of the relation of a collective mode and an individual project – and these are the only categories we can initially presume – is a recognition of related practices. That is to say, the irreducibly individual projects that particular works are, may come in experience and in analysis to show resemblances which allow us to group them into collective modes. These are by no means always genres. They may exist as resemblances within and across genres. They may be the practice of a group in a period, rather than the practice of a phase in a genre.[23]

Williams is telling us that genre study, which has traditionally dealt with the relations between texts, must include the notion of practice. To accomplish this task not only takes a different methodological approach from that most historians used in their panoramic histories but a much larger mass of evidence than they could realistically gather. Such a mass of data will allow us to discern practices associated with a particular film or period. This will not only affect the history we write but our enjoyment of the films we watch.

Notes

First published in *Iris* vol. 2 no. 1, 1984.

1. Not only the documentation cited in these notes. See, for instance, American Mutoscope and Biograph Company, *Film Catalogue, Supplement No. 1* (New York, April 1903), 30 pp. Xerox at MOMA.
2. American Vitagraph Company, *New Vitagraph Features* (New York: Cameron Print, *c.* June 1903). Academy of Motion Picture Arts and Sciences Library.
3. Lyman H. Howe, Program, 17th Semi-Annual Tour (Fall 1903), Wyoming Geological and Historical Society.
4. Edison Manufacturing Company, *Edison Films* (Orange, NJ, October 1903), p. 16.
5. Selig Polyscope Company, *Special Supplement of Colorado Films* (Chicago, 1 November 1902), p. 3.
6. The Edison Company offered two different descriptions of *Life of an American Fireman* in its advertisements, one emphasizing the 'documentary' aspects of the film while the other played up its story potential. The exhibitor could take either extreme or some middle ground in his lecture. See Charles Musser, 'The early cinema of Edwin S. Porter', *Cinema Journal*, Fall 1979, pp. 28–9. French version: 'Les débuts d'Edwin S. Porter', *Les Cahiers de la Cinémathèque*, no. 29, Hiver 1979, Perpignan, pp. 127–46.
7. Lyman Howe Moving Picture Company, Program, 30 August 1905, at the Casino in Vandergrift, Pennsylvania.
8. Wolfgang Schivelbusch, *The Railway Journey: Trains and Travel in the 19th Century* (New York: Urizen Books, 1980), p. 25.
9. John L. Stoddard, *John L. Stoddard Lectures*, 10 vols (Boston: Balch Brothers Co., 1907), particularly his lecture on Mexico (Vol. 7).
10. Burton Holmes, *Burton Holmes Travelogues with Illustrations from Photographs by the Author* (New York: the Mc Clure Company, 1908), 10 volumes.
11. Schivelbusch, *The Railway Journey*, p. 59.
12. *New York Dramatic Mirror*, 22 June 1896. The film was shown at Bergen Beach and elsewhere in New York City.
13. *New York Mail Express*, 21 September 1897, p. 2.
14. A slight revision of Lubin's *Love in a Railroad Train* (1902).
15. See Raymond Fielding, 'Hale's Tours: ultra-realism in the pre-1910 motion picture', *Cinema Journal*, vol. 10 no. 1, Fall 1970.
16. 'Chief Hale's new concession at Election Park', *Kansas City Star*, 28 May 1905, p. 73.
17. *New York Clipper*, 28 April 1906, p. 287.
18. The important function of this shot has been misunderstood by historians since Lewis Jacobs saw it as an extraneous trick, unconnected to the film's narrative.
19. Kenneth MacGowan, *Behind the Screen* (New York: Delacorte, 1965), p. 114.
20. George Fenin and William K. Everson, *The Western: From Silents to Cinerama* (New York: Bonanza Books, 1962), p. 49.
21. Noël Burch, 'Porter or ambivalence', *Screen*, Winter 1978/79, pp. 91–105. Appeared in French in Raymond Bellour (ed.), *Le Cinéma américain* (Paris, Flammarion, 1980).
22. See, for example, André Gaudreault, 'Detours in Film Narrative: The Development of Cross-Cutting', (pp. 133–50 of this volume); David Levy, 'Re-constituted newsreels, re-enactments and the American narrative film', in Roger Holman (ed), *Cinema 1900–1906*. Both papers appeared in French in *Les Cahiers de la Cinémathèque*, no. 29.
23. Raymond Williams, *Problems in Materialism and Culture* (London: Verso Editions, 1980), pp. 47–8.

Detours in Film Narrative
The Development of Cross-Cutting

ANDRÉ GAUDREAULT

For some time now the appearance of cross-cutting has been a problem for film historians. An earlier generation of historians traced it to the Brighton 'school' (*Attack on a China Mission*, among other films) and the films of Edwin Porter. Many of them agreed that Porter discovered this form of editorial construction, relying on certain documents to suggest its presence in *Life of an American Fireman* (1903). They were, however, unable to see the film itself, which was lost. Since its rediscovery, various investigators have made attempts to get to the bottom of the problem, but controversy still continues, for there now exist two contradictory versions of the film.

One of these versions employs cross-cutting, the other does not. Which one is closer to Porter's original? Champions for each version have not been lacking. Several years ago, for instance, readers of the French periodical *Cahiers de la Cinémathèque* opened its pages to find two separate articles on *Life of an American Fireman*, each defending one of the two versions in terms that no doubt typify a controversy that has fascinated and challenged the historians of two continents.[1] Roman Gubern argued for the authenticity of what we shall call the Cross-Cut Version, finding it, if not a masterly instance of parallel editing, then at least an early example of it, and quite possibly *the* earliest. This is the version that can be seen in the Film Department of the Museum of Modern Art, and I will discuss its origins further on. Barthelemy Amengual, on the other hand, gave persuasive reasons for believing that the so-called Copyright Version – that is, the version of the film that in 1903 was deposited by the Edison Company at the Library of Congress for copyright – was authentic. I believe that this controversy is of the utmost importance, hinging as it does on the genesis of filmic expression, on the convergence of narrativity and cinema, and on the evolution of narrative constructions at which first Griffith and then other film-makers would excel a few years later. For the sake of clarity, here (adapted from the one given by Roman Gubern) is a shot-by-shot breakdown of the two versions of the film which specifies the differences between them.

A Comparison of the Two Existing Versions of 'Life of an American Fireman'

1. Long shot (L.S.) of the fireman asleep. At his left appears a dream balloon showing a mother putting her child to bed. The fireman wakes up suddenly and anxiously walks about the room.

   Dissolve to

2. Close-up of a hand activating an automatic fire alarm.

(*Dissolve in the Copyright Version*)

3. L.S. of the firemen in their sleeping quarters. Hearing the alarm, the men spring from their beds and slide down a fire pole placed in the centre of the room, to the first floor.

Dissolve to

4. L.S. of the firehouse interior. The men jump into their fire engines which then approach the camera and exit offscreen right.

Dissolve to

5. L.S. of the firehouse exterior. The outside doors are flung open to let the fire engines emerge and, turning to the right, they exit offscreen right.

Dissolve to

6. L.S. of a suburban street. Eight fire engines race across the screen from right to left, passing a gathering of onlookers. (Although the camera remains stationary, there are jump-cuts in the action, probably to shorten the distance between vehicles.)

(*Dissolve in the Copyright Version*)

7. L.S. of four fire engines in succession racing down a street, moving from right to left. The camera follows the fourth one, panning to reveal the front of a burning house, where the firemen have already set to work.

COPYRIGHT VERSION
Library of Congress,
Washington

Fade-in

8. L.S. of a room filled with smoke. The mother, in her nightgown, rises from her bed and goes to the window at the back of the room. She faints on her bed. The fireman enters through the door at right and breaks the window to let in air. The fireman lifts the woman into his arms and carries her through the window to the outside. *After a pause he re-enters the room through the window, seizes the child and exits with it through the window. Finally two firemen come through the same window with a hose and extinguish the fire.**

Dissolve to

9. L.S. of the front exterior of the house. *The woman appears at the upstairs window and calls for help. A fireman pounds on the front door*

CROSS-CUT VERSION
Museum of Modern Art,
New York

Fade-in

8. L.S. of room filled with smoke. Mother, in nightgown, gets up and goes to window at back of room.
9. L.S. of front exterior of the house; the woman appears at the upstairs window and calls for help.
10. L.S. of room (shot 8). The woman faints on the bed.
11. L.S. exterior (shot 9). A fireman pounds on the front door and runs into the house.
12. L.S. of the room. Fireman enters through the door at right and breaks the window to let in air.
13. L.S. of the exterior of the house. Some fireman place a ladder against the window to rescue the victims, while others spray the house with water.
14. L.S. of the room. The fireman

and runs into the house. Some firemen place a ladder against a window to rescue the victims, while others spray the house with water. The fireman carries the woman down the ladder to safety. Reviving, she pleads with him to save her child. He remounts the ladder and disappears into the room again, while the woman gives vent to her despair. He reappears with the child almost immediately and descends the ladder. The mother receives and hugs her child.

* I have italicized those portions of the action which are unmentioned in the description of the film printed in Edison's 1903 catalogue (see below). In the Cross-Cut Version these correspond to shots 9, 11, 13, part of 15, 16, 18, 20.

picks up the woman and carries her through the window to the outside.

15. L.S. of the exterior. Fireman carries the woman down the ladder to safety.
16. L.S. of the room. The fireman enters at the window and seizes the child.
17. L.S. of the exterior. The woman gives vent to her despair.
18. L.S. of the room. The fireman goes out of the window with the child.
19. L.S. of the exterior. The fireman emerges from the window with the child and descends the ladder. The mother receives and hugs her child.
20. L.S. of the room. Firemen come through the open window with a hose and extinguish the fire.

There is a real problem here. This is no mere question of attributing priority or authorship to some film-maker, but of trying to determine the actual evolution of filmic expression: whether there was ever a time when film-makers did not know how to express the simultaneity of two actions or whether this ability was inherent from the beginning; and of obtaining a clearer understanding of the relationship that exists between cinema and narrativity. And these, surely, are not the only problems whose resolution will depend on a clarification of the various stages through which filmic expression has passed. Yet, if parallel editing did not in fact make so early an appearance, by what means did early film-makers express the simultaneity of two actions? In cinema as we now know it, this simultaneity can be expressed by at least four basic techniques.

1. *Simultaneous actions coexisting in the same field*: By a sufficiently wide shot or by using depth of field, two simultaneous actions can be shown taking place in the same field – or in effect the same field, for the latter might conceivably be enlarged by camera movement. Obviously this solution is impracticable as soon as the two actions occur at too great a distance from each other.
2. *Simultaneous actions coexisting in the same frame*: If for any reason the first solution is impracticable, the two actions might still be set in the same frame by such techniques as double exposure or split-screen. Porter does this in the opening shot of *Life of an American Fireman*.
3. *Simultaneous actions presented in succession*: Showing first one and then the other on the screen – that is, not showing the second until the first has been

seen in its entirety – and establishing their simultaneity either by means of a title ('In the meantime . . .') or in a narrator's commentary on the action. This is what Porter did if the Copyright Version significantly resembles the original release print. And later we will see that he did this in at least one other film.

4. *Cross-cutting of simultaneous actions*: By the sustained intercutting of two actions, A and B, presented successively but alternately on the screen, as: A-B-A-B-A-B, etc. This is what Porter did if the Cross-Cut Version corresponds to the original. It is the procedure which, in a few years, Griffith would be following systematically.

These, then, are the techniques, and this is the question: did *Life of an American Fireman* actually introduce cross-cutting? Which of the two versions is in fact the original? While the evidence that presently exists is insufficient to determine this for certain, we can at least give an account of the factors for and against the authenticity of each.

A) The Copyright Version (which can be seen at the Library of Congress)

Let us consider the possibility that the print sent to Washington for copyright does not correspond to the final version but merely represents the order in which the scenes were shot. This argument is sometimes heard, but it works both ways; for if some of the copyright prints consist obviously of unedited footage, others just as obviously represent a completed release print. Which leaves us where we were before, although the argument cannot be dismissed out of hand: the prints do disagree. Yet to prove that the Copyright Version is not authentic is not automatically to establish the authenticity of the Cross-Cut Version.[2]

It may be instructive to notice the incongruencies in the Cross-Cut Version. In shots 8 to 12 the following are to be found:

8. Interior. The window is closed.
9. Exterior. The woman opens the window.
10. Interior. The window is still closed.
11. Exterior. The window is open.
12. Interior. The window is closed. The fireman breaks it open with his axe.

In addition, both versions of the film present another instance of 'illogicality' by showing specific action from two different viewpoints – that is, by overlapping them in time. It is possible, however, that these 'bad' cuts reproduce in miniature what, in the Copyright Version, may be the conscious technique of showing the rescue of a woman and her child first from the interior and then from the exterior. We find this example in shots 3 and 4:

3. L.S. of the firemen in their sleeping quarters. On being awakened by the

alarm, the men jump up and slide down the fire pole to the first floor, all of them leaving the picture via the fire pole.

Dissolve to

4. L.S. of firehouse. One by one the men enter the picture by sliding down the fire pole from the ceiling. They get into their fire engines which then move towards the camera, exiting off right.

Thus, in shot 3, all the firemen slide down the pole out of the picture below the floorline, while in shot 4 nevertheless we see each one of them come down through the hole in the ceiling. This is another factor which gives weight to the authenticity of the Copyright Version: it is a reasonable assumption that the editorial 'mistake' made between shots 3 and 4 was duplicated between shots 8 and 9.

B) The Cross-Cut Version (which can be seen at the Museum of Modern Art)

Once again, let us keep in mind that even if it should be disproved that the Copyright Version is the original, it would not follow that the Cross-Cut Version is authentic. But what exactly are the origins of this other version? We learned from Charles Silver of the Museum of Modern Art's Film Study Center that the Museum acquired this copy through the intermediacy of the Pathé Company in 1944.[3] As for the authenticity of either version, until investigators with proof in hand have resolved this question, we have no choice but to confine ourselves to simple logic. Attentive study of another Porter film may bring us, if not a definitive answer, then at least the suggestion of one. Certain considerations, taken together, invite the conclusion that the Cross-Cut Version does not correspond to the original and that the Copyright Version may well be more accurate. What are these considerations?

First of all let us rephrase the question we are trying to answer: was Porter really able to express the simultaneity of separate actions in any other way than by the successive presentation of these same actions on the screen? Is it reasonable, in other words, to suppose that he might have edited the rescue sequence by systematically applying the procedure of alternating scenes? I think it is not.

To see why it is not, let us look for a moment at another film by Porter, as well known and as important as *Life of an American Fireman* (1902–3): *The Great Train Robbery* (1903). The scenario of this later film is somewhat ambiguous, allowing us, as we'll see further on, an interpretation that may be quite different from what Porter intended to express and which I think he did express. Indeed the ambiguity of the scenario is such that among the many studies that have been made of the film it is difficult to find a sound, or at least clearly stated, understanding of its temporality. If anything, the opposite has been the case, for the film itself offers little help to those who approach it without some prior inkling of Porter's handling of temporality at this period.

And here we may be approaching an answer. Let us show the two possible interpretations of *The Great Train Robbery* by using two synopses, each representing a different way of seeing the film. It may be useful to precede these synopses with the description of the film given in Edison's catalogue:[4]

> *Scene 1: Interior of railroad telegraph office.* Two masked robbers enter and compel the operator to set the 'signal block' to stop the approaching train, and make him write a fictitious order to the engineer to take water at this station instead of 'Red Lodge', the regular watering stop. The train comes to a standstill (seen through window of office); the conductor comes to the window, and the frightened operator delivers the order while the bandits crouch out of sight, at the same time keeping him covered with their revolvers. As soon as the conductor leaves, they fall upon the operator, bind and gag him, and hastily depart to catch the moving train.
>
> *Scene 2: Railroad water tower.* The bandits are hiding behind the tank as the train, under the false order, stops to take water. Just before she pulls out they stealthily board the train between the express car and the tender.
>
> *Scene 3: Interior of express car.* Messenger is busily engaged. An unusual sound alarms him. He goes to the door, peeps through the keyhole and discovers two men trying to break in. He starts back bewildered, but, quickly recovering, he hastily locks the strong box containing the valuables and throws the key through the open side door. Drawing his revolver, he crouches behind a desk. In the meantime the two robbers have succeeded in breaking in the door and enter cautiously. The messenger opens fire, and a desperate pistol duel takes place in which the messenger is killed. One of the robbers stands watch while the other tries to open the treasure box. Finding it locked, he vainly searches the messenger for the key, and blows the safe open with dynamite. Securing the valuables and mail bags they leave the car.
>
> *Scene 4: This thrilling scene shows the tender and interior of the locomotive cab, while the train is running at forty miles an hour.* While two of the bandits have been robbing the mail car, two others climb over the tender. One of them holds up the engineer while the other covers the fireman, who seizes a coal shovel and climbs up on the tender, where a desperate fight takes place. They struggle fiercely all over the tank and narrowly escape being hurled over the side of the tender. Finally they fall, with the robber on top. He seizes a lump of coal, and strikes the fireman on the head until he becomes senseless. He then hurls the body from the swiftly moving train. The bandits then compel the engineer to bring the train to a stop.
>
> *Scene 5: Shows the train coming to a stop.* The engineer leaves the locomotive, uncouples it from the train, and pulls ahead about 100 feet while the robbers hold their pistols to his face.
>
> *Scene 6: Exterior scene showing train.* The bandits compel the passengers to leave the coaches, 'hands up', and line up along the tracks. One of the robbers covers them with a revolver in each hand, while the others relieve the passengers of their valuables. A passenger attempts to escape, and is instantly shot down. Securing everything of value, the band

terrorize the passengers by firing their revolvers in the air, while they make their escape to the locomotive.

Scene 7: The desperadoes board the locomotive with this booty, compel the engineer to start, and disappear in the distance.

Scene 8: The robbers bring the engine to a stop several miles from the scene of the 'hold up', and take to the mountains.

Scene 9: A beautiful scene in a valley. The bandits come down the side of a hill, across a narrow stream, mounting their horses, and make for the wilderness.

Scene 10: Interior of telegraph office. The operator lies bound and gagged on the floor. After struggling to his feet, he leans on the table, and telegraphs for assistance by manipulating the key with his chin, and then faints from exhaustion. His little daughter enters with his dinner pail. She cuts the rope, throws a glass of water in his face and restores him to consciousness, and, recalling his thrilling experience, he rushes out to give the alarm.

Scene 11: Interior of a typical Western dance hall. Shows a number of men and women in a lively quadrille. A 'tenderfoot' is quickly spotted and pushed to the centre of the hall, and compelled to do a jig, while bystanders amuse themselves by shooting dangerously close to his feet. Suddenly the door opens and the half-dead telegraph operator staggers in. The dance breaks up in confusion. The men secure their rifles and hastily leave the room.

Scene 12: Shows the mounted robbers dashing down a rugged hill at a terrific pace, followed closely by a large posse, both parties firing as they ride. One of the desperadoes is shot and plunges headlong from his horse. Staggering to his feet, he fires at the nearest pursuer, only to be shot dead a moment later.

Scene 13: The three remaining bandits, thinking they have eluded the pursuers, have dismounted from their horses, and after carefully surveying their surroundings, they start to examine the contents of the mail pouches. They are so grossly engaged in their work that they do not realize the approaching danger until too late. The pursuers, having left their horses, steal noiselessly down upon them until they are completely surrounded. A desperate battle then takes place, and after a brave stand all the robbers and some of the posse bite the dust.

Scene 14: A life-size [close-up] *picture of Barnes*, leader of the outlaw band, taking aim and firing point-blank at the audience. The resulting excitement is great. This scene can be used to begin or end the picture.

Here is the first of the two interpretations it is possible to make of the film:

As the train pulls into the station, four bandits attack the telegraph operator and knock him unconscious. Having tied him up they board the train which has stopped to take on water. When it is once again in motion, two of them hold up the mail car while the other two take control of the locomotive and halt the train. The passengers are forced off the train and robbed at gunpoint. The bandits return to the locomotive, which has been uncoupled from the rest of the train, and use it to reach their horses, which await them in the underbrush. They then continue their getaway on horseback. *At this moment* the telegrapher *revives* and *is untied*. He runs to warn the posse-to-be, who *are dancing* in a saloon. Hearing of the robbery all dash out in pursuit. *Shortly afterwards* the bandits are overtaken by the posse and shot dead as they divide the loot.

If we compare this synopsis to the actual cutting of the film, we must admit that the two apparently agree. Most viewers who see *The Great Train Robbery* take this interpretation of it; we projected the film for more than 200 students and not one of them disagreed with it. No doubt many who read this and who have seen the film would also agree with it. Indeed the vast majority of its original viewers may well have understood the film in this way, for in its temporal linearity it is still visibly influenced by the practices of literature. In the novel it is possible and even usual to express simultaneous actions by successive descriptions of these actions in the text. But for many reasons (among them, that cinematic time is always perceived as the present) in film it is difficult to express simultaneity by means of successiveness except by developing an alternating succession of bits of the two lines of action. *The Great Train Robbery* cries out for cross-cutting; a synopsis that would more satisfactorily render the temporality of its story-line is this one:

The four bandits subdue and tie up the telegraph operator, rob the train and escape in the locomotive to the hiding place of their horses, continuing their getaway on horseback. *In the meantime* the telegrapher *has been revived* and *untied*. He *has run* to warn the posse-to-be, who *were dancing* in a saloon. On hearing the news, they *had set out* in pursuit of the bandits, and now, *encountering them*, they kill them as they divide the loot.[5]

Reading the two versions it becomes evident that the differences are essentially those of the tense of the verbs. Porter here shows us two simultaneous actions which unravel concurrently from shot 2 to shot 11 (see the catalogue description). Those lines of action which diverge in shot 1 converge again in shot 12. To express the simultaneity of these lines of action Porter might have inserted a title ('Meanwhile ...') between shots 11 and 12, or he might have edited these lines of action by cross-cutting. He did neither, perhaps considering it unhelpful to add a title and *perhaps being unfamiliar with the practice of cross-cutting*. If the latter was the case, then we might have a strong and important perspective on the validity of one of the two versions of *Life of an American Fireman*, though more about that in a moment.

Porter could have made a more effective film by cross-cutting. Once we have understood the temporality of *The Great Train Robbery* we see that the subject was ideally suited to that kind of construction. Griffith of course would later use it exactly this way, and if he had made this film around 1910 he might have edited the sequence of shots as follows: 1–2–3–10–4–5–6–7–11–8–9–12–13–(14). In any event, as the film stands it evinces a degree of cross-cutting that is close to zero.[6]

The point is that, working with a subject that was ideally suited to cross-cutting, Porter did not use it, and I think there is nothing of chance or coincidence in this. In fact, a few conclusions can be drawn from it which I submit as tentative for the time being. 1) He did not use it because he had no knowledge of it, and this being the case, he could hardly have invented it the previous year in *Life of an American Fireman*. 2) If Porter, whose business it was to see a good many films, was ignorant of cross-cutting, this could well mean that it did not exist at the time he made his film. 3) Given the above, we can conclude that cross-cutting probably did not exist at the end of 1903 when *The Great Train Robbery* was released.

Even so, it would not be strictly correct to say that Porter had no grasp of the nature of cinematic time, as one French writer has done:

> Porter did not fully understand the principles of narrative cinema, and there is a detail which proves this and which has strangely escaped the notice of film historians: in the first scene, the clock in the railroad station reads nine o'clock sharp. *After the robbery has taken place,*[7] scene 10 shows a new shot of the station where the clock still reads nine o'clock sharp. This incoherency, attributable to the fact that the clock is painted on the backdrop, still reveals, more than carelessness or clumsiness, a deep misunderstanding of the nature of cinematographic time.[8]

Actually, however, when we return to the railroad station in shot 10 the assault on the telegrapher has only just been completed. That is to say, it could easily be no more than a few moments later when we are taken back to it, and I believe it is because of some such brief span of time that Porter thought it unnecessary to show an advance of the minute hand.

Returning once again to *Life of an American Fireman* and pursuing the hypothesis that the Cross-Cut Version is a counterfeit, still, if it is one, how did it come into being? There is certainly one plausible answer: that the unedited negative was years afterwards recovered and the film reassembled by someone unfamiliar with the original version. This individual could have been following some sort of written description of the film, such as the one implicit in the so-called 'Jamison continuity' given as an illustration in Lewis Jacobs' *The Rise of the American Film*. Indeed, one French writer, Jacques Deslandes, has accused Jacobs of having cut up the photographs of the plate at the Museum of Modern Art to make them conform to his thesis. And, whatever his intentions, the 'Jamison continuity' reproduced by Jacobs does not correspond with the original plate.[9] There is only one change, but it is an important one: in the final 'scene' the sequence of pictures is as follows (referring to the numbers attached to the frame enlargements printed below): 13–15–14–16. Thus, given the fact that *The Rise of the American Film*, published in 1939, contained the first printed reproduction of the 'Jamison continuity', and the additional fact that the Cross-Cut Version came to the Museum of Modern Art just five years later, in 1944, it is understandable that some might see a connection between the two.[10]

At all events, the maker of the Cross-Cut Version, guided though he may have been by some unknown text, was certainly not following literally the detailed scenario of the film printed in Edison's 1903 catalogue, which is reproduced here from Jacobs' *The Rise of the American Film*:

> *Scene 1*: THE FIREMAN'S VISION OF AN IMPERILED WOMAN AND CHILD
> The fire chief is seated at his office desk. He has just finished reading his evening paper and has fallen asleep. The rays of an incandescent light rest upon his features with a subdued light, yet leaving his figure strongly silhouetted against the walls of his office. The fire chief is dreaming, and the vision of his dream appears in a circular portrait on the wall. It is a mother putting her baby to bed, and the impression is that he dreams of his own wife and child. He suddenly awakens and paces the floor in a nervous state of mind, doubtless thinking of the various people who may be in danger from fire at the moment.
> *Here we dissolve the picture to the second scene.*
>
> *Scene 2*: CLOSE VIEW OF A NEW YORK FIRE-ALARM BOX
> Shows lettering and every detail in the door and apparatus for turning in an alarm. A figure then steps in front of the box, hastily opens the door and pulls the hook, thus sending the electric current which alarms hundreds of firemen and brings to the scene of the fire the wonderful apparatus of a great city's Fire Department.
> *Again dissolving the picture, we show the third scene.*
>
> *Scene 3*: SLEEPING QUARTERS
> A row of beds, each containing a fireman peacefully sleeping, is shown. Instantly upon the ringing of the alarm the firemen leap from their beds and, putting on their clothes in the record time of five seconds, a grand rush is made for a large circular opening in the floor through the center of which runs a brass pole. The first fireman to reach the pole seizes it and, like a flash, disappears through the opening. He is instantly followed by the remainder of the force. This in itself makes a most stirring scene.
> *We again dissolve the scene to the interior of the apparatus house.*
>
> *Scene 4*: INTERIOR OF ENGINE HOUSE
> Shows horses dashing from their stalls and being hitched to the apparatus. This is perhaps the most thrilling and in all the most wonderful of the seven scenes of the series, it being absolutely the first moving pictures ever made of a genuine interior hitch. As the men come down the pole and land upon the floor in lightning-like rapidity, six doors in the rear of the engine house, each heading a horse-stall, burst open simultaneously and a huge fire horse, with head erect and eager for the dash to the scene of the conflagration, rushes from each opening. Going immediately to their respective harness, they are hitched in the almost unbelievable time of five seconds and are ready for their dash to the fire. The men hastily scamper upon the trucks and hose carts and one by one the fire machines leave the house, drawn by eager, prancing horses.
> *Here we again dissolve to the fifth scene.*
>
> *Scene 5*: APPARATUS LEAVING ENGINE HOUSE
> We show a fine exterior view of the engine house, the great door swinging open and the apparatus coming out. This is the most imposing scene. The great horses leap to their work, the men adjust their fire hats

and coats, and smoke begins pouring from the engines as they pass our camera.
Here we dissolve and show the sixth scene.

Scene 6: OFF TO THE FIRE
In this scene we present the best fire run ever shown. Almost the entire fire department of the large city of Newark, New Jersey, was placed at our disposal, and we show countless pieces of apparatus, engines, hook-and-ladders, hose towers, hose carriages, etc., rushing down a broad street at top speed, the horses straining every nerve and evidently eager to make a record run. Great clouds of smoke pour from the stacks of the engines, thus giving an impression of genuineness to the entire series.
Dissolving again we show the seventh scene.

Scene 7: ARRIVAL AT THE FIRE
In this wonderful scene we show the entire fire department as described above, arriving at the scene of action. An actual burning building is in the center foreground. On the right background the fire department is seen coming at great speed. Upon the arrival of the different apparatus, the engines are ordered to their places, hose is quickly run out from the carriages, ladders are adjusted to the windows, and streams of water are poured into the burning structure. At this crucial moment comes the great climax of the series. We dissolve to the interior of the building and show a bed chamber with a woman and child enveloped in flame and suffocating smoke. The woman rushes back and forth in the room endeavoring to escape, and in her desperation throws open the window and appeals to the crowd below. She is finally overcome by the smoke and falls upon the bed. At this moment the door is smashed in by an ax in the hands of a powerful fire hero. Rushing into the room, he tears the burning draperies from the window and smashes out the entire window frame, ordering his comrades to run un a ladder. Immediately the ladder appears, he seizes the prostrate form of the woman and throws it over his shoulders as if it were an infant and quickly descends to the ground. We now dissolve to the exterior of the burning building. The frantic mother having returned to consciousness, and clad only in her night clothes, is kneeling on the ground imploring the fireman to return for her child. Volunteers are called for and the same fireman who rescued the mother quickly steps out and offers to return for the babe. He is given permission to once more enter the doomed building and without hesitation rushes up the ladder, enters the window and after a breathless wait, in which it appears he must have been overcome with smoke, he appears with the child in his arms and returns safely to the ground. The child, being released and upon seeing its mother, rushes to her and is clasped in her arms, thus making a most realistic and touching ending of the series.

Comparing this scenario to both existing versions of the film, one is surprised to find that it does not exactly correspond to either. Missing are shots 9–11–13, the first half of shot 15, as well as shots 16–18–20 in the Cross-Cut Version, and of course the corresponding parts of shots 8 and 9 in the Copyright Version.

Here is what *Life of an American Fireman* would be like if we follow the scenario in Edison's catalogue while substituting a description of what is actually visible on the film in the Cross-Cut Version. The first seven shots being, as we know, practically identical in all versions, we shall go directly to:

Dissolve to

8. L.S. of a room filled with smoke. The mother, in her nightgown, rises from the bed and goes to the window at the rear wall of the room. She leans out of the window, evidently to call for help. She then faints on her bed. The fireman enters at the door on the right and breaks the windows to let in air. Carrying the woman in his arms the fireman exits through the window to the exterior.

Dissolve to

9. L.S. of the front exterior of the house. The woman dramatically begs the fireman to save her child. The fireman goes back up the ladder and through the window as the mother expresses her despair. The fireman comes out with the child and descends the ladder. The mother receives and hugs her child.

As far as anyone knows, this version does not exist anywhere. It is of course possible that the film was edited this way, yet any attempt to establish that the original release print was not identical with the catalogue scenario should, however, offer to explain why that text, written in 1903 and so fond of details, says not a word about certain bits of action and describes suspense effects that simply do not exist in the Copyright Version. For it becomes impossible to claim that 'after a breathless wait in which it appears that he must be overcome with smoke, he appears with the child in his arms', if one is referring to the Copyright Version, for in that version we saw him perform that rescue just a few moments earlier. If the catalogue is faithful to the original, then both of the existing versions of the film would have to be re-edited to make them conform to it. Many writers believe that the catalogue is inaccurate, however. As the French writer Barthelemy Amengual puts it:

> It is obvious that the catalogue – primarily for the purpose of ballyhoo but certainly also with a view to furnishing adequate material to the lecturer for an 'artistic' commentary on the image – elaborates and embellishes on the visible action, adding pathos and suggesting details ... which might escape the notice of even a fairly perceptive eye; and most of all rationalizing it (to borrow a term from the psychology of dreams) by endowing it with a logic that is possibly more vigorous than the one it actually possesses.[11]

Let us go to the heart of the matter: Porter was apparently able to elaborate at least the initial stage of cross-cutting, a stage that was rudimentary but essential. He did not carry the construction to its logical conclusion, as Griffith would do several years later. It is this 'preparatory' stage of cross-cutting that we find in the Copyright Version of *Life of an American Fireman*. This is also the stage of it that appears in the unique (for how long?) existing version of *The Great Train Robbery*.[12] The final step into actual cross-cutting is one that Porter may have taken in *Life of an American Fireman* and did take, if the Cross-Cut Version is authentic. He might have done the same in *The Great Train Robbery*, whose shots could be combined as 1–2–3–10–4–5–6–7–11–8–9–12–13, as we saw earlier. This final step into cross-cutting, whoever took it, made possible such later feats of editing as Griffith's *The Lonely Villa* (1909) and *The Lonedale Operator* (1911).

Let us briefly review this initial or 'preparatory' stage of editing as developed in the Catalogue Version of *Life of an American Fireman* and in *The Great Train Robbery*. The Catalogue Version contains short overlaps which try to express simultaneity except that the interjoining of the series is made only after the complete (or nearly complete) exposition of each scene. It is much easier to see this when we examine *The Great Train Robbery*, where this initial state of parallel editing is more easily discernible. Let us consider that the film contains two simultaneous lines of action: line-of-action A, the bandits; and line-of-action B, the telegraph operator and his surrogates, the posse. The film is constructed as follows: AB–A–B–AB–I, with the first AB containing only one element: 'Scene' 1 (see the Edison Catalogue, just before the two lines of action diverge. Sequence A consists of shots 2 to 9 and shows us in these eight shots how the train is robbed and the bandits make their getaway. Sequence B, in two scenes (10 and 11), shows how the operator gets free and gives the alarm. Finally, sequence AB, containing scenes 12 and 13, shows how the operator's surrogates track the bandits down, followed by an insert (I), the close-up referred to in the catalogue as 'Barnes, leader of the outlaw band', firing at the audience. This structure of AB–A–B–AB, simple though advanced for its time, forms the very rudiments of parallel editing. We cannot go so far as to use the term cross-cutting to describe this structure, for that would be proper only if the editing consisted of systematic alternation, which is not the case here. Of course the film's structure might also be read as follows: aB–A–B–Ab, where the opening and closing incidents of the sequence could be reduced in importance as properly belonging to the adjoining sequences until they are left out altogether, thus creating a structure worthy to be called a cross-cut sequence: B–A–B–A. But I think that doing so would be invalid for the reason that in those two sequences, the presence of both series is essential to our understanding of the film. Actually, 'alternation' is limited to the joint exposition of each of the two series A and B. In such a case I feel it is proper to speak of parallel editing though not of cross-cutting, the minimal requirement for which would be, in my opinion, a structure of four terms: A–B–A–B.[13] As previously mentioned, Griffith would make his speciality the systematic development of parallel editing by means of cross-cutting. Porter did not progress beyond its brink, either in *The Great Train Robbery* or, as we'll see in what follows, in *Life of an American Fireman*, Catalogue or Copyright Versions.

Studying the latter one finds the alternation of two simultaneous lines of action organized much as they are in *The Great Train Robbery*. But instead of AB–A–B–AB–I, we have AB–I–A–B–AB – a strikingly similar construction just the same. The only real difference between them is the different position of the I in each film. To illustrate:

AB: The two lines of action are united in the same shot, though by trick effect rather than by any real coexistence. The line of action 'firemen' is represented by their chief, who sleeps and dreams, while the line of action 'citizens in danger' is shown by his dream, which is pictured in the dream balloon (the people in the dream being to all appearances the ones who will later be seen in the burning house). This section consists only of the first scene of the film (see Edison Catalogue 1904).
I: Insert. This single shot consists of the film's second 'scene', the close-up of the fire alarm box.
A: The firemen sequence. It includes scenes 3, 4, 5, 6, and the first part of 7 in the Edison Catalogue description. Or, if we follow the versions given in this article of the Cross-Cut, Copyright and Catalogue versions, this sequence contains shots 3 to 7 inclusive.
B: The sequence 'citizens in danger', consisting of the second part of the catalogue's scene 7, or, in our Copyright and Catalogue versions, the beginning of shot 8 (up to where the fireman comes through the door).
AB: The two lines of action converge, being the third portion of the catalogue's scene 7, or the last portion of shot 8 and the whole of shot 9 in the two film versions.[14]

If it should eventually be shown that the Cross-Cut Version is a fake, and the authenticity of the Copyright or Catalogue versions is established – and provided of course that the above breakdown into sequences is based on sound assumptions – it will then appear: 1) that *The Great Train Robbery* and *Life of an American Fireman* are constructed along identical principles, with the single difference of the placement of the I shot in each – copresence, divergence, convergence; and 2) that they present a structure of parallelism much like the figure AB–A–B–AB though without actual cross-cutting. The first stage of cross-cutting would then appear to be the 'literary' mode of expression by which Porter tried to express the simultaneity of two series of events and beyond whose limits he, and probably other film-makers of the period, could not go. Of the second stage of parallel editing we could say that it was inevitable that it should later be discovered and utilized, by someone else if not by Griffith.[15]

Postscript

Since this article was written I have had the opportunity to examine the recently discovered print referred to in Note 3. During a visit to Washington in August 1978, Paul Spehr, of the Library of Congress, generously allowed me access to this print with its original perforations, which only the previous week Larry Karr, of the American Film Institute, had passed along to him for examination. As the film's perforations are not the standard ones and as it had suffered some shrinkage, the film had to be examined on a pair of reels. With the aid of a Steenbeck, however, I was able to view the duplicate negative made from this print. Needless to say, I had been eagerly awaiting this chance to determine whether this copy, probably an early release print, corresponds with the Cross-

Cut Version, the Copyright Version or even the Catalogue Version. The answer is that it does not correspond exactly with any of them!

Are we now to be obliged to juggle with one more version, which will have to be labelled the Recovered Version? Happily not. For this print roughly conforms to the Copyright Version. Their differences are, all things considered, minor. If this print can be authenticated it will give credence to the Copyright Version and for all purposes relegate the other two versions to oblivion; for just as in the Copyright Version, the recovered print includes bits of footage that do not appear in the Cross-Cut Version (whose unknown editor cut away the final moments of certain shots in order to smooth out the action which alternates between interior and exterior). For the Catalogue Version (which remains hypothetical, for not a foot of film has ever been found to support its existence), the missing portions are those of the rescue of the child as seen from the inside, and that of the mother as seen from the outside. Yet if it was possible to re-edit the film by pruning away unwanted bits of shots, it is inadmissible that the opposite may have occurred: that a forger (whatever his intentions) might have taken a film that had been edited in a continuous manner (as in the Cross-Cut Version) and, after successfully unearthing the bits of shots missing from it, re-edited it in a non-continuous manner (to use a distinction of Tom Gunning's).

Everything leads to the conclusion that the recently recovered print is a release print of the epoch. The various tests it is undergoing will presently be completed, and from these more will be known on the matter. If it is determined that this print is original, we will have learned at least one thing: to put no faith in catalogue descriptions! It would not of course be the first time that a catalogue was guilty of misrepresentation, though it is still somewhat surprising to see how far, in this case, Edison's catalogue was allowed to go.

Let us return to the differences we noted between the Copyright Version and this recovered print. They are six in number but they concern only three aspects of the film, one of which (the second) is of minor importance, and one other (the third) is external to the film; while the remaining one is for the moment inexplicable:

1st The manner in which the shots are joined: the Copyright Version has a dissolve between each shot except in the case of the last two, which are as follows: the next-to-the-last shot ends with a fully densified image and the final shot begins with a fade-in. The recovered print (except in three cases) shows the first image fading out, followed, without any superimposition, by a gradual fade-in of the second image. The three other cases, between shots 3 and 4, 4 and 5, 6 and 7, show a clean cut between them with no fading. There are thus no superimposed fades in the recovered print.

2nd A portion of shot 7 is missing in the recovered print. Here, in place of the tilt-up shot which rises from the view of the fire engine halted in front of the house to the upper portions of the house, there is a jump-cut. This is probably due to a break in the film which happened in the course of the numerous projections to which it was necessarily subjected.

3rd The film is preceded by a title signed 'Thomas A. Edison', which asserts the producer's rights:

> *Patented March 14, 1893*
>
> September 30, 1902
>
> This film is sold subject to the restriction that it shall not be used for duplicating or printing other films from it. Any use of it for those purposes is an infringement of the patents under which it is made and sold.

It remains to be explained how it happens that the shots of the film sent to the Copyright Office are connected by dissolves which are missing in the other, the presumed release print. This question must be left open for the present as I lack the materials needed to resolve it and as I believe that, in any case, its resolution will have no real bearing on the present study.

Translated by Charles Musser and Martin Sopocy.

Notes

First published in *Cinema Journal* vol. 19 no. 1, Fall 1979.

1. Roman Gubern, 'David Wark Griffith et l'articulation cinématographique', *Cahiers de la Cinémathèque*, no. 17, Christmas 1975; and Barthelemy Amengual, '*The Life of an American Fireman* et la naissance du montage', same issue. Translated quotations from these articles are ours – C.M. and M.S.
2. Especially since, comparing the Cross-Cut Version to other films of the time, one can't help being surprised, if not actually astonished, by the editor's precocious skill. Such virtuosity seems unlikely in a film-maker who never exhibited it again. Consider shot 17, whose sole function is to build suspense by getting the audience to identify with the frantic mother and her fear that the fireman may not be in time to save her child.
3. After this article was completed I obtained some additional information from Eileen Bowser, Curator of the Film Department at the Museum of Modern Art. Concerning the Cross-Cut Version of the film she writes, in a letter dated 8 November 1977: 'No, I don't understand why Gubern assumes ours is an original print; I am sure we have never claimed that. We acquired a 35 mm nitrate print from Pathé News Inc. in 1944 and have no knowledge of its previous history. . . . I am not completely convinced, but I am tending more and more to believe that the [Library of Congress Version] is the correct one. . . . We are considering the possibility of preparing a circulating program which would give both versions of *Life of an American Fireman* for scholars to study.'

   According to another source, who presently prefers to remain anonymous, another copy of *Life of an American Fireman* has recently been discovered, and it could well prove to be original since it has the small perforations characteristic of the epoch. This copy will soon be available for study and the truth may then be known once and for all.
4. Edison Catalogue of 1904 – C.M.
5. While researching a revision of this article I located a study which exhibits a good understanding of the film's temporality: A. Nicholas Vardac's *Stage to Screen: Theatrical Method from Garrick to Griffith*. In it Vardac describes the film in detail, including its temporal dimension: 'three scenes follow a single pictorial continuity, showing three phases of the bandits' escape: the locomotive run, the race over the hills to the waiting horses, and finally the dash into the wilderness on horseback. This continuity is broken to flashback to the uncompleted line of action stemming from the original attack of the

bandits upon the telegraph officer and their successful departure. The operator's daughter releases and revives him. He rushes out to give the alarm.' (p. 183)

I also found a similar description of the film by Adolph Zukor in *The Public Is Never Wrong*: 'Boarding the engine, the desperadoes force its driver to take them to a point several miles up the track, where they take to the mountains. Their horses are tethered in a valley. They mount hurriedly and ride into the wilderness. Now for the revolutionary flashback. In the telegraph office the bound-and-gagged operator struggles to his feet and calls for assistance by manipulating the telegraph key with his chin' (p. 26). By his own reckoning Zukor had seen the film almost a thousand times.

6. The Danish film *Et Drama fra Riddertiden, eller For en Kvindes Skyld* ('A Drama from the Age of Chivalry, or For a Woman's Sake'), directed by Viggo Larsen in 1907, is interesting in this connection. A late example of pre-Griffith treatment of a suspense situation simultaneously located in the interior and exterior of the same building, it exhibits a structure that is hardly more advanced than that of the Copyright Version of *Life of an American Fireman*, and indeed is strikingly similar to it, despite its greater complexity. In the final episode of this 152-metre film, a jealous knight murders his rival by cutting the rope on which the latter is climbing to a rendezvous in the chamber of the woman they both love. The editing of the film presents the scene in this way: 1. Medium long shot. A room in the castle. The woman kneels at prayer. Rising, she goes to the window and looks down at the ground below. Seeing something there, she begins to fasten bedsheets together into a rope. M.L.S. The jealous knight is seen in a room on a lower floor of the castle. He looks out of the window and opens it. 3. M.L.S. Same setting as 1. The woman finishes tying the sheets. She opens the window, attaches the joined sheets to the window's central pole, and lets the rope fall. 4. M.L.S. Same setting as 2. The jealous knight sees the rope fall directly in front of his window. He unsheathes his sword and cuts the rope of joined sheets. 5. M.L.S. Same as 1. The woman looks outdoors and is seized with horror. 6. M.L.S. Same as 2. The jealous knight exits at right. 7. M.L.S. The castle exterior, below the windows. The lover enters and looks upward. 8. M.L.S. Castle exterior, outside the woman's window. She lets the sheet fall along the wall. 9. M.L.S. Same as 7. The lover begins to climb the rope of sheets. 10. M.L.S. Castle exterior at a point between the woman's window and the ground. A body is seen falling. 11. M.L.S. Same as 8. The woman looks down and is seized with horror. 12. M.L.S. Same as 7. The lover's body lies on the ground as the sequence ends. More complex than the Copyright Version of *Life of an American Fireman*, the film's action originates in several interior and exterior locations at once. But as in the earlier film, it is the contiguity of the locations that calls forth these complexities.
7. My italics.
8. Gubern, 'David Wark Griffith', p. 11 – C.M.
9. When I asked Jacobs why he had reversed the order of the stills, he responded, in a letter dated 10 December 1977: 'Because the Edison Catalogue listed the order differently than the published photos, I followed the Catalogue order.' This explanation seems somewhat inadequate, however, as there is, in fact, more alternation in the 'Jamison continuity' as Jacobs gives it than is indicated in the catalogue scenario.
10. It should be made absolutely clear that the imputation in this context is of naive opinionation or a lapse in a methodology that was usually more rigorous, rather than of any conscious wrongdoing. Lewis Jacobs – a writer of such pre-eminence in his field that a later generation of historians stands squarely on his shoulders even while disagreeing with him – needs no defending. Yet I cannot resist commenting that, given the success of what might be called 'the cross-cutting revolution' in having shaped and conditioned our basic concepts of film narrative, it would have taken a superhuman effort indeed to imagine in 1939 that footage of two simultaneous actions interrelated in a suspense situation would *not* have been cross-cut. Given, further, the closest thing to hard evidence that then existed – the Edison Catalogue which, to our hindsight anyway, certainly appears to imply some degree of cross-cutting – the no doubt independently arrived at assumption by both Jacobs and by the assembler of the Pathé print (at whatever date prior to 1944 he may have worked) that the original version must have been cross-cut was inevitable – M.S.

11. Amengual, '*Life of an American Fireman*', p. 24.
12. There are some grounds for doubting the uniqueness of the version which I have seen at the Museum of Modern Art, and which is identical with the copies in the Canadian Film Institute at Toronto and in the Laval University Film Library at Quebec. Consider this description of the film by Jean Mitry in his *Histoire du cinéma*, vol. 1, p. 240. 'In the last scene we have lost sight of the pursuers but we see the bandits dividing up the booty in a clearing. The question that immediately comes to the viewer's mind is: 'Have they shaken the posse off?' At the same time, as if to answer the question, the camera pans slowly to the left, revealing the pursuers in the foreground. Hidden by tall trees from the bandits, they have just arrived and are dismounting. The last reverse angle shows the bandits in the foreground. The pursuers appear in the background on the right, moving towards the camera, and after a short struggle they capture the villains.' In our copies there is no trace of the first shot Mitry describes, a pan with pursuers in the foreground; there is only the 'reverse angle'. Our bafflement mounts as a few lines later Mitry writes: '... the fourteen scenes in *The Great Train Robbery* contain about thirty shots.' This is totally mystifying. The three copies I have seen consist of fourteen scenes corresponding to as many shots, unless account is taken of the jump-cuts which can easily vary in number from one print to the next. We might almost assume he was mistaken except that Amengual, in *Clefs pour le cinéma* (Paris: Seghers, 1971, p. 73), refers to the same pan shot.
13. Another factor to be taken into consideration relates to the type of continuities created by the kind of editing involved. In the terms of our analysis, parallel editing produces inter-sequential continuities and cross-cutting intra-sequential ones. We see this clearly in *The Great Train Robbery*, where there is continuity between the first and second sequences (between scenes 9 and 10) and between the second and third (scenes 11 and 12). In *Life of an American Fireman* the situation is less clear. First comes the 'firemen' sequence, in which the fire alarm shot has been inserted. This sequence is linked to a scene of the rescue seen from the inside of the house, which in turn is linked either to a shot of the exterior in which we are shown the successful conclusion of the rescue (Catalogue Version), or to another shot of the same rescue, seen this time from the outside, but repeated (Copyright Version). The ambiguity is to be found in the contiguity of the last two sequences. A wall is the only thing that separates them.
14. It may be objected that it is arbitrary to label the second sequence of *Life of an American Fireman* as 'I' instead of 'B' and that this sequence is part of the line of action B, 'citizens in danger', as the alarm was sounded by someone who was aware of the fire. Indeed, I felt some hesitation before eliminating this division which would have produced the sequence AB–B–A–B–AB. Of course, either way, the film's structure fails to go beyond the stage of parallel editing that just precedes cross-cutting. This is quite apparent in the Cross-Cut Version (whose authenticity is in question), which has a structure of AB–B (or I)–AB–Ab–B–A–aB–A–aB–AB–aB, where the small letter signifies an intruding series for the shot in question – and, incidentally, brings us up once again to the problem of the parallel editing of contiguous events.

    If we hesitate to identify 'scene' 2 (the close-up of the fire alarm box) with the line-of-action B, this may well be because we sense that it is properly neither. If this shot had shown the mother in distress calling for help we could not hesitate to identify it with line-of-action B. On the other hand, if it were replaced with another shot showing a close-up of an alarm-receiver in the fire station, we would then have to identify it with line-of-action A. As neither is the case, I see no validity in identifying it with either one.
15. One further direction which research could take to validate one of the versions of *Life of an American Fireman* would be that of the film's length. Edison's catalogue gives its length as 425 feet (with or without credits?), whereas the Copyright Version is 400 feet long without credits, and the Cross-Cut Version, again without the credits, is only 378 feet long. Converted to 16 mm (in the ratio 2 to 5) these figures become 170, 160 and 151 feet. If the Catalogue's figure is correct, the Cross-Cut Version is much too short, while the missing footage of the Copyright Version could conceivably be the credits.

II

THE INSTITUTION CINEMA

Industry, Commodity, Audiences

Introduction

Once More: Narrative

In the previous section, it was argued that the history of film form is bound up with the development of 'narrative', though in a more special sense than that given in traditional accounts. Not as the inevitable destiny of the cinema, in its drive for realism and verisimilitude, but understood as the most 'economical' solution to a number of contending exigencies involved in the representation of space and time, but also in the representation of the spectator within this space-time.

The compromise hinged on what one might call a logic of commutation or substitution, which in turn depended on the cinema severing two kinds of bond with the represented: the (ontological) one between the filmic and the pro-filmic, and the (physical) one between spectator and the screen. At first, films were presentations in the sense of reproducing situations already existing elsewhere: as self-contained actions, as topical events, as scenic views, as vaudeville sketches, jokes or gags – brought before a 'live' audience. But the historical dynamics was such that cinema developed its autonomy by working out how to convert this double 'reality' (that of the pro-filmic occasion and that of the spectator-screen relation) into a single one, in which each is somehow contained, yet also drastically refigured. The spectator had to be bound not to the screen (as a performative space) nor to the event or spectacle, but to their representations: this implied changing both the logic of the event represented and the place of the spectator *vis à vis* the event. If we recall the way the films of Lumière are read by Deutelbaum, Vaughan, deCordova, we can see that each emphasises the emergence of a new viewing subject (which we recognise as essentially that of classical cinema); by contrast, the readings of Burch, Gunning and Gaudreault all insist, for early cinema, on the autonomy of the events/actions as 'attractions', addressed to a collective audience who experience the viewing situation as external to and separate from the views represented. For the latter it is only when more complex actions are being put on screen (the multi-shot film and the beginnings of analytical editing) that a change occurred in the way spectators experienced the event or action: the history of the insert shot and the point-of-view shot, of overlaps and cross cutting being the most obvious instances of this change from presentation to representation, from monstration to narration.[1] The cinema's turn to 'narrative' appears thus as the consequence, rather than as the cause of turning audiences into isolated spectators, bound to the representation by the spectacle of seeing space and time as variables of another logic which we perhaps too unproblematically identify with narrative.[2]

But why did the cinema have to convert collective audiences into isolated spectators? In order to answer this, we must look to the so-called institution cinema, a term naming a number of apparently very heterogeneous aspects: the social spaces needed to gather audiences and the practices regulating their admission; the production companies' competition for access to and control of technology; the changes in distribution from selling to exchanging and renting, and most fundamental of all, the standardisation of an agreed commodity, recognised by producers and audiences alike. At first glance, none of this appears to have to do with questions of film form and the development of narrative as outlined above.[3] Yet what is emerging from work done on early cinema's institutional context is how crucially the emergence of narrative as the dominant mode is inflected if not outright determined by the particular definition which the viewing spaces, the mode of production and the distribution of product received. Thus, from the institutional perspective, too, narrative represents a compromise of different factors dovetailing in practice while nonetheless remaining contradictory in their effects.

This reminder seems the more necessary since little of the cinema's subsequent history was implied in the invention itself: the recording and projection of moving images first appeared to be primarily of scientific interest, and of little use commercially beyond its novelty value and appeal as a toy.[4] As a scientific invention the cinematograph was mainly an 'extension' of existing techniques,[5] and only when its attraction and attractiveness to very large and very diverse audiences became manifest did the commercial potential dawn on the inventors, in contrast to the showmen. But especially as an entertainment form, the cinema raises a number of questions about the technological, economic and social environment from which it emerged and where it consolidated itself. Economically, there is little doubt that it inexorably came under the sway of capitalism. To grasp this in a non-reductive way, though, we need to investigate how it resolved or managed the changes between artisanal and industrial organisation, between entrepreneurial and managerial business practice, between the craft ethic of the workshop and the mass-production factory system. Such an economic perspective draws attention to the forces that decide and define the sort of commodity film actually is, and how it circulates. Yet these forces turn out also to be social and demographic, which is why questions of audiences and spectatorship loom large in the study of early cinema. Technology, on the other hand, which used to be regarded as the royal road to an understanding of early film history, now finds itself firmly embedded in other histories, mainly economic and legal.

Within the institutional development of early cinema we can distinguish at least two separate periods. The first comprises the years 1896–1907,[6] and the other, the period up to 1917, by which time classical continuity cinema was fully in place. The most obvious moment in this history is the 'Nickelodeon boom', in other words, the fixed siting of exhibition outlets. This radically transformed the cinema, not only in the United States. But the Nickelodeon boom is both cause (in that it gave rise to a reshaping of film production and film distribution), and effect (in that it responded to the tremendous increase in popularity and demand). The second most momentous event is the transition from single reel to multi-reel film, and the changes this brought in the structure of the industry, the textual organisation of the film, and the commodity form of the product.

Film before Commodity: From Artisanal to Industrial Production

For the study of the primitive cinema's mode of production several directions have opened up. First, how did the 'pioneers' acquire the technology involved in making pictures, and secondly, how did they control its use through legal battles around copyright protection and patents: what one might call the *intellectual* property relations involved. Thirdly, a more thorough investigation is needed of the *industrial* property relations. What was the character of film production from the turn of the century to the mid-1910s? Was it artisanal, industrial or entrepreneurial? When did it become fully capitalist and under what pressures did its monopolistic phase emerge? Defining the cinema's mode of production also means having insight into the corporate strategies used to dominate an industry, of which the most prominent was the move of individual producers to form interest groups and associations – either for the purpose of sharing resources, like patents (cross-licensing) or to ensure the exclusion of other producers (the formation of cartels and the calculated increase in production values and costs).

Film-making began in the artisanal environment of professional inventors, showmen and small precision engineering firms. But already during the very early period, different strategies emerge.[7] Michael Chanan in 'Economic Conditions of Early Cinema' reminds us that 'an invention is brought about by a particular conjunction of technological opportunity with the exploitation of economic conditions'. By looking at the reasons behind Edison's omission to take out overseas patents on the kinetoscope and comparing them to the business practices of British manufacturers, Chanan can already identify one key feature of all subsequent development: competition and the struggle for control. But the basic mechanism of control during the first period was the camera and projection equipment, deliberately designed so as to make it incompatible with other manufacturers'. Edison, Lumiére, R.W. Paul and Messter (the so-called 'inventors' of the cinema) all became producers of films mainly in order to establish dominance in the equipment market (format, perforation, etc. of the films obliging a client to use only their machines). The films themselves, however, were priced purely by quantity, as so many feet of celluloid. We are at a stage where the producers regarded the 'software' (the films) as the necessary inducement for establishing a monopoly on the production, sale or leasing of the hardware, which was the chief commodity.[8]

However, as soon as films entered an already established entertainment medium, such as vaudeville, music hall or the variety theatre, replacing integrally one act of the show, the balance of forces changes and another set of determinants takes over. The fact that film technology is used to reproduce mechanically and more profitably the show- and entertainment values of another medium, ends up changing this medium itself: in terms of its acts and numbers as well as in its exhibition practices and economic organisation, vaudeville becomes the proverbial dog wagged by its tail. Thus, what distinguished the cinema from vaudeville up to 1907 was not so much the types of films shown (hence the appropriateness of Gunning's term 'spectacle attractions'), but the cinema's rapid development of separate and distinct business operations to cover production, distribution and exhibition.[9] What Robert Allen has called 'industrial autonomy' is based on just such a rigid separation, and it emerges as the precondition for the rise of the storefront theatres and nickelodeons.[10] The historical alternatives outlined by Michael Chanan – either show the same film to different people (itinerant projection/Lumière) or show different films to the same people (fixed exhibition site/permanently installed projection equipment) – were already by 1905 resolved in favour of the latter.[11] The change from selling to renting, and the emergence of fixed sites other than vaudeville theatres are thus interdependent factors. As we shall see, fixed siting will in turn become the focus for change, having an effect on, but also being determined by, the institution's *technical* ability to produce longer films as well as its *aesthetic and formal* ability to create longer, self-contained narratives.

Chanan's discussion of the 'special character of the commodity film' compared to other commodities is thus particularly useful in detailing how to understand the change from selling to renting, and the introduction of film exchanges. His remarks on standardisation (of equipment and film stock) outlines a competitive logic which in due course was to bring about the decisive division of the film industry into its separate spheres, along with the various shifts of control which these entailed. The fact that film is a different kind of commodity in respect of use value and exchange value (as Benjamin would say, a commodity produced directly for exhibition value) begins to explain its 'immaterial materiality', where no physical act of exchange takes place in order for the commodity to realise its exchange value. Chanan also underlines that production is in the case of film even less separable from questions of ideology, of social relations and social spaces than in the circulation and consumption of more directly 'material' commodities. The economic expansion of the cinema was related to the fact that especially in the United States (but in Europe, too), people in increasing numbers were prepared to pay for a particular kind of pleasure. Understanding early cinema as a specific mode of production means to see 'production' not just taking place at the sites of manufacture, but also at the sites of consumption, requiring a business practice, capable of organising capital so as to ensure its circulation as well as orchestrating discourses that could legitimate this pleasure socially, by purging it of certain associations and fostering others.

Control Through Patents and Litigation: The MPPC and the Independents

These general reflections might help to understand why film production had to follow the practice of other factory systems,[12] but also why and in what ways it had to break new ground. As Janet Staiger's 'Combination and Litigation: 1896–

1917' shows, the film industry needed to find a way of dividing labour and defining separate tasks; it needed management structures and forms of production control; and as a diverse technological apparatus, involving engineering, optics, chemistry, the electrical industry, and supplying a mass market, it needed standardisation of both manufacturing processes and of product.[13] Companies able to impose their norms on an industry and thus on the market have always been at a competitive advantage.[14] Yet while vigorously pursuing standardisation, firms would also aim to control access to the market by controlling invention, and thereby prevent other producers from copying either patents or products. Staiger details the meshing of different strategies among early producers, calling 'litigation' and 'combination' the twin objectives of American capitalism in the sphere of film production and distribution.[15]

A tell-tale index, as Staiger points out, is the increase in the size of legal departments attached to production houses, fighting cases of litigation, infringement of patent rights, and working out cross-licensing agreements. These actions were all part of the same strategy: creating a legal monopoly. By using 'patent infringement suits as a legal weapon for collecting royalties'[16] the film industry followed the example of the textile industry. But in the fight for the protection of product, existing copyright laws came under severe strain when trying to decide authorship and originality in the case of photography and film. Paul Levy[17] and André Gaudreault[18], as we saw, have looked at sales policy and film piracy in order to demonstrate how, especially in the period between 1900 and 1906, international film production tried to meet demand for film by, for instance, copying films that had proved successful for a competitor. Thus Méliès' *A Trip to the Moon* was duped and widely distributed in the United States 'without Méliès ever being able to collect a single cent' because he had failed to register his films under US copyright.[19] Levy, Gaudreault, and also Gunning have analysed in detail the ramifications of one particular case, Porter copying the BBBBiograph film *Personal* (1904) for the Edison Company, itself copied by the Lubin Company, and then by Pathé in France.[20]

If legal arguments frame the film-text at one end of the institution, the internal exigencies of organising production determine it at another end. Supporting Staiger's arguments about the photoplay as industrial blueprint,[21] Patrick Loughney's 'In the Beginning was the Word' shows how carefully pre-Griffith Biograph scenarios were constructed and written with the production needs in mind. For Loughney, their sophistication is particularly noticeable when compared with Selig scripts from the same period, which gave priority to dialogue continuity. Not only does Loughney confirm that scenario writing at Biograph was influenced by the fact that several production teams were working simultaneously, but given that the practice can be traced back to 1904, he can suggest that division of labour and the separation of production stages already existed well before Ince and Griffith.

What emerges from these essays is a twofold struggle: one that focuses on regulating the development of the basic film technology and rationalising production capacity, the other on the ideologically as well as logistically complex issue of the exploitation right of the product itself. The different cartels and the emergence of the studio system itself need thus to be understood also as successive and simultaneous moves towards an 'optimal' management of problems that are neither purely technological nor strictly economic, but once again, a matter of different kinds of control: control over the technology and the right to exploit it; control over the sites of exhibition and thus access to markets; control over labour, personnel, story-properties. In the case of the United States, the most prominent interest group engaged in this struggle during the period between 1897 and 1907 was the Motion Picture Patent Company (the so-called Trust). Staiger's essay (as well as one by Jeanne Thomas Allen already referred to) have detailed the strategies of Edison trying to control the emerging film industry. They show how his company either forced competitors out of business through litigation, patent wars and other legal steps, or by obliging them to join the Trust, the first cartel specifically set up to restrict legally the use of the basic film technology in a way that would exclude rivals from entering the market. Edison, who is often cited as the inventor of the cinema, could therefore with more justification be called the inventor of the film industry.

Equally important, however, is the fact that the MPPC, by combining most of the major film producers, was able to promote through cross-licensing, under the name of the General Film Company, the drive towards standardisation in the industry, thereby not only cutting down on costly duplication in the technological sphere, but greatly increasing and accelerating the circulation of the product film.[22] Contrary to legend, the Independents who moved West and founded Hollywood, also formed a trust; they, too, were an oligopoly which would, within a decade or so, become the nucleus of one of the most successful cartels: the Hollywood studio system. In this respect, the beginnings of the American film industry are roughly similar to developments in other areas of the capitalist economy, moving from a competitive phase to one in which a small group of producers form cartel-like organisations, to protect themselves from outsiders and to control a specific market.[23]

Mode of Representation or Mode of Production: The Logic of Production Companies

The Trust, however, also took on a self-policing role, being in charge of censorship of film content and concerning itself with the improvement of the quality of film theatres. It is an index of the film industry's own awareness of an ideological role, and thus an awareness that in some important respects, the cinema is quite unlike other capitalist industries, involving factors which a strictly economic model cannot adequately account for. For what needs to be underlined is the way industrial practices and ideological-textual ones are interdependent (an interdependence implied by Burch's term 'mode of representation').[24] Such an emphasis on the ideological, textual and legal dimension of the commodity in conjunction with the mode of production in the industrial sense requires a more detailed study of the various film production companies.[25] For even though the formation of the Trust, and later, of the cartel set up by the Independents, ensured that companies developed in their business practices and outlook in similar fashion,[26] this by no means resulted in identical products. As Janet Staiger argues, the dynamic of standardisation was only one of the imperatives underlying the development. Equally significant was the need for product differentiation, the styling of films in a way that allowed companies to compete with each other by offering choice to the consumer, and attach to their products signifiers of value differentiating them from the products of other companies. As Staiger also argues, the system that resulted from the introduction of factory-type practices, the division of labour and managerial hierarchies 'was by no means the cheapest film-making procedure'.[27] In other words, for the film industry such manufacturing priorities as unit cost or rationalisation may well have had to be balanced against other priorities in the contest for brand recognition, respectability, or penetration of specific markets, raising again the issue whether the cinema's commodity can be treated as material (product) or immaterial (service), and what might be the industrial organisation most appropriate to this double status.[28] This in turn underlines the fact that individual production companies tried to gain an advantage by manipulating or creating particular kinds of assets or 'properties' such as stars[29] or production values identifiable by the public.[30]

The clearest case of a pre-Hollywood company self-consciously playing on all available registers in order to market its image along with its product is the Vitagraph company.[31] Although more detailed research into production methods has probably been done on the Edison and Biograph companies (not least because an unusual wealth of documents and primary material has survived in archives and special collections), it is Vitagraph, despite the paucity of business records and even of surviving films, that has caught the attention of the new historians.[32] Driven by thinking of economic priorities in terms of product differentiation and the rapid internationalisation of film distribution[33], Vitagraph stylistic peculiarities, such as its pioneering of the 'nine foot line' (or *plan americain*), come to be seen in a different light. No other company showed such an astute assessment of the economic development of film production and such a clear understanding of how success in overseas markets required stylistic changes or the raising of production values. As Salt has remarked:

> After 1907 the films of the Vitagraph Company force themselves on the attention of the informed eye. Long ignored because of their lack of fast cutting, the films of this major company which had the widest distribution in Europe of any American producer, developed qualities within the individual shots which were quite inaccessible to D.W. Griffith.[34]

Media Intertexts: Early Cinema and Vaudeville

Before such stylistic strategies could fully emerge as part of an economic and competitive context, the cinema had to have not only established an autonomous institutional basis, but also a notion of its audiences. If one looks at some of the many precedents cited for the cinema: magic lanterns or dioramas, optical toys or Hale's Tours, they suggest, as entertainment forms, a predominantly middle-class audience. In 'Porter or Ambivalence' Burch had tried to relate these precedents to the development of the cinema in a more dialectical fashion, speculating that early cinema catered for and was frequented by working-class audiences, and therefore, that the primitive mode constitutes a more radical break with bourgeois modes of self-representation. Burch had based his view partly on formal features (the scanned image, the absence of an individual hero, the types of closure) and partly on accounts of how popular and populist the cinema originally was (Ramsaye, Agee, Wagenknecht, Jacobs[35]). But as Robert Allen's comparative study of the Lumières' and Edison's exhibition policy shows,[36] both early film technology and early cinema audiences, at least in the United States, need to be seen in a very precise historical context – what Allen calls the 'media intertext' of vaudeville.[37] According to Allen, up to at least 1906 films depended for their exhibition almost exclusively on the already existing vaudeville theatres, which with an admission fee of 25 cents, were outside a working-class budget. Kristin Thompson, in an analysis of the formal features of early cinema[38] comes to the conclusion that the media intertext does allow us to distinguish between early film form and classical cinema, but that many of the features singled out by Burch as evidence of a 'proletarian' mode of representation can be directly attributed to films fitting themselves into vaudeville programmes. According to her, early cinema is not only economically dependent on vaudeville but also for subject matter. She cites single shot films; verbal and sight gags, films with a 'pay-off' ending, playlets, skits, episodic sketches, condensed novel/tableau films and visual newspapers as film forms and genres typical of cinema imitating vaudeville acts.[39]

The weakness of Burch's argument is thus its indebtedness to theoretical speculations of the kind that have always compared the cinema and its mode of representation to either stage theatre or the bourgeois novel. To this approach, Allen provides a most detailed historical corrective, which especially for the decade 1890–1900 requires us to be much more cautious about the cinema's first audiences. Similarly, for the Nickelodeons and covering the period until 1911, Russell Merritt's 'Building an Audience for the Movies' confirms that films had economically and ethnically very diverse and heterogeneous audiences, just as vaudeville theatres (in contrast to burlesque) had always been aiming to attract a middle-class audience.[40] Allen, Merritt and also Gomery's evidence tends to point in the opposite direction of Burch's thesis, suggesting that only with the victory of the 'institutional mode of narration' and the exhibition situation associated with it did the working class frequent the cinemas in appreciable numbers.[41]

The mutual but uneven relations between cinema and vaudeville can also be documented by looking at the kinds of promotion and self-representation of the two media, and at their exhibition practices. The nickelodeons – the economic victors – borrowed directly from their vanquished competitor:

> Vaudeville had in effect provided the unwilling model of exhibition for the energetic new rival. Just as five years later, movie exhibitors would use the legitimate theatre as a guide to learn how to exhibit feature films,

so, in 1908, nickelodeon owners preyed on vaudeville houses for methods of exhibiting movie shorts.[42]

What emerges is a kind of piggy-backing, whereby films, at first featured as one kind of attraction among others in the vaudeville or variety programmes, emancipated themselves by finding fixed sites, larger audiences and by lowering admission prices (hence the name 'nickelodeons'). By the same logic, but in reverse, the nickelodeons came under pressure from stage theatres, which converted into cinemas, and in the drive for higher profits, began separating and dividing audiences, thus raising admission prices and aiming at more respectability, that is to say, a middle-class audience. Merritt tries to understand the 'embourgeoisement' of the cinema and its audiences in terms of the shifts from vaudeville to the nickelodeons, and from the nickelodeons to the large picture palaces, arguing that the demise of the nickelodeons began with legitimate theatres showing films and thus making movies respectable.[43] Higher prices allowed them to screen films censored or forbidden to the 5 and 10c theatres, which in turn initiated the practice of exclusive deals with distributors, what came to be known as zoning and clearance agreements. Unlike conventional wisdom, which sees the latter as a sign of the power of the production side of industry over exhibition, these agreements originated from the exhibition sector itself, and pitted one of its branches, the first-run houses (admittedly, increasingly owned and controlled by the production companies and studios) against another.

Thus, whatever effect vaudeville and stage drama may have had on film *forms*, their physical spaces and audiences were at different times formative for the amenities and class-associations which the cinema-going experience began to foster. Merritt suggests 1905–1911 as the period when a noticeable upward shift in audiences occurred, and when in trade journals one can discover signs of discrimination against 'rough trade' like sailors or enlisted men; when theatres were discouraged from catering to one national group alone, from booking ethnic vaudeville acts or foreign language songs; and when, finally, new theatres began to be sited not in working-class areas and instead at the periphery of a city's business district or white-collar shopping streets.[44] There is thus extensive evidence that the co-presence of different audiences was decisive in the development of early cinema, but that this co-presence began to be stratified in several ways: a point of capital importance when one begins to assess the economic factors in the growth of the cinema as an industry.

Audiences and Gendered Spectatorship

According to Merritt, what brought the affluent into the cinemas was a massive appeal to the 'new American Woman and her children'. Theatres wooed her, and censorship boards professed to protect her.[45] These arguments around gendered spectatorship have been taken up by feminist film historians[46] who have tried to supply both empirical and textual evidence for the impact which women, immigrants and children may have had on the development of the cinema as a leisure industry. Judith Mayne and Miriam Hansen have focused on issues of early cinema and gender, by looking simultaneously at how exhibitors targeted women and children as audiences, while social reformers singled them out as vulnerable to seduction and victims of corruption. Hansen's 'Early Cinema: Whose Public Sphere' returns to the issue of a proletarian audience, but via a highly original and interesting route. Seeing the notion of a proletarian early cinema either as 'yet another projection of leftists media theory' or, in the American version of the 'democratic art', as 'one of American mass-culture's most powerful myths of its own origins', she nonetheless suggests that one can reconstruct the notion of the cinema as a non-hegemonic, subversive public sphere in the United States from the 'efforts – documented by Merritt and other historians – to rid the institution of its class-specific stigma', and in Germany, from the very virulence and contradictions generated by the reformers' efforts to bring the cinema under control. However, instead of identifying the working class as the object of concern, she argues that the reformers' zeal and outrage was aimed at women, whose presence in the cinemas was felt to be a threat to the family and a provocation to public morality. In the very language used by the reformers she discovers a familiar 'fear of femininity ... on both a pragmatic and metaphoric level'.[47]

However, Hansen's conclusions are quite cautious when it comes to gendering the spectators of early cinema. Mindful perhaps of Merritt's point, namely that there is a difference between women and children being wooed as spectators or becoming the cause of public concern, and their statistical numbers (they were, according to Merritt, outnumbered by adult males 3 to 1), she points to the fact that the industry was neither concerned with the ideology of the democratic art, nor did it worry about 'women's conformity to traditional roles', but – rather as Mayne had already suggested – the institution cinema was busy addressing women as possessors of disposable incomes and as consumers, while trying to construct a new social consensus (repressing differences of class, of ethnic origin, and possibly even of gender) around a new culture of consumption, convenience and leisure.[48] This is in line with an argument that theorises audiences by asking what exactly a spectator pays for when buying admission. Referring to John Ellis' formula about 'paying for the possibility of pleasure',[49] Chanan has suggested amending this to 'paying for a view', in order to focus on another dialectic involved in the development of early cinema. Since economically, the cinema became profitable when it separated production from exhibition, and distribution from either, the introduction of film exchanges meant that the right of admission represented the right to a view, as opposed to possessing, or even renting a viewing copy. Brewster has pointed out that the zoning and clearance agreements were only a logical extension of a development beginning already with the nickelodeon boom, namely that a film's movement through time and space enters into the question of pleasure. An admission ticket effectively buys a class position, because it gives access to a location advantage and a time advantage. The emergence of first-run theatres thus means a division and standardisation of both exhibition time and exhibition space, with direct consequences for the (economic value of the) product itself.

Exhibition-Led History and the Creation of a Stable Commodity

Emerging from these discussions of audiences and spectatorship is a certain corrective perspective on the institution as a whole. On the one hand, Burch's notion of the 'mode of representation' privileges the ideological and the textual operations of early cinema at the expense of industrial and economic determinations. On the other hand, by concentrating on the mode of production, and making it the major force of change, there is a danger of collapsing the history of the cinema with a general history of American capitalism. Yet a history conceived 'from the bottom up' as it were, around audiences and spectatorship also runs into serious difficulties: as we saw, the issue of class is more complex than Burch at first conjectured. But if film history cautions against too readily theorising the textual spectator, then film theory has alerted us to the contradictions involved in sociological models of gendered spectatorship. What seems to be needed is a more historically informed account of the site at which product and spectator interact with and construct each other in the act of exchange. This justifies the emphasis given by Merritt and others to the role of the nickelodeons. Yet their importance is still underestimated, if we see them mainly as the 'first permanent home' for the cinema, 'building an audience for the movies'. They were just as important for significantly redefining the cinema's basic commodity.

Charles Musser is one of the historians of the early cinema most aware of this point, arguing for a more 'dialectical' conception of the history of the film industry, and for locating the dynamics of change neither in film form and technology, nor in technology or business practice, but in what he calls 'the history of screen practice'.[50] In a series of articles investigating the cinema of Porter, the Nickelodeon boom and patterns of exhibition Musser has tried to demonstrate the interdependence of production and exhibition, and the relation operating between these spheres. Also taking the case of Vitagraph, Musser argues[51] how changes in the mode of production also changed the product. Indeed, Vitagraph according to Musser offers itself particularly well as a test case for examining the formation of a production company as the site of convergence for a number of determinants in which the economic factors enter into a dynamic interplay with non-economic factors. To Musser the crucial aspect in Vitagraph's early history is that the partners Blackton and Smith understood 'the possibilities inherent in the interaction and interdependence between film-production and exhibition',[52] which meant above all, the rationalisation of the product itself.

In 'The Nickelodeon Era Begins: Establishing the Framework for Hollywood's Mode of Representation'[53] Musser returns to specific films, regarding the changes from *Life of an American Fireman*, 1903 (exemplifying a form of film-making associated with vaudeville) to *The Lonely Villa*, 1909 (a recognisable example of storytelling cinema of the kind still with us today) as symptomatic of a shift in paradigm, for which neither their proximity in time nor traditional accounts of progress (attributing the development to technical sophistication or the genius of Griffith) prepare us adequately. Musser sees the difference historically grounded in a radical transformation of the circumstances of film exhibition. Whereas up to about 1904, vaudeville owners would buy single-shot films and arrange them into programmes, by the end of 1904 large chains like the Keith Circuit had changed to installing projectors, exhibiting the films with their own staff and merely hiring the films.[54] As Allen had already pointed out, these were the essential conditions for the 'nickelodeon boom', with its very rapid growth and expansion of store-front theatres exclusively devoted to showing films. But, according to Musser, the nickelodeon boom was not merely the result of improved technology (e.g. the possibility of flicker-free projection through the reframing device over which Edison fought so hard to gain control); it depended on the existence of 'longer films used interchangeably by theatres'.[55]

Thus, the importance of the shift from the films shown in vaudeville theatres to the multi-shot films shown in nickelodeons, beyond any effect it may have had on genres (such as the predominance of acted fiction films over 'scenics' and 'topicals'), lay in the creation of a unified product, the reel of film as 'the basic industry commodity'.[56] By standardising length and fitting both form and content around this standardisation, the groundwork for film-making to become a mass-producing industry had been laid. But for this to happen, films had to have entered into a regulated circuit of distribution and exchange which in turn depended on the existence of distributors and exhibitors supplying fixed sites and a constant rate of turnover of product.[57]

Musser's point is that it was the exhibition mode which determined this drive towards the reel of film as the standard commodity, with the mode of production (the manufacturing processes) and the mode of representation (film form) lagging behind: 'film-making remained a cottage industry while exhibition had become a form of mass-production'.[58] This latter point was also made by Allen and Gomery, in their studies of cinema chains in Chicago and New York. They looked at company records, town planning ordinances, fire regulations in order to clarify not only the question of the cinema's class nature, but how presentation, marketing, advertising became professionalised and geared towards educating audiences into appreciating the new commodity. The concept of deluxe films, with coordinated release dates and longer exhibition periods can also be seen as part of this new consumer industry, which in due course would include cartel-like agreements to artificially restrict access to the product (the zoning and clearance regulations already mentioned).

The Question of Editorial Control

By specifying the conditions under which the reel of film became the standardised commodity form for the institution cinema in all its aspects, Musser has isolated processes of far-reaching consequences, since these emerge as the necessary preconditions for the establishment of the IMR. Stressing the commodity forms and focusing on the material elements in the exhibition process – the reel of film, projection techniques, and other material aspects of the viewing experience – Musser pursues a similar objective to that of Burch, tracing the contradictory impulses within early cinema. However, Musser's thesis of an exhibition-led history for early cinema is able to account more coherently for an aspect of the PMR which in Burch remains largely unsupported by historically verifiable evidence. For a central element of Burch's case for the PMR was the role he attributed to the lecturer commenting on a film or explaining the action, and thus serving as the extra-textual element guiding the viewer's perception of the events. For Burch, the lecturer assumed an anti-illusionist function *vis à vis* the representation. This argument was strongly based on the importance of the benshi in Japanese cinema, whose commentary remained a frequent feature of film showings well into the 1930s. Burch, as in other aspects of the PMR, tried to ground historically an oppositional or alternative practice occurring at a given stage in the cinema's development by treating it paradigmatically, laying himself open to 'factual' challenges, such as Salt's who doubted the widespread use of the lecturer, arguing that already by 1906 films were comprehensible on their own and that Burch's claims were both exaggerated and incorrect, insofar as Burch had claimed that the lecturer contributed to 'respectability'.[59]

Musser, in a sense, restores to Burch's insight its proper place: as an example of what he calls 'editorial control'[60]. Seen from the perspective of a history of screen practice, the lecturer not only becomes a specific instance of an exhibition mode in which the showman/exhibitor exerted control over the film by having control over its mode of reception, but the commentator also become only one instance among a whole number of other ways in which the exhibition mode exerts editorial control: the variable projection speed (to compensate for uneven hand-cranking, but also used to speed up a film for comic effect),[61] actors placed behind a screen who lent the characters voices and dialogue, the 'interpretation' of an action through the accompanying music, whether played on a piano or by an orchestra, or even the amenities and services offered by the movie theatres. Included in the Reader are therefore articles by Gaudreault on the lecturer, music and sound effects in early film, and by Kevin Brownlow on 'Silent Cinema – What Was the Right Speed?', not least because they lend additional evidence to Musser's thesis.

Just as the famous example of the shot of the outlaw firing point blank at the audience which could be placed at the beginning or the end of Porter's *The Great Train Robbery* demonstrates for Musser the non-closure of the filmic text at this historical juncture (since it indicates the exhibitor's control over the film's projection and thus the audience's viewing experience), Yuri Tsivian's article about the historical context of the Kuleshov experiment raises the same issues in a nationally specific context: that of early Russian cinema and its culturally conditioned reception. Tsivian makes a strong case for the need to see theories of montage historically and within the institutional framework of early cinema. The notion of a period of editorial control thus puts the debate about the PMR, about open and closed form, context dependent and self-sufficient films, paratactic or linearised narratives on a wider and more historically verifiable footing.

Musser's analysis of the nature, causes and consequences of this shift of control seems at this stage to offer the most promising account of the relationship between the PMR and the IMR, providing a suitable model for recasting a number of issues that have emerged around the question of the PMR and its historical supercession. Not unlike Staiger, in her discussion of the mode of production, what interests Musser is the process of standardisation underlying the transformations of the PMR into the IMR. But while Staiger concentrates on standardisation of production and managerial processes, Musser adds to this the standardisation of film length, viewing conditions and spatio-temporal articulations, seeing these as vital in the struggle by which the textual and editorial control exercised by the showmen, the vaudeville owners and the exhibitors shifted, paradoxically under the pressure of the nickelodeons, to another part of the institution cinema. One of the conditions of classical cinema is that control became more and more firmly concentrated in the hands of the producers at the textual level, while at another level – the delivering and processing of audiences – it has remained in the hands of the distribution and exhibition sector ever since.[62]

Towards the Institutional Mode and The Continuity System

'The Nickelodeon Era Begins' thus represents perhaps the most ambitious attempt to analyse the emergence of narrative, the question of spectatorship, the pressure of exhibition on production, and the changes from artisanal to mass production in the American cinema within one coherent theoretical framework, that of the reel as the basic commodity. The Nickelodeon period ends when production switches to multi-reel films and exhibitors seek to attract a well-to-do audience by moving to better locations. It is the division into first- and second-run theatres which inaugurates another major period of rapid change, by dramatically altering the shape of the emergent film industry. The picture palaces demanded longer films, and by providing more comfortable surroundings and better seating, they starved the nickelodeons of both product and patrons. These re-emerged as neighbourhood cinemas, catering for the less affluent among the urban population: as already mentioned, segregation of audiences would therefore seem to be the result of a particular exhibition strategy rather than its cause, and thus represent a relatively late phenomenon in the development of the cinema. In this context, Gunning's arguments about the transition from one-reelers to longer films[63] are also relevant. For if it was the exhibition structure which changed the product and also brought about the changes of production methods (factory system and division of labour), then Gunning's theses, as Musser points out, about respectability and middle-class audiences need to be refined, insofar as pressure for longer and more complex narratives would then come from changes in the industry's standard commodity, itself a consequence of a new strategy for maximising profits, rather than being related to pressures of morality, gender, or class. By erecting barriers to admission through zoning and clearing agreements, the cinema experience became not text-dependent, but context-based, valorising the location advantage and the time advantage, and thus shifting, as Brewster had also recognised, the question of privilege from being rooted in the class content or class appeal of the films to a question of status: one's position and participation in a particular act of consumption.

For a crucial period then, between primitive cinema and the institutional mode, the struggle for editorial control within an exhibition-led history might be the formula that usefully mediates between technological determinism, industrial-managerial determinism or any other version of a production-led history. This editorial control, which was to a large extent based on local kinds of knowledge, aimed at building audiences and spectatorship on the basis of ethnic identity, region or familiarity with the subject matter, had to be broken for the cinema to become 'universal'. Thus, while in one sense totally shifting the grounds of the argument, Musser is able to make the case for or against the PMR as an autonomous mode in historical terms which, though modifying Burch's argument in almost every detail, end up by lending his speculations a certain kind of support.[64] In the light of Musser, Burch's account of generic and stylistic changes – the 'externality' of the PMR – tries to explain the move to continuity editing – 'linearisation' of the IMR – as a way of detaching, unhooking filmic representation and the viewing situation from any form of material presence, such as it might exist when editorial control is located outside the text, in the viewing situation (whose coherence is not dependent on an internalised narrational instance or self-generated form of closure). With the IMR, the spectator-screen relationship is radically transformed, de-materialised and de-contextualised, made abstract to the point where the burden of making it 'real' and 'physical' shifts to the film-text: a task for which, as we shall see, Griffithian narrative construction was eminently suited.

Presentation, Representation, Narration

Thus, although this section of the Reader highlights the importance of taking into account extra-textual features, notably the cultural, legal and demographic factors alongside the more narrowly economic ones in explaining the rate and direction of change, or the diffusion and mass-impact of the cinema between 1900 and 1917, it has not been without implications for the study of narrative, and the shift towards 'interiorisation'. For the very pressure towards longer narratives coming from the exhibition sector meant that the struggle for control once more shifted away from the mode of presentation to the mode of representation, though defined by the new commodity-form embodied in the multi-reel film, which required self-sufficient fictional narratives.

While in the previous section, scholars like Gaudreault and Gunning came to the conclusion that in formal terms, the distinction between the early cinema and the classical cinema has to be sought in the difference between monstration and narration, by positing different conceptions of how a cinematic presentation constructs the relation between screen and spectator, the present section concludes with Musser reminding us of the importance of the exact conditions of exhibition. He thus underscores and reformulates in terms of the cinematic institution and its history the approach which Gaudreault and Gunning have taken in respect of narration: Musser, too, sees the distinction between the PMR and the IMR as ultimately one that revolves around 'presentation' and control over the rapport between screen space and spectator space, regulated by different forms of closure, the interiorisation of the narrating instance, the pressures towards narratives purged of contextual foreknowledge or shared cultural, ethnic or regional assumptions.[65] As Musser shows, the importance of Porter and of his innovations in the articulation of temporal as well as spatial relations must be seen in this context.

In the following section, this isolation of the spectator and his/her placement within the film will be further investigated, notably through the example of Griffith, but in the context of a more general theory of cinematic space and its significance for the emergence of a more complex conception of narrative, in which the presentational aspects of early cinema gradually disappear, in order to develop into a wholly context-free, imaginary relation between the spectator and the screen. The classical text will emerge as one with multiple uses, as opposed to the early text, context bound and local, saturated and therefore also fixed by particularities.

Longer narratives, multi-reel films and status advantage thus produce not only respectability, continuity editing and narrative integration, but an institution dedicated to processing a large number of paying spectators through the product outlets in the minimum time and with maximum efficiency. The classical text becomes one that can most effectively convey meaning and pleasure, in different locations at different times, to audiences of very different cultural and educational background. It is an accumulation of values generated at the point of consumption and at the moment of commodification, rather than innate textual ones determined at the point of production. This capacity destines narrative film to become the successful prototype of virtually all popular culture this century.

Thomas Elsaesser

Notes

1. A more linguistic way of expressing the shift would be to say that a syntactic (syntagmatic) logic of implication and hierarchy supersedes the paratactic succession of views.
2. Noël Burch prefers to call it the 'diegetic effect' (see, for instance, 'Narrative Diegesis – Thresholds, Limits', *Screen* vol. 23, no. 2, July/August 1982, p. 18). André Gaudreault's neologism of monstration, part of and yet different from narration, also acknowledges the difficulties of simply talking about 'narrative'. See 'Showing and Telling', below, pp. 274–81 and also, 'Narration et monstration au cinéma' *Hors-Cadre*, no. 2, April 1984, pp. 87–98.
3. It is one of the virtues of Yuri Tsivian's article on the 'Kuleshov Experiment' (see below, pp. 247–55) that it links signification and narrative (more particularly, montage and the diegetic effect) to a context fashioned by cultural norms and historically specific exhibition practices.
4. Both Edison and the Lumières are on record for considering the cinema as 'an invention without a future'.
5. This scientific view of the cinema could mark the point of departure for another history of the cinema, to do with surveillance, with the technologies of penetration and visibility. See Paul Virilio, *Guerre et cinéma: logistique de la perception* (Paris: Editions de l'Etoile, 1984).
6. Kristin Thompson locates the break around 1908: 'We may usefully consider the primitive cinema to have been dominant up to about 1908. ... The period from

approximately 1909 to 1916 involved a transition between the two approaches. During those years, devices and functions from the primitive period continued to exist alongside newer classical strategies, often within the same film.' Kristin Thompson, 'Narration in three Early-Teen Vitagraph films', in Paolo Cherchi Usai (ed.), *Vitagraph Co. of America: il cinema prima di Hollywood* (Pordenone: Edizioni Biblioteca dell'Immagine, 1987), quoted from the author's manuscript, p. 1.

7. For a consideration of the ideology of invention, see Michael Chanan, *The Dream that Kicks* (London: Routledge and Kegan Paul, 1980), esp. chs. 3–8.
8. A good illustration of Chanan's general argument, stressing the pre-industrial production context as a decisive feature, can be found in Alan Williams, 'The Lumière Organization and "documentary Realism"', in John Fell, ed., film before Griffith (Berkeley: University of California Press), pp. 153–61.
9. In Alan Williams' account of the Lumière organisation, the fact that it was not rigidly divided between production and exhibition was its initial strength in the field of reportage and actuality, but it characterises their family business as artisanal and preindustrial. See Williams, 'The Lumière Organisation', p. 161.
10. See Robert C. Allen, 'Vitascope/Cinématographe: Initial Patterns of American Film Industrial Practice', *Journal of the University Film Association*, vol. 31, no. 2 (Spring 1979), pp. 13–18 (reprinted in Fell, *Film before Griffith*, pp. 144–52). Allen's case study also interestingly compares with Williams' argument about the Lumière organisation. Allen argues that vitascope (a licensee of Edison) and the Lumière Company pursued two quite distinct forms of exhibition, at least in the period examined (the year 1986-7), because of the technical apparatus at their disposal and their approach to production. While Vitascope developed along the lines of the Kinetoscope and built a projector to be serviced by a showman/magician, the lightweight Lumière Cinematographe was ideally suited for being incorporated into the vaudeville performance, since it could be delivered and hired out to the theatres as a package: projector, operator, film. Thus, as long as film found its most profitable home on the vaudeville circuit, the Lumière apparatus was the most progressive. It emerged as the loser as soon as film exchanges and a distribution system developed to service fixed site cinemas.
11. See Michael Chanan, quoting Peter Bächlin's *Der Film als Ware*, in Roy Armes (ed.), *Problems of Film History* (London: BFI/Middlesex Polytechnic, 1981), pp. 35–6.
12. For a detailed discussion of the notion of interchangeable parts, of Taylorization in film production, the how-to approach to the screenplay, the type of collective work it represents, and the emergence of a production line system, see Janet Staiger's chapters in David Bordwell, Janet Staiger, Kristin Thompson, *The Classical Hollywood Cinema: Film Style and Mode of Production to 1960* (London: Routledge and Kegan Paul, 1985). See also Janet Staiger, 'Mass-produced Photoplays: Economic and Signifying Practice in the First Years of Hollywood', *Wide Angle* vol. 4, no. 3, Fall 1980, pp. 12–27 and Jeanne Thomas Allen, 'The Industrial Context of Film Technology: Standardization and Patents' in S. Heath and T. de Lauretis (eds.), *The Cinematic Apparatus* (London: Macmillan, 1980), pp. 26–36.
13. It is interesting to note that standardisation and the factory system 'developed in the United States within the fire-arms industry and as a response to the demands of government contracts of armaments'. Jeanne Thomas Allen, 'The Industrial Context of Film Technology: Standardization and Patents', p. 29.
14. Jeanne Thomas Allen discusses the 'necessity of interchangeable parts to service a mass market' and mentions the case of 'John Murdock, who sought to enter the film market from vaudeville through a series of innovations which were neither interchangeable with existing products nor mass produced widely enough to gain hegemony.' (Ibid., p. 31). She also cites Paul Strassmann, *Risk and Technological Innovation: American Manufacturing Methods During the Nineteenth Century* (Ithaca: Cornell UP, 1959), pp. 7–19, who draws attention to 'the promise of invention as a means of lowering the cost of production, thereby affording a competitive edge, and the cost of accommodating the industrial process to a change in machinery'.
15. Jeanne Thomas Allen comments on 'the ability of patented inventions to provide a patent monopoly serving both as a barrier of entry to competitors and a means of collecting income through royalties' (ibid., p. 33).

16. Jeanne Thomas Allen, p. 33.
17. 'Edison's Sales Policy and the Continuous Action Film, 1904–1906' in John L. Fell (ed.), *Film before Griffith* (Berkeley: California University Press, 1983), pp. 207–22.
18. See André Gaudreault, 'The Infringement of Copyright', above, pp. 114–22.
19. André Gaudreault, pp. 114–22 above. For this reason, Méliès founded an American company, Star Film, and sent his brother to the United States to look after his interests. See Patrick McInroy, 'The American Méliès', *Sight and Sound*, Autumn 1979, pp. 250–54.
20. See Levy, 'Edison's Sales Policy', Gaudreault, 'Infringement of Copyright', and Gunning, 'The Cinema of Attractions' (pp. 56–62 above). Levy and Gaudreault in particular do not simply detail instances of copyright violation or film piracy. Quite generally, legal files and court records of infringements allow one to study the arguments by which a certain practice was legitimised. Levy shows how a particular constraint coming from the definition of copyright can have major implications, on the one hand, for distribution and exhibition practice, and onnn07 the other, for film form and the development of longer narratives. Gaudreault, in a similar vein, argues that the judgment in the court case between Lubin and Edison over the copyright of a documentary gives us a clear insight into whether the law regarded a film as a coherent whole, irrespective of how many frames or shots it contained, or whether it endorsed the view that each frame or shot constituted a separate entity. Levy and Gaudreault both aim at reconstructing a certain discursive reality which materially affected films as legal objects and economic entities, but also as texts.
21. See Janet Staiger, 'Mass-produced Photoplays'.
22. Jeanne Thomas Allen quotes C. Francis Jenkins, who patented the first American projector (the Phantascope) with Thomas Armat: 'the process which will succeed is that which fits standard machines without change' and comments 'an observation which the Motion Picture Patents Company took to heart in making the patents of each member available to all'. ('The Industrial Context of Film Technology', p. 31).
23. The decline and demise of the Trust is usually attributed to the buccaneering spirit of the Independents, who broke with the Trust in order to be able to make more innovative films (apart from moving West and escape law-enforcement officers hunting them down for copyright infringement and pirating). But as Jeanne Allen and Janet Staiger have shown (see also Robert Sklar, *Movie-Made America* (New York: Random House, 1975, pp. 37–42), this is itself part of the mythology and lore of Hollywood.
24. Jeanne Thomas Allen has pointed out that the decline of the MPPC, for instance, may to some extent have been due to members enforcing economic priorities too rigidly, and she cites Robert Allen about the temporary unpopularity of film in vaudeville (the so-called Chaser theory) as having to do with producers trying to 'minimise product differentiation (hence audience response) and maximise product supply through studio-controlled production'. 'The Industrial Context of Film Technology: Standardisation and Patents', p. 32.
25. For the early period, it is the Pathé company in France that pioneered the practice of an industrialised basis for film-making, the model so successfully adopted by American firms. Although work has been done on Edison, Biograph, Vitagraph in the United States, and on Svenska Biografteatren in Sweden, production company history is perhaps the area most in need of more detailed historical scholarship.
26. But see Robert Sklar, *Movie-Made America*, for discussing differences in management style and objectives among the major studios.
27. Janet Staiger, 'The Hollywood Mode of Production: Conditions of Existence', *The Classical Hollywood Cinema*, p. 89.
28. Staiger, for example, has proposed a periodisation for different historical stages, based on the type of management structure prevalent at the time. For the period between 1907 to 1909 she identifies what she calls the 'director' system; from 1909 to 1914 the 'director unit system' and beginning around 1914 the 'central producer' system which remained in place roughly until the coming of sound (*Classical Hollywood Cinema*, pp. 93–6).
29. Janet Staiger sees the star system in the cinema as a direct carry-over from vaudeville and theatre, but agrees that from around 1912 onwards, the star system became one of

the most important 'means to differentiate product to achieve monopoly profits'. ('Standardization and Differentiation', *Classical Hollywood Cinema*, p. 101). For more detailed historical and theoretical account of the early star system, see Richard de Cordova, 'The Emergence of the Star System in America', *Wide Angle* vol. 6, no. 4, 1984, pp. 4–13, and Charles Musser, 'The Changing Status of the Film Actor' in Leyda and Musser (eds.), *Before Hollywood* (New York: American Federation of Arts, 1987), pp. 57–62.

30. Janet Staiger makes the point that production company catalogues from as early as 1903 'exhibit many of the exchange-values the industry has consistently promoted as the qualities in their films: novelty, specific popular genres, brand names, "realism", authenticity, spectacle, stars and certain creators of the products whose skills as artists were considered acknowledged' ('Standardization and Differentiation', p. 99).
31. See Anthony Slide, *The Big V: A History of the Vitagraph Company* (Metuchen, NJ: Scarecrow Press, 1987) and Paolo Cherchi Usai (ed.), *Vitagraph Co of America: il cinema prima di Hollywood* (Pordenone: Edizioni Biblioteca dell'Immagine, 1987).
32. See Charles Musser's 'Vitagraph 1894–1902', Jon Gartenberg's 'Vitagraph before Griffith', Salt's 'Vitagraph Films – A Touch of Class' (for details, see Bibliography).
33. In Britain, the 'Putting Narrative in Place: 1906–1916' Conference at Derby in 1982 also looked at the production policy of Vitagraph, with unpublished papers by Noël Burch and Ben Brewster, and the Vitagraph retrospective in 1988 at Pordenone have greatly contributed to knowledge about the company.
34. Barry Salt, 'Fresh Eyes', *BFI News*, 24 July 1976, p. 4.
35. James Agee: '... the searing redolence of peanuts and demirep perfumery, tobacco and feet, and sweat; the laughter of unrespectable people having a hell of a fine time' (quoted by Russell Merritt, along with passages from Ramsaye, Wagenknecht, Jacobs in 'Nickelodeon Theatres 1905–1914: Building an Audience for the Movies', in T. Balio (ed.), *The American Film Industry*, p. 59.
36. See Allen, 'Vitascope/Cinematographe', pp. 146–8.
37. See Robert C. Allen, *Vaudeville and film 1895–1915: A study in media interaction* (New York: Arno Press, 1980).
38. See Bordwell, Staiger, Thompson, *Classical Hollywood Cinema*, chs. 3–5.
39. According to Thompson, the chief influence on the classical mode is neither the theatre nor, as is often claimed, the C19th European novel, but the more recent, American practice of the short story. The shift away from vaudeville type material, however, has to be seen as the consequence of pressures from the production sector which required more industrial and systematic production processes (and thereby drawing on freelance writers to supply story material) in order to respond to the exponential expansion of the market and its demand for ever more footage. More footage meant longer narratives, longer narratives required more psychologically conceived protagonists, which in turn meant a more complex organisation of time and space and thus more elaborate editing techniques. See Bordwell, Staiger, Thompson, *Classical Hollywood Cinema*, pp. 163–73.
40. Merritt, 'Building an Audience'.
41. See Douglas Gomery, 'Movie Audiences, Urban Geography, and the History of the American Film', *The Velvet Light Trap* no. 19, 1982, pp. 23–9; 'The Growth of Movie Monopolies: the Case of Balaban and Katz', *Wide Angle*, vol. 3, no. 1, 1979, pp. 54–63; 'The Picture Palace: Economic Sense or Hollywood Nonsense?', *Quarterly Review of Film Studies*, vol. 3, no. 1, Winter 1978, pp. 23–36.
42. Merritt, 'Building an Audience', p. 72.
43. The whole question of the theatrical influence can be reopened around this economic development. Not only did film-makers adapt well-known plays for the screen in order to cater to already established expectations, but many of what we now think of as the great C19th novels, circulated as stage (and staged) dramatisations. For an extensive examination of this, in relation to both Griffith and classical narrative, see Rick Altman, 'Griffith, Dickens and Film Theory Today', *The South Atlantic Quarterly*, vol. 88/2, Spring 1989, 321–59.
44. See especially the articles by Gomery, fn. 41.
45. Merritt, 'Building an Audience', p. 73. The strong ties of the movie industry to a consumer culture have been a feature since the very beginnings of the Nickelodeon era.

46. See Miriam Hansen, below pp. 228–46 (first published as 'Early Silent Cinema: Whose Public Sphere?', *New German Critique* no. 29, Spring/Summer 1983, pp. 147–84) and Judith Mayne, 'Immigrants and Spectators', *Wide Angle* vol. 5, no. 2, 1982, pp. 32–41.
47. While Hansen argues for the existence of a female public sphere by reference to a male hysterical discourse about the cinema as institution, which she contrasts with Emilie Altenloh's 1914 empirical enquiry into women's preferences, Heide Schlüpmann has used Tom Gunning's 'cinema of attractions' to argue that particular genres of early cinema (in Germany the social film and melodramas) inscribe forms of exhibitionism and collusion with the spectator into the representation which would appear to make sense only if one thinks of the audience as female. See Heide Schlüpmann, *Frühes Kino zwischen Emanzipation und Reform* (Frankfurt am Main: Roter Stern, 1990).
48. Questions of class and spectatorship have also featured in the debate in Britain. At a conference held at Dartington in 1980, Michael Chanan argued for greater attention to the class-nature not so much of spectators but of the modes of production (artisanal or industrial, individual or collective). He also drew attention to the function of early newsreel and the quest for the exotic as an ideological category. By bringing the periphery to the centre in the form of spectacle and consumption, actualities in the Lumière tradition can be seen perhaps less as part of a bourgeois notion of property ('showing off *their* wives, *their* children ...' as Noël Burch had put it in 'Porter or Ambivalence') but as an early indication of media-imperialism: possessing the world in the act of making it visible (what Burch himself had called 'celluloid tourism'). See Paul Kerr, 'Re-inventing the Cinema', *Screen* vol. 21, no. 4, 1980/81, pp. 80–84.
49. See John Ellis, 'Art, Culture and Quality', *Screen* vol. 19, no. 3, Autumn 1978, p. 34.
50. Charles Musser, 'A History of Screen Practice', *Quarterly Review of Film Studies*, vol. 9, no. 1, Winter 1984, pp. 59–69.
51. Charles Musser, 'American Vitagraph 1897–1901', in John L. Fell (ed.), *Film Before Griffith* (Berkeley: University of California Press, 1983), pp. 22–66.
52. Musser, 'American Vitagraph 1897–1901', p. 69. Among other things, Musser argues that the struggle for control within the emergent film industry did not limit itself to the recording and reproduction apparatus, nor to the right to exploit spectacle attractions, but developed along lines, where technologically-based invention, innovation, diffusion as conceived by Douglas Gomery has to be analysed in a wider context. See Douglas Gomery, 'The Coming of the Talkies: Invention, Innovation and Diffusion', in Tino Balio (ed.), *The American Film Industry* (Madison: Wisconsin University Press, 1976), pp. 193–211.
53. See below, pp. 256–73 (originally published in *Framework*, no. 22/23, pp. 4–11).
54. See Robert C. Allen, 'Vitascope/Cinematographe' and the differences between the exhibition practice of the Lumières (renting out projector, projectionist and films as a package) and Edison's (sale and installation of fixed projectors).
55. Musser, 'The Nickelodeon Era Begins', below, p. 256.
56. Ibid.
57. In this context, the question arises, whether the cinema provides a product or a set of services. What needs to be shown, perhaps, is why the cinema business is not like, say, the motor industry. The cinema deals with 'pleasure' in a much more overt way than in the case of the motor-car (which still has a use-value). However, as commodity production in general has moved further and further away from use-values into the area of pleasure-and-status values, the difference of the cinema may seem less clear. Many consumer goods, in the way they promote self-images, life-styles and attitudes, are involved in a 'mode of representation'.
58. Musser, 'The Nickelodeon Era Begins', p. 257.
59. Unpublished transcripts from the 'Putting Narrative in Place' Conference at Derby in December 1982.
60. 'The Nickelodeon Era Begins', p. 256. Other instances of editorial control are discussed in Charles Musser, 'The Eden Musee: Exhibitor as Creator', *Film and History* vol. 11, no. 4, December 1981, pp. 73–83.
61. See Kevin Brownlow, 'Silent Cinema – What Was the Right Speed?', below, pp. 282–90.
62. Post-classical cinema once again shows how textual control is shifting: to the ties-ins

and spin-offs, the peripheral rights and merchandising which define the block-buster film.

63. See Tom Gunning, 'Weaving a Narrative', below, pp. 336–47.
64. In 'A Primitive Mode of Representation?' Burch restates his belief that the early cinema had its own stable system of representation, and was at the same time the outcome of contradictory forces. Acknowledging that the uneven development of the American and the European cinema further complicates both the period-break and the ideological-epistemological interpretation given, he also distances himself from seeing the PMR as modernist, or as the avant garde's lost paradise, underscoring but also modifying his assertion about an alternative practice which has itself a tradition and a history, as he had in some sense claimed (see Noël Burch, Jorge Dana, 'Propositions', *Afterimage* no. 5, Spring 1974, pp. 40–60).
65. Burch notes that the passion play genre poses a further issue, fundamental to early cinema, as distinct from classical: spectatorial foreknowledge is the most important extra-textual element of continuity within non-continuous film forms. This applies *a fortiori* to a whole class of early genres other than the passions, such as the filmed novel and theatre play, or scenes from American history. Griffith's *Enoch Arden*, *Edgar Allen Poe*, and others can usefully be compared with films like Porter's *Uncle Tom's Cabin* or *The McKinley Assassination*, for all of which foreknowledge is indeed crucial to an understanding of the story. It also distinguishes, as we shall see, the Nickelodeon multi-reeler from the 'genuine' multi-reel feature film, for the advance of, say *Birth of a Nation* over *Quo Vadis* or *Uncle Tom's Cabin* lies not least in the greater autonomy that the diegesis has vis à vis the referential foreknowledge of the source material. See Noël Burch, 'Passion, pursuite', *Communications* no. 38, 1983, pp. 30–50.

Economic Conditions of Early Cinema

MICHAEL CHANAN

At the very beginning, films were treated as straightforward commodities to be sold on the open market like pieces of cloth, at a uniform price of so much per foot. Indeed different kinds of film were all treated in the same way – no distinction was made between lengths of different quality, or between the different types of subject matter. The price of new films was determined primarily by the cost of raw film stock. This condition is registered in the fact that at this stage film production was simply called manufacture; and that the price of films fell during the first couple of years following the famous first film shows in late 1895, early 1896, as the supply of ready-coated celluloid film increased.

Yet film is not an ordinary commodity. It has a number of peculiarities. Since it took time for the film business to discover what these consisted in, so the history of the early economic development of cinema is in large part the history of this process of discovery.

Consider first the unexpected fact that Edison neglected to patent his original peep-show machine, the Kinetoscope, outside the United States. Was this an oversight? Or was it that he didn't believe it worth the expense for something he doubted would be more than a short-term money spinner (a common enough view at the time)? Some writers have suggested it was probably the latter, since he wasn't normally careless about patents. After all, as early as 1881, the British *Electrical Review* described him as 'the young man who keeps the road to the Patent Office hot with his footsteps', and explained:

> His plan appears to be to patent all the ideas that occur to him, whether tried or untried, and to trust to future labours to select and combine those which prove themselves the fittest. The result is that the great bulk of his patents are valueless in point of practicability; but they serve to fence the ground in from other competitors.[1]

All historical evidence supports this type of reading of Edison's business sense. We cannot go on thinking of him as a naïve 'eureka' type of inventor. In fact he was one of the first to organise a proper research laboratory, to treat invention as a business like any other, to deal in patents systematically as pieces of property which can be bought and sold, which can yield royalties, can be offered up as securities against investments, and so forth. All this has been obscured, however, by popular historical accounts which hardly deserve to be called historical at all, because they pander to ideological notions of genius and inspiration.

Edison's contemporaries did not always suffer from such illusions, even though he had successfully manufactured for himself a popular reputation as 'the wizard of Menlo Park' (the site of his 'invention factory'). As the English trade journal *Photographic Work* said in 1894:

> The exhibition of Mr Edison's Kinetoscope in London is disappointing, as when it is announced that Mr Edison has 'invented' something, we at least expect that he will carry refinement, completeness and perfection of construction a long way beyond what has previously been done. Mr Edison should, perhaps, rather rank as a careful and laborious constructor than as an inventor – that is to say, if a man may be called a constructor of articles which are made by others under his control.[2]

One explanation of why Edison took out no patent on the Kinetoscope outside the United States is provided by the English film pioneer Birt Acres, who said in a letter to the *British Journal of Photography* in 1896:

> I believe that no patents were taken out on the Edison machine [in Britain], the Company relying on the difficulty of the successful making of films, and, as machines were of no use without films, they made it a stipulation with the sale of films that they were only to be used with their own machines.[3]

If this was indeed Edison's policy, what we know is that it didn't work, and not only because of lack of patents protection abroad. At the same time, it is in the nature of things that such inventions are rarely unique. Again we must depart from conventional popular history, which is forever remarking on the strange coincidences of discovery and invention. The fact is, an invention is brought about by a particular conjunction of technological opportunity with the exploitation of economic conditions. If such conditions exist, then it would be surprising if the same invention, more or less, were *not* achieved simultaneously and independently by different people; hence the claims of rival inventors, like William Friese-Greene in England and the Lumières in France. This too is one of the reasons for Edison's failure to control the market which he played a part in opening up, in spite of the extensive experience he and his associates had acquired in patents litigation in connection with other inventions.

Technological opportunity is the consequence of the historical stage of development which has been reached by the material forces of production. In the case of cinematography, the main factors were the improvement of photographic emulsions; the development of precision engineering and instruments, and their application to the problem of the intermittent drive mechanism; the development of the chemicals industry involved in the quite unconnected invention of celluloid – the first of the plastics – and the improvement of its production techniques to the point where it became available as a thin film, durable, flexible and transparent enough to provide the base for the film strip.

Economic conditions then provide the mechanisms whereby any particular invention may be financed, developed and tested, and finally marketed. Here the legal superstructure, which defines property rights in certain forms of knowledge through the patents laws, comes into play. The story is well known whereby the London precision instrument maker R. W. Paul was asked to copy an Edison Kinetoscope and at first refused because he assumed it would be subject to patent; and how he then undertook to manufacture his own version when he discovered that it wasn't. These machines he sold to travelling showmen, and in his own words, 'in conjunction with business friends installed fifteen at the Exhibition at Earls Court, London, showing some of the first of our British films, including the Boat Race and Derby of 1895.'[4]

But this is already to skip over certain intermediate stages. Paul was able to copy the Kinetoscope easily enough, and at first he and his associates relied on the supply of Edison's own films. When Edison heard what was going on he of course tried to cut off the supply. This made it necessary for Paul to devise a camera to make films of his own in order for the enterprise to succeed. Moreover, Paul was soon struck with the commercial limitations of the coin-in-the-slot peep-show machine, and resolved to devise a method of projection. His project for a camera was also necessary to expand the supply of films for this further enterprise.

Should Paul perhaps be counted as one of the inventors of cinema? As a precision instrument maker he was well equipped for the tasks he set himself, and his achievement in producing both a camera and a projector cannot be discounted (apart from the question of the role played by Birt Acres as his collaborator). Moreover the intermittent drive mechanism he developed was an improvement on Edison's. He employed an established technique with which he was well familiar, the Maltese Cross, and the application of this device was enough at the time to ensure the grant of his own patent. Nevertheless, the question of whether he should be called an inventor is in some respects misconceived, and there is no unequivocal answer. From the time of the industrial revolution to the era of corporate capitalism and the systematic application of large funds to research and development, historically successful inventors tended to be master craftsmen with an ability to combine their technological skills with a capacity to play the economic game. What produced success in those conditions was the astuteness to turn an invention – one's own or somebody else's – into the means of achieving a technological rent. A technological rent is an advantage gained from the monopolistic exploitation of a particular process or technique. What counts here as a monopolistic practice? In *The Beginnings of the Cinema in England*, John Barnes remarks that information about Paul's first camera is hard to come by, but that this is not surprising:

> Cameras generally are the least documented of early cinematograph equipment, since it was usually the practice of the first film-makers to supply films exclusively for use in projectors of their own make. The camera was thus regarded as the fountainhead of their success and its details were kept secret.[5]

An important clue about these conditions was the absence of standardisation during the first few years in the perforation of raw film stock. It was a while before major suppliers like Eastman emerged, who produced film stock ready perforated. The reason for this delay was the nature of early competition in the manufacture of both celluloid and film equipment. Until the process of continuous casting on rotating drums was introduced in 1899, no single manufacture could achieve a monopolistic position, either by capturing a sufficiently large section of the market, or in terms of sufficiently consistent quality. The evidence is unclear as to whether priority for continuous casting belongs to Eastman or the Celluloid Manufacturing Company, but in any case the method gave much greater lengths and a uniform thickness, it eliminated the static electricity markings which sometimes resulted from casting on a flat surface, and it was operable twenty-four hours a day.

Until then, the structure of the market allowed for competition in the supply of celluloid by small-scale producers who lacked as yet the expertise to supply a fully finished product – raw film stock, coated and perforated and ready to go straight into the camera or the printer. Indeed, because of the unreliability of the supply, the earliest film-makers not only equipped themselves to make their own perforations, but often bought their celluloid in sheets and cut and coated it themselves as well. The reason why early conditions produced this effect was not only insufficient supply but also the competition which existed between producers of cameras and projectors, who were still mostly small entrepreneurs. As long as this form of competition existed, each producer of these instruments was jealous of his own techniques, and standardisation was delayed. One of the contributory factors to this situation, at least in Britain, was the state of the patent laws. It was not until 1907 that as a result of increasing technological competition in a wide range of fields, not to mention the ensuing wrangles, a new Patents Act instigated an official search for novelty on the part of the Patents Office before a patent could be granted. Many of the early patents in respect of moving pictures would very likely not have been granted if this provision had been in operation earlier.

These early conditions should also be understood in terms of the absence as yet of the compartmentalisation of the business into the various specialised sectors which later came to characterise the structure of the film industry. Such specialisation took time to develop, like the division of labour among the film crew in film production itself. Of the firms which took the leadership in the first few years, many of them made films as well as manufacturing equipment, but the former were secondary to the latter. That is to say, they did not make equipment in order to be able to sell films, they made and sold films in order to promote their primary business of making equipment. Thus it would happen that in order to gain an edge over competitors, the maker of a projector would incorporate an idiosyncratic design, for example in the perforations, corresponding to their own camera, requiring purchasers of the projector to purchase films from the same source. The object of this strategy was not to capture the market in films, but to support the market for what we would nowadays call the 'hardware'.

This explains the pattern taken by such businesses as Paul's: a primary undertaking in the manufacture first of kinetoscopes and then of projectors, and a secondary one in the production and sale of films. Such a pattern was far from unique. Elsewhere too, several companies which dominated the film business right up to the First World War began by manufacturing equipment. These included Pathé and Gaumont in France, Edison, Biograph and Vitagraph in the United States, and Messter in Germany. Their situation may be likened to leading companies in radio broadcasting in the United States in the early 20s, before the establishment of the commercial broadcasting system. The radio stations were initially set up by equipment manufacturers for the simple reason that without the transmission of programmes, the public radio enterprise was pointless. There are significant differences, of course, between radio and films, but the comparison helps us understand the peculiarity of film as a commodity. In both cases, there is a crucial distinction between hardware and software. Hardware indicates the means of production, diffusion and reception in radio, production and exhibition in cinema. Software refers in both cases to the programming, the content which is broadcast and received, or exhibited.

It has frequently escaped attention that in the case of broadcasting, the programmes themselves are not commodities in the strict sense of the term. A commodity is something which constitutes both a use-value and an exchange-value. The use-value *carries* the exchange-value, and there can be no exchange-value unless purchasers expect to find a use-value in their purchase. But there *can* be use-value without exchange-value – in which case the object is not a commodity. Therefore broadcast programmes are not commodities from the point of view of the human receiver, who does not have to pay for them (except for special cases like pay-TV). All that is needed is to buy a set and turn it on. This was perfectly clear to the early manufacturers of radio equipment, who regarded the provision of programmes as a necessary expense in the establishment of the market in which the sets were the principal commodities – until it became evident that there were different ways of providing programmes other than at their direct expense.

By way of further comparison, notice that the products in another new medium, the gramophone, which is similarly divided into hardware and software, are none the less proper commodities; though if a record contains a piece of music which is in the public domain, it is the record but not the music which is the commodity – or rather, to be accurate, the recorded performance. But just as records turn something into a commodity which previously had no permanent material form, in broadcasting there is also a commodity of a new order, one might say a non-material commodity, which nevertheless can be sold for the purpose of financing the enterprise: air-space. (Of course there are other ways to finance broadcasting, such as licence fees or simple government subvention.) Air-space takes the form of time for commercials or programmes for sponsorship. It is nowadays measured in terms of the size and profile of the audience attested by means of market research. Indeed this form of market research was a technique directly stimulated by radio, for such information was never needed before.

Turning back to cinema, it emerges that while the film is indeed an object of exchange-value, which produces a direct income from the consumer, at the same time it has other peculiarities. According to Marx, 'the use-values of commodities *become* use-values by a mutual exchange of places: they pass from the hands of those for whom they were means of exchange into the hands of those for whom they serve as consumer goods.'[6] The peculiarity of film is that this physical exchange need not take place. Those for whom the film serves as an exchange-value need never *let go* of it in order for that exchange-value to be realised. The film as a material object does not pass into the hands of the consumer. What the viewer receives and takes away is, in Stanley Cavell's felicitous phrase, 'a projection as light as light'.[7] What the exhibitor sells is the right of admission to view the film, in the same way as the performing arts: through the box office.

This is what accounts for the whole structure of ownership and control in the film industry. If there is no need for the film as commodity to pass physically into the hands of the consumer, it turns out there is also no reason why its ownership should pass into the hands of the exhibitor – where the exhibitor and the distributor are not the same entity – when a contractual agreement will do instead, which gives the exhibitor the right of exhibition without the rights of ownership, just as the exhibitor sells the viewer the right to consume the film without physical possession. What early cinema history reveals is that the domination of the distributor over both exhibition and production began when they hit on the device of exclusive film rental, by which they became the principal bankers for production money. This process began to occur around 1906 and was effectively complete by the time of the First World War. The remainder of this chapter will examine the changing circumstances of production, distribution and exhibition which led up to this development.

Although films were initially sold on the open market, a brisk second-hand trade developed quickly. It was initiated by enterprising showmen wanting to shift their accumulating stock of films. The pioneers of this development in Britain seem to have been J. D. Walker and E. G. Turner, whose company was called Walturdaw. They were already exploiting the Edison Kinetoscope (as well as the same inventor's phonograph) early in 1896, and in July they bought a film projector, the first to be manufactured by one of Paul's early rivals, Wrench. They toured the country under the name of the North American Entertainment Company, at first using Edison films and films by the Lumières. By the end of 1897 they had three machines in operation and a mounting stock of films. Turner himself later explained what happened then:

> The price of films quickly dropped from 1s to 8d per foot, and then became standard at 6d per foot; this allowed us to increase our store, but it soon became evident that to have to provide new films every time we took a repeat engagement was too expensive. So we conceived the idea, first of all, of an interchange with other exhibitors, who experienced the same difficulty in regard to new supplies. From this we eventually

> evolved the renting of films to other people, because we found that we had by far a larger stock than any of the other men. By buying films regularly we could use them ourselves and hire them to other people, and so from such small beginnings was evolved the great renting system as we know it today . . . We would buy as many as ten or twelve prints of an interesting subject, and on one occasion we actually bought eight prints of a film, which was entitled *Landing an Old Lady from a Small Boat* . . . We then extended operations to the entertainment bureaus . . . [8]

What was discovered here? In the first place, that while audiences demanded novelty, the film was not used up in a single act of consumption; celluloid was relatively durable, and the film continued to be available for further exploitation. However, since there are various types of relatively durable commodity (from clothes to washing machines), this in itself does not account for the peculiarity of film. The peculiarity discovered by the likes of Walker and Turner was the consequent rentability of the product. In other words, where goods usually pass from the producer or manufacturer to the wholesaler, from the wholesaler to the retailer, and thence to the consumer, the terms 'producer', 'distributor', 'exhibitor' and 'audience' which we now apply to the film industry do not signify quite the same set of relations, and this difference already existed embryonically even before the rationalisation of the film industry into its present structure. When this is related to the relative material durability of the film, its peculiar character as a commodity begins to emerge more clearly, and the evolution and structure of the industry can be better understood. It is like a performing art in some regards but not in others – a synthetic performing art. It comes to depend mainly on narrative forms and personalities, but by reproducing their image it extends and intensifies their exploitation beyond the reach of the stage. The means by which its prices are fixed, and the manner in which market domination is achieved, is therefore different. It is also different from ordinary commodities, including other cultural commodities like the gramophone record and the book, whose sale removes them from the market. Each copy of a film *remains within the market* until it has deteriorated physically from so many showings that it is no longer viewable.

If exhibition was at first the business of itinerant showmen, then as Peter Bachlin pointed out in his pioneering (and still almost unique) economic study of cinema, that was effectively the only way it could be. 'The exhibitors were able, thanks to their continual change of location, to present their programmes until the films were totally used up, and in this way to amortise the cost price through numerous showings.'[9] As he also points out, the itinerant shows were usually family businesses. One of the outstanding examples in Britain was Walter Haggar, who illustrates both the link between early film and the tradition of itinerant popular theatre, and also the rapidly evolving dependency of the film-maker upon the dealer.

Haggar was drawn into film in the summer of 1897.[10] He was playing a highly successful theatrical season in Aberafon to the hundreds of migrant workers who formed the labour force building the new docks at Margam. He already had a photographic side-show, and now he bought a film projector out of the profits. The following year he handed the theatre over to his son and went on tour as a film showman. He opened at the Aberafon fair on 5 April 1899, and collected £15 in twopences and threepences. The following week at Pontypridd he took nothing at all, owing to a combination of rain and a strike. Such were the tribulations of the itinerant.

There were also tribulations for the dealers they obtained their films from A. C. Bromhead said of the fairground showmen that:

> a certain directness characterised their methods, but they were full of good hard common sense and were shrewd hands at a bargain. Sometimes it was difficult to collect accounts from them. A representative meeting a showman who was behind with his account was immediately invited to 'come and collect it yourself'. That representative spent a couple of days on the roundabouts collecting the amount due, in twopences. It was not at all unusual to wait all day until the money for the film just sold had been collected and to stay put in the pay box or round the show while it was coming in.[11]

Haggar soon encountered competition. Faced with the example of a competitor called Wadbrooks who scored a huge success in 1901 with a film of their own of a Wales-England football international at Cardiff, he decided to improve his position by making films as well, and naturally turned to the theatre troupe in order to do so. One of his first productions, *The Maid of Cefn Ydfa*, made in 1902, proved particularly successful. He took £40 at the ticket office in the course of its first presentation alone. What makes him an aesthetically interesting figure is the speed with which he realised that plays and films were different, and not just because the latter were mute. His *Life of Charles Peace*, the story of a notorious criminal of the day in eleven scenes and running just under ten minutes, is already conceived for the camera, not the stage, and uses exterior locations.

An itinerant like Haggar could shoot his own films, but had no facilities for developing and printing them. Haggar made an agreement with the Gaumont company in London. They bore the costs of developing and printing the film in return for countrywide rights except for the area which Haggar covered himself. Bromhead, who ran Gaumont's London business, later said that he seemed to remember also supplying Haggar with negative stock. Nevertheless the deal was basically in Gaumont's favour. Bromhead recalled that he made 480 prints of Haggar's *The Poachers*, of which well over one hundred were exported to Europe.

Bromhead himself, who later became one of the leading figures in the British film industry, began as an urban showman, in partnership with T. A. Welsh, but like other early showmen quickly developed interests in film dealing. He recalled how he and Welsh were astonished when a competitor by the name of A. D. Thomas bought a hundred copies of a film made for Gaumont in Paris of the Seaforth Highlanders marching through Cairo *en route* to the Battle of Omdurman in 1898. He then discovered that Thomas had bought them for the film dealers McGuire and Baucas, which at that time was run by Charles Urban before he set up his own company; McGuire and Baucas, with headquarters in New York, was the firm which had opened the first Kinetoscope Parlour in London in 1894. This discovery made Bromhead realise, he said, what business potential there was in importing films. He therefore proceeded to obtain British sales rights on items listed in the Gaumont catalogue, which included films made by people who had bought cameras from them. This was how Bromhead's association with Gaumont began. Some film histories record that Gaumont opened a London office in 1898. In effect it was Bromhead and Walsh who set themselves up as agents for the French company, and then began to do the same for producers like Haggar in Britain. They were not only Haggar's agents but also Cecil Hepworth's, until Hepworth opened his own sales office.

Within a few years, Bromhead began to expand into both production and exhibition. In 1902 he opened a studio at Loughborough Junction in South London, for which he obtained backing from Gaumont, and then in 1904 began operating what was probably the first permanent cinema in the country, the Daily Bioscope in Bishopsgate. An installation not unlike the music hall 'penny gaff', the term was soon taken over and applied to all such operations. Long before this, urban showmen used to take over empty shops or other suitable premises but only on a temporary basis, introducing films in new locales and then moving on. This was one of the effects of the sale of films on the open market: these small-time operators could not afford to keep replenishing their stock, so they moved on to find new audiences instead. It was a satisfactory system only in the early days while the thing was still a novelty and the business chaotic.

Over the next few years, Bromhead's most significant interventions lay in the organisation of distribution. It was he, at any rate in Britain, who seems to have initiated the system of exclusive booking contracts whereby the highest bidder in each locality secured the sole rights for a particular development – a development which could hardly have taken place until fixed cinemas amounted to a significant part of the market. According to Bromhead's own account, he took this step in order to try and insert some order into the somewhat chaotic conditions which prevailed at the time. He was concerned not only that often the same films came to be simultaneously available on both open sale and rental, but also with various malpractices whereby, for example, showmen receiving copies of films on approval were able to show them first, and then return them saying they didn't want to take them, a situation to be averted later by the institution of the preview. We should not regard these malpractices as merely incidental. The history of the film industry is so riddled with a succession of various different types of malpractice that they should be regarded as an inherent result of the peculiarity of film as a commodity, and of the contradictions thus entailed in a capitalist film industry (much like the malpractices rampant today in the computer industry, similarly inherent in the peculiarities of its products as commodities).

Peter Bachlin has explained the broad rationale behind the appearance of rental like this:

> The distributor took the risk of purchasing films on his own account, while the exhibitor did no more than rent them; and the distributor's intervention improved economic conditions for the exhibitor by allowing more frequent programme changes. This created a growth in the market for the producer: films could reach the consumer in greater number and more rapidly; moreover the new system constituted a kind of sales guarantee for their films. In general, the distributor bought copies of one or several films from one or several producers and rented them to many exhibitors; by doing this it was possible to obtain for them a greater sum than their cost price. The old system of selling the individual copy, which meant ceding a piece of property, was replaced by *the temporary concession of the right to exhibit.*[12]

It is undeniable, he adds, that the birth of the branch of distribution accelerated the development of the film industry: the rationalisation of costs, and the more effective and rapid diffusion of films led to an increase in the number of cinemas.

As for Bromhead, he quickly realised that permanent cinemas, like the one he established in Bishopsgate, would obviously prefer the rental system, so as not to be lumbered with copies of films which they could only repeat a limited number of times. Yet initially the introduction of rental had the effect of increasing the chaos because of the way it intensified competition. For example, exhibitors of the 'town hall' type, who moved from one fixed location to another, were forced to purchase a greater number of new films for fear that otherwise someone else would already have shown the same films in the same locality that they were about to play themselves. This wrought havoc with their custom of calculating their costs partly on the basis of the rental for the location in relation to the costs of the films they were showing. At the same time, fairground showmen were forced to spend more on dolling up their tents and trailers, and engaging more splendid musical accompaniment, to try to hold on to their audience.

If producers were gradually forced to abandon open sale, which meant losing a certain amount of control over their product (a frequent subject of litigation in the film industry), it is true the distributors were the ones to be faced with the greater risks. It was they who had to keep track of itinerant showmen, and recoup their money from exhibitors who now not only fell behind in their payments but were even forced out of business. It was therefore the distributor who took the next step of instituting exclusive rental. A new form of monopoly, the system took time to establish, but reduced the distributor's risk. It also offered another advantage: it reduced the number of copies of a film that were needed, because it made the exploitation of each copy more efficient.

Turning, then, to production, we first observe that in Britain it quickly became a cottage industry – or more precisely, a suburban one. Even before Bromhead opened his studio in Loughborough Junction, Paul had opened one in New Southgate in North London in 1899, while Hepworth, a year later, had built a studio in the back garden of a house he rented west of London, in Walton-on-Thames, the year after he left the employ of Charles Urban.

Before joining Urban, Hepworth ran, according to his own account unsuccessfully, a small shop selling cameras and dry-plates for still photography, but he had already begun to tinker with cinematography.[13] After designing an arc-lamp, originally intended for magic-lantern projection, which brought him into contact with Paul, he bought a film projector which he proceeded to modify. He made his own first film while working for Urban, who employed him to print and process the films which the company handled. He also developed a semi-automatic process for developing and printing in which the film was cranked through the baths in the same way it was cranked through the camera and the projector. Without such a device, the strips of film had to be dealt with by individual handling, which was one of the reasons for their short length. Urban agreed to pay him a farthing per foot for all films processed on the new machine, but evidently soon found this an uneconomic proposition, and gave Hepworth the sack. Thereupon Hepworth took his machine away with him and set up on his own in the house at Walton-on-Thames. He soon found that processing other people's films provided too little work to sustain his business, so he decided he had better make his own, and built the stage in his back garden. Naturally, he also followed general practice and filmed the usual public events. In August 1902, on the occasion of Edward VII's coronation, his developing and printing machine paid off most handsomely. He and his staff spent a week solid, non-stop, trying to satisfy the demand for prints of the coronation film. His advantage in the manufacture of copies thus gave him a leading position in production, which he maintained for nigh on twenty years. He was one of the few producers who managed to stay in business in Britain during the First World War, though he finally went bankrupt in the early 20s when he tried to float a public company in the middle of a highly apathetic money market, with the result that it was seriously undersubscribed. In the early 1900s, when his business first began to expand, he too was an important aesthetic innovator, who in the interests of better photography converted his open-air stage into a glass-covered studio; he also seems to have been one of the first British producers to have set up a distribution office in New York.

If it took about ten or fifteen years for the special character of film as a commodity to emerge, this also means that it took this long for film to take on what we now think of as the first real hues of art. There was nothing mysterious in this process – we have just seen how it began. What happened, to put it crudely, was that film-makers began to develop greater sensitivity towards the expressive possibilities of the new medium; audiences then began to demonstrate preferences which pointed the film-makers in certain directions, reinforcing certain tendencies; and then dealers began to realise the consequences of these developments – to realise, in other words, that for aesthetic reasons too – though that is not a word they would have used – the film was no ordinary commodity. This meant not just developing more efficient methods for its exploitation, but also learning to trade on audience taste, learning how to entice them.

It was in taking on the hues of art that film began to develop the intricate and hierarchical division of labour which subsequently became one of the chief characteristics of the labour process involved in production. In the beginning, the division of labour in film production hardly existed. Since the earliest films were scarcely more than moving photographs, short scenes ranging from public events to comic sketches, they were produced with little sophistication and at ridiculously little cost – scarcely more than the cost of the film stock, if you discount the cost of the camera itself. What this actually means is that the various overheads were not counted in the costs of production. Not just the overheads included in property company accounts, but also the incidental costs involved in staging scenes especially for the camera. This is just another way of saying that at first there was no real concept of what were later called production values, only of simple manufacture. Put this way, it is clear, firstly, that the discovery of production values was part and parcel of the emergence of film production as a capital-intensive industry, and secondly, that the process whereby film became an art was conditioned by capitalist processes.

Among the unpaid overheads in this first stage of film manufacture was the labour of the actors. We can surmise, for example, that Haggar had no need to pay his actors when he made *The Maid of Cefn Ydfa* in 1902, since they were members of his own theatre company. Hepworth says in his autobiography that the 'actors' in his earliest films were generally members of his company, family or friends, who remained uncredited. The camera was operated by someone who wasn't appearing in front of it. Other jobs – printing, processing and so forth – were also shared. The first time Hepworth paid actors a fee was in 1905, for the film *Rescued by Rover*. The principals, who came down from London to augment a cast which included Hepworth himself, his wife, his baby and his dog, were paid half a guinea each, including travelling expenses. Even so, the total cost of the film was £7 13s 6d. The film ran 425 feet, about seven minutes, and prints sold for £10 13s 9d (6d per foot). A total of 395 prints were sold, and this required two remakes of the film because the negative wore out in the printing. Even considering the remake costs and the cost of the film stock, it is clear that the profits must have been enormous.

Soon people began to show individual aptitudes for particular jobs. One of the first specialised jobs to emerge, as the techniques of filming developed their first real elements of judgment, was that of the cameraman (there is no evidence that there was ever at this time a camera-woman). In the early stages this job also included the functions that were later ascribed to the director (such as deciding where to place the camera and how to divide the film set up into its constituent shots), as well as combining technical responsibilities which were later divided up between the several members of the crew working as a unit, as both *mise en scène* and the technology grew more complex. But to begin with, the cameraman was the film-maker. And even when the operation of the camera began to evolve its distinctive traits, everyone in a company like Hepworth's still constituted a general pool of labour. It would have been impossible otherwise to fulfil the tasks of manufacturing the hundreds of copies needed of the more successful films, using the primitive equipment then available. Hepworth says as much in his autobiography, and he himself had partly mechanised the process.

The rough-and-ready conditions of early film-making depended on similar attributes to those of the *bricoleur*, the figure described by the anthropologist Lévi-Strauss as 'someone who works with his hands and uses devious means compared to those of a craftsman', to which his translator adds the footnote: 'The "bricoleur" has no precise equivalent in English. He is a man who undertakes odd jobs and is a Jack of all trades or a kind of professional do-it-yourself man, but, as the text makes clear, he is of a different standing from, for instance, the English "odd job man" or handyman.'[14] A question therefore interposes itself: what is the connection between the evolution of a more sophisticated kind of craft knowledge – the kind which always lies at the roots of real aesthetic production – and the development of the more efficient capitalist relations of production that were necessary to intensify the exploitation of the film as a commodity (especially given its peculiarities)?

It emerges that the aesthetic conditions of early film were intimately bound up with its particular form of entry into the market – at the bottom, unlike most technological innovations which enter at the top. At the same time, it appears that the peculiarities of film as a commodity began to take effect before the aesthetic issues were posed in any way articulately. Indeed it was several more years before anyone took film seriously as an art form, and a Hollywood major adopted the famous slogan *Ars gratia artis*. By then, in terms of economics it had already long outstripped the classical patterns of capitalist development. However, at the end of the first stage of development, covering roughly the first decade of cinema's history, there was still little advance from the aesthetic point of view in the relations of production. In the branches of distribution and exhibition, on the other hand, the industry was growing up fast. This is why the first moves towards unionisation in the British film industry took place not in the production sector but in the cinemas themselves, with the formation in 1907 of the National Association of Cinematograph Operators.[15] In the ensuing period, these economic developments will begin to affect the aesthetic dimension, and force it into a shape which corresponded more closely to economic demands.

The economic conditions of early cinema and the characteristics which governed early film production can be summarised as follows. Firstly, the initial conditions favoured the manufacturers of equipment, and gave them a dominant position as film producers which they were never to enjoy again. But because the production of films needed little capitalisation, a large part of the catalogues of companies like Pathé and Gaumont were actually made up of films produced by the purchasers of their cameras, which they naturally agreed to market because it was in their interests to do so. Their own production efforts were always a smaller proportion of their business than the manufacture and sale of equipment, while they used the sale of films at a low and uniform price to open up and extend the market for their hardware. At this point there was no standardisation.

Secondly, standardisation was the result primarily of advances by the manufacturers not of equipment but of film stock. Equipment manufacturers accepted standardisation because the market had grown sufficiently that it was no longer in their interests to resist it; otherwise they would find themselves unnecessarily limiting their access to the market. This also means that it was the dedicated manufacturers of film stock who were the first to introduce mass production techniques and acquire the status of monopoly producers.

Thirdly, a separate distribution sector began to appear, as the idosyncratic nature of film as a commodity began to make itself felt, and dealers began to exploit the film's rentability. At this point the film industry begins to show signs of departing from the classical patterns of capitalist development.

The situation now shaped up like this. As long as exhibition venues remained small and films short, the possibilities of surplus profit – the kind of profit that attracts extra investment – resided mainly in a large turnover of both showings and films. If an exhibitor was to remain in the same place, frequent programme changes were necessary. Since many showmen could not afford this, they remained itinerants, following the well-established itineraries of traditional popular entertainment; but these were already in decline for other reasons. Overall, however, the film market was growing in extent and penetration, and production was expanding and becoming more organised. Indeed the audience was growing to such an extent that the new film 'factories', as the first studios were often called, only managed to satisfy the demand with difficulty, and in every country film importers flourished. Indeed the film business was international from the very beginning.

The conditions of free competition, as yet without any trade bodies to regulate business practices, made the business anarchic, and invited promotion by ballyhoo and hype. Competition intensified on every level. Distributors began to charge differential prices. Exhibitors who started paying rental charges ran after the newest and therefore most expensive films. In order to obtain the films they rented, the distributors were still in competition with each other, maintaining simultaneous relations with the pool of producers until the institution of exclusive distribution contracts; and this was one of the developments which in the United States, already the largest single market in the world, began to attract the interest of finance capital in a big way. As for the producers, they were increasingly obliged to go through the renters in order to reach the exhibition market, because they were progressively less able to sell directly to exhibitors who were less and less inclined to buy where they could rent.

By going over to the rental system, the dealers became distributors, and strengthened their position of control over the market. A process began to unfold which step by step propelled them towards better control over the terms and conditions of supply and demand than either producers or exhibitors. The exhibitors were made to bark at their orders, while the producers bore the brunt of the risks. The aesthetic development of cinema came to depend in very large part on either the distributors' lead or their acquiescence. This stage was accomplished during the course of the 1920s. We are still suffering from the consequences.

Notes

Revised version of an article first published in Roger Holman (ed), *Cinema 1900–1906* (Brussels: FIAF, 1982).

1. Quoted in Gordon Hendricks, *The Edison Motion Picture Myth* (Berkeley and Los Angeles: University of California Press, 1961).
2. *Photographic Work*, vol. 3 no. 132, 9 November 1984, p. 534.
3. Quoted in John Barnes, *The Beginnings of the Cinema in England* (David & Charles, 1976), p. 35.
4. Paul in W. G. Barker, R. W. Paul and Cecil Hepworth, 'Before 1910: Kinematograph experiences', in *Proceedings of the British Kinematograph Society*, no. 38, 3 February 1936.
5. Barnes, *Beginnings of the Cinema*, p. 19.
6. Karl Marx, *A Contribution to the Critique of Political Economy* (London: Lawrence and Wishart, 1971), p. 42.
7. Stanley Cavell, *The World Viewed* (Cambridge, Mass.: Harvard University Press, 1979), p. 24.
8. Quoted in Rachael Low (with Roger Manvell), *The History of the British Film*, Vol. 1 (London: Allen & Unwin, 1948), p. 34.
9. Peter Bachlin, *Histoire économique du cinéma* (Paris: La Nouvelle Edition, 1947), pp. 14–15.
10. See Will Aaron, 'Walter Haggar', *Barn*, October 1975. (I am grateful to Michael Engelhard for translating this article from the Welsh.)
11. A. C. Bromhead, 'Reminiscences of the British film trade', *Proceedings of the B. K. S.*, No. 21, 11 December 1933.
12. Bachlin, *Histoire économique*, p. 21.
13. Cecil Hepworth, *Came the Dawn, Memories of a Film Pioneer* (Phoenix House, 1951).
14. Claude Lévi-Strauss, *The Savage Mind* (London: Weidenfeld and Nicolson, 1972), p. 17.
15. For the history of the unions in the British film industry up to the end of the Second World War, see my monograph *Labour Power in the British Film Industry* (London: British Film Institute, 1976); for the continuation, my article 'Labour power and aesthetic labour in film and television in Britain', in Mattelart and Siegelaub, eds, *Communication and Class Struggle*, Vol. 2 (International General/IMMRC, 1983).

Combination and Litigation
Structures of US Film Distribution, 1896–1917

JANET STAIGER

Every history of the early US film industry is obliged to account for the appearance and disappearance of the first major attempt at monopoly: the Motion Picture Patents Company (MPPC), organized in 1908. In these histories, the federal antitrust suit and the competitive techniques of the independents are generally determined to have been the causes of the Patents Company's failure. This essay will disagree with those accounts, showing that the legal system was not just sporadically used but consistently part and parcel of the business strategies of several of the companies. Additionally, because competitive product practices of the Patents Company members and the independents do not differ significantly, while the Patents Company may have ceased operating, not all of its members did. Rather, some MPPC firms, some independents, and several new companies are those firms emerging around 1915 as the dominant producer-distributors. Former histories have relied on neo-classical economics to explain events; by using Marxist assumptions, this study provides a new understanding of this period.[1]

The Patent Wars, 1891–1908

Thomas Edison filed a patent application on a moving picture camera and film in August 1891. Having set up a systematic organization for research and development in 1876, he was well versed in the use and value of patents.[2]

The initial (1790) form of US patent law required no examination of originality at the filing of the request. Courts decided novelty (and hence the patent right) once a patent holder filed an infringement suit. In 1836 examination for originality became part of the application procedure, but disagreements over priority of invention might be brought to court, and any alleged overlapping of rights or claims of infringement had to be settled there. If a patent holder did not actively pursue the right by instigating suits, the alleged infringers could use the invention with impunity. The cost of litigation hampered patent holders who might file test cases rather than seeing legal action in every case of suspected violation of the right.[3]

When Edison's patent application was granted in August 1897, he wasted little time in protecting his rights. Between December 1897 and September 1901, his lawyers filed twenty-three infringement suits. Some suits resulted in settlements. Others awaited a test case against American Mutoscope and Biograph. In July 1901, a lower court ruled in favour of Edison. Biograph, which appealed, continued to produce films but under court surveillance in the event that a higher court might affirm the decision.[4]

The higher court did not. In March 1902, it reversed the lower court, arguing that the claims in the original application were too broad. Edison responded by applying for reissues, splitting the original patent into one on the camera and one on the film stock. The reissues were granted in September 1902.[5]

Within a month, Edison filed new suits based on the camera patent reissue. A suit against Biograph was again a test case. In 1906, the lower court decided generally in favour of Biograph, but on appeal the higher court reversed the decision in part (March 1907). Since this seemed to determine that Edison possessed the right to manufacture cameras with a particular design, almost every camera generally used then would probably have been guilty of infringement. Thus, in early 1907 litigation started ten years earlier was terminating with an apparent resolution in favour of Edison's control over the dominant (and almost only practical) design of camera technology.[6]

Besides the camera patent, four other patents were crucial to film production: Edison's film stock patent reissue, a projector patent, the Latham loop patent and the Pross patent on projector shutters. Edison's lawyers filed suits on the film stock reissue, but they did not press resolution because of involvement with other appeals.[7]

Armat Moving Picture Company claimed ownership of the Jenkins and Armat projecting machine patent, dated July 1897. Eventually filing ten suits, the firm received a favourable decision in October 1902 that enjoined Biograph from using the device, so Biograph took out a licence. Edison also lost a lower court case against it, but on appeal the court held that the right of possession was in doubt. Because of lack of funds, the Armat Company did not vigorously pursue the case, and it neared completion in late 1908.[8]

The Latham loop patent was granted in August 1902. This invention was necessary in projectors and useful in cameras. Having insufficient funds to conduct suits, Latham's company sold the patent to Biograph in February 1908. Biograph then filed nine suits. Biograph also owned the Pross patent on projector shutters (dated March 1903), and between May and June 1908 the firm filed three suits on its claims.[9]

What are the implications of this struggle over patent rights? Technically, patent law suggests that the value issuing from an invention should go to its originator. However, access to legal restitution is not equal. Unless the inventor has sufficient capital to pursue rights, they are unenforceable. As Edison's lawyers later put it: 'The expense of these suits would have financially ruined any inventor who did not have the large resources of Edison. . . .'[10] Thus, economic strength was one factor in the outcome. The Armat Company and the Latham firm were both handicapped by lack of capital. Latham's firm followed a common capitulation: it sold its patent, obtaining some restitution.

Another implication of the patent rights struggle is how firms used the practice of manoeuvring for time to their advantage. Firms commonly continued to engage in profit-making activities while legal appeals were made.[11] In fact, because of the system and time of litigation, no firm was absolutely in violation of any patent rights until the March 1907 decision in favour of Edison's camera patent reissue.

Furthermore, firms secured additional profits through the possession of patents. In March 1907, the demand for films was rapidly expanding: the nickelodeon boom was on. Rather than being able to supply films and compete in the growing market-place, the manufacturing firms found themselves facing Edison's possession of the design of most practical cameras in use.[12] On the basis of the camera patent reissue, the Edison Company proceeded to take advantage of its legal victory. In February 1908 Edison licensed Lubin, Selig, Vitagraph, George Méliès, Pathé Frères, Kalem, and Essanay to use the patent.[13]

Several months earlier, in November 1907, manufacturers and distributors had held the first of a series of industry meetings to stop a rash of price-cutting (note the emergence of informal collusion). In December 1907, the exchanges formed the Film Service Association. Once Edison licensed most of the manufacturers, the Film Service Association contracted in March 1908 to buy exclusively from that production combination. This initial production-distribution alliance effectively dominated the industry, and combination practices began.[14]

Biograph, however, did not sign up as an Edison licensee, apparently because of a failure to resolve how royalties would be split. Instead, Biograph purchased the Latham patent in February 1908 and filed suits on that and the Pross patent. Owning these key patents provided a counterweight to Edison's patent strength. Furthermore, Biograph constructed its own alliance of firms, also competing by increasing its size and share of the industry. Licensing the use of its patents to several equipment manufacturers and film importers (including George Kleine), Biograph attempted to compete with Edison's alliance.[15]

Thus, at this point, the battle for industrial control was not conducted through competitive products (perhaps because, from what is known, demand exceeded supply) but through legal and structural practices. Firms attempted through patent law and the strategy of combination to secure an anticipated legal monopoly with its profits. Litigation and combination immediately typified the industry's early conduct.

The Formation of the Patents Company and General Film, 1908–12

By mid-1908, the US film industry's production structure boiled down to two equipment and film manufacturing combinations and sets of patents – Edison's, which were important for the camera and film stock, and Biograph's, which were essential in the projector and useful in the camera. What the companies did in order to do business 'lawfully' (i.e. to avoid further litigation with its costs and doubtful outcome) was to cross-license each other.[16] They went a step further, however; they followed the example of big business and organized a combination, the Motion Picture Patents Company. Because no firm could secure an immediate control of the business, this alternative enabled them to avoid wasteful market competition.

Collusion through one of the various forms of combination allowed them to set prices at an optimum level.[17] Furthermore, current law seemed to support the legality of such a combination. In late 1908 Standard Oil, US Steel and other firms, while under attack, had successfully maintained consolidated organizations. Moreover, patents had special protection. In defending the Patents Company, lawyers cited numerous precedents for patent pools.[18]

The structure of the Patents Company was that of a patent pool. It incorporated in September 1908 for the purpose of acquiring inventions and patent rights related to the technology of moving pictures. It would then license the right to use that technology. Edison and Biograph owners purchased all the stock in the Patents Company except for four shares that qualified the directors. In December 1908, the company formally started by accepting the assignment of sixteen patents from Edison, Biograph, Armat and Vitagraph. Under a specified system royalties from manufacturers of equipment, from producers making films, and from theatres using projectors were to be collected and distributed to the four companies. The Patents Company also organized the licensing and contracting of various other segments of the industry. It signed a three-year, exclusive contract with the principal domestic raw film producers, Eastman-Kodak, and licensed equipment manufacturers. In addition, it licensed all significant film manufacturers and importers, fixing rental prices at a minimum level. Licences ran until June 1910, with yearly renewals thereafter until the expiration of one of the patents in August 1919. Furthermore, in a move to eliminate a substantial foreign competition, the Patents Company restricted the amount of imported footage.[19]

The Patents Company moved to control distribution. Of the 130 to 140 exchanges in the US, approximately 100 received licences. Not franchises, the licences did not allocate geographical rights but did prohibit an exchange from dealing with an exhibitor served by another licensed exchange. Exchanges were required to handle a minimum number of films monthly. Finally, the Patents Company licensed exhibitors.

The pool constructed a combination with potential monopoly power in all three levels of the industry. While competition was not totally eliminated (exchanges might compete for the business of the exhibitors, and exhibitors for customers), the members of the pool envisioned cessation of litigation and competition. They had assured routes of wholesaling and distributing, a sure level of rental income, and a nationwide market that appeared to be expanding. Foreign competition would be controlled. The Patents Company expected excellent earnings from film and equipment manufacture and royalties.

That their plans went awry is common knowledge. But at the outset, the strategy of the Patents Company promised to stabilize the industry and make a solid improvement in films and service to exhibitors. Prior to the formation of the company, a single negative from a Chicago or New York manufacturer might reach only a limited locale or receive spotty distribution because of the expense of setting up a nationwide distribution system with a regular schedule of releases. With the new structure, larger numbers of prints could be efficiently distributed. Economies of scale could be realized. One of the immediate results was the investment of capital into production.[20]

Also sensitive to relations among distributors, exhibitors and customers, the Patents Company inserted stipulations in the licences to improve business practices. Included were clauses requiring the recall of old prints and prohibiting duped films. With an improvement in the industry's image, increased consumption might occur.

The Patents Company later argued that a general attempt to upgrade the films and service motivated the subsequent organization of the General Film Company (GF) in 1910.[21] Between early 1909 and April 1910 when General Film was organized, the number of licensed exchanges dwindled to sixty-nine. Some voluntarily withdrew; of the thirty-two licences the Patents Company revoked, most of the cancellations were due to violations of contractual agreements.[22]

General Film was not legally connected to the Patents Company although the manufacturers who organized the Patents Company formed it. An interlocking directorate of the Patents Company, General Film, and the licensed manufacturers is a more accurate description. The Patents Company licensed General Film as its distributor, including contractual stipulations that prevented losses at the distribution level.[23]

General Film promptly instituted standing orders (an early form of block booking) and zoning. It classified theatres and began purchasing exchanges. Acquiring these small businesses as corporations do in mergers, General Film paid in cash and preferred stock in General Film. (The licensed manufacturers held the common voting stock.) Thus, as exchanges merged into General Film, their owners became stockholders in the firm and often managers of their previously owned company. Within eighteen months, General Film had purchased fifty-eight exchanges, cancelled the licences of ten others, and reduced its operations to a streamlined, nationwide system of forty-two outlets.[24] With General Film, system and efficiency were evident, with a regular, varied supply of films to exhibitors and customers. As in the case of combinations in other industries, the structure of the combination reduced loss and provided better returns, without necessarily increasing the cost of the product.

The formation of the Patents Company in 1908 seems consistent with US economic history. Failing to secure a legal monopoly through ownership of all necessary patents, Edison agreed to a truce and constructed a legal monopoly through a business structure, combining the various patent rights. The Patents Company proceeded to monopolize the industry informally via General Film, an interlocking directorate among manufacturers and distributors. Eventually, the Patents Company failed to maintain that monopoly. The reasons for this involve the impermanence of informal combinations, the changing interpretation of what constituted legal collusion, and varying success by members of the Patents combine in responding to transitions in the grounds of product competition.

Counter-Practices by the Independents, 1909–12

The ink was barely dry on the Patents Company licences when resistance to the company's formation began. The opposition was less at the film manufacturers' end; only very minor producing firms were excluded in the company's formation. Response came primarily, and more forcibly, from distributors and exhibitors.[25]

In January 1909, the unlicensed firms founded a counter-organization, the Independent Film Protective Association, which was actually an informal combination in its own right – a trade association. Besides the rhetoric of condemning 'any monopoly striving to control the moving picture business', the organization promised financial and legal support to exhibitors that fought the Patents Company. It also supplied information about litigation filed against the Patents Company and suggested optional non-infringing technology. Finally, it sought an alternate supply of product from excluded European companies and from non-licensed domestic manufacturers, newly formed by independents.[26]

The independents never had the stability of a long-term organization such as the Patents Company, which is perhaps why subsequent representations of the independents romanticize them as individualists struggling against big business and monopoly capital. In fact, the independents cultivated such an image, advertising themselves as fighting the 'trust'.[27] Such rhetoric, however, belied the allied status of the independents. Actually, the independents practise similar methods of combination and litigation, although it might be argued that at first the independents did so out of necessity.

In autumn 1909, the independents reorganized their trade association. The National Independent Moving Picture Alliance planned legal protection against patent suits, lobbying for favourable legislation, methods to prevent salacious films, and the prohibition of unethical business practices. Initiation fees, membership dues and an assessment for legal defence financed the Alliance.[28]

While the Alliance had some effect, some members opted for a more powerful and formal combination – a distribution alliance. Organized in December 1909, the Motion Picture Distributing and Sales Co. officially began in May 1910, three weeks after General Film incorporated. The Sales Co. purchased its members' films and then distributed them in a standing order. However, it did not buy exchanges as General Film did.[29]

Independents did not immediately flock to the Sales Co.; a new rival organization, the Associated Independent Film Manufacturers, urged an 'open market', arguing that films were more likely to be quality product when exhibitors could selectively choose from either licensed or independent manufacturers. Some exhibitors even accused the Sales Co. of stooping to General Film's practices, arguing that both combinations tried to foist off films of inferior quality.[30] However, the economic advantages of standing orders were apparent; neither the Sales Co. nor General Film moved to an open market.

Eventually, the Sales Co.'s approach won out over objections. By mid-1910, it served forty-seven exchanges in twenty-seven cities, supplying 4,000 theatres.[31] The Sales Co. argued:

> Would the Trust manufacturers and the manufacturers marketing

through the Sales Company have attained anything like their present [April 1911] standard of quality without organizations whose aims have been to eliminate the evils and so regulate the business as to encourage the manufacturers to make the investments necessary to improve the quality of their products . . .

Any exhibitor or exchange can prove beyond a doubt that dividing the visible supply of films and restricting their use to certain houses as under the present system is the only way in which the present large number of houses could have been opened and furnished a non-conflicting service.[32]

This is a blatant statement of the economic advantages of combination and cartelization. By 1911 the economic structure of the production and distribution sectors of the industry was that of an oligopoly. Two distribution firms representing two sets of manufacturers and exhibitors virtually split the US film business.

Furthermore, once these two alliances set up their nationwide distribution system, they considered multinational distribution.[33] The movement into other nations has historically occurred after nationwide expansion. The first step was exportation of excess product.[34] In film's case, additional positive prints and distribution costs are justified if distribution is efficiently organized. Although the Patents Company members were first to consider exporting movies, by 1911 both MPPC firms and independents were selling abroad. Such an expansion was possible because both alliances practised combination to increase their size, providing sufficient conditions for moving into multinational marketing.[35]

The history of the independents for the next few years is one of disintegration of alliances and formation of new ones.

Following the pattern already established, some companies organized, hoping to break into the industrial structure. Some combinations broke up when members calculated that different practices would produce greater profits. A report in May 1911 listed five independent distribution groups including the Sales Co.[36]

One example of a major realignment in the independents will indicate the cyclical nature of these combinations. The break-up of the Sales Co. apparently resulted from a conflict over profits. Harry E. Aitken owned a chain of exchanges in the Midwest when General Film organized. Joining the Sales Co., Aitken helped form American Film Manufacturing Company and Majestic Film Manufacturing Company; he also later bought control of Carlton Motion Picture Laboratories which made Reliance films. According to one historian, after Aitken hired Mary Pickford away from Carl Laemmle's Independent Motion Picture Company (IMP), Laemmle (in charge of the Sales Co.) retaliated by doubling Majestic's fee for distribution. Majestic announced in March 1912 that it was leaving the Sales Co. and that it was suing that company for restraint of trade.[37]

Aitken then set up two firms. In April 1912 Livingston & Co., members of the New York Stock Exchange, financed Mutual Film Company, capitalized at $2,500,000. Aitken became president, with the board of directors including Crawford Livingston and a treasurer of Guaranty Trust Co. According to Aitken, Mutual would only purchase exchanges. In May 1912 the other new firm, the Film Supply Company of America, announced that it would distribute single and multiple-reel films for several manufacturers (Reliance, Majestic, Thanhouser, Gaumont, American, Great Northern, Solax, Lux and Comet). Thus, the Film Supply Company had lured away a number of the Sales Co.'s suppliers. The remaining Sales firms (the New York Motion Picture Company, IMP, Powers, Rex, Champion, Republic and Nestor) announced they would remain allied with the Sales Co., but the first four also indicated that they were creating Universal Film Manufacturing Company which would only be a trade organization.[38]

By June, however, it was clear that Universal was splitting from the Sales Co., leaving little. Universal promised to organize exclusive territories for exchanges, create an efficient production system, make multiple-reel films, and provide a full service of twenty-four reels per week. Stories conflict as to what happened next. One owner, Fred Balshofer, later said that 'everyone in the combine wanted to be the permanent president.' Contemporary trade reports suggested that the problem was disagreement over a capital purchase. In either case, policy discord caused the New York Motion Picture Company to indicate that it was leaving the organization. Universal went to court for an injunction to prevent the removal of New York's assets, and Pat Powers of Universal directed an attempt to physically take over one of New York's manufacturing plants. (Ironically, the only well-documented, armed battle of this period was not between the Patents Company and the independents but between warring factions of independents.) In July 1912 New York Motion Picture Company went to Mutual's alliance. Then in late 1912, the Mutual-Film Supply tie split with Mutual taking Reliance, Majestic, Thanhouser, American, Kay-Bee, Broncho and Keystone. Film Supply said it would add new brands.[39]

In summary, at the end of 1912, four distribution combinations – General Film, Mutual, Film Supply and Universal – split the exhibition business. General Film had approximately 60 per cent of the exhibitors, with the others controlling the rest.[40] While the independents, more properly considered alternative combinations, had not yet broken General Film's solid control of the market, they did have a respectable share of the business and profits. By using the practice of combination, the independents competed nationally and did some multinational distribution.

More Independent Counter-Strategies

The early success of the independents was not entirely due to the formation of alliances. Another major practice was to use property law regarding patents and combination methods. At the formation of the Patents Company, the members had achieved favourable – but not clear-cut or final – court decisions on the various patents. The vagaries of legislation and adjudication could be counted on as well as the time to hear suits. In addition, antitrust sentiment provided another legal support since the trends in legislation, if not adjudication, were favourable to the independents. In other words, the independents had reason to hope for decisions that would allow them to continue in business. In addition, laws aimed against patent pools were advantageous to them, and their trade associations lobbied for this in the federal Congress.

The Patents Company, of course, attempted to enforce their patent rights. Between 1909 and 1911 more suits were filed. Adverse temporary effects to the independents included injunctions against and impoundment of allegedly infringing equipment. However, the independents responded by using the form of the law against the Patents Company: they had to be caught infringing to be required to make restitution. So cameramen kept several cameras on a set, and when detectives arrived, they would pull out non-infringing equipment. Cameramen also installed infringing mechanisms in non-infringing exteriors.

For the Patents Company, costs of pursuing infringers must have been more than any court-ordered repayment. For the independents, fines for patent violation were less than profits from film-making. In addition, the independents often shared the costs of defence rather than let the burden fall on a single company. The Sales Co., for instance, allocated part of its income for litigation and hired a patent attorney to fight suits. Contrary to some stories, one thing they did not do was hide out in California; patents companies preceded independents there, and trade papers freely reported the whereabouts of motion picture production units.[41]

Some important patent cases went the independents' way. In a key case on the Latham loop patent, *Motion Picture Patents Co.* v. *Independent Moving Picture Company* (1912), the district court judge directed the bill of complaint dismissed. He found that while the Latham loop was usable on cameras, it was invented for projectors, so the patent claim did not apply to cameras. Furthermore, if the patent was claimed for projectors it would be held invalid because the device was anticipated in an earlier projector. The Patents Company also lost on the film stock patent reissue.[42]

The independents were not so fortunate in two cases that considered combination methods. In *Motion Picture Patents Co.* v. *Ullman et al.* (1910), the court declared that companies could not infringe on patents even though the patents might be held by an illegal combination.[43]

The more famous case is *Greater New York Film Rental Company* v. *Motion Picture Patents Company* (1912). By October 1911, General Film had purchased fifty-eight exchanges and cancelled the licences of ten others. Of the originally licensed exchanges, one was left: the Greater New York Film Rental Company owned by William Fox. In September 1911, General Film offered Fox $150,000 for his exchange. Fox refused to sell, claiming he deserved a better price. General Film had a contractual right to cancel any exchange's licence without cause, and in November it served cancellation notice. Fox vacillated but eventually refused to sell. When Fox did not receive his regular supply of films in December, his attorney filed suit, seeking an injunction against the Patents Company and General Film. In February 1912, a lower court held that General Film had a contractual right to cancel Fox's licence. Although the judge granted a temporary injunction, intimating that the Patents Company's combination 'may constitute an illegal monopoly and become a restraint of trade', the lower court's ruling was affirmed on appeal in February 1913. However, the notoriety of the case attracted the attention of the US Department of Justice, and in August 1912 it filed a federal charge of antitrust violation against the Patents Company.[44] By late 1912, independents had prevented the termination of their business through patent suit defences. While the legality of the patent pool and its conduct would now be determined, the outcome was uncertain.

The Innovation of the Multiple-Reel Film

Discussion as to causes for the decline of the Patents Company often attribute its lack of success to an inability or unwillingness to respond to two forms of product competition – stars and multiple-reel films. However, elsewhere I have shown how the licensed firm, Edison, was early to publicize hiring famous writers, and MPPC members Vitagraph and Kalem were particularly energetic in promoting stars.[45] More significant as a possible point of comparison is the two factions' response to the multiple-reel film. While not every participant in the Patents Company or the independent alliances was astute enough to recognize the advantages of longer films, parts of each combination did perceive their potentialities. Those firms that did survived.

From 1911, the film industry increasingly turned to multiple-reel films as its major product. These longer films had significant profit advantages over the one-reel film. Their length and production values permitted higher admission prices and longer runs, which bolstered profits; multiple-reelers were also easier to advertise, improving the exhibitors' chances of luring customers into theatres.

In July 1912, one trade writer called for a 'scientific management' of film distribution. Multiple-reel films were changing the production and distribution needs of the industry. Because higher costs for stories, stars, elaborate sets and costumes went with the multiple-reeler, a geometrical increase in the cost per foot of negative occurred, affecting those manufacturers making features. As a result, companies that made longer films but still distributed through the single-reel services were at an economic disadvantage. Working in a standing order system, the single-reel distributors charged a uniform price per foot, regardless of the negative cost per foot. Thus, multiple-reel film-makers received the same as those who made less expensive films. As one exhibitor put it, 'the manufacturers of first-class films must get discouraged'.[46] Distribution of multiple-reelers was another problem. Longer films disrupted the exchange schedules, particularly if exhibitors requested longer runs. Early alternatives to the single-reel distribution alliances were states-rights distribution and road-shows.[47]

In November 1912, eight small manufacturers that produced mainly multiple-reel films announced the organization of a nationwide feature film distribution alliance. These producers would distribute their films to over 200 theatres. Although this alliance never produced important results, it did indicate that states' rights and road showing were inadequate distribution methods.

First-class exhibitors who wanted to show multiple-reelers routinely required a regular schedule of films rather than a sporadic supply. In addition, producers needed the assurance of a return on costs and a revolving flow of incoming and outgoing funds.[48]

Not until 1914 were national feature film distribution alliances organized and maintained. One of the earliest was Warners' Features. By 1914, Warners handled three features per week for eleven manufacturers. Another early one was Paramount. In May 1914 it contracted with four production firms, Famous Players, Jesse L. Lasky Feature Film Company, Pallas and Morasco Films. The alliance promised exhibitors two films per week. Providing a full-feature complement, the firm argued exhibitors would no longer need to deal with half a dozen feature firms to fill out a year's supply. In June 1914 another big feature distribution alliance organized. Louis Selznick and Arthur Spiegal (of Spiegal, May and Stern, Chicago mail-order merchants) reorganized World Film Company as a distribution firm, and Philadelphia bankers underwrote the stock issues, with World capitalized at $3,000,000.[49]

In July 1914, a trade paper split the major distribution alliances into three regular (General Film, Universal and Mutual) and four feature distributors (Warners, Paramount, World and Fox's Box Office). Despite the promise of these new feature film distributors, however, a trade commentator wrote several months later that the feature-release system was not yet regularized and that exhibitors ought not give up their standard service.[50]

The Patents Company: A Period of Uncertainty, 1913–15

In the middle of 1913, one trade paper credited General Film with 60 per cent of the film market. The company had also won several legal victories. But in retrospect, major questions about some of its practices were only then being posed.

One question was what the results of the Department of Justice's antitrust suit would be. In August 1912, the federal government filed suit under the Sherman Act, charging that the Patents Company had garnered control of 70 to 80 per cent of the business, which by then had $100 million invested in it. The government also claimed that the Patents' licensing procedures determined which theatres could be open, that General Film had acquired a distribution monopoly, and that General Film had prevented all but a small amount of import competition.[51] According to the trade papers, 'The suit is regarded by the Department of Justice as one of the most important moves under the Sherman law, as it squarely asks for a judicial determination of the relation of that statute to the patent laws.'[52] Clearly the suit was to be a test case on patents and permissible structures of combination, affecting not only the film industry but US law in general. In January 1913, hearings started in *United States* v. *The Motion Picture Patents Co.*

Within one month, Richard Rowland, a preferred stockholder in General Film, filed the first of several suits as a result of information from the antitrust hearings. The suit argued that if the antitrust case resulted in the dissolving of General Film, preferred stockholders might not get a return on their shares equal to their value, while common stockholders already had. The courts reserved a decision, and hearings continued in the main case.[53]

Not until December 1914, after two years of taking testimony, did the court hear closing arguments in the case. The government contended points of fact and law. It charged that, through licensing and royalty contracts, the Patents Company and General Film had acted unlawfully in all three sectors of the industry, 'terrorizing exchanges and exhibitors' and forcing others out of business by 'arbitrary, oppressive and high-handed methods'. Regarding law and following the most recent (1911) Supreme Court interpretations of the Sherman Act, the government argued that no longer were intent and motives for combination a justifiable defence: 'the direct effect of the acts involved is the criterion by which it is to be determined whether the combination is a restraint of trade within the intendment of the law. Therefore, reason becomes the guide.'

The defendants responded under the earlier interpretation that their motives justified the combination; their purposes had been to constitute a legal business (which required cross-licensing the patents) and to improve the quality and service of the industry. (Perhaps they hoped for a favourable clarification of the recent reinterpretation.) They then proposed an additional defence. They argued that motion pictures 'are not articles of commerce like lumber, cheese, beef or turpentine. They are works of fine art and of a literary and dramatic essence.' As such, films would not be subject to interstate trade regulations or, hence, the Act. Both sides expected an early decision from the court, but it did not come until October 1915, ten months later.[54]

While awaiting the decision, the Patents Company tried another legal manoeuvre based on then-current patent law. It filed a suit against Universal in March 1915, appealing to a law that allowed 'typing' arrangements. In a typing arrangement, manufacturers of a patented invention could require that only certain supplies, which were not necessarily patented, be used on that invention. The Patents Company accused Universal of renting films to be used on a projector bearing an engraved notification prohibiting use of unlicensed films on the equipment.[55]

The legal history of this business practice suggested that it might compensate for any unfavourable decision in the antitrust case. Tying as a common practice began about 1896 after a lower court approved it in the 'Button Fastener' case. A manufacturer of a patented stapler inscribed a notice on the stapler that it could only be used with the manufacturer's staples. Although many observers expected the Supreme Court to overthrow this lower court ruling eventually, other lower courts followed the precedent. The surprise came in 1912 in *Henry* v. *A. B. Dick Co.* when the Supreme Court upheld Dick's right to restrict the use of ink, paper and other supplies on its duplicating machines. The decision was a four-to-three vote with one new member not participating and one court seat unfilled. Public response to the decision was negative. In a film trade paper, for instance, the editor pointed out that the bench was not full, that such a decision could be quickly changed, and that US Congressmen were introducing bills to limit such patent powers. In 1913 the Supreme Court voted five to four (with the minority comprising the same four as had been the majority in the Dick case) that a manufacturer could not control the resale price of an invention; the disparity between precedents was evident. A US House committee studying revisions in the form of patent law in 1914 urged a change in law to resolve the contradictions. As a response to this and difficulties with the Sherman Act, Congress passed the Clayton Act (1914) which expressly forbade such tying arrangements. Thus, when the Patents Company filed its suit against Universal, the suit was a test case of the Clayton Act and tying. The suit was also a delaying strategy that could extend the practical lifetime of the patent pool.[56]

If the question of the legal status of the Patents combination was being posed between 1913 and 1915, a second question was what the Patents members' positions would be on the manufacture and distribution of multiple-reel films. As a review of the early multiple-reel films indicates, some of the Patents Company manufacturers moved into their production although they did not neglect the regular product. General Film also licensed and distributed multiple-reels so that its exhibitors could share in the profits.[57] Some General Film manufacturers, at least, seemed interested in the longer films.

The Patents alliance did hesitate to make a consistent policy regarding the increasing diffusion of multiple-reelers. In October 1913, as feature film operations throughout the industry began increasing, General Film announced a new distribution plan for any interested exhibitors. It would initiate an exclusive ninety-day territory for any exhibitor who would pay for it. One two-reeler and two one-reelers would be provided three times a week. With this exclusive service, General Film pointed out, an exhibitor could take full advantage of advertising and 'charge a fairly high rate of admission'. In December, however, General Film abandoned this strategy for a 'series of special features ranging from three to eight reels' to meet what it termed exhibitors' demands for large features.[58]

Despite these attempts to respond to the changing market, conservative elements were strong. Most exchanges still changed films daily and set a standard fee for all films regardless of their negative cost. Edison announced in early 1914 that its response to the multiple-reeler would not be longer films but more serials like its success *What Happened to Mary?* At a time when multiple-reel distribution alliances were just starting to form, creating national feature distribution systems, Selig and Kalem were predicting in trade papers that the trend towards making longer films would end with films of two or three reels. Whether this prediction was for show or whether it was in fact their calculation, these manufacturers generally continued to hold film lengths at the two- or three-reel level while others in the industry moved to and stabilized at five- and six-reel lengths.[59]

This policy of discord and indecision regarding the multiple-reel film evoked a predictable response: some licensed manufacturers quietly began to dissociate themselves from General Film within a year of the forming of the Paramount and World alliances. In April 1915 Vitagraph, Lubin, Selig and Essanay announced a new distribution combination called V-L-S-E, which would distribute the multiple-reelers for these manufacturers. General Film, however, would continue to distribute their regular product. The ostensible reason for the alliance was that General Film had never handled the longer film satisfactorily: the product did not get 'proper remuneration when thus distributed'. Facing competition with such feature distributors as Paramount and World Film, V-L-S-E advertised an open-booking policy. It condemned its competitors' closed systems which required exhibitors to pay for all of the films regardless of whether or not they wanted the product. In July 1915, Kleine and Edison also organized a multiple-reel distribution firm, Kleine-Edison Feature Film Service. Of the US-based licensed manufacturers, only Biograph (already virtually inactive), Kalem and David Horseley's Ace Films, which had only recently been admitted to General Film, were still without an alternative distribution unit.[60]

Since both the Patents Company and General Film were separate corporations formed by the product manufacturers, neither firm's economic life was bound to the other's. As has been seen, the history of the alliances is one of combination and disintegration as each member calculates what policy will yield optimum profits. The member firms of the Patents Company and General Film did not abandon General Film outright, an action that might have brought further stockholder suits; and, in fact, they sought legal sanction for their alliance. The manufacturers did, however, seek alternatives to a threatened dissolution of their form of alliance which, in the case of feature product, was proving inadequate to the market situation. In fact, one of Kleine's lawyers noted in early 1914 that some Patents manufacturers were already willing to give up the Patents Company and General Film.[61] The period from 1913 to 1915 was one of uncertainty for the licensed manufacturers as they gambled on several strategies, waiting to see which would yield the best results.

The End of the Patents Alliance

In October 1915, ten months after the hearings concluded in the antitrust case, the district judge announced his decision. He agreed with the government that the Patents Company *et al.* had violated the Sherman Act, and he ordered the combination, but not the firms, dissolved. In explaining his decision, the judge pointed out that the motion picture business was commerce and subject to interstate and business regulation. In addition, patent and antitrust law limited property rights. Moreover, the judge applied the rule of reason. No matter what the defendants' motives, the effects of the combinatory structure had been a restraint of trade. The court directed the Department of Justice (in consultation with the defendants, the preferred stockholders of General Film, and the Greater New York Rental Company) to write a decree. Furthermore, as a stipulation of the recent Clayton Act, any firm that believed the acts of the defendants had hurt its business could sue for treble damages, using the decree as *prima facie* evidence.

Trade paper opinion was that the individual defendants were all liable and that all royalties paid by exhibitors on projectors purchased prior to the formation of the pool, for instance, might be recoverable. It was, of course, clear what effect this would have on the Patents members. The Greater New York Film Rental Company had already filed suit in January 1915 asking

$1,800,000 in damages.[62]

The decree was presented in January 1916. Although it permitted the patent holders to license the use of the patents and to collect royalties, the decree forbade combination through a pool. The decree was stayed because the Patents Company entered an appeal, which it eventually requested dismissed in 1918.

Another legal setback also came in January 1916. The US district court ruled against the Patents Company in the test case on tying arrangements. Arguing that the tying clause was contrary to the Clayton Act, the judge held that a licence notice on patented equipment would not prevent the use of other manufacturers' supplies. The Patents Company appealed. In April 1917, in a key decision on US patent law, the Supreme Court held that the form of the law only allocated the right to restrain the manufacture, use or selling of patented inventions. No other rights were included. Arguing from patent law, the court ruled that the purpose of patent law 'is not to create private fortunes but is to promote the progress of science and the useful arts'. In overruling the Dick case, the landmark decision initiated an era of increasing judicial disapproval of attempts to extend the use of patents beyond the scope of their claims.[63]

Facing the Patents Company and General Film were numerous ancillary cases developing out of the two major ones. Although the Patents Company and General Film defended themselves in these suits and filed appeals in the major cases, several other responses occurred. Even before the antitrust decree's directives in January 1916, General Film reorganized its business practices. Having already eliminated a form of block booking, General Film abolished in November 1915 the 'old "standing order" plan' although it would book in small blocks of five or six reels. It also reduced the number of offerings, allowing manufacturers to expend more money on 'good plays' and 'well-known actors and better directors'. General Film's new policies seemed to imitate the successful practices of the feature films: block book and increase negative costs.[64]

An even more significant strategy, however, was the steady abandonment of the troubled combine. In December 1915, Edison announced that it was completely withdrawing from General Film and would only release five-reel films through its feature distribution alliance, Kleine-Edison. Edison seems to have been attempting to move with the industry in its shift to multiple-reelers as well as to cut losses from the General Film fiasco.[65]

This was not lost on General Film stockholders. In June 1916, several stockholders requested a receiver for General Film, charging that the defendant manufacturers had eliminated feature films from the company to its detriment. Indeed, V-L-S-E and Kleine-Edison had formed after the antitrust hearings, although they were in tune with other industrial developments. After the January 1916 decision, most of the manufacturers steadily left General Film, giving General Film only the less profitable single-reelers to distribute. Finally, General Film went into receivership in April 1919 after the last of the stockholders' suits was decided.[66]

Furthermore, V-L-S-E pursued recent combination practices. In 1915, feature alliances began organizing in a new, more permanent and legal way: they started merging into vertically and horizontally integrated firms. In July 1915, Triangle Film incorporated. Acting as a distributor for its merged producers, Triangle's 'ambitious plans' included leasing showcase theatres. Controlling first run and franchising subsequent run, Triangle was early and aggressive in vertical integration.[67]

In early 1916, the V-L-S-E manufacturers flirted with Paramount over a merger, but that deal fell through. Benjamin Hampton, a vice-president of the prototypical 'big business', the American Tobacco Company, had proposed the merger on the grounds that such a consolidation would 'create efficiency, render better service ... improve quality, and reduce waste'. With American Tobacco Company money to invest, Hampton then engineered Vitagraph's reorganization into Greater Vitagraph, capitalized in May 1916 at $25 million. American Tobacco received four seats on the board of directors, with one going to Hampton. In September 1916 Vitagraph purchased the Lubin, Selig and Essanay interests in V-L-S-E, so that Greater Vitagraph was now vertically integrated with its own nationwide exchange system for feature film distribution. During September, Selig and Essanay signed with Kleine-Edison, forming K-E-S-E, which distributed the features of the four firms, while some of the firms continued to release short subjects through General Film.[68]

Vitagraph's activities from May to September 1916 were noted by its competitors. In May 1916, trade papers reported rumours of a horizontal merger between Triangle, Triangle's subsidiaries, the Lasky Company and Famous Players. It did not go through. Instead, in July 1916, the holding company, Famous Players-Lasky Corporation, was formed and acquired the stock of its predecessors. In October Morosco and Pallas merged as well, as horizontal integration increased the size of Famous Players-Lasky. In December the firm vertically integrated, adding the assets of its distributor, Paramount, for a new capital value of $22,500,000.[69]

All of these mergers were instances of a major structural change in the film industry. Such permanent combinations were symptomatic of the transition to monopoly capitalism. Thus, both Vitagraph, once a licensed manufacturer, and Famous Players-Lasky, once distributing with the Patents Company approval but also deriving from the independent faction, were early industry leaders in using organizational structure and size as a wedge to dominate the industry.

Conclusions

The implications of this analysis to US film history in general are to suggest that the strategies of the Patent members and independents were not dissimilar. Differences in notions of how to compete through product (e.g. stars and multiple-reel films) cannot be linked in any systematic way to the 'monopolists' versus the 'independents'. Licensed and unlicensed firms that stayed with short films eventually were dominated by those companies from both groups that moved to feature film-making *and to vertical and horizontal integration*. In addition, contradictions between sites of legal decision-making allowed firms to continue to operate while litigation delayed the closing of their business. In fact, exploiting such gaps among the form and places of law became a business practice (e.g. the independents' manoeuvres against the patent infringement suits; the Patents Company's institution of the test case on tying arrangements). Furthermore, production profits were linked to distribution access as early as 1907: firms needed distribution alliances in order to organize the industry efficiently and to return better profits. Finally, expansion into foreign markets came as early as 1911, and both groups were involved.

The end of the Patents alliance, then, was a complex event, better understood when the implications and use of the law, the various forms of combination, and the responses to new technologies (stars, feature films) are considered. While the federal government's antitrust suit might have had some effect in encouraging independents to fight 'the trust', it was only one factor and needs consideration in the context of the other legal battles also occurring. Although the innovation of new technology affected General Film, it appears that licensed manufacturers abandoned that combination in favour of other distribution alliances. Thus, while General Film 'died', the histories of the licensed manufacturers take various turns in the rest of the decade. Nor did feature film-making mark the demise of monopolistic tendencies; companies merely found new, legal ways to combine in the move towards monopoly capital. Only the participants and combinations changed.

In reality, while the Patents pool lost its hope for a monopoly, its disintegration came from competition (General Film was allowed to remain a short film distributor), from litigation (the court ruled that form of combination illegal) and from economic causes (members sought more profitable alliances). In the case of individual Patents pool members, some firms responded better than others. Faced with damage suits and the obvious shift to feature films, some firms cut their losses and let the corporate entities cease active production. This did not mean that former stockholders necessarily retired with their capital, although many did. William Selig, for example, continued in independent production until 1923. Some firms tried to compete in the market place by continuing to produce the shorter product which was still used to fill out theatre programmes. But shorter films never reaped the return that features did. Other firms moved to new business practices. Vitagraph led the industry when it reorganized, increased capital, and vertically integrated. Vitagraph remained active longer than any other former Patents pool firm. In 1925 Warner Bros purchased it during Warner's expansion activities. Thus, the end of the Patents alliance was a response to changing property law, to changing technology and, most importantly to changing practices in the burgeoning tactic of combination.

Notes

1. This essay is a shortened and revised version of an article published in *Cinema Journal*, vol. 23 no. 2, Winter 1983. The theoretical models are outlined there as well as important historical context. I would like to thank Tino Balio for his help and comments.
2. Motion Picture Patents Co. (hereafter MPPC), 'Memorandum for the Motion Picture

Patents Company and the General Film Company concerning the investigation of their business by the Department of Justice', submitted by M. B. Phillipp and Francis T. Homer, 18 May 1912, TS (New York: Museum of Modern Art).

3. Floyd Vaughan, *Economics of our Patents System* (New York: The Macmillan Company, 1925), pp.16–23; Alex Groner, *The American Heritage History of American Business and Industry* (New York: American Heritage Publishing Co., 1972), p. 97; Harry N. Scheiber, Harold G. Vatter and Harold Underwood Faulkner, *American Economic History*, 9th rev. edn. (New York: Harper & Row, 1976), p.162.
4. MPPC, 'Memorandum', p. 7; Charles Musser, 'The early cinema of Edwin Porter', *Cinema Journal*, vol. 19 no. 1, Fall 1979, pp. 12–13, 20–1; Ralph Cassady, Jr, 'Monopoly in motion picture production and distribution: 1908–1915', *Southern California Law Review*, vol. 32 no. 4, Summer 1959, p. 25n.
5. MPPC, 'Memorandum', pp.7–8.
6. Ibid., pp. 8–10.
7. Ibid.
8. Ibid., pp. 16–17.
9. Ibid., pp. 13–16.
10. Ibid., p. 9.
11. According to one historian, the Armour meat-packing plant financed Selig Polyscope's defence in one appeal. The Armour firm exchanged its support for public relations films that countered attacks on Armour's business practices. While the Selig defence was eventually unsuccessful, Selig stayed in operation during the litigation period. Kalton C. Lahue, *Motion Picture Pioneer: The Selig Polyscope Company* (Cranbury: A. S. Barnes & Co., 1973), pp. 12–13.
12. Cassady concludes: 'While the decisions were far from clear-cut evaluations of the strength of Edison's patent rights, the early decisions [1897–1907] were favourable enough to attract most of the manufacturers, distributors, and exhibitors into the Edison camp' ('Monopoly', p. 25).
13. MPPC, 'Memorandum', p. 12; Cassady, 'Monopoly', p. 25; George Kleine Papers, TS, Box 33 (Washington, DC: Library of Congress Manuscript Division).
14. Kleine Papers, TS, Box 33.
15. Cassady, 'Monopoly', pp. 25–6.
16. MPPC, 'Memorandum', pp. 2–3.
17. Janet Staiger and Douglas Gomery, 'The history of world cinema: models for economic analysis', *Film Reader*, no. 4, 1979, pp. 35–44. I would like to thank Douglas Gomery for his help in general theory.
18. In a 1902 case, six manufacturers organized the National Harrow Company of New York, assigned eighty-five patents to it, and received individual, pre-arranged licences to manufacture equipment. Then National Harrow charged one of the manufacturer/licensees, Bement, with failure to meet the licence's conditions. Bement responded that the contract was null and void because the pool was a combination that illegally restrained trade. The US Supreme Court ruled in favour of National Harrow and the patent pool, arguing, 'the general rule is absolute freedom in the use or sale of patent rights under the patent laws of the United States. The very object of these laws is monopoly.... The fact that the conditions in the contract keep up the monopoly or fix prices does not render them illegal.' (MPPC. 'Memorandum', 17; Vaughan, *Economics* pp. 36–9)
19. Vaughan, *Economics*, pp. 52–8, 106–8; Cassady, 'Monopoly', pp. 27–37; MPPC, 'Memorandum'.
20. Price, Waterhouse & Company, *Memorandum on Moving Picture Accounts* (New York: Price, Waterhouse & Company, 1916), p. 17; Lahue, *Motion Picture Pioneer*. p. 13; Benjamin Hampton, *History of the American Film Industry* (New York: Dover Publications, Inc., 1970 [1931]), p. 96.
21. Among other problems, some exchanges failed to organize their territories well, which sometimes resulted in competing theatres simultaneously having the same films. Poorly organized exchanges also hampered effective advertising: with no assurance of a film's availability, exhibitors could not capitalize on advance advertising. Finally, the Patents Company could not easily audit the exchanges' activities. Some exchanges were

negligent in collecting royalties, and under-the-counter rentals were difficult to detect.

22. MPPC, 'Memorandum', pp. 42–6, 56–9.
23. Cassady, 'Monopoly', pp. 41–4.
24. Ibid., pp. 44–9; MPPC, 'Memorandum', pp. 56–9.
25. Cassady, 'Monopoly', p. 49; 'The independent movement,' NKL, vol. 1 no. 1, February 1909, pp. 39–40.
26. 'The independent movement', NKL, vol. 1 no. 1, February 1909, pp. 39–40. Cassady notes a Patents Company versus independents lobbying effort over US tariff duties on imported raw and finished film; the independents succeeded in having the duty lowered ('Monopoly', p. 50n).
27. Jeanne Thomas Allen, 'The image of big business and theater, vaudeville and film competition', Athens, Ohio, 1980 Ohio University Film Conference, 30 April–4 May 1980.
28. Laurence F. Cook, 'Convention of the independent alliance', NKL, vol. 2 no. 4, October 1909, pp. 105–10.
29. 'Motion Picture Distributing and Sales Co.', *Motion Picture News* (hereafter MPNews), vol. 4 no. 15, 15 April 1911, pp. 25–6; Cassady, 'Monopoly', pp. 53–4.
30. 'The open market', MPW, vol. 8 no. 8, 25 February 1911, p. 403; see also John M. Bradlet, 'Exhibitors' meeting at Columbus, Ohio – national league proposed', MPW, vol. 8 no. 20, 20 May 1911, p.1124; 'Motion Picture Distributing and Sales Co.', MPNews, vol. 4 no. 15, 15 April 1911, pp. 25–6; Cassady, 'Monopoly', pp. 53–4; 'The Goat Man', 'On the outside looking in', NKL, vol. 6 no. 5, November 1911, pp. 237–8; Epes Winthrop Sargent, 'The new Townsend bill', MPW, vol. 12 no. 2, 13 April 1912, p. 125.
31. 'Motion Picture Distributing and Sales Co.', MPNews, vol.4 no. 15, 15 April 1911, p.26; Cassady, 'Monopoly', pp. 53–4.
32. 'Motion Picture Distributing and Sales Co.', MPNews, vol. 4 no. 15, 15 April 1911, p. 26.
33. Ibid.
34. Staiger and Gomery, 'History', p. 38.
35. 'Mr. Dyer returns and discusses the moving picture situation', *The Edison Kinetogram*, vol. 1 no. 6, 15 October 1909, p. 11; 'Spectator', 'Spectator's comments', *New York Dramatic Mirror* (hereafter NYDM), vol. 65 no. 1677, 8 February 1911, p. 28; 'Casting the horoscope', MPW, vol. 8 no. 11, 13 May 1911, pp. 1053–4; 'American films abroad', MPW, vol. 10 no. 5, 4 November 1911, p. 357; 'Extraordinary official report on the influence of cinematography', MPW, vol. 14 no. 6, 9 November 1912, p. 532; J. J. Robinson, 'From the other side of the world', MPW, vol. 8 no. 5, 4 February 1911, pp. 237–8; 'Picture trade in other lands', MPW, vol. 9 no. 9, 9 September 1911, p. 703.
36. 'Spectator', 'Spectator's Comments', NYDM, vol. 65 no. 1691, 17 May 1911, p. 28.
37. Kalton C. Lahue, *Dreams for Sale: The Rise and Fall of the Triangle Film Corporation* (South Brunswick and New York: A. S. Barnes & Company, 1971), p. 20; 'H. E. Aitken', *Reel Life*, vol. 3 no. 16, 14 March 1914, pp. 17–18; 'Majestic Leaves Sales Company', NYDM, vol. 67 no. 1736, 27 March 1912, p. 25.
38. 'Financing the moving picture/Wall Street's latest move', *Reel Life*, vol. 3 no. 22, 14 February 1914, p. 34; 'Mutual Film Corporation', MPW, vol. 12 no. 1, 6 April 1912, p. 34; ad, Film Supply Company of America, MPNews, vol. 5 no. 20, 18 May 1912, p. 48; 'Independent factions organize', MPW, vol. 12 no. 9, 1 June 1912, pp. 807–8; James S. McQuade, 'Break in the ranks of the Sales Company', MPW, vol. 12 no. 8, 25 May 1912, p. 707.
39. 'Independent factions organize', MPW, vol. 12 no. 9, 1 June 1912, pp. 807–8; Fred F. Balshofer and Arthur C. Miller, *One Reel a Week* (Berkeley: University of California Press, 1967), pp. 83–90; 'Another "independent" split', MPW, vol. 13, no. 2, 13 July 1912, p. 129; 'Mutual gets Empire film exchanges', MPW, vol.13 no. 6, 10 August 1912, p. 1280; 'Doings in Los Angeles', MPW, vol. 13 no. 3, 20 July 1912, p. 235; 'Doings in Los Angeles', MPW, vol. 13 no. 4, 27 July 1912, p. 335; 'Bison plant attached', MPW, vol. 13, no. 5, 10 August 1912, p. 533.
40. Alfred H. Saunders, 'The film industry in America today', MPNews, vol. 7 no. 15, 12 April 1913, p. 10.

41. Ad, Motion Picture Distributing & Sales Co., MPW, vol. 9 no. 4, 5 August 1911, p.304; William Horsley, 'From pigs to pictures', Part II, *International Photographer*, vol. 6 no. 3, April 1934, p. 2; Janet Staiger, 'The director-unit system', in David Bordwell, Janet Staiger and Kristin Thompson, *The Classical Hollywood Cinema: Film Style and Mode of Production to 1960* (London: Routledge & Kegan Paul, 1985), pp. 122–3.
42. *Motion Picture Patents Co.* v. *Independent Moving Picture Company*, 200 Fed. 441 (2nd Circ. 1912); 'Important patent decision', MPW, vol. 11 no. 7, 17 February 1912, p. 560; 'Latham loop patent adjudicated', MPW, vol. 13 no. 8, 24 August 1912, p. 747; Francis Jenkins, 'Trust vs. independents', MPNews, vol. 4 no. 4, 28 January 1911, pp. 6–8; 'Edison film patent declared void', MPW, vol. 14 no. 11, 14 December 1912, p. 1060.
43. *MPPC* v. *Ullman et al.*, 186 Fed Rep. 174 (Circuit Court, S. D. New York, 27 September 1910); John L. Lott and Roger Shale, *Federal Anti-Trust Decisions, 1890–1917* (Washington, DC: Government Printing Office, 1917), vol. IV, pp. 46–7.
44. Note that at the start of the case, Fox was in the licensed camp. Anthony Slide, *Early American Cinema* (New York: A. S. Barnes & Co., 1970), p. 84; '*United States* vs. *Motion Picture Patents Company*', MPW, vol. 15 no. 11, 15 March 1913, pp. 1082–3; Cassady, 'Monopoly', pp. 46–7; Vaughan, *Economics*, p. 55; 'Factors and comments', MPW, vol. 11 no. 6, 10 February 1912, pp. 464, 470; 'Fox combination granted injunction', NYDM, vol. 68 no. 1753, 24 July 1912, p. 25; 'Spectator', 'Spectator's comments', NYDM, vol. 68 no. 1754, 31 July 1912, p. 24; 'Motion Picture Patents Co. wins', MPW, vol. 15 no. 7, 15 February 1913, p.685; 'Doings in Los Angeles', MPW, vol. 13 no. 2, 13 July 1912, p. 133; 'Fox starts feature exchange', MPW, vol. 19 no. 2, 10 January 1914, p. 182; 'Box office attractions company', MPW, vol. 21 no. 2, 11 July 1914, pp. 260–1.
45. Staiger, 'Standardization and differentiation', in Bordwell, Staiger and Thompson, *The Classical Hollywood Cinema*, pp. 101–2; Janet Staiger, 'Seeing stars', *The Velvet Light Trap*, no. 20, 1983, pp. 10–14.
46. 'Spectator', 'Spectator's comments', NYDM, vol. 68 no. 1754, 31 July 1912, p. 24; 'Spectator', 'Spectator's comments', NYDM, vol. 68 no. 1756, 14 August 1912, p. 21; Price Waterhouse, 'Memorandum', pp. 7–8; Frederick James Smith, 'The evolution of the motion picture, IX: from the standpoint of the exhibitor', NYDM, vol. 70 no. 1809, 20 August 1913, p. 27; 'The Open Market', MPW, vol. 8 no. 8, 25 February 1911, p. 403.
47. Cassady, 'Monopoly', pp. 57–9; Hampton, *History*, p. 118.
48. 'Feature film manufacturers organise', MPNews, vol. 6 no. 22, 30 November 1912, p. 10; 'State of Missouri sues Mutual', MPW, vol. 19 no. 8, 21 February 1914, p. 929.
49. 'Warners' Features, Inc.', MPW, vol. 21 no. 2, 11 July 1914, p. 262; Cassady, 'Monopoly', pp. 60–2; 'Famous players anniversary', MPW, vol. 21 no. 10, 5 September 1914, p.1384; William Henry Irwin, *The House That Shadows Built* (Garden City, New York: Doubleday, Doran & Company, 1928), pp. 28–91; Hampton, *History*, pp. 99, 118–20; 'Feature producers affiliate', MPW, vol. 20 no. 9, 30 May 1914, p. 1268; W. Stephen Bush, 'New blood in new programs', MPW, vol. 20 no. 10, 6 June 1914, p. 1394; 'Paramount program', MPW, vol. 22 no. 3, 17 October 1914, p. 345; 'Shuberts and world film in big deal', MPW, vol. 20 no. 12, 20 June 1914, p. 1700; Lahue, *Dreams*, p.89; 'World film reorganizes', MPW, vol. 27 no. 6, 12 February 1916, p.931.
50. 'Kinematography in the United States', MPW, vol. 21 no. 2, 14 July 1914, pp. 175–80; W. Stephen Bush, 'The regular program', MPW, vol. 21 no. 10, 5 September 1914, p. 1345.
51. Cassady, 'Monopoly', p.64; 'Suit against the Patents Company', MPW, vol. 13 no. 9, 31 August 1912, p. 868; 'Hearings in government's suit', MPW, vol. 15 no. 5, 1 February 1913, p.450; 'United States vs. Motion Picture Patents Co.', MPW, vol. 22 no. 13, 26 December 1914, p. 1815.
52. 'Suit against the Patents Company', MPW, vol. 13 no. 9, 31 August 1912, p. 868.
53. Requesting a temporary injunction, Rowland's suit sought to prevent the distribution of a dividend to the common stockholders (the owners of the manufacturing firms) and requested a return of earlier distributions totalling over $844,000; 'General Film

Company enjoined', MPW, vol. 15 no. 8, 22 February 1913, p.793; 'Decision reserved', MPW, vol.15 no. 10, 8 March 1913, p. 981.

54. 'United States vs. Motion Picture Patents Co.', MPW, 22 no. 13, 26 December 1914, pp. 1816–17.
55. *Motion Picture Patents Co.* v. *Universal Film Mfg. Co.*, 243 US 502, 11 (9 April 1917).
56. US Patents Committee, House, 'Revision of Patent Laws, Report of Committee on House R. 15989', 63rd Cong., 2nd sess. (Washington, DC: Government Printing Office, 1914), 3; Floyd L. Vaughan, *The United States Patent System: Legal and Economic Conflicts in American Patent History* (Norman, Oklahoma: University of Oklahoma Press, 1956), pp. 168–95; 'Facts and comments', MPW, vol. 11 no. 13, 30 March 1912, p. 114; Scheiber *et al., American Economics*, p. 315.
57. General Film permitted licensed theatres to show *Dante's Inferno* (1911) and *Queen Elizabeth* (1912). When the Selig three-reeler *The Coming of Christ* (1912) went on the market, General Film provided extensive advertising and music. Kleine financed his own feature-film distribution system in 1913 and road-showed *Quo Vadis* (1913). In April 1914, Selig's *The Spoilers* (nine reels) opened at the new Strand Theater, an early picture palace. 'Dante's Inferno', MPW, vol. 9 no. 6, 19 August 1911, p. 459; 'Facts and comments', MPW, vol. 9 no. 12, 30 September 1911, p. 948; Hampton, *History*, p. 107; James S. McQuade, 'The coming of Columbus', MPW, vol. 13, September 1912, pp. 407–10; Kleine Paper, TS, Box 26.
58. Kleine Papers, TS, Box 26; 'General Film exclusive service', MPW, vol. 8 no. 2, 11 October 1913, p. 139; 'Report on General Film exclusive service', MPW, vol. 18 no. 4, 25 October 1913, p. 385; 'Change in General Film service', MPW, vol. 18 no. 11, 13 December 1913, p. 1266.
59. Hampton, *History*, pp. 98–9; 'Edison touches popular chord', MPW, vol. 19 no. 1, 3 January 1914, pp. 28–9; 'Pathe opens exchanges', MPW, vol. 20 no. 7, 16 May 1914, p. 975; William N. Selig, 'Present day trend in film lengths', MPW, vol. 21 no. 2, 11 July 1914, pp. 181–2; 'Kalem finds business excellent', MPW, vol. 21 no. 8, 22 August 1914, p. 1084.
60. 'New feature combination', MPW, vol. 24 no. 1, 3 April 1915, p. 44; 'Big feature exchange launched', MPW, vol. 24 no. 3, 17 April 1915, p. 366; 'Ouch!', *V-L-S-E Pals*, vol. 4 no. 16, 15 April 1916, p. 1; 'William N. Selig perfects strong organization', MPNews, vol. 12 no. 4, 31 July 1915, p. 55; 'Kleine-Edison merger formed', MPW, vol. 25 no. 4, 24 July 1915, p.626; 'Horsley in licensed group', MPW, vol. 22 no. 1, 3 October 1914, p. 71.
61. Kleine Papers, Letter from Henry Melville to Kleine, 12 March 1914, TS, Box 37.
62. *United States* v. *Motion Picture Patents Co.*, 225 Fed. Rep. 800–11 (1 October 1915); W. Stephen Bush, 'Uncle Sam orders dissolution of Motion Picture Patents Co. and others', MPW, vol. 26 no. 3, 16 October 1915, pp. 414–16; W. Stephen Bush, 'The Federal decision', MPW, vol. 26 no. 3, 16 October 1915, p. 413; Vaughan, *Economics*, pp. 52–8; 'Sues for $1,800,000 damages', MPW, vol. 23 no. 2, 9 January 1915, p. 206; 'Government enjoins Patents Company', MPW, vol. 27 no. 5, 5 February 1916, p. 753; Cassady, 'Monopoly', pp. 64–6; Kleine Papers, Annual Report on Litigation, 25 June 1918, TS, Box 36.
63. 'Victory for Universal', MPW, vol. 27 no. 2, 8 January 1916, p. 250; 235 Fed. 398 (2nd Circuit, 1916); 243 US 502, 510–11, 9 April 1917; Vaughan, *United States*, pp. 168–80.
64. 'The General Film Company reorganized', MPW, vol. 26 no. 8, 20 November 1915, p. 1458; 'Co-operation keynote of General Film', MPW, vol. 26 no. 9, 27 November 1915, p. 1635; 'Unit program basis of General Film's new policy', MP News, vol. 12 no. 22, 4 December 1915, p. 45; 'Kalem announces plans', MPW, vol. 26 no. 10, 4 December 1915, p. 1804; 'General Film policy', MPW, vol. 26 no. 10, 4 December 1915, p. 1806.
65. 'Edison leaves General Film program', MPW, vol. 26 no. 13, 25 December 1915, p.2333; 'Edison five reel masterfeatures now available at the rate of two per month through the Kleine-Edison Features Service', *The Edison Kinetogram*, vol. 12 no. 7, 1 January 1916, p. 3.
66. 'Asks receiver for General Film', MPW, vol. 28 no. 13, 24 June 1916, p. 2211; Kleine Papers, TS, Boxes 24, 37.

67. Lahue, *Dreams*, pp. 48–53, 78; 'Triangle Film Incorporated', MPW, vol 25 no. 5, 31 July 1915, p. 824.
68. Hampton, *History*, p. 150; 'Millions for Vitagraph', MPW, vol. 28 no. 8, 20 May 1916, pp. 1305–6; Lahue, *Dreams*, p. 109; 'New and greater Vitagraph Company of America succeeds V-L-S-E Inc.', *V-L-S-E Pals*, vol. 5 no. 5, 9 September 1916, p. 3; 'Greater Vitagraph absorbs V-L-S-E Organization', MPW, vol. 26 no. 11, 16 September 1916, p.1808; 'Kleine, Edison, Selig and Essanay in combination', MPW, vol. 26 no. 11, 16 September 1916, p. 1807; Kleine Papers, TS, Boxes 16, 26.
69. 'Merger of several manufacturers and distributors in formation', *The Triangle*, vol. 2 no. 3, 6 May 1916, p. 1; Hampton, *History*, pp. 149–59; Lahue, *Dreams*, p. 108; 'Two large feature companies combine', MPW, vol. 29 no. 3, 15 July 1916, p. 434; 'Another combination of picture companies', MPW, vol. 30 no. 3, 21 October 1916, p. 376; Famous Players-Lasky Corporation, *The Story of Famous Players-Lasky* Corporation (New York: Famous Players-Lasky, 1919), p. 65.

In the Beginning Was the Word:
Six Pre-Griffith Motion Picture Scenarios

PATRICK G. LOUGHNEY

There are many unquestioned assumptions about the origins of the American narrative film, but the most interesting and durable of these is the idea that its development was free of meaningful influence from popular entertainment forms in vogue at the end of the 19th century. A direct outgrowth of this is the belief that dramatic and comic motion pictures, of the period 1900 to 1915, were universally produced, with little or no prior planning, using story ideas improvised to accommodate available actors, locations and props.

The reasons for the persistence of this view are many. Most obvious is the scarcity of non-film records that document the first motion picture companies. While, at the opposite extreme, is the mountainous accumulation of conflicting 'history' that has been left to us by the first generations of participants in the industry. But most important, to those who take a scholarly interest, is the added factor of the prevailing academic adherence to an investigative methodology that relies primarily on historical proofs found exclusively in the internal or 'cinematographic' evidence of early films.

Recent years have produced some developments beyond this narrow methodological approach. But the fact remains that few important efforts have been made to place the general phenomenon of motion pictures within the spectrum of turn-of-the century American popular entertainment.[1] And equally important, no extended writings have appeared which trace the relationship of well-known early narrative films to their *direct* antecedents in works of popular fiction, or other entertainments that first achieved popularity on dramatic and variety stages, in vaudeville and burlesque houses, and the many lesser forms of middle-class entertainment that have passed from the American scene.

One of the best ways to understand the development of the American narrative film prior to 1915 is to study the history of the American stage for the same period. To be more precise, it lies in knowing the 'theatrical writing' forms of the *playscript* and *scenario* that evolved as *the* organizational elements essential to the production of all performing media decades before the advent of motion pictures.[2] Their importance cannot be overestimated for it is to these already established written forms that early film-makers turned as they developed production methods for narrative films longer than one or two minutes. It is also important to realize that they also provided, by their ubiquitous existence, the *main* source for the 'content' of narrative motion pictures until a large new group of writers could be trained for the industry. More than 60,000 of these 'non-film' scripts and scenarios were copyrighted in the United States between the years

1870 and 1916 and many, legally or otherwise, found their way on to the screen in the years after 1900.[3]

It is disconcerting, perhaps, to think that the Edison and Biograph companies may have been using rudimentary screenplays as early as 1902. Or to discover that the simple chase comedies of 1904, which we now consider to have been completely improvisational, were, in fact, based on written forms quite similar to present-day motion picture source documents. These suggestions are not as far-fetched as they seem, especially if one considers a few of the many historiographic references that cite the early appearance of direct written sources for individual motion pictures.

Terry Ramsaye, in *A Million and One Nights*, reports that Edwin Porter made *The Great Train Robbery* from a scenario he wrote himself.[4] He also records that one of the McCutcheons at Biograph (he does not say which) first created written versions of *Personal* and *The Moonshiners* that were subsequently filmed during June and July of 1904.[5] An independent corroboration of this statement was recorded by Nicholas Vardac in a 1941 interview with Frank J. Marion, who worked at Biograph as a director and scenario writer through 1906. It was Marion's claim that *Personal* was made by Biograph from that company's 'earliest photoplay' and that its success inspired many chase comedies of a similar type.[6]

It should be noted, however, that Ramsaye's historical continuity is not without its flaws. After discussing McCutcheon's early work at Biograph he goes on to mention Kalem's copyright-infringing treatment of *Ben Hur* (1907), and the fact that it was made from a 'working synopsis' written earlier by Gene Gauntier.[7] Later, however, in a summary statement on the first appearance of motion picture scenarios, he writes that 'the technique of scenario writing began to evolve parallel to Griffith's development of pictorial narration', and that Frank Woods was 'among the first and most famous' of scenario writers.[8] He also adds that George Terwilliger, a colleague of Woods at the *Dramatic Mirror*, was among the first who recognized the coming craze in 1908.[9]

Benjamin Hampton, in his *History of the American Film Industry*, remembered the facts of a somewhat contradictory version. He declares that Henry Marvin of Biograph was the first 'to organize the writing of scenarios as a separate branch of production'.[10] He further states that this took place 'early in *1900*', and that newspaperman Roy McCardell soon began making $200 a week as a regular employee of Biograph.[11] McCardell's success was so newsworthy, according to Hampton, that 'scribes of the press ... buzzed about the headquarters of film makers like flies around sugar barrels, and scenario writing soon became an occupation as definite as reporting'.[12]

It is also important to note that several first-hand sources report that Griffith's first contact with the film industry was his attempted sale of a scenario to Edwin Porter. The scenario was not purchased but Griffith was hired for an acting part in *Rescued from an Eagle's Nest* (1907) and, shortly thereafter, began his career at Biograph as an actor *and* scenario writer. Billy Bitzer recalled that it was 'Lee Dougherty, *the Biograph scenario writer*. . . to whom Griffith really owed the chance to become a director'.[13] (It is interesting to remember, in this context, that Dougherty started working for Biograph in 1896. Though it is unclear when he began writing scenarios, it seems safe to assume that he was regularly employed in this capacity before the arrival of Griffith.) Bitzer, in the same source, also makes references to scenario writing by other members of the Biograph Company, such as Mary Pickford and Mack Sennett.

The earliest known specimens of the motion picture scenario/screenplay exist in the archives of the US Copyright Office, in the Library of Congress. These documents were found during a general search for copyright records of motion picture companies that registered works during the years 1893 to 1916. They were registered separately from the thousands of Paper Prints (legally defined as 'photographs') deposited during these years and were specifically categorized as 'dramatic compositions' in the copyright records. Only a few have been positively identified, but they are fascinating evidence of the complex origins of the narrative film.

The following is a title list of those documents including, for the Biograph materials, known production information preserved in the Biograph Camera Register, at the Museum of Modern Art.[14]

The Suburbanite
Filmed in Asbury Park, NJ, and the studio on 21 and 22 October 1904, by A. E. Weed. Biograph production no. 2975. Total footage exposed – 734 feet. 'Corrected length' – 690 feet.[15] Paper Print copyrighted 11 November 1904.[16] Copyrighted as a Dramatic Composition, on 25 November 1904, by the American Mutoscope and Biograph Company. Author: Frank J. Marion. Document actually received for registration was a copy of the Biograph advertising bulletin for the film.

The Chicken Thief
Filmed in Asbury Park, NJ, and the studio on 16 and 26 November 1904, by Billy Bitzer. Biograph production no. 2977. Total footage exposed – 786¾ feet. 'Corrected length' – 763½ feet. Paper Print not copyrighted despite claim printed in advertising bulletin no. 39, 27 December 1904.[17] Copyrighted as a Dramatic Composition on 17 December 1904, by the American Mutoscope and Biograph Company. Authors: Frank J. Marion and Wallace McCutcheon.

Tom, Tom, the Piper's Son
Filmed in the studio on 12 February 1905 by Billy Bitzer. Biograph production no. 2987. Total footage exposed – 850 feet. 'Corrected length' – 506 feet. Paper Print copyrighted 9 March 1905. Copyrighted as a Dramatic Composition on 6 March 1905 by the American Mutoscope and Biograph Company. Authors: Frank J. Marion and Wallace McCutcheon. Copyright record bears the explanatory notation 'Scenario'.

The Nihilists
Filmed in Grantwood, NJ, and the studio on 28 February 1905 by Armitage. Biograph production no. 2992. Total footage exposed – not listed. 'Corrected length' – 850 feet. Paper Print copyrighted on 28 March 1905. Copyrighted as a Dramatic Composition on 20 March 1905 by the American Mutoscope and Biograph Company. Authors: Frank J. Marion and Wallace McCutcheon. Copyright record bears the explanatory notation 'Scenario'.

Wanted, a Dog
Filmed in Deal Beach, NJ, and the studio on 22 and 28 March 1905, by Armitage and McCutcheon. Biograph production no. 2997. Total footage exposed – 786¾ feet. 'Corrected length' – 693¾ feet. Paper Print copyrighted on 7 April 1905. Copyrighted as a Dramatic Composition on 12 April 1905 by the American Mutoscope and Biograph Company. Authors: Frank J. Marion and Wallace McCutcheon.

The Wedding
Filmed in Brick Church, NJ, and the studio on 3, 4 and 5 May 1905, by Billy Bitzer. Biograph production no. 3005. Total footage exposed – 524¼ ft. 'Corrected length' – 482¼ feet. Paper Print copyrighted on 19 May 1905. Copyrighted as a Dramatic Composition on 20 May 1905 by the American Mutoscope and Biograph Company. Authors: Frank J. Marion and Wallace McCutcheon.

The Serenade
'A Dramatic Composition in Four Scenes by W. N. Selig, 43 Peck Court, Chicago, Ill.' Copyrighted as a Dramatic Composition on 1 May 1905 by William N. Selig. No known print of this film survives. Page two of the document bears the following statement: 'Caution – Stage representation, Moving Pictures, etc. positively prohibited, without the written consent of the author'.

Six of the documents were copyrighted by the Biograph Company between November 1904 and May 1905, and another was registered by W. N. Selig, of Chicago, on 1 May 1905. All are for films that have been considered, until now, as unworthy of special notice. The authenticity of the Biograph materials is confirmed in several sources. First, the legal notice of copyright (the right to display the '©' mark in connection with the work) was issued to the American Mutoscope and Biograph Company, not the authors. This means that Biograph paid the 50 cent fee for registering the works on behalf of the acknowledged authors, Frank Marion and Wallace McCutcheon. That fact is confirmed on the title pages of the typewritten manuscripts that were received at the time of registration. Second, the corresponding Biograph advertising bulletins, issued in advance of the release of each title, specifically state that those films had been copyrighted 'both as a Picture and as a Play'.[18]

Proof of the direct relationship of these written materials to the films of the same title – other than the internal evidence of the extreme similarity of their narrative structures – has been lacking. That is, until the recent discovery of original correspondence between the Register of Copyrights and the law firm retained by Biograph, concerning the nature of *The Suburbanite,* the first of the scenarios to be copyrighted as dramatic compositions.

The exchange of letters was initiated by the Copyright Office because it did not understand the reason for Biograph's wanting to identify Marion's first work as a 'dramatic composition'. The confusion arose because the document registered was simply a copy of the regular Biograph bulletin for that title. Wrote the Registrar,

> the article sent consists of a four-page folder describing a series of moving pictures. The term 'dramatic composition' as used in the copyright law has the originary meaning of that term, that is, a play consisting of dialogue and action. Your article is apparently not a dramatic composition as the term is used in the law, and it would not be permissible to make entry as a dramatic composition.

The reply, written by Drury B. Cooper of the firm of Kerr, Page and Cooper, on behalf of American Mutoscope and Biograph, contains a clear statement of the nature of the documents registered, and a defence of their claim for the registration of the work as a dramatic composition.

> As we understand, your position is that the term 'dramatic composition' as used in the copyright law means a play consisting of dialogue and action, and that the composition in question is not dramatic in that it has no dialogue. [Legal citation follows.]
>
> Referring to the composition in question, it is obviously within the definition of this case. It is a representation or exhibition consisting of 7 scenes and 16 characters. The action is to depict the story described in the composition itself. It is the sole purpose of the composition that this narrative or story shall be represented dramatically by action, posture and gesture. [Legal citation follows.]
>
> Something of a novelty may be presented by the fact that *this particular dramatic composition has been photographed in a series of living pictures,* and is susceptible of being represented thereby. That, however, is true of substantially every drama, or at least of every drama which depends in larger part for its portrayal upon an appeal to the eye than to the ear ... [emphasis mine].[19]

Biograph won its argument with the Copyright Office but no longer submitted copies of their bulletins as documents of registration. Apparently hoping to avoid the confusion they had found with *The Suburbanite,* the company sent in typed manuscript copies of the actual dramatic compositions for the remaining five titles which they copyrighted in this manner.

There is no satisfactory answer, to date, as to why Biograph decided to copyright these particular compositions in two forms. The fact that they seem to boastfully mention the dual registration in the corresponding bulletins might mean that it was part of an effort to promote the narrative quality of their films. It is possible that these scenarios were created as part of a short-lived experiment in co-ordinating the schedules of several different production units. The Camera Register for the time shows that the film lab and studio were being kept quite busy. It is equally possible that the experiment was successful and permanent, but that Biograph simply decided, as a cost saving, to forgo the separate copyrighting of scenarios as unnecessary to the legal protection of their films.

No trace of *The Serenade* is known to this writer other than the document which Selig wrote and copyrighted. It does seem plain, however, from the cautionary statement, that Lubin intended it primarily as a 'screenplay' for a comedy film. This conclusion is reinforced by the fact that the scenario is less than thirteen pages in length, including dialogue and stage directions, but is divided into four full scenes. It is unlikely that any stage representation of this work, even a full vaudeville staging, would include four full scene changes. Especially for settings that call for: (1) garden scene – with balcony projecting from upper part of house; (2) street scene (with only six exchanges of dialogue); (3) exterior wood scene, and artificial lake, covering half of stage (scene contains only three exchanges of dialogue); (4) street scene, same as Scene 2 but with an automobile which arrives and departs in such a way as to be seen disappearing in the distance.[20]

The Serenade seems to have been written from the point of view of a live performance. It is a script with full dialogue and a minimum of stage directions. The bulk of Selig's creative effort was devoted to the one part of the performance (the dialogue) that would not have an effect on viewers of the film. The Biograph scenarios were constructed from an opposite point of view. They include no dialogue and are concerned almost exclusively with set descriptions and character actions. The impression one has after reading them is that they were conceived with a great deal more thought and experimentation than Selig's effort.

The arrangement of information, in the works by Marion and McCutcheon, reflect their logical approach to the problems that lay before them. Each of the scenarios is divided into sections which clearly address different elements of the film production. The first section, on page one of each document, is the 'Cast of Characters'. This is followed by general information for the scene painters and costumers. The next segment gives specific descriptions of the sets required for each scene in the film.

There is also a definite statement of the period of time which the production is meant to represent. *Wanted, a Dog,* for example, is a well-made comedy about the difficulties a young widow encounters while trying to buy a watch dog. The plot covers a complicated sequence of actions but the 'time' statement for that scenario reads, 'The action of the first three scenes occurs on the afternoon of one day, and the action of the remaining nine scenes, during the morning of the following day.'[21] This is an essential piece of information about the production. It defines the chronology of the narrative and provides the necessary conceptual framework in which all the actions are to be performed. The narrative chronologies of the Biograph scenarios vary widely and indicate that complexity of narrative structure was not a principal concern. *Tom, Tom, the Piper's Son* covers the shortest narrative period: 'The action is continuous, taking place at consecutive periods on the afternoon of one day.'[22] The most intricate is *The Nihilists*, in which the actions occur through seven scenes in eleven camera positions, and a time period of more than three months.

The preliminary segments of the scenarios deal exclusively with the sort of pre-production information that would have been essential to anyone charged with preparing for the production of a narrative film. *Tom, Tom, the Piper's Son,* for example, was filmed on Sunday 12 February 1905.[23] It required 'Costumes, Properties, and Scenic Effects of about the time of Shakespeare' for sixteen actors and seven scenes.[24] (About fifty chickens and geese were added to the atmosphere in the final barnyard scene alone.) If the Camera Register is accurate, all of these preparations were assembled and ready for the single day that it took to make the film. Logic suggests that some mechanism of regular co-ordination had to be in place that would provide for the hiring of actors, the construction and painting of flats, the measuring and assignment of costumes, the selection of a camera operator, the lighting of the studio, the rehearsal of the cast, and the completion of a split-reel film in one day. The starting point for that mechanism, regardless of the hierarchy of studio command, had to have been an idea or document capable of effectively co-ordinating the independent activities required in preparation for the completion of even the simplest narrative film in one day. The introductory portions of the Biograph scenarios were created to fill that function.

The remaining parts of the scenarios describe, in minute detail for each scene of each film, *how* the actors, costumes, sets and props were to be used in front of the camera. The following is the text for the first scene of *Tom, Tom, the Piper's Son.*

> Scene 1. At Chatsworth Fair. At the opening of the scene, a typical English country fair of the Shakesperian [sic] period is in full swing. Booths are erected at the back of the stage offering various catch-penny attractions. A female tight rope walker is giving an exhibition of her skill. A buffoon juggler is attracting the crowd with his tricks, and a fakir with a shell and pea game is also bidding for attention. A crowd of rustics wander about amusing themselves with the various attractions of the fair.
>
> Time: Early Afternoon.
>
> The opening scene is laid in a typical old English Fair with a primitive 'midway' in full swing. There is a lady tight rope walker, a clown juggler, a fakir with a shell and pea game, a goose girl, and a great crowd of rustics. Among the latter appears Simple Simon trying to sample the pieman's wares, and at one side, the old blind piper is blowing merrily on his pipe while Tom, his son, is on the watch for pennies. A bumpkin strolls in, leading a small pig by a string. He stops to watch the shell game, over which a fight ensues. The village constable arrests the gambler and there is great excitement. The bumpkin has in the meanwhile handed his pig over to a small boy who also is greatly interested in the turmoil and drops the string. Tom seizes the opportunity, and catching the pig, darts away. The owner sets up a shout, and starts after him, followed by the entire crowd.[25]

The redundant style is characteristic of all of the Biograph scenarios. The action of each scene is always described on two levels. The first provides a general outline of the scene, followed, when necessary, by a specific statement of its 'time' relationship to other scenes. The second is devoted to an extended, more detailed narrative of actions to be portrayed. The first level 'sets' the scene and develops the atmosphere that the secondary characters are to create. The second descriptive level elaborates on that function, then quickly narrows to concentrate on the actions of the principal characters in the scene.

The division of narrative levels probably facilitated scene rehearsals.

It is probable that these portions of the scenario were read aloud to the ensemble of actors to inform them of what the scene was about and to provide them with initial rehearsal directions. The close co-ordination of interior and exterior actions and the complexity of plots, as they appear in the the films, argue strongly for the conclusion that rehearsal activity preceded the filming of every scene.

The future importance of the Biograph and Selig scenarios depends largely on the continuing search for a much wider sample of similar manuscripts, and their interpretative correlation with whatever archival materials already exist. But these few examples, particularly those from Biograph, provide valuable documentary evidence from the first crucial phase of motion picture history – the period when narrative motion pictures overtook the production of all other types of film. The Biograph documents, when analysed in conjunction with the Paper Print Collection and the Biograph Camera Register, reveal extremely important information about that company's first efforts to begin the regular production of split-reel length narrative films. The collation of this information has produced the first solid evidence of the appearance of several important innovations either invented or adopted by that company. For example, through a comparative study of these sources, it can now be determined:

a. when Biograph shifted to the weekly production of narrative films of more than one or two scenes, in a split-reel format of three to five minutes;
b. how, in 1904, Biograph directors were able to maintain visual and narrative 'continuity' between 'interior' scenes, shot in the New York City studio, and 'exterior' scenes filmed as much as a week later, in locations as far as 60 miles away;
c. who was involved in the writing of scenarios in 1904 and 1905, and who may have been the first film directors responsible for the sustained experimental use of scenarios in the making of narrative films.
d. when, in 1904, the practice of filming 'retakes' arose, and when the 'editing' of a 'release version' became a standard practice.

Elaboration of these points (and others) will have to wait for explanation in a longer format but one conclusion is certain. The future of scholarship in early narrative film is tied directly to the need for further documentary evidence of written sources. The many early references to their existence, and the examples presented above, clearly suggest that early film-makers relied on some basic types of theatrical scenario form to give organization to their longer productions. The first examples have been found and the job now is to look for more.

Notes

First published in *Iris* vol. 2 no. 1, 1984.

1. The most notable works are Nicholas Vardac's *Stage to Screen* (Cambridge: Harvard University Press, 1949), and John Fell's *Film and the Narrative Tradition* (1974).

2. The evolution of the terms 'scenario', 'screenplay', 'script', 'photoplay', etc., all demand an extensive study of their own. There is evidence that indicates that some of these words had well-defined meanings – in and out of the motion picture business – much earlier than is often supposed. It is fairly common practice among writers on early film to use all of these words interchangeably, or to give them a meaning which they did not originally have. For example, the principal current meaning of the word *scenario* is an 'outline' or 'synopsis'. Modern writers, when discussing the plots of early films, usually have this meaning in mind when they write of the 'scenario' found in contemporary publications; that is, predominantly in the sense of an outline or synopsis, such as those that abound in early motion picture-related sources (advertising bulletins, newspaper accounts and trade journals), and which are assumed to be derivations of plots and actions taken from complete films.

   Ramsaye, Hampton and other writers of the early period, who comment on the writing of scenarios for motion pictures, use the word with a meaning much closer to 'screenplay' than to 'outline' or 'synopsis'. This is also the sense in which the word was used within the motion picture business until it was replaced by the later, more functional term. A practical definition of the older meaning of 'scenario' is in the sense of a written description of a plot, with or without dialogue, often divided into scenes, and written with the intent of being the direct source of a motion picture.
3. *Dramatic Compositions Copyrighted in the United States, 1870 to 1916*, 2 vols (Washington, DC: Government Printing Office, 1918).
4. Terry Ramsaye, *A Million and One Nights* (London: Frank Cass & Co. Ltd, 1964), pp. 416–22.
5. Ibid., p. 189.
6. Nicholas Vardac, *Stage to Screen* (Cambridge, Mass.: Harvard University Press, 1949), p. 189.
7. Ramsaye, *A Million and One Nights*, p. 512.
8. Ibid., p. 513.
9. Ibid.
10. Benjamin Hampton, *History of the American Film Industry* (New York: Dover Publications, 1970), p. 31.
11. Ibid. (emphasis mine).
12. Ibid., p. 30.
13. G. W. Bitzer, *Billy Bitzer, His Story* (New York: Farrar, Straus & Giroux, 1973), p. 64 (emphasis mine).
14. Documents registered, by title and date, in the US Copyright Office, The Library of Congress, Washington DC, 20540.
15. The term 'Corrected Length' is quoted from the Biograph Camera Register, located at MOMA, New York, and refers to the length of the film as it was sold to exhibitors.
16. The standard early method of copyrighting motion pictures, used by most American companies, was to make a positive 'paper print' of part or all of the production negative. This print was then sent to the Copyright Office along with the application requesting copyright protection for the film.
17. Kemp Niver, *Biograph Bulletins, 1896–1908* (Los Angeles: Artisan Press, 1971), p. 140.
18. Ibid., pp. 136, 140, 150, 153, 156, 160.
19. Correspondence in the archives of the US Copyright Office pertaining to the copyright registration of *The Suburbanite*.
20. W. N. Selig, *The Serenade*. Unpublished script in the archives of the US Copyright Office, pp. 4, 6, 8 & 12.
21. Frank J. Marion and Wallace McCutcheon, *Wanted, a Dog*. Unpublished motion picture scenario in the archives of the US Copyright Office.
22. Frank J. Marion and Wallace McCutcheon, *Tom, Tom, the Piper's Son*. Unpublished motion picture scenario in the archives of the US Copyright Office.
23. Biograph Camera Register. Unpublished. Located in the Film Study Center of the Museum of Modern Art, New York, p. 50.
24. Marion and McCutcheon, *Tom, Tom, the Piper's Son*, p. 2.
25. Ibid., pp. 4–6.

A Primitive Mode of Representation?

NOËL BURCH

Before turning to what is an essential aspect of the institutional mode of representation (IMR), the unity–ubiquity of the spectator subject, I must address the earliest period of cinema history from another direction. If it is true that after twenty or thirty years of cinema an IMR appeared, what then was the precise status of the period preceding its earliest manifestations? Was that 'simply' a transitional period whose peculiarities can be attributed to the contradictory forces pulling in various directions – the influence of popular spectacle and popular audiences on the one hand, bourgeois economic and symbolic aspirations on the other? Or was there a 'primitive mode of representation' (PMR) in the same sense as there is an IMR, a stable system with its own inherent logic and durability?

My answer is clear. It was both these things at once.

There really was, I believe, a genuine PMR, detectable in very many films in certain characteristic features, capable of a certain development but unquestionably semantically poorer than the IMR. It is illustrated by some very remarkable films, from Zecca's *Histoire d'un crime* or Méliès' *Voyage dans la lune* to Gad's *Afgrunden* ('The Abyss' or 'Woman Always Pays', 1910) or Feuillade's *Fantômas* (1913–14). But after 1906 it began to be slowly displaced, particularly under the influence of a conception of editing born in primitive films of a different, more 'experimental' sort which coexisted with the 'pure' system, often in the work of the same film-makers, but which was profoundly ambivalent. This was the case with a few rare French films,[1] several British ones, and above all a large number of Porter's films (*Life of an American Fireman, The Gay Shoe Clerk, The Great Train Robbery, A Subject for the Rogues' Gallery*, etc.) which upset the primitive equilibrium by introducing one or other procedure betraying characteristic aspirations to linearity, centring, etc. But these same films are still massively implicated in the primitive system, a fact which often makes them seductive monsters, seductive, that is, when viewed from the standpoint of the institutional normality yet to be achieved, our normality.

What then constitutes this primitive mode of representation? I have discussed some of its main features at length: autarky of the tableau (even after the introduction of the syntagma of succession, horizontal and frontal camera placement, maintenance of long shot[2] and 'centrifugality'. These are features that can be detected in the text of a typical film, and they, the ambience of the theatres and the possible presence of a lecturer interact to produce what I have tried to define as the experience of *primitive externality*.

But there is another characteristic of the primitive film – really a whole cluster of characteristics – which I have hardly touched on as yet, although it will help us to understand an aspect of the IMR which has been so completely internalised that it is now very difficult to approach it directly. This is what I shall call *the non-closure of the PMR* (in contrast, in other words, to the closure of the IMR).

But I should make it clear that while this feature is found in various forms in a large number of films, many others, especially after 1900, already present a formal semblance of institutional closure. Hence, in so far as this feature can be registered in certain films as narrative non-closure (in the sense defined below), it is not constitutive of the PMR in general. But if institutional closure is taken to be more than narrative self-sufficiency and a certain way of bringing the narrative to an end, if, on the contrary, it is treated as the sum of all the signifying systems that centre the subject and lay the basis for a full diegetic effect, including even the context of projection, then the primitive cinema is indeed non-closed as a whole.

However, the most acute manifestations of this non-closure do concern the narrative, its structure and its status.

Is the potential or actual presence of a lecturer alongside the primitive screen[3] the only explanation for the existence of films like Porter's *Uncle Tom's Cabin; or Slavery Days* (1903), a fifteen-minute, twenty-tableau digest of a bulky novel? In any case, the extraordinary ellipses implied by such a procedure are hardly filled by the captions to the different tableaux ('Eliza's Escape Across the River on the Floating Ice', 'Eva and Tom in the Garden'). It is as if story and characters were assumed to be familiar to the audience, or this knowledge was to be provided for them during the projection.

Initiated with the Passion films, this setting aside of the narrative instance, this tacit affirmation that the narrative discourse is located outside the picture – in the spectator's mind or the lecturer's mouth – was to inform the cinema for twenty years and more. Vitagraph's early 'art films' (e.g. *Francesca da Rimini* (1907), *Richelieu; or The Conspiracy* (1910) and the Vitagraph version of *Uncle Tom's Cabin* (1910)) still appealed to an external narrative instance. It is so self-evident today that a film must tell its own story[4] that we are often unable to read such narratives. To our eyes, *L'Assassinat du duc de Guise*, for example, is incomplete as a film without some knowledge of history, whereas *Intolerance*, eight years later, is 'self-sufficient'.

From the simple headings they started as, insert titles changed around 1905 into summaries of the action preceding each tableau. But this did not make any basic difference; the externality of the narrative was now simply inscribed into the film. When in 1905 Bitzer made *The Kentucky Feud*, based on a celebrated feud between two subsequently famous families, the Hatfields and the McCoys,[5] he introduced each tableau with a long intertitle summarising in dry telegraphese all the bloody peripeteia of the shot that follows ('Home of the McCoys. The Auction. Buddy McCoy shoots at Jim Hatfield and kills Hatfield's mother'). Such intertitles, systematically anticipating the narrative content of the following shot and thus eliminating any possible suspense, were to constitute a major obstacle to the linearisation of narrative for a further ten years at least, and their traces can be detected right through the 1920s, though with connotations that were ironic (Sennett), cultural (Gance) or distancing (Vertov). There was clearly *no discontinuity* between this use of the intertitle and the lecturer's commentary. One more example of a 'step forward' that brought with it a retreat (until around 1914). One more example, too, of a primitive feature that was to be successfully integrated into 'cultural' cinema.

I should add that this externality of the narrative instance in the primitive cinema only existed for 'serious' subjects: Passion films, digests of famous plays or novels, melodramas and, of course, scenics. It was hardly perceptible in trick films or burlesques, during which the bourgeois lecturer was at a loss for words.[6] Yet while these films with their very rudimentary stories, ritual rather than narrative, were sufficient unto themselves, it seems to me that they manifest the other, 'visible' face of what I call non-closure.

Let us therefore examine the history of *the ending* in the cinema, if only briefly and schematically.

The general rule in the Lumière films and in the subsequent 'Lumière school' was that the film (the shot) ended when there was no film left in the camera. Most of these films were actualities, which gave them the implicit signification that the action went on outside the film (before and after). But once we turn to Lumière's first entirely staged film we discover an initiatory feature.

L'*Arroseur arrosé* concludes, more or less,[7] with a punishment: the mischievous boy is spanked by the angry gardener. Such *punitive endings* are legion throughout the primitive period: the voyeur in innumerable 'The Bride Retires' films is caught and beaten, or the bed canopy falls on him as he is about to substitute deeds for looks; as for the countless tramps and other outlaws of American and British films, they are invariably caught at the end of a spectacular chase and beaten black and blue, until the film runs out.[8] All sorts of variations are possible, from the umbrella blows a New York chaperone rains on the back of Porter's unlucky *Gay Shoe Clerk* (1903) to *The Ingenious Soubrette* in Zecca's film (1902) kicking offscreen a cloddish valet. The symbolic import of these 'infantile', 'innocent' aggressions, these castratory endings (it is remarkable how often women have the punitive part, especially in the USA), is part of the overall symbolism of the primitive cinema that I must leave it to others to elucidate. But the extreme contrast between these endings and what we would recognise as an 'end' in the cinema today should draw our attention to the process whereby the 'satisfactory' endings of the institution were constructed. For the institutional ending was not self-evident, it was more than ten years before film-makers knew how to end their films in a way allowing the spectator to withdraw 'gently' from the diegetic experience, convinced that he or she had no more business in it and not feeling that the dream had been interrupted by a beating or by being kicked out of it.

The punitive ending came straight from the circus (the clown's closing kick in the behind) and from certain music-hall turns that themselves probably have the same source. The other main primitive ending was just as mechanical and arbitrary: the Méliès *apothéose*, adopted from the variety theatre and becoming almost obligatory in all French *féeries* and trick films[9] until the exhaustion of these genres around 1912. Punishment and *apothéose* have at least one thing in common: they are both open endings, associated with the primitive forms that were self-sufficient enough (popular enough?) to be able to dispense with either lecturers or intertitles – the chase and the *féerie*.

The next stage in the *history of the ending* had a life of its own and then an afterlife, both surprisingly long. It represented a decisive step towards closure – in particular because this new invention could involve both the end and the beginning of the film. This was the emblematic shot. The best-known example today is surely the famous shot of the leader of the outlaws in *The Great Train Robbery* shooting at the audience to end (or begin) Porter's film. Deriving directly from the autonomous genre of the primitive medium close-up – which died out between 1903 and 1906 as the emblematic shot became established – this kind of portrait could thus appear either at the beginning or at the end of a film, or both. As a general rule its semantic function was either to introduce the film's main concern (at the beginning of *Rescued by Rover* the baby is asleep, watched over by the dog) or to summarise the film's 'point', e.g. its moral (at the end of *How a British Bulldog Saved the Union Jack* the dog is filmed from close to with the flag between its teeth) or its 'joke' (at the end of *Le Bailleur*, 'The Yawner' (Pathé, 1907)), the protagonist's irrepressible yawning, the sole source of the film's humour, breaks a strap that has been fastened round his jaws, in close-up).

Emerging around 1903 – and partly determined by the search for character presence and the establishment of eye contact between actors and spectators – emblematic shots continued to be used for six or seven years. After 1906 they often became a way to present, usually as an '*apothéose*', the smiling face of the heroine, at last seen from close to.[10] But at the same time more far-sighted spirits began to forge more consistent links between the emblematic shot and the main body of the narrative. One of these innovators was a notorious 'plagiarist', Sigmund Lubin. In his *Bold Bank Robbery* (1904), the initial presentation of the three gentlemen-crooks is made by a portrait shot which, although it is not matched with the succeeding action, is shot on the same set with the same characters dressed in the same costumes and in the same positions; they are simply 'posing' for the cameraman. The same is true of the final picture, in which the three pose once again, but this time in their convict's uniforms.

In its presentational and often extra-narrative dimension, the emblematic shot was still a rejection of closure. At the beginning of the film it ultimately metamorphosed into a 'live' introduction of the characters (e.g. *The Cheat*), a practice that persisted throughout the silent cinema, in which it constituted a clear primitive survival. But the terminal emblematic shot, especially in so far as it was the repository of the 'point' of the film (for Lubin: 'Crime does not pay'), is particularly revealing about the future Institution.

The notion of an 'ideological point' (not always a 'message') that each spectator should be able to take away at the end of a film seems to me to be an essential aspect of institutional centring. Linked to the notion of a central character anchoring diegetic production, this point was displayed in the last picture for a long time, like the primitive emblem: think of the hand clasp of Labour and Capital at the end of *Metropolis*, or the corpse of *Little Caesar* lying in the rubbish behind an enormous billboard. Think, too, of the final kiss in so many Hollywood happy ends. The Institution has become more sophisticated today, but this practice is still alive: consider the two workers, one white, the other black, attacking one another in a freeze frame at the end of Paul Schrader's pernicious *Blue Collar*.

One more characteristic of the primitive cinema taken as a whole:[11] the prodigious 'circulation of signs' that went on in it. Att the time, of course, it was more common to speak of plagiarism or piracy. In the absence of appropriate legal provisions (an absence with its own history and its own lessons)[12] or international legal recourse, films could easily be copied in a laboratory and distributed without the producer-proprietor's agreement. But more interesting to us here is the fact that films could also be copied in their substance, their staging and their editing, by any other film-maker, whether a foreigner or a rival compatriot, and without any possible retaliation.[13] It seems even that, unlike the printing of pirated copies, the practice was hardly thought of objectionable among film-makers. The first major trial involving the cinema in France that centred on artistic property occurred in 1908, when Georges Courteline sued Pathé for the unauthorised adaptation of his play *Boubourache*. Courteline's success established a precedent. For, in the primitive period, the notion of artistic property had not been felt to apply to the cinema: these pictures belonged more or less to everyone. Thus film-makers as important as Porter or Zecca could acquire subjects and conceptions of direction by unconcernedly stealing from each other and their English colleagues, who did not hesitate to repay them in kind.

Finally there is the characteristic of primitive cinema most obvious to modern eyes, a characteristic both of its peculiar forms of narrative and of the rules of direction then in force. I mean the absence of the *classical persona*.

In *The Great Train Robbery*, as in all narrative films up to that point (a few milestones as a reminder: Williamson's *Fire!*, Mottershaw's *A Daring Daylight Burglary*, Méliès' *L'Affaire Dreyfus*), although a certain linearisation is beginning to appear, the actors are still seen from very far away. Their faces are hardly visible, their presence on screen is only a bodily presence, they only have at their disposal a *language of gestures*. The essential supports of 'human presence' – the language of the face and above all of the voice – are still completely lacking. The addition to *The Great Train Robbery* by Porter and his collaborators at Edison of a mobile close-up – which could be shown at the beginning or at the end of the film, as the exhibitor chose[14] – was intended, among other things, to give the film this dimension, which they presumably felt it sadly lacked. I speak of an addition to the film rather than an insert because at this time the introduction of inserts was almost inconceivable.[15] That is why it wanders about the margins of the diegesis, with no fixed abode. And that was how the emblematic shot began. But more was needed to make the cinema leave the field of a strictly external 'behaviourism' and embark for the continent of *psychology*.

One last word on the very notion of a primitive mode of representation. Unlike some English and American writers, overinfluenced by modernist ideology, perhaps, I no longer really see the primitive cinema as a 'good object' on the grounds that it contains countless 'prefigurations' of modernism's rejection of classical readerly representation. These prefigurations are clearly no accident: it is not surprising that the obstacles that blocked the rise of the Institution in its 'prehistory' should appear as strategies in the works of creators seeking explicitly or implicitly to deconstruct classical vision. But to see the primitive cinema as a lost paradise and to fail to see the emergence of the IMR as an objective advance is to flirt with obscurantism.

Nevertheless, the primitive cinema did produce some films that strike us today as 'minor masterpieces', either in a certain archaic perfect – as in Méliès finest films, *Voyage dans la lune, Voyage à travers l'impossible, L'Affaire Dreyfus, Barbe Bleue, Le Royaume des fées*, and in certain films of Zecca's. But there are other very different films in which primitive otherness produces a strange poetry all of its own, irreducible either to the codes of the popular arts of the period or to some anticipation of modernist strategies.

I have already discussed the magnificent British film *Charles Peace*, in which the combination of two systems of representation of space, of elements taken from the circus and from the serial novel, produce a poetry of this kind. *Tom, Tom, the Piper's Son* and *The Kentucky Feud*, two Biograph films Bitzer worked on, also seem to me to have this 'primitive originality'.

But I would like especially to evoke a little French film of 1905, of uncertain genre and only two minutes long, called *L'Envers du théâtre* (*Behind the Stage*), which is a condensation of primitive otherness. It consists of three shots, stencil-tinted in the version I have seen, which gives a slight impression of having been taken from very different sources. (This is not completely impossible, what we would call collage having been a common technique at that time.)

1. A cab deposits some night owls in front of a theatre.
2. A tableau of a teeming crowd of people in a theatre dressing room; a flirtation, jealousy (all barely adumbrated).
3. The camera is at the back of the stage facing the auditorium (a painted backdrop glimpsed in the distance), the curtain is up. A prima donna is standing with her back to the camera. She finishes her song; flowers are tossed to her; the curtain falls; a fireman crosses the stage; the stage manager(?) comes and peeps through the spyhole in the curtain; a bit of the scenery falls on his head and breaks to pieces.

Whatever may have been thought when this film was 'rediscovered' at the FIAF Congress in Brighton in 1978, this really is a complete film: the *punitive ending* – punishing a voyeur into the bargain – so highly codified at the time, signifies without any shadow of doubt the end of a 'narrative' (which I see as an abstract and generalised résumé of the gossip columnist's write-up), a narrative as open and on-centred as is conceivable, a kind of *haiku* produced in the Pathé factory, why and how we will probably never know.[16] Here is a jewel buried in a 'heap of rubbish' that deserves to be dug into.

Notes

Originally published in *Iris* vol. 2 no. 1, 1984, and reprinted here as revised for publication in Noel Burch, *Life to those Shadows* (London: BFI Publishing and Berkeley: University of California, 1990).

1. For example, the astonishing *The Dialogue of Legs* (a French film of 1902?), an attempt to establish the cinematic equivalent of the 'synechdoche' (adumbrated in the same period by Porter in the close-up of the fire alarm box in *Life of an American Fireman*). The film tells a 'dirty story' in several concatenated shots unashamedly showing an assignation with a prostitute in the grass of a Parisian wood. After a tableau presenting the situation in long shot (the streetwalker meets her client on a café terrace), we only see the characters' legs. But as this film was made at a time when the articulation of a series of close-ups was still inconceivable, the truncation of the bodies is achieved by a series of extraordinary off-centre long shots placing the legs at the very top or bottom of the screen. The ambivalence of primitive 'advances' is admirably represented by this film, which was remade in 1914 in Italy, in accordance with the new codes of editing.
2. The genre (which in fact comprises several sub-genres) of the 'portrait' in medium close-up also seems to have been a stable form until its absorption into the emblematic shot.
3. It is not impossible that there was a lecturer on hand for film projections in certain vaudeville houses in the USA, but I have no evidence of this.
4. To understand *All the President's Men* one does, it is true, have to have some general knowledge about the political situation in the USA in 1973 and 1974, for example. But the kind of cultural competence demanded by any modern film is one thing, the basically lacunary structure on the screen of these primitives is quite another.
5. There is a famous ballad about them.
6. 'Comic films as a rule require no explanation, it is in dramatic and historical pictures that the need for some brief synopsis is most felt,' wrote an anonymous author in 1909. By contrast, a 'comic' film that adopted the form of the political cartoon such as Porter's curious *Terrible Teddy, the Grizzly King* (1901) certainly needed a spoken 'caption'.
7. In fact the film ends a few seconds after the spanking with little going on (the gardener is about to return to work and the scapegrace is running off). But it is interesting that the series of 'popular' engravings of 1887 that is strikingly similar to Lumière's film (see Sadoul, *Histoire générale du cinéma*, Vol. I, pp.296–7) ended with the actual punishment. The film goes on after this because the 17 metres in the magazine had to be completely used up!
8. In other words, the film ends with a kind of 'closed groove' like a gramophone record, it does not terminate, it is arbitrarily stopped in a perpetual motion which is simply a condensation of the repetitive character of the chase as a whole.
9. It seems also to have been extended to more 'modern' genres in which the institutional narrative is already in gestation. At the end of the astonishing *composite* film *Tour du monde d'un policier* ('A detective's tour of the world' (Pathé, 1906)) – it alternates scenic shots and composed views – the end of the story strictly speaking (the pursued fraud settles his debt and sets up in business with the detective as his partner!) is followed in due form by an *apothéose*, a series of tableaux vivants evoking the different countries visited during the film, in the manner of a variety show.
10. 1906 or thereabouts was also the time at which female parts ceased to be played by men: the world the cinema was entering was that of the close-up, in which such 'frauds' were no longer acceptable; but the world it was leaving was primarily that of the music-hall where this was a standard practice.
11. At this level I have discussed the characteristic opposition between interiors and exteriors, flatness and depth.
12. For a first, incomplete approach to this question, see Edelman, *Le Droit saisi par la photographie*, 1979.
13. I need only mention the countless versions of *L'Arroseur arrosé* and *Le Coucher de la mariée* ('The bride retires') or Porter's copy of *Rêve à la lune* ('Moon lover' or 'Drunkard's dream' or 'Why you should sign the pledge?') in *Dream of a Rarebit Fiend*, only the title of which was taken from McCay's cartoons.

14. Charles Musser (see pp. 123–32 above) sees this latitude conceded to the exhibitor as a vestige of the period when, in the USA especially, it seems, the film-maker's job consisted essentially of shooting raw material that he did not really know how to work up but preferred to hand over to the exhibitor to sort it, arrange it and establish its articulations. For example, *Execution of Czolgosz* (Porter, 1901) was sold both with and without the descriptive track along the outside of Auburn Prison (*Panorama of Auburn Prison*) that Porter also shot.
15. The situation shown in *The Gay Shoe Clerk* which permitted the insertion of the close-up, still quite exceptional in 1903, was itself rather exceptional: static, with few characters, a restricted set, etc. One has a feeling that this film, like other analogous ones (*A Subject for the Rogues' Gallery*), was shot with the sole aim of introducing this close-up.
16. This description of the film is my decipherment after three viewings of it (projected, not on an editing table). Ben Brewster has pointed out to me that the Pathé Catalogue talks of an old stage-door Johnny snubbed by a dancing girl (?), obliged to give the bouquet intended for her to the stage fireman, and the butt of practical jokes from the stage hands. The example is, I believe, evidence both of the difficulties we often experience in deciphering the films of this remote period, and of the 'externality of the narrative instance', which, as is so often the case, is better articulated in the catalogues than it is on the screen. But however accidental, the poetry remains.

Translated by Ben Brewster

Early Cinema: Whose Public Sphere?

MIRIAM HANSEN

The reclamation of early silent cinema as a proletarian public sphere, as attempted for example by Dieter Prokop inevitably raises questions as to the epistemological status of such a concept.[1] Does it correspond to any empirical constellation that would substantiate the claim? Or are we dealing with yet another projection of leftist media theory in the tradition of Brecht and Benjamin, motivated by the desperate desire to redeem the cinema as a 'good object' in the face of so much evidence to the contrary? A closer look at film history may indeed require revisions on the level of theory; but we may also need a more differentiated discussion of the concept of the public sphere if this category is to have any impact on the critical practice of film history.

Before I direct these questions to the cinema of Imperial Germany, I will briefly discuss some problems arising from the study of its American counterpart, focusing on methodological perspectives developed in current research of the period.[2]

Cinematic Acculturation

When barely in its second decade, American cinema began to be discussed in terms of its class-specific, public functions. Whether with conservative or liberal intent, the rhetoric surrounding the novelty of the motion picture, particularly following the rise of the nickelodeon (1905ff.), acknowledged its appeal to the urban poor and working class, to 'new' immigrants from Southern and Eastern Europe, to sailors and to recently uprooted migrants from rural areas in the US – people, as was remarked, who had never before been considered an audience on a massive scale. With the pathos of uplift characteristic of the Progressive Era, the nickelodeon was hailed (or condemned for not fulfilling its proper function) as 'democracy's theatre', 'the labouring man's university' or – in a more sober vein – at least 'a worthy rival of the saloon'.[3] The democratic appeal of the new medium was attributed to the power of moving images to speak to everyone – the poor and illiterate, women and children, foreigners and country folk. As haphazard speculation grew into a full-fledged mythology, this notion of film as a new universal language became one of the key metaphors in public discourse on the cinema, drawing legitimacy from its lower-class distinction which the figuration itself functioned to mask and deny.[4]

Film historians of later decades, notably Lewis Jacobs in *The Rise of the American Film* (1939), further perpetuated the image of the nickelodeon as a genuinely democratic – and genuinely American – institution, thus validating one of American mass culture's most powerful myths of its own origin. By and large, historiography of early American cinema reiterated the working-class spectator's relation to the cinema as a scenario of integration.[5] Besides offering escape from the burdens of sweatshop labour and tenement life – as well as a chance to learn English by way of titles or lectures – the function of the cinema for its spectator was seen as that of an agency of acculturation, introducing newcomers to the social topography of the great melting pot. Jacobs – who serves as Prokop's authority on 'structural references' – supports this view with a description of what he calls 'story films with a social theme', i.e. films dealing with poverty, crime, alcoholism, capital/labour conflicts, clashes with police and other authorities. Although the plots of these films usually drift towards sentimental and affirmative solutions, Jacobs argues that they at least acknowledged the plight of the so-called Common Man and thus provided him with a sense of identity and community. This idyllic state of affairs came to an end in 1914, 'with a suddenness and finality that startled even its backers';[6] the feature film conquered the market, accompanied by the downtown palace and admission charges so prohibitive that they effectively displaced the working class as the cinema's allegedly primary spectator/subject.

As recent studies of trade journals, exhibition patterns and programming guidelines as well as sociographic analyses of theatre locations have shown, this account has to be thoroughly revised. While thriving on working-class patronage, exhibitors could not have cared less about the nickelodeon's democratic mission. To the more ambitious among them – in particular men of similar immigrant background who were working their way up to eventually challenging the Edison Trust as 'independent' producers – the 'labouring man's' support not only presented immediate problems of hygiene and discipline but above all an obstacle to a long-range economic goal: attracting the better-paying middle-class clientele. 'The seduction of the affluent occurred', as Russell Merritt documents, 'between 1905 and 1912, in precisely that theatre supposedly reserved for the blue-collar workers.' Merritt also deflates the myth of the watershed as it had been dramatized by earlier film-historians: 'By 1914, the middle-class audiences were, in fact, already in the theatres waiting for the spectacles and movie stars that would follow.'[7]

Part of the seduction strategy was the marketing of film as (high) art. Griffith's ambition 'to translate a manufacturing industry into an art, and meet the ideals of cultivated audiences' is nothing but a more idealistic phrasing of Adolph Zukor's resolution 'to kill the slum tradition in the movies.'[8] The bid for cultural respectability (literary adaptations, casting of stage celebrities, gentrification of exhibition) coincided with the rise to hegemony of the narrative film,[9] with its debt to the 18th and 19th century novel, its claim to both realism and universality, its inscriptions of the close-up with connotations of intimacy, interiority, individuality. With regard to the public status of the cinema, these moves suggest a systematic appropriation of characters of the classical, bourgeois public sphere or rather, more specifically, of forms of literary subjectivity which, rooted in the intimacy of the privatized, nuclear family, had provided a medium for public discourse in the 18th century, thus giving rise to a literary public sphere that prepared the ground for the political one.[10]

In the effort to (re-)align itself with the cultural standards of the bourgeois public sphere, the cinema implicitly adapted the mechanisms of exclusion and abstract identity characteristic of the paradigm. Dispensing with the detours of literary and artistic ambition, the leading forces in the industry tried to implement these mechanisms in a rather more straightforward way. Exhibitors keen on attracting a broader, 'mixed' audience were advised to avoid ethnic vaudeville acts as well as nationally slanted programmes and to eliminate sing-alongs in foreign languages. On the level of film production, the suppression of ethnic difference was imperative: no actor with distinctive ethnic features was to be cast in a leading role.[11]

Among the few films that ostensibly dealt with the problems of the immigrant and other urban poor,[12] one of Griffith's Biograph shorts, *Musketeers of Pig Alley* (1912), seems to capture some of the contradictions involved in the process of transformation. Shot partly on location in Lower Manhattan, the film has been celebrated for its realism of milieu, plot and character, as exemplifying the early cinema's symbiotic relationship with its working-class audience. The action takes place in a tenement district, swiftly moving between a living-room, a hallway, a saloon and outdoor settings, the systematic use of offscreen space suggesting rather fluid, tenuous (if not insufficient) demarcations between public and private spaces. Streets and back alleys are teeming with bystanders and passers-by; with prostitutes, loiterers, children shoppers, and – privileged just enough to catch the spectator's eye – a Chinese launderer and a Jewish street-vendor. Against the haphazard contingency and diversity of this backdrop, the protagonists – led by the blonde and blue-eyed Lillian Gish – are set off by means of casting, acting style and more intimate camera ranges, thus ensuring identification on the basis of individual character traits. As usual, plot conventions of romance, rivalry and reconciliation take the sting out of the representation of working-class experience; poverty, violence and alienation are muted in social compromise, which in turn is naturalized by the final embrace of the reconsolidated couple. The source of the money that stabilizes social conflict (title: 'lins in the system') remains mysterious – a hand reaches into the frame presenting a pay-off to the Snapper Kid; offscreen space comes to signify tacit yet public condonement of methods of private appropriation, linking its excesses to the system as a whole.

From the start, the spectator's position is split between inside and outside, between participant in and consumer of the spectacle. With the opening title, 'New York's Other Side',[13] Griffith projects an audience already removed from the social environment the film purports to represent, to whom he tenders picturesque values from a nostalgic or touristic vantage point. Complementing visual pleasure with the illusion of intimacy, however, he offers his projected audience a way back into the film, setting into play voyeuristic mechanisms of separation and identification that, even in this rudimentary form, advance the process by which empirical spectators were to be transformed into the meta-spectator constructed by the classical text.[14] By the same token, the image of the immigrant in *Musketeers*, safely relegated to the status of decor, no longer simply denotes (did it ever?) a specific social experience but rather serves to authenticate the 'reality' of the narrative as a whole, following well-worn practices of literary realism.[15]

If the suppression of class and ethnic diversity was in keeping with the cinema's pretension to a bourgeois public sphere, the effort to co-opt such diversity into a generalized aesthetic appeal was more in touch with large-scale transformations in the capitalist economy. The film industry's aim was not, as Jacobs implies, to exclude the working class but to integrate them, allegedly into the democratic melting pot, yet more effectively into a consumer society of which mass culture was to become both agent and object.[16]

Consumerism, offering 'the image of a homogeneous population pursuing the same goals',[17] not only became the ticket to full American citizenship, but fundamentally affected the relation of public and private spheres, especially for immigrants and their families. As Judith Mayne argues, the cinema served to redefine this relationship, organizing private consumption on a massive, public scale. In its mediation of public and private spheres, Mayne compares the function of spectatorship for immigrant audiences with another cultural response to capitalist development, two centuries before: the emergence of the middle-class novel in England, with its appeal to a predominantly female reading public. While the novel gave women readers the illusion of social participation in the privacy of domestic space, the cinema re-enacted a similar mediation in inverted form, 'offering an imaginary private sphere from the vantage point of public space'.[18]

Paradigms of the Public Sphere

The analogy between twentieth-century spectatorship and eighteenth-century readership, as Mayne herself remarks, is a precarious one – on historical as well as theoretical grounds. The bourgeois public sphere that had established itself in opposition to – though crucially dependent on – the privately owned sphere of appropriation and commodity circulation had been in a process of disintegration since the mid-nineteenth century; its American variant, moreover, never quite possessed the same degree of autonomy as its European prototypes. A new type of public sphere was beginning to take shape in the modern mass media which turned the raw material of human experience into an object of capitalist production. Lacking in substance and stability, these new 'public spheres of production' (*Produktionsöffentlichkeiten*) – in the analysis of Negt and Kluge[19] – tend to absorb the remnants of the classical public sphere, grafting themselves on to its persistent semblance of coherence and legitimacy. As could be seen with the film industry's bid for the middle-class trade, such grafting entails a perpetuation of the formal mechanisms of exclusion and abstract identity, of artificial divisions of public and private. At the same time, since the 'public spheres of production' depend upon maximum marketability of their products, they necessarily aim for a more direct and totalizing use of human needs and qualities than their bourgeois predecessor. These contradictory tendencies, however, suggest a shift of focus; rather than emphasize historical parallels in the cinema's integration into the dominant public sphere, one might consider the potential of the gap created by a historically changed constellation, i.e. the possibility that early silent cinema – *because* of and *counter* to its commercial orientation – may have contained elements of a public sphere radically different in kind.

According to Negt/Kluge, the possibility of an antithethical concept of the public sphere cannot be derived from a critical analysis of the classical public sphere (redemption of its ideals against its ideology) but has to be sought in the contradictory make-up of the late-capitalist public spheres of production. Even in their parasitic and illusory grasp of human needs and qualities, these new public spheres make visible a substantially different function of the public sphere in general, i.e. to provide a medium for the organization of human experience[20] in relation to – rather than, as in the classical model, separation from – the material sphere of everyday life, the social conditions of production. As a historical counter-concept to the bourgeois public sphere, Negt/Kluge assert that this type of public sphere already emerged in rudimentary shape – and not acknowledged as 'public' – in the intestices of contradictory and non-linear social and political processes. (Their examples include the independent communication media developed by the English working class in the early 19th century; Lenin's concept of 'self-expression of the masses' as opposed to party propaganda; Italian Maximalism in 1919; certain groupings in the protest movements of the 1960s.) As a fundamentally new structure opposed to both classical-representative and market-oriented types of public sphere, this counter-concept entails principles of inclusion and multiplicity, an emphasis on concrete interests and self-organization and, most crucially, an insistence on the connectedness of human experience across dominant divisions of public and private, including the experience of fragmentation and specific blockages (cf. the chapters on the role of phantasy in the production of experience; on time patterns and biographical rhythms of learning; on language barriers; on the fate of the human senses (*Sinnlichkeit*)).

If Negt/Kluge have designated this type of public sphere as 'proletarian', then they do so primarily in opposition to Habermas who dismisses any deviations from the classical bourgeois model as merely a 'repressed variant of a plebeian public sphere'.[21] Although focusing on the working class as the historical subject of production, the term 'proletarian' transcends its empirical reference point, not to mention the political scope of the traditional labour movements. Even if there were nothing in the history and living situation of the working class that corresponded to a proletarian public sphere, Negt/Kluge argue, this category would have to be – and could be – developed in its negative determination: on the basis of hegemonic efforts to suppress, repress, destroy, isolate, split or assimilate any formation of a potential proletarian public sphere and to appropriate its material substance, experience, in the interest of private profit-maximization.[22]

Early cinema would qualify as an instance of a proletarian public sphere in Negt/Kluge's sense, if only for the comprehensive efforts – as documented by Merritt and other historians – to rid the institution of its class-specific stigma, in the same measure as public exaltation of its democratic virtues began to flourish. The cinema's transition from an anarchic cottage industry to a monopolostic branch of American Business, however, was not as streamlined as its eventual success suggests; the unequal development of productive relations, spectatorship and individual authorship left traces of resistance in the films themselves. Yet these traces can hardly be defined with recourse to Prokop's 'structural references', a notion that ignores the structure of cinematic representation along with the mechanisms by which the image of proletarian life was increasingly co-opted into democratic mythology and aesthetic consumerism, a process almost synonymous with its becoming an 'image'.

In a more radical sense, as a medium for a fundamentally different organization of public experience, the cinema's potential of resistance hinges on the formal organization of spectatorship, the study of which has been developed, among others, by Noël Burch and Ben Brewster.[23] On this level, the integration of a relatively autonomous public sphere into a universalized, homogenized mass culture can be observed in the systematic improvement of cinematic techniques that guarantee the complete absorption of the spectator into the fictional world of the film and the imaginary flow of linear narrative; the absolute division of screen space and theatre space; the institutionalization of private voyeurism in a public space. Conversely, the relative imperfections of 'primitive' cinema – tableau style that may require a lecturer, disregard for continuity in editing – suggest that the experience in front of the screen was at least as significant as the actions depicted on the screen.

More than just 'a chance to come in from the cold and sit in the dark' (as Merritt contends in deliberate provocation), early cinema also provided a social space, a place apart from the domestic and work spheres, where people of similar background and status could find company (not necessarily of their own kin), where young working women would seek escape from the fate of their mothers.[24] Yet it was not merely the space that constitutes a new public sphere, a public sphere of a new type; it was the interaction between the films on the screen and the 'film in the head of the spectator' (Kluge) that allowed individual experience to be articulated and thus organized in a participatory, social and public mode. As cinematic experience was progressively subordinated to the reality-effect of the 'other scene', the narrative space of the film, the space of the spectator became increasingly de-realized, reduced to specularity, privatized. This process was not completed until the 1930s – which gives the entire silent era its moments of alterity – yet as a normative tendency it manifests itself almost from the start: in the systematic elimination of genres, modes of address and peripheral activities that provided the potential for an alternative organization of public experience.[25]

I hope to have elucidated the precarious status of the notion of early cinema as a proletarian public sphere. As a theoretical construct, this notion is useful only in so far as it acknowledges the contradictory dynamics of its historical reference point – which calls for empirical studies and textual analyses in the direction indicated by recent contributions to the American debate. Above all, the reclamation of early cinema for a theory/politics of the public sphere requires a revisionist attitude towards the rhetoric of cultural criticism and historiography; short of that, the theoretical project is bound to collapse into the reified mythologies that co-opted the proletarian characteristics of early cinema in the name of uplift and integration.

Wilhelmine Cinema

German cinema cultivated its own myths of origin, corresponding to significant peculiarities in the development of the institution. One of the major factors in this development was the virtual absence of a native film production until about 1910, when German banking capital overcame its initial reservations and began to invest in the motion picture business. Shortly before 1914, Germany's share in the total number of films distributed was still barely 15 per cent; the rest were supplied by France (30 per cent), the United States (25 per cent), Italy (20 per cent), Denmark and England, mostly by way of imports but also through local subsidiaries (e.g. Pathé Frères and Nordisk). While all of these countries, before asserting hegemony on their domestic markets, depended upon foreign imports to a greater or lesser degree (the US more than France, for instance), Germany – ironically – preserved the international profile of early cinema longer than any of them, until it was nationalized, as it were, by World War I.[26]

Despite – and most likely because of – this peculiar weakness in the realm of production, cinematic forms, exhibition patterns and economic structures seem to have developed along similar lines to other national cinemas. Shortly after the establishment of mutoscope and kinetoscope arcades in major German cities, the first screening of films in public – for an admission charge – took place in the Berlin 'Wintergarten', a variety theatre, on 1 November 1895, nearly two months prior to the Lumières' opening on the Boulevard des Capucines in Paris. Yet the films the Brothers Skladanowsky presented on this occasion rather resembled the Edison kinetoscope productions in choice of subject matter and mode of representation, though avoiding the claustrophobic intimacy of the peep-show perspective: short one-shot numbers like 'Italian Peasant Dance' (two children), 'The Boxing Kanagaroo' (Mr Delaware), 'Wrestling Match' (Greiner and Sandow), 'Acrobatic Potpourri' (eight persons), 'Serpentine Dance' (Mlle Ancion), and 'Apotheosis' (featuring the Skladanowskys themselves). Staged on a platform and isolating their figures against a white or greyish background, these films appealed to the spectator's interest in physical skills and disciplined body movement, extraordinary personality, exotic sights and folkloristic customs, not unlike the circus and vaudeville programmes in the context of which they were to be scheduled. In subsequent years, Oskar Messter, inventor and pioneer film-maker, added a variety of genres to this repertoire: urban street scenes à la Lumière; travelogues and actualities (including the first appearance of the Kaiser on film), trick films, faked catastrophes in the Edison tradition, comic chases, and humorous sketches in the vein of *L'Arroseur arrosé*, and – between 1903 and 1913 – a cycle of musical films utilizing the invention of synchronized sound-image projection.

During the first decade of German cinema, films were primarily shown in the *Wanderkino* (travelling shows); around 1904 the establishment of permanent facilities gained momentum and the *Laden* – and/or *Vorstadtkino* (comparable to the nickelodeon) became the most popular locale of exhibition.

In the years following 1910, the theatres designed specially for motion picture shows were going up in Berlin and elsewhere, paralleling the conversion of small-time vaudeville houses and the construction of downtown picture palaces in the United States.[27] The expansion of the exhibition sector coincided with increased efforts to consolidate the industry as a whole, a strategy intended to counter foreign control of the German market and culminating in the formation of the UFA in 1917. The impulse towards vertical integration, in distinction to the American development, came primarily from the producers, an important exception being the Produktions – A.G. Union (PAGU) that had started out as a theatre chain.

Other deviations from the American model clearly derive from the different dynamics of culture and the public sphere. The relative underdevelopment of bourgeois democratic ideology and the concomitant problems of German working-class identity gave the cinema a different position in relation to existing public spheres; consequently, it steered budding mythologies in a direction quite divergent from its American counterpart. With hierarchic class structures persisting alongside industrialization and modernization, the egalitarian appeal of the new medium was more likely to be perceived as a threat than a foil for democratic mythology. While American critics were preoccupied with the cinema's power – and task – of integration, German commentators tended to discuss the cinema's social, collective function – if they acknowledged it as such – in terms of crowd psychology at best. Typically, only its almost adamant enemies would grant the cinema a political potential with radical implications, inasmuch as they accused it of 'dulling the sense for law and order', fostering idleness and instigating strikes, and further demanded that all films be banned that might 'stir up hatred between the classes *(den Klassenhass zu schüren)*'.[28][. . .]

The Cinema Reform Movement

The cinema reform movement not only represents the arena in which public discourse on the cinema was first taking shape but also offers implicit statements concerning the status and the makeup of early cinema as a public sphere. One of the many reform movements of the Wilhelmine era, the first organized efforts to influence the course of the cinema – in and following 1907 – were sponsored by teachers' associations and groups devoted to popular and continuing education (e.g. Gesellschaft der Freunde des vaterländischen Schul- und Erziehungswesens, Gesellschaft für Verbreitung von Volksbildung). Warning against the moral dangers of the entertainment film – humorous sketches and, in particular, the mushrooming genre of melodramatic narrative – the proponents of *Kinoreform* emphasized the educational potential of the new medium, prescribing a fare of scientific and geographical documentaries and other teaching films.[29]

While these efforts towards a *Reformkino* were supported to some extent by the recently (1905–8 ff.) established trade journals (e. g. *Der Kinematograph, Licht-Bild-Bühne*), such concern has to be viewed in relation to the growing threat of censorship. Following a Prussian police order of 1906 (and its amendment in 1908) censorship was introduced on the local level; in practice, censors in the provinces and in other states in most cases endorsed the decisions of the Berlin authorities. Challenged by exhibitors, the police order was subsequently affirmed by a superior administrative court. Besides showing a remarkable degree of sophistication in analysing the peculiarities of the cinematic apparatus, the legal arguments in defence of censorship testify to the cinema's potential as a public sphere even as they attempt to deny it the status and the political prerogatives of a public formation in the traditional sense. Apologists for censorship asserted its legality by claiming that it did not violate freedom of trade, or infringe upon freedom of the press or on freedom of assembly. The exclusion of the cinema from constitutional protection of expression in print involved elaborate speculations as to the process of exhibition and individual reception, focusing on the distinction between the celluloid product – marked by separate fixed frames (the 'body' of the print as protected by law) – and the moving image on the screen, which obliterates the scriptural character of the 'body'.[30] The justification for denying film showings the prerogative of a public gathering was the alleged lack of a 'public cause' (*öffentliche Angelegenheit*) to convene the spectators, as contrasted with events of a 'serious' – i.e. scholarly, religious, political – nature that served the 'interest of the general public' (*Interesse der Allgemeinheit*). Subsumed under the category of entertainment (*Lustbarkeiten*), 'diversion', 'pleasure', 'socializing' in the cinema were relegated to the status of the 'merely' private.[31]

The public/private configurations invoked by the legal defenders of censorship may account for whatever ideological support the trade press might have given to the educational ('serious') goals of the former; it seems unlikely that anyone even loosely connected with the film business would have considered scientific and educational documentaries a drawing card at the box-office. When narrative-dramatic films conquered the market and marginalized most other genres – a tendency already perceived in 1907 but overwhelmingly asserted between 1910 and 1912[32] – publicity strategies changed course and veered towards Art, a category conspicuously absent from the early censorship debate. If the pleasures of fiction and theatricality were to define cinematic consumption in any event, then only a professed aspiration to aesthetic standards could have hoped to disembarrass the cinema from the stigma – and legal vulnerability – of 'merely private' entertainment.

The second wave of the cinema reform movement, which reached its peak between 1912 and the outbreak of the war, crystallized around issues of artistic quality and cultural value and involved, as mentioned before, an increasing number of literary intellectuals in the debate. Public concern about the cinema had never ceased, continuity being maintained by individual reformers,[33] recurrent stereotypes such as the cinema's threat to mental and physical health (especially of the young), and a generally moralistic tone; yet the emphasis seems to have shifted, within a few years, from the mission of popular education to a more abstract ethics of culture. The cinema's poaching on the domain of high art was considered reprehensible only in so far as it violated the authority and integrity of the literary classics. Thus a 1910 adaptation of Schiller's *Don Carlos* which omitted the characters of Marquis Posa and Princess

Eboli raised storms of moral indignation and general discussion on tampering with the cultural heritage of the nation.[34] Phrased somewhat differently, the anxiety over cultural values also moved members of the avant-garde. To Franz Pfempfert, editor of the expressionist journal *Die Aktion*, the cinema symbolized the blend of triviality and genius, the lack of soul and individuality characteristic of the age: '"Edison" is the war-cry of a culture-killing epoch, the war-cry of barbarism (*Unkultur*).'[35]

Once distinctions between culture and barbarism began to dominate the discussion, it was only a short step to blaming the allegedly inferior quality of the standard cinematic fare on its mostly foreign origins. Art historian Konrad Lange, probably one of the most hostile cinema reformers, epitomized the nationalist-conservative slant of the movement which, with the outbreak of the war, gave ideological cover to the effective banning of imports and nationalization of foreign subsidiaries: 'Away with this cheap and artless trash! Away with this disgusting potion that poisons the soul of the German folk! Let us impose severe economic sanctions against the foreign and international film capital, the canker that blights the tree of German culture.'[36] [. . .]

Attitudes towards the cinema ranging from neglect and hostility to reformist purism, as they were articulated from within the public sphere of the traditional labour movement, urge us to take a closer look at the displacement of social and political terms into those of morality, hygiene and high culture and to consider the particular qualities that were being repressed in the process of displacement. The lower-class patronage, whatever its actual proportion, appeared as the cinema's cultural stigma or, conversely, accounted for its bohemian appeal in so far as literary intellectuals liked to go slumming. Although the public sphere that mushroomed outside the gates of legitimate culture was clearly non-bourgeois, it did not have the overwhelming working-class profile attached to the American nickelodeon. Nor did the German cinema attract any group comparable in size, cultural difference and class dynamics to the immigrant contingent among American movie-goers, which would have endowed a random leisure-time activity with a specific social meaning and implicit teleology (comparative to that of acculturation). While American writers could readily unfold the myth of the 'laboring man's theatre', German writers had to resort to phrases like 'the theatre of the small people' (the title of Alfred Döblin's 1909 essay, 'Das Theater der Kleinen Leute'). Moreover, the word 'proletarian', in the context of the cinema, was used to refer to the actors who, unless they were stars, received about the lowest wages paid to anyone in the industry.[37]

The Threat to Patriarchal Divisions of Public and Private: Women's Passion for the Cinema

This characteristically German constellation poses the issue of early cinema as a proletarian public sphere at an angle somewhat diverging from the American case. Tentatively, I would argue that the block of resistance in the cinema's path to cultural respectability (and thus acceptance into the dominant public sphere) was sexual and gender related, rather than primarily class-related. If the potential for a radically different public sphere (in Negt/Kluge's sense) can be inferred from widespread and systematic efforts to render it illegitimate, then the high percentage of women in early audiences must have presented a more fundamental threat to the dominant organization of public experience than the cinema's appeal to any particular class, least of all to the traditional working class.

This is not to say that American discourse on early cinema was free of patriarchal bias, nor do I mean to dismiss the significance of female spectatorship for the development of the American institution – by no means. The comparative lack of democratic mythology in German writings on the cinema, however, foregrounds the sexual subtext in a peculiarly intense and pervasive manner. Whatever political interest in class-specificity there might have been was diffused in an aesthetic evocation of plebeian diversity, especially by literary commentators who found the physical appearance of the audience and the whole ambience clearly more fascinating than the films that were shown.

> Inside the pitch-black, low-ceilinged space a rectangular screen glares over a monster of an audience, a white eye fixating the mass with a monotonous gaze. Couples making out in the background are carried away and withdraw their undisciplined fingers. Children wheezing with consumption quietly shake with the chills of evening fever; badly smelling workers with bulging eyes; women in musty clothes, heavily made-up prostitutes leaning forward, forgetting to adjust their scarves. Here you can see 'panem et circenses' fulfilled; spectacle as essential as bread; the bullfight a popular need.[38]

A plebeian gathering indeed and quite a spectacle to writer and reader alike. Even in such a self-consciously hyperbolic text, one cannot help perceiving an echo of the sexual fears that bourgeois and leftist reformers projected on to the plebeian screen. It is no coincidence that literary intellectuals fascinated by the whiff of Otherness that emanated from the movies hardly even failed to mention the presence of prostitutes in the audience. The image of the prostitute was actually used as an epithet for the cinema as a whole – typical of the opportunistic double standard that characterized the attitude of the cultural bourgeoisie towards an openly commercial ('venal') art. The censors' attack on 'mere pleasure' had its counterpart in literary intellectuals' phrasing of their contempt ('soul-lessness') for – and simultaneous fascination (stark sensuality, exotic vitality) with – cinema in terms that invoked the idealistic dichotomy of body and soul along patriarchal lines of sexual difference.[39]

Much of the reformers' (as well as the literary intellectuals') rhetoric – if literalized the way Klaus Theweleit treats sources relating to proto-fascists' biographies and politics[40] – translates into fear of femininity in general, of female presence on both a pragmatic and metaphoric level. Cinema reformers cautioning against the suggestive appeal of film to the 'irrational' tendencies of the 'mass' described the cinema as a vortex of confusion and force of intoxication. Objections to the cinema on hygienic grounds – the unhealthy effects of dark and stuffy rooms, the danger of contagion – carried overtones of hysteria inspired by the uncontrollable mingling of people of different age,[41] class and sex. With its irresistible pull, the cinema as an institution threatened to blur not only the boundaries maintaining hierarchic distinctions of class but also the boundaries between public and private, between individuals with access to social representation by virtue of their economic position and those traditionally confined to the domestic sphere. The high percentage of women in cinema audiences was perceived as an alarming phenomenon:

> Quickly the benches fill up with workers of both sexes, young shop assistants and sales-girls, clerical employees and their female rivals on the labor market – people, in short, whose lungs must be starved for fresh air and whose eyes and nerves need rest, rest, and rest. Housewives drop in as 'neighbors', greeted by the staff as if they were old acquaintances. Their conversations suggest that they never miss a single new release. One would rather see these mothers around the family dinner table, tending to the fold – their children.[42]

In the eyes of a social-democratic reformer like Noack, female moviegoers seem to fall into two categories: those who neglect their duties and home and those who compete with men for white-collar jobs.

The film industry, less concerned with women's conformity to traditional roles than with their economic potential as consumers,[43] soon began to cater to female audiences with particular genres and stars. Adapting patriarchal ideology to changes in sexual-social divisions of labour, the cinema was to become a crucial mediator between women's experience and the dominant public sphere in the 1920s. (Siegfried Kracauer, one of the critics to perceive this link, nonetheless perpetuates its patriarchal inscription with condescending authority, when he defines the salesgirl – or the typist, the '*Tippmamsell*' – as the linchpin of the false correspondence between film and society.[44])

A remarkable exception to the patriarchal undercurrent in discourse on early German cinema is Emilie Altenloh's study, *Sociology of the Cinema* (1914), a dissertation written with Alfred Weber in Heidelberg. With all scepticism due to empirical studies, Altenloh's close analysis of theatre statistics and 2,400 questionnaires has to be considered one of the most differentiated sources on spectator stratification available. A major advantage of Altenloh's sociological approach is that she has little investment in the commercial/high art controversy of her time and largely abstains from cultural value judgments (with the exception of a few stabs at the elitism of modern drama). Instead, she focuses on patterns of interaction between the film industry and its audience, both of whom she sees as determined by a capitalist mode of production. Most important, Altenloh recognized the cinema as a public sphere in its own right, constituted by people who had previously been indifferent to spectacles of any degree of absorption, people who had never before been perceived as an audience in the proper sense of the German word '*Publikum*'.[45]

Dismissing the poets' services to the medium as largely irrelevant if not opportunistic, Altenloh explains the transformation that set in about 1910 as a result of a combination of factors, e.g. the rise of the melodramatic narrative

('*Sensationsdrama*') and the establishment of larger, more comfortable and luxurious theatres in the city centres. Picture palaces, masquerading as respectable theatres displaying cloakrooms, bars, programme notes, ushers and orchestras) and films that appropriated the epithet 'social' as an advertising cliché were the decisive factors – according to Altenloh – in making the cinema a fad among the urban upper and upper middle classes, bringing them up to date on fashions and sentiments and linking them to the international world of cultural consumption.

In Altenloh's analysis of spectator stratification, however, these new audiences play a relatively marginal role. Focusing on a cross-section of moviegoers in the city of Mannheim, her survey differentiates between class, age, sex and professional backgrounds. Subproletarian interviewees of all age groups represented the largest constituency of cinema enthusiasts, with preferences for cowboys and Indians, cops and robbers, and other adventure films. Proletarian spectators, mainly metal workers, professed a similar penchant, at least in their youth, combined with a stronger interest in erotic films as well as a more pragmatic usage of the movie theatre as a dating place; young workers of petty-bourgeois and patriotic family background tended to prefer military and historical spectacles. Status-conscious sales assistants and clerical employees were primarily concerned about the respectability of the particular movie theatre and its location and frequently ranked the cinema second after the theatre, the opera (predominantly Wagner), concerts and educational lectures. Like the upwardly mobile and/or politically active blue-collar workers, employees seemed to abandon the cinema in later years, while the subproletarian element remained faithful to it even as adults. The more meaningful and promising the interviewees' professional and political lives, Altenloh concludes, the less significant the role of the cinema for their leisure time.

While responses from the male interviewees were differentiated along the lines of occupation, class background and social aspiration, female moviegoers of varying class and marital status tended to express a remarkably homogeneous attitude towards the cinema. Many attributed their pleasure in film-viewing to the combination of image and music, a preference that Altenloh relates to their equally strong interest in opera (especially Wagner – as in the case of male employees – but also Mozart, Bizet, Verdi, Flotow and Massenet). Romances and 'social' dramas with female protagonists were indisputable favourites with female spectators, in particular employees, many of whom confessed to a special adoration for Asta Nielsen in the title roles of such films. The only other genre given a modicum of attention was the geographical documentary or natural spectacle (*Nataraufnahme*). Unlike male employees who emphasized this genre's informational and educational value, women primarily responded to its 'aesthetic' – i.e. more precisely, its kinetic – appeal, in particular if the films were featuring waterfalls, ocean waves or drifting ice-floes.

The synaesthetic involvement of women spectators and their tendency to get emotionally absorbed (to the point of usually not remembering the title or content of individual films) leads Altenloh to somewhat essentialist speculations concerning the alleged affinity between the workings of the female mind and the techniques of cinematic representation, invoking the opposition of female intuition and male intellect. Such speculations are contextualized, however, by references to the social and economic situation of female spectators as well as more specific considerations of the function that movie going had for women in their everyday lives. In her chapter on working-class women, mainly workers' wives (*Arbeiterfrauen*), Altenloh remarks on their comparative lack of interest in educational and political (primarily social-democratic) activities such as occupied the leisure time of their male counterparts:

> In this context, the cinema plays an important role, especially for those women who do not have a job of their own. Once they are done with their house-work, they have very few options for filling out their free time. More often they will go to the movies because they are bored than for any real interest in the program. While the men are attending political meetings, women visit the movie theater next door where they'll be met by their spouses when the screening is over. Gradually, however, this stop-gap activity becomes an essential part of their daily lives. Before long, they are seized by a veritable passion for the cinema, and more than half of them try to gratify that passion at least once a week. During the screening they live in another world, a world of luxury and extravagance which makes them forget the monotony of the everyday. (pp. 78–9)

For upper-class women who supposedly had access to this other world by virtue of their socio-economic status, the cinema added a slightly risqué titillation to daily consumer activities – a convenient way-station on shopping trips as well as a source of information on the latest fashions from Paris and elsewhere. In married couples of all social strata, Altenloh further observes women would usually initiate the visit to the movie theatre, dragging along a husband either deadened from work or deeming himself superior to his wife's emotional absorption in the events on screen.

While Altenloh's conception of female spectatorship in terms of an addiction (*Kinosucht*) seems to echo similar tropes in Noack's tract, her analysis of the escapist and regressive functions of the cinema is largely free of the moralistic tone found in the latter. Rather, Altenloh considers the cinema's appeal in the context of social processes concomitant with capitalist development, such as the alienation inflicted by mechanized work processes and wage labour, the fragmentation of social experience, the isolation and attrition of domestic space and – related to all these aspects – the constitution of a new type of public sphere. While Altenloh tends to idealize – in the manner of romantic anti-capitalism – the function of pre-industrial popular culture (as a creation/expression of the folk's body-psyche), she opens up a perspective on the cinema which is neither nostalgic nor blindly utopian. Remarking on the sparsity of moviegoers' responses when asked *why* they felt drawn to the cinema, Altenloh quotes one 'lady' as saying, '*faute de mieux*'. 'This "*mieux*", however,' Altenloh goes on,

> has as many different faces as individual spectators. In any case, the cinema succeeds in addressing just enough of those individuals' needs to

> provide a substitute for what would really be 'better,' thus assuming a powerful reality in relation to which all questions as to whether the cinema is good or evil or has any right to exist appear useless. (p. 94)

In its indefinite and heterogeneous appeal, this substitute is not merely and simply a result of strategies of mass-marketing; it also contains elements that run against the grain of capitalist modes of production and consumption.

Notes

1. Dieter Prokop, *Soziologie des Films* (Frankfurt am Main: Fischer Verlag, rev. ed. 1982; and 'Versuch über Massenkultur und Spontaneität' (1971), repr. in Prokop, *Massenkultur und Spontaneität: Zur veränderten Warenform der Massenkommunikation im Spätkapitalismus* (Frankfurt am Main: Suhrkamp, 1974), pp. 44–101; esp. 58 ff.
2. What follows is an abridged version of the essay which first appeared in *New German Critique*, no. 29, 1983.
3. Myron Lounsbury, *The Origins of American Film Criticism, 1909–39* (unpublished dissertation, 1966; New York: Arno Press, 1973). For easily accessible selections of sources, see George C. Pratt (ed.), *Spellbound in Darkness* (Greenwich, Ct: New York Graphic Society, 1973), and Gerald Mast (ed.), *The Movies in Our Midst* (Chicago: The University of Chicago Press, 1982). For an instance of the temperance argument, see Vachel Lindsay, *The Art of the Moving Picture* (1915; rev. ed. 1922; New York: Liverright, 1970), ch. XV.
4. Used in a variety of pragmatic contexts, the universal language metaphor inevitably reproduces the ideological contradictions of its sources. While Vachel Lindsay's celebration of moving pictures as the new 'hieroglyphics' is mediated by the context of modernist poetics (Imagism, the paradigm of the ideogram (Pound/Eisenstein), Griffith's insistence on the transcendent truth of moving images more directly taps connotations of nineteenth-century positivism and its Enlightenment antecedents (q.v. his defence of *Birth of a Nation*) as well as millenarian underpinnings of concepts of American Democracy and its Manifest Destiny (q.v.*Intolerance*. 'A picture is the universal symbol, and a *picture that moves* is a universal language. Moving pictures, someone suggests, "might have saved the situation when the Tower of Babel was built"' (*Focus on D. W. Griffith*, ed. Harry M. Geduld (Englewood Cliffs, NJ: Prentice Hall, 1971), p. 56, (Gish reports 'Mr. Griffith once heard one of his actresses call a film a 'flicker.' He told her never to use that word. She was working in the universal language that had been predicted in the Bible, which was to make all men brothers because they would understand each other. This could end wars and bring about the millennium. We were all to remember that the next time we faced a camera'. (*Dorothy and Lillian Gish* (New York: Charles Scribner's Sons, 1973), p. 60)

   The millenarian-utopian connotations of the universal-language metaphor were pervasively invoked by social reformers and journalists discussing the cinema's emancipatory function for a working-class immigrant audience (for a graphic example, see Garth Jowett, *Film: The Democratic Art* (Boston: Little, Brown & Co., 1976), p. 42). The destiny of the democratic spirit, however, was to manifest itself primarily in terms of commercial success: advertisements for Carl Laemmle's Universal (*sic*) Film Manufacturing Co. (founded in 1912) which fuse the inherently totalitarian bias of the eponymic trope with the economic imperative that homogenizes all products of consumer culture. For a rather late, apologetic elaboration of the universal language metaphor ('The Esperanto of the eye'), prefaced by Will H. Hays, see Edward S. Van Zile, *The Marvel – The Movie: A Glance at Its Reckless Past, Its Promising Present, and Its Significant Future* (New York and London: G. P. Putnam's Sons, 1923).
5. An amazingly uncritical yet comprehensive celebration of the cinema as an agency of Americanization (acculturation as homogenization) can be found in Jowett, *Film: The*

Democratic Art (n. 4, above). For a reading of Jacobs' work in the context of 30s radicalism, see Myron Lounsbury, 'The Gathered Light': history, criticism and the Rise of American Film', *Quarterly Review of Film Studies*, 5/1, Winter 1980, pp. 49–85.

6. Jacobs, *The Rise of American Film: A Critical History* (1939; New York: Teachers College Press, 1968), p. 160.
7. Russell Merritt, 'Nickelodeon theaters, 1905–1914: building an audience for the movies', in Tino Balio (ed.), *The American Film Industry* (Madison: University of Wisconsin Press, 1976), pp. 59–70; p. 60. Robert Allen's research of early exhibition practices suggests that the middle class had actually been catered to from the start, since prior to – and even continuing through – the nickelodeon boom films were programmed in vaudeville shows: *Vaudeville and Film, 1895–1915: A Study in Media Interaction* (New York: Arno Press, 1980); on the role of vaudeville theatres in upgrading exhibition in a specific community, see Robert Allen, 'Motion picture exhibition in Manhattan 1906–1912: beyond the nickelodeon', *Cinema Journal*, 18/2, Spring 1979, pp. 2–15.
8. Geduld, *Focus on D. W. Griffith*, p.57; Zukor, according to his biographer, Will Irwin (*The House That Shadows Built*, 1928), quoted in Robert Sklar, *Movie-Made America* (New York: Random House, 1975), p. 46.
9. Robert Allen, 'Film history: the narrow discourse', *The 1977 Film Studies Annual: Part Two* (Pleasantville: Redgrave, 1977), pp. 9–17; 'Contra the Chaser Theory', *Wide Angle*, 3/1 9, 1979), pp. 4–11; course file in *AFI Education Newsletter*, 3/3, January–February 1980).
10. Jürgen Habermas, *Strukturwandel der Öffentlichkeit* (Neuwied, Berlin: Luchterhand, 1962; 1967), chaps I and II.
11. Merritt, 'Nickelodeon theaters', pp. 67, 72.
12. Ibid., p. 72, cites a total of eight films listed in *Motion Picture World* between March 1907 and December 1908 that might qualify; the standard fare at the beginning of the nickelodeon period consisted of comic chases (mostly French), native scenes of knockabout humour and moderate pornography, sporting events, especially prize fights; further, increasingly marginalized, trick films *à la* Méliès, historical enactments, travelogues and disaster films (Allen's essays on cinematic diversity before 1907–8; n. 9, above).
13. While a paternalistic fascination with the 'other' side in general could perhaps be expected in a Kentucky Victorian like Griffith, *Musketeers* appears to be tapping a more specific source, i.e. the representation of immigrant working-class milieux in contemporary still photography, most notably Jacob Riis, *How the Other Half Lives* (New York: Charles Scribner's Sons, 1890; republished with better prints 1901). The connotation of still photography as a medium is also invoked by the film's segregation of characters into those who move and act (the protagonists and their 'helpers') and those who seem to be frozen in decorative postures and gestures, abandoning their positions only to clear the stage for the carefully choreographed shootout.
14. It is no coincidence that the first systematic attempt to theorize spectatorship was published in 1916 when the techniques (primarily of continuity editing) that supported this transformation were being established as rules in production: Hugo Münsterberg, *The Photoplay: A Psychological Study* (republished New York: Dover, 1970). The conditions and techniques by which the cinematic apparatus puts the spectator in the position of 'transcendental subject' have been explored, in considerable depth, by semiological-psychoanalytic directions in film theory. Cf. seminal essays by Christian Metz, in *The Imaginary Signifier* (Bloomington: University of Indiana Press, 1981); Jean-Louis Baudry, 'Ideological effects of the basic cinematographic apparatus' and 'The apparatus', repr. in Theresa Hak Kyung Cha (ed.), *Apparatus* (New York: Tanam Press, 1980); also pertinent here is the debate on 'suture', summarized by Stephen Heath in *Questions of Cinema* (Bloomington: University of Indiana Press, 1981), ch. 3.
15. Roland Barthes, 'The realistic effect', trans. Gerald Mead, *Film Reader*, no. 3, February 1978, pp. 131–5; Barthes' concept of myth as a second-order system of signification is also extremely relevant here (*Mythologies* (London: Paladin, 1973)). Chaplin, a film-maker not generally praised for critical reflexivity towards his own medium, shows an acute awareness of the cinema's appropriation of the immigrant as image and

in *The Immigrant* (1917), Charlie's survival and founding of a family with a fellow immigrant (Edna Purviance) hinges upon the discovery of the two by a painter, i.e. on turning the immigrant image into an aesthetic/commercial value. In a similar vein, Chaplin's *Easy Street* (1917) can be read as a sarcastic comment on the immigrant-lower-class/nickelodeon mythology.

16. Stuart and Elizabeth Ewen, *Channels of Desire, Mass Images and the Shaping of American Consciousness* (New York: McGraw Hill, 1982), esp. pt. III; Lary May, *Screening Out the Past: The Birth of Mass Culture and the Motion Picture Industry* (New York: Oxford University Press, 1980), chaps 5–8. Both these books offer interesting arguments towards a revisionist analysis of cinema in the larger context of mass culture and consumer society, yet cannot be relied upon as far as textual evidence is concerned, especially May's study. More useful from a film-historical point of view are the following: Jeanne Allen, 'The film viewer as consumer', *Quarterly Review of Film Studies*, 5/4, Fall 1980, pp. 481–99; Charles Eckert, 'The Carole Lombard in Macy's window', *Quarterly Review of Film Studies*, 3/1, Winter 1978, pp. 1–23; Douglas Gomery, 'The movies become big business: public theatres and the chain store strategy', *Cinema Journal*, 18/2, Spring 1979, pp. 26–40, and 'The economics of US exhibition policy and practice', *Ciné-Tracts*, no. 12, Winter 1981, pp. 36–40.
17. Judith Mayne, 'Immigrants and spectators', *Wide Angle*, 5/2, 1982, pp. 32–41; 34.
18. Ibid., p. 38. Also Judith Mayne, 'Mediation, the novelistic, and film narrative', in S.M. Conger and J. R. Welsch (eds), *Narrative Strategies* (Macomb, Ill.: Western Illinois University Press, 1980), and her introduction to *Ciné-Tracts*, no. 13, Spring 1981, issue on *Film/Narrative/The Novel*; Margaret Morse, 'Paradoxes of realism: the rise of film in the train of the novel'. *Cine-Tracts*, no. 13, Spring 1981, pp. 27–37.
19. Oskar Negt/Alexander Kluge, *Öffentlichkeit und Erfahrung: Zur Organisationsanalyse von bürgerlicher und proletarischer Öffentlichkeit* (Frankfurt am Main: Suhrkamp, 1972). For an introductory review in English, see Eberhard Knödler-Bunte, 'The proletarian public sphere and political organization', *New German Critique*, no. 4, Winter 1975, pp. 51–75.
20. 'In strict opposition to a technocratic concept of organization, the concept of an organization tied to a proletarian public sphere indicates a concrete dialectic of spontaneity and organization, of immediate experience and insight into the social totality' (Knödler-Bunte, 'The proletarian public sphere', p.55).
21. *Öffentlichkeit und Erfahrung*, p. 8. Negt/Kluge refer here to Habermas, *Strukturwandel der Öffentlichkeit*, p. 8. Habermas himself appears to be revising some of his earlier positions on the fate of the public sphere in 'postliberal' societies in *Theorie des kommunikativen Handelns*, vol. 2 (Frankfurt am Main; Suhrkamp, 1981), pp. 571 ff.
22. Negt/Kluge, *Öffentlichkeit und Erfahrung*, p. 65 f. The last sentence of the book illuminates their use of the term 'proletarian' as oscillating between literal-historical and metaphorical-utopian meanings: 'Proletarian public sphere is the name of a socially collective process of production, the object of which is the redemption of the integrity of the human senses (*Sinnlichkeit*) (p.486). In recent years, Kluge who – as a film-maker – is concerned with the cinema's position between a self-reducing bourgeois public sphere and the all-absorbing public spheres of production (the privately owned new media) has abandoned the epithet 'proletarian' or even 'counter' (*Gegenöffentlichkeit*) in favour of the notion of a public sphere in the authentic sense (as opposed to the dominant pseudo-public spheres), as a medium for the integral organization of human experience, hence the production site of radical politics; see Klaus Eder/Alexander Kluge, *Ulmer Dramaturgien: Reibungsverluste* (München: Hanser, 1980), transl. in *New German Critique*, no. 24–25, Fall/Winter 1981–2, pp. 211–14. Since then, Kluge is even considering a reallotment of the cinema to the notion of the classical public sphere, arguing – in a revision of Benjamin's reproduction thesis – that the break between the aesthetics of film and the traditional arts was not as significant as that between the cinema and the privately owned and privately distributing consciousness industries (*Bestandsaufnahme: Utopie Film*, ed. A. Kluge (Frankfurt am Main: Zweitausendeins, 1983), pp. 49 ff.); this suggests a turn towards Habermas' position(s) on the public sphere.
23. Ben Brewster, 'A Scene at the Movies', pp. 318–25 of this volume; Noël Burch,

'Narrative/diegesis – threshold, limits', *Screen*, vol. 23 no. 2, July-August 1982, pp. 16–34; 'Porter, or ambivalence', *Screen*, 19/4, Winter 1978–9, pp. 91–105; Noël Burch, *To the Distant Observer: Form and Meaning in the Japanese Cinema* (Berkeley: University of California Press, 1979), pp. 61–6 *et passim*; and other writings. For a critique of Burch's approach see Paul Kerr, 'Re-inventing the cinema', *Screen*, vol. 21 no. 4, 1980/81, pp. 80–4, and Kristin Thompson and David Bordwell, 'Linearity, materialism and the study of early American cinema', *Wide Angle*, 5/3, 1983, pp. 4–15. Besides pointing out a series of factual errors in Burch's work, Thompson and Bordwell criticize him for falling back into the same type of linear narrative (relying on metaphors of evolution and teleology) which a 'materialist' history of film sets out to subvert. While they raise important issues concerning the relationship between film history and film theory, their advocacy of 'verification' and 'validity' as essential standards of any non-linear historiography strikes me as remarkably untouched by methodological and theoretical debates in the humanities and social sciences over the past decades – from Critical Theory to Deconstruction.

24. Elizabeth Ewen, 'City lights: immigrant women and the rise of the movies'. *Signs*, 5/3, suppl. 1980, S45–S65; repr. in Ewen and Ewen, *Channels of Desire*, pp. 81–105 (problematic in her reliance on Jacobs' book).
25. Allen, essays cited in n. 9, above; Burch and Brewster, n. 23, above.
26. On the history of this transition, from a nationalistic perspective, see Hans Traub, *Die UFA: Ein Beitrag zur Entwicklungsgeschichte des deutschen Filmschaffens* (Berlin: UFA Buchverlag, 1943). The most detailed account of the whole period can be found in Friedrich von Zglinicki, *Der Weg des Films: Die Geschichte der Kinematographie und ihrer Vorläufer* (Berlin: Rembrandt Verlag, 1956). Also see Wilfred von Bredow and Rolf Zurek (eds), *Film und Gesellschaft in Deutschland: Dokumente und Materialien* (Hamburg: Hoffmann und Campe, 1975), pp. 17 ff. An invaluable collection of documents relating to early German cinema was published as an exhibition catalogue by the Schiller-Nationalmuseum, Marbach a. N.: *Hätte ich das Kino!* (Stuttgart: Klett, 1976).
27. Sklar, *Movie-Made America*, p. 45, argues that the construction of respectable movie theatres in Germany (Berlin) preceded the American vogue of such theatres by two years. Neglecting the role of the vaudeville business in mediating this vogue (see note 7, above) and other factors, Sklar too easily links this argument to the different class composition of the respective audiences, disregarding the significance of coexisting forms of exhibition and their functional place within the public sphere. The *Wanderkino*, for instance, stigmatized by its affiliation with circus and fairground entertainment, continued to exist beyond 1904 when permanent exhibition locales were becoming the rule, and was even revived and appropriated briefly by the cinema reform movement following 1907 (Zglinicki, *Der Weg des Films*, p. 373). Moreover, distinctions between city and country and, even more so, between Berlin and other cities appear to be crucial to an assessment of the dynamics of exhibition practices and film production (see E Altenloh, *Zur Soziologie des Kino: Die Kino-Unternehmung und die sozialen Schichten ihrer Besucher* (Leipzig: Spamersche Buchdruckerei, 1914), pp. 18 ff.).
28. Konrad Lange, *Das Kino in Gegenwart und Zukunft* (Stuttgart, 1920); earlier sources quoted in Zglinicki, *Der Weg des Films*, p.367. For an example of the influence of LeBon's concept of the crowd, see H. Künschmann, 'Kinematograph und Psychologie der Volksmenge', *Konservative Monatsschrift*, 69 (1911/12), pp.920–30; see also Altenloh, *Zur Soziologie des Kino*, p. 94.
29. *Hätte ich das Kino*, pp. 67 ff.; Gerhard Zaddach, *Der literarische Film* (Berlin: Paul Funk, 1929), pp. 12 f., 16.
30. Hans Müller-Sanders, *Die Kinematographenzensur in Preussen*, diss. Heidelberg (Borna-Leipzig, 1912), pp. 57 f. Also see Regierungsrat Griebel, 'Die Kinematographenzensur' (1913), repr. in von Bredow and Zurek, *Film und Gesellschaft*, pp. 67–72.
31. Müller-Sanders, *Die Kinematographenzensur*, pp. 100–10.
32. By 1912, the share of narrative-dramatic films in the total production had reached 58%, clearly ranking comedies (20%) and 'actualities' (5%) as secondary genres; the remaining part consisted of scientific (2%) and other films (15%) (*Licht-Bild-Bühne*, no. 9, 1913).

33. E.g. Hermann Häfker, editor of the journal *Bild und Film* (1912 ff.) and author of a pamphlet on film aesthetics, *Kino und Kunst* (Mönchen-Gladbach: Volksvereins-Verlag, 1913). Häfker was active in the reform movement from the start and advocated a system of self-censorship as early as 1909.
34. Zaddach, *Der literarische Film*, p. 31 ff.
35. Pfemfert, 'Kino als Erzieher', *Die Aktion*, I, 19 June 1911, pp. 560–3; repr. in Anton Kaes (ed.), *Kino-Debatte: Literatur und Film, 1909–29* (Tübingen: Niemeyer, 1978), pp. 59–62; p. 60.
36. Lange, *Nationale Kinoreform*, based on a lecture of 1916 (Mönchen-Gladbach: Volksvereins-Verlag, 1918), excerpt in *Hätte ich das Kino*, p. 72.
37. Victor Noack, *Der Kino* (Gautzch b. Leipzig: Felix Dietrich, 1913), pp. 29 f.
38. Döblin, in *Kino-Debatte*, p. 38.
39. Curt Moreck, *Sittengeschichte des Kinos* (Dresden: Paul Aretz Verlag, 1926), defends the cinema against charges of harlotry and venality by claiming that a desire for anonymous sexuality is inherent in all art (Zglinicki, *Der Weg des Films*, p. 367). Intellectual attempts of aesthetic distancing, however hysterical and misogynous, have to be credited for acknowledging visual pleasure ('*Schaulust*', Freud's term for scopophilia) as a sexual drive; see Walter Serner, 'Kino und Schaulust' (1913), *Kino-Debatte*, pp. 53–8. Even Georg Lukács' relatively sober reflections (compared to those of his Expressionist contemporaries) invoke the body/soul dichotomy, applying it to the rivalry between cinema and theatre: 'Gedanken zu einer Ästhetik des Kinos' (1913), *Kino-Debatte*, pp. 112–18; Engl. transl. in *Framework*, no. 14, Spring 1981, pp. 2–4. On the patriarchal undercurrent linking intellectual attitudes of contempt/fascination/exploitation towards the cinema with the cultural repression of sexuality and physicality, see Heide Schlüpmann, 'Kinosucht', *Frauen und Film*, no. 33, October 1982, pp. 45–52; see also Gertrud Koch, 'Schattenreich der Körper: Zum pornographischen Kino', in *Lust und Elend: Das erotische Kino* (Munich: Bucher, 1981), pp. 16–39, 134–7.
40. Theweleit, *Männerphantasien*, 2 vols (Frankfurt am Main: Verlag Roter Stern, 1977/78).
41. As in the United States (Sklar, *Movie-Made America*, ch. 8; Jowett, *Film*, pp. 77 ff.), the high number of children frequenting the motion picture shows was observed with great alarm by reformers and educators, resulting in a wave of legal and administrative measures on the regional and local level. The concern about the cinema's effect on the physical and mental health of children – as well as on their sense of morality – was usually spiced with detailed descriptions of the sexual dangers lurking in the dark of the crowded theatre (Noack, *Der Kino*, pp. 3–7; Dr Albert Hellwig, 'Die Schundfilme, ihr Wesen, ihre Gefahren und ihre Bekämpfung' (1911), repr. in: von Bredow and Zurek, *Film und Gesellschaft*, pp. 60–6).
42. Noack, *Der Kino*, p. 8.
43. The link between spectatorship and other consumer activities was established early on: one of the first films, still produced for the mutoscope, shows Max Skladanowsky's six-year-old daughter advertising 'Liebigs Fleischextrat'; by 1911, department stores in Berlin (as in Vienna and Paris) were using films for advertising purposes (Traud, UGA; cited in Zglinicki, *Der Weg des Films*, p. 325). In the transition from kinetoscope and mutoscope to public exhibition, automat stores – e.g. Stollwerck (chocolate and candy) and Pritzkow (pickled herring *Rollmöpse* – played an important role: ibid., pp. 313–16).
44. Kracauer, 'Die kleinen Ladenmädchen gehen ins Kino' (1927), in *Das Ornament der Masse* (Frankfurt am Main: Suhrkamp, 1963), pp. 279–94; 280. Schlüpmann ('Kinosucht', p. 47) criticizes Kracauer for exempting his *own* passion for the cinema from the scrutiny of cultural criticism; Adorno may have anticipated that charge when he argues that Kracauer, even as he makes fun of the 'little salesgirl', discovers in her reactions a part of his own naive pleasure in cinematic spectacle ('Der wunderliche Realist', p. 397).
45. Altenloh, *Zur Soziologie des Kino*, p. 55 *et passim*; in the following, page numbers in parentheses refer to this publication. Closer to the conservative tenor of the reform movement is Altenloh's article, 'Die Stellung des jugendlichen Arbeiters zum Kino', *Die Hochwart-Monats-Schrift zur Bekämpfung des Schundes*, 4/8, 1913/14, pp. 198–203.

Some Historical Footnotes to the Kuleshov Experiment

YURI TSIVIAN

In a now classic article of 1968, Naum Kleiman drew the distinction between the Kuleshov *experiment* and the Kuleshov *effect*. Kuleshov's experiment lent this effect, now familiar to the cinematographer, the appearance of a proved theorem.[1] Indeed if theoreticians regard Kuleshov as the initiator of the cinema, one can only wonder why the workings of the effect he canonised were so belatedly recognised. Kleiman showed this by analysing the work of the montage mechanisms which were already popular in the decade preceding Kuleshov's experiment. What I shall attempt to deal with here is another, rather more archaic mechanism, connected not to the inception of montage images, but to their reception.

The *coup monté* of Kuleshov's experiment is a misreading of two contiguous pictures. Its author deliberately appeals to the 'uninitiated viewer',[2] who will see three identical shots of the faces of Mozzhukin as three different ones. It is clear that only someone used to reading films syntagmatically would be deceived by the face's expression – anyone with the slightest experience of watching films would identify the actor's expression in the various sequences with a plate, a grave, or a playing child. To borrow an analogy from phonetics, one might say that the effect of reciprocal assimilation means that the first of each pair of sequences is comprehended retrospectively, in the context of the second. In other words, the mechanism works by forcing us to read two contiguous texts as one.

In the history of the cinema, this mechanism was observed long before it was consciously used in narrative montage structures.[3] Indeed during the first decades of this century in Russia, we see the apparently paradoxical situation whereby cinema and its reception in the cultural consciousness of the epoch developed along autonomous lines. This relates partly to the way the boundaries of the cinematic text are defined, for this text was differently understood by the early film-maker and by the viewer. Whereas for its creator, the film was of course *par excellence* text, the viewer experienced the actual, tangible text in the form of the film-show itself. In the 1900s, one went not 'to a film', but 'to the cinematograph', performances consisted of a selection of short, unconnected films, and the differences between the various scenes appeared less striking than the similarity of all belonging to this new visual genre.

In these conditions, a certain semiotic skill was required of viewers in order to differentiate between the consecutive images, while the organisers of the show were required to separate the scenes within the performance. In the first years of cinema's existence in Russia, the pictures in the Lumière brothers' programme were separated by short intervals, for instance, whereas in a programme of 1898, described by Vladimir Turin, the pictures were separated by 'acoustic' methods:

> The master of ceremonies *rings*; the first animated picture disappears and we see another: before us, in place of the station, is a broad forest clearing, filled with cavalry and artillery ... The master of ceremonies *rings* again, and in place of the clearing there appears a long alley, with an old gentleman on a bench reading a newspaper.[4]

The proliferation of cinematographs in the early 1900s conspired to weaken the internal coherence of the performance. In drawing up their programmes, cinema managers generally observed neither the rules of composition nor the need to separate the pictures. A torrent of films would be shown without intervals, and the selection of scenes was generally a matter of chance. This had its effect on audiences' perceptions of the cinematograph: the impressions from one picture were involuntarily transferred to the next, to which it was connected only by its random adjacence in the programme. These were the origins of the effect subsequently used in Kuleshov's experiment.

Let us take an example. In the 1900s, the censors in Russia issued a ban against all pictures of an evangelical or spiritual nature, as well as those depicting members of the imperial family. The first ban caused no surprise, since the profane representation of sacred images was already prohibited elsewhere, on the stage of the theatre, for instance. It is harder to explain the ban on the cinematic representation of royal figures, firstly since Russian state tradition held that the tsar was not a sacred figure and his depiction was not taboo, and secondly since it is well known that the first film-operators to come to Russia – B. Matuszewski, M. Promio, F. Boublier and others – had been invited to take pictures of Nicholas II, so that the film collection of the imperial court contains a large number of reels portraying the tsar. The censors' ban applied not to photographs but to their projection on the screen. What worried them was the semiotic disruption which the films preceding and following them might introduce into the chronicle of the court. It was the inadequately hierarchical nature of the average film show to which N. Karzhansky objected, for instance, recalling in 1915 a cinematograph he had seen earlier in Paris, in which

> The Spanish monarch and the British king jumped out after each other on a piece of white sheet, a dozen Moroccan landscapes flashed past, followed by some marching Italian cuirassiers and a German dreadnought thundering into the water.[5]

In the early years of the century, when Russian cinema firms received permission to show members of the imperial family, the censors tried to block the semantic interference of contiguous films with a special circular which set out the conditions of public projection, and demanded

> a) that these images be shown without music, and always in a *special part*

of the programme, not connected to or interspersed with the showing of other images. In other words, that a curtain be lowered before a picture of one or another event is shown, then just a few episodes from these events should be shown, after which the curtain should be lowered again.

> And b) that these pictures be *separated by a short interval from pictures of a different content.* All this on condition that the showing of these films takes place under the special supervision of the chief cinematographer, by his own hand and at such a speed that the movements and gestures of the figures depicted in the film may evoke no comment.[6]

In attempting to stifle the aleatory syntagmatic of the show and to isolate the chronicle of the court from films of a less official content, the censors demanded that viewers interpret each film as an autonomous text with its own semiotic boundaries. One might accuse them of a certain lack of evolutionary wisdom in this: the structural tension between the clearly delineated boundaries of the performance, and the diffuse, precarious boundaries between the films of which it consisted, was a mainspring of the development of a film language in those years. It was this that made possible the improvised transfer – to paraphrase Roman Jakobson's famous formulation – of contiguity to similarity, whose results were visible in the Kuleshov experiment. From various contemporary sources we may conclude that true films of ideas, devised by associatively linking the content of consecutive pictures, were familiar to many early cinema spectators. M. A. Kuzmin's story 'Mark of Distinction' contains a description of

> . . . silken horses whisking their tails, *crawling butterflies magnified to the dimensions of a carriage*, and the alarmingly juicy dark-red of the cut pomegranate.[7]

We see here the spontaneous montage-like association of images which was so characteristic of viewers in those years. Two consecutive images impose their own system of scale on each other. The butterflies are clearly compared to a carriage because their relative dimensions automatically derive from those of the horses in the preceding picture. The contiguity of films produced a common semantic field – even the semblance of some larger connection.

The rapid alternation of disparate pictures during a performance fractured the boundaries of these pictures. But not only this, apparently. We have already mentioned the utterly unpredictable nature of early films' reception, which appeared determined by neither their content nor their creators' intentions. This was chiefly because a film's reception, as opposed to its conception, took in a wide cultural background, which overshadowed the originality of the film text, and which generally interpreted this originality as a fault. The more one investigates the history of film, the less part the film itself appears to play in the mode of its reception, and the greater the role of unconscious cultural stereotypes, which dictate to the viewer a whole system of perception. The numerous responses in the Russian press to the first Lumière film, *L'Arrivée d'un train*, unexpectedly reveal that the cultural background dominating the film's reception was not photography, but literature. This did not mean merely that most Russian audiences – and writers such as Gorky, for instance, or Stasov – almost automatically associated an approaching train and the attendant atmosphere of tension with some earlier literary experience, such as the tragic finale to Tolstoy's *Anna Karenina*; it was also a matter of their perception of the semiotic boundaries of Lumière's picture. In most journalistic accounts of this film, special attention is paid to its beginning and end. But whereas the beginning is described correctly – an empty railway track, a dot appearing on the horizon, the dot growing into a train, and so on – most descriptions of the conclusion are quite wrong. In contrast to the beginning, there is no clearly marked ending,[8] and the film breaks off at the point when the gentleman in the dark suit alights from the carriage, and stretches out his hand to help a woman lift out a little girl. The newspaper accounts of this reveal a clear, and doubtless unconscious, desire to give the film the appearance of a completed text. I shall quote from the middle of one of these accounts:

> ... the passengers departing on the train hurry to take their seats, anxiously looking around for the best places. A ragged fellow who has slipped into a first-class carriage is marched back, and is now back on the platform again, looking around distractedly, not knowing what to do with himself. At last everyone takes their seats; at a sign from the guard the train moves off, and one suddenly feels alarmed, as though it were about to crush us.[9]

This article was written from Paris, with the Lumière show still fresh in the author's mind, and it would be hard to suspect him of forgetfulness or a conscious desire to misrepresent the contents of the picture. Yet we see here two essential displacements. One introduces a novelettish quality into the events: there is indeed a poorly-dressed man holding a bundle, who does indeed look about him distractedly, and walk hesitantly into the camera. But he leaves the screen long before the train stops, so that he could not possibly be suspected of 'slipping into a first-class carriage'. The other displacement involves tidying up the construction of the film. The above article, like several others, concludes with the scene in which the train departs – a scene which is in fact is missing from the film. The cultural stereotype forces the writer to replace the film's unusual ending, which seems to hang in the air, with the finale of a basically circular construction – arrival/departure. This stereotype is so powerful that even a recent researcher, in a work specially dedicated to Lumière, inadvertently repeats the mistake of audiences in the nineteenth century: if one is to believe A. Gaudreault, the train appears to cut into the camera as it approaches the station, and as it departs, it cuts into the audience ('. . . en partant, sur les spectateurs').[10]

In its relation to early cinema, therefore, the internal semiotics of culture become a sort of metalanguage, whose role is constantly to effect a hypercorrection of each film. In the case of *L'Arrivée d'un train*, this reads into the man with the bundle the desire to live beyond his means, and into the face of Mosjoukine it reads expressions of grief, hunger or tenderness.

Nevertheless we should not think that early cinema's culturally determined reception encouraged its unhindered evolution from fragmentary to montage forms. If it had, we would have to agree that the tension and reluctance with which montage structures entered into the narrative equipment of the cinematograph lay entirely on the conscience of the early film-makers. The situation is in fact quite the reverse. Several works of Noël Burch,[11] as well as the preliminary results of new research on the early cinema carried out in the State Film Archive (Mikhail Yampolsky's work and my own on the early western cinema and the early Russian cinema), have shown that highly advanced and complex montage images had emerged with startling regularity when the language of the cinema was still at the 'babbling stage'. Further study of the reception of cinematography reveals the inertia, and even resistance, with which viewers greeted these experiments in the twenty years following the discovery of cinema. Research also reveals, with unwavering regularity, that the higher the general cultural level of the spectators, the more unwillingly they accept the innovations offered to them. The shifts in scale, for example, which the uneducated public in Russia had more or less assimilated by the end of the 1900s, were continuing to provoke serious aesthetic objections among Russian theatre-going circles as late as 1913. The theatre critic E. Stark wrote thus about the problems of enlarged scale:

> The makers of the film, clearly deprived of the most elementary artistic taste, alight briefly on a scene of some pathos, then for some reason present these faces and figures magnified by almost twice their normal size. Judge for yourselves what happens when you see before you a huge nose, a vast mouth, the monstrous whites of eyes and unnaturally protruding lips; when these features of some creature from another planet start to move, reflecting emotions which seize the soul, the result is excessively ugly, and comical in the very places which are meant to be sad.[12]

Here once again we come up against the inertness of the cultural reception of film, which has formed such an obstruction to the coherence of montage sequences. The fact is that in contrast to the examples cited, montage as a narrative (or expressive) strategy of the text manifestly contributed to violation of culture's internal stratification. Borrowing ready-made forms of narrative culture from the pre-cinema period,[13] the cinematograph was compelled to deal with several cultural topoi simultaneously. No single aspect of traditional art known to culture could provide the language of cinema with everything it needed for a coherent narrative. This language was created at the beginning of the century by the tension between the various separate cultural strata on which it rested. The results were a counter-balancing of several forces: the cinematograph, claiming its right to create a new cultural topos, aimed to hybridise all these genealogically diverse elements, which in turn displayed a semantic resistance, so that for contemporary cinema-viewers each element remained attached to its own source – the medium shot to the theatre stage, the close-up to portrait-painting and photography, the titles to literature, and so on. The struggle was waged on the terrain of each new film, and the conflict between the various sub-languages of culture focused on the point of collision between the montage images. This at least partly explains the prevailing culture's unwillingness to accept some of the rules of film language. Just as difficulties of absorbing a foreign language are determined not by a low intellectual level but by the degree of structural interference from the native tongue, so early cinema audiences' grudging response to montage was not a matter of unintelligence, but on the contrary, of the refinement of their cultural sensibility: for cinema-viewers at the turn of the century, the centrifugal tendency of various images of diverse origin far outweighed the unity imposed by their inclusion within the boundaries of one text – the film.

These difficulties of perception were intensified by the fact that Russian culture was fundamentally unfamiliar with such developed pre-cinematic forms of figurative narrative as the comic-strip. It was the absence of comic strips which discouraged the adaptation in Russia of those basic elements of montage with which the Pathé directors, say, were so at ease. Take this 1908 newspaper article about the cinematograph, presumably written by the music scholar Yuri Engel. In it he reveals part of the plot of a French farce:

> Having sent off her husband, 'she' sends an invitation to Paul. This letter, with all the amorous enticements of 'Letter-writing for the Young', is then shown separately on the screen. Paul instantly appears'.[14]

We can easily reconstruct the montage structure of the above episode:

1. Medium shot: 'She' writes the letter.
2. Close-up: The text of the letter to Paul.
3. Medium shot: Paul enters 'her' room.

Yet a glance at the account of this montage phrase makes plain what a poor command its author has of the language of narrative montage. The words 'separately' and 'instantly' are particularly striking. They both refer to the collision between montage images, encoding the simplest of narrative shifts: spatial shifts, from the woman writing the letter to the letter itself (magnification), and temporal ones, such as the sending of the letter, Paul receiving the letter, and so on, which are all omitted (ellipse). Engel signifies this ellipse by the word 'instantly' and although he has clearly not completely failed to understand what is happening, he is describing a discursive, rather than a diegetic level of montage composition. Even more interesting is Engel's phrase 'shown separately on the screen', referring to the close-up of the letter, and the striking way in which he omits this close-up from his diegesis of the film bears witness to the cultural incompatibility of their differing textures. The author regards the letter as belonging to a separate figurative category – more precisely literature: it is no coincidence that he provides it with its own genealogy by alluding to the style of 'Letter-writing for the Young' – and he resists all attempts to draw him into the theatrical context of a farce.

We may thus observe two contradictory tendencies in the reception of film language. We see the desire to unite dispersed fragments, and to provide them with a common context. Yet as soon as film-makers themselves attempt to construct such a context, we see them meeting serious resistance from these very mechanisms of cultural reception. At the turn of the century, there was a temporary but fundamental equilibrium between these two tendencies. The growing numbers of films, the proliferation and increasing complexity of themes, the developing experiments in the narrative use of montage – all this was later to transform the structure of the cinema show. In the meantime, however, new montage forms in Russia existed side by side with the old conception of the performance, which continued to consist of a string of disparate pictures. In this transitional period in the consciousness of film language, both layers remained similarly active, with both the new, contrived, montage sequences, and the old, haphazard ones perceived in the context of each other.

This parodically embellished description of a film show in a short story by Sergei Gorodetsky, for instance, faithfully reflects both the state of montage language in that period, and the cultural reception of that language:

> The Rajah is riding on tall elephants, under date palms and bananas. His face grows suddenly vast, the skin is whipped off a giant banana, and the fruit slips between his thick lips. A river. People are jumping into the water. A staircase. A room. A man with St Vitus' dance reads a newspaper, plunging into it, tearing himself away, turning somersaults. Hamlet sings over a skull, his voice shrouded in a whining hiss. Suddenly two Pathé cocks appear. It becomes dark. A little boy runs across a field, through a wood, into the water, to a tree, away from the tree, into a house, the house is on fire, he escapes out of the chimney, followed head-over-heels by some crazy fat men, one after another. They can't keep up with an old woman wearing thick trousers with no laces, but the little boy can't get away. . . .[15]

One's attention is drawn to the exaggerated diffuseness of the boundaries between the separate pictures. Only in one place does Gorodetsky locate the end of one film and the beginning of another: 'Suddenly two Pathé cocks appear, it grows dark, a little boy runs . . .' But here too we see a deliberate discontinuity in the account, for the Pathé film's trademark – the two cocks – concludes the first, but does not open the second. Yet Gorodetsky appropriates this as a pause between two subjects ('it becomes dark'), displacing the break and emphasising it with the barrier word 'suddenly'. His entire account of the show plays with the way in which the subjects blend together, as the contents of one film seem to roll on the same intonational wave into that of the next. This creates the impression of a single context, within which separate subjects exist as discrete pieces. In the light of this, the other appearance in the text of the word 'suddenly' is even more striking: 'his face grows suddenly vast . . .' The montage transition from middle-ground to close-up is described as a sudden leap – the magnification is experienced as an event which seems to burst open the frame of the subject, and this collision of perspectives proves a sharper semiotic boundary than the actual boundaries of the film.

This brings us back to the general problematic of the evolution of film language. The tension which accompanied it during its first twenty years had little to do with problems of a heuristic character. The development of the narrative structures of the cinematograph was not a series of discoveries and improvements, rather the complicated sum of the contest between various concealed and differently directed forces. The problem is not the development of a new language, but the extent of this language's cultural adaptability. The dramatic effect of the evolution of montage in the cinema lies in the confrontation between generally understood notions of the semiotic boundaries of the text, and the notions which the cinematograph suggests in relation to it. On the one hand, the early films flouted the conventional semiotic constraints on the text – the observation of a beginning and an end, the rules of semantic composition, spatial autonomy, and so on. On the other, in the transition from one perspective to another (or several others), the cinematograph helped to destroy existing cultural boundaries. The association of montage images was seen as a cross-cultural phenomenon, and the attempt to create a unified spatial articulation of the world, secured behind the various sub-languages of culture, resulted in the cultural-semiotic boundaries appearing at the very centre of the film, permanently disturbing its already precarious identity.

In the early stages of its development, therefore, the language of film may be regarded as a communications network, striving for an isomorphic relationship with culture. None the less the adaptation was mutual. Film language has not merely appropriated the semiotics of these intertextual boundaries, but has taught culture the semiotics of their destruction. Rising above the former stratification of culture appears a language whose rationale is its mobility. To quote Arkadii Arkatov's definition, the service this language has rendered is to 'replace the individual moving and gesticulating in space with alternating, flying spaces'.[16] This brilliant formulation dates from 1922, almost at the same time as, and independently from, Kuleshov's experiment. But it describes the same essential character of the film language of that experiment, and may successfully serve as an adequate description of it.

Notes

First published in French in *Iris* vol. 1 no. 4, 1986.

1. *Kadr kak yackeika montazha. Voprosy kinoisskustva* (The sequence as the cell of montage. Questions of film art), Moscow, 1968, 2nd edn, pp. 112–13.
2. V. Pudovkin, *Complete Works* (Moscow, 1974), vol. 1, pp. 182, 252.
3. We shall leave aside here the complex question of how to date the point at which narrative structures were translated into montage. For the present we shall date the origins of montage from the point at which it became universal. In Russia this was at the beginning of the first decade of the century.
4. V. Turin, *Zhivaya fotografiya* (Living photography) (St Petersburg, 1898), p. 4. It is conceivable that by 'ring' Turin meant the click in the camera mechanism, to which Gorky also referred in an article in Nizhegorodskii listok (The Nizhnenovgorod Leaflet), 4 July 1986, no. 182.
5. 'V kinematografe: Iz knigi "Paris"', *Rampa i zhizn* no. 32, 1915, p. 6.
6. Circular of 21 March 1911. Central State Historical Archive, 776–22–33.
8. I am assuming that our copy of the film is complete.

9. V. Yakovlev, *Son nayavu* (Waking dream), *Novoe vremya* (New Times), 29 January (Old Style) 1896. The atmosphere of alarm, to which others too refer, is before the train stops.
10. André Gaudreault, 'De "L'Arrivée d'un train" à "The Lonedale Operator": une trajectoire à parcourir', in *D. W. Griffith* (Paris, 1984).
11. See e.g. Noël Burch, 'Porter, or Ambivalence', *Screen*, Winter 1978/9, vol. 19 no. 4, pp. 91–100.
12. E. Stark, 'S nogami na stole' (Feet on the table), *Teatr i iskusstvo* (Theatre and Art), no. 39, p. 770.
13. J. L. Fell, *Film and the Narrative Tradition* (University of Oklahoma Press, 1974).
14. Yuri Engel, 'O kinematografe' (On the cinematograph), *Russkie vedomosti* (Russian Gazette), no. 275, 27 November 1908.
15. S. Gorodetsky. 'Volf' (Wolf), *Povesti is rasskazy* (Tales & Stories) (St Petersburg, 1910), pp. 146–7.
16. 'Sevodnyashnee kino' (The Modern Cinema), *Teatr i zhisn* (Theatre and Life), Berlin, 1922, no. 11, p. 10.

Translated from Russian by Kathy Porter

The Nickelodeon Era Begins
Establishing the Framework for Hollywood's Mode of Representation

CHARLES MUSSER

The year 1907 was pivotal for the institution of American cinema. While crises and fundamental changes occurred at almost every level of the industry, perhaps the most important transformations involved the interrelated modes of production and representation. In effect, this article attempts to establish how and why cinema moved from *Life of an American Fireman* to *The Lonely Villa*.

A pertinent historical model is based on dialectical materialism and focuses on the interaction between cinema's modes of production and representation. In cinema, the mode of production involves three essential practices or groups: film production, exhibition and reception (the production companies, the showmen and the spectators). While the mode of film production is responsible for the films, these can only be understood within a changing framework involving additional elements: the mode of exhibition, concerned with the showman's method of presentation and his relation to the films made by the production companies, and the mode of appreciation, concerned with the audience's strategies for understanding/enjoying, and with their relationship to, the exhibited films. Although this mode of cinema production, modified by other socio-economic and cultural factors, determines the framework for possible representational strategies, it is, of course, also determined by them.

A brief overview of the first ten years of American cinema is perhaps useful. During the late 1890s, after a short novelty period, exhibitors usually purchased one-shot films from producers and often arranged/edited these into sequences and programmes – often accompanying them with narration, music and sound effects. During the early 1900s, editorial control shifted increasingly to the production companies, coinciding to some degree with the rising popularity of story films.[1] By the end of 1904, two further developments had taken place. First, 'features', usually acted films of one-half to one reel in length, had become the industry's dominant product. This does not mean that more acted films were made than actualities, but the production companies' profits were based principally on the sales of longer fictional films.[2] Second, the reel of film became the basic industry commodity. Previously, exhibitors like Biograph, American Vitagraph and Percival Waters' Kinetograph Company rented an exhibition service to vaudeville theatres, which included a projector, a motion picture operator and a reel of film. In late 1903, Waters, recognizing that the exhibition process had become quite simple, trained theatre electricians to operate a projector and rented a reel of film to these vaudeville houses for a lower price.[3] This was one reason why he was able to win the Keith Circuit from

Biograph in the fall of 1904. Exhibitors now became renters or film exchanges, while the theatres became the actual exhibitors. Vitagraph and other services followed suit, and by the beginning of 1905, the necessary preconditions for the nickelodeon era had been met.

The nickelodeon era required a certain number of exhibition outlets devoted primarily to moving pictures (store-front theatres) plus an essentially interchangeable commodity (the reel of film) plus sufficient variety in its supply (a certain number of new fictional 'headliners'). The onset of this era, however, had little immediate impact on the rate of film production and the mode of representation – at least at the Edison, Biograph and Lubin companies. At Edison, the number of fictional features actually declined during 1906 and the first six months of 1907 relative to 1905. The Edison films which Edwin Porter made in 1906 became more elaborate and sophisticated within the representational system constructed in previous years. Only Vitagraph and Pathé quickly recognized the implications of the nickelodeon era to any degree. Vitagraph moved into production and film sales in the fall of 1905 and both companies rapidly increased the number of films they produced. A gap soon developed between the modes of film production and representation on one hand, and the mode of exhibition and the system of distribution on the other. Film-making remained a cottage industry while exhibition had become a form of mass production. This contradiction was masked at first by the success and rapid expansion of the nickel theatres. If the Edison Company sold 71 prints of *How a French Nobleman Got a Wife Through the New York Herald 'Personal' Columns* in 1904, it sold 182 copies of *Dreams of a Rarebit Fiend* in 1906. Such growth at first appeared to affirm the existing methods of making films, a situation which continued until approximately mid-1907.

Prior to mid-1907, the early or 'pre-Griffith' mode of representation dominated the film industry. The films of this period were non-linear. The narrative construction of *Life of an American Fireman* or *The Great Train Robbery*, with their overlapping actions and returnings to earlier points in time, continued to be used although rarely in such extreme forms (see Biograph's *Wanted, a Dog* or Edison's *Lost in the Alps* (1907)). The tensions between scenes perceived as self-contained wholes on the one hand and their potential as part of a more complex sequence on the other is a partial explanation for these narrative structures. While early cinema generally moved from the first extreme to the second, it was not until the foundations for Hollywood's mode of representation had been laid that this contradiction was superseded.

The mode of appreciation (reception) remained fundamentally unchanged between 1898 and mid-1907. Strategies for making film narratives comprehensible to audiences fell into three basic complementary and interdependent categories, centred within the spectator, the exhibitor or the film.

Audience Familiarity

When films were based on well-known stories, comic strips or popular songs, this meant a different relationship between audience and cultural object than in most contemporaneous literature and theatre, where it was assumed that audiences had no foreknowledge of the narrative's plot, characters, etc. Porter's *Night Before Christmas* (December 1905) 'closely follows the time honored Christmas legend by Clement Clarke Moore, and is sure to appeal to everyone young and old'.[4] Biograph and Edison both made films based on the hit song 'Everybody Works but Father' popularized by Lew Dockstader in 1905. Porter's *Waiting at the Church* (July 1906) assumed spectator familiarity with the lyrics of the hit song 'Waiting at the Church', written by Fred W. Leigh and popularized by Vesta Victoria. Porter did not simply illustrate the song: a discrepancy between the lyrics and the film narrative is an essential element of the film's humour.

The 'Teddy' Bears (February 1907), one of Porter's personal favourites, manipulated audience familiarity in particularly sophisticated ways and demonstrated Porter's mastery of a mode of representation about to be fragmented. The juxtaposition of two different referents was an important element of its humour and success. The film begins as an adaptation of *Goldilocks and the Three Bears* and functions for the first two-thirds as a fairy-tale film for children, with the life-sized Teddy Bears as the subject. Suddenly the film moves outside the studio, changing moods and referents. The bears chase Goldilocks across a snowy landscape until a hunter, Teddy Roosevelt, intervenes, kills the two full-grown pursuers and captures the baby bear. The sudden appearance of 'Teddy' was based on a well-known incident when President Roosevelt, on a hunting expedition in Mississippi, refused to shoot a bear cub. This was in November 1902. Shortly thereafter, Morris Michtom, a Russian immigrant who ran a small toy store and would eventually start the Ideal Toy Corporation, began to make and sell 'Teddy's Bear' – a stuffed version of the spared cub. The novelty became a craze by 1906–7, when thousands of toy bears were being sold each week and music like 'The Teddy Bear March' (copyrighted 1907) was popular.'[5] Unless audiences appreciated this shift in referents, the killing of the two endearing bears would seem bizarre and at odds with the earlier part of the film. Simi somewhat wilfully missed the point in his *Variety* review when he wrote:

> The closing pictures showing the pursuit of the *child* by the bear family is spoiled through a hunter appearing on the scene and shooting two. Children will rebel against this position. Considerable comedy is had through a chase in the snow, but the live bears seemed so domesticated that the deliberate murder in an obviously 'faked' series left a wrong taste of the picture as a whole.[6]

It is the shift in referents which reveals to the audience that *The 'Teddy' Bears* is not simply a children's film but was aimed at adults under the guise of a children's story. By judging the film from the viewpoint of a child who could not be expected to grasp a range of contemporary adult references, Simi postulated a relationship between viewer and cultural object that would be applicable to later cinema. In fact, Simi's review indicates that criteria for assessing films were changing and that films relying on a prescient audience were received with less sympathy.

The extent to which the antecedents of American films can be found in newspapers from this period suggests that most films worked within a highly specific, well-known cultural framework. Biograph's *Love Microbes* (September 1907), in which Professor Cupido isolates the love microbe and injects it into unsuspecting victims, was inspired by Ella Wheeler Wilcox's headline pronouncement that 'The Love Microbe Did It'. This precursor to Dear Abby asserted that 'I am thoroughly convinced that love is composed of microbes, good and bad, "benign" and "pernicious"'. Her amused colleagues followed her editorial with cartoons that literalized and burlesqued it.[7] The Biograph Company soon picked up the idea and knowledge of the antecedent enhanced, but was not essential to, an understanding of the film.

Self-sufficient Narrative and Intra-textual Redundancy

A second group of strategies for facilitating audience understanding involved the production company. During the 1890s, a few simple gag films and the magical films of producers like Georges Méliès were among the few kinds of 'self-sufficient' films. After 1903, two common structuring principles using narrative redundancy proved efficacious in creating readily accessible subjects: the accumulation of discrete scenes built around a unifying theme, character or gag, and its corollary – the chase. Redundancy of situation, which Porter had used in *The Buster Brown Series* (February 1904) and *The Seven Ages* (February 1905), continued to provide structuring principles for comedies like *Nine Lives of a Cat* (July 1907), which showed nine attempts to dispose of an uncooperative feline, and *The Rivals* (August 1907), which, like many films of this type, was based on a comic strip by T. E. Powers which ran in the *New York American*. The film and the comic strip show two rivals fighting over the desirable woman. In each scene, the rival escorting the girl is outwitted by his opponent, who then takes possession of the beloved object. The situation is then repeated with the characters reversed. When Porter had enough scenes and wanted to achieve closure, he had the woman leave both rivals for a third. This structuring principle of repetition with slight variation was deeply indebted to the repetitive structures of daily and weekly strips and was used in most films where a humorous effect was desired. Biograph's *Mr Butt-In* (released February 1906), based on a cartoon series in the *New York World*, uses a similar structure. After the requisite number of incidents in which Mr Butt-In interferes with other people's business, he is taken to an insane asylum, ending the succession of disruptions and the film. Other surviving films utilizing this structure include Biograph's *If You Had a Wife Like This* (February 1907), Hepworth's *That Fatal Sneeze* (June 1907), Urban's *Diablo Nightmare* (October 1907), Eclipse's *Short-Sighted Cyclist* and Gaumont's *Une Femme vraiment bien* (1908).

While the chase also utilized a repetitive structure, it achieved new levels of clarity through a simple opposition between pursuers and pursued which could be expressed compositionally, by foregrounding first one group then the next, and through movement, as the pursued and pursuers came towards and past the camera. Biograph's *Personal* (1904), *The Escaped Lunatic* (1903) and *The Lost Child* (1904) are pure chase films. By 1906–7 chase sequences were often integrated into longer narratives: Biograph's *The Elopement* (released December 1907) and Edison's *Kathleen Mavourneen* (May 1906) are two examples. Porter, like many of his contemporaries, combined the chase with other forms of narrative redundancy in comedies like *The Terrible Kids* (April 1906) and *Getting Evidence* (September 1906). *The Terrible Kids* begins with a series of scenes in which two unsocialized boys and their dog harass various adults, until society (the local police and the victims of the pranksters) responds by chasing and eventually catching the culprits. In *Getting Evidence*, a detective is beaten each time he tries to photograph a young couple kissing. When he succeeds, the private eye is 'pursued by a crowd, caught and ducked thoroughly in the surf'.[8] This method of narrative construction was simple, effective and allowed for the production of one-reel features without complex stories.

Severe limitations were placed on other kinds of self-sufficient narratives in the pre-1907 period. If a story was unfamiliar and complicated, how was the spectator to know if the succeeding shot was backwards or forwards in time? The temporal/spatial and narrative relationships between different characters and lines of action were often vague, or worse – confusing. Visual cues like repeated action were helpful, but often not possible. The producer occasionally used intertitles but this practice was not universally accepted. Generally the film-maker had to tell a relatively simple story or count on the exhibitor's intervention to clarify the narrative.

The Problem of Complex Narrative

A third group of representational strategies was used by the exhibitor to clarify screen narratives. One way to facilitate audience comprehension, as *Views and Film Index* pointed out with regard to *Kathleen Mavourneen*, was through sound effects:

> Recently a film was seen in which a young couple were coming across a field. They stopped and stood with bowed heads for a few seconds, then proceeded on their way, much to the mystification of the audience. But when the same picture was shown at another theatre, the mystery was solved; for a second before they stopped a church bell tolled; as they seemed to hear it they stood with lowered heads. The realism was pretty and very touching – it made a hit and occasioned comment among the audience.[9]

Sound effects alone could not solve the problem of narrative clarity in most instances. *Kathleen Mavourneen* and other ambitious Edison projects challenge Nicholas Vardac's assertion in *Stage and Screen* that stage melodrama could be readily adapted to silent film because dialogue was a non-essential part of the play. The standard version of the script for the play *Kathleen Mavourneen* is wordy, relying on dialogue for essential information and the story line: the absence of words was strongly felt by producers, exhibitors and viewers.

The lecture accompanying a film continued to be an option used by many travelling exhibitors. At least one such exhibitor considered the lecture to be essential for Porter's *Daniel Boone* (December 1906), a 1,000 ft dramatic film starring Florence Lawrence.[10] This form of assistance, however, was not offered in all theatres. Perhaps Porter assumed audience familiarity with these plots since *Kathleen Mavourneen* and *Daniel Boone* were both based on well-known stage plays. Whether Porter misjudged this, wanted the film to be shown with a commentary or failed to achieve the level of self-sufficient clarity he originally intended is difficult to determine. This problem (faced by many film-makers) was underscored by a writer for *Views and Film Index* in September 1906:

> *Moving Pictures – for Audiences, not for Makers*
>
> Regardless of the fact that there are a number of good moving pictures brought out, it is true that there are some which, although photographically good, are poor because the manufacturer, being familiar with the picture and the plot, does not take into consideration that the film was not made for him, but for the audience. A subject recently seen was very good photographically, and the plot also seemed to be good, but could not be understood by the audience.
>
> If there were a number of headings on the film it would have made the story more tangible. The effect of the picture was that some people in the audience tired of following a picture which they did not understand, and left their seats. Although the picture which followed was fairly good, the people did not wait to see it.
>
> Manufacturers should produce films which can be easily understood by the public. It is not sufficient that the makers understand the plot – the pictures are made for the public.[11]

The need to respond to such criticism, however, was not strongly felt by production companies, which were then experiencing unprecedented prosperity. This soon changed.

By mid-1907 the nickelodeon frontier was disappearing, as almost every town and city had its local movie theatre. In many areas the number of movie houses had reached saturation point as competition for patrons intensified. Heady optimism and seemingly unlimited growth were giving way to new insecurities. For the producers, the contradictions between the established modes of representation and the new system of mass entertainment were becoming inescapable. New production companies were created each month to profit from the demand for story films. Production had to expand at companies like Edison, Biograph and Lubin if they were to maintain their standing in the industry. Here production efficiency and maximum profits were directly and indirectly related to the problem of narrative efficiency and cinematic strategies.

The repertoire of cinematic strategies in use at the beginning of the nickelodeon era proved inadequate. Narrative redundancy did not provide enough diversity to generate sufficient stories without boring audiences. While companies continued to use simple stories and variations on a single gag as the basis for film narratives during 1908–9, producers had to turn to more complex stories.

The explosion in film production and the rapidly expanding audience, however, meant that reliance on prescient spectators was becoming outmoded. When Kalem produced *The Merry Widow* in late 1907, it presented a condensed, silent version of the Broadway hit. *Variety* observed that

> The film is photographically excellent, but the *Merry Widow* would seem to have its greatest value in the advertising opportunities it affords, in cities where the vogue of the Savage productions, in New York and Chicago, is a matter of general knowledge; but it is a question whether it would be of any value whatever to an exhibitor in the average city or town.[12]

Subsequent Kalem films were provided to the exhibitor with lectures which eventually ran in *The Moving Picture World*. These were not always used, however, and the *New York Dramatic Mirror* continued to criticize films like Kalem's *Lady Audley's Secret* (June 1908) because 'unless one has read the book and knows the plot he finds it difficult to understand'. Such criticism was also levelled at Pathé's *L'Affaire Dreyfus*.[13] While there was a general rejection of precognition as a mode of appreciation by 1908, a few directors continued to rely on audience foreknowledge in some circumstances. A textbook demonstration of consequent problems was offered by Arthur Honig who analysed the viewer's reaction to Porter's *The Devil* (September 1908). Honig had seen the play on which the film was based and was able to follow the film's narrative, imagining the spoken lines and judging the acting and sets in relation to the play which for five cents he was able to re-experience. While Honig was very pleased with the film, he was accompanied by an 'intelligent friend' who had never seen the play and who started asking Honig questions about the story line, forcing him into the role of personal narrator. Without the necessary frame of reference the friend's enjoyment of the film was spoiled.[14]

Reliance on audience foreknowledge was doomed in two respects. First, there was a limited number of specific stories, hit songs, successful plays and crazes familiar to most Americans and these had in most instances already been used. Secondly, these items usually had a more limited audience than the films which were inspired by them. This created problems for renters and exhibitors who served a mass audience. This gap between what the film-maker expected the audience to know and what the audience actually knew was either filled by the exhibitor or led to confusion. There were two possible solutions. First, narrative clarity could be facilitated by the exhibitor introducing live sound through a lecture or behind-the-screen dialogue. Secondly, the producer could employ cinematic strategies which made the narrative more accessible without involving the exhibitor.

The Lecture

The lecture, always an important strategy in the exhibitor's repertoire, was the focus of renewed interest by early 1908. This was encouraged by the breakdown of the strategies relying on a prescient audience and facilitated by the theatre's new role as exhibitor. The manager or someone else connected with the theatre could interpret the film without necessarily adding to the overhead. In fact, the competition between small theatres encouraged up-to-date showmen to clarify inaccessible films. It was a way to personalize their theatres and turn grateful patrons into steady customers. W. Stephen Bush, former travelling exhibitor and frequent contributor of articles and reviews to *Moving Picture World*, considered the lecture 'a creative aid to the moving picture entertainment'. Often lecturing at church functions, his approach to cinema was that of the traditionalist who wanted to instruct as well as entertain. Bush condemned the uneducated exhibitor who showed a Shakespeare play on film without a lecture and 'bewildered his patrons who might have been thrilled and delighted with a proper presentation of the work'. To combat these and similar failings, Bush prepared and offered to sell 'special lectures with suggestions as to music and effects for every feature turned out by the Edison Licensees'.[15]

Beginning with *Evangeline* (released in February 1908), the Kalem Company, an Edison licensee, began to issue lectures to be read with its films. Referring to *Evangeline*, *Show World* observed that, 'Shown as a straight picture this film is certain to be of interest; but it presents excellent opportunities for a lecturer of ability to further increase its interest by the recitation of those portions of the poem (which naturally accompany the scene depicted)'.[16] Porter's *Colonial Virginia* (made in May 1907 but not released by Edison until November 1908) was gently praised by the *Dramatic Mirror* as 'an interesting and instructive representation of early Colonial life in Virginia'. A more critical review in *Moving Picture World* felt the film needed 'to be presented with a lecture for the spectator to fully understand and appreciate the scenes that are presented'.[17]

Stephen Bush argued that a skilled lecturer would more than offset the cost of his salary by increasing patronage and turnover. He asked exhibitors,

> Why do many people remain in the moving picture theatre and look at the same pictures two or even three times? Simply because they do not understand it the first time; and this is by no means a reflection of their intelligence. Once it is made plain to them, their curiosity is gratified and they are pleased to go.[18]

In another article on 'The value of the lecture', Van C. Lee claimed surprise that 'the managers are just awakening to the fact that a lecture adds much to the realism of a moving picture'. Like Bush he asked his readers, 'Of what interest is a picture at all if it is not understood?'[19] Bush and Van C. Lee's arguments, at least on a financial level, were overly facile given the rapid turnover of subject matter, the exhibitor's narrow profit margin and the substantial number of films which were intelligible without such aid. Their position was an attempt to expand those traditional strategies of screen presentation which had been frequently used among travelling lectures, to this new form of mass exhibition.

Talking Pictures – Actors Behind the Screen

'Talking pictures', the technique of endowing screen characters with live dialogue went back, at least, to stereopticon 'picture plays' like *Miss Jerry* for which Alexander Black changed his voice as he assumed different parts. As early as

1897, Lyman Howe's success was 'largely due to his well-trained assistants who presented dialogue behind the screen'.[20] Porter, who had become familiar with this procedure at the Eden Musée while projecting the *Opera of Martha* (1899), photographed a minstrel performance for Havez and Youngson's show, *Spook Minstrels*. The resulting film was never copyrighted but recently turned up at the Museum of Modern Art as part of its collection. Havez and Youngson's act opened in Pittsburgh on 9 January 1905 at the Grand Opera House and reached New York City's Circle Theatre a month later where it was reviewed:

> A distinct novelty on the bill was the first appearance here of Havez and Youngson's *Spooks Minstrels*, in which moving pictures are used in a novel way. The pictures show a minstrel company going through a performance, and as the various numbers are presented the songs, jokes and dances are given by men who stand behind the screen and follow the motions of the men in the picture very accurately. The act is original and novel and was highly appreciated.[21]

The same principle was used in January 1907 when Porter filmed another version of *Waiting at the Church* for the Novelty Song Company. Vesta Victoria was photographed singing 'Waiting at the Church' in a wedding gown that was part of her vaudeville act. Afterwards she sang 'Poor John'. The song was used in the novelty company's theatres, where a singer would stand behind the screen and sing synchronously with the picture, giving audiences the impression of witnessing an amazingly life-like performance by Vesta Victoria.[22]

Talking pictures, however, did not become a 'craze' in New York until the spring of 1908. Advocates felt that 'the dialogue helps the less intelligent to fully understand the plot, for no matter how skillfully worked out, there are always passages which require something more than mere pantomime to fully explain the situation'.[23] By July 1908, at least three businesses were supplying behind-the-screen actors and films to theatres. Len Spenser, a 'pioneer' in supplying slides, singers and operators to moving picture managers on a systematic basis could now also furnish trained competent screen actors to do the talking behind the screen.[24] – The Humanovo Producing Company, run by Will H. Stevens and owned by Adolph Zukor, had as many as twenty-two companies on the road.[25] One of the groups Stevens hired included J. Frank Mackey and Theressa Rollins. Before they moved into talking pictures, the two had often travelled with road shows doing theatrical comedies like *Raffles the Burglar*. Mackey had also done vaudeville routines as part of Mackey and Clark, and also Quigg, Mackey and Nickerson – in both cases as comedy musical artists. Starting off with Zukor's Humanovo Company, Mackey broke off and formed his own 'original' Humanova Company with a stock of old films, including either Porter's *Uncle Tom's Cabin* or the Lubin imitation. A programme in one theatre[26] included:

1. Bennett's Orchestra
2. Silent Pictures
3. Illustrated Songs

4. Silent Pictures
5. Talking Pictures
   Intermission – 5 minutes
6. Silent Pictures
7. Illustrated Songs
8. Talking Pictures
9. Bennett's Orchestra

The third major company, the Actologue Company, was owned by the National Film Company of Detroit and the Lake Shore Film and Supply Company of Cleveland. Edison films, particularly *College Chums* (November 1907) and *Gentlemanly Burglar* (May 1908), were among the most commonly used.[27] Porter's film of Molnar's *The Devil* was particularly suited for this exhibition strategy which avoided the need for prescient audiences.[28]

Talking pictures had several limitations. There was a lack of standardization: quality and effectiveness varied from theatre to theatre. The *Dramatic Mirror* felt that

> The possibilities of this sort of thing with trained actors and painstaking rehearsals are admitted, but the manner in which the idea was carried out in the houses visited by *The Mirror* representative were grotesque and a drawback to the pictures themselves. The odd effect of the voice of a barker trying to represent several voices, some of them women and children, and in one case a dog, may be amusing as a freak exhibition, but can hardly add to the drawing power of the house.[29]

If trained actors and lecturers were expensive and their aid was not always necessary or even desirable, the customary daily change of programmes prevented the local exhibitor from becoming sufficiently familiar with his material. Nor were many people up to performing 12 to 16 times a day. High-class talking picture companies and many of the more experienced lecturers worked outside the renting system set up by the exchanges. They provided a speciality service that toured different towns with films, as the travelling exhibitor had done. While additional expenses may have been recouped by higher admission prices, as middle-class audiences were drawn to a more customized and 'refined' entertainment, these talking pictures were never a realistic option for most storefront nickel theatres.

Mechanical Talking Pictures – Synchronous Sound

Another kind of talking pictures relied exclusively on the mechanical reproduction of image and sound. These early sound films had reached new levels of technical sophistication and commercial success in the nickelodeon era beginning with Gaumont's Chronophone which had its American début in May 1907 at Cleveland's Family Theatre. The Chronophone presented a programme of eight numbers including Zanetello, singing an aria from Pagliacci, Saheret, the dancer, and the Hogan Colored Quartette. *Billboard* declared, 'the tone reproduction and movement of the picture is absolutely perfect.'[30] Although the invention was praised by many, only four machines were in use in the United States at the beginning of 1908.[31] The National Cameraphone Company, a concern based in Bridgeport, Connecticut, with a studio at 43rd Street and 11th Avenue in New York, was a domestic competitor that was started by J. A. Whitman and became active in the winter of 1908. A private exhibition of the Cameraphone in February created considerable excitement.[32] By July, the enterprise was exhibiting sound films in forty-five first-class houses and claimed to have contracts for 140 more. Subjects generally consisted of vaudeville acts, bits of dramatic plays and musical numbers.[33] One critic remarked that

> For the reproduction of vaudeville acts and burlesque musical numbers, [the cameraphone] is a valuable addition to the moving picture program, but for the presentation of feature films of the melodramatic variety, and the description of foreign travel pictures, it can never replace the lecture, especially the lecture by the educative and impressive talker.[34]

But by the summer, the Cameraphone company was producing versions of *Quo Vadis*, *The Corsican Brothers*, *The Count of Monte Cristo* and other plays. The dialogue facilitated the audience's ability to follow the narrative much as it had with actors behind the screen. The need for dialogue to clarify actions and narrative was addressed from within the production company.

The Cameraphone Company did not play in New York City until late November 1908 when it opened at the Cameraphone Theatre in Brooklyn.[35] It also opened at several Keith Theatres in December.[36] In these situations the Cameraphone presented top vaudeville stars who had performed for its cameras and phonographs for fees as high as $2,500.[37] Singing acts, often serving as a kind of substitute for the illustrated song, were most successful. Exhibitors never attempted to replace regular moving pictures with them.

The Chronophone and Cameraphone competed with numerous rivals: the Auxetophone, the American Theaterphone, Spoor's Phoneidograph and the Synchroscope. Although synchronized recorded sound and image had been one of Thomas Edison's dreams from the time of his peep-hole kinetoscope, his company did not become actively involved in this new phase until late 1909 when it began a series of experiments at the old 21st Street studio. The resulting Kinetophone began to play in large vaudeville theatres during February 1913 to an enthusiastic response but had a short commercial vogue – like the Chronophone and the Cameraphone before it.

The diffusion of these sound systems was restricted by several factors. Technical limitations often impinged on production practices:

> The difficulty that attends to the advance preparation of phonograph talking moving pictures makes it evident that the art cannot, at present at least, be extended beyond short scenes, sketches and songs with any success. The trouble lies in the fact that the phonograph record of the words spoken or sung cannot be made at the same time that the moving picture is taken with the camera. Phonograph records are spoken into the phonograph at close hand which would be entirely impossible with

people moving about as they must do for the film. It is therefore the custom to make the phonograph record first and afterwards repeat the same scene for the camera. In some cases, perhaps in all, the person who talks into the phonograph is not the one who represents the same character for the camera. The result then is often an incongruous coupling of a robust voice and a diminutive figure or the contrary.

However the actor or actress employed in posing for the camera must have become letter perfect in the words of the phonograph record and must go through the actual motions of speaking the words in concert with the record, while the picture is taken. The result is a perfect timing of words and lip motions, but the process, which is practical with one or two characters, increases tremendously in difficulty with the addition of each extra character. It can readily be seen how it would be well nigh impossible to produce with fidelity a dramatic or operatic scene that was at all complicated and contained any considerable number of characters.

If the phonograph could be made to record words and other sounds at the same time the camera was at work, it would be plain sailing, but until something of that sort is accomplished theatrical producers and actors need not lie awake at nights dreading the time when talking moving pictures will drive them out of the field.[38]

Exhibition also presented problems for mechanical talking pictures. The quality of reproduction was often poor and tinny, undercutting the illusion of reality that synchronous sound was designed to push to new heights. This was painfully apparent when a film was projected out of synchronization – a relatively common occurrence.

Cost was another factor. The Miles Brothers offered to sell the Auxetophone for $550 while the Cronophone went for $1,000.[39] The Cameraphone did not sell its machine but offered a complete service including projector, sound system, operator and films. None the less, the cost of materials and the limitations on the market meant that mechanical talking pictures were integrated into the system of production, distribution and exhibition established by the Edison and Biograph licensees. Furthermore, mechanical pictures were limited to fairly simple, short situations at the very moment that mainstream producers were making more frequent use of complex narratives. The alternative of actors behind the screen may have offered greater flexibility and been as inexpensive as mechanical talking pictures. Once again, it was never a realistic alternative for most nickelodeons.

Both types of talking pictures were part of an emphasis on heightened verisimilitude which was particularly intense during 1906–8. Hale's Tours, which suddenly became successful early in 1906, placed the viewer in a mock railway car with simulated train rocking and appropriate sound effects. (Adolph Zukor's capitalization on talking pictures was perhaps not so coincidental given his initial involvement in cinema through Hale's Tours.) Pathé's hand colouring process using stencils and the slightly later Smith/Urban Kinemacolor, with its first public showing in May 1908, achieved startlingly naturalistic effects – in contrast to earlier uses of hand-tinting which heightened the fantastic elements of films like *Ali Baba and the Forty Thieves* and *Voyage à travers l'impossible.*[40]

These attempts to expand the range of perception to include sound, colour and bodily sensation further heightened the illusion of film as a transparent medium. The popular perception of film was shifting from an emphasis on the filmic elements to a preoccupation with the profilmic, from a conception of cinema as a special kind of magic lantern show to cinema as a special kind of theatre.

Talking pictures combined a notion of film as a transparent medium with profilmic theatrical elements to highlight cinema's potential similarities with the stage. Illusionism and theatricality were thus parallel currents in cinema which converged in this particular mode of exhibition. As one enthusiast wrote,

> The illusion of life which it is the mission of moving pictures to present to the best of its ability, must always be incomplete, but there is no reason why the complete illusion should not be sought after, to a much greater degree than at present, by the means of stage effects.[41]

This rise of talking pictures reveals much about the changes occurring within the institution of the screen during this period. It coincided with an initial influx of theatre-trained directors like J. Searle Dawley, D. W. Griffith and Sidney Olcott. It occurred as cinema was taking over legitimate theatres for exhibitions and as a theatrical newspaper like the *Dramatic Mirror* began to review films. In 1907–9 these elements redefined cinema as a kind of theatre – superior to the traditional stage in some respects (diversity of locale) though deficient in others (sound, colour and three-dimensional space).

The move towards increased verisimilitude and transparency in cinema, however, remained subservient to the narrative requirements of entertainment and the need for an efficient mode of film production and exhibition. Strategies to achieve a super-realism were abandoned or remained a speciality service because they limited the film-maker's freedom to tell a story or increased admission prices – or both. Intertitles were the most artificial representational strategy but, because they were an inexpensive and extremely effective way to clarify a narrative, they quickly became standard.

Titles were placed originally on lantern slides and were often made by the exhibitor to announce the titles of individual films. While Edwin Porter, following the lead of European producers, integrated titles into his films between 1903 and 1905, he virtually abandoned this practice in 1906–7. Biograph's *A Kentucky Feud* (October 1905) used intertitles to introduce scenes, outlining their action: without them the film would have been incomprehensible. Pathé appears to have relied on intertitles more than other companies during 1906–7. Since Pathé films were sold throughout the world, the company supplied intertitles in many different languages. Although intertitles were urged on film producers as a standard procedure by the *Film Index* in September 1906, these urgings became more frequent and insistent by 1908.

The Edison Company began to use brief intertitles on a consistent basis with *Fireside Reminiscences* (January 1908). The *Dramatic Mirror*, however, demanded even more elaborate titles if they were deemed necessary. The Edison film *Romance of a War Nurse* (July 1908) was strongly criticized because it 'is not as clearly told in the pictures as we would like to see . . . love wins in the end and all are reconciled though how they do it and what was at the bottom of the story we must confess our inability to discover'. It was suggested that 'The Edison Company would do well in producing complicated dramatic stories of this kind if it would insert descriptive paragraphs at the proper points in the films so the spectators might gain a knowledge of what the actors are about'.[42] The *Mirror* actually represented the most advanced trends in the industry. More traditional critics like Stephen Bush often praised a film like *Romance of a War Nurse*. What the *Mirror* found confusing, others might praise for the opportunities they offered exhibitors to intervene. Thus the *Mirror* faulted Porter's *The Devil* for inadequate titling: 'In producing this film an attempt is made to make it intelligible by inserting descriptive paragraphs, but these are not numerous enough to be of much assistance.'[43] Edison's *Ingomar* and Vitagraph's *Richard III* (both September 1908) were criticized along similar lines.[44] Although Griffith's effective use of titles was rarely singled out for specific praise, it was an important factor which contributed to the clarity of his films. His *Barbarian Ingomar* (September 1908) was praised because it 'reads to the spectator like a printed book'.[45]

The motion picture industry was moving towards a relationship between film production and exhibition in which the showman was acting as a businessman/programmer who simply presented the already complete works of the production companies. To the extent that Porter's films resisted this trend, he had come to represent the industry's old guard. His continued reliance on the exhibitor and a mode of representation associated with the pre-nickelodeon era is perhaps most apparent in his refusal to abandon a conception of temporality which was being jettisoned by his contemporaries.

An exhaustive retrospective of films made in 1907 and early 1908 by a full range of production companies (organized by Eileen Bowser at the Museum of Modern Art) revealed a remarkable shift in the conception of temporality during this period. At the beginning of 1907, Porter's *The 'Teddy' Bears* or *Lost in the Alps* reflected the state of cinematic storytelling. Shots were still discrete units, overlapping action was frequent, temporal repetition common, and the narrative often loosely constructed. By mid-1907 the most advanced production companies began to observe a strict linear time frame. This involved two phases. First, there was an elimination of retrogressive elements like overlapping action. In Vitagraph's *The Boy, the Bust and the Bath* (July 1907) or Pathé's *Doings of a Poodle* (1907) there is rapid cutting between proximate spaces and, in many instances, a strong suggestion of a seamless linear temporality across shots. This, however, is not made explicit by strategies like a match cut on action. In these films the inevitable forward movement of time, often in conjunction with intertitles, meant that viewers no longer had to wonder if action shown in a given scene occurred before or after a previously shown action. This is the foundation on which the mode of representation associated with Hollywood would be constructed.

A second phase employed new representational strategies based on this new form of temporality. Pathé's *The Runaway Horse* (*Cheval emballé*), made in late 1907, explicitly acknowledged a linear temporality through its use of parallel editing. At this stage, however, the procedure served as the basis for a series of tricks:

Shot 1 Exterior – man with horse cart arrives outside city apartment building.
Shot 2 Man goes up the stairs.
Shot 3 A very scrawny horse begins to eat from a bag of oats.
Shot 4 Man goes up the stairs.
Shot 5 Man goes into family dining room and makes a delivery.
Shot 6 Horse eating – less oats in bag.
Shot 7 Delivery man talks to man and woman (same as shot 5) and leaves.
Shot 8 Delivery man goes down the stairs.
Shot 9 Delivery man stops to talk to concierge.
Shot 10 Horse eating – much less grain in bag.
Shot 11 Man says goodbye to concierge.
Shot 12 Delivery man comes outside – horse attached to cart is strong, healthy and well-fed – the delivery man and cart quickly leave as owner comes out and chases them away.

By cutting back and forth between two lines of action, the French director was able to manipulate the size of the bag of oats and substitute a dashing steed for a scrawny nag without having to resort to stop action. There is a rigorous advancement in time and a rapid alternation between activities in two spaces, which provided the basis for effective comedy. Nothing so extensive happens in other available films made in late 1907 or early 1908 but Biograph's *Old Isaacs, the Pawnbroker* (written by Griffith, directed by McCutcheon in March 1908) cuts away from a sequence in which a girl is visiting the offices of the Amalgamated Association of Charities, to her sick mother at home – and then back again to the offices. McCutcheon (and Griffith) conveyed a strong sense of linear temporality as simultaneous actions are shown in a parallel rather than successive manner. *Old Isaacs* stops short, however, of the rigorous A-B-A-B structure which is the paradigm for parallel editing.

The limited selection of surviving films from late 1907 and early 1908 none the less suggests that *The Runaway Horse* and *Old Isaacs* anticipate the period when strategies of parallel editing or matching action could be executed readily by film-makers and accepted by spectators. This moment seems to have come in the summer of 1908 around the time Griffith was making *The Fatal Hour* (July 1908). *The Fatal Hour* involves a last-minute rescue where the forward march of time becomes the subject of the film, as a pistol is mounted on a clock that will shoot the heroine when the minute hand reaches twelve. The *Mirror* described *The Fatal Hour* as 'a wholly impossible story, with a series of inconsistent situations, and yet the wild drive to the rescue, while the clock slowly approaches the hour of twelve, brings a thrill that redeems the picture'.[46] The emotional intensity here is much greater than in *Lost in the Alps* which has a similar rescue but lacked a narrative structure based on cross-cutting and the pressure of time moving inevitably forward.

In films like *Life of an American Fireman* and *Lost in the Alps*, time was primarily manipulated profilmically, through the contraction of action occurring offscreen. In *The Fatal Hour* time was accelerated by filmic manipulation through cross-cutting. Griffith was able to move the clock forward whenever he cut to the rescue party (just as Zecca greatly reduced the sack of oats whenever he cut to the driver in the apartment house). While both strategies for condensation (filmic and profilmic) appear frequently in Griffith's films of 1908 – as one might expect of this transitional period – Griffith increasingly elaborated on the former and gradually eliminated the latter.

Griffith's films from the summer and fall of 1908, particularly *Betrayed by a Handprint* (August 1908) and *The Guerilla* (October 1908), give an increasingly strong impression of matching action between contiguous spaces.[47] By *The Lonely Villa* (April–May 1909), Griffith was matching action in most situations with comparative ease. His use of such procedures specified a rigorous linear temporality. In such films, the shot ceased to act as a discrete unit on any level. The shot is completely subservient to the one-reel feature, to the narrative and linear flow of events. Action moves across shots, not within them.

The use of linear temporality, parallel editing and matching action both demanded and created a more efficient narrative structure. The dances, rodeo tricks and peripheral incidents common to so many films of the pre-1907 period were disappearing or being pushed into the background. In the terminology of Sergei Eisenstein, film-makers were editing on the *dominant* (orthodox montage), making editorial choices that emphasized the drama of the narrative. From late 1907 onward, directors at Pathé, Vitagraph, Biograph and elsewhere were developing strategies which would provide the basic framework for classic narrative cinema. Porter, however, barely participated in this shift towards a seamless, self-sufficient, linear narrative structure.

Parallel editing and match cuts were not incompatible with the lecture or behind-the-screen dialogue. As these editorial strategies were elaborated by procedures, however, the exhibitor's intervention was less essential. Given the economic and cultural system in which American and European cinema were operating, the decline of these exhibitor-initiated strategies was gradual but inevitable. As a result, the reel of film came much closer to being a pure commodity – a goal which would be achieved only when all exhibition procedures (music, projection speed) were completely standardized and dictated by the production companies. This final event, of course, only happened at the beginning of the sound era.

A few observations can be made from this historical framework. First, Hollywood cinema has its basis in the nickelodeon era, in cinema's rapid emergence after 1905 as a form of mass entertainment. I must disagree with my colleague Tom Gunning in certain important details.[48] He tends to see the transformation from pre-1907 to post-1907 representational strategies as principally influenced by the desire for respectability and the wooing of potential middle-class patrons. Gunning, like Noel Burch,[49] sees a shift towards a bourgeois cinema as fundamental to this period. Without wanting to dismiss the influence exerted by reformers insisting on respectability and producers hoping to attract a better class of spectators, I feel their influence was not nearly as important as Gunning suggests. The desire and need for respectability cannot account for the increasing popularity of complex narrative, although such pressures did affect the types and treatment of subject matter, encouraging the adaptation of plays, poetry and high culture. Nor can these pressures account for the cinematic strategies exploited most effectively by Griffith. The lecture, for instance, had the support of critics and reformers: it gave the exhibitor opportunities to underline a clear moral lesson. In fact, film-makers in 1908 were exploring many different ways of making cinema. While the approach associated with Griffith won out for many reasons, standardization, narrative efficiency and maximization of profits were among the most crucial determinants.

In my analysis, the transformation in the mode of representation was dialectically related to the changing mode of production inaugurated by the rise of the nickelodeon. There was a shift from an industrial (petit bourgeois) mode to one based on mass production. Before and after 1907, the viewpoints expressed by the cinema's system of representation are primarily those of the middle classes: what Harry Braverman calls the old middle class for the pre-1907 period and the new middle class in the post-1907 period.[50] At the risk of being somewhat reductive, this is the major difference between the films of Porter and those of Griffith, between their respective methods of work and their distinctive representational strategies.

Notes

First published in *Framework*, Autumn 1984.

1. Charles Musser, 'The early cinema of Edwin Porter', *Cinema Journal*, Fall 1979, pp. 1–38; Charles Musser, 'The Edwin Musée in 1898: The exhibitor as creator', *Film and History*, December 1981, pp. 73–83. These developments are also explored in Charles Musser's film *Before the Nickelodeon*.
2. In 1904 the Edison Company sold two prints of *Inter-Collegiate Regatta* (750 ft), 34 prints of *Elephants Shooting the Chutes No. 2* (75 ft), 29 prints of *Fire and Flames, Luna Park* (165 ft), one print of *Parade, N.Y. Fire Department* (290 ft), 6 prints of *Opening Ceremonies, New York Subway* (300 ft), but 71 prints of *How a French Nobleman Got a Wife Through the New York Herald 'Personal' Columns* (675 ft). Using Robert Allen's method of analysis, actuality subjects dominated Edison's production (Robert C. Allen, 'Film history: the narrow discourse', *Film Studies Annual*, Part 2, 1977, pp. 9–17). In fact the company sold 47,925 feet of *French Nobleman* and only 10,925 feet of the other five films.
3. Albert E. Smith, Testimony, 14 November 1913, Equity No. 5–167, US Circuit Court, Southern District of New York, Printed Record, p. 1702.
4. *Edison Films* (Orange, NJ: Edison Manufacturing Company, July 1906), p. 70.
5. Peter Bull, *The Teddy Bear Book* (New York: Random House, 1970).
6. *Variety*, 9 March 1907, p. 8.
7. *New York Evening Journal*, 3, 4 and 13 May 1907.
8. *Views and Film Index*, 10 November 1906, p. 3.
9. *Film Index*, 13 October 1906, p. 3.

10. Van C. Lee, 'The value of a lecture', *Moving Picture World*, 8 February 1908, p. 9.
11. *Film Index*, 1 September 1906, p. 10.
12. 'The Merry Widow', *Variety*, 25 January 1911, p. 11.
13. *New York Dramatic Mirror*, 4 and 11 July 1908.
14. *Film Index*, 3 October 1908, p. 4.
15. Stephen Bush, 'Lecture on moving pictures', *Moving Picture World*, 22 August 1908, pp. 136–7; and Stephen Bush, advertisement, *Dramatic Mirror*, 9 January 1909.
16. *Show World*, 8 February 1908, p. 12.
17. *Dramatic Mirror*, 28 November 1908; *Moving Picture World*, December 1908, p. 398.
18. Bush, *Moving Picture World*, 27 August 1908, p. 137.
19. Van C. Lee, *Moving Picture World*, 8 February 1908, p. 93.
20. *Moving Picture World*, 16 May 1908, p. 431; and *Dramatic Mirror*, 14 November 1908, p. 11.
21. *Dramatic Mirror*, 25 February 1905, p. 18.
22. *New York Clipper*, 20 August 1907, p. 246.
23. *Moving Picture World*, 16 May 1908.
24. *Dramatic Mirror*, 13 June 1908, p. 10.
25. *Dramatic Mirror*, 18 July 1908, p. 10.
26. Bennett Theatre, Programme, 1 March 1909 (?), Mackey and Rollins Collection, Harvard Theatre Collection.
27. *Moving Picture World*, 4 July 1908, p. 9. See also 'Motion Picture Notes' in the *Dramatic Mirror* for this period.
28. *Dramatic Mirror*, 19 September 1908.
29. *Dramatic Mirror*, 6 June 1908.
30. *Billboard*, 25 May 1907, pp. 14, 28.
31. 'The Chronophone', *Moving Picture World*, 14 September 1907, p. 440; *Billboard*, 25 January 1908, p. 17.
32. *Billboard*, 14 March 1908, p. 11.
33. 'Cameraphone Development', *Dramatic Mirror*, 4 July 1908, p. 7.
34. *Billboard*, 21 March 1908, p. 30.
35. *Variety*, 28 November 1908, p. 10.
36. *Billboard*, 2 January 1909, p. 32.
37. 'Talking pictures in New York', *Variety*, 28 November 1908, p. 10.
38. *Dramatic Mirror*, 26 December 1908, p. 8.
39. *Billboard*, 25 January 1908, p. 11.
40. 'Clippings', Charles Urban Papers, Vol. 1, Science Museum Library, Imperial College.
41. *Film Index*, 1 August 1907, p. 3.
42. *Dramatic Mirror*, 5 September 1908, p. 8.
43. *Dramatic Mirror*, 19 September 1908.
44. *Dramatic Mirror*, 26 September and 10 October 1908.
45. *Dramatic Mirror*, 24 October 1908.
46. *Dramatic Mirror*, 29 August 1908.
47. From about 1903, film-makers occasionally employed match cuts in highly specialized situations (cut-ins, changing camera angle, etc.). Such early instances of linear temporality coexisted with many other examples of non-linear narrative construction.
48. Tom Gunning, 'Weaving a Narrative', pp. 336–47 of this volume.
49. Noël Burch, 'Porter or ambivalence', *Screen*, Winter 1978/79, pp. 11–15.
50. By this I do not mean a shift in subject matter *per se*, for Griffith's ideology on the level of the story is as 'old middle class' as Porter's. Likewise Biograph films made before Griffith's arrival generally espouse the values of some groups within the new urban middle class.

Showing and Telling
Image and Word in Early Cinema
ANDRÉ GAUDREAULT

> Descended from the fairground barker, and more specifically from the magic lantern lecturer, the film lecturer had, it seems, particular importance during the first decade of film exhibition. He furnished audiences with an oral commentary accompanying the projection of the film ... and influenced in a crucial manner the way films were experienced during the earliest period of film history. (Tom Gunning, *David Wark Griffith*, p. 84.)

We know that the so-called silent period of the cinema was rich in varied experiments in the use of the three audible components of cinematic expression (in the sense used by Metz); sound effects, words and music. Less well known, or too often ignored, is the absolutely basic importance of this phenomenon: it was quite exceptional, in the silent period, for a film to be projected in complete silence.[1] One of the fundamentals of the early cinema, although it is often ignored, is that the filmic spectacle, even in those days, was nearly always an *audio*-visual one like (for example) circus or theatre. Of course it is difficult today to analyse the sound aspect of the early days of cinematic spectacle with all the thoroughness one would wish, since all that remains of it are traces whose most notable qualities are their rarity and incompleteness. Nevertheless sound is a fundamental component of the silent cinema which must be taken into account by those seeking a comprehensive understanding of the cinema phenomenon. The more so as one manifestation of this sound aspect, the narrative commentary of a lecturer is of basic importance to anyone trying to grasp the varied expressions of filmic narrativity.

The essential difference between the sound of the silent period and that of the talking period is obviously that the former, with a few exceptions, was not recorded but produced on the spot in a one-off performance. This phenomenon gave the spectator's experience a strong element of directness and uncertainty, making it completely different from the experience which came to dominate the consumption of recorded images and sounds after the 'talking revolution'. In effect, despite their superficial and momentary belief in the actuality of the filmic image and sound, modern cinema spectators know that in principle the performance to which they are exposed is immutable from one showing to the next. They know that someone sitting in the same seat for the next showing will have the same experience. Only a technical problem in the projection room or a random incident among the audience can disturb the sequence of events on screen. Everything (or almost everything) has been foreseen from the vantage-point of an 'elsewhere' which is, first and foremost, a 'before'. Cinema spectators are thus always aware that they are not taking part in a 'happening' of any kind, unless the film happens to be *The Rocky Horror Picture Show* (Jim Sharman, 1975). Active participation is certainly demanded, but it is first and foremost a psychic participation. Whereas (to get to the crux of the matter) the sound aspect of the 'silent' cinema, a unique performance actualised anew for each spectacle, worked in a completely different way. As Norman King so excellently puts it, the execution of sound during that period 'produced effects in the cinema that recorded sound could not, a sense of immediacy and participation. Live sound actualised the image and, merging with it, emphasised the presentness of the performance and of the audience.'[2]

Under these conditions the 'showing' of a film was not just a simple *re-run* of a spectacle already put in the can elsewhere and earlier, as it was to become in the talking era. This is probably true of the majority of public screenings between 1895 and 1927 which were accompanied by live music, sometimes by timed sound effects, in some cases by dialogue spoken behind the screen by flesh-and-blood actors, and even – quite frequently before 1910 – by the commentary of a lecturer who explained the narrative line of the film or, to fill out what was seen . . . and heard, improvised a discourse based on the images shown. The sound aspect was so much a part of the so-called silent cinema that there can be no doubt that the spectator was familiar with this dimension. The histories are full of examples proving beyond any doubt that the filmic experience of the time was an auditory one as well. As a result much attention was given to words and to the possibility that they might be recorded. Even before the invention of the Lumière Cinematograph, Edison and Dickson had made various attempts to achieve synchronisation of images and (recorded) sounds for the kinetoscope. Georges Demenÿ's experiments, carried out before the turn of the century, have left us the famous talking (self-) portraits, which show him in close-up articulating for posterity the two famous phrases '*Je vous aime*' and '*Vive la France*'. We know too that Chronophone Gaumont's 'Phonoscènes' later enjoyed a longish run in Paris between 1906 and 1912.

Beside these examples, it should not be forgotten that the Lumière Cinematograph was accompanied by piano music from the very first showings. It was probably felt from the beginning that the screen's uneasy, flickering silence represented a *lack*.

So the cinema was an audio-visual spectacle even in its infancy. But live instrumental music from a pianist (or quite often a whole orchestra) was just one of many ways in which the use of sound was explored in the early cinema. At the beginning of the century, for example, it was not unusual for the singing human voice to be used for (among other things) 'Picture Songs', particularly interesting for their use of the live human voice in juxtaposition with delayed images.[3] We should also recall the quite frequent experiments in the use of flesh-and-blood actors concealed behind the screen, speaking their dialogue in synchronisation with the projected images. *College Chums* (Edison, 1907) is one of the films made expressly with this technique in mind.

For us, of course, the most central of these different uses of sound is the figure of the lecturer, which remained unknown and neglected until very recently. It has already been suggested that the use of this voice-over commentator, part visualised and part acousmatic (to use the terms suggested by Michel Chion[4]), is directly descended from the magic lantern. Indeed the cinema can be said to constitute a sort of extension of an existing tradition in the use of the screen for purposes which are usually narrative.[5] But narrativity, in the stories recounted by magic lantern operators, owed a great deal more to the contribution of the speaker-presenter, the lecturer, who acted as narrator or storyteller, than to the short succession of immobile images contained in the set of slides. Given their relatively small number (often no more than a dozen) and more particularly the absence of movement, the narrativity contained in the bare succession of slides was comparatively weak and certainly not very legible: the inevitable breaks, numerous and abrupt, could not but produce a very disturbing effect of discontinuity. For this reason it seems to me more accurate to regard magic lantern shows as oral narratives supplemented by illustrations on screen. It is not difficult to see that the lecturer's text has priority over that of the slides despite the latter's 'spectacular' (in the literal sense) aspect. To tell a story, in effect, one has to use one of two fundamental modes of narrative communication: narration, and what I call monstration. One must either narrate the different events which constitute the story (narration), as the lecturer does; or show them (monstration), as the glass slides attempt to do. The narrative 'weakness' of still images, within which the characters seem to have no autonomy, probably best explains this recourse to verbal narration. With a magic lantern, monstration could not support a narrative project on any scale. This is because the images are immobile and the 'actor' mute. In the theatre, by contrast, monstration comes into its own and there is no need for a superimposed narration: the characters 'move' and 'speak'. Through their performance (their acting) they tell the story by living it, right there in front of the audience. The need for intervention by a narrator does not arise.

Being modelled on both the magic lantern and the theatre, the cinema is positioned exactly between the two: beyond the spectacle of the magic lantern (the cinema's more 'real' characters 'act' like those of the theatre) but more limited than the theatrical spectacle (the cinema's less 'real' characters, like those of the magic lantern, do not 'talk'). This absence of the spoken word meant that the monstration of the early cinema was soon felt to be relatively deficient. This probably explains in part[6] the hybrid form of the cinematic spectacle in the first years of the cinema which, through the movement inherent in the images, borrows the theatre's 'acting' characters, while conserving the magic lantern's lecturer to fill the void left by these characters' inability to be heard.

Lecturers seem to have been used in this way intermittently between 1895 and 1910. But their presence was certainly not obligatory in all cinemas, even at the times when they were most in fashion. This was itself a source of problems, as some films were produced expressly to be understood with the aid of the lecturer's,[7] the external narrator's, meta-diegetic voice. But what exactly was the lecturer's role? Why were his services required?

The lecturer's explanations were originally needed to resolve certain problems of legibility. Until about 1901 there was no great need to make the story being told more comprehensible, since most films were relatively simple and easy to read. The great majority consisted of a single shot and they usually aspired to nothing beyond visual pleasure: the stories were of restricted scope and could be read as much through topological parameters as through chronological ones. So all that the spectators had to do was to see, to look, something for which they had no need of a lecturer-adjuvant. Which is not to say – far from it – that the lecturer was never used during this period. It should not be forgotten that at that time the operator was solely responsible for the shows he *edited* (for the order in which films were shown, the music played in the auditorium, the final multi-media mix): in some cases part of his job was to advertise the show in the street, acting as a public barker to bring in the largest possible number of spectators (especially as there were still very few fixed and permanent cinemas, therefore virtually no regular audiences). There was nothing to stop him from keeping up the flow of patter as the lights went down and mutating effortlessly into a speaker-lecturer, a commentator, with the slightly different object of maintaining and supporting his audience's interest.

From 1902, however, films began to get longer, their stories became more complex and, above all, the number of shots increased. With the appearance of films consisting of several shots (very few were made before that date), narrative continuity – quite easily achieved by the filmic mega-monstrator who had been responsible for the single-shot piece – came under threat: every camera hiatus could cause spatial or temporal hiatuses, knock a hole in the narrative thread and leave room for interpretation – or incomprehension. Hence the difficulty of producing a clear and intelligible narrative (so long as editing remained rudimentary) unless someone was designated to take charge of arranging the shots: the filmographic narrator whose appearances until about 1910 were, to quote Tom Gunning, 'sporadic, an occasional phantom, more than a unified presence'.[8]

Meanwhile, there were only two ways of ensuring some sort of continuity between the shots and enabling the spectator to grasp the meaning of what lay behind the cuts (camera hiatuses) on the screen: either to turn control of the story over to the *narrative voice of the lecturer*, or to use *intertitles* (which, incidentally, appeared in 1903). As there was no dialogue to help the spectator grasp what was happening in the diegetic universe, the need for a *narrator* began to be felt when films became longer and more complex. And – until the narrative faculties of *editing* had been further developed – this narrator would carry out the work of narration through the use of words, of articulated language, either in written form (intertitles) or oral form (speaker).

The need to include a narrative voice external to the images of the film seems to have been felt, in the United States at least, in two distinct phases before 1910, the first time – for the reasons I have just mentioned – between 1902 and 1904. The second phase began in 1908 during a series of important changes in the cinema industry. Between these two peaks the need for the lecturer (who of course never disappeared completely) seemed much less pressing.[9] From about 1904, there began to develop a very simple form of editing (the syntagmatic juxtaposition of shots linked by spatial and temporal proximity) which made it possible to render with great clarity a narrative form then entering its hour of glory: the chase sequence. Thanks to a thematic presupposing the relatively linear movement of two groups of actors (pursuers and pursued), this very popular genre – as well as giving a fillip to 'montagist' thought – provided a sort of apprenticeship in the mental connections which have to be made in order to link two shots separated by some spatio-temporal hiatus. In any case most of the chases shot between 1904 and 1907 were very simple to understand and could easily do without an external narrative voice, either in intertitle or lecturer form. We may presume that the growing popularity of this genre contributed to the apparent decline of the lecturer between 1904 and 1907.

But from 1908, as we know, the cinema industry underwent profound changes, one result of which was that it began to attract bourgeois and petty-bourgeois audiences more or less new to the dark auditoriums where, it was claimed, an amusement fit only for Helots was presented. This overt quest for new audiences brought about a series of consequences which it would be impossible to analyse here in depth. It is evident, however, that such attempts to 'upgrade' audiences must have involved a parallel 'upgrading' of subjects. This explains why the cinema at this time began systematically turning towards established literary and theatrical values, of which the *Film d'art* was an early manifestation in France. But the systematic adaptation of great literary works was not to be achieved without problems since, as Tom Gunning writes: 'This ambition was the cause, at the same time, of a crisis in film narrative; faced with the adaptation of verbal works, presented without sound, audiences found them incomprehensible.'[10]

We must add that the filmic narrative – adaptation or not – was beginning to expand (especially in running time) and to display increasing complexity. Film-makers were taking liberties and producing narratives which were much more difficult to understand. During 1908 and 1909 the corporate magazines often carried critics' articles and readers' letters complaining of the total illegibility of some films and the difficulty experienced in deciphering many others. As early as September 1906 *Views and Films Index* had published something close to an indictment of this tendency entitled 'Moving pictures – for audiences, not for makers': 'Manufacturers should produce films which can be easily understood by the public. It is not sufficient that the makers understand the plot – the pictures are made for the public.'[11]

The author of an important article which appeared in February 1908[12] states in all seriousness that only one film in fifty could be understood properly by the spectator without a lecturer's explanation either before or during the projection. This makes it easy to see why at about this time producers began pressing film-makers to find a way of communicating ambitious narratives without resorting to that useful but very cumbersome adjunct, the lecturer. There was of course a way of making the stories intelligible without using the lecturer's actual voice: to condense the commentaries he might make as far as possible, print them on cards, and punctuate the filmic narrative with the resulting intertitles. This solution had the advantages of uniformising the exterior narration and, more importantly, of restoring total control of the work – too long in the hands of the operator – to the producer, but was still so inconvenient as to prove, finally, inadequate. To be really effective in practice, this method required cards to be inserted at frequent intervals ('at every place on film wherein an explanation is necessary', demanded an Iowa operator),[13] which raised two major objections on the part of those concerned: intertitles caused a very noticeable increase in the cost of films (which were then sold by the metre or foot), and they interrupted the continuity of the images.

The solution which, as we learn from the history of the cinema, finally came to predominate over all the others, was the integration of the narrator into the picture itself. The work of one David Wark Griffith, which began in 1908, was to result in the establishment of a narrator who no longer needed the *human voice* to impose his *narrative voice*, who used editing to interpolate himself *between the images* to present them, arrange them, even comment on them. As Tom Gunning writes:

> The *narrator-system* could be described as an interiorized film lecturer. . . . However, this narrator was not located off-screen, but was absorbed into the images themselves and the way they are joined. The *narrator-system* seems to 'read' the images to the audience in the very act of presenting them. The narrator is invisible, revealing his presence only in the way he reveals the images on the screen.

It is in this context that the development of the cinema, as a result of the many factors I have just mentioned (and a few others which I have not), seems to have led to the emergence of the *filmographic narrator*, the entity I have stated to be responsible for editing or, to be more exact, for all the operations involving the manipulation through production processes of images already shot, produced by the activity of the mega-monstrator. This would mean that it is a collusion between the *filmographic narrator* and the *filmic mega-monstrator* (himself the product of a collusion between the *profilmic monstrator* and the *filmographic monstrator*) which gave birth to the entity I have called the *filmic mega-narrator*, ultimately responsible for communication of the filmic mega-narrative. And it would be in the same context, one which saw the speaker, that flesh-and-blood narrator, 'absorbed' by the very phenomenon he described from a distance, that the spectator himself may finally have aspired to enter the fiction in his turn.[15] This would have facilitated the passage from one mode of filmic consumption to another: from an early cinema which presupposed relations of *exhibitionist confrontation* between the spectator and the screen, to another – still dominant today – which presupposes rather a form of *diegetic absorption* into the universe presented by the sequence of animated images which, having achieved a measure of balance and autonomy, is at last liberated from the heavy, cumbersome presence of the lecturer, that literal 'explainer of films'.[16] Thus was the human voice banished from the dark auditoria for nearly twenty years, although it remained on the picture in written form, in the shape of cards placed to represent sometimes the actors' dialogue and sometimes the voice of the mega-narrator. Only when title-cards fell into disuse with the appearance of recorded and synchronised sound during the 'talking revolution' did the lecturer make a sort of comeback through the restoration – this time recorded on a track alongside the picture – of a commentator in voice-off, or rather in *voice-over*. With the difference, however, that the spectator would now be listening to a voice actorialised by being recorded, subjected to a sound *take*, and that to make itself heard the entity controlling this voice, quite unlike the turn-of-the-century lecturer, would have had to force a passage into the interior of the profilmic 'world' (albeit only on the sound level). Narratologically speaking, this intrusion into the kingdom of diegesis by a narrator – apparently more legitimate, in any case better integrated, than the simultaneous lecturer of the early days – clouded the issue considerably. Because now the filmic narrative, so close in appearance to stage narrative, was in a position to imitate in even more euphoric fashion the written narrative, or rather, one genre of written narrative: the kind which *pretends* to have been distilled, word by word, phrase by phrase, by an explicit and actorialised (therefore representative and secondary) narrator, whose strength nevertheless is precisely that he has convinced the narratologist that *he is the original narrator*. Hardly surprising, then, especially as filmic narratology is inevitably modelled on literary narratology, that this apparently extra-diegetic narrator should have succeeded in throwing the same kind of dust in the eyes of the cinema field's 'indigenous' narratologists and helped tangle the skein of narrative threads from which even the least complex filmic narratives are woven. These questions are of fundamental importance in the attempt to fashion tools to understand the narrative working of the cinema through all its periods. A number of films (for example, the recent *Les Yeux noirs*) deftly combine different narrative levels, and our efforts so far should also enable us to evaluate the role in the narrative fabric of that human voice which, sometimes throughout the whole film, reports and describes various events and is often used to launch narrative advances; that voice which 'tricks' us by convincing spectators and filmic narratologists alike that it is the original source of the imaged '*novel*'[17] it offers us to see . . . and hear.

Notes

1. I refer here to many of the ideas put forward in my article 'Bruitage, musique et commentaires aux débuts du cinéma' which appeared in *Protée*, vol. 13 no. 2, Summer 1985, pp. 25–9 (Chicoutimi, University of Quebec at Chicoutimi).
2. Norman King, 'The Sound of Silents', *Screen* vol. 25 no. 3, May–June 1984, p. 15.
3. We are concerned here mainly with use of the speaker-narrator. For more detailed discussion of the other experiments in the use of sound, see my article in *Protée* (Note 1 above) and also Charles Musser's 'The Nickelodeon Era Begins: Establishing the Framework for Hollywood's Mode of Representation', pp. 256–73 of this volume.
4. Michel Chion, *La Voix au cinéma* (Paris: Éditions de l'Étoile, 1982).
5. The narrative aspect was not always dominant, however, since magic lantern slides were often used to illustrate lectures. Even the cinema was sometimes used in this way.

Some 'exhibitors of films' tried to make their activity seem more respectable by giving their own discourse priority over that of the moving pictures they showed. This could be important in ensuring the survival of moving picture shows in places like French Canada where the Catholic church wielded excessive influence and was inclined to see the Cinematograph as an invention of the devil. A pioneer of the Quebec cinema business, Breton by origin, advertised her 'show' in 1901 as follows: 'Illustrated lectures. The Comtesse de Grandsaignes d'Hauterives . . . whose illustrated lectures offer their support to all religious enterprises, begs all who . . .' (*La Presse*, 22 April 1901, quoted by Germain Lacasse with Serge Duigou in *L'Historiographe (Les débuts du spectacle cinématographique au Québec)*, Cinémathèque québécoise, Montreal ('Les Dossiers de la Cinémathèque' no. 15, 1985, p. 29).

6. But only in part as there were a number of other factors. Many of the first 'exhibitors' of the films seem to have started as magic lantern operators, so it is hardly surprising that the figure of the speaker was carried over. Especially as the cinema was regarded as a technical improvement of the magic lantern (it should not be forgotten that the apparatus used for projecting films included a magic lantern which did duty as a light source), and the shows at which films were displayed, for the first few years, were often multi-media events in which films were mixed haphazardly with lantern slides among other 'turns'.
7. According to Martin Sopocy, these include most of James Williamson's films. See 'Un cinéma avec narrateur. Les premiers films narratifs de James A. Williamson', *Les Cahiers de la Cinémathèque*, Perpignan, no. 29, Winter 1979, pp. 108–26. The author is working on a book *James A. Williamson*, in which these ideas are further developed.
8. Tom Gunning, 'D. W. Griffith and the narrator-system', p. 34 of a draft version which I have read, but absent from the published work.
9. Especially as, in David Levy's words: 'With the arrival of nickelodeon exhibition, the need for a major modification in the mode of commercial display required of the manufacturers a lecturer-independent experience based on a stricter codification of spatio-temporal convention and a tighter sequential arrangement of focused visual detail.' See 'Edwin S. Porter and the origins of the American narrative film, 1894–1907', unpublished doctoral thesis, McGill University, Montreal, 1983, pp. 333–4.
10. Tom Gunning, 'D. W. Griffith', p. 117 of draft version (my emphasis).
11. *Views and Films Index*, September 1906, p. 10, quoted in Charles Musser, 'The Nickelodeon Era Begins', pp. 256–73.
12. Van C. Lee, 'The value of a lecture', *Moving Picture World*, 8 February 1908.
13. *Moving Picture World*, 22 February 1908. Letter to the editor from one W. M. Rhoads, in reply to Van C. Lee's earlier article.
14. Tom Gunning, 'D. W. Griffith', pp. 304–5 of the published version.
15. A reference to the title of Roger Odin's article 'L'entrée du spectateur dans la fiction' in *Théorie du film*, ed Jacques Aumont and Jean-Louis Leutrat (Paris: Albatros), pp. 198–213.
16. This is how the speaker was often perceived, as this contemporary description of a cinema show illustrates: 'A strip filled with juxtaposed photographs passes rapidly between a lens which magnifies them and a bright light produced by an arc between two carbon rods. Add the continuous murmur which arises from the audience, eyes widened beyond measure, heads atop stretched necks and, to cap it all, a man who explains what you are seeing in a bored tone, to whom you do not listen although he patters on imperturbably to the very end!' (Quoted in Lacasse, *L'Historiographe*, p. 26). It is to be hoped that this 1900 spectator, clearly fascinated by the images, paid more attention to the patter during any subsequent visits to the cinema!
17. I allude here to one of the first models of this kind of film, *Le Roman d'un tricheur*, made by Sacha Guitry in 1936.

Translated by John Howe

Silent Films – What Was the Right Speed?[1]

KEVIN BROWNLOW

The silent film died, commercially, fifty years ago. Since then a swarm of misconceptions have obscured a great deal of fascinating history. Ask people to describe a silent film, and they'll tell you they were 'jerky', like the Chaplins they've seen on television, or they'll talk about 'flicker' and 'bad photography'. The last two charges can often be laid at the door of modern laboratories, for the original prints were generally superior to the black and white they produce today. But the idea that silent films were 'jerky' is less easily dismissed. Shown at the right speed, of course, they move as smoothly as a modern film – but what *was* the right speed?

Silent films have more mechanical drawbacks than other antiques – you can't even look at them without the right equipment. And the 'right' equipment is generally wrong: 16mm sound projectors are fitted with a switch marked 'silent' and 'sound'. The latter indicates the standard speed for sound films – 24 frames per second (fps). 'Silent' is supposed to do the same for silent films. But it doesn't. It merely indicates the speed for films photographed on clockwork home-movie cameras – 16 or 18 fps. The fact that some silents were photographed at this speed is a happy coincidence. But it has given rise to the illusion that *all* silent films, professional and amateur, were photographed at 16 fps. And they weren't. I have interviewed many cameramen who worked on silent pictures, and I have asked them, again and again, about the question of speeds. They always give me the same answer. 'The standard speed was sixteen.' When confronted by evidence that it wasn't, they look puzzled. But they never shift from their position. And hardly any of them has offered a satisfactory explanation.

To try to sort it out, I have done research in the trade papers of the time. I discovered the controversy popping up throughout the silent era. For the silent film placed responsibility on the projectionist in a way the sound film never did.

This came into sharp relief when I began work with David Gill on the *Hollywood* series for Thames Television. We were faced with doing the programmes on film, and initial tests with various laboratories proved very disappointing. Laboratories could reproduce neither the tonal range nor the sharpness of the original nitrate prints. What was worse, they could not alter the speed satisfactorily. They could stretch-print the film – by using an optical printer, they could print every third frame twice to give the equivalent of 16 fps – but this only increased the problem: 16 fps was too slow for most silent films, and the stretching tended to give the action a hiccup effect which was most distracting.

After further tests, and long discussions with our supervising editor, Trevor Waite, we decided to abandon the conventional approach and to make the series on videotape. This gave us complications galore, but at least it preserved as much of the photographic quality as the television line system would allow and, even more important, it enabled us to alter the speed without destroying the action. We used a variable speed telecine machine called a Polygon. Because they are virtually obsolete, suitable Polygons in Britain exist only at the BBC – which has both 16mm and 35mm models. Fitted with a 28-sided prism – 'The Flying Ashtray' – the Polygon enables you to transfer film to videotape at any speed from 4 fps to 35 fps.

The Polygon has a deficiency of its own; under about 16 fps any lateral movement is subject to 'image drag'. The Polygon prism actually 'mixes' from frame to frame, so that at slow speeds one's persistence of vision tends to retain the double image, giving the 'drag' effect. This was a drawback we had to accept to a certain degree (no doubt people will blame *that* on the crudity of the early films, too!). There was also a loss of picture quality compared to other telecinés. In other respects, the Polygon was a godsend. It was particularly fascinating to run the early films, altering the speed until the movement seemed absolutely right. A pattern emerged that seemed related to the year of production, the studio and, of course, the cameraman.

Yet these speeds seldom corresponded with the speeds at which the films were shown in the theatres. It is possible to check these because they were specified on the cue sheets. These cue sheets were issued to the musical directors of the theatres, and contained musical suggestions. The same sheets were available for the projectionists. 'Examination of hundreds of cue sheets for silent films,' said James Card, former curator of George Eastman House, 'has failed to turn up a single one which indicates a film should be projected at 16 frames a second.'

The cue sheets were often quite emphatic. For *The Four Horsemen* they insisted: 'The correct speed is 12½ minutes per 1,000 ft – not any slower – and mark off, then make sure and hold it. Speedometer should be used and film should be run registering 86 revolutions per minute.' Speed: 21½ fps. The chart overleaf offers some fascinating comparisons.

The Polygon method is not definite proof of the original camera speed, for it is entirely dependent on the eye of the person in charge. Everyone has a slightly different sense of rhythm; I tended to favour a frame or two faster than David Gill, for instance. And one can check back at our Polygon sheets and see that a film transferred at 22 fps at one session might run at 21 or 23 at another. But while it may not be scientific, the Polygon is the best guide to film speed since projectors abandoned tachometers.

The opportunity for television film-makers to achieve the correct speed will soon be widely available. The new generation of Ampex VPR tape machines – with variable speed capacity – will give even greater control, for they permit a reduction to the equivalent of 4–5 fps without image drag, and with no loss of definition.

Controversy over speed dogged silent films from the start. Thomas

TABLE I

Comparison of probable camera speeds (as indicated by Polygon) and projection speeds (as specified by cue sheets)

		Camera	*Projector*	*Cameraman*	*Studio*
		fps	*fps*		
Blind Husbands	1919	16	?	Ben Reynolds	Universal
Foolish Wives	1921	16	18	Reynolds/Wm Daniels	Universal
The Four Horsemen of the Apocalypse	1921	20	21	John Seitz	Metro
Monsieur Beaucaire	1924	18	24*	Harry Fischbeck	FP-Lasky
Robin Hood	1922	19	22	Arthur Edeson	United Artists
Scaramouche	1923	19	22	John Seitz	Metro
Merry Widow	1925	19	24	Oliver Marsh	MGM
Ben-Hur	1925	19	22	Various	MGM
The Crowd	1928	20	24	John Arnold	MGM
Show People	1928	20	24	John Arnold	MGM
Flesh and the Devil	1926	20	23	Wm Daniels	MGM
Mysterious Lady	1928	20	24	Wm Daniels	MGM
The Black Pirate	1926	20	24	Henry Sharp	United Artists
Lilac Time	1928	20	24	Sid Hickox	First National
Love	1927	20	24	Wm Daniels	MGM
The Eagle	1925	22	24	Geo Barnes	United Artists
Wedding March	1928	22	24	Hal Mohr	Paramount
The Strong Man	1926	22	24	Elgin Lesley	First National
What Price Glory?	1926	22	24	Barney McGill	Fox
Trail of 98	1928	22	24	John Seitz	MGM
Woman of Affairs	1928	24	24	Wm Daniels	MGM
The General†	1926	24	24	Dev Jennings	United Artists
Docks of New York	1928	24	24	Hal Rosson	Paramount
Queen Kelly	1928	24	24	Paul Ivano/G. Pollock	United Artists

* Cue sheet specifies: 'Do not run at normal speed of 85 feet per minute, but 90 as we feel the film requires it.'

† H. A. V. Bulleid, who knows this film well, is convinced its ideal screening speed is 20 fps.

Edison recommended a speed of 46 frames per second – 'anything less will strain the eye.' As historian Gordon Hendricks wrote in his book *The Edison Motion Picture Myth*: 'There would seem to be no good reason for it. This rate was far above any rate necessary for gaining the persistence of vision.'[2] H. A. V. Bulleid points out, however, that Edison's decision was a sensible one: 'To obviate flicker from white light projected on a bright surface requires about 48 obscurations per second.'[3] Nevertheless, Edison films did not follow this recommendation for long. Apart from anything else, it used too much film. It also reduced the exposure, and film stock was not fast. But Edison films were photographed much faster than the films of most other companies – although Hendricks found them varying as much as 15 fps in a single day. An Edison film of 1900 will generally project satisfactorily at 24 fps. Edison's rival, the American Mutoscope and Biograph Company, used a camera which weighed 1,700 lbs. This camera had a motor, and it turned at a speed of 40 fps. Billy Bitzer operated one. (Curiously, his later films were characterised by a remarkably slow camera speed.)

During the nickelodeon period, films were projected at whatever speed suited the management. The standard was supposed to be 16½ fps. 'I remember running a full 1,000 ft reel in 12 minutes at the eight o'clock show,' recalled Victor Milner, who later became a leading Hollywood cameraman, 'and in the afternoon I used to project the same reel so slow it took Maurice Costello ages to cross the set. Those were my manager's orders.' Projected at the 'correct' speed of 16 fps, a full 1,000 ft reel of 35 mm film would last 16 minutes. The Essanay Film Company of Chicago tried to beat wily exhibitors by printing the running time of the films on the posters. The exhibitors retaliated by pasting a strip of paper over the line. Some unscrupulous theatre managers could get through a full reel in six minutes! Ten minutes was acknowledged to be 'more usual'. Yet, even today, on standard 24 fps sound projectors, 1,000 feet takes eleven minutes . . .

> There is no hard and fast rule that can be laid down governing speed. It may, however, be said that 70 feet per minute is about as fast as a film should be run under any circumstances, with 45 as the limit the other way. Slower than 40 feet would not be safe. In general, the film should be run at the speed that will produce a minimum of flicker, combined with the lifelike, natural motion of the figures. . . . It is as likely as not that the speed should be changed several times in different portions of the same film. With most standard machines, one turn of the crank runs off exactly one foot of film, so that normal speed is about 66 turns of the crank per minute, and by counting turns you know just how fast you are running.[4]

Projectionists might speed up Edison one- and- two-reelers with relative impunity. But Biographs looked ridiculous at anything above the so-called standard 16. By 1913, even that speed was too fast. The chief Biograph director, D. W. Griffith, appeared to be struggling against the limitations of the one- and-two-reeler. (The following year, he would embark on his epic *The Birth of a Nation* in twelve reels.) By slowing the speed of the camera (and therefore the projector) he could squeeze in extra sequences and extend his story. Biograph instructed exhibitors to project their films so that a full 1,000 ft reel lasted *eighteen minutes* – 15 fps.

The highly inflammable nitrate film had to move slowly past the searing heat of the arc lamp. On most projectors, the fire shutter would descend and cut off the light if they moved below 40 ft per minute. Projectionists often ignored the 18 minute-per-thousand rule. One might assume that reports that his actors were zipping across the screen would horrify Griffith, and he would increase the speed of his camera to suit the standard projection speed. Not at all. Some sequences of *The Birth of a Nation* are so under-cranked that they need to be shown at 12 fps. Griffith, and his cameraman Billy Bitzer, continued to crank slower than average on all the major features they made together. And because Griffith's films are the most frequently revived of all American silent films, film societies religiously switch their projectors to 'silent' for Griffith films – and all other silent pictures. The speed is not slow enough for Griffith – and is ruinously slow for other films.

But not even Griffith was consistent. His instructions for *Home Sweet Home* (1914) recommended 16 minutes for the first reel (16.6 fps), 14–15 minutes for the second (17.8–19 fps), and 13–14 for each of the other reels (19–20.5 fps). 'The last reel, however, should be run slowly from the beginning of the allegorical part to the end.'[5] 'The projectionist,' said Griffith, 'in a large measure is compelled to redirect the photoplay.'

A 1915 projectionist's handbook declared – in emphatic capitals – 'THERE IS NO SUCH THING AS A SET CAMERA SPEED.' 'The correct speed of projection, it added, is the speed at which each individual scene was taken – which may – and often does – vary wildly.' And it declared: 'One of the highest functions of projection is to watch the screen and regulate the speed of projection to synchronise with the speed of taking.'

The reason that films of this period were sometimes shown too fast was that exhibitors worked to iron-bound schedules. For a seven-reel show lasting 1 hour 50 minutes, each reel could be run at an average 15.7 minutes per reel (around 17 fps). But if there were nine reels, the projectionist had to speed up to 12.2 mins (about 22 fps) in order that the show could end precisely on time. Nevertheless, the fact that silent pictures were invariably shown slightly faster than they were shot was confirmed by historian David Shepard. When for example he worked on the restoration of *Nanook of the North* (1922), he found that Flaherty had shot the film at 16 fps – 'but the pace and rhythm of the edited feature was completely destroyed by so slow a speed.'

Exhibitors declared in the 1920s that the standard speed was much faster than it used to be, because cameramen varied their rate of cranking so much. The Hollywood cameramen were indignant. Victor Milner stated in the *American Cinematographer*, in July 1923, that the average camera speed was still 16 fps, sixteen minutes, forty seconds per thousand. 'To achieve smoothness of tempo, projection should also be at this speed.' He pointed out that rushes were shown every day at the studios, on the most modern projectors. The operator had an indicator, and there was another indicator on the director's desk. It was set between 65 and 72 feet per minute. 'If a scene shows the wrong speed, it is retaken.' Already, Milner has weakened his argument. For he has admitted that films, allegedly photographed at 16, were being checked at a speed approaching 19. In the same article, Milner enlisted the support of director Rex Ingram; he declared that he was very careful to achieve perfect speed. Yet the films of Rex Ingram, photographed by John Seitz, registered between 19 fps and 22 fps on the Polygon, and his cue sheets specified from 21 to 24 fps.

In 1925, director Al Rogell wrote in *Director* magazine:

> At a recent meeting, the Society of Motion Picture Engineers advocated a universal set speed for projection of 80 feet per minute (21.3 frames per second). As a matter of fact, most theatres show pictures at a speed of 85–90 ft. per minute (22.6 fps–24 fps) in these days of long shows with 10–11 reels of film and various entertainment acts.

That same year (1925) the head of a theatre chain in Indiana claimed that 24 fps was now the standard speed. Again the cameramen denied it. Paul Perry, in the *American Cinematographer*, claimed that he had checked with his colleagues and found the majority cranking at – you've guessed it – 16 fps, 60 feet per minute. The Polygon may not be a definitive scientific instrument, but no film of 1925 we put through had been shot at 16 fps. Yet Perry let slip a hint that cameramen *had* been asked to turn faster: 'If the theatres insist on faster projection, it is only natural that some of the producers request that their film be exposed more rapidly to offset the increased speed of projection.'

Karl Malkames, the son of silent-era cameraman Don Malkames, and a cameraman himself, wrote to me recently:

> The practice of cranking from 20 to 24 to compensate for rising theatrical projection speeds was common while my father was at Fox in 1924. Bell and Howell equipment continued to reflect the idea of 16 fps as 'normal'. The shutter speed plate on my later model Bell and Howell, circa 1930, is still calibrated for 16 fps.

The Bell and Howell 2709 camera became the standard studio model of the 1920s. Two turns of the handle sent one foot of film through the gate – one foot of film contained sixteen frames of picture, so two turns per second equalled sixteen frames, the 'standard' speed. Cameramen prided themselves on their even rate of cranking. To achieve it you said 'One hundred and one' to yourself, over and over, until the speed came naturally. One cameraman hummed the 'Anvil Chorus' from *Il Trovatore*. While the speed was undoubtedly even, how could they know precisely *what* their speed was? Could they honestly say they were cranking at 16 and not 18 frames per second? *For there was no speed indicator on the Bell and Howell.*

Kemp Niver has interviewed a number of silent-era cameramen for the American Society of Cinematographers.

> To a man, they said that unless there was some specific reason . . . they tried to maintain 16 fps. No cameraman could make a statement that he cranked at a specific speed and prove it unless he had a stop watch at the start and end of a given number of feet of film. Even then he couldn't guarantee that he wasn't under-cranking or over-cranking as the tension on the take-up magazine increased.

A motor was available for the Bell and Howell, with a speed indicator. Predictably, 16 fps is marked 'Normal'. The top speed is 22 fps. In production stills, this motor appears more and more often towards the end of the 20s. In the old days, they said they *preferred* hand cranking. So why the motor? Perhaps because of the increased demands of the mobile camera – now far more common – which needed more manipulation than the static camera. And perhaps because a standard speed had at last arrived. In October 1927 *The Jazz Singer* had been premièred, and theatres were being wired for sound. The standard speed of sound films was 24 fps. It is interesting to discover how that speed was arrived at.

According to Stanley Watkins, head engineer for Western Electric, he and his team checked with the Warner Theatre for the average speed of projection in 1926. They were told 'between 80 and 90 feet per minute' in the big theatres – between 20 and 24 fps – and around 26 fps in the smaller theatres. They settled on 90 feet a minute (24 fps) as a reasonable compromise for the Vitaphone process.[6] The other sound systems began at slower speeds (Fox-Case's first tests were shot at 21 fps), but they, too, adopted 24 fps as standard in November 1926.

If Hollywood cameramen were still working rigidly at 16 fps their work would have looked ludicrous in the public theatres. The fact that they *were* cranking the films slower than they were projected is borne out by *The Jazz Singer*: Al Jolson walks to the stage at a slightly accelerated pace, and when the Vitaphone section begins, he is filmed at 24 fps. Filmgoers often remarked that the early talkies seemed leaden-footed.

While filming *Annapolis* in 1928, cameraman Arthur Miller received a wire from the studio to crank at 24 fps. He did so, and everyone complained that the speed slowed everything down too much – it was particularly noticeable in a dress parade scene of midshipmen.

Walter Kerr, in his brilliant book *The Silent Clowns*,[7] puts forward his theory: silent films were photographed at 16 or 18 frames a second, but projected at a rate closer to sound speed. 'The result was not only faster than life, it was cleaner, less effortful, more dynamic.' Kerr illustrates his theory with a photograph of the instructions printed on the leader for the 1922 *Down to the Sea in Ships*: 'Operator: please run eleven minutes for 1,000 ft' – or 24 fps, the speed of sound. I have projected the film, and found two or three sections too fast at that speed (although the remainder is satisfactory). But that was how audiences saw it at the time. Other, later films such as *The Winning of Barbara Worth*, were shot at a speed so close to 24 fps that they are wrecked by being shown at 16 fps. I have even seen an occasional silent, such as *The Blood Ship* (1928), apparently designed to be projected at 26 fps, since sound speed is too slow for them. (Poverty Row producers like Columbia, who made *The Blood Ship*, ordered cameras to be cranked faster to fill their reels more economically!)

Talking about comedies, Walter Kerr writes: 'Silent films *chose*, by control of the camera and through instructions to projectionists, to move at an unreal, stylised, in effect fantasised rate.' And he quotes as examples the last two silent Chaplins – both films designed to be shown at sound speed, but photographed at silent speed (whatever that was!).

> The least glance at *Modern Times* reveals instantly that all of Chaplin's work in the film . . . has been filmed at a rate that puts springs in his heels and makes unleashed jack-knives of his elbows. This is how the films looked when they were projected as their creators intended.

One can only have sympathy for those who programme silent films. But sympathy evaporates as soon as one has to endure slow projection. It's bad enough to be deprived of the sound of the symphony orchestra (which accompanied all first-run films in the big theatres), but to be forced to watch the films in dead silence at an equally deadly pace is too much to ask of anyone. William Wellman's spectacular war film *Wings* (1927) moves at an exhilarating pace when projected at the speed at which it was shown originally – 24 fps – but it drags miserably when shown at 16. At one of its last major showings in Britain, a few years ago, the audience emerged complaining of its slowness. Their complaints were not aimed at the projectionist, for they thought it was an inherent fault of all silent films. Yet it had been shown at 16 fps – and had lasted nearly an hour longer than in 1927. That attitude shows no respect towards the films of the past. It does them a grave disservice. David Gill says:

> Ideally, projectors should have variable speeds from at least 14 to 24 fps. There was no standard for the normal camera speed in the silent days, and for commercial reasons, the recommended projection speeds do not necessarily match the camera speed. We could recommend that most silents be shown at 24 – but that means that silent film actors will always move in crisp, sharp movements – never smooth and languorous ones. This is fine for actors in comedies, war films and some Westerns. But it's sad for the others – especially the Great Lovers!

Postscript

Since the above was written, it has become much easier to ensure the right speed on videotape – thanks to new models of telecine with variable speeds – and on the screen – thanks to a machine called a Microverter. Manufactured by AEG of West Germany, this machine can be used with most projectors and can handle virtually any speed.

And yet surprisingly few makers of television programmes using archive film bother to correct the speed. The First World War continues to be fought by troops with St Vitus' Dance. And few projectionists, alas, seem to know of the existence of the Microverter.

And the Cinémathèque at Bois d'Arcy, near Paris, continues to ruin its restorations of silent films by stretch-printing them. *La Merveilleuse Vie de Jeanne d'Arc* had to be 'restored' twice, once in stretch-printed form, by Bois D'Arcy, then more conventionally (and much more successfully) by the Cinémathèque Française in Paris. Since the film was made in 1928/9, after the introduction of sound in America, it was photographed close to 24 fps. Stretch-printing added redundant footage and slowed the pace. L'Herbier's *L'Argent* should run 150 minutes; Bois D'Arcy's print runs 195 minutes.

European silent films tended to be shot at slower speeds than American, and shown closer to 20 fps than 24 fps. *Napoleon* is projected at 20 fps in its fully restored version; the shorter American version is projected at 24 fps with ruinous results.

After I had written the article, I came upon a 1926 book called *The Mind and the Film* by Gerard Fort Buckle which noted that camera speeds today – the mid-20s – were worked at 22 to 28 pictures per second. And I was sent the cue sheets for *Old Ironsides* (1927) for which the slowest speed was 20 fps, the fastest 25.33 (95 feet per minute – faster than sound).

I rest my case.

Notes

First published in *Sight and Sound*, Summer 1980.

1. Grateful thanks for invaluable help in the preparation of this chapter to David Gill, George Pratt, H. A. V. Bulleid, David Shepard, Karl Malkames, Kemp Niver.
2. G. Hendricks, *The Edison Motion Picture Myth* (Berkeley and Los Angeles: University of California Press, 1961).
3. This was later achieved, of course, by the design of the shutter.
4. *Moving Picture World*, 9 May 1908, p.3.
5. Ibid., 20 June 1914, p. 652.
6. One reason for world standards accepting 24 fps was that it permitted flickerless projection with a 2–blade shutter (H. A. V. Bulleid).
7. W. Kerr, *The Silent Clowns* (New York: Knopf, 1975).

III

THE CONTINUITY SYSTEM

Griffith and Beyond

Introduction

Griffith and Film Form

Griffith's work will always provide the ultimate challenge to the student of early cinema, if only because for so long, his was virtually the only historiographically examined manifestation of the period, often the sum total of what was known about early cinema.[1] In a corrective counter-move, the toppling of Griffith as the father of classical cinema and inventor of narrative film-making has become a ritual act of parricide among film scholars. However, such obligatory revisionism is itself giving way to a more historically and textually informed view of Griffith's work, with the result that we now have a body of knowledge establishing quite specifically the terms of Griffithian film practice.

In the essays on Griffith collected here, one can witness a shift from traditional assertions of his importance as the founder of the feature film, to a recognition of the relative autonomy of his work from both the early and classical modes. This shift has been facilitated by the acceptance of norms, in contrast to 'firsts' and 'inventions', as the touchstone in the history of film. Consequently, there has been a willingness to surrender the notion of Griffith as originator of the basic techniques of filmic narration,[2] in favour of trying to reconstruct the idea of film form and the practice of cinema underpinning his work. Attention has moved from Griffith's epics to his earlier work at Biograph where the fundamentals of a unique approach to filmic form, as well as the pressures emanating from the 'institution' can be studied in the process of coming into being.

As argued in previous introductions, the turn to narrative in the cinema cannot simply be seen as the consequence of the urge for storytelling. It involves the contradictory articulation of a logic of space and time, within the context of a new industrial commodity, the reel of film, itself standing for new experiences of spectatorship. Film narrative and classical continuity cinema emerge, in this model, as the 'solution' to the problem of how spatial representation can be inflected with a certain linearity (itself a compromise between a temporality and a causal chain), while serving as the optimal textual form of creating a commodity amenable to industrial production and capitalist exploitation. Griffith's films, as a consequence, seem even more extraordinary, complex and symptomatic, just as his influence becomes more puzzling, unexpected and multidimensional.

Before arguing this more fully, it may be helpful to recall in what ways

Griffith's work stands at the points of intersection and poses questions for students of early cinema and its transformations. To begin with, there is Griffith's relation to early film form, and the reasons why he must be regarded as belonging to a transitional rather than the primitive or the institutional mode. Although shot relations, formal linkages and a very sophisticated use of space make him a consummate example of continuity cinema and the IMR (in his use of alternation and repetition, for instance), there are enough features of the PMR even in Griffith's 'mature' work (frontal staging, rare close-ups, little scene dissection, relative absence of point-of-view structure) which make the retention of these features not so much a sign of retardedneeeess (as some of the iconoclasts had first argued), but evidence of a different conception of filmic form. In this respect similar to Porter during the first decade, Griffith is a Janus-faced figure among the directors of the second decade, looking both backwards and to the future. Hence, the possibility of treating, for instance, Griffith's Biograph films either *sui generis*, or as evidence of a transitional period where he is joined by other directors, such as Ralph Ince, Maurice Tourneur or George Loane Tucker (director of the remarkable *Traffic in Souls*), all of whom developed features of the different modes in idiosyncratic ways, helping to make especially the first half of the 1910s in the United States a much more diverse period stylistically than had been suspected as long as Griffith's remained the only body of films accessible or examined.

The retention of frontal staging, both in Griffith and Ralph Ince, for example, made possible a narrative space which in its complexity is almost incomprehensible to the modern eye. Open towards the audience (and thus 'primitive'), but nevertheless emphatically part of a cinema of narrative integration (where the space occupied by the camera is supposed to be 'invisible'), this 'frontal space' in films like *An Unseen Enemy* or *The Right Girl?* is fundamental to the progression and thus the logic of the narrative itself.[3] In particular, Griffith's use of frontality well into the 1920s does not spring from ignorance, but is more likely evidence that the PMR could be developed, and was developed, in sophisticated and still little understood ways, which were lost to the institutional mode when it abandoned frontal staging and the spectator-positioning it connoted. At the same time, it indicates that, from a certain point onwards, Griffith and so-called classical cinema parted company, obliging us to consider his influence elsewhere (in the European cinema, for instance). In fact, it is probably more useful to see Griffith as a representative of non-continuity cinema, elaborating the most extraordinary forms of continuity within that mode, rather than practicing a cinema of discontinuity, but retaining features of the non-continuous mode.

This is not to deny that Griffith remained an important source for instituting a 'cinema of discontinuity' in the sense used by Salt,[4] by developing techniques for transforming visually disparate locations (switching from place to place, or by juxtaposing scenes) into the impression of an overall unified narrative space. But instead of, say, the cut on action, which will become the most common form of shot transition, in Griffith it is character movement between spaces, frame cuts (shot transition as a character exits the frame) and a manipulation of screen direction which serve as the key principles of Griffithian continuity. Jacques Aumont is therefore right to focus on the spatial articulations of Griffith's Biograph films, in order to emphasise their non-naturalistic qualities. Griffith's shallow frontal stagings create enclosed spaces, since in his conception of film drama, these spaces are crucial to the development of the narrative trajectory, almost as important as (and working in tandem with) parallel editing. One only has to remember in how many films the setting up of self-enclosed spaces within the frame and discrete action spaces are the starting points for narratives that drive towards an eventual bringing together of all the elements within one frame – the usual moment of closure in a Griffith film. It is in this context, and beyond the economic exigencies of film-making at Biograph, or the speed at which shooting took place, that one must see what Aumont calls the 'poverty of the referential store of locations'. However, Aumont insists, it is also indicative of 'figurative closure', another feature different from classical continuity cinema, which developed 'more fictional, thematic, indeed spatial' modes of closure, compared with the degree of figurative abstraction achieved by Griffith. Spatial closure thus becomes the symptom of a cinema allied to the theatre – the edges of the frame are used as wings (rather than continuing into off-screen space), *as well as* of a kind of abstract use of space quite unlike anything possible in the theatre.

Symmetry, Doubling and Alternation

Similarly multi-faceted is Griffith's most outstanding contribution to the development of narrative and continuity cinema, namely parallel editing which, although he did not invent it, he explored more fully than anyone else. Semiological models of filmic signification, such as Metz' 'grande syntagmatique' and its elaboration and application by Raymond Bellour to specific films have given us a much better understanding of parallel editing as only one instance of that more general principle – alternation – which, according to Bellour has a crucial function for both classical and non-classical modes of film-making.[5] What is only beginning to be appreciated is how deeply the principles of segmentation, division and alternation penetrate not only Griffith's formal procedures, but structure his very conception of the diegetic material, including his view of the family, of morality, sexual difference and history.[6]

Gunning recognised this feature when he distinguishes the formal principle of parallel editing and the diegetic principle of doubling the narrative interest (running two separate plot-lines together). Thus, in a film like *An Unseen Enemy*, the story of the two sisters alone in the house is joined to the story of the maid 'doubling herself' by calling on a crony to carry out the robbery. Put another way, Griffith's narratives are always based on an act of splitting the narrative core or cell, and obtaining several narrative threads which could then be woven together again. By this act of separation, and his ability to subdivide even the smallest of episodes, Griffith was able to insert further plot-lines and complications, opening up potentially infinite series, as in his epics, where the 'expansive' tendency of the narrative stands in a highly dramatic relation to its resolution and the bringing about of closure. Thus, analytical story-telling and the breakdown of the linear narrative flow (parallel editing at the macro-level of the scene, juxtaposition and alternation at the micro-level of the shot) makes possible a certain 'formalisation' in Griffith's treatment of the referential material, quite different from the kind of scene-dissection of classical cinema, which Griffith uses so sparingly. Again, it would appear that the retention of a 'retarded' style gives the director a repertoire not available in the classical mode, such as the freedom to manipulate the pro-filmic, cutting it up and reassembling it according to formal procedures: in Griffith, the 'constructed' nature of cinematic realism is inescapable. This supports Aumont's point that 'Griffithian representation, just as coherent and systematic [as classical narrative] uses other means, thus obtaining very specific effects of reality, often very disconcerting.'

An equally non-naturalistic view of Griffith's *mise en scène* is taken by Bellour in his meticulous analysis of *The Lonedale Operator*. He is able to show that patterns of alternation structure both cinematic and non-cinematic codes, the narrative level (with its emphasis on sexual difference and the formation of the couple) and the formal level (different patterns of symmetry and asymmetry in the composition of the frame, in figure movement and visual rhymes), generating what Bellour calls 'textual volume'. Closure is brought to this proliferation of echoes and reduplications by 'that particular effect which superimposes repetition on resolution', identified by Bellour as one of the most typical traits of the classical Hollywood cinema. Bellour's analysis demonstrates a rigorous textual system at work even in this most simple of Griffith's race-to-the-rescue films. Yet perhaps he assimilates this system too categorically to the classical paradigm, given other possibilities inherent in alternation, also present in Griffith's work and explored by the avant garde.[7]

Within early cinema, alternation is itself a consequence of the kind of succession typical of the chase film, except that a succession of two shots had to be read not only as signifying temporal successiveness and relative spatial proximity, but as potentially signifying also an inverse relation: that of temporal simultaneity and spatial distance.[8] The example of the chase film best illustrates Griffith's different conception of spatio-temporal relations. In the early chase films, as already mentioned, pursuer and pursued were always in the same shot, due to the absolute priority of spatial coherence in the representation of causal relations or sequential action. By contrast, Griffith divided the pursuer and pursued, or more often, the attacker, victim, and rescuer into separate shots, and then intercut between them, creating emotional suspense and formal-dynamic patterning, but also a quite different conception of cinematic/diegetic space: one only has to look at Griffith's *The Curtain Pole* to realise its particular deviations from other chase films, which developed their own form, only remotely similar to Griffith's use. Parallel editing in the classical cinema (and to some extent this is true of *The Lonedale Operator*), increasingly came to connote temporal simultaneity/spatial distance. As film-makers began to favour the paradigm temporal succession/spatial proximity, the practice of analytical editing – i.e. classical cinema – generally came to mean articulating shots according to a form of alternation which privileged temporal successiveness (exemplified in shot-reverse shot) over spatial coherence, the former eventually absorbing the latter, and subsuming both under the new narrational logic. But there are other formal systems (the European art cinema of the 1920s: so-called German Expressionism, notably the films of Murnau and Lang) where some of the other spatial possibilities of Griffith's editing are taken up or developed further,[9] and of course, Soviet montage cinema, where spatial coherence and temporality are played off against each other, without classical narration unifying either, and where instead, film-makers elaborate different principles of coherence.[10]

Aumont's article reminds us that Griffith has often been celebrated as the precursor of the classical cinema, because he led the cinema towards the novelistic. Yet this emphasis limits him to being an exponent of a Bazinian cinema of transparency, and must be balanced, as Aumont implies, against Eisenstein's acknowledgment of Griffith as the inventor of montage. The busy backgrounds in so many of his Biograph films (for example, the scenes in the tavern of *An Unseen Enemy*) with so many narratively insignificant figures moving deep in the frame are not only there to give a 'realist' effect. For Aumont, 'all these supplementary figures, these scraps of the imaginary appear by the very excess of their inscription as what they are: patchwork, collage, montage, . . . the famous "montage within the frame" so dear to Eisenstein'.

Griffith, the Storyteller

Finally, another feature of Griffith's system which is different from both early and classical cinema needs to be mentioned: the insert, the close-up and the point-of-view shot, as they make up a particular mode of narration. The exploitation of framing and depth, of the close-up and the look is, in Griffith as elsewhere, integral to, and indeed constitutive of narration itself, and thus requiring (the implied presence of) both a narrator and a narratee. Much of the discussion around narration and the diegetic effect in early cinema has thus focused on the status of the insert (cut-in): is it a monstrational or a narrational device? Burch, as we have seen, regards the history of the close-up as crucial for the 'linearisation of the iconic signifier',[11] a history in which Griffith (Burch's example is from *Musketeers of Pig Alley*) retains 'spatial coherence and topological complexity' as an alternative to the close-up. Parallel editing, cross-cutting, and the insert in Griffith thus can be read either (from the vantage point of the PMR) as elements of 'external' narration, or (from the vantage point of the IMR) as already part of a strictly narrational logic (overriding spatial coherence and temporal logic): only in the latter case will the close-up be read as an internally motivated, diegetically integrated element of a scene. This in turn shifts the emphasis from the active intervention of the film-maker to the capacity of the viewer to construct different kinds of difference as 'motivated'. Thus, Brewster in his article on *Gold is not all* ('A Scene at the Movies') points out that one of the crucial differences between the point-of-view shot as insert (and signifier of pure visual curiosity), and the technical point-of-view cut-in as narrational device depends on the kind of motivation the point-of-view shot has within hierarchies of knowledge organised according to the narrative's hermeneutic code.[12] In this respect too, then, Griffith stands both at the margins of the classical mode and exceeds it. As Aumont argues, the close-up in Griffith very often functions not as internally motivated, but has a disruptive function. Instead of giving the illustrative detail or directing viewer attention, the Griffith close-up is often 'of the order of hyper-articulated writing, almost caricatural, in a sense the grimace of the film text'.

The question of 'externality' v. 'integration' with respect to narration is one of the key issues in Griffith, since his ambiguous place in this development sharply focuses attention on the extra-textual and institutional aspects of narrative cinema. When looking at Griffith the story-teller, traditional Griffith studies are in something of a dilemma: on the one hand, his consummate skill in putting across a story is the very basis of his reputation, but on the other hand, it has been difficult to locate this genius in anything more precise than his cross-cutting and parallel action. From the perspective of classical narrative, with its invisible story-teller and omniscient narration, Griffith's use of cross-cutting, together with the moralism of his intertitles would indicate a more 'primitive' instance of narration, with a didactic narrator making his presence felt, perhaps even pointing to the lecturer in a lantern slide show. From the perspective of 'primitive' monstration, however, as we have seen when discussing frontality, Griffith's films are, at least from 1911 onwards, the very epitome of 'narrative integration'. Aumont also addresses this issue, but perhaps too formalistically, from the perspective of Eisenstein and the avant garde.

In a sense, none of the available models had adequately described Griffith's mode of story-telling, his narrational procedures and strategies, until Brewster's 'A Scene at the Movies'. His contribution to the debate about narration in Griffith is first of all that he differentiates clearly between what he calls a 'technical' point of view (or optical point of view) and 'narrative' point of view (or 'focalisation', if one adopts Genette's literary terminology), linking technical point of view, as Salt had already done, with inserts, and thus with 'primitive' rather than classical use of cutting. As Gaudreault was also to argue, narration in primitive cinema functions perfectly well without the optical point of view. In Brewster's words, 'even when a narrative hinges on what a character sees, this will often be conveyed without pov structures'. Conversely, precisely because Griffith does not use the optical point of view, he can create situations where characters 'see' each other across an imaginary space. Aumont refers to this when he says that the economy of Griffith's locations, as in *Enoch Arden* (when Annie waits, then 'sees' Enoch, who eventually lands, on the 'same' beach where Annie had waited), greatly helps establish these forms of spatial continuity. In this example the different spaces are cut together on the basis of a 'homology of the two situations' which creates a space they both share and at the same time, reduces the imaginary distance between them. Gunning, when discussing point of view in early cinema calls such indirect point-of-view structures 'sight-links', and their presence in Griffith (he mentions *The Lonedale Operator*), alongside other features, makes him a representative of the 'cinema of narrative integration'.[13]

An example that comes to mind from *Drive for a Life* involves the use of close-up when a box of candy is injected with poison and then gift-wrapped. The scene proceeds by cross-cutting between the hero discovering the plot and driving towards the house of his fiancée, and the fiancée unwrapping the candy and passing it round to her women friends. In this alternating structure, the various interruptions delaying the eating of the candy are now motivated both from within the diegesis (the women joke and tease each other) and also via the narrational agency of cross-cutting, establishing the spatial alternation between the scene of the candy being passed round and the car approaching the house. *Drive for a Life* could serve as an example of two kinds of narration, internal and external, coexisting and naturalising each other, with intermittence and delay diegetically motivated (by resorting psychological and gender clichés of the protagonists) and extra-diegetically motivated (by cross cutting, as sign of an external narrator intervening).

Yet Gunning's concept of narrative integration and Bellour's notion of alternation and textual volume ignore to some extent what to Brewster is perhaps the most important feature of Griffith's narrational perspective 'without point-of-view shots', namely, that it has as its necessary third term the spectators' plane of vision, his/her presence within the (imaginary) field of the diegetic space. This particular way of situating the spectator could be said to form the bridge between showing and telling, monstrative and integrated narrational modes, and thereby shifts attention to the processes of intelligibility as well as specular seduction. Brewster makes the important distinction between two types of knowledge, both crucial to an understanding of Griffith and early film form: narrative knowledge and knowledge dependent on the visual field. The opposition would be between the information given in and through the visual field, and the 'narrative knowledge' accumulated by the filmic process and its temporality, which can be signalled, albeit ambiguously, by off-screen space,[14] of which one dimension or direction would be the frontal space already referred to.[15]

Multi-scene films were to give off-screen space a new significance, and it is not until his full-length features that Griffith thoroughly 'reinvents' frontality and combines it with an active use of off-screen space (as opposed to the off-screen space involved in the 'sight-links' or the narrative point of views), in order to create inferential structures of sight and knowledge far in excess of and unparallelled by the kind of hierarchisation of knowledge which we recognise as suspense and usually identify with classical cinema.[16] Brewster locates this inferential knowledge already in the Biograph films: 'the narrative (and the titles) provide a third perspective: the rich are ignorant of the poor; the poor see the rich and envy them; the spectator knows rich and poor *and knows the poor do not know how unhappy the rich really are*' (author's emphasis). This additional layer of contrast and dramatic irony is a powerful narrational device, because it relativises the positions of knowledge between characters and spectators. Differentiation in the hierarchies of knowledge thus becomes a sophisticated and specifically Griffithian mark of narration, without however contributing towards the dominance and narrative importance of the look as practiced in classical continuity editing. Since Griffith draws attention more often to off-frame space (the characters' movement from room to room, for instance) than to off-screen space, the separation of these spaces builds up a very particular 'spatialisation of

knowledge'. Such narrative knowledge is in Griffith more detailed in the way it not only relies heavily on recognition/repetition and the effects of irony this produces, but on an extension of the visual field (the space in front) to include the spectator as an active component of that visual field, a kind of mirror around which spectatorship is reflected back into the diegetic space.[17]

Griffith and the Multi-Reel Film

In order, however, to situate Griffith's role more precisely, we need to look at the way his narrational procedures were both shaped by and, in all probability, finally marginalised by the institutional context in which he found himself. The greatest change, and perhaps still the least understood aspect of early cinema transforming itself into the institutional mode is the switch from single reel to multi-reel film, and Griffith's perhaps exaggerated reputation as inventor and pioneer has at its core a basically sound intuition of his importance for the development of the feature-length film and of complex narratives. Gunning's 'Weaving a Narrative'[18] argues persuasively that there exists a relationship between the emergence of longer films, of which Griffith's work is still exemplary, and socio-economic changes in the institution cinema, such as the need to attract middle-class patrons and give film-going cultural respectability. In Gunning's argument, the changes required were of a quite distinct and diverse kind, coming together around the figure of Griffith, or rather, around a number of practices we usually associate with Griffith. Firstly, there are the formal features described above, and in particular his ability to subdivide plot-lines, locations and to cross-cut action spaces, within a form that could linearise them, and lead them to satisfactory narrative resolutions. Secondly, Griffith's involvement in the contemporary theatre and the melodramatic tradition, which at the most obvious level greatly assisted in what Gunning identifies as the chief economic necessity: the attraction of a middle-class public, used to stage plays and melodramas, and demanding longer films in order to accept the show at the cinema as an adequate definition of an 'evening out'. Thirdly, there was Griffith's own 'Victorianism', his concern for public issues of the day, such as alcoholism, mental health, the institution of the family, which made him a perfect figurehead for the institution to protest its respectability and counter accusations of depravity and immorality. Finally, there is what Gunning sees as the glue that holds all the elements together, namely Griffith's handling of spatial and temporal non-continuity which is the very premise for this ability to use parallel editing in order 'to provide one of the most basic desiderata of a bourgeois narrative – psychological motivation'.

Gunning's argument is a subtle and far-reaching one, putting forward the thesis that Griffith's stylistic developments are determined not by individual genius, but by the pressures on the emergent cinematic institution. Griffith's contribution to the history of the cinema was to have found an (institutionally and textually) economic way of overcoming a crisis, the transition from single reel to multi-reel films, by solving the problem of the longer narrative, via parallel editing. For Gunning, class-bias becomes a determining factor not at the level of the producer nor even at the level of public opinion or ideology, but because it is inherent in the exhibition situation: since the aim is to attract a better class of patrons, longer narratives are necessary in order to equal and imitate bourgeois forms of entertainment.

Brewster, in a paper on *Traffic in Souls*,[19] has drawn attention to the very complex history underpinning the institutional and technical developments of the multi-reel film. *Traffic in Souls* (George Loane Tucker, 1913) in some ways is one of the first films to utilise the resources of alternation as developed in Griffith's Biograph shorts (symmetry, doubling, mirror-relation between the characters and the dramatic situations), in order to generate a full-length feature of the kind we now think of as classical. Unlike Griffith's *Birth of a Nation* or *Intolerance*, however, *Traffic in Souls* plots its action on a much more transparently linear time scheme and builds up a particular tight interlocking of episodes, expertly developing cross-cutting and parallel action for the purposes of suspense and spectator identification. Brewster, in retracing the history of the multi-reel film from European models (*Quo Vadis*, *Last Days of Pompey*, *Cabiria*) to American productions of the literary classics (*Uncle Tom's Cabin*) and biblical epics (*Life of Moses*), convincingly argues that in many cases these were shot as single-reel films made up of separate episodes but released and shown as continuous programmes. He refers to them as nickelodeon multi-reelers, to distinguish them from true feature films, such as *Traffic in Souls*, where the reel ends do not coincide with the narrative breaks, thus making it a film structurally different from European models or nickelodeon three-reelers, but also different from Griffith's own multi-reel films of the mid-1910s. Furthermore, *Traffic in Souls* is unashamedly sensationalist, indeed it was notorious for its explicitness,[20] making concessions to middle-class respectability only insofar as its narrative virtually inverts one of the social subtexts that made the topic 'hot': police corruption and collusion in the New York white slave trade.

If we grant that the thesis of the increasingly middle-class bias of the cinema has had to be modified (not least by Gunning himself, in light of more recent research both on exhibition practice and on the demographics of film viewing and film theatre siting during the 1910s by Allen, Gomery, Staiger and Musser), Gunning's case for Griffith's editing going hand in hand with the need to produce more novelistic effects in the cinema, remains a convincingly 'materialist' argument, for the close interweaving if not of class and narrative, then of the cinematic institution and narrative. Although this argument, too, needs to be balanced by Aumont's caution against assimilating Griffith's cinema too quickly to an ideal of novelistic transparency. The point is echoed by Rick Altman who has restated Griffith's relation to melodrama and the theatre, by pointing to the widespread practice of adapting popular novels for the stage, in order to argue against the now prevalent view of seeing the classical mode quite divorced from theatrical practice.[21] Likewise, as Anne Friedberg's essay shows, the concern with moral and health issues in Griffith's films is not only part of a shrewd calculation of what might arouse topical interest, it is also – as referential subject matter – totally integrated into the differing stylistic strategies. Friedberg draws attention to a major shift in the representation of madness in Griffith around a certain date, which we might want to see in connection with what was suggested earlier, namely the need to rearticulate not only the basic commodity of the industry as a different temporality (the long narrative), but also the position of the spectator *vis à vis* the representation, that is the severing of the quasi-existential bond with the reality of the viewing situation and the collectivity of the audience gathered there.

Griffith's 'discovery' of the infinite divisibility of the signifying material of cinema, when mapped onto narrative is in some sense the key to his filmic system, but it also indicates the constraints and limits facing the integration of his methods into the emerging film industry. Division becomes one of the preconditions for there to be a narrating instance, as well as for there to be an industrial mode of production. But Griffith's cinema is a kind of orgy of metaphor: everything can be combined with everything else, stand for everything else, rhyme with everything else. Within the filmic image, anything can become the basis for an analogy, the premise for a parallel, for structuring the narrative around similarity and juxtaposition. Divisibility and decontextualisation so important for the economic and technological organisation of film-making, but also for constituting context-free spectatorship, thus enters into textual articulation as the power of substitution and equivalence which in the classical system will emerge as the very order of cinematic narrative. Divisibility thus allows the filmic discourse to take on both a metaphoric and a metonymic function, to allow for 'linearisation' and 'topographical complexity'.

Griffith's feature films can be typified by their tendency to expand enormously in the topographical sense, while the classical cinema will put limits on these metaphoric orgies, in favour of a more strictly linear, overtly causal and to that extent metonymic logic, for economic (division of labour, calculation of budgets) and ideological reasons (standardise intelligibility and spectator orientation). In this sense, one can reconcile the fact that Griffith appears to be at once a 'modernist' in his approach to form (attracting the attention of German and Russian film-makers), and quintessentially 'Victorian' in his subject matter (putting the family or the couple at the centre of classical narrative). For the preference for family conflicts or for stories that deal with family separations is heavily overdetermined: however much it might have related to public concern about the decline of family values or the need of the cinema to woo a family audience, his choice was eminently sensible, insofar as a family separated, a house divided already imply the narrative's eventual goal and the terms of its formal closure. In most of Griffith's films we therefore find a preference for (1) dividing and doubling action spaces (almost all of the Biograph shorts), (2) dividing and doubling of families (e.g. *Way Down East*), (3) dividing and doubling characters (the Gish sisters in *Orphans of the Storm*), (4) dividing and hierarchising narrative knowledge (*Gold is not All*), (5) temporal division (across the movement of eventual recognition: (*Enoch Arden*) and (6) division of visual field, as in the typical Griffith frame, where frame left and frame right are crowded with action and detail, while the middle is usually left bare until the crucial moment, creating a tension between the narrative levels (and their divisions) and the visual levels (and their particular geometry).

By contrast, directors of a more 'classical' style, such as King (*Tol'able*

David) or DeMille (*The Squaw Man*) develop the narrative divisions towards the effects of repetition/resolution described by Bellour, organising the material in ways that will 'use up' the narrative (or condense the functions of the characters). The reason why in Griffith, there is, by the end, so often a feeling of excess and asymmetry, comes from the fact that narrative divisions (male/female, aristocrat/commoner, departure/landing, Babylonian story/Huguenot story/Modern story/Judaic story) are never quite exhausted by the visual resolutions, which are dovetailed and superimposed in ways that give rise to all manner of *en-abyme* effects. It has been argued that this can be directly related to the text's unconscious, its articulation of femininity (threatening and desired) and the way the race-to-the-rescue scenario is called upon to enact but also to disguise relations of sexual exchange.[22] This of course, also foreshadows later both classical and non-classical developments, as they become typical of Lang, Hitchcock or Welles, all of whom were in love with the intricacies of their films' designs, which crucially depended on the exchange of women.[23]

Inscribing the Spectator: Griffith and Imaginary Space

Just as the issue of narrative and narration cannot be seen separately from that of the spectator in respect of film form, so the institutional issue cannot be divorced from questions of spectatorship. The effort to specify the modes of textual address of early cinema is a relatively new endeavour, which must be situated between two other more established fields of enquiry – the first focusing on the fundamental nature of the cinematic apparatus, the second on the textual characteristics of the films produced within the IMR. Both these discourses assert powerful claims towards all-inclusiveness: the first has tended to subsume all modes of cinematic spectatorship under Metz and Baudry's formulation of the Imaginary Signifier, while the second has tended to assimilate every operation of filmic signification to the paradigm of the IMR. The specifications of the modes of address of early cinema and Griffith in particular involves a complex process of engagement and disengagement with these two competing fields of inquiry and theorisation.

This in turn implies that our discussion of early cinema needs to confront the fact that at a certain point in its history, but perhaps implicit since its beginning, the cinema was instrumental in the development of what today is often referred to as 'a media reality', a regime of verisimilitude both hyper-real and non-referential. The very fact that continuity editing made possible the concatenation of images or views, and the construction of an imaginary space/time 'continuum', turned the cinema into a species of discourse, of which narrative became the privileged support. More concretely, the cinema's ability to establish an imaginary relation between the spectator and the represented relies not only on the semiotic process whereby space and time become effects of a discourse (the 'diegetic effect' or 'impression of reality'), but on objects and people being perceived as signs: meaningful or 'expressive' only in relation to other signs and as part of a specular geometry, binding camera, screen and spectator into a fixed set of articulations. That is to say, through the cinema, photographic representations of reality become involved in the constitution of human subjectivity, while the real, and the significance that might be attached to it, is at the mercy of the filmic discourse. The camera, as a recording device of the visible, abstracts the visible from all contexts, all causality, all agency. Narrative and narration become the textual forms by which causality, agency and context are, as it were, reinserted into the representation, thus 'motivating' the filmic chain.

The consequences of this move were momentous, and yet the shifts are themselves embedded in the historical conditions of the filmic apparatus and the cinematic institution. Once again Griffith's work occupies a special place in these developments,[24] powerfully adding to the semiotisation of cinematic representation (in the sense of 'causing something to stand for something else, in such a way that both the relationship of "standing for", and that which is intended to be represented, can be recognised'),[25] while differing from the way this semiotisation was later elaborated: whether in the classical mode, or montage cinema or the German cinema of the 1920s.

We can now return to Aumont's and Brewster's case for saying that in Griffith the spectator needs to be thought of as part of the representation and separate at the same time. Aumont's reluctance to see Griffith as the master and precursor of the classical cinema of Bazinian realist transparency is closely connected to his perception that in Griffith's cinema the spectator plays a different role: 'One could say that the spectator's position is designated in an infinitely more explicit way'. Griffith's shots are rarely sutured classically, but mark the space of the absent field, leaving that space to be claimed by the spectator.[26]

Especially in the multi-reel feature films is this spectator required as the axis around which the system pivots. In contrast to the extra-diegetic audience, implied in a 'cinema of attractions', a dramatisation occurs of the spectator's space (now located not somewhere in the auditorium, and instead at the imaginary apex of a textual geometry). With it, Griffith builds on and radically transforms the PMR, to the extent that the spectator position is no longer a fixed place, but one that undergoes constant transformation in the course of the narrative trajectory.[27] In fact, one could say that in Griffith the characters only see and know each other, because the spectator sees and knows them, and thus, relaying that knowledge and linking the spaces that separate them, it is the spectator who introduces them to each other. Only hindsight or teleological reasoning would therefore want to subsume Griffith's mode under that of the IMR. The most one can say is that through Griffith we can thematise the difference and begin to understand historically the transformations between the two systems. This appears to be the direction of Brewster's work, which differentiates on the one hand, between the constitution of a physical audience (exhibition practice) through the film performance, and the constitution of an imaginary spectator (taken out of the auditorium 'into' the text) through the various hierarchies of knowledge and vision.

If in some sense, the spectator had to become 'mobile' and 'monadic' in the transition from PMR to IMR, it points to the institutional developments underlying these changes. For the film industry, once embarked on the need to 'commodify' and standardise the product, and under pressure from the exhibition situation to generate longer films, endeavoured not only to provide these films, but to counteract the various forms of editorial control which in the transitional phase had belonged to the exhibition sector or the exhibition site (and to that extent, to the collective audience). In this process, too, Griffith occupies an ambiguous position. On the one hand, his longer narratives were fundamentally beneficial to the institution, in that they bound a better paying public to the cinema. Textually, on the other hand, his films showed quite a number of features associated with non-continuous cinema, in which causality was often extremely opaque, complex and indirect, testimony of that 'spatial' or 'topographical' way of thinking about narrative, alongside the emergent psychological one. It was the latter which was most sought after by the institution in wresting editorial control from the exhibition site and exhibition circumstances. What the institution had to adapt to was a new commodity – not the reel of film, but the more immaterial and yet nonetheless standardised film experience, located in the coherence of the narrative, its interlocking mechanisms of resolution and closure, and the 'centering' of the spectator via equally interlocking levels of knowledge, via 'foreshadowing' (Brewster), ellipsis and the motivation of coincidence. That this was itself an intricate historical process is indicated by the trade press, where the practice of uninterrupted screenings of multi-reel films was for some time regarded as a health-hazard, because of eye-strain: another indication that 'respectability' may not have been the driving force in the change from nickelodeon multi-reeler to picture palace narrative feature film.

Continuity and the question of control can thus be seen to be linked, becoming crucial aspects of the story-telling process, since as Musser pointed out, the most effective way in which the production side of film-making can acquire control over the text as a fixed sequence of scenes is to develop forms of continuity and narrative complexity which make irreversibility of the scenes a function of the narrative's intelligibility. This suggests that non-continuous forms, as one finds them in Griffith and others even after 1915 are, once again, not a sign of backwardness or primitivity, but reflect a precise historical moment in the balance of power and economic rapport of forces within the emerging film industry. Conversely, continuity becomes not the attainment of an ideal of narrative efficiency as much as it is a 'weapon' in a struggle over control, in which textual authority is the expression of authorship as product control and the ability to impose standards and standardisation.

Yet by the same token, once the historical and economic reasons for imposing continuity have disappeared, with the stabilisation of the institution around the unified product (multi-reel film and narrative complexity), non-continuity can develop in quite different directions and assume different narrational functions, as it does in Griffith's later films, where the multi-reel non-continuous film generates an extraordinary narrative complexity far greater than the contemporaneous continuity film. Non-continuity as a structural principle culminated in Griffith with *Intolerance*, a film which falls right outside any linear development between non-continuous film and classical continuity editing. Miriam Hansen has offered a very challenging reading of this fact, seeing *Intolerance* and its deviation from an increasingly streamlined, monocausal, psychological model of narrative continuity in terms of a twofold crisis. Griffith's 'cultural' ambitions to retain for the cinema the prestige of an essentially literary mode (emblematically represented by Whitman's democratic universalism) made him strive for an elaborate allegorical mode of hieroglyphics (perhaps also in the sense of the cinema as the 'script of life' alluded to earlier), rather than the visual transparency of the emergent classical style. The second crisis is the representation of femininity, in particular, the moral problem (which is also a structural one) of the unmarried woman: 'the fate – and the fatal power of unmarried female characters throughout the ages, especially the closer they get to modernity'.[28] Hansen sees an inverse symmetry between working woman and prostitute (which bears the traces of a whole history of feminism in the 1910s and the 'new woman' of the early 1920s), in relation to Griffith's own concerns about 'his personal investment in the cinema's bid for cultural respectability'.[29] Griffith saw his status as an artist threatened not only by the growing industrialisation of film-making, but also by the 'feminisation' of that consumer culture to which the cinema had become inextricably tied. Male narrative authority in *Intolerance* is only reasserted by playing out that most persistent of Victorian sexual fantasies, the rescue scenario, to which Griffith adheres in so many of his films. *Intolerance* could be said to represent a particularly complex response to the liberal, anti-racist protest against *Birth of a Nation* in which the former is a (sexist) middle-brow reply to sensationalist low-brow potboilers like *Traffic in Souls*, 'white slave trade' being itself a condensation of other social concerns, such as immigration and race, overcrowding and female factory work. While *Intolerance*, according to Hansen, tries to represent social tensions, racial and sexual difference in the allegorical mode of a literary culture, one could argue that *Traffic in Souls* was already simplifying the moral issues of social order, women's rights and prostitution, in favour of a very 'classically' narrative oedipal story of suspense, action and voyeurism, thus pointing the way to a much smoother operation of the cinematic institution in its treatment of social conflict and ideological contradiction.

Griffith, Non-Continuity and the European Cinema

One of the paradoxes of Griffith's place within and between early and classical cinema is the relative 'failure' of his films after *Birth of a Nation* in America, and his enormous influence – during the same period and with the same films, notably *Intolerance* – among European film-makers. The conventional answer is that his film-making system was retarded in relation to the imposition of the classical norms of continuity cinema. But an equally probably argument – and one that suggests itself if one follows the perspective taken above – is that his filmic system was too complex, sophisticated and eccentric for the emergent institution, and failed because of its inadaptability to the industrial norms, even more than because of its moral Victorianism and overtly patriarchal values.[30] If Griffith 'failed' in the late 1910s and 20s, it may be because his systems of divisibility – the elaboration of homologies, oppositions and symmetrical relations – implied the coexistence of several distinct levels of textual work, which in the films are often played off against each other: the formal level (division of visual field and the frame), the fantasy level (sexuality and the use of the rescue scenario), the thematic level (the doubling of families and characters), the narrational level (hierarchising narrative knowledge and playing off external against integrated narration), the temporal level (the use of melodrama and the recognition scenario). This echoing and responding of levels with each other is of course the specifically Griffithian way of generating longer narratives out of basic conflicts and opposition usually rooted in the family. What the institution took from Griffith (though as we saw, by briefly looking at *Traffic in Souls*, not only from him) was the family melodrama and its oedipal emplotting of conflict and sexual difference. What it did not take was the formal complexity by which this emplotting is worked out, which in turn seems crucially related to the institutional need, with the establishment of the feature film as the basic commodity, to further push and develop the division of labour in the production process, the imposition of a production schedule and the agreement of release dates as its way of regulating production while maintaining a hold over the exhibition context. The multiple levels at which a Griffith film operates does not lend itself so readily to the breakdown which scripting in the industrial mode demanded. Thus, Griffith's model of alternation had to be greatly simplified in order to become the basis of the institutional mode, and in particular, impose a strictly unilinear cause and effect logic on events, which in turn would enable the shooting of scenes out of sequence, just as extensive scene dissection would enable editing to play the role it has had ever since: 'linearising' filmic narrative. Griffith's way of implicating the spectator – the other revolutionary aspect of his work in the early 1910s – relied on the perception of correspondences, of 'sight links', of empathetic, antithetic relations, of mental and moral parallels. This feature of his cinema which I characterised as 'metaphoric', the institutional mode abandoned in favour of plotting spatial contiguity, narrational cogency, the suppression (or motivation) of coincidence, in short a metonymic cinema, or a cinema of discontinuity, against Griffith's obstinate adherence to a cinema of non-continuity.

If we now look at Griffith's impact in Europe, we need to be careful to distinguish two moments, possibly even two quite distinct phases. The first would be the elaboration – parallel to Griffith, but quite possibly independent from his work – of a cinema of non-continuity. This we can see happen in France, but also in the Scandinavian countries and in German art cinema. The second phase would be the post-WWI period, when Griffith's films, and indeed the American cinema generally, became well-known to both film-makers and audiences, and directors needed to differentiate themselves from the American cinema (be it for competitive reasons, be it as part of an avant garde counter-cinema), by reinventing or further elaborating a cinema of non-continuity. Griffith's formal complexity and his non-industrial mode of production could thus be seen as the very condition of his success in Europe, where both mainstream and alternative film-making had to come to terms with the increasing dominance of the Hollywood mode of production, as well as its strategies of occupying and colonizing foreign film-markets. Formally, once the cinema of discontinuity had established itself as the norm, non-continuity could become the hallmark of an 'alternative' to the classical cinema, as I believe it did in both the national art cinemas and the international avant garde cinemas of the 1920s, for directors as differently placed within their respective film industries as Fritz Lang and F.W. Murnau, Sergei Eisenstein, Vsevolod Pudovkin and Dziga Vertov, Marcel L'Herbier, Abel Gance, Jean Renoir and Luis Buñuel.

While the notion of a connection between early cinema and the contemporary avant garde is riddled with problems of historical periodisation, it is worth recalling that efforts such as Burch's to elucidate the peculiarity of early cinema have been marked by an acute awareness of what one might call a tradition of the cinematic avant garde. As Rod Stoneman has argued, studies of early cinema and the avant garde 'both function to relativise and counter the naturalisation of [the classical] mode of representation'.[31] The discovery of textual parallels between early and avant garde films (non-closure, non-perspectival space, material/spatial coherence over narrational coherence, the preference of non-continuous forms over analytical editing) depends, of course, on a particular reading of both types of films, a reading which Aumont already warns against as a-historical.[32] Stoneman's notion of autonomy for both early and avant garde cinema foregoes the fertile ambiguity of Burch's formulations about the 'fundamentally contradictory nature of primitive cinema . . . in which each gesture – in the direction of linearisation or closure, for example could contribute . . . to the creation of objects, whose other major attributes tended to impede the implicit project which underpinned those gestures'.[33]

From the work that has been done since on the European cinema of the 'teens, it is possible to go beyond Burch's formulation, and situate the question of an alternative practice more historically, both within the institutional framework and the textually specific forms of cinema that emerged in European countries. Informed by the historical perspective indicated by this Reader, namely the need to develop a framework which is capable of understanding the changes between the early and classical cinema in a non-reductive, non-linear way, it is possible, at least in outline, to grasp within the same terms that have been developed for early cinema and its multiple transformations into the classical cinema, the peculiarities of European cinema in the 1910s as well as in the 1920s. For reasons of space, this has to be sketchy, provisional and incomplete.

Some generalisations might nonetheless be in order. The American style could be said to have developed a spatio-temporal articulation in view of a certain type of (character-centred and psychological) causality, of a narration in view of a subject position/knowledge position, and a mode of representation in view of a single diegesis, and achieved via editing, scene dissection, cutting rate, point-of-view structure and changing shot-scales.[34]

The European cinema could be said to have developed the 'primitive' style of narrativity, mainly by preserving a greater flexibility of narrational stances, whether this is explained in terms of monstration rather than narrative integration, a multiplicity of narrators and narrative authorities (both intra-textual and extra-textual), an emphasis on performative styles, a greater interplay of knowingness between spectator and character. Formally the European cinema seems to adhere to spatial coherence and spatial integrity, at the expense of unilinear causality determining spatio-temporal relations. Instead of scene dissection, fast cutting, and reverse field editing, the European cinema developed its systems of causality, its temporality and narration by a division of space into different playing areas, by deep staging, by action overlap, by 'editing within the frame' via door frames, apertures, by figure composition and frontality, and by a use of the look to generate off-screen space as an indeterminate space, rather than one folded back into the diegesis via point-of-view structure. By necessity, such a style implies longer takes and a greater degree of autonomy for the shot, and the consequences are a different way of reading the frame, different skills in 'following' the narrative, and a different mode of spectatorial address.

Non-Continuous Cinema in the 1910s

To substantiate these generalisations in detail would require a volume to itself. However, a start has been made, and the final remarks of this introduction are no more than pointers to this research.[35] During the 'primitive period', the developments in different countries were relatively non-specific to that country, and more part of the 'international' developments of film form. This might apply to France, Britain and the United States, all of them simultaneously even if on different fronts, exploring aspects of film form and heavily plagiarising each other's subject matter.[36] Only with the rise of the nickelodeons and their European equivalents – it is the increase in demand, as well as the feedback via audiences/reviewers which leads to competition – does differentiation in style or genre emerge along possibly 'national' lines.[37]

A striking case is the Scandinavian cinema, traditionally considered very 'advanced'[38] and also nationally specific in its genres,[39] its treatment of women,[40] its stylistic complexity.[41] John Fullerton, in 'Spatial and temporal articulation in pre-classical Swedish film' is challenging some of the assumptions underlying these models of stylistic differentiation, as they might apply to national cinemas, and also as they distinguish between 'spectacle attraction' and 'narrative integration'. Fullerton's main point is that, whereas Gunning and others have focused on spatial and temporal organisation as the key to understanding modes of continuity in early cinema, in the Swedish cinema there is a need to look to other factors as well. He juxtaposes filmic continuity (i.e. space/time) to narrational continuity, which, he says, must involve, apart from the relation between images, the relation between image and intertitle. And not only image/intertitle, but the way intertitles cue the spectator in terms of tense, tone or mode (e.g. irony) to read the images both preceding and following them. *Trädgårdmästaren*, the 1912 Sjöström film he discusses, might at first glance appear to belong to a cinema of attraction, because of its elements of non-continuity. Yet if we redefine what we understand by 'narrative integration', then the film can be seen as highly integrated, narration hinging on the retrospective and prospective placing of the spectator, with tension and ellipsis marking the gap between what the intertitles communicate and what the images present. Thus, despite the fact that the Swedish cinema, which according to Brewster, gives priority to spatial coherence and uses lighting cues for organising its deep spaces, belongs to the European paradigm, its emphasis on narrational coherence over spatio-temporal coherence makes it closer to American models, although visually, Swedish films up to 1917 look 'retarded' when judged by the fast cutting/shallow staging yardstick of Salt and Brewster. For Fullerton, Swedish films show signs of 'external' narration (the reliance on intertitles), but of a degree of sophistication in tone and mode that distinguishes them from the more didactic commentary of, say, Griffith. Unified narratively by assuming a good deal of implied (cultural) foreknowledge, Swedish films were clearly addressing themselves to a 'literate' and possibly even 'literary' public.

A similar assertion can be made about a certain group of German films, the self-consciously literary 'author's cinema' inaugurated around 1913 by directors like Max Mack, Max Reinhardt and Stellan Rye, actor-directors like Paul Wegener and writers like Hanns Heinz Ewers, Paul Lindau, Heinrich Lautensack. But in contrast to Fullerton's article on early Swedish films, Leon Hunt's analysis of *The Student of Prague* (1913) concentrates primarily on the codification of space, and discovers that within the non-continuous mode and the primacy of spatial coherence, Wegener's film is particularly remarkable for systematically transgressing the norm (thereby showing its importance) in ways which no subsequent film practice has taken up (except that we might compare it to Ince's treatment of space in *The Right Girl?*). With its left/right near/far oppositions *The Student of Prague* is both very Griffithian and yet very different from Griffith, in its use of trick shots and special effect, or indeed its evocation of the uncanny. On the other hand, formally it is quite different from subsequent German films of the same genre, including the remake of 1926, which relies on much more classical shot-reverse shot structures, on point of view and off-screen space, precisely the features which the 1913 original avoids in order to articulate power relations *within* the frame.

This raises the question of how one might account for such variations as Fullerton and Hunt identify. In the case of the French *film d'art* (the most thoroughly discussed example of deviation and differentiation for the period up to 1911),[42] we can already recognise the complex process of cultural legitimation and product differentiation which characterises European film-makers' response to competition and foreign imports. For instance, the preference for deep space staging can by analysed, as Brewster does, within the context of traditional 'art' forms (whose codicity is painting and theatre) but also of increased production values aiming at a competitive edge both domestically and internationally. Given the importance of staged theatre in France, Sweden, Denmark and Germany, it is possible to argue that during the crucial years of fixed site cinemas gentrifying themselves in the bid for better paying audiences, the media intertext (the legitimate theatre, but also operetta and music theatre[43]) and entertainment context (the pressures of censorship or social reform[44]) are more decisive than stylistic differences, bringing us back to the European variant of 'exhibition-led' film history.[45] Another possible cause for differentiation for the early period might have to do with the availability of certain items of film technology,[46] but this too, became a factor of diminishing importance by the late 1910s.

What the comparative stylistic analyses of Salt or Brewster and the detailed historical research of Kristin Thompson regarding film export[47] indicate is that the economic and stylistic interchange between European and US film-making is more important, more pervasive and begins earlier than had been assumed, which can be demonstrated when one studies the cases of plagiarism and copyright infringements, the output of a company like Vitagraph,[48] in addition to the well-known import of 'art films' into America.[49] The promotion of a 'national' film industry in this perspective becomes a retrospective, defensive, ideological move, so that by the early 1920s, the European response to Hollywood's policy of importing, poaching, loaning talent, in order to control the competition,[50] is to play up 'difference', national character, and the search for national subjects. In light of this, one can posit either that the notion of an autonomous film style/film form/national cinema derives from a different socio-cultural context or a different mode of representation[51] taking account of political and demographic factors, or different media intertexts, audience expectations and national markets (which includes the reception by critics, the intervention of reform movements or the role of the literary establishment). But this is a problematic argument, for what strikes one in this respect is the gradual Americanisation of all the European markets from 1919 onwards. Less contentious is the fact that this gives rise to counter-moves, either by launching self-consciously 'alternative' modes to Hollywood (in terms of an art cinema, of an avant garde, or as part of a product differentiation), or by marketing strategies that promote a 'national' film industry, to rival and compete with Hollywood.

Non-Continuous Cinema as Counter-Cinema

It is in these contexts that the earlier remark about the Janus-faced character of Griffith can be placed. Looking at his work during the late 1910s from the vantage point of the 1920s, he appears a director whose role was crucial because, for reasons we have tried to sketch, his work could be (and has been) inherited by very different traditions of film-making, from continuity cinema to art cinema, from the Russian montage school to the French avant garde, in each case for very different ideological reasons.

One of the reasons why German and Russian cinema in particular could learn from and refine the Griffithian model was that, effectively, both film industries – though for different reasons – were for some time protected from the world market. While in the classical Hollywood system we see a greater and greater convergence between narrative economy and industrial efficiency, in Germany, the kinds of narrative economy directors were interested in (or were driven towards in their battle for artistic legitimation and respectability) stood in an intriguing tension with the practical ways of producing it. This, if you like, more 'experimental' mode, was possible because, unlike the American system (which by the mid-1910s is market-driven, and thus for economic reasons as well as for reasons of intelligibility and universality, works towards efficiency in narrative and narration), the German model, at least for some companies, is still film-maker driven, and does not have the same feedback as the American industry with its public. A similar case can be made for Eisenstein, Kuleshov and Pudovkin in the Soviet Union, though the ideological legitimation is as much political as it is artistic. If these ideological constraints of having to establish themselves domestically as 'artists' (or 'revolutionary artists') made them lean towards Griffithian models (himself an embattled director *vis à vis* his 'artistic pedigree'), in the German case, research into special effects and technological innovation (in prestige superproductions like *The Nibelungen*, *Faust*, *The Last Laugh*, *Metropolis*) was part of another strategy: penetrating European and overseas markets where they could compete with the Americans, with the ultimate goal being the US market itself. In this dual strategy of the German cinema we can study the prototype of a consumer oriented industry and its hazards. While the American film industry modelled itself directly around consumer demand, and the most economical way of satisfying and stimulating it, the German situation was distorted by this intermediary level of a taste elite, demanding cinema to be art, a demand which the film industry had to take seriously, since it was actively promoting a 'quality' market at an international level. At the same time, the industrial basis of the German film industry could not come to terms with what was effectively an avant garde ideology, where production schedules were uncertain, budgets open-ended and release dates volatile.[52]

Towards the 1920s: Avant Garde or Popular Cinema

In keeping with the focus of the Reader, we have concentrated in this section on a more pragmatic, but also tighter approach than is usually taken when discussing European cinema. By investigating the different deployment of the characteristics of early cinema generally a significantly more diverse, but also potentially more comprehensive picture emerges, in which the differences between American practice and European practice appear in the traditional histories to have been exaggerated, or at least not analysed within a historical, and instead a primarily ideological context. The handling of space and spatial coherence; the use of continuity, discontinuity, non-continuity; patterns of alternation, point-of-view structure, the look and off-screen space; narrational stances as they emerge out of the interplay of these parameters, but also the use of intertitles, commentary, sound and other marks of discursiveness (degree and modes of narrative integration, alternation/integration of diegetic and non-diegetic spaces) all bear features that can be usefully compared to American practice and historically differentiated. The Griffithian concept of several action spaces gradually coming together into a unified space is used by European directors of the 1920s for a more complex articulation of causal relations, and for developing narrational forms which put in crisis the relations between seeing and knowing, or for constructing quite different imaginary spaces. The uncanny of Murnau, the *en-abyme* constructions of Lang, their use of off-screen space vs. off-frame space and the importance of the frontal look without reverse-field cutting; French Impressionist cinema's adoption of the continuity style, relying heavily on the point-of-view shot and camera movement, motivated diegetically by subjective states of mind rather than by spatio-temporal causality; Eisenstein's 'reinvention' of Griffithian non-continuity for a more oblique and multi-level causality; Gance's combination of non-continuity and the point-of-view shot; Renoir's use of off-screen space in *Nana*, and finally Buñuel's 'deconstruction' of classical continuity editing, heavily relying on point of view and the glance/glance, glance/object structure, but violating spatial continuity and contiguity, while parodying Impressionist subjectivity; all can be usefully analysed in terms of the formal problems and options raised in this section of the Reader around Griffith and his place within the emergent continuity cinema.[53] German Expressionist cinema, Soviet montage cinema, French Surrealist cinema thus reinvent certain aspects of a cinema of non-continuity and spatial coherence, but only in order to violate its norms, and playing them off against the narrational rule of classical American cinema (the dominance of the optical point of view) which in turn it renders discontinuous by frustrating the causal and narrational logic that classical cinema imposes on the material.

Although, for reasons of space, such assertions have to remain speculative, the idea has been to suggest that even the better known work of the late 1910s and 1920s (the first avant garde) can be fruitfully examined by the new film history, so that this most intense period of reflection on the cinema can be seen to emerge out of an often very careful study and familiarity with what went before, rather than constituting a radical break, and of being determined by institutional questions and choices, just like the commercial cinema. At the same time, a possibly even more urgent task will be the re-examination of European popular cinema during the 1910s, for it is there that our ignorance is directly proportional to the contempt and neglect which the old history has shown to productions deemed to lack 'artistic ambition'. Not only the preservationist and archival agenda of the new film history demands that we look at these films with fresh eyes: the temper of the times, with its love of the heterotopic, the parodic, the melodramatic, the carnivalesque and the multi-cultural, will find in the survivors of a hitherto largely despised cinema if not documents of history then documents of a sensibility with which rightly or wrongly, we today in our televisual culture feel a curious kinship.

Thomas Elsaesser and Adam Barker

Notes

1. 'The years from 1903 to 1907 are the most obscure part of film history, as far as nearly everyone is concerned occupied only by the films of Griffith . . . Griffith may have been the best director working in the years from 1908 to 1915, but that does not prove that he invented everything.' Barry Salt, 'The Early Development of Film Form', in John L. Fell (ed.), *Film Before Griffith*, p. 284.
2. See, for instance, William Johnson, 'Early Griffith: A Wider View', *Film Quarterly* vol. 29 no. 3, Spring 1976, pp. 2–13.

3. See Martin Shingler, 'The Right Girl?', unpublished paper, UEA Film Studies, 1989. Also of interest in this context is Noël Burch's discussion of frontality in Renoir's *Nana*. Noël Burch, *Theory of Film Practice* (New York: Praeger, 1970), pp. 17–31.
4. Barry Salt, 'Fresh Eyes', *BFI News*, 24 July 1976, p. 4.
5. It could be argued that Griffith, rather than 'leading up to' the IMR, actually 'goes beyond' the IMR, which represents a drastic simplification of the possibilities of alternation. It is Fritz Lang and Eisenstein, among others, who 'rediscovered' those other possibilities. For elaboration of this argument, see below.
6. See, for instance, how alternation and its resolution structure both the syntax and the semantics of a Griffith passage: 'Man is a moving animal. The bigger the man, the more he has need for activity. It isn't so with women. Their natures are different. The motion pictures give a man a place to go besides a saloon. He drops in to see a picture. He has been somewhere. He has seen something. He comes out and goes home in a different state than if he had gone to a saloon. The domestic unities are preserved.' (quoted by Anne Friedberg, below, pp. 326–35).
7. Bellour's reading of *The Lonedale Operator* concentrates on the features which make this Griffith film a paradigm of classical cinema, reading its modes of alternation and doubling primarily as pointing to the American cinema of the 1920s and beyond. Elsewhere, Bellour insists that alternation is also a crucial feature of non-classical styles. See Janet Bergstrom, 'Interview with Raymond Bellour', *Camera Obscura* no. 3/4, 1979, pp. 79–81.
8. Noël Burch has pointed this out in 'Passion, pursuite', where he argues that the chase film provided the crucible in which the technique of parallel editing, the means by which two events could be signified to be 'diegetically simultaneous and spatially distant' was forged. For Burch, this feature is fundamental to the IMR.
9. Such a perspective is implied in Noël Burch, 'Fritz Lang: The German Period' and Jean-André Fieschi, 'F.W. Murnau', both in R. Roud (ed.), *Cinema A Critical Dictionary* (London: Secker and Warburg, 1980), pp. 583–609. See also my 'Secret Affinities: F. W. Murnau', *Sight and Sound* vol. 58, no. 1, Winter 1988/89, pp. 33–42.
10. See recent discussions, notably around Eisenstein's *October*: Mary Claire Ropars' use of Bellour's principle of alternation ('The Ouverture of *October*', *Enclitic* vol. 2 no. 2, Fall 1978, pp. 50–72), David Bordwell's discussion of *October* in *Narration and the Fiction Film* (Madison: Wisconsin University Press, 1985, pp. 236–40, and Yuri Tsivian, 'Eisenstein's *October* and Russian Symbolist Culture' (unpublished paper, 'Eisenstein at 90', conference, Oxford, 1988).
11. See Noël Burch, 'Passion, poursuite', *Communications* no. 38, 1983, p. 40.
12. See Ben Brewster, 'A Scene at the "Movies"' (first published in *Screen* vol. 15, no. 3, May/June 1982), reprinted below, pp. 318–25.
13. Tom Gunning, 'What I saw from the Rear Window of the Hotel des Folies-Dramatiques', in André Gaudreault (ed.), *Ce que je vois de mon ciné* (Paris: Meridiens Klincksieck, 1988), p. 42 (see fn. 16).
14. Although at first all relevant action was contained/staged within frame, from Lumière onwards the dramatic possibilities of off-screen space were known. Its use in early films can be very sophisticated, as in Haggar's *Life of Charles Peace*, where five out of the six possible off-screen spaces detailed by Burch are being used. See also de Cordova's article above, and Barry Salt, 'The Space next Door' (in French, in Pierre Gibbert, (ed.), *Les premiers ans du cinéma français* (Perpignan: Institut Jean Vigo, 1985), pp. 198–203.
15. See, again, Noël Burch in *Theory of Film Practice*, where he discusses frontality as 'off-screen space' (pp. 20–1).
16. Tom Gunning has challenged Brewster's differentiation of Griffith's use of point of view: 'Brewster does not take account of what I call "sight links" in Griffith's films, an edited relation between two spaces which is motivated by a character's glance. . . . Sight links occur frequently in Griffith after 1909 and are conspicuous in *The Lonedale Operator*, for instance . . . The theoretical distinction between ocularisation and focalisation offered by [François] Jost helps untangle this . . . The importance of focalisation in Griffith, compared to its relative absence in early cinema, is a clear mark of the cinema of narrative integration that Griffith represents, and the foundation of his use of suspense.' Tom Gunning, 'What I saw from the Rear Window of the Hotel des

Folies-Dramatiques, or The Story Point of View Films Told', in André Gaudreault, (ed.), *Ce que je vois de mon ciné* (Paris: Meridiens Klincksieck, 1988), p. 42, note 15.

17. See Michael Allen, 'The Three Systems of the Look in Griffith's *Orphans of the Storm*', unpublished M.A. thesis, University of East Anglia, 1988.
18. Tom Gunning, 'Weaving a Narrative: Style and Economic Background in Griffith's Biograph Films', below, pp. 336–47 (first published in *Quarterly Review of Film Studies*, Winter 1981, pp. 11–25).
19. '*Traffic in Souls*: A Formal Experiment in Feature-length Narrative Construction', Society for Cinema Studies Annual Conference, Iowa City, May 1989.
20. See Kevin Brownlow, '*Traffic in Souls*' in Cherchi Usai/Jacob (eds.), *Vitagraph Co of America: il cinema prima di Hollywood* (Pordenone: Edizioni Biblioteca dell'Immagine, 1987), pp. 227–37, and Robert C. Allen, '*Traffic in Souls*', *Sight and Sound* vol. 44 no. 1, Winter 1974/5, pp. 50–52.
21. See Rick Altman, 'Dickens, Griffith and Film Theory Today,' *South Atlantic Quarterly*, vol. 88/2, Spring 1989, 321–59.
22. See Miriam Hansen, 'The Hieroglyph and the Whore: D.W. Griffith's *Intolerance*', *South Atlantic Quarterly*, vol. 88/2, Spring 1989, p. 385. More generally, Brewster's formal argument about the different narrational hierarchies of knowing and seeing also carries ideological implications: the spectator's superiority of knowledge ('the spectator knows the poor do not know how unhappy the rich are') is also a superiority of moral judgment, equally secure in its didacticism and sentimentality.
23. Hitchcock, talking about the structure of *Strangers on a Train*: 'isn't it a fascinating design? One could study it forever' in François Truffaut, *Hitchcock on Hitchcock* (London: Secker and Warburg, 1968), p. 164. For Welles, see Stephen Heath, 'Film and System: Terms of Analysis: *Touch of Evil*,' *Screen*, vol. 16 no. 1 and vol. 16 no. 2, 1975. And for Lang, see Steve Jenkins (ed.), *The Image and the Look* (London: BFI Publishing, 1975), especially Raymond Bellour, 'On Fritz Lang'.
24. See Klaus Wyborny, 'Random Notes on the Conventional Narrative Film', *Afterimage* no. 8/9, Spring 1981, where Griffith is the villain of the piece (pp. 120–8).
25. This definition is taken from 'The Dialectics of Representation' in Chris Sinha, *Language and Representation* (Hemel Hempsted: Harvester Press, 1988), p. 37.
26. An example that comes to mind occurs in *Drive for a Life*, in the scene in which the jealous (evil) woman follows the lovers in a coach. Griffith is able to suggest the different relationships between the individual characters by creating several distinct spaces within the diegetic space (Central Park), by the way the camera is mounted on a motor car, but then, without a cut, detaches itself from the car, to follow the carriage. At a certain point after having followed (though in truth preceded) the lovers, the camera follows the jealous woman. The horses are at first in frame, giving us the impression of the camera being fixed on the carriage, the camera than lets the horses go out of frame, and we realise the camera is on another vehicle. We suddenly become very aware of the presence of the camera, but since Griffith does not motivate it through a point-of-view structure, there is no effect of suture, and instead, an active 'reading' of the different subject positions of seeing, knowing, feeling as they structure the emotional drama of the characters.
27. See Michael Allen, *Spatial Articulation and Melodramatic Form in Griffith's Early Twenties Feature Films*, unpublished PhD thesis, University of East Anglia, 1990.
28. Hansen, 'The Hieroglyph and the Whore', p. 370.
29. 'Griffith entered the newly created market place of the cinema, ostensibly surveying it for its artistic possibilities, though already in search of customers. The image of the prostitute, vendor and commodity in one, encapsulated this historical ambiguity. Likewise, as a phenomenon of urban society and mass production, the prostitute came to personify the artist's ambivalence towards the urban masses whom he embraced as consumers but also blamed for the alienation which linked their fate to his own. In other words, the metaphorical debasement of the woman who works betrays both fear of and desire for the woman who has money to spend – the consumer.' Hansen, p. 385.
30. '. . . with its fantastically complex construction, *Intolerance* exhausted 1916 audiences; they were shattered by its power, worn out by its tempo, and they just did not

understand the idea behind it; audiences no longer fail to understand it, but it remains an unavoidably exhausting film to sit through' (William K. Everson, quoted by Vlada Petric, 'David Wark Griffith' in Richard Roud ed., *Cinema A Critical Dictionary*, London: Secker and Warburg, 1980). The reasons for Griffith's merely intermittent success in the 1920s are obviously very complex: if his difficulties with Hollywood are well-documented (see, for instance, Richard Schickel, *D. W. Griffith*, London: Pavilion Books, 1984, pp. 395ff, and Janet Wasko, 'D. W. Griffith and the banks: a case study in film financing', *Journal of the University Film Association*, vol. 30, no. 1, Winter 1978), the relation between formal complexity and industrial organisation of production in Griffith's case awaits to be explored further.

31. Rod Stoneman, 'Perspective correction: Early Film to the Avantgarde,' *Afterimage* no. 8/9, Winter 1980/1, p. 63.
32. See the final paragraph of Aumont's essay, below, pp. 348–59, and his tendency to read Griffith with Eisenstein in mind, rather than Bazin. More generally, the polemical assertion of a mode of avant garde film practice separate and wholly distinct from the institutional mode is itself profoundly inflected by historical concerns, and may once more impose itself, as avant garde film and video-makers reassess their ideological and institutional role.
33. Noël Burch, 'Primitivism and the Avant-Gardes: A Dialectical Approach', in P. Rosen (ed.), *Narrative, Apparatus, Ideology* (New York: Columbia University Press, 1986), pp. 483–505, 'The IMR and the Soviet Response', *October* no. 11, pp. 77–98 and also 'A Primitive Mode of Representation' above, pp. 220–7.
34. For a useful summary of the classical model, see David Bordwell, Kristin Thompson, *Film Art* (2nd ed.).
35. The main comparatists for the period up to the mid-teens are Barry Salt and Ben Brewster. But see also essays by Tom Gunning, André Gaudreault, Donald Crafton and Richard Abel listed in the bibliography.
36. Barry Salt explains the international nature of the earliest period by the fact that film-making is still 'producer-driven'. See *Film Style and Technology: History and Analysis* (London: Starword, 1985), p. 83.
37. Salt has argued that in France, Pathé films from 1907 onwards regularly used cross-cutting, and inserted close shots, though without 'fully developing the use of cross-cutting between parallel action'. He has also shown that at least two Pathé films (*The Physician of the Castle* and *Le Cheval Emballé*) were seen by Griffith, who based *The Lonely Villa* and *The Curtain Pole*, respectively, on these French models. Griffith, according to Salt, also took from Pathé films the transfer of parts of the action to adjoining rooms or hallways, what Salt calls 'the space next door'. But whereas in Pathé films, this seems mostly in order to generate longer films out of repeated situations (e.g. the keyhole films), Griffith was able 'to split the same amount of action into a greater number of shots, and this greater number of shots within the same length of film was undoubtedly the major feature of the dynamics of his films, with the extra cuts giving a visual impulse at each transition'. Barry Salt, 'The Space Next Door' (English version supplied by the author, French version in Pierre Guibbert (ed.), *Les premiers ans du cinéma français* (Perpignan, Institut Jean Vigo, 1985), pp. 198–203.
38. See Barry Salt, 'White Slaves and Circuses – The Pursuit of Sensation' (in Italian in Paolo Cherchi Usai (ed.), *Schiave bianche allo specchio, Le origini del cinema in Scandinavia* (Pordenone, Edizioni Studio Tesi, 1986, pp. 61–78).
39. See Cherchi Usai (ed.), *Schiave bianche allo specchio.*
40. This is a point also made in Noël Burch, *What do these old films mean?* (Great Britain: Channel Four, 1988).
41. Using both Scandinavian and French examples, Ben Brewster has shown that in early European cinema there is evidence of fundamental stylistic and technical choices, working as variables within a number of priorities. See 'Deep Staging in French Films', above, pp. 45–55.
42. Tom Gunning has looked at the French film d'art in its influence on Griffith: 'Filmed Narrative and the Theatrical Ideal: Griffith and the film d'art' (in French in P. Guibbert (ed.), *Les premiers ans du cinéma français*, pp. 123–9).
43. See a paper given by Barry Salt at the 'Space Frame Narrative Conference, University of

East Anglia, 1983, on the relation between the early films of Ernst Lubitsch and the operetta, 'The World inside Ernst Lubitsch'.

44. See Yuri Tsivian 'Notes on the Margins of the Kuleshov Experience,' above, pp. 247–55.
45. Richard Abel has discussed early French cinema, especially Pathé films, classifying them by using Gunning's 'cinema of attraction', and charting the emergence of integrated narratives. Looking at the melodramatic conventions in the subject matter (criminality and socialisation, motherhood and gender), he concludes that 'a number of Pathé domestic melodramas, beginning in the summer of 1906, seem specifically to address a female spectator' and that one can discern 'certain strategies of representation and narration intersected with particular social relations of difference in terms of class and gender', although they 'ultimately proved less crucial than the developments of extended parallel editing and especially of analytical editing'. Richard Abel, 'Scenes from Domestic Life in Early French Cinema', *Screen* vol. 29 no. 3, 1989, pp. 4–28.
46. Peter Baxter, 'On the History and Ideology of Film Lighting', *Screen* vol. 16 no. 3, Autumn 1975, pp. 83–106 (see also Barry Salt's reply in *Screen* vol. 16 no. 4, Winter 1975, pp. 119–23).
47. See Kristin Thompson, *Exporting Entertainment* (London: British Film Institute, 1985).
48. See Cherchi Usai (ed.), *Vitagraph Co of America*, especially the essay by Charles Musser.
49. Adolph Zukor's distribution of *Queen Elizabeth* (1912) and his setting up of the 'Famous Players' production company, resulting in the 'Famous Players in Famous Plays' campaign. See Kenneth MacGowan, *Behind the Screen* (New York: Dell Publishing, 1965), pp. 155–70.
50. See Jan-Christopher Horak, 'Rin-Tin-Tin in Berlin', paper given at the Clark Luxembourg Weimar conference, May 1989.
51. See Noël Burch's brilliant but problematic case history of Japan in *To the Distant Observer* (London: Scolar Press, 1979).
52. *The Nibelungen*, for instance, had to premiere without its final act, because Lang was unable to finish editing in time, and the opening date could not be postponed, after the massive budget that had been spent on press promotion and cinema advertising. Ufa and other German companies appear to have taken these risks with its creative personnel in order to develop prototypes and encourage experiment.
53. Buñuel's *Un Chien Andalou* in this respect opposes itself to French Impressionist cinema by parodying the American style (fast cutting, shallow staging, camera angles, proximity to the camera), and Yuri Tsivian has argued that Eisenstein developed certain principles of symbolist poetics in the direction of surrealism. Yuri Tsivian, 'Eisenstein's *October* and Russian Symbolist Culture' (unpublished paper, 'Eisenstein at 90' conference, Oxford, 1988).

A Scene at the 'Movies'

BEN BREWSTER

> She stole noiselessly down the broad staircase ... and noiselessly approached the door of the big room where she had left her father.... Nobody saw her, nobody heard her, and she had a moment to gaze unobserved at the scene before her. It was like a scene at the 'movies', with all those books, and the piano, and the comfortable chairs, and the big portrait hanging over the fireplace, and the pretty lady behind the steaming tea-kettle, and the dog and the boys.... Only it was real! There were real bindings on the books, real reading in them, there was real tea in the teapot. The people were real, and their feelings for each other were real, too. She, standing on the outside, was the only unreal thing in this home scene. She looked at her father. Suddenly the room faded, disappeared, and a close-up of his face dawned on the screen before her, as it were. Why, her father was gazing at the lady behind the tea-kettle, as if – as if! – Laurel had seen too many close-ups of faces not to recognise that look! She drew in her breath sharply. It flashed over Laurel that perhaps this man wasn't really her father after all! She stirred, moved a foot: Mrs Morrison glanced over her shoulder. 'Oh! come here Laurel,' she exclaimed at the sight of her, and stretched out her arm, and kept it stretched out until Laurel had stepped within its circle.[1]

In this passage from a popular novel first published in 1923, the cinema is functioning as a metaphor for a kind of experience, or rather as the vehicle for a kind of phantasy. It is invoked for the segregation of the audience and the screen, the division between a place 'down here' outside, from which one can watch unobserved, and a place 'up there' inside where what one sees is fictional, obviously, and yet seemingly more real than what is down here: Laurel Dallas outside the door is the 'only unreal thing in this home scene'. The segregation involves a reversal of the opposition between reality and illusion, and the projection of the spectator into the scene. And the novel goes on to move Laurel (despite her pangs of conscience: 'How could she – oh how could she have become a part of the picture on the screen, while her mother was still in the audience, out there, in the dark, looking on')[2] decisively into the world of Helen Morrison, shifting its point of identification to Laurel's mother Stella Dallas, who abolishes herself as visible to her daughter so as to be able to contemplate her in that world. Near the end, Stella out in the dark streets sees Laurel looking towards her from the lighted window of the Morrisons' house, but 'Laurel didn't know it. Laurel had no idea that her mother's eyes were in the depth of the mirror she had gazed into, at her own reflection'.[3] (The scene is faithfully reproduced in the 1925 film version of the novel. The 1937 version, far more uneasy about the phantasy, locates the cinema itself as one of its sources.)

What was the cinema, so that by 1923 it could provide such a metaphor? Fifteen years earlier, such a cinema did not exist. It is a specifically English usage that makes the same term, the name for the movie house and for the whole institution of the production, distribution and exhibition of films (*Stella Dallas*, being American, uses 'movies'). But it is appropriate to the institution we know, so appropriate that we read it back into the whole history of the invention and utilisation of moving pictures. But the movie house as the apparent centre of moving picture-related activity only emerges in the decade after 1905; only then is there a hierarchisation of the experience of moving pictures into the cinematic (primary) and the non-cinematic (peripheral). Before this decade there is no such division – apparatuses for the reproduction of an illusion of movement are integrated into a whole series of other practices, of science, education, religion and entertainment. There are a few specialised film-show houses, but films are shown in vaudeville, music-hall or *caf' conc'* programmes, in fairground booths, in peep shows, in church halls, accompanying popular lectures, and so on. Even as entertainment, they constitute one among a variety of attractions.

After 1905, however, marked most spectacularly by the nickelodeon boom in the USA, specialised houses devoted exclusively or principally to the viewing of films appear and are integrated more and more into a national and international network, containing its own hierarchy of first-, second- and nth-run houses, seat prices, publicity channels, fan magazines, press criticism, etc., which is the cinema we know, the 'movies' Laurel can refer to so casually. Of course, all sorts of other uses of moving pictures continue – blue movies, educational films, films for religious use, scientific films, commercial films; but they are not seen in movie houses (except for a few rare occasions when they obtain the accolade of being real cinema, as with the transfer of some training films for the armed forces into the cinema during the Second World War), so they are not cinema, just a kind of poor relation. Correspondingly, activities inside the movie house are hierarchised under the film – stage interludes, sing-songs, Brenograph displays, in the auditorium; coffee, dinner, even steam baths in the building. And the film is hierarchised – main film, newsreel, travelogue, later A and B feature and high and low genres. In one sense this cinema is just as heterogeneous as the pre-cinematic uses of film were, but the heterogeneity is now held in a more or less peripheral location under the very specialised use of film described by Laurel in the universal form of 'a scene at the "movies"'. And the audiences, too, with all their differences of class, income, education, culture and nationality, consume a single product in a social and geographical hierarchy measured by the interval between release date and their viewing.

But what about the combination of exclusion and projection that characterise that 'scene'? The movies are a form of visual entertainment – pleasure is obtained from what is seen up on the screen. However, for the curious reversal of reality and unreality noted by Laurel, more is required – the articulation of the look from spectator to screen with the looks from character to object and character on the screen. This is the field of what are known as point-of-view structures.

Films had been using point-of-view structures of the type analysed by Edward Branigan[4] for a long time before *Stella Dallas* was published. In the POV structure we see somebody see, then we see what they see from somewhere approaching their viewpoint (less commonly it is the other way round); vision is marked in the first of these shots, and often in the second, too. The simplest form of this is a type of insert. The scene with insert(s) is probably the earliest form of cutting within the scene; in it, some detail of the scene presented in long shot is shown in a 'magnified view' – not necessarily what would now be called a close-up, but a less inclusive camera set-up than the main scene. In *Falsely Accused* we are given magnified views of bank-notes, a key being pressed into wax, and so on;[5] in *Mary Jane's Mishap* we have closer shots of the heroine's face. These are taken from the same angle as the main shots, but with a less inclusive view. They do not represent any fictional character's view, they are there for the audience. Even in *The Gay Shoe Clerk*, where what we see in the magnified view (the heroine lifting her skirts for the shoe clerk to see her underwear) is undoubtedly the object of a look, it is still taken from the side, not from the clerk's own viewpoint.

In the true POV pattern, however, the second shot purports to be (and, more rarely, actually is) photographed from the place where the looking character is fictionally located. In *Grandma's Reading Glass* we see a boy with a magnifying glass looking through it at a newspaper, a watch, a bird in a cage, his grandmother's eye, a kitten, and these shots alternate with magnified views in a black circular mask (representing the glass and the look) of the print of the newspaper, the watch mechanism, the bird, the eye, the kitten's head. In *As Seen Through a Telescope* a peeping Tom with a telescope spies on a young man tying a girl cyclist's shoe-lace, but the view, much the same as that in *The Gay Shoe Clerk*, is now in a circular mask and represents the peeping Tom's point of view.[6]

POV here is, as I say, a special case of the magnified insert. But it would be wrong to see it as a development from the simple insert, leading on to more sophisticated uses of POV in later films. On the contrary, if anything the development is the other way round. In *Grandma's Reading Glass*, the POV structure is the pleasure point of the film, its attraction – to make the break in continuity implicit in a cut within one represented space, the cut has to be made into the end of the film, not its means; in *As Seen Through a Telescope* (and many other films such as *Ce que l'on voit de mon sixième* and *A Search for Evidence*), the structure is serving a simple pornographic narrative, the voyeuristic pleasure in the extra vision still explicitly thematised; in *The Gay Shoe Clerk* the pornographic insert is no longer a strict POV shot; in *Falsely Accused*, conveying straightforward narrative information has become the function of the insert, which function survives as the main role for the insert (and the cut within the same interior space) until the early 1910s (the other role, more especially in comedies, is the complicit closer shot of a character winking or grinning at the audience, as in *Mary Jane's Mishap* and many others).

This pattern, from pure spectacle via pornography to simple narrative, is a common one for the introduction of filmic devices, and the association of POV with the first two stages in the introduction of the insert suggests that POV begins as a primitive rather than as a sophisticated use of cutting. Even when a narrative hinges on what a character sees, this will often be conveyed without POV structures, even if a falsification of the diegetic space is implied: in *The Voice of the Child* a character is shown looking down at a picture and there follows a magnified insert of him holding the picture up in front of him to the camera so the audience can see what, in the fiction, he is supposed to be seeing.[7] By this time, of course, spatially more adventurous directors than Griffith were using POV structures where their narratives gave them the opportunity in much the way that later became standard – for example, in *A Friendly Marriage*, where the wife sees her husband and the vicar's daughter apparently lovers. But this 'reintroduction' of POV seems independent of and secondary to another sense of point of view in film narratives much more significant for the experience of segregation and projection described by Laurel Dallas. This is the sense in which changes of viewpoint not necessarily involving true POV make possible hierarchies of relative knowledge for characters and spectators.

A number of early films exploit the change in what can be seen produced by shifting the camera through 180 degrees. In *Ladies' Skirts Nailed to a Fence*, the first shot shows two ladies gossiping by a fence, the second, from the 'other side' of the fence (in fact the film-makers, with what seems now a misplaced confidence in the Kuleshov effect, use the same camera set-up and simply move the characters round to the other side of the fence), shows two young men creep up, pull the ends of their skirts through the fence and nail them to it, and the third, back on the 'original side', shows the ladies struggling to escape. This really hardly differs in its narrative effect from the gardener's turned back in *L'Arroseur arrosé*, which of course consists of a single shot.

The Other Side of the Hedge uses a two-shot pattern round a hedge not unlike the three-shot one in *Ladies' Skirts*, but to greater effect. In shot one, a courting couple sitting in front of a hedge are kept apart by a chaperone. The chaperone settles down for a nap between them. The couple then disappear behind the hedge, but the spectators, and the chaperone when she wakes momentarily and looks anxiously for her charges, can see their hats sticking up over the hedge a decent distance apart. Shot two is the 180-degree shot from the other side of the hedge: the hats, the spectator now sees, are attached to sticks and the couple are kissing in between them. The gap between the image given in one shot, and the truth given in the second, a truth denied the censorious chaperone, creates an irony out of the change in viewpoint. (It is interesting that two out of three contemporary accounts of this film – in *Biography Bulletin*, no. 38, 1904, and *The Optical Lantern and Kinematograph Journal*, 1905, as opposed to the manufacturers' 1906 'Hepwix' Catalogue entry – cannot describe it properly, because they cannot separate a description of the shots from a version of the story being told, when the point of the film is the eventually resolved discrepancy between them; this failure suggests an important threshold in the development of film narration.) On the other hand, neither shot is a true POV shot. In the first, although we see no more of the other side of the hedge than the chaperone, we see more than she does in that we see her. In the second, we are put into complicity with the couple who are assumed to know what we have seen, that the chaperone has been duped.

This kind of simple irony of differing viewpoints held together by narrative positioning can of course be linked to true POV. In *A Friendly Marriage*, the wife sees the husband and vicar's daughter apparently lovers, whereas we already know that the husband loves the wife and is secretly earning a living, with secretarial help from the vicar's daughter; but the irony is resolved for the characters in the next shot, when the wife accuses him and he explains. More is at stake here than a mere wifely misunderstanding (as sexuality enters this Platonic marriage, money and initiative in it shift from the wife to the husband), but the discrepancy between characters' and spectator's knowledge is only incidental to the narrative structure as a whole.

Narratives entirely constructed around these discrepancies are in fact to be found in the films Griffith made for Biograph between 1909 and 1912, despite the consistent refusal of POV structures in these films, and their reluctance to cut within the same space, especially in interiors. *The Drive for a Life* has one non-POV insert of an action and one insert of a letter, *Gold Is Not All* one; otherwise they consist of one-shot scenes and ordinary or alternating sequences. Yet both depend on hierarchies of relative knowledge and deception.

In *The Drive for a Life*, a man abandons his mistress in order to marry a respectable girl. (The *Biograph Bulletin*, no. 233, 1909, insists the former relationship is completely innocent and the 'mistress' French and a widow into the bargain, but the titles leave the precise relationships so vague as to make mistress the most obvious reading; moreover, it provides a better motivation for her subsequent actions and more powerful identification with her.) After he has said goodbye, the ex-mistress goes out on an errand, riding in a horse-cab. Meanwhile the man is showing off his motor car to his new fiancée. The two routes intersect, and the ex-mistress in her cab sees the couple in the car; but they do not see her. Driven into a jealous rage by this sight, she puts poison in some sweets (insert of this) and sends them with a forged covering note by special messenger to the fiancée. The man arrives at her house to reclaim his love-letters, discovers what she has done, and races in his car to arrive in the nick of time to prevent the fiancée eating the poisoned sweets.

The switchback that ends the film, between shots of the speeding car and the obstacles to its arrival on the one hand, and shots of the delivery, unwrapping and preparation for eating of the sweets on the other, is the device for which Griffith is most famous (although he probably did not invent it), so it is worth emphasising that it too depends for its suspense on the discrepancy of knowledge between the spectator and the fiancée receiving, opening and preparing to eat the sweets supposedly sent by her lover. But more interesting for my purposes in the scene where the ex-mistress oversees the man with his new fiancée. It is filmed in one shot from the back of an unseen car travelling in front of the chauffeur-driven car in the back seat of which the man and his fiancée are seated. After a while, the cab enters left from a side road and drives along behind the couple's car. Finally the couple's car leaves frame right, and the mistress orders the cab to turn back the way it had come. The murderous jealousy which constitutes the narrative is set up in this one complex shot, through the spectator's sharing in the greater knowledge of the ex-mistress and recognition of the vulnerable ignorance of the couple.

Gold Is Not All adds a third layer to these two. It tells the parallel stories of two couples, a poor couple and a rich couple. They court and marry more or less simultaneously and both couples have children. The only direct link between them, apart from living in the same neighbourhood, is that the poor girl does the rich couple's laundry. The narrative alternates between the two stories, and we learn, not surprisingly, that one couple is poor but happy, the other rich but unhappy. But the symmetry between the two couples is deceptive: in fact the spaces they occupy are segregated into an inside, occupied by the rich couple, and an outside, occupied by the poor couple. This is marked not only by the fact that, whereas the rich couple's life takes place largely in interiors (sets), the poor couple are never seen inside their humble cottage; but also, and more significantly, by the fact that the rich couple live on an estate bounded by a wall. The key scene in the film, while both couples are courting, is filmed looking along this wall, with the street outside on the left and the park inside on the right. Both couples appear, initially each couple absorbed in itself. Then the poor couple see the rich couple over the wall and gaze at them in envy. The rich couple, oblivious, leave right, the poor couple shake their heads in sad resignation and leave left. This asymmetry of awareness is repeated throughout the film. Even in their own space, the poor cast many a backward glance towards the rich estate. The rich couple, on the other hand, are oblivious of the poor, until they intrude directly on them, when they (the rich) behave with embarrassed and uncomprehending condescension (in the first scene the poor girl picks up the handkerchief the rich girl has dropped and hands it to her; during the climactic party at the rich house, the poor girl arrives with the laundry at the wrong door and has to be hurriedly redirected). But the narrative (and the titles) provide a third perspective: the rich are ignorant of the poor; the poor see the rich and envy them; the spectator knows rich and poor, and knows the poor do not realise how unhappy the rich really are. Inside and outside on the screen duplicate inside and outside in the movie house.

This is the structure of Laurel's 'scene at the "movies"'. Point of view, in the sense of narrative perspective, the measurement of the relative perceptions and knowledge of the characters by the development of the narrative, is here achieved without point-of-view shots. This is done by finding narrative actions and settings where the look and its object can be staged in one shot, or by dividing the narrative space into contrasting sections linked by much more generalised or even metaphorical looks (when the poor heroine of *Gold Is Not All* looks back over her shoulder 'at' the rich estate as she stands by the door of her cottage, it is not what she *physically* sees that concerns the narrative or the spectator). Notoriously, Griffith did not develop or ever really acclimatise himself to the 'just-off-the-eyeline-shot-reverse-shot' system which became the 'classical' method of scene editing by the end of the First World War. *True Heart Susie*, which is an extension of the pyramid of knowledge of *Gold Is Not All* to feature length (Susie knows more than William, but the spectator knows that and what she knows, and also what neither knows), still prefers long shots and 'concertina' cut-ins to close-ups from the same angle. Early examples of that system I have seen – *The Loafer*, *His Last Fight*, *The Bank Burglar's Fate* – all use it in the context of fights, whereas the 'point-of-view' structure of the Griffith films is essentially passive (although it can give rise to subsequent aggression – the poisoned sweets). Although I cannot trace the process in detail, it seems clear that when the 'classical' system came to incorporate less aggressive contexts, it absorbed the Griffithian point-of-view structure, and combined together technical and narrative point of view.

One final characteristic of the establishment of this cinema: what might be called the extra twist of fictionality it brought with it. Many American films made before 1910 involve a plot where a worker hero (usually a foreman rather than a simple workman) is in conflict, usually over his girlfriend or wife, sometimes herself a worker, with another higher-ranking blackguardly employee – a supervisor (e.g. *The Mill Girl*, *The Paymaster*). The foreman displaces the supervisor in the mill-girl's affections, or rescues her from his unwelcome attentions, and is then the victim of some conspiracy on the supervisor's part, which is finally uncovered, the happy couple are united and the villain punished – or the girl is unjustly suspected of infidelity with a (less blackguardly) supervisor, leading to friction between the men, finally resolved by the opportunity for selfless heroism presented by an accident at work (*The Tunnel Workers*). The sets in these films are typically sketchy functional ones, providing a space for the action and painted décor indicating the milieu; but exteriors and a few interiors are filmed in 'real' surroundings – *The Paymaster* in a real (though disused) New England mill, *The Tunnel Workers*, spectacularly, at the top of the shafts of the works for the Pennsylvania Tunnel from New York City to Long Island. Thus the films can be said to have a naive realism: made for the nickelodeon market when it was already becoming reasonably unified but was still confined to a lower-middle- and working-class clientèle, they reflect that milieu in the most direct possible way, confining themselves largely to it and filming directly in its real surroundings.

The films of the early 1910s I have been principally discussing have changed this. Their heroes and heroines are from the respectable, even rich middle class, and the locations and especially the sets are chosen, designed and furnished to convey luxury and fashion. Even more strikingly, the poor have become a picture-book poor, living a carefree life in little cottages with roses round the porch. A shift in the centre of the fiction from the presentation of scenes to the presentation of differing character perspectives on scenes, and a displacement of point of view from a mechanism for articulating diegetic space to one for articulating characters' knowledge, go with a move from the direct photography of real environments to the presentation of a world much more penetrated by phantasy. The American cinema, not yet in Hollywood (although *Gold Is Not All* was filmed in Pasadena), is becoming a dream factory. The remark is not made either in a spirit of civically responsible condemnation, or one of surrealist celebration – the examples hardly suit either response: the story of *The*

Mill Girl is no more socially responsible than that of *Gold Is Not All*, and by 1925 the latter seemed embarrassingly naive to Linda Arvidson, who played the poor girl in it[8] – but in order to re-emphasise the cinematicity of the 'scene at the "movies"' that, by 1923, could be reappropriated by popular literature.

Notes

This chapter was first published as an article in *Screen* vol. 23 no. 2, July/August 1982, and is reprinted here with the addition of a note correcting a mis-description of *The Voice of a Child*.

1. Olive Higgins Prouty, *Stella Dallas* (New York: Paperback Library, 1967), pp. 38–9.
2. Ibid., p. 53.
3. Ibid., p. 251.
4. Edward Branigan, 'Formal permutations of the point-of-view shot', *Screen*, vol. 16 no. 3, Autumn 1975, pp. 54–64,
5. For a still, see Barry Salt, 'Film Form 1900–1906', *Sight & Sound*, Summer 1978.
6. For a still, see p. 36 above.
7. I now realise this is a partial mis-description, and there is no falsification of the space involved. In the main scene, the office typist gives the clerk, her boyfriend, a picture. He looks at the picture and gestures to the effect 'It's you.' In the cut-in, we see first the back of the picture as he is looking at the front. Inscribed on it are the words 'To my sweetheart'. He then turns it round to read the message on the back, and now we see the picture of the typist on the front. Thus, the shot never purports to be a POV shot. It is also worth mentioning that these are secondary characters whose motivations are of no concern to the narrative; the point of the shot is to establish the inscribed photograph, which the false friend will later slip into the coat pocket of the boss of these two characters, the hero of the story, so that it will be found by his wife and interpreted as a sign of infidelity.
8. See Mrs D. W. Griffith (Linda Arvidson), *When the Movies Were Young* (New York: Dutton & Co., 1925), p. 147.

'A Properly Adjusted Window'
Vision and Sanity in D. W. Griffith's 1908–1909 Biograph Films

ANNE FRIEDBERG

This chapter offers the residue of an earlier study, one conducted in 1977, when I was simultaneously reading Michel Foucault's *Madness and Civilization* and taking Jay Leyda's Seminar on Griffith's Biograph films, in which we viewed and analysed every film that Griffith made in the years 1908 and 1909. The project that follows emerged from that convergence, the product of something quite frequent in graduate school: a superimposition of two dual and seemingly contradictory enquiries. The double question of 'how does one speak of madness in the language of reason?' and 'how does one establish the *range* of a culture by its *derangement*?' seemed to pose itself almost naturally to the point when cinematic conventions were not yet 'reasoned' themselves. What is provided here is not a history of D.W. Griffith at Biograph, but an observation on a particular turning point in his film style.

Between 1908 and 1909, Griffith made a total of 202 one-reel films for the Biograph Company. When viewing them consecutively, one cannot but notice that the Biograph films were a remarkable laboratory for narrative technique. An abundance of scholarship on Griffith has focused on the development of his narrative strategies and on their ideological implications. The observation which I wish to put forth here is in many ways a small one. Of the 1908–9 films, Griffith's villains – necessary catalysts for family melodramas of threat and reconstitution – were, from the gypsies in Griffith's first film *Adventures of Dolly*, racially stereotyped figures with exaggerated, telegraphed gesticulations – they were gypsies, Italians (usually Sicilians), Mexicans or blacks. But one other figure appeared, with what seemed to me a striking insistence, as a threat: the 'lunatic', 'maniac' or 'mentally deranged'. Struck with a malady of the mental condition, the 'lunatic' figure poses direct questions about the public notion of 'mental disorder' in 1908 and 1909. I originally isolated ten Biograph films which had villain/threat figures with some form of *mental* aberration. At some point in the middle of 1909, a change occurs in Griffith's representation of mental disease (somewhere between *Where the Breakers Roar*, Griffith's eighteenth Biograph film shot in August 1908 – his first with a clearly denoted 'lunatic' – and *The Rocky Road*, his 192nd film at Biograph, shot in late November 1909). This chapter intends to address this change, relate it to the development of character subjectivity in Griffith's work, to the Reform crusades of 1908 and 1909 called the Mental Hygiene Movement, and to the campaign to win a middle-class audience for the cinema: three separate but in no way independent factors in Griffith's work.

A Properly Adjusted Window

> Imagine a public library of the near future, for instance. There will be long rows of boxes or pillars, properly classified and indexed of course. At each box a push button and before each box a seat. Suppose you wish to 'read up' on a certain episode in Napoleon's life. Instead of consulting all the authorities, wading through a host of books, and ending bewildered without a clear idea of exactly what did happen, you will merely seat yourself at a *properly adjusted window* in a scientifically prepared room, press the button, and actually see what happened. ... There will be no opinions expressed. You will merely be present at the making of history.[1] [emphasis mine]

Such was the version of the 'near future' which D. W. Griffith envisioned in the year 1915. It was a prophecy for the cinema, an apparatus with a power as apocryphal as 'writing history with lightning': *you will merely seat yourself at a properly adjusted window in a scientifically prepared room. ... You will merely be present at the making of history*.

It is, of course, easy to cast doubt on D. W. Griffith's version of *what did happen*. Griffith, as we know, waxed certain about cinema's potential to render historical 'truth'. (That he offered $10,000 to anyone who could prove distortion in *Birth of a Nation* is just one indication of such certainty – even if it was never spelled out how he intended to accept proof.[2]) His fantasy of the cinema of the future with 'no opinions expressed' is clearly an idealist one, effacing all consequences of the interventions of re-presentation, cinematic or otherwise. But it was less a projection of the Holy Grail of 'total cinema' in the Bazinian sense, than it was related to Griffith's determination that the cinema should function as an educational and reformational tool. Griffith's above statement serves witness to the consolidation of efforts to employ the still-fledgling *pictograph* in a socially redeemable manner. 'I believe in the motion picture not only as a means of amusement,' said Griffith in an interview in 1915:

> but as a moral and educational force. Do you know that there has been less drinking in the past five years and that it is because of the motion pictures? It is absolutely true. ... No man drinks for the sake of drinking. He drinks because he has no place to go. Man is a moving animal. The bigger the man the more he has need of activity. It isn't so with women. Their natures are different. The motion pictures give a man a place to go beside a saloon. He drops in to see a picture. He has been somewhere. He has seen something. He comes out and goes home in a different state than if he had gone to a saloon. The domestic unities are preserved.[3]

The cinema here is to function as a saloon-surrogate, displacing one site of consumption with another. The *picture* serves a twofold purpose ('He has been *somewhere*. He has *seen something*.'): a transformation incurred as much by the activity of getting out of the house as by what is *seen* in the theatre. Of course, Griffith's tone is not surprising. (Nor are his assumptions about women – leaving the female spectator, and the female alcoholic, simply unaddressed. The 'moral and educational force' is aimed, here, at a male subject.) His quasi-theoretical speculations about the relation of cinema to alcoholism (the concomitant similarities of incorporation, habituation, desire for loss of self, replacement with other) are twisted into a suggestion of the cinema as *cure*, an effective substitute for drinking and vice, a potential superintendent of domestic unity. In making an argument for the cinema as an instrument of social reform, Griffith does not defend it in terms of narrative content, but describes instead the sense of *destination* offered, a place, a *somewhere* outside the home. But Griffith also used the family and its unity as a regulatory narrative force – all threats to its sanctity were central devices for catalysing his one-reel dramas; the restoration of its hold central to his ideas of narrative closure.

The Griffith statements I have just cited are from 1915, a year which marks a point of assurance in the campaign for the cinema's legitimacy. Hugo Munsterberg described the reform potential of the cinema vividly in that same year: 'Intellectually the world has been divided into two classes – the "highbrows" and the "lowbrows". The Pictograph will bring these two brows together.'[4]

The aspirations of Griffith and Munsterberg in 1915 were projections towards a spectatorial homogeny – the cinema as unifier of an aggregate audience; to Americanize the immigrant, maintain and stabilize the family; to create, in the logical extension of Munsterberg's vision, an intellectual 'monobrow'.[5] The notion that the cinema could unify its public around any consensus would have seemed ludicrous a few years earlier, in 1908, when Lawrence Griffith, the young actor afraid to taint his stage name with his movie credits, first arrived at the 14th Street Studios of the American Mutoscope and Biograph Company.

In fact, to consider the cinema capable of influencing any social reforms, it first had to be re-formed. Between 1908 and 1915, there were vast changes in the public's conception of the cinema, the structure of the film industry, the style and content of films produced. Explicit accounts of the vice-crusader's attack on cinema (culminating in the dramatic Christmas Day closing of 550 New York City movie houses in 1908), of the attempt by producers and exhibitors to lure a middle-class audience (aided by the economic advantages of the Patents Trust formed in September 1908), have been provided elsewhere,[6] along with historiographical debates about the complex motivations and goals in the reform and progressive movements' relation to an emerging mass culture.[7] Suffice it to say that despite the competing interests of cinema reformers and producers, there was a common impetus to 'upgrade' the audience *for* and the content *of* motion pictures. If one reformist's rhetoric could summarize such a transition, Reverend Charles Parkhurst of the Madison Avenue Presbyterian Church in New York City, a vocal opponent of the cinema in 1908 – instrumental in Mayor McLellan's Christmas closing – was, by 1915, praising the latest film by D. W. Griffith, *Birth of a Nation*: 'A boy can learn more pure history and more atmosphere of the period by sitting down three hours before the films which Mr Griffith has produced with such artist's skill than by weeks and months of study in the classroom.'[8]

While Griffith's relation to reformers was at best ambivalent, he was not averse to being endorsed by them. (The anti-reformist modern layer of the palimpsest *Intolerance* would seem to have been a reaction to his disappointment that social workers such as Jane Addams and Frederic Howe vehemently attacked *Birth of a Nation*.[9])

Even so, the transformative power of the cinema was apparent by 1915. In Munsterberg's remarkably anti-psychoanalytic *Film: A Psychological Study*, he describes the effect on the film spectator:

> The intensity with which the [photoplays] take hold of the audience cannot remain without strong social effects. . . . The associations become as vivid as realities because the mind is so completely given up to the moving pictures. The possibilities of psychical infection and destruction cannot be overlooked.[10]

But the threat of 'psychical infection' was counter-balanced by the regulatory potential of the photoplay: 'Any wholesome influence emanating from the photoplay must have an incomparable power for the re-molding and up-building of the national soul.'[11]

Griffith's work at Biograph hangs precisely in this balance – staving off the cinema of 'psychical infection' and using, instead, the cinema's 'incomparable power' to 'up-build' and 'remold'.

A Mind That Found Itself: The Mental Hygiene Movement of 1908

While the vices and virtues of the cinema were being debated in 1908, a single-minded reformer, Clifford Whittingham Beers, was conducting a determined campaign to change public attitudes towards mental disease. Exposés of asylum treatment were not unique to reform movements of the beginning of this century. But Beers' *A Mind That Found Itself*, published in March 1908, was the cornerstone of a new reform movement in America. Beers, who had suffered brutal treatment in a series of mental institutions between 1900 and 1903, deemed his crusade the Mental Hygiene Movement. 'Hygiene' was rhetorically linked to the germ theory-spawned association of health with the clean, uninfected, undisturbed. Beers' autobiographical account was unique not only because he was well-born and Yale-educated before the onset of mental disturbance, but also because he enlisted endorsements from such notable figures as William James, Jane Addams, Dr Adolf Meyer and Jacob Riis. Messianic in tone, Beers was stridently intent on making his cause nationally (or at best internationally) known: 'Why cannot a book be written which will free the helpless slaves of all creeds and colors confined today in the asylums and sanitariums throughout the world?'[12] In February 1909, the National Committee for Mental Hygiene was officially formed. Its goals were to change the public conception of mental illness, and to provide some intermediary between the ongoing discourse among specialists and an uninformed public.

A reading of the popular magazines in 1908 – *Harper's Weekly*,

Everybody's, *Arena* – supports an impression that the popular press addressed Beers' concern for the changing care and treatment of the mentally ill. A May 1908 article in *Harper's* claimed: 'Lunatics have been treated with great brutality in the past, but happily those days are over. There is no stronger proof of human progress than the modern treatment of the insane.'[13] In October 1908, an article in *Everybody's* called 'Insanity is not a Brain Disease' pointed to the nosographic difference between disease and the mental disturbance called insanity: 'Insanity may exist with a brain perfectly healthy.'[14]

But madness has always been judged from the position of reason. Posed as a negation – the absence of reason – madness has a diagnostic history which reads as a series of reformulations of the perimeters of sanity.[15] In American medical psychology, a simple semantic substitution indicated the beginning of the change in treatment of the mentally ill. The New York State Care Act of 1890 stipulated that the mentally disturbed were wards of the State and that State-sponsored institutions be established to care for them. But it also prescribed that these institutions were to be called *hospitals*, suggesting a possible cure, not *asylums*, which indicated confinement without hope of transformation.

Nathan Hale, in his account of the beginnings of psychoanalysis in the United States,[16] refers to the wide reception of the Beers' book as 'one of the best measures of informed opinion about insanity'[17] and places the impact of the Mental Hygiene Movement, a crusade very much in the public press in 1908 and 1909, as an important factor in the general ambience of Freud's reception at the Clark University in September 1909.

A Mind That Found Itself at Biograph

As reform crusades raged separately in the public discourses around the cinema and the treatment of insanity, D. W. Griffith was busy producing several one-reel narratives per week. Without constructing these events in a set of grand historiographical switchbacks – an elaborate Griffithian narrative device for the writing of history – how does one reconcile these discursive debates which form a backdrop to the conventions that Griffith developed for representing character and point of view?

Where the Breakers Roar, Griffith's eighteenth film at Biograph (August 1908), is the first of his films with a clearly marked 'lunatic' figure. A film of fifteen shots, it opens with two shots of well-dressed young couples, first on a veranda, then in a park. The third shot, with no apparent proximity to or continuity with the first two, shows uniformed officers escorting a man towards an arched doorway bearing the sign: 'Lunatic Asylum'. The man struggles with the police, knocks them down, emerges brandishing a gun. In the fourth shot, the escaped man walks along a large brick building towards the camera, menacingly. As he leaves the frame, the police follow. In the fifth shot, the 'lunatic' is hiding in bushes next to an empty road. He ambushes a man, steals his knife, and then wobbles towards the camera falling back and forth across the frame, now threatening with a knife. The opening five shots of *Where the*

Breakers Roar establish two separate spaces: the playful couples in one, a 'lunatic' loose and dangerous in another. A simple narrative is set into motion.

The next three shots (shots 6, 7, 8) continue this parallel construction. The couples at the beach change into bathing attire, play in the waves; two lovers court under a beach umbrella until they are interrupted by the teasing of the other bathers. In the ninth shot, the two stories reach their inevitable intersection. A young woman runs away from her friends who plan to duck here teasingly in the water. She runs along the shoreline, away from the group. She turns towards the camera and runs towards it, alone in the frame. After she runs past the camera, the other laughing couples run through giving chase, followed by her boyfriend. For a moment the shot of the beach is empty until the 'lunatic' enters with the knife and runs through the same space. This type of one-shot chase was not uncommon for Griffith and others – the threat is *unseen* by the characters but *known* by the spectators. All of the characters have run towards the camera, into a close-up that magnifies their facial expressions momentarily before they leave the shot. In the tenth shot, the 'lunatic' intercepts the young woman as she jumps into a boat at the water's edge. As he jumps aboard, she is trapped with him. Shot 11 isolates the threat: shot from slightly above, the two are struggling in the boat completely surrounded by water, the water she was running from in the first place. Shot 12: the friends get into another boat and head out after her. Shot 13: the two boats chase each other. Shot 14: the friends intercept the frightened woman, rescuing her and catching the 'lunatic'. The film concludes with the friends embracing on the beach, the 'lunatic' in custody, the threat resolved, the woman surrounded and secure, centre frame.

While a shot description may seem quite tedious here, it supplies the basic structure of the one-reel chase. The woman runs further and further away from the safety of civilization and, as she crosses into the empty frame of the beach, enters the dangerous, liminal space of the 'lunatic'. The 'lunatic' is given no motivation for his derangement, for his custody in shot 3, for his aggression in subsequent shots. The implication is simply that he is harmful if unconfined – his wild, frenzied gestures directed at both the characters and the spectator (in his run-in close-ups). The narrative closes with the woman returned to the protective presence of the crowded frame full of her friends. The 'lunatic' is a villain, not psychologically detailed, but broadly sketched.

In several other 1908–9 films (*Money Mad*, released December 1908, *The Maniac Cook*, released January 1909, *The Cord of Life*, released January 1909), a mentally disturbed character is denoted as dangerous by exaggerated pantomimic gestures of disturbance – often a clutching of the head, aggressive invasion of the *mise en scène*. The threat is directed at the usual vulnerable victims in Griffith's work, the lone woman or child. (In *Where the Breakers Roar*, the woman-victim was played by Linda Arvidson, Griffith's wife; in *The Maniac Cook*, an infant is put in the oven; in *Cord of Life* a child is hung out of a tenement window by a rope.) These films consistently demonstrate that madness needs to be contained and the insurgent must be placed in, or returned to, custody. Madness, as a disturbance that needs to be textually contained, may be metaphoric for textual regulation itself, an acting-out of Griffith's own struggle with narrative conventions. Cinematic narrative, as Griffith was refining it, was constructed by establishing a momentarily safe and static world, threatening its fragile security, and then constructing a narrative resolution to the threat. The lunatic character, in this way, is more than just a villain. Madness is also a metaphor for narrative incoherence, a text which needs to be controlled.

But later in 1909, Griffith changes his portrait of mental disturbance. An important transitional film is *The Drunkard's Reformation* (shot in February 1909, released in April 1909). *The Drunkard's Reformation* contains a character who is 're-formed' in the course of the film rather than remaining an agent of harm to be caught, kept in custody or destroyed. The film has a striking shot structure, supplying a direct point-of-view shot for the character who is to be re-formed, collapsing what the spectator *sees* with what the character *sees*. The drunkard and his daughter attend a play about a drunkard and his family. In alternating shots, we see a temperance play from the audience's point of view and then the father and daughter in the audience, seen from a camera placed in the position of the stage. By alternating the shot of the father in the audience with the 180 degree reverse-field counter-shot of the play that he is seeing, Griffith places the film spectator in a unique position, complicit with the characters' view. The spectator also witnesses the father's straightforward transformation: the father in the audience reacts to the father in the play who abuses his family. The character has been *cured* of drinking through *seeing* the temperance play. But the significance of *The Drunkard's Reformation* extends beyond the character's transformation. Griffith had hit upon a technique that welded character subjectivity with that of the spectators', even if this is done within a hierarchy of knowledge where the spectator knows more, has seen more, than the character.

The Broken Locket (released in September 1909), *The Expiation* (released in October 1909), *The Restoration* (released in November 1909), *The Rocky Road* (released at the end of December 1909) all contain characters whose mental condition is determined by what they see. These films include motivations for the 'loss of reason'. Madness is no longer regulated by simple containment, but is given its own reason. (In *The Broken Locket*, a woman suffers hysterical blindness when her husband disappears; in *The Expiation* and *The Restoration*, a jealous husband misperceives his wife's attention to another man.) Sanity is tied to vision in all of these films. In fact, as a brief description of *The Restoration* demonstrates, the restoration of the husband's sanity is conducted by an exercise in re-seeing.

The Restoration is an elaborate example of the calamitous consequences of misconstrued vision. The film, almost twice as long as *Where the Breakers Roar* (964 feet compared to 556), has twenty-six shots. Two separate couples – a husband and wife, a cousin and her suitor – are introduced in two separate spaces. The intertitles make the complicated family relations quite clear. The husband is a landowner; seen with his wife, he wears riding clothes on the grounds of his large estate. Elsewhere in the garden, the cousin and her suitor are seen courting. They have a fight and separate. *Moving Picture World* provides this account:

> Wrong impression, converted ideas, hallucinations, have formed the stronger part of the causes of calamity and there is no stronger ideological force than jealousy and jealousy thrives most in the fagged brain. Henry Morley was suffering from what seemed to be an attack of hypochondriasis. He was low-spirited, irresolute of purpose and in fact, on the verge of a nervous collapse.[18]

But even without an explanation of the husband's fragile mental state, the film contains four incidents which justify his suspicious assumptions. The husband sees the wife and the suitor on a bench in the garden, intercepts a note intended for the cousin, sees the suitor and his wife in the parlour, and finally sees the cousin and the suitor embrace and mistakenly thinks his wife is in the embrace. His transformation towards derangement is clear to the spectator who knows that he has mis-seen these events. After the husband lunges towards the suitor, a title explains: 'His mind is affected and imagines his victim pursuing him.' The husband returns to previous locations, the garden bench, a leafy bush, gesturing wildly and stopping to see if he is pursued. He runs through the garden, alternately hiding and looking back, rubbing his hands together. He talks to the bush, waves his arms in front of his face, grabs at his hair. But these exaggerated actions, similar to those of the 'lunatic' in *Where the Breakers Roar*, are not threatening to others. He is, instead (like the dipsomaniac husband in *The Expiation*), cared for and understood by his family.

The suitor, the cousin and the wife call a doctor to the house. The doctor brings the husband back into the parlour, the scene of his previous trauma. The title reads: 'The doctor's plan. Has them re-enact the episode thereby inducing the restoration of his mind.' In the final tableaux, the doctor directs the action. The husband is placed in the same position in the parlour facing the embracing couple. The doctor points to the couple kissing and the husband, in anger, repeats his earlier action, throwing the suitor aside. This time, of course, he *sees* that it is not his wife. The film ends: the husband shakes hands with the suitor, the doctor is congratulated, the husband and wife embrace, centre frame.

The simplicity of the doctor's cure is in its repetition of the earlier scenario. Not unlike the talking cure, this doctor enforces a *seeing* cure. The character who sees things correctly, aided, for example, by a doctor, is the character whose disorder is not merely contained but *cured*. For the spectator, Griffith has constructed something different from the narrative of containment: a narrative of transformation. Griffith's knowledge of medical psychology was quite limited. Once he provided his characters with some psychological depth, he was no more a sophisticated psychological *metteur en scène* than the doctor in *The Restoration*. His characters had an investment in the image, limited to the locus of appearance which that image defined. Madness was an error in *seeing*; a delirium curable by reinvesting the same image with a different meaning. For the characters and the spectator this is not a strictly perceptual change, but rather is a retrospective rewriting of the mental, cognitive frame through which the image was first seen.

In 1909, Griffith changes the image of madness in his one-reel narratives. Madness is no longer a narrative device for disruption requiring containment; madness becomes a character's reaction to an *image*, is a disturbance of vision, which, if properly corrected, can be cured. For Griffith, whose famous statement, 'my task is above all to make you see', meant *see* through his 'properly adjusted window'. If carried to polemical extremes, Griffith's own *history lessons*, his certainty of the image's 'truth', seem to restate the madman's delirious relation to the image. In Foucault's words: 'While before the eyes of the madman, drunk on a light which is darkness, rise and multiply images incapable of criticizing themselves (since madmen *see* them), but irreparably separated from being (since the madman *sees nothing*).'[19]

D. W. Griffith was not a madman. But his aspirations for the cinema were bound to his conviction that vision was a determining factor in mental health; its regulation a potential form of mind control. From here, it would not take much to add that D. W. Griffith is also often remembered as the 'father' of cinema style, as patriarch in command of vision. The cinema: *a properly adjusted window in a scientifically prepared room*.

Notes

1. D. W. Griffith, 'Five dollar "movies" prophesied', *The Editor* (24 April 1915), excerpted as 'Some prophecies: film and theatre, screenwriting, education', in Harry M. Geduld (ed.), *Focus on D. W. Griffith* (Englewood Cliffs, NJ: Prentice-Hall, Inc., 1971), p. 35.
2. Thomas Cripps, *Slow Fade to Black* (New York: Oxford University Press, 1977), p. 59.
3. Originally published in *New York American*, 28 February 1915, City Life and Dramatic section, p. 9. Reprinted as 'D. W. Griffith, producer of the worrld's biggest picture', in Geduld, *Focus on D. W. Griffith*, p. 2229.
4. Richard Griffith quotes this in his foreword to Hugo Munsterberg's *Film: A Psychological Study* (New York: Dover Press, 1970), p. ix.
5. In Tom Gunning's portrait of economic context in 'Weaving a Narrative: Style and Economic Background in Griffith's Biograph Films', pp. 336–47 of this volume, the turning point in the drive for a middle-class audience was 1908–9: 'All of this defines the years 1908–9 as the origin of a unified effort to attract the middle class to motion pictures, an effort that extends over the whole span of Griffith's work at Biograph (1908–13).'

   Judith Mayne provides an excellent account of the cinema as 'socializing machine' for immigrant spectators in her book, *Private Novels, Public Films* (Athens, Georgia: University of Georgia Press, 1988). Mayne also points out that the cinema not only provided a cross-class cultural phenomenon, but also cross-gendered. The immigrant audience was not exclusively male but also included immigrant women.
6. See Russell Merritt, 'Nickelodeon theaters 1905–1914: building an audience for the movies', and Jeanne Thomas Allen, 'The decay of the Motion Picture Patents Company', in Tino Balio (ed.), *The American Film Industry* (Madison: University of Wisconsin Press, 1976).
7. See also Robert Sklar, *Movie-Made America* (New York: Vintage Books, 1975) and Lary May, *Screening Out the Past* (New York: Oxford University Press, 1980).
8. Reverend Dr Charles H. Parkhurst, 'The Birth of a Nation', review reprinted in Fred Silva (ed.), *Focus on Birth of a Nation* (Englewood Cliffs, NJ: Prentice-Hall, 1971), pp. 101–3.
9. Jane Addams gave a detailed interview to the *New York Post*, which complained about the film's glorification of the Ku Klux Klan and its selective use of historical events to

justify its racist premises: 'You can use history to demonstrate anything when you take certain of its facts and emphasize them to the exclusion of others' (*New York Post*, 10 March 1915). The National Association for the Advancement of Colored Peoples sent Addams' review to newspapers across the country and included it in their pamphlet 'Fighting a Vicious Film'. Frederic Howe, a member of the National Board of Censorship, dissented with the Board's approval of *Birth of a Nation*. At the National Board of Censorship hearing on 30 March 1915, Howe declared that the nation's black population was 'degraded' by Griffith's portrait of Negroes. (Quoted in Richard Shickel, *D. W. Griffith: An American Life* (New York: Simon & Schuster, 1984), pp. 283–5.)

10. Munsterberg, *Film*, p. 95.
11. Ibid., p. 96.
12. Clifford Beers, *A Mind That Found Itself* (New York: Longmans, Green & Company, 1908).
13. 'The Past-times of Madmen', *Harper's Weekly*, May 1908.
14. W. H. Thomson, 'Insanity is not a brain disease', *Everybody's*, October 1908, vol. 19, pp. 563–4.
15. As Michel Foucault traces in *Madness and Civilization*, the explanatory discourses for madness have, through the centuries, struggled with a precise account of the causes of mental disorder. Yet managerial responses to the condition of madness have consistently leaned towards confinement, isolation, expulsion from the social whole, even if this was intended as part of the cure.
16. Nathan Hale, *Freud and the Americans* (New York: Oxford University Press, 1971).
17. Ibid., p. 234.
18. *Moving Picture World*, vol. 5 no. 20, 13 November 1909, p. 691.
19. Michel Foucault, *Madness and Civilization*, trans. Richard Howard (New York: Vintage Books, 1973), p. 109.

Weaving a Narrative
Style and Economic Background in Griffith's Biograph Films

TOM GUNNING

The spectre of D. W. Griffith, the mythical 'father' of film as an art form, haunts film history. All too often Griffith has been an excuse for a lack of scholarship on early film. To relieve film scholars of the burden and anxiety of wading into the morass of anonymous or little-known films that mark the early years of the cinema, Griffith has been labelled as the 'beginning' of film as an art form. A whole barrage of techniques have been identified as Griffith 'discoveries'. Or when this myth of actual invention could not be maintained, Griffith was seen as the man who first gave these techniques meaning; or used them in an artistic context. A radical inversion of this myth has also appeared. In this counter-myth, Griffith is seen as the betrayer of a purer idea of film found in the work of Méliès and Lumière, as the man who introduced the fatal element of bourgeois narrative, the Adam from whose fall film is yet to recover.

Like any myth of a father's role, both these approaches carry something of the significance and paradox of Griffith's place in film history. Yet some attempt to demythologize Griffith's contribution is necessary, if only to help us understand the myth more fully. An examination of the economic factors at the time of Griffith's entrance into film shows the extent to which they determined the transformations of film form that appear in Griffith's first films. Griffith's early work must be seen as a paradigm of the development demanded by the new economic identity film was establishing, rather than as the magical creation of a semi-mythical culture hero. At the same time, Griffith's work appears curiously overdetermined, fulfilling certain expectations and aspirations of the film industry of the time, and yet also running into conflict with them – exceeding them. I feel that this excess created a tension between his work and the film industry as an economic entity that was to pursue Griffith throughout his career. The way Griffith's early style resulted from certain demands within film economics will be shown by an examination of the film industry in 1908–9 and the treatment of one aspect of his style – parallel editing – during these years. We may also find within the use of parallel editing something of the tension that would develop between Griffith and the very conditions which allowed his film style to appear.

Griffith Films in Economic Context: The Years 1908–1909

Any close examination of the early period of film reveals its non-monolithic nature. The period from 1895 to 1915, that is, from Lumière to *The Birth of a*

Nation, is not a uniform slice of film history that can be labelled simply 'early' or 'primitive' film. Our task must be to find the points of articulation within this period, the breaks and reroutings in film practice. Practically every year in this twenty-year period provides something of a milestone in the development of cinema. But the years 1908–9 are of a peculiar nature worth defining. The changes that begin in these years mark the nature of film until 1913, when other factors begin to dominate.

1908 is a year not so much of innovation as of crystallization. It is not the year of the first story film, or of the first full reel (1,000-foot) or the first film exchanges or nickelodeons. Rather, it is the year when the film industry tried to knit all these developments into a stable industry. Permanent film theatres, built for the showing of films, had begun appearing in 1905. A large number of steady theatres had allowed for the growth of film exchanges as a means of distribution. The film of one-reel length had become common by 1906. And by 1908 the heads of the film industry saw economic organization as a way to unite all these factors into an assured profit-making system.

The formation in December of 1908 of the Motion Picture Patents Company (MPPC) was to be the means of this stabilization. The combine was an agreement between the Edison Film Company and the other principal American producing companies to end the decade of lawsuits over patent infringements, by acknowledging Edison's priority. The American Mutoscope and Biograph Company felt confident in the strength of its own patents (and the financial support of the powerful Empire Trust Company) and held back from joining the combine. However, at the end of 1908, Biograph was admitted on an equal basis with Edison, and the MPPC was officially formed.

The MPPC brought to the film industry the kind of organization that had been dominating American business since before the turn of the century. Industry had moved away from a system of competition between rival firms towards a variety of pooling agreements and 'trusts' which would limit competition. This process had encountered opposition from the government, the strongest being the Sherman Anti-Trust Law of 1890. However, control of patents seemed a way to circumvent those restrictions, and it was on this basis that the MPPC was formed.

Control of patents was only a means to an end. The aim of the MPPC was total control of the film industry in all its aspects. All of the major American producing companies were included in the group (as well as the American representatives of several foreign companies: Pathé, Méliès, Gaumont and Eclipse). A few inconsequential American firms and a large number of European manufacturers were excluded. To further sew up its control of the production end of the industry, MPPC worked out a contract with Eastman Kodak, the world's largest supplier of film stock, for exclusive use of their product. With the company pool of patents, the MPPC hoped to restrict the American use of any existent motion picture camera.

Exerting control over the various aspects of the film industry was as important a motivation for the establishment of the new film combine as the regulation of competition among film production companies. In 1909 the MPPC abolished Edison's previous exclusive contract with the Film Service Association, an organization of independently owned exchanges which had distributed the films of the Edison combine. Instituting a new series of licences for the exchanges handling their films, the MPPC also exerted a large measure of control over the methods of film distribution, setting release dates for films and firm price schedules for rentals. This led the way for a new unified distribution corporation directly under the control of the MPPC, General Film, which was introduced in 1910. With its patents for projectors and control of the major sources of American films, the MPPC could also exert pressure on film exhibitors, instituting restrictive licences and a collection of royalties. Under the MPPC the film industry was reorganized both vertically and horizontally under a central controlling body.

Ultimately, the 'Film Trust' (as it was called by its rivals) failed, for a number of reasons. But what is important for our purposes is not the economic defeat of the combine, but rather the desire in 1908–9 to create a centralized, permanent and stable industry. The MPPC claimed its economic control of the film industry would 'uplift' the motion pictures, improving their content and the means of exhibition. In July 1909 the *Moving Picture World* praised its success in this direction.[1] If we look carefully behind the Film Trust's rhetoric of reform, we discover a major purpose of the MPPC – the wooing of a middle-class audience. In most film histories, this phenomenon is assigned a later date. But it begins (as Russell Merritt has pointed out[2]) during Griffith's work at Biograph. It is difficult to understand Griffith's early work without being aware of this background.

The push to make film respectable (i.e. acceptable to the middle class) opened on two basic fronts: censorship of film content, and improvement of the theatres in which the films were shown. Both of these issues had been inflammatory in the hands of anti-film reformists. These groups had shown their ability to convince authorities that films were an undesirable anti-social force when, in December 1908, Mayor McClellan of New York City had ordered all nickelodeons shut down as a threat to the city's physical and moral well-being. To succeed in capturing a new audience, the MPPC had to defuse the criticisms of the reform groups. In 1909 the People's Institute, a liberal-minded reform organization, set up the National Board of Censorship in association with the MPPC. The MPPC submitted all films made by its ten-member companies to this board for review. This support of film censorship had two aims: to 'improve' film content and therefore attract a 'better class' of audience, and to keep censorship out of the hands of the police and clergy who might deal more harshly with the films than the producers wanted.

MPPC's drive to improve theatres centred on an issue now almost forgotten – fear of the dark. The darkness of the motion picture theatre blackened film's image for the respectable classes. In that darkness, anything could (and perhaps *did*) happen. Crawling with real or imagined 'mashers', the darkened theatre was a place a middle-class patron hesitated to enter (unless, of course, he was a masher). The MPPC stressed the possibility of lighting set-ups whereby the theatre could be light enough to read a newspaper while the film was projected.[3] In an official announcement, the MPPC declared 'the light theater is one of the most desirable changes that can be made toward the elevation of the motion picture business.'[4]

The MPPC did not single-handedly father this desire to elevate film to the level of middle-class entertainment. The film trade journals reflect this longing for middle-class respectability as well. We find this in their discussion of the film theatres. The trade journals encouraged exhibitors to cater to the creature comforts of their customers, providing such things as iced water,[5] comfortable chairs and proper ventilation.[6] The *Moving Picture World* advised against using sidewalk barkers for film shows, saying 'this sort of thing jars the nerves of refined people.'[7]

The terms 'educational', 'instructive' or 'a moral lesson' appear again and again in the trade journals as a justification of the film medium. The claim that entertainment was in fact educational has long been an important ploy in American culture to justify (or disguise) frivolous pastimes to a middle class still dominated by a puritan ethic. The need for films whose outlook would be acceptable to 'refined people' became a constant theme in trade journals during this period. The National Board of Censorship addressed itself to this issue, but the journals emphasized its finer points. 'Improve your pictures', said *Nickelodeon*, 'and you will improve the class of patrons who come to your theater'.[8] *Moving Picture World* noted that Biograph's *Confidence*, a film without a chase or murder, would appeal to the 'higher class' audience.[9]

Along with the drive to eliminate gruesome melodrama or vulgar comedy, we find during this period a lobbying for the happy ending as a requisite for all films. This enforced optimism seems in tune with the pursuit of a middle-class audience. An editorial in *Nickelodeon* states, 'We are living in a happy, beautiful, virile age ... we do not want sighs or tears. ... We are all seeking happiness – whether through money or position or imagination. It is our privilege to resent any attempts to force unhappy thoughts on us.'[10] The *Moving Picture World* also sounded this theme, saying in one review, 'We object to being made sad in motion picture houses.'[11]

All of this defines the years 1908–9 as the origin of a unified effort to attract the middle class to motion pictures, an effort that extends over the whole span of Griffith's work at Biograph (1908–13). As Russell Merritt has pointed out, these are transition years, when film was still catering to the working class, while wooing the bourgeois.[12] This is the context within which Griffith's Biograph work must be seen: a period of, on the one hand, the economic stabilization of a large industry reaching a mass audience, and on the other hand the decision of that industry that its ultimate stability lay in its attaining social respectability.

Attracting a middle-class audience entailed more than lighting the theatre and brightening the content of the films. The narrative structure of the films would have to be brought more in line with the traditions of bourgeois representation. One of the clearest signs of this is the films made in 1908–9 based on famous plays, novels and poems. Before 1908, the primary sources for films seem to have been vaudeville and burlesque sketches, fairy-tales, comic strips and popular songs. These forms stressed spectacular effects or physical action, rather than psychological motivation. Although still in an elementary form, film now looked towards more respectable narrative models and the problems they entailed.

Many of the adaptations that appeared were greeted with the same complaints by trade journals: the audience did not understand them.[13] Film had not yet developed a narrative style suited to the bourgeois traditions it wished to emulate. The emphasis of earlier films had been on the technical mastery of magical effects (as in the 'trick' films of Méliès and Pathé) and the creation of a unified geography from shot to shot in the chase films. The need now appeared for a series of film techniques that could articulate the narrative elements and involve the audience in their unfolding.

Parallel editing, with its fracturing of the natural continuity of the actions, is one of the most important of these new techniques and the film technique with which the name of Griffith is most clearly tied. Through parallel editing we sense the hand of the storyteller as he moves us from place to place, weaving a new continuity of narrative logic. The development of parallel editing can be seen not simply as the product of Griffith's individual genius, but as a response to the demand for a more complex narrative style. More investigation is needed of the use of parallel editing by other film-makers during this period. It may be that what I have to say about Griffith's style is that it is merely typical of film style of the period. However, my preliminary investigation of other film-makers seems to indicate that Griffith's use of the technique exceeds that of other film-makers and has a larger variety of meanings. This excess and variety of meanings may represent Griffith's movement beyond the style demanded by the times.

Parallel Editing at Biograph: Meanings and Implications

In a lecture at New York University, Noël Burch gave a handy schema for describing the editing of early film. He pointed out that there are three basic spatial relations possible between any two shots. The first, which he called *alterity*, is the movement from one location to an entirely different one (for instance, in Porter's *The Great Train Robbery*, the edit from the girl untying the telegraph operator in his office to the interior of the dance hall). The next possibility – *proximity* – is an edit from one space to a space very near yet different from it. This obviously shades into *alterity*, but a clear example of it would be an edit from a character opening a door in an interior to an exterior shot of the character emerging from the door. Most shot/counter-shot patterns would be examples of *proximity*. The third spatial relation would be for a shot to include part of the space of the preceding shot. The classical example of this would be a cut-in to a close-up of something previously seen in the preceding master shot (e.g. the close-up of the wrench near the end of *The Lonedale Operator*). The cut from such a close-up back to the master shot would also be included in this category. Although Burch does not use this term, I will call this spatial articulation *overlap*.

Parallel editing is a subclass of *alterity*. The traditional definition of the term would be *alterity* with the qualification of simultaneous time for the events within the shots. The classical examples of parallel editing are sequences of shots which alternate from one location, or group of characters, to another, with the indication that the actions are occurring at the same time. Closely related to this strict definition of parallel editing – and in Griffith's Biograph films at points difficult to separate from it – are alternating patterns of shots which do not necessarily happen simultaneously. (Christian Metz's term 'alternating syntagm' in his essay 'Some points in the semiotics of cinema', which would include both patterns, might be useful here. However, Metz later separated the patterns more completely into 'parallel syntagm' and 'alternating syntagm'.[14] The basic structure underlying much of Griffith's editing at Biograph is this pattern of interweaving one location or action with another, of interrupting one line of narrative development by a separate one.

The history of parallel editing before 1908 still needs to be written. Although isolated examples of it appear before 1908 (particularly in European films), it is extremely rare in American films before Griffith. Further research may reveal that the role of Griffith in making it a common element in film narrative will be his strongest claim as one of the fathers of the narrative film style. In any case, by 1909 Griffith structures parallel editing in such a way that the pattern overrides the unfolding of action within individual shots. In 1908 Griffith had already cut between two threads of actions (from rescuers speeding to save victims from some imminent disaster, such as a lynching about to take place, or a mechanically rigged pistol about to go off) to build suspense. With *The Drive for a Life* (1909), Griffith begins to place his edits so that they interrupt the action at a crucial point, in the middle of a gesture. In this film a woman scorned has sent her ex-lover's fiancée a box of poisoned chocolates. The lover finds out and rushes off in a car to warn his fiancée. Griffith cuts from the speeding automobile to the innocent girl at home about to eat the chocolates. At the end of each shot of the fiancée, she is in the middle of an action: holding the chocolate to her lips or opening her mouth. Of course when we cut back to her, she hasn't eaten the chocolate (she is interrupted by her sisters, or drops it, or merely kisses it). Griffith builds suspense, then, not only by cutting away from the dangerous situation, but also by placing his edit at a point where the action is incomplete. The pattern of the editing overrides the natural unfolding of the action. The action's continuity is noticeably interrupted, its unity sliced and its development suspended, by the structure of the shots. One senses, then, the intervention of the storyteller, the manipulator of narrative signs, who directly invokes the audience's participation by withholding – for a moment – the desired information.

Griffith used a structure similar to parallel editing in non-suspense sequences as well. The most famous example of this is in *A Corner in Wheat* (1909). In this film Griffith cuts from the financial gain of the Wheat King to the suffering he causes farmers and the poor. In this case the primary thrust of Griffith's editing is not simultaneity (though that is not ruled out) but contrast (Metz's 'parallel syntagm'). This contrast pattern of editing, alternating rich with poor, is found in a number of Griffith's Biograph films. First sketched in *The*

Song of the Shirt (1908), it also appears in *The Usurer* (1910), *Gold Is Not All* (1910) and *One Is Business, the Other Is Crime* (1912). The interweaving in these films of rich and poor, exploiters and exploited, is articulated by pairs of shots that sharply contrast. The death of a poverty-stricken woman is cut with bosses eating heartily at a restaurant (*The Song of the Shirt*); the Wheat King's lavish entertainment is contrasted with poor people unable to buy bread (*A Corner in Wheat*); a poor couple play with their children while a rich woman's daughter dies (*Gold Is Not All*). The intervention here of the storyteller allows the creation of a moral voice, who not only involves the audience in reading the narrative signs – recognizing the contrast – but also instructs them by causing them to draw a moral conclusion.

It is interesting to note that, in *The Usurer*, a 1910 near remake of *A Corner in Wheat*, Griffith combines this contrast pattern with the practice of suspending the outcome of an action by an edit. In one shot we see Henry Walthall as a poor man ruined by the Usurer's greed. He stands alone in his apartment, points a gun to his breast, and shuts his eyes. We cut to the Usurer at a lavish party raising his glass. We return to Walthall staggering and falling dead on the floor. The pattern here is very interesting. On the one hand we have the structure, already established in the film, of contrasting the evil joys of the rich with the miseries of the poor. In addition, we have the intensification given by interrupting actions (both the pistol shot and the Usurer's raised glass; in the shot following Walthall's death we return to the Usurer as he drinks). The editing pattern (and particularly the ellipses of the actual firing of the gun, which presumably occurs while we see the usurer raise his glass) certainly seems to indicate simultaneity. The edit involves a degree of suspense, but since no rescue is attempted this is not the main effect of the edit. The ironic juxtaposition with its indication of cause and effect becomes the principal meaning. Later in the film, Griffith cuts from the Usurer, accidentally locked in his own safe and beginning to suffocate, to Walthall's dead body, underscoring the irony.

In Griffith's later Biograph films, some form of alternating pattern increasingly underlies the narrative form, even in cases that don't involve suspense or contrast. In 1912 and 1913, the first two shots frequently introduce two characters (or two groups of characters) before they have actually met. The characters' stories will be intercut in the opening sections of the film until a scene where they are finally narratively linked. Such interweaving seems to be Griffith's basic narrative schema. Griffith also further articulates its use for dramatic effects. In *A Woman Scorned* (1911), Griffith uses interruption of an action and contrast to accent an act of violence. A doctor (Wilfred Lucas) has been lured to an apartment by a gang of thieves who knock him unconscious. As he falls, we cut from this action to his wife and child at home sitting down to supper. In this shot, the father's empty place at the table is prominent in the left foreground. Although one might be dubious that this is intentional (similar structuring of space across edits in other Biograph films leads me to think that it is), it is worth pointing out that this empty place occupies the same area of the frame that Lucas collapsed into in the previous shot.

Later in the same film, Griffith enhances a contrast edit by presenting two radically opposed but visually similar actions. He cuts from the mother untying her daughter's shoes as she lies on her bed to the thieves tying a gag on Lucas, who is also lying in bed. By this kind of visual rhyming, Griffith develops a visual structure that overlays and articulates the narrative action taking place in the shots themselves. This elaboration of the formal elements of the shots beyond the necessary narrative information is one of the clearest examples of Griffith's tendency to make the storyteller evident to the audience. The act of arranging narrative information becomes as important as simply conveying it.

During the Biograph period, Griffith's use of patterns of alternating shots takes on several meanings, usually distinguishable from each other, but at points shading into one another, as though not yet moulded into rigid formulas. The meanings of parallel editing patterns become particularly complex when they are used in relation to the psychological development of characters. Very early in his career appears a type of parallel editing based on the thoughts of his characters. Here we can see Griffith using parallel editing to provide one of the most basic *desiderata* of a bourgeois narrative – psychological motivation. By the intercutting of disparate locations and characters within certain narrative contexts, Griffith creates, as it were, a sort of psychological space. Significantly, its first use is in an adaptation of a respected literary source, his 1908 version of Tennyson's *Enoch Arden, After Many Years*.

The intercutting of the faithful wife at home with her distant shipwrecked husband provides one of Griffith's first cuts on action. As the husband on his desert island kisses his wife's locket, we cut back to her standing on her porch, arms outstretched, as if yearning for her absent husband; the splicing together of the gestures metaphorically unites the characters across vast space. Later in the Biograph period, Griffith's editing frequently joins characters separated in space. The vehicle of these connections is often a prayer (*The Fugitive*, *The Broken Locket*, *The Last Deal*, *A Pueblo Legend*). Many shots of this sort include a token of the absent person, a locket or necklace, which the characters gaze at as they long for reunion (*Rose of Salem Town*, *The Broken Locket*, *After Many Years*). This pattern is often combined not only with an interrupted action (like the kiss in *After Many Years*), but also with a contrast. In *The Fugitive*, for instance, we cut from a mother praying, to her son's death on the battlefield. The defining quality of the parallel editing in these instances is its participation in the characters' desires; the motive for the editing springs from their desire to cross space and join their loved ones. Through the editing their emotional union is stressed along with their physical separation.

There are films in which the expression of an emotional sympathy between separated characters takes on a nearly supernatural overtone. This is especially true in those cuts where the simultaneity of events is stressed. In both *As It Is in Life* (1910) and *In Life's Cycle* (1910), Griffith cuts from a pair of lovers embracing to a male relative of the girl far removed from the scene. The relatives (who in both films disapprove of their girl's lover) suddenly look very disturbed or shiver involuntarily. When we return in the following shot to the couple of *In Life's Cycle*, the girl too suddenly looks upset, as if aware of her brother's distant disapproval.

In *Sunshine Sue* (1910), Griffith expresses this type of emotional connection over distances through composition as well as editing. A beloved daughter (Marion Sunshine) is first introduced playing the piano for her parents. Later in the film she is stranded, penniless, in a big city. Getting a job at a music store, she is preyed upon by the store's manager. Upset, she leans against a piano in the left foreground of the shot and weeps. Griffith cuts to her father in the family parlour looking at a piano (which is associated with the daughter from the first shot) and patting it fondly. Not only do both shots contain pianos, both pianos occupy the left foreground of the frame. Through this edit and the similar arrangement of space in each shot, Griffith transfers the father's caress from the piano to his distant daughter who occupies the same area of the frame in the preceding shot.

Less dramatic than these shots of emotional union, but perhaps more revealing of the psychological meanings Griffith derived from parallel editing, is what I will call the 'motive shot'. An early example of this kind of editing appears in *A Salvation Army Lass* (1908). A tough (Harry Salter) has scorned his girlfriend's (Florence Lawrence) attempt to dissuade him from joining a burglary with his cronies, and has knocked her down. As he and his gang creep along the edge of a building, he suddenly stops and looks offscreen. Griffith cuts to a brief shot of Lawrence still on the ground. In the next shot we return to Salter, who changes his mind about the burglary, hands his gun back to his companions, and leaves the frame. The editing pattern articulates and explains Salter's decision. It splits in two the moment when Salter changes his course of action, interrupting it with a shot of the factor that causes the change. The editing portrays a mental act and supplies a motive for the action ('He thinks of his true love . . .').

However, it is the double nature of this shot which reveals the still fluid stage in the evolution of film syntax which characterizes Griffith's Biograph films. The shot of Lawrence is not univocally defined as a mental image, released from the objective space and time of the diegesis. The use of parallel editing remains an intervention of the storyteller who 'points out' the character's motivation, rather than assigning the shot unambiguously to the subjectivity of the character. Salter's offscreen look could define the shot of Lawrence as an awkward sort of point-of-view shot. Or we could stress the simultaneity of the shot and see it as a strict parallel edit, conveying the information of what is happening to Lawrence as Salter sets off on the burglary. But since it neither offers new narrative information (at most it tells us that Lawrence is *still* lying there), nor develops a suspense situation, its articulation of Salter's decision remains its primary effect.

This three-shot pattern frequently recurs in Griffith's Biograph films to portray a decision by a character. Its appearance in *A Plain Song* (1910) is typical. A girl (Mary Pickford) is leaving her aged parents and running off with a carnival man. At the train station, she sees a group of old people being taken off to the poor house. Struck by the scene, Pickford stands motionless in the foreground. Griffith cuts to her parents at home. We then return to Pickford, still frozen in her previous position. The carnival man approaches with the train tickets, but she turns away from him and runs home. Again the interpolated shot of the parents articulates and motivates a decision. In this case there is no possibility of its being a point-of-view shot. Mary's frozen stance, as if she were in deep thought, also stresses the psychological nature of the shot. We can find the same pattern in *The Sands O'Dee* (1912). Mae Marsh has decided not to keep an arranged meeting with an artist on the beach. She stands motionless by her window. We cut to a shot of the artist wrapped in a shawl, waiting at the beach. We cut back to Mae, who apparently has changed her mind and climbs out of her window to keep the assignation.

In both these instances, we must hesitate before we describe the interpolated shot purely as a mental image. Pickford's parents *are* waiting at home for her, and the artist *is* waiting on the beach for Mae. The shot of the artist includes details that Mae could not 'imagine', such as his paisley shawl. The shots therefore are also parallel edits to events occurring at the same time. This dual role of expressions of the characters' thoughts and parallel edits to autonomous events shows the still pliable nature of Griffith's film syntax at this point.

Interestingly, in 1913, we find Griffith modifying this pattern, probably in order to present the interpolated shot more unequivocally as a mental image. In the opening of *Death's Marathon* (1913), a clerk (Walter Miller) looks up from his work with a dreamy expression. The next shot begins extremely underexposed and then brightens in a camera-made 'fade-in'. We see a girl (Blanche Sweet) seated on a bench in a garden facing the camera in a rather static posture (this is her first appearance in the film). The shot fades and we return to Miller, who rouses himself as if to shake off his reverie and return to work. The use of fades and the actionless shot of Sweet seem to signal the shot as Miller's mental image, rather than a parallel edit which indicates that Sweet is sitting in a garden at this precise moment. It is in this way that Griffith presents memories in *The Birth of a Nation*, by a thoughtful look of a character and an interpolated shot bracketed by fades. The fades signal an entrance into another dimension, that of unequivocal mental images. However, even this example is not an unambiguous image of a single character's subjectivity. The three shots from *Death's Marathon* just described are themselves bracketed by two shots of Walthall, who plays a co-worker of Miller. Walthall too is in love with Sweet, and this rivalry forms the basic dynamic of the plot. At the end of the first shot of Walthall he pauses. When we return to him after the shots of Miller and Sweet, he too seems to be emerging from a daydream. The shot of Sweet, then, could be interpreted as a shared mental image. Again the pattern seems to be a gesture of the storyteller unwilling to relinquish the authority of the image to the subjectivity of any one character.

Griffith's use of parallel editing in the films at Biograph created not only a narrative form, but a form of narration, a storyteller to tell the story. Through parallel editing Griffith could create suspense by interrupting action and delaying information, make moral judgments, underscore characters' desires, and reveal motivation. All of these techniques fulfilled essential conditions for a new bourgeois narrative form, the rival of theatre and the novel.

However, the process of fulfilling these demands does not explain away all effects of the technique. The multiple meanings gained from this one technique in different situations show something of its enormous power and far-reaching implications. By breaking the continuity of actions, by composing similar frames that are separated in space, by interpolating shots in the middle of decisions, Griffith both creates a fissure in the continuity of the narrative and forms a synthesis on a new level. Griffith's editing becomes a noticeable force which suspends, interrupts and yet knits together actions within his narratives. What is sensed behind this narrative labour is the storyteller. This invisible but sensed hand will reach its apogee in Griffith's commercial disaster *Intolerance*. The 'uniter of here and hereafter' will prove an obstacle to much of his audience, a frustration rather than a guide. Already towards the end of his tenure at Biograph the trade journals (which had praised some of his earlier films for their 'high class' appeal) were finding his style too disjoined, too brutal, and were complaining about the large number of shots in Biograph films, the disorienting nature of their editing.[15] This kind of dissatisfaction may have had a role in the tension between company executives and Griffith that led to his leaving Biograph in 1913.

Increasingly in the feature era, the storyteller would blend indistinguishably into the unfolding of the action of the narrative, and Griffith's style would be found old-fashioned or clumsy. Writing the history of this process and the many factors that contribute to it – the rise of the studio style as pioneered by Ince, the importance of film stars, and a new economic organization of the film industry – will require a great deal of new research. Griffith's place within that history is complex. But it is clear that Griffith's development of parallel editing during the Biograph years opens a tradition that not only moves towards the invisible editing of the classical Hollywood narrative, but also to (as he was the first to admit) the radical understanding of montage in the films of Sergei Eisenstein.

Notes

First published in *Quarterly Review of Film Studies*, Winter 1981.

1. *Moving Picture World*, vol. 5, pp. 82, 84.
2. Russell Merritt, 'The films of D. W. Griffith and their social impact (1908–1915)', unpublished Ph.D. dissertation, Harvard University, p. 196.
3. *The Edison Kinetogram*, 15 October 1909, p. 2.
4. *Moving Picture World*, vol. 4, p. 631.
5. *Nickelodeon*, vol. 2, p. 5.
6. Ibid. vol. 2, p. 101.
7. *Moving Picture World*, vol. 5, p. 443.
8. *Nickelodeon*, vol. 2, p. 13.
9. *Moving Picture World*, vol. 4, p. 476.
10. *Nickelodeon*, vol. 2, p. 135.
11. *Moving Picture World*, vol. 5, p. 278.
12. Merritt, 'The films of D. W. Griffith', pp. 196–8.

13. See, for example, the reviews of Edison's productions of Molnar's *The Devil* and Halm's *Ingomar* in the *New York Dramatic Mirror*, 19 September 1908, p. 9, and *Moving Picture World*, vol. 3, p. 231, respectively.
14. Christian Metz, *Film Language* (New York: Oxford University Press, 1974), p. 104.
15. Samples of such reviews can be found in George Pratt, *Spellbound in Darkness* (Greenwich, Conn., 1973), pp. 95–105.

Griffith: the Frame, the Figure

JACQUES AUMONT

I am constantly told that Griffith is a film-maker who is nothing less than the inventor of the art of cinema. Who tells me this? Jean Mitry, for instance:

> Without exaggerating in the least, one can say that if the cinema owes its existence as a means of analysis and reproduction of movement (and therefore as an entertainment form and an entertainment industry) to Louis Lumière, it is to Griffith that it owes its existence as an art form, as a means of expression and of signification.[1]

But these words could just as easily have come from any historian of the cinema, even from Eisenstein, who, in a famous passage,[2] put Griffith forward as the inventor of film montage and the inheritor of the great literary and novelistic traditions of narrative.

I do not intend to reiterate the critique of such a view of history, or of the cinema, written around the exploits of great men. But among the mythologies of Griffith, I am struck by one constant feature, which I think may be the principal reason for the limited number of serious studies (and to be honest, for their generally low theoretical standard) written on Griffith in France, at least before 1980. I am of course referring to the absolutely teleological predication of these descriptions. There is virtually nothing in the Griffith myths that is not determined by what he is supposed to have founded: the 'classical' narrative cinema, the cinema of transparency, naturalisation (and the industrial mode). This Griffith, inventor of narrative forms, embodiment of a sort of 'golden age' of narrative, is to the various histories of the cinema what Abraham is to the Bible – the necessary Patriarch.

Of course, I do not want to risk toppling this monument too hastily. First, I am not a Griffith 'specialist' (for one thing, I do not know all of his 450-odd films). Second, there is probably an element of truth in this image, however simplistic and limiting it may be: as Pierre Baudry puts it so well,

> [Griffith's inventions] represent a transformation of cinematographic fiction as such, that is, basically, a displacement of its intertextual status: that which the short films of D.W.G. inaugurate and *Intolerance* rearticulates, is, roughly speaking, the formation of a rhetorical machinery which uses the cinema for effects analogous no longer to those of photography and the theatre, but of the novel.[3]

What are these 'inventions'? To name a few at random: alternating editing and parallel editing, the latter culminating in the interweaving of the episodes of *Intolerance*, the former constituting the veritable system of closure in the shorts; the rigorous coding of the procedures of the happy ending; the hierarchisation of shot-scales, and notably the close-up itself, functioning as a signifying link in the representative chain, and no longer merely as a descriptive insert, etc. etc. Not only are these techniques far from negligible, but it is indisputable that in Griffith's work one finds them truly exploited, refined and perfected.

Nonetheless, whatever caution one employs in the formulation, it seems to me that by discussing Griffith from this single point of view, one always ends up limiting his cinema to that of being the *pre*cursor, or the *pre*monition of another cinema, that of evidence and of immediacy, whose theorisation will later be promoted under the name of Bazin, with his idea of 'transparency' – and which years of cinephilia have accustomed us to associating 'spontaneously' with *the* cinema. This attitude freezes Griffith's work, and, among other consequences, leads to the position (absurd as it may seem) of making us defend his films *despite* and *against* their own stories,[4] and only appreciate them for their value as formal narrative models. As if this gradual establishing of a narrative apparatus, and the fairly strictly circumscribed fictional themes accompanying it, did not mutually determine one another: the happy ending is the microstructure of the story, and as such is overcoded. But it is also the necessary form of an ideology of reconciliation. Likewise, variations in the scale of shots, as is well known, bring about a *humanist* marking of the human figure, while alternating editing functions as a demonstration of the law of causality (no effect without a cause, and often, no cause without an effect) which organises these stories.

What actually strikes me when watching Griffith's films again is less this narrative apparatus and these themes, and instead the truly quite stupendous (stupendous, too, in that it has attracted so little attention) work on the framing, the placing of the actors, their gestures, in short, on what used to be called the *mise en scène* and which affects the representation.[5]

Without wishing to replace one mythical image by another, and without claiming to give a definitive answer to this question (which would amount to having finally written the history of the cinema), I propose to show in what ways this work of representation in Griffith forces us to reconsider the generally held view about his work, starting with remarks on the treatment of space in some of the Biograph shorts.

Locations

In Griffith's films, there is an ostensible, indeed ostentatious, paradigmatic paucity of locations; the shorts with which I am dealing (those that I have seen) are usually content with two or three different locations.

I shall take the first example which comes to mind. The basis of the story in *Friends* (1912) consists of a series of encounters between three protagonists, two people at a time. All except one of the encounters take place in or in front of the saloon. Pushing this economy still further, *The Battle* (1911) stages its story by a series of back-and-forths between the inside and outside of Blanche

Sweet's house. Thus the battle which gives the film its title takes place in front of this house, where previously (in diegetic time) soldiers had paraded before leaving for war.[6] Even more striking is the beach in *Enoch Arden* (the 1911 version) where, from angles which hardly vary, successively both Annie Lee's waiting takes place and Enoch's landing on the shores that shipwrecked him: the height of narrative economy, with a single profilmic location serving two diegetically distinct story spaces.

This play of quotations could be extended without introducing major variations to the principle (no doubt, there are exceptions . . .). I can see an obvious objection: that this is due to the production conditions of the films, and nothing else. Wedged between the four walls of the studio, and the four days of filming, Griffith scarcely had the leisure to refine the set-ups – it is already quite something that from time to time he took his camera outside! I am not underestimating this determining factor, in the last instance an economic one. However, if I insist on the significance of this poverty of the referential stock of locations in Griffith's work, it is because it seems to me part of what I would term the *figurative closure* of the film (of each film).

The idea needs supporting, if only statistically, and deepening. But even as it stands, it does, I believe, show how in this type of cinema, everything basically happens as if a single location (a small number of locations) were sufficient to contain a whole fiction (all the fictions in the world), demonstrating the profoundly anti-naturalistic character of this *mise en scène*. We will see in what follows how this figurative closure could be described in more detail, but here I would merely underline that for me it is the polar opposite of what the cinema of 'transparency' leads to when taken to its logical extreme: so-called *cinéma-vérité*, which is very precisely defined by the search for a relationship with 'the world' in which every profilmic element must be represented as unique. This does not mean that the classical cinema could not also be described as 'closed' in its turn (moreover, with a 'closure' more fictional, thematic, indeed spatial, than properly figurative). But it seems to me that it is never archetypal to the same degree in its representations, which means that Griffith's representations foreground the adventures of the scenery rather than the adventures of the characters.

Irrespective of the deep and essential artifice which is the foundation of classical cinema, its distinctive feature is always to maintain the impression that we are looking at the characters, and that their 'life' permits us, at least potentially, to go and 'occupy' any space whatever. It is not a question of denying that this attachment to the characters happens when we watch Griffith's films: but the prevailing impression here is always – and it is undoubtedly accentuated by the way the codes, notably those of gesture and mimicry, have dated – of a kind of centripetal force which insists on aligning the character with a framing, itself defined according to a certain conformity with the décor. Is this figurative primacy of the set over the character a mere figment of my imagination? Of course. But no more than another illusion, its inverse, into which the classical cinema lulls us – that the 'hero' exists prior to his setting, indeed, that he chooses it.[7]

With Griffith's work at Biograph[8] we are in a cinema where the theatre (as far as a certain theatre can be conceived of as a spatial receptacle functioning universally) is still quite close, where the set is only a set, where the scene does not have to appear real and can calmly refer only to itself.

Closure

Let us take this a step further. I will go as far as to say that almost all these places of fiction and figuration present themselves as closed, which has the effect of closing space not just at the level of the film, but of each frame. This is clear in the interior sequences (more numerous, it would appear), filmed as if 'in the theatre', from the point of view of the missing fourth wall, the point of view of the 'spectator in the stalls', of whom we know that he is also the person whose place was determined once and for all with the invention of the laws of pictorial perspective.

But still more striking, because still less 'natural', is this effect when it produces itself (or when it foregrounds itself, since for me it is never absent) in exterior shots. The first point to be made is that these 'exteriors' are often shot in the studio, which gives them a certain deliberate falseness, a delimitation often marked *within* the frame by crowds or buildings. But, even when this frame pretends to open on to an outside world, we remember that there are, so to speak, never any master shots in Griffith's work at Biograph as if, perhaps to put it a little sketchily, everything was always measured by the human figure, as if, in the manner of the 'American' medium shot, everything was always seen from that kind of distance.

Let's take a closer look. I will pick (not at random, but almost) *An Unseen Enemy*, a lovely short film of 1912, fairly typical of the 'Biograph system' and, moreover, famous. As is the rule, the end of the film comprises a 'rescue': the brother of the two girls held captive by the villains rushes to the rescue in a car with two other men. A series of shots shows us the car moving at full speed: suddenly, there is a medium shot of the three men, filmed frontally (as are all interior shots), a shot which abstracts the three figures from their pursuit, a shot closed in on itself, with no horizon, coming at an unexpected moment to remind us, as it were, of this centring of the representation on the human figures.[9]

It seems to me that the oddity of the effect which this insistent closure produces is not laid to rest by referring us back to its theatrical origin. The frame, for instance, is underlined and marked as such, by innumerable figurative artifices (starting with the systematic exploration of the interior of the shots by the protagonists themselves, who cross it in every direction, stopping of their own accord just at its edges, as if to show these edges even more clearly, unless they go as far as actually scanning the edges[10]). This frame is of course a metaphor of the proscenium arch of classical theatre in the Italian style. Let us extend the metaphor – it lends itself to it. The lateral edges of the frame are constantly used as true wings, permitting exits and entrances from the field (not, as will be the obsession of 'classical' cinema, to ensure a perfect and reversible communication with an imaginary offscreen space, as a homogeneous and isotropic extension of the screen, but as a simple 'putting the actors on hold':

that is, as theatrical wings).

Let's test this with specific examples, a shot from the above-mentioned *Unseen Enemy*. The frame in question occurs in the film on three occasions, punctuating it by its appearances, playing the role of a sort of fulcrum. This is the frame that the brother appears in for the first time (at this stage bringing the money), but the second time it occurs, its use is more complex. The two girls come in with their brother, from the left: the brother goes off to the right, and immediately (he was waiting in the wings), Robert Harron, the somewhat silly suitor of Dorothy Gish, enters also from the left: exits and entrances (I haven't described everything) which unequivocally denote their status, precisely, as exits and entrances: that is, as a movement from a certain type of space (the area where the play takes place, where a narration is inscribed) to another (offscreen: the wings, where another action takes place, that of production, radically different from the preceding one). Let us look at this frame again: the slight tilting of the camera (a remarkably constant feature in this type of scene in Griffith) has, among others, the effect of lowering the top edge of the frame. No more 'air', no horizon, only a sort of line (the crest of trees) which comes to reinforce and designate this edge. At the bottom of the frame we notice a symmetrically related phenomenon: a daringly arbitrary framing eliminates from the scene all trace of what, referentially speaking, might explain and naturalise the entrances and exits. There is no road, not even any ground, despite the tilting of the camera. Totally blocked off, top and bottom, open, but not transparent at the sides, this is the kind of frame which, despite its 'external' referent, typifies the closure I am referring to.[11]

The Double Space

> When Mr. Griffith suggested a scene showing Annie Lee waiting for her husband's return to be followed by a scene of Enoch cast away on a desert island, it was altogether too distracting. 'How can you tell a story jumping about like that? The people won't know what it's about.'
>
> 'Well,' said Mr. Griffith, 'doesn't Dickens write that way?'
>
> 'Yes, but that's Dickens, that's novel-writing; that's different.'
>
> 'Oh, not so much, these are picture stories: not so different.'[12]

For the film historian this cinematic copying of an avowedly novelistic method (something which 'started' with Griffith) is indeed remarkable. But let's look at it again; let's see, for example, how this juxtaposition of scenes functions in the famous *Enoch Arden* (the 1911 version):

Shot 1: Annie Lee, pacing up and down on the beach, where Enoch had set sail much earlier on. Suddenly, she has a kind of premonition, her expression changes completely, she stares wide-eyed and fixedly.

Shot 2: Enoch and his companions are swimming in the midst of rocks which have just sunk their ship, in a raging sea.

Or, again, a little further on:

Shot 1: Annie Lee is waiting on the same beach, telescope in hand. She is scanning the horizon.
Shot 2: Enoch, on the beach of his desert island, glimpses in the distance the boat which is to save him.

One could add further examples. What do they show? I believe that for a modern reader, the really surprising thing in this 'link' between the two spaces is less the jump than the continuity. Here is the film text showing me two spaces which are diegetically heterogeneous (England and far-off islands) not only as similar (and with reason, since they were shot in exactly the same place!), but as *contiguous*: a contiguity which in the first case is marked by the relationship between the look of Annie Lee and what she cannot see, but which she lets us see, literally; in the second case by the similarity between the two situations, as if the homology between the situations reduces their imaginary distance. (A variant of the same effect should be mentioned here: the absolute similarity, of framing and location, between the respective shots in which Enoch first embarks on his long journey, then sees his rescuers, and finally sets foot again on English soil.)

My attention thus returns again to the fact that Griffith here fully dons the mantle of his role as precursor, and even, in this respect, kills two birds with one stone: he 'invents' nothing less than parallel editing, while he undeniably lays down the principles of what is to become perhaps the essential basis of the treatment of space in Hollywood narrative cinema. Heterogeneous out of necessity (the fragmentation of a profilmic continuity which is also, phantasmatically, referential, as the exigencies of narrative production demand it); and ceaselessly rehomogenised by a thousand tricks: as is well known, this, amongst other things, is the meaning of the famous notion of 'continuity' which still holds sway in editing rooms.

But there remains the fact that Griffith does nothing to hide the white threads which sew the frames together: on the contrary, he makes much of them, flaunts them, puts a great deal of emphasis on them, marks them with a whole signifying apparatus. Just think of Annie Lee's expression, bulging eyes, fixed, 'Expressionist'.

The *code* which here is still in the early stages of constituting itself, this code of continuity, has since become familiar to us to the point of nausea, because it is the code in charge of naturalising figurative space. Griffith, who marks the film with conscious, articulated traces of his stylistic signature, is therefore in a way (still) beyond the code: for us, too, he is thus outside the code. To convince oneself of this, it would be sufficient to search out the traces of an undoubted *return of Griffith* in certain modern films. Return *of* Griffith, that is of an entire scenic system for a long time repressed by the dominant ideology, that of the classic *mise en scène*, and now taken up again in view of 'overcoming' or 'deconstructing' this same classic cinema:[13] but this is in no way, of course, a return *to* Griffith (understood regressively, as a step backwards).

Once More

In *An Unseen Enemy*, the two young heroines, recently orphaned, are locked in a room for the whole of the end of the film, while in the next room a burglar, brought in by the treacherous maid, is trying to open the safe. The gag of the film (which has been a major factor in its celebrity) is the famous circular hole which establishes, arbitrarily with regard to verisimilitude, a connection between the two rooms, one through which the maid passes her hand, armed with a revolver. One of the two sisters nevertheless succeeds, after many a setback, which are the brakes and catalysts of the story, in calling their brother on the telephone for help, thus setting in motion the ending according to the model of the high-speed chase.

It is more than tempting to read this as a fairly transparent metaphor of Griffith's own *mise en scène*. The scene is closed, it literally encloses its characters (the two girls, locked up by the maid) who, during the fifteen or twenty shots they will spend there, will, moreover, have the time to explore the whole width of the frame, and the whole depth of the scene, thereby physically marking the closure of their living space. There is, however, one way out of this prison of the frame: the telephone. It will in fact, as in many of the short Biograph films, be used to raise the alarm.[14] But not any old way: the scene has a system to its spatial orientation. If at the start of the film it was still possible to leave the frame to the left, to go into the 'contiguous' room, one will easily see the logic of the telephone, means of communication with the 'exterior' of the house, being situated on the right of the same frame – and that, extending the system, the character at the other end of the line will occupy the extreme left of his own frame. This is another example of communications from one frame to another, and more generally, from a frame to what is outside it, which are, as can be seen, anything but instances of classical continuity.

And perhaps, by way of parenthesis, one might permit oneself to give an interpretation of this astonishing intrusion of offscreen space, represented by the revolver. It has been remarked,[15] in the context of *Intolerance*: in Griffith's cinema, 'partir, c'est toujours mourir un peu' ('to leave is always to die a little') and leaving the scene signifies at least potentially the death of the character. What closes the scene, via the frame, is in a sense this threat of death, always implicitly and metaphorically proffered from beyond the frame. The revolver of *An Unseen Enemy* can, God knows, be read in more ways than one, but besides its thematic value (signifying the villains), and its symbolic value (a phallic symbol, if ever there was one),[16] plastic, scenic (with close-up – see below), can we not still see in it the literal agent of this threat, openly articulated in this way?

Depth

Let's take once more some 'fragments' (in Eisenstein's terminology) from two Griffith texts: two shots from *Friends* and one from *The Lonely Villa* (1909). What happens in them? Among other things, that the heroes at one point pass directly in front of an opening, deep, perspectivally marked, and above all inhabited. Extras, busy dancing, driving in stakes, pushing wheelbarrows, are gesticulating energetically in this space. Thus for a moment, superimposed on the principal fictional trajectory, a second fiction appears, erratic and mysterious, of which we will never know more than what we see here – which is, nothing.

The clear value, from the point of view of the code, of this opening up of a beyond on the 'principal' fictional line, is to lend weight to the idea that this 'background noise' is not just that, that it has its own laws, that it too could form the object of a narration. In short, its value, in a movement which is fairly familiar to us, trained by Hollywood, is to anchor the founding illusion of all filmic representation a little more firmly in a supposed reality – according to the banal idea that film is a representation of 'life', where events are not dissociated from their background. The inter-text here is well established: we know that Lumière's single-shot films often conjoined, arising from the vagaries of the shooting, a counterpoint of independent events: and later on, as we know too, the Bazinian discourse of the 'more than real' served to justify the 'ontological' vocation of the cinema towards a certain analogical realism.

Once again here is a Griffith pulled by his 'successors' on to the side of transparency, to an immediate reflection of the 'world out there'. And yet, even here, I can't really believe in the naturalness of it all. Everything holds me back: the gestural excesses of the actors (which are far from being solely attributable to the so-called 'failings' of the silent cinema); the compressed nature of the composition which carefully superimposes the 'principal' intrigue and the 'secondary' actions; the systematic relegation of the latter to the back of the tableau, whose perspective they designate at the same time as they block it; the equally systematic surveying of the fictional depth by the protagonist (staking it out as one stakes out a territory); and last but not least, their sheer quantity. It is impossible to consider all these figures, packed into the enclosure of the frame, as characters. They are the teeming, arabesque part of the set. Nowhere can this over-occupation of the scenic space (the frame) be better observed than in a composition from *Musketeers of Pig Alley*, shared by several shots, but at one moment empty of players, and in the next shot full to bursting point.[17] One could not dream of a more convincing illustration of what was said earlier about the primacy, the priority of the décor. This set, with its all-embracing frame and its depth, is a sort of apparatus for swallowing up, devouring and trapping the characters.

Be that as it may, all this is more than enough to stop the work of production from effacing itself, the indispensable condition of our notion of verisimilitude. These supplementary elements of figuration, these excessive scraps of the imaginary, appear by the very excess of their inscription for what they are: patchwork, collage, montage. (If you like, the famous 'montage within the frame' so dear to Eisenstein – although the link is a little strained, despite Eisenstein's explicit reference to Griffith, since as we know, montage within the frame has a completely different function for Eisenstein. But at least the reference has the advantage of distancing us radically from Bazin.) Once again, therefore, and as we have already noted in respect of 'continuity', we find a highly coded work of representation, and above all one which declares its coded nature, designating itself expressly as a convention, as writing.

The Close-up

It is banal to include the close-up amongst Griffith's inventions, or at least a certain use of the close-up, since, as Mitry pointed out, Griffith was not the first person to use it. But it is in his work all the same (and in that of Ince) that it begins to escape from the role of pure functional repetition of a detail supposedly not clearly seen in the shot as a whole, to become a fully signifying unit in the narrative discourse (acquiring, as Mitry says, dramatic value).

So be it. Griffith, promoter of the close-up which carries dramatic function and value, why not – to the extent that it has been inserted as an indubitable link into the chain of transformations of this so-called 'cinematographic language'. However, the close-up in Griffith's work, as elsewhere, is that which functions precisely as *extra-* (extra-scenic, for example) and, as such, is a sign of the discontinuity of the discourse, at once already perforated in order to facilitate the fetishistic cutting up of the body of the text, and an index, in the narrative fabric itself, of the principle of discontinuity enshrined in editing.

The close-up is used, firstly, as an excess of representation, sometimes unbearable (think of the mouth, distorted to the limits of the possible, of Brown Eyes, the heroine of the 'Saint-Bartholomew' episode in *Intolerance*, at the moment when she is about to die – think of her eyes, those of a strangled rabbit, rolling in the corners of their sockets), sometimes loaded with a certain 'obscenity' (like the round and dirty end of the shoe pressing on the accelerator in *Intolerance*[18]) but always, in any case, interpellating the spectator directly and brutally. This interpellation of course takes on the most diverse forms – we are simply looked at by the photograph of Lionel Barrymore, itself contemplated by Mary Pickford in *Friends*; one is stared at by the famous revolver of *An Unseen Enemy* which, having hesitated for a long time, suddenly turns its black and threatening muzzle towards us; we are transfixed by the slow and continuous advance, into a big close-up, of the face of the 'Musketeer' of Pig Alley, which invades, now horribly ugly, the whole height of the screen.

And, more generally, Griffith uses the close-up as an excess of writing; the close-up, like the juxtaposition within the frame of which we have already spoken, is a rhetorical figure of montage, making sense outside the causal and naturalising chain[19] (however much one tries to re-attach it). It is of the order of an almost caricatural hyper-articulated writing, in a sense the grimace of the filmic text (grimace: alteration to the continuity and homogeneity of the most quietly expressive text, the face).

It is therefore not without good reason that I propose to read in the same vein, but in long shot this time (that is, at the level of textual figuration generally), the grimaces which affect, not the representational discourse, but those who figure in it: nervous tics (Battling Butler in *Broken Blossoms*), distortions (the mouth of Brown Eyes), excessive make-up (the brother in *An Unseen Enemy*), deformations (the villain's head in *Musketeers of Pig Alley*), etc. The grimace (*grimage*/make-up – the slip is tempting) might have as its eponymous figure the smile which *advertises* itself, producing itself artificially before our very eyes, like Lillian Gish's in *Broken Blossoms*: a heavy, opaque and manufactured display.

Griffith and Us

What is basically at issue in the whole 'narrative-representational' cinema? It is to make an imaginary world come to life by way of an illusion, and in order to do this, to build out of certain figurative elements a representational chain, to provide for and to articulate the place of the spectator-subject somewhere in this chain.

We know, moreover, how the cinema to which we are overwhelmingly accustomed, goes about it: what has been called *suture* is nothing other than the trick of allowing the spectator precisely to be included in the chain as subject, by the device of the look.

Griffithian representation, whilst just as coherent and systematic, uses other means, thus obtaining very specific reality effects, often very disconcerting. Generally speaking, one could say that in his work the spectator's position is designated in an infinitely more explicit way. We have seen a major example of this with the 'interpellations' produced by the close-ups. But without doubt the succession of closed tableaux which is so typical of his shots is, paradoxically (since to us who read it retrospectively, it has the effect of fragmenting the discourse), the most constant means of this inclusion of the spectator, even if it is only the frontal nature of the filming, and the insistent focusing on the absent fourth wall which it brings about (faces turned in towards the camera, participants moving, on the contrary, according to a rigorous laterality, sweeping against the surface of the screen). What is thus drawn, whether directly or not, is the imaginary line running from our eye to the screen.

This line is all the more perceptible for being underlined still further by Griffith's staging in depth. We have seen how this depth was described, in both senses of the word, by certain figures. We must add here that depth, quite frequently, is moreover literally polarised and orientated towards the spectator-eye. I will give just one example, to illustrate what I mean. In *An Unseen Enemy*, the rescuers' car must, in a first frame, 'move away from us' (by leaving the brother's office to disappear into the depth of the shot), then in a series of other frames, 'come towards us' (approach us at the same time as the – fictional – place of the rescue). Without mentioning the even clearer instances where this polarisation is combined with the effects of the close-up (the villain who leaves the frame 'under our very eyes', the revolver pointing at us).

To sum up then. We have, all along the way, pointed out that Griffith's cinema could not care less about that 'unique' moment which, by contrast, is the pride and glory of the cinema for someone like Bazin – the moment in *Louisiana Story* when the crocodile devours the heron, or when an unexpected and authentic tear rolls down the actor's face. . . . In Griffith's work, the actor must not be moved to tears: it would spoil the make-up; the wild beast can be stuffed or tamed – and the location is merely a simulacrum which can be reused an infinite number of times: a tool, and nothing more. The figurative closure of the text is obviously for us a closure on the text – like the production of a sort of less-than-real, in the last instance sacrificing the 'immanent ambiguity of the real'[20] for a direct representation, without the alibi of cosmic realism, or of the grand sentiments of petty-bourgeois ideology.

Griffith, a precursor of genius. Without a doubt. But a precursor of what, and of whom?

Perhaps it is finally time to stop relegating him to a prehistory of the cinema (even if it is the Utopian prehistory of the birth of an art-form), where the simple fact of christening it prehistory amounts to, it should be noted, a limiting of the history of the cinema to that of its 'classical' period.

It has not escaped me that in these notes I have not really suggested another, more authentically historical way of reading Griffith. The danger which attends this type of formal approach is even, very clearly, an ahistoricity from which I could not absolve myself completely by arguing that the history of the cinema is yet to be written.... Thus, it was not at all my intention here to anticipate the works of a more directly historical reflection which are being undertaken in some places, but rather to assume this relative ahistoricity, with the thought at the back of my mind, on which I shall end, that having already explored the classic cinema at length, it is now from its fringes (its ancestors and predecessors, but also all those who, from Godard to Bunuel, have worked from within the classic paradigm) that film theory can draw new inspiration.

Notes

First published in Raymond Bellour (ed.), *Le Cinéma Américain* Vol. I (Paris: Flammarion, 1980).

1. Jean Mitry, *Griffith*, coll. Anthologie du cinéma (Paris: Editions de l'Avant-scène, 1965), vol. 1, p. 68.
2. 'Dickens, Griffith et nous', 1940; text revised 1946. French translation: *Cahiers du cinéma*, no. 232. In English: 'Dickens, Griffith and the film today', *Film Form* (New York: Harcourt Brace, 1949), pp. 195–255.
3. Pierre Baudry, 'Les aventures de l'idée (sur *Intolerance*)', *Cahiers du cinéma*, nos 240 (July–August 1972) and 241 (September–October 1972). Unless I am mistaken, this is, by the way, the first densely theoretical work on Griffith.
4. An example: 'It is only from 1912 . . . that he begins to show the true extent of his talent, his brilliant discoveries having until then merely been at the service of puerile anecdotes' (Mitry, *Griffith*, p. 75).
5. Here, as in the rest of the text, I shall adopt the terminology suggested by Jean-Pierre Oudart, despite the problems it poses. He distinguishes figuration (product of specific pictorial codes, in particular those of figurative analogy) from representation (which makes this figuration into a fiction, and notably leads to judgments about the existence of the figures produced, as having their referent in reality). See Oudart, 'Eléments pour une théorie de la représentation', *Cahiers du cinéma*, no. 228, March–April 1971.
6. Here one can usefully consult the shot-by-shot breakdown of the film, done by Pierre Sorlin, in *L'Avant-scène du cinéma*, no. 193–194, October 1977.
7. Nothing makes this specificity of the system used by Griffith at Biograph clearer than a comparison with other reputedly 'theatrical' films, for example those of Sacha Guitry, in which, whatever the paucity of locations, it is always the characters (and their words) that rule and move the dramatic space.
8. The hypotheses put forward here should clearly be checked against Griffith's later films, without, however, I think, risking complete invalidation, if I go by a recent viewing of *Broken Blossoms*.
9. Similarly, I don't think I am fantasising too much in reading the swing bridge which cuts the rescuers off from their route for some time as a more or less controlled metaphor for this phenomenon of spatial closure/fragmentation.

10. Cf., in another context, 'Zaroff "rolls" his eyes in hyper-theatrical fashion. Not any old way: he looks down, to the left, upwards, to the right, straight ahead. What more radical way could there be, of marking out, mirror-fashion, the frame of my vision, than framing it?' (Thierry Kuntzel, 'Savoir, pouvoir, voir', *Ça* no. 7, p. 165).
11. The only notable exception to this form of closure: the exit of the protagonists towards the front of the screen, rather than by its sides. Two examples: in *The Battle*, the parade of soldiers leaves the frame on the right, but with a clear turn to the camera, brushing past it (this is shot no. 11 in Sorlin's shot breakdown (*L'Avant-scène du cinéma*); in *The Musketeers of Pig Alley*, the villain advances towards us, as if pulled forward – see below.
12. Exchange reported by Linda Arvidson Griffith in her biographical memoirs (*When the Movies Were Young* (New York: Dutton & Co., 1925)); I am quoting after a footnote by Armand Panigel on p. 407 of his French edition of *Film Form*.
13. I am thinking particularly of Godard: a film like *La Chinoise*, for instance, clearly shows this return in the form of a rewriting. See my analysis of a sequence from the film, 'This is not a textual analysis', *Camera Obscura*, nos 8/9/10, pp. 131–56.
14. Let us recall that the first short of Griffith which film historians single out for its use of parallel editing is *The Lonely Villa* where the telephone plays the same role, and whose scenario is taken from a piece of Grand-Guignol, called *On the Telephone*.
15. By Pierre Baudry, in the second part of his article, 'Les aventures de l'idée'.
16. More generally, it is no doubt possible to develop this literally sexual value of closed spaces: to put it briefly, in the Griffith–Biograph system, the dispersal of a space, for instance, is almost always the equivalent, barely metaphoric, of rape; see also the gestures of Mary Pickford in *Friends*, as she opens or closes her door, which are a sort of instant translation of the feelings (the desire) aroused in her by the two men. All this could be linked, in a more rigorous way, to the symbolism of the chamber (*Frauenzimmer*) that Freud talks about.
17. This frame has been commented on by Jean-Louis Comolli in 'Technique et idéologie', *Cahiers du cinéma*, no. 230, July 1971, pp. 51–3, a text I can only recommend, for a more concise discussion of this question of 'primitive' depth of field.
18. These two shots are reproduced on the margins of Baudry's article 'Les aventures de l'idée'.
19. 'Speaking generally, the close-up is neither more nor less fragmentary than any other shot, but in contrast to other types of shot, it is almost always *read* as fragmentary . . .' (Pascal Bonitzer, 'Le gros orteil', *Cahiers du cinéma*, no. 232, October 1971).
20. This phrase, need one add, is Bazin's, who also said: 'some reality needs always to be sacrificed for reality'.

Translated by Judith Ayling and Thomas Elsaesser

To Alternate/To Narrate

RAYMOND BELLOUR

We shall see here how the systematicity at the heart of the great American classicism is elaborated, proceeding from the reduction of a fundamental form of cinematographic discourse: *alternation*. I shall not pause to define either the nature or especially the multiple determinations of a formal principle whose first general formulation – before returning to it more fully – I have already outlined.[1] It will emerge, as in most of my earlier analyses, from a step-by-step textual analysis whose systematic organisation it very largely regulates (even if, of course, the organisation cannot be reduced simply to this): within limits, but with the effect of insistence and almost deliberate abstraction which often characterise primitive works.

In order to follow this process which sets out to reconstruct (because it is short) an entire film (*The Lonedale Operator*, D. W. Griffith[2]), it will be necessary to try to imagine the deployment of this principle of alternation, its extension, its dispersion and its diversification, from shot to shot, from segment to segment: in short its *mise en abyme*, its *mise en volume*, in films by Hitchcock or Lang, Mann or Curtiz, Wyler or Thorpe. There where it is at work, orchestrated, orchestrating all levels, the classical cinema.

It will be remembered that in *The Lonedale Operator*: all the shots are fixed; thus the description will need to specify, when necessary, only the movement of the characters and the objects inside the frame, with regard to the frame enlargements chosen for each shot; the shots are always strictly regulated according to the immediate exigencies of the performance and its dramatisation, which alone determine the sometimes noticeable shifts in duration between the shots; there are no intertitles, at least not in the copy to which I had access.

It would be well to remember, finally, that in regard to this exemplarily simple film, even if it already brings into play textual operations of a certain degree of complexity, we will not really be concerned with an analysis as such here: that is to say, an underlying logic which a commentary would come to enlighten. Rather, I see these pages as an ordered description whose insistence seeks to draw forth an *additional* knowledge which gives force to the knowledge which one acquires more directly.

He/She/He/She, she and he. At the beginning of the narrative, the diegetic couple, the mainstay of the fiction. It sustains the first alternation, and sets the film under the sign of the changing form which will be its basic law. This first alternation is of course made in order to be broken, to reunite (shot 4) its two terms in the same frame, the man and the woman, the train driver and the telegraphist. The displacement of the hero, which consequently brings about, from shot 1 to shot 3, a slight variation on his body (from medium shot to close-up) inside an identically arranged frame, produces this break in alternation by making the first term penetrate the frame which until then had been given over to the second. After which, from shot 4 to shot 7, the action continues by repeated shots of the couple, where according to the purest romantic code, the pressing tenderness of the hero and the affectionate reserve of the heroine are asserted. One will note only (but in order to show it we would need many more frame enlargements: you always need too many) that the displacements of the characters play, in a graduated way, on an opposition between near and far: leaving the field of vision on the right, in shot 4 (according to a placing similar to that in shot 3), they are framed in tighter and tighter close-up, before disappearing, to appear again in shot 5 far back on the right and to be framed exactly as they were at the end of shot 4. This operation is more or less repeated in shot 6 (except that the trajectory is inverted: the couple this time arrives on the left of the frame), helping to sustain the systematicity of the narrative. This is sometimes done, as here, in a pure and insistent way: in these less complex films the filmic writing seems ceaselessly to put to work, as though for their own sake, the potentialities of cinematographic language.

6–9, 9–13. A sequence of frames which the narrative lays out in order to take them up again later, according to a partly invariable succession, which will give its strength to the repetition. The separation, in shot 7, prepares for the second alternation which arises from it between shots 9 and 10: she/he again. But this time with the effect of a liaison implied by the exchange of looks, which makes of shot 10 a semi-implicit subjective shot. A specifically cinematographic code (that of point of view) obliquely takes up the diegetic alternation and incorporates it: their superimposition (which could be layered with other specific codes and is already half done by the shifts in framing) is the body of the fiction itself.

This alternation continues: shot 11 effects a return to the first term; it develops in this way right up to shot 13. And it is only interrupted to make way for a new alternation, apparently more loose, but no less distinct, which aids in establishing on a greater scale the alternating distribution of the succession of actions.

Another office, in another station. Another train (so identical are they that for a moment one could think it is the same train we saw leaving in shot 10; but when it stops in shot 15 after a lengthy forward climb, some passengers get out and others board the train, whereas the train driven by the hero consists of only one locomotive). Another action: a man enters an office, holding a satchel, stops near a cashier who hides two bags of money in it, then goes out again by the same door on the left, on the platform, where he holds out the satchel to a second man who is leaning out of the train we have just seen pulling into the station (15), and which we see leaving again, at the end of this very lengthy shot (31 seconds).

This time it is by groups of shots (thirteen shots, from 1 to 13, then two, 14–15, then x shots, according to the way in which one decides to divide up the rest of the action), that is to say by units corresponding to segments or supra-segments, and no longer only from shot to shot, that the alternation of actions, within a more or less sutured continuity, is fused. In this sense we can speak of a superior alternation, since it integrates, at least in the first of its terms, earlier alternations; but superior in extension, not in nature: whether close by, or further on, it is never other than the same displaced process operating between the spaces.

In effect we return to the office of the telegraphist. By means of a closer framing, at first in close-up (16), then in medium shot (17), which returns to the earlier framing (9, 11, 13). These two frames thus draft a sketch, not developed, of an alternation within the alternation of actions, which models itself on the latter and develops out on its own. Let us note that, as with other configurations, this alternation cannot be resolved by the fusion of its two terms: no shot can maintain two framings at the same time (unless it be the perfect superimposition of the two shots), whilst it mingles for example the subject and the object of its vision. One could thus consider classifying the alternations according to this first criterion, doubled back on itself by taking into consideration the specificity or the non-specificity of the codes put into play.

Thus there are four shots (16–19) of the telegraphist. After having glanced out the window – analogous to the glance which determined the earlier alternation with the first train – she gets up and goes out of her office in shot 17 (let us never forget that the shots remain invariably fixed), and very exactly repeats in the opposite direction, according to an equivalent number of shots, the same walk which she accomplished from shots 7 to 9. Shifts in fiction, in the repetition effects which carry it (the fiction): there is no longer anyone in the office in shot 18, and it is in shot 19 that we see her reappear alone in the doorway, there where in shot 9 she was saying goodbye to her lover.

The train which arrives in shot 20 (the second train, having left from the other station) continues this alternation of actions, which has been set up between the two stations, when it enters the field of the first, in the frame where already through two occasions the motifs of the action have been inscribed. This alternation, initiated in shot 17 by the look of the telegraphist (which recalls the goodbye to the first train), materialises between shots 19 and 20; but it disappears forthwith in the very shot which constitutes its second term, in the latter part of the shot: there the telegraphist receives from the person who himself had received them in shot 15 (by a left-right inversion in the arrangement of the characters, determined by that of the trains and the platforms) the bags filled with money which she hides in her own satchel. By a very subtle arrangement, the framing of shot 20, which reiterates that of shot 10 (departure of the first train), also repeats very nearly (more or less floor or roof coming into view) the framing of shot 6 where the couple were crossing the tracks, thus further accentuating the effect of inversion between the series which leads the young woman from the platform to her office (6–9), and that which leads her from her office to the platform (17–20). Micro-condensation of the textual system, which integrates into one of its units components of several earlier units,

and thus constructs itself, by means of displaced similarities which constitute its repeated difference.

20–21. New motif, third term: the thieves who emerge from between the rails, under the carriage, and cross the field from left to right, in shot 20. They open an alternation (20/21/22: she–he/thieves/she–he) which, as with that of the two stations, is going to arrange itself from then on, at first, according to groups of shots (she/22–25/thieves/26–27). It will be noticed that: the three shots 23–25 reiterate, in the strict succession of their three settings, the first entrance and the exit of shots 7–9 and 17–19; shot 27, of the thieves, repeats the framing of where they emerge in shot 20, which combined the terms of the previous alternation (the telegraphist/the train from the other station), thus imbricating, through both obvious and subtle interlocking, the two alternating movements, before the second systematises itself through a relationship determined from shot to shot.

28–42. This time it is not her lover, but the thieves whom the telegraphist sees, or rather guesses at, as from the end of shot 28, which reiterates so exactly, even to the position of the chair, shots 9, 11 and 13. The alternation from shot to shot will be broken four times in different ways, without interrupting itself for all that, thus showing that it is the same serial movement, varied according to the dictates of the diegesis, following on from shots 20–21, between the two thieves and the telegraphist.

a) 32–34. From the second office to the exit door, three shots of the telegraphist once again repeat 7–9, 17–19, 23–25.

b) In shot 34 alternation is established not from shot to shot, but by means of the door which the telegraphist closes again, which serves as a shutter, in the very shot (thus divided, 34*a*/34*b*) where the thieves appear (this framing, succeeding that of the window, 29 and 31, will from then on be given over to the thieves, right up to shot 70). This example shows very well that diegetic alternation (to show this *or* that, in order to show this *and* that) merely coincides, through a kind of massive coding, with the limits of the shot; but it shows too that it spills over continually, either by dividing, as here, the shot on to itself, or as shown elsewhere by continuing through diverse regroupings of shots, according to the continuous variation of a single principle.

c) The same again, for shots 37–38, 40–41.

d) It will be noticed how the movement of the telegraphist is this time accomplished: shot 34, the third occasion of her displacement, from her desk to the door, becomes the first of an inverse displacement, from the door to the desk, the duration of a half-shot which serves the theatrical dictates of the action; the second shot assigned to the displacement (first office) is in contrast repeated twice, conforming to the build-up of suspense, of which alternation, by the internal breaking up of motifs, is one of the major instruments (35 and 37: she closes the door, then runs across the room).

40–41. From the medium shot to the close-up: this inverse placing, again for the benefit of the suspense and the future alternation which serves it, of shots 16–17, by identical framings and positions, but according to a strict logic which assigns the telegraphic activity to the close-up.

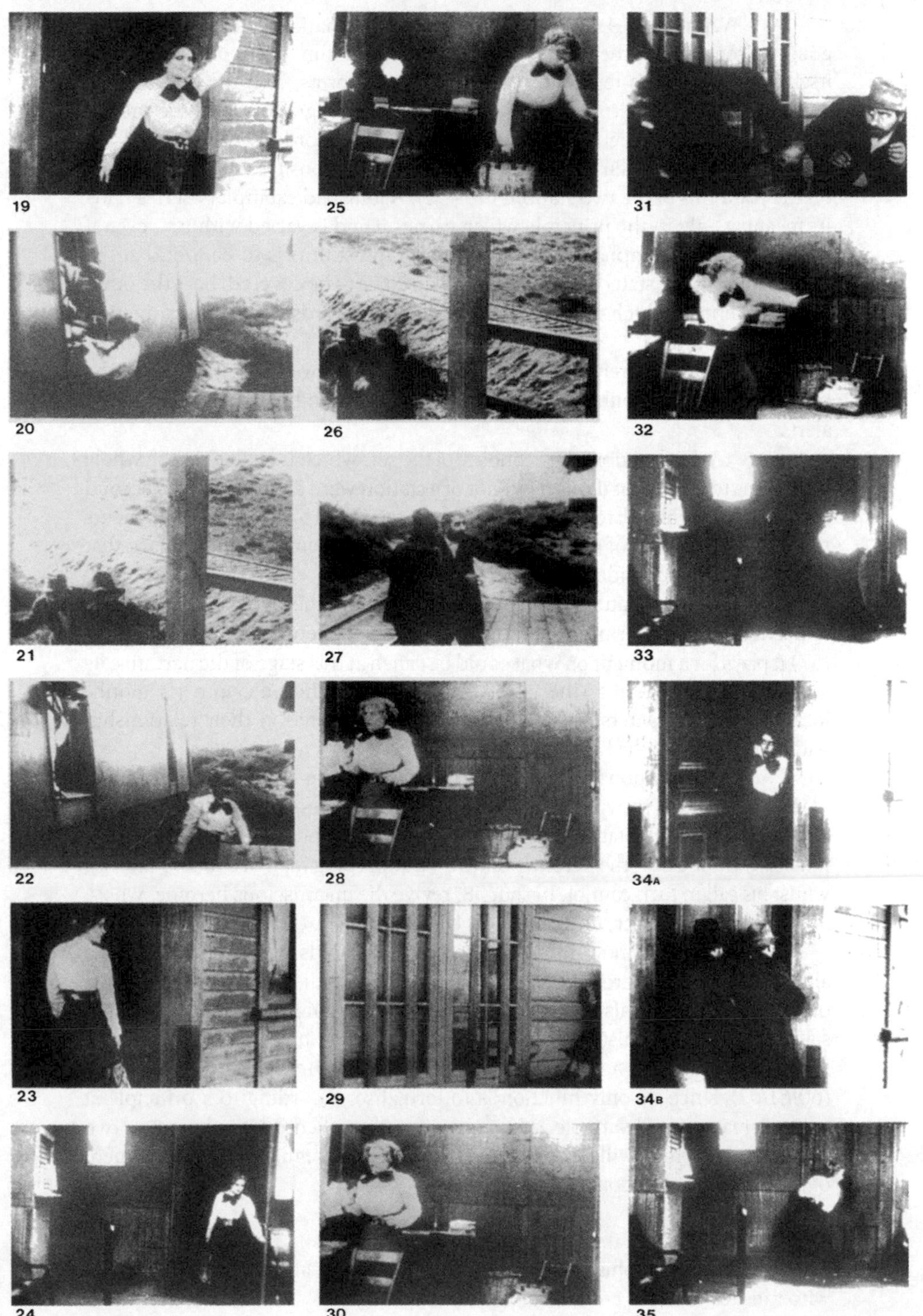

19 20 21 22 23 24 25 26 27 28 29 30 31 32 33 34A 34B 35

With shots 42 and 43 a three-term alternation is set up, which is going to continue further, almost to the end of the film, more or less effacing itself behind the two-term alternations which it forms, and the alternations within each of these terms. The heroine, the other telegraphist and the thieves form a movement which immediately focuses on the orderly exchange of the two telegraphists at their desks, arranged in mirror opposites as were the trains on the platforms of the two stations (42–52). A long and exemplary series finds its meaning only in the principle which carries it and is varied within it, even if the principle is triumphant. The (male) telegraphist thus is to be found at the other station as the stated second term of a distance to be covered, he is the other of a same term of which the heroine is the centre, towards which all disjunction does and will return.

In an apparently third station, shot 55 allows us to meet again the hero (from now on doubled by a second driver), whom the (male) telegraphist alerts.

(A third station: the economy of the sets which is evident in the whole film seems to attest that if this new shot of a station were to designate the second station, it would have been more or less similar to shot 15. Now, all the elements regrouped on the left of the frame are different, and seem to want to mark that difference, due to the identity of the angles.)

The alternation, which is continued in the action, immediately reinscribes its third term (the thieves, 56); thus, by a return to the telegraphist (57) it plays for a moment on what could be called at this stage of the narrative its second and third terms (the other station – itself divisible into its motifs, locations and characters – and the thieves) at first stated in their relationship with the first term (the heroine).

A continuous variation of the diegesis: the fainting of the young woman in shot 54 provides the fiction with one of these oppositions which it relishes, when it reinstates (57/58/59) the alternation between the two telegraphists: by calling out, the heroine wakes up the sleeping man in shots 45 and 47; whilst his call in turn cannot, in shot 58, revive the unconscious heroine, whose awakening is held over, until ten shots later, purely for the sake of the drama.

This repetition, of shot 55, at shot 60, holds over the shot-by-shot alternation with the heroine whose sleep is used by the diegesis to put to work its other terms. The motifs of the second term, converging in shot 60 (the other station: the telegraphist, the driver(s)) divide up at first in order to weave together the motif of an internal alternation, almost immediately interrupted (60/61/62), since its only function is to formalise, according to a principle at once permanent and variable, an acceleration of the fiction. It is based on two frames, one of which will disappear, and the other will regulate the development of the alternations to come:

a) a wide frame, which regroups the whole of the action; the station platform, the telegraphist who holds out the message and a gun to the driver who runs towards his engine;

b) a closer frame: the driver on his engine which is starting off (with

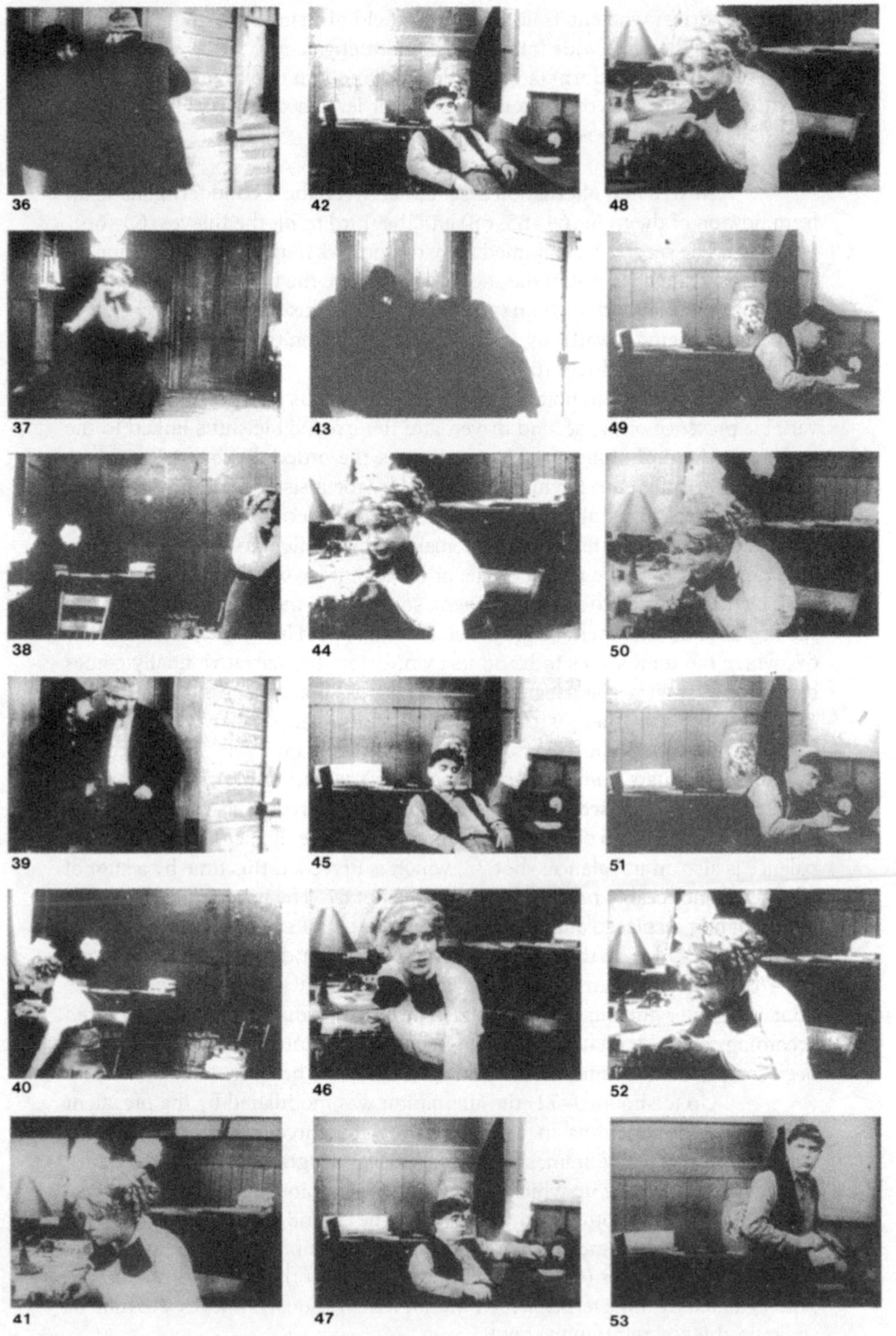

the second driver who enters and leaves the field of vision (61)).

a') the same wide frame; the train leaving, facing the screen, and the telegraphist on the platform (a title added into modern copies justly notes that the driver runs towards the back in shot 60 in order to board his engine which in shot 62 is seen the opposite way, turned towards us).

Next, a new alternation is set up, between the second term, made up from now on of the train (64–65, 68) and the third term, the thieves (63–66).

The second term immediately reproduces in this new alternation an arrangement sketched out in the shots which assure the transition between the telegraphist's office and the train (59–62). Division, this time, between a shot of the train advancing towards us, front on, and leaving on the right of frame (64), and a close-up of the driver (65).

Two things to note. This shot strictly repeats shot 61 (except for the variable presence of the second driver, and the irreducible shifts linked to the realism of the performance): it thus assumes the ordered progression of the narrative, the difference having been settled by the insistence of the repetition. These two shots, in the alternate weaving of the three terms, open up a potential sub-alternation: this latter can either remain at this elementary embryonic stage, or it can develop by the return of one or other of its two elements, or reabsorb itself by limiting itself to a single element, so as to fuse more rigorously with the shot-by-shot development of the general alternation. This is the case with shot 67, where the train seems to be on its own, before the narrative finally comes back to its first term: the telegraphist who regains consciousness.

But also, there is the balance of spatio-temporal masses: shot 64, followed by a shot of the drivers, shows the train only on a very short stretch of its journey (it enters from the back and advances to mid-frame); shot 67, which by itself upholds the second term, positions the train at a distance, makes it come right up to us, go out on right of frame, and leave the field empty. But this balance is also an imbalance: shot 73, which is preceded this time by a shot of the drivers, noticeably repeats the course of shot 67. The narrative is thus built up by slightly displaced analogies, an accumulation of small differences.

68–71. She/the thieves. This time the shot doubles up on this pair (69–70), following their movement, when they finally succeed in opening the door and enter the first office, thus repeating, through fragments ordered according to the dramatisation of the diegesis, the course which has already been completed five times (in both directions) by the heroine.

Up to shots 70–71, the alternation was modulated by the prevalent insistence of the two terms, in turns taken out of the three possible relationships (she/telegraphist or she/train, she/thieves, thieves/telegraphist or thieves/train). The alternate doubling up which operates on the heroine, opposing her successively to each of the other two terms (train/she: 67/68; thief/she: 69–70/71), whilst at the same time renewing an alternation a/b/a' between the young woman and the thieves (68/69–70/71), is resolved for the benefit of an alternation regulated by three terms, which we can write variously: thieves/she/train or she/train/thieves, right up to shot 83.

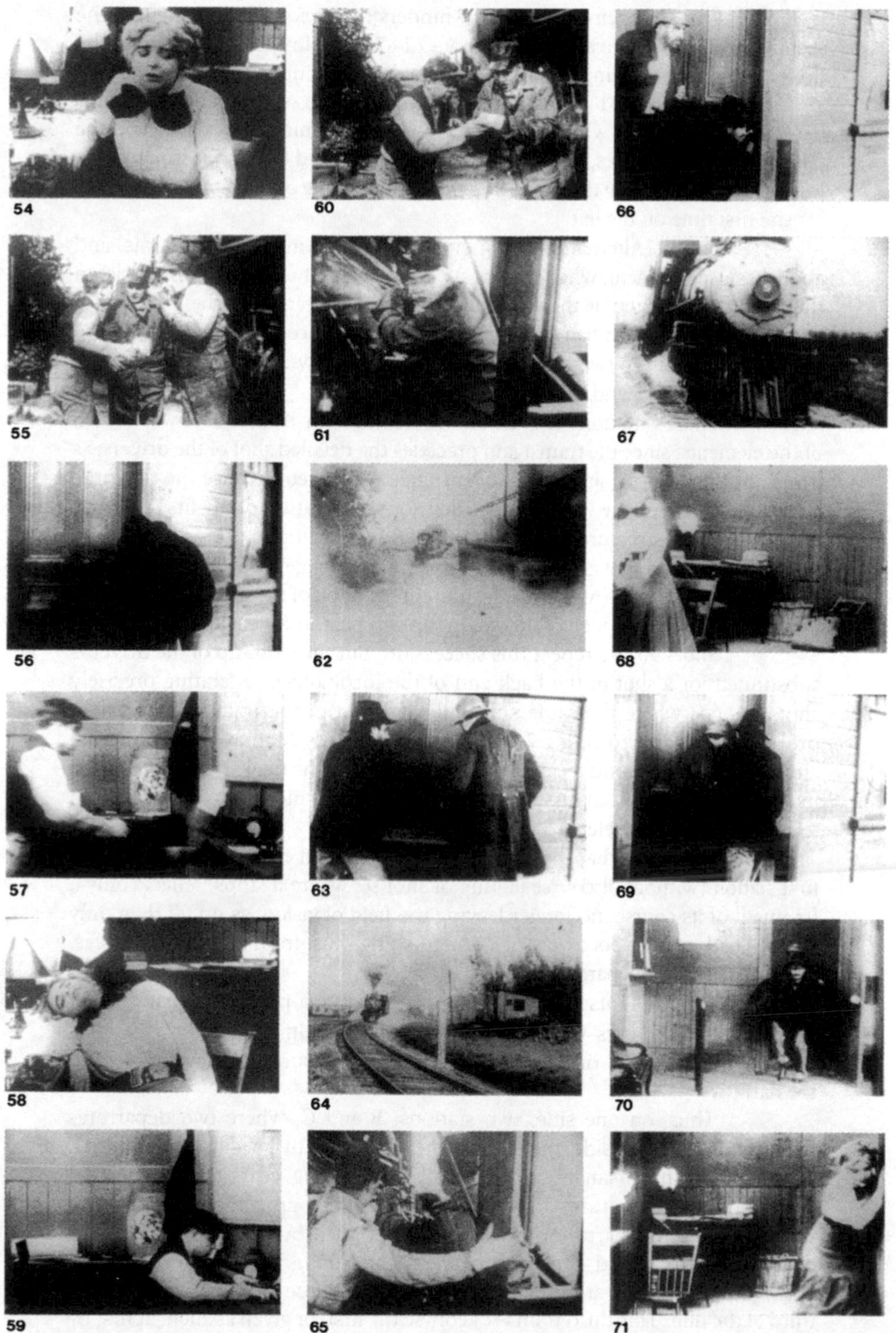

This arrangement in no way hinders the divided arrangement of the second term, which is reaffirmed in shots 72–73, but inversely: the shot of the driver this time preceding that of the train, which is contrary to shots 64–65.

76/77–80/81. Same arrangement, with the only notable variations being: the countryside which the train crosses still coming towards us, and the path which it completes, arriving in these shots 77 and 81; rather from a little less of a distance than in the preceding frames and going out of frame, in shot 77, for the first time on the left.

82–85. Alternation again crystallizes itself in two of its terms, and abolishes itself in them, when in shot 85 the thieves, after having broken down the door, finally penetrate the office of the telegraphist, and take their place with her in this frame which had been given over to her since frame 9.

It is thus a two-term alternation which now continues between the telegraphist–thieves and the train.

Three variations operate on the second term. At first, a new inversion of the elements, since the train again precedes the detailed shot of the drivers, as it did in shots 64–65, at the first occurrence. And then because the potential alternation between the two elements develops, by a return of the first element, the train, which structures the shots 86/87/88 according to the schema a/b/a'. Lastly, the detailed shot changes (87) – this time no longer showing the driver in close-up on his engine (with the intermittent eruption of the second driver), but the back of the engine, each of the two men at his post, and a background of sky.

Shots 90–91 repeat this succession. But the close-up of the driver is substituted for a shot of the back end of the locomotive: reiterating precisely shots 64–65, where the same shot followed that of the train which it then precedes in the micro-series 71–72, 76–77, 80–81. Moreover, this internal alternation of the second term which continues with the final arrival of the train in shot 92, is thwarted in this very shot where the two men jump from the train to hurry towards the telegraphist's office.

Let us add that the train, in shot 90 where it enters the setting of the first station (without of course talking of shot 92 where it stops), effects only a fragment of its course, no longer leaving the field of vision, as up till then only shot 64 had made it do: a way of distinguishing thus, from other occurrences, the arrival and the departure.

Finally, shots 90 and 92 happen to close a paradigm: that of train arrivals and departures which structure the whole film, according to a logic where symmetry gives rise to dissymmetry and so assures the development of the narrative.

Thus, on one side, two stations, B and C, where two departures operate. On the other side, the station where the narrative begins and ends (A), where, according to an arrangement of interlocking cross-referencing and alternation, two departures and two arrivals are lined up: almost at the beginning of the film, departure of the first train, driven by the lover; the almost consecutive arrival and departure of the second train, with an ellipsis of the entire journey; arrival, at the end, of the last train, whose journey covers the last third of the film. This third train is of course the first, or given as such: at first by

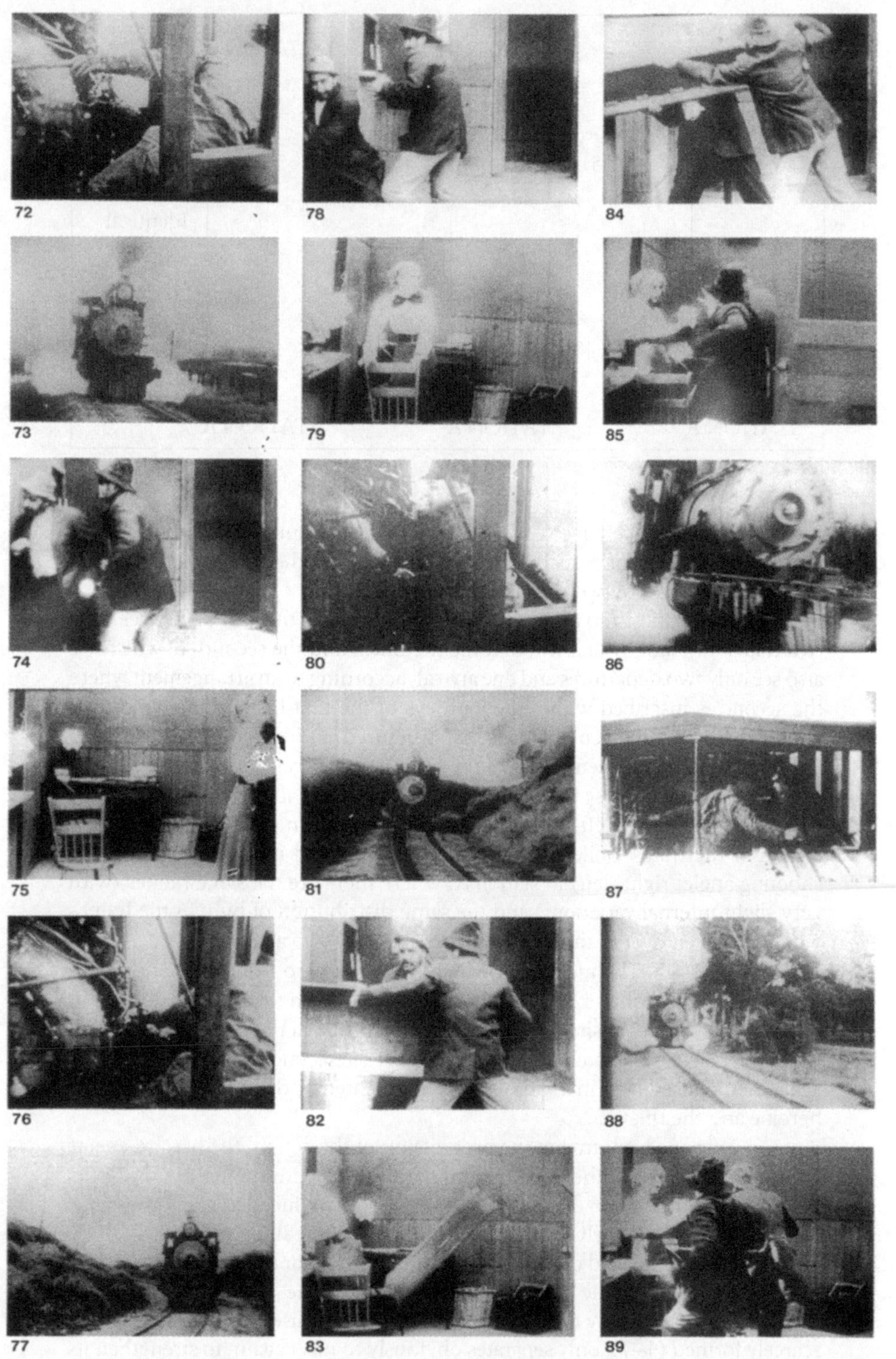

72 78 84
73 79 85
74 80 86
75 81 87
76 82 88
77 83 89

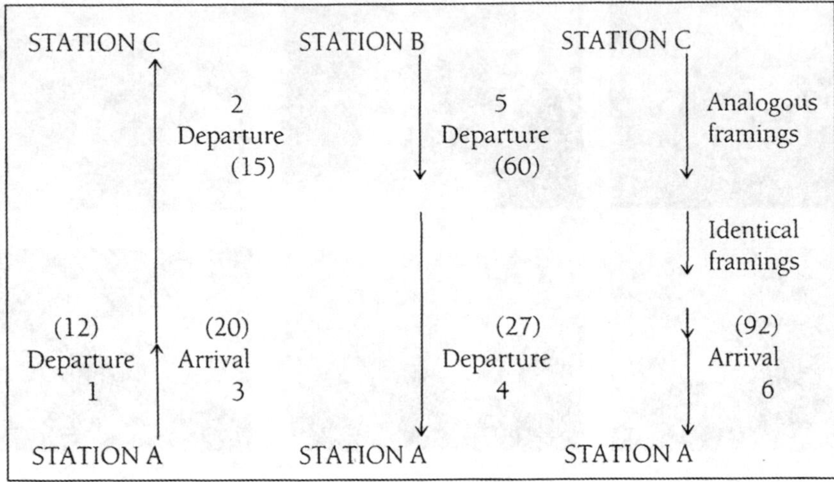

its driver; then, as we have seen, because at its departure from station A, this train only consists of a locomotive, in contrast to the second train which apparently consists of two carriages.

A relationship of symmetry–dissymmetry is thus set up between the two trains: the first, which will become the third, and the second, of which we also see only two departures and one arrival, according to an arrangement where the second is inscribed within the journeys of the first like a double motif by which the architecture of suspense is structured and refined. One will also appreciate the neat systematicity of the framing: *analogous*, it could be said, in stations B and C, because the train pulls into the station in the same way, filmed from the same angle (left–right), in spite of the shift in setting and the distribution of the trains' bulk in the frames; *identical* (and inverted, in respect of shooting angle: right–left) in station A, where there are the same frames (with very slight internal variations) and the same distribution of bulk in the frames which are given over to the two departures and the two arrivals.

92–95. The movement which leads the hero from the station platform to the telegraphist's office reiterates with precision the path she follows at his side, then alone, in shots 6–9, which she repeats, in the opposite direction, when she receives the satchel after the arrival of the second train, and which will again be traversed later in a more or less fragmented or divided fashion, by the heroine and the thieves.

In one leap, true to the progression of the action, the hero re-enacts the course followed in the initially calm period of the pre-drama. He thus puts an end to the alternation of the three terms (already reduced to two terms since shot 85, and inordinately concentrated on the second since shots 92–93), by penetrating into the field of vision reserved until then for the first term, then for its conjunction with the third. Thus the terms of the narrative come to be combined, and to resolve the division posed by its premises: the diegetic couple, scarcely formed (4–7), only separates obviously to meet again, to strengthen its

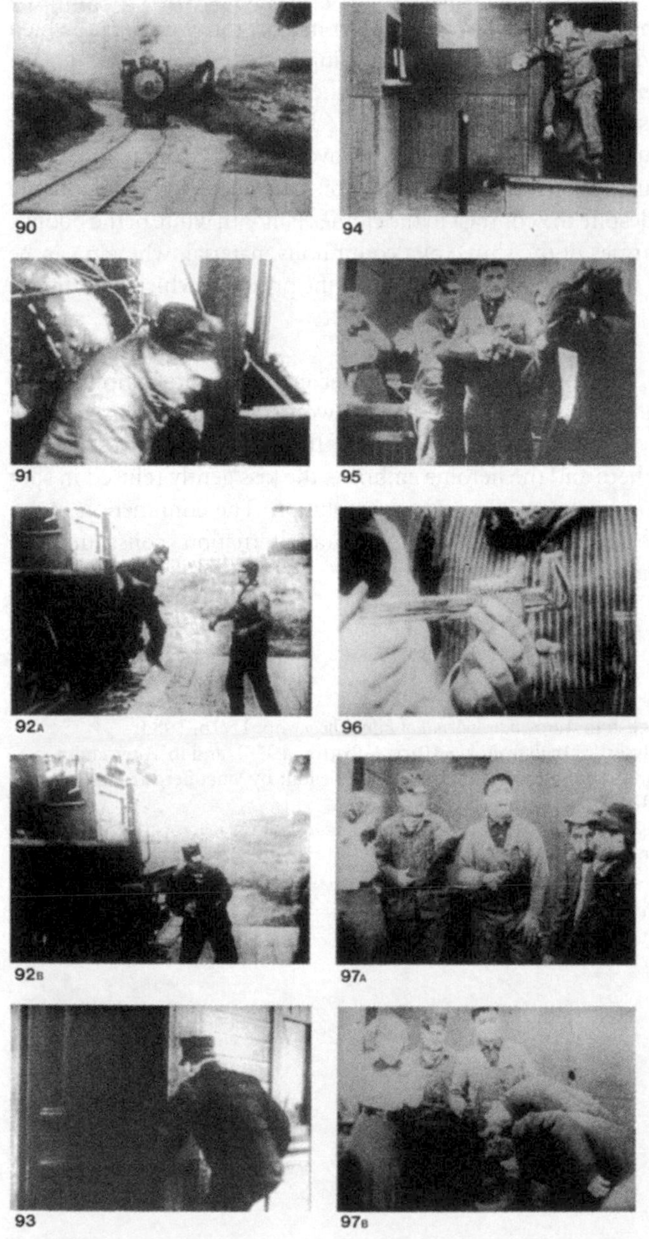
90
94
91
95
92A
96
92B
97A
93
97B

image by the test of a dramatised separation whose internal form is alternation, orchestrated at its multiple levels in order to serve the principle which carries the narrative, by its repetition, towards its resolution.

Shot 96 refines this terminal movement by means of a final alternation: the alternation of frames which places, between the two shots which reunite the five protagonists (95 and 97), a close-up of the object with which the heroine held the two thieves in check. Hermeneutic resolution. The non-seen, or the badly-seen, appears in its true colours: a monkey-wrench instead of a revolver. A rhyming effect, too: with the revolver held by the young man, which re-establishes the distribution of objects according to that of sex.

But this close-up, the only one in the film, also acknowledges an added meaning, stemming from the rhymed difference which it inscribes between the man and the woman: it unites, as if over and above the action which reforms it, the couple, by isolating fragments of their bodies which suddenly seem to be made, despite the contrast in the clothes (smooth white of the bodice, black and white stripes of the shirt), of a continuous material, wherein can be read the subject of the fiction, in the meaning of the principle which determines it.

NB Another print has since shown me another ending (quite simply ten to twenty seconds cut from the copy on which I worked), which completes the perfection of the system. Same shot, same frame: the two thieves leave, then the second driver; the hero and the heroine embrace: the kiss gently refused in shot 4 is accepted in the final shot. Repetition–resolution. The conjunction of the couple, of the two terms posed by the inaugural alternation, constitutes the substance of the narrative.

Notes

First published in English in *Australian Journal of Film Theory* no. 15/16, 1983.

1. In 'Segmenter/analyser', *L'Analyse du film* (Paris: Albatros, 1979); and in 'Alternation, enunciation, hypnosis', an interview with Raymond Bellour by Janet Bergstrom, *Camera Obscura*, No. 3, 1979.
2. Production Biograph, 1911; 998 feet (16.30 to 16 images/second); actors: Blanche Sweet (telegraphist); Frank Grandon (driver).

Translated by Inge Pruks

Spatial and Temporal Articulation in Pre-classical Swedish Film

JOHN FULLERTON

In an article concerned with narration in early film, Tom Gunning identified four syntagmatic principles.[1] He notes that each syntagmatic type not only represented different and successive responses to the issue of temporal and spatial organisation, but constituted genre-specific narrative forms. Towards the end of the article, he goes on to propose that the cut-in inaugurated, in rudimentary fashion, the development of scene dissection.[2]

In establishing his narrational paradigms, Gunning privileged spatial and temporal articulation. While these priorities established with regard to the classical style are appropriate for the analysis of prototypical and pre-classical film, they should not be seen as the only analytic criteria available to us for films where intertitles were a standard narrational device. Given that pre-classical narration incorporated the written word (almost certainly the mark of a narrator inherited from the lecturer), it can be argued that the status of spatio-temporal articulation is problematic. The examination of this issue in pre-classical Swedish film will lead us to question the apparently self-evident notion that filmic (as opposed to narrational) continuity constituted a major organising principle in pre-classical film. The point I wish to make is that questions of editing and staging in early cinema should be extended to include a consideration of the role of language in narration. The argument in this chapter will be based largely on a three-reel film, *Trädgårdsmästaren* (Victor Sjöström, Svenska Biografteatern, 1912).[3]

Why select Swedish film in this period for investigation? The answer involves the comparative history of early cinema, for, while there is much to confirm Gunning's proposition that the cut-in, the eyeline match and the shot/reverse-shot system constituted a series of successive formal innovations in American and Danish film, Swedish film is notable if only because there are no cut-ins in surviving films before 1913,[4] and scene dissection does not occur until 1917,[5] when, on a comparative basis, its incidence is very late. This may suggest that Swedish film was stylistically 'retarded'. However, given that the example of American and Danish practice was available to film-makers in Sweden, Swedish film may constitute a practice which, different to that of the classical paradigm, requires us to question the model's pertinence also in a more general account of the development of narrative film.

More specifically, since Swedish film is overwhelmingly concerned with the autonomy of profilmic space, it raises three fundamental issues. First, if Sweden developed a divergent practice to that of America during this period, are its modes of narration nationally specific? Second, given that Swedish films are formally different, what logic determines their narratives, and how do they address the spectator? Third, how do intertitles and image interact in its narrational system? Although the last point forms the subject of this chapter, the two former questions will necessarily be touched upon. My central argument can be formulated as follows: if intertitles (particularly narrative intertitles) are part of a narrational system based on spatio-temporal continuity, then Swedish films are comparable to those Gunning calls continuous in the American context. If, however, intertitles in Swedish films have discontinuous[6] or other narrational functions, then spatio-temporal continuity might not have had the same stylistic priority.[7] In arguing for the latter, close attention will be paid to shot transition (to determine the appropriateness of spatial and temporal criteria) and the modes of address of intertitles. In this discussion, narration will be taken to imply, as David Bordwell and Edward Branigan have argued, two distinct operations: the filmic inscription of specific spatio-temporal relations between a given series of shots and the cognitive, active process of meaning construction undertaken by the viewer across larger segments of the film.[8] As we shall see, the latter can overdetermine and thus render continuous what at the filmic level is discontinuous. A segment from *Trädgårdsmästaren* which can serve as an example of how shot transition constitutes a rudimentary form of filmic continuity occurs early in the first reel of the film:

Title 7 'In the tea gardens.' *Cut to*

Shot 8 Exterior, long shot (L.S.), the tea gardens. As the shot opens, Cedric's mother (the head gardener's wife, towards mid-field, frame left) is serving students seated at a table, foreground centre, with drinks. The head gardener enters from foreground right, crosses over to her, and they converse. The gardener points towards off-frame right (see Plate 1), whereupon his wife leaves the garden at rear right. As the gardener begins to walk towards rear left, *cut to*

Shot 9 Exterior, L.S., yard. Rose, Cedric's girlfriend, left of centre and with back to camera, is feeding chickens. Shortly, a gate at foreground left swings open, and Cedric's mother, holding an apron, comes into the yard. She walks towards Rose as Rose turns to greet her. While they converse, Cedric's mother, turning towards camera, points towards off-frame left (see Plate 2), hands Rose the apron, and, as Rose begins to put apron on, *cut to*

Title 8 'An energetic help.' *Cut to*

Shot 10 Exterior, L.S., the tea gardens, same camera set-up as in shot 8. A waitress carries drinks on a tray to a group of students seated at mid-field left of centre. As she serves them, Rose enters at rear right, comes towards frame left, and, as she approaches the group of students seated around the table at foreground right, she ties up her apron. Rose picks up the ice bucket on the table, places it on a tray, and leaves the shot, rear left. *Cut to*

Title 9 'A noble patron.' *Cut to*

Shot 11 Exterior, L.S., another location in the tea gardens with shrubs towards foreground right framing right-hand half of shot. Rose, without a tray, is walking across the foreground of the shot towards foreground left. The General (the noble patron referred to in intertitle 9) advances towards her. As they approach one another, the camera pans slightly left to reframe them at left and centre of the shot. They converse. Rose points towards off-frame right (see Plate 3). As Rose turns away from camera and walks away from the General, the General walks towards front right and leaves the shot at medium (M.) L.S. The shot is held without Rose and the General for a moment before *cut to*

Shot 12 Exterior, M.L.S., a table at foreground centre, behind and to the right of which, a bench screened from the rest of the tea gardens by shrubbery. The General is seated on the bench, and appears to be talking to himself. As the film cuts to the next shot, a woman's arm is visible entering at frame right (when projected, this imminent entry into shot of Rose (see Plate 4) is not registered by the viewer). *Cut to*

Shot 13 Exterior, L.S., tea gardens with shrubs, same camera set-up as at the conclusion of shot 11. Shortly, Rose enters from behind shrubbery carrying a tray. She crosses towards foreground right, and exits at frame right. The shot is held for a moment. *Cut to*

Shot 14 Exterior, M.L.S., a table, same camera set-up as in shot 12. As shot opens, Rose enters from foreground right, crosses over to left of shot, and serves the General his drink. He pays her for the drink, and, as Rose makes to leave, he, much to her surprise, offers her more money (a not inconsiderable sum for he paid for the drink with coins, but here (see Plate 5) offers her a note). Taking the money, Rose tries to kiss the General's hand, but he makes to halt her and, in turn, kisses her hand. Turning towards the foreground, Rose, with a quizzical expression on her face (see Plate 6), crosses the shot and begins to exit at frame right close to camera. *Cut to*

Title 10 'A troubled idyll.' *Cut to*

Shot 15 Exterior, L.S., the veranda of Rose's cottage.

If one considers the spatio-temporal relations which obtain in this extract, one notices that at the end of shot 8, Cedric's mother, at the request of her husband (i.e. prompted by his gesture), leaves the shot at rear right. Shortly, she enters shot 9 from frame left. Although a brief temporal ellipsis may be inferred between shots 8 and 9 (sufficient, in diegetic terms, for Cedric's mother to get an apron to give to Rose), the manner in which her exit from shot 8 matches, in directional terms, her entry into shot 9 establishes, through action, a strong causal link and inscribes spatio-temporal continuity. Similarly, though an intertitle separates shots 9 and 10, Rose's entry in shot 10, motivated by Cedric's mother's gesture towards off-frame left in the preceding shot, reinscribes spatial contiguity, while the action of putting on the apron, accomplished over both shots, secures a near-continuous sense of temporal progression. In the context, then, of these three shots, unity of action together with directional matching define the extract's spatio-temporal relations despite the insertion of intertitle 8.

However, while continuity of action secures temporal coherence in the remaining part of the extract, spatial relations are more problematic. First, the spatial coherence between the two parts of the extract is only loosely inscribed. Rose leaves shot 10 at rear left. After intertitle 9, she enters shot 11 at frame right and crosses the picture plane in the direction of the General. Though action across shots 10 and 11 secures a sense of spatial contiguity with the first part of the extract, the precise relationship of shot 11 to the previous action is not specified. An indeterminate temporal ellipsis occurs between shots 10 and 11 (evidenced in the fact that Rose leaves shot 10 carrying a tray, but enters shot 11 without it), and the location of action, though still set in the tea gardens, does not match any details seen in the two previous locations. Second, the space between shots 11 and 14 is ambiguous. Rose points towards off-frame right in shot 11, and the General exits in that direction at the end of the shot. Given, however, that shot 12 opens with the General seated on the bench, the continuity of action across the shots which is necessary to define the spatial relationship of shot 11 to shot 12 is not inscribed. As a result, it is difficult to determine whether Rose's entry into shot 14 (from frame right) is consistent with her exit at frame right in shot 13. If the two spaces are parallel (see Fig. 1), the relationship between the two shots is spatially inconsistent. If, on the other hand, shots 12 and 14 denote an adjacent though reverse field to that of shots 11 and 13 (see Fig. 2), Rose's entry into shot 14 is spatially coherent, though it should be noted that such an inscription of space is not typical of the later classical style.

The problem of the film's spatial coherence, however, does not end here. Given that Rose's entry into shot 14 is anticipated in the last few frames of shot 12 (as close inspection of the 35 mm viewing copy held at Svenska Filminstitutet reveals), we can assume that this scene was filmed as a two-shot sequence. Shots currently numbered 11 and 13 would have constituted the first shot of the sequence, and shots numbered 12 and 14, the second shot of the sequence. After filming, the two shots were edited, so that they now constitute a four-shot alternating syntagm, with a degree of temporal simultaneity between shots 12 and 13, but, overall, temporal succession between shots 11, 12/13, and 14. Although, therefore, temporal progression and a certain spatial coherence characterise this part of the extract, why was the film edited in this fashion, why was action thus intercalated? The answer points towards a different conception of screen space to that of the classical period, so different that it calls into question our conception of spatio-temporal continuity for this period.

At the end of shot 11, Rose exits behind the shrubbery. If shot 13 was actually a continuation of shot 11, Rose would have left the shot only to reappear, sooner or later, with a drink for the General. Given this description of action, Rose's reappearance would either have been too early to be plausible, or entailed a considerable lapse of time. Whichever narrative logic guided the film-makers, Rose's absence, it would appear, was perceived to violate a fundamental principle regarding screen space. Hence, the pressure to edit the sequence in its present form. By so doing, a single and developing narrative line, accomplished

Figure 1. Relationship of exits and entry into shot within parallel fields

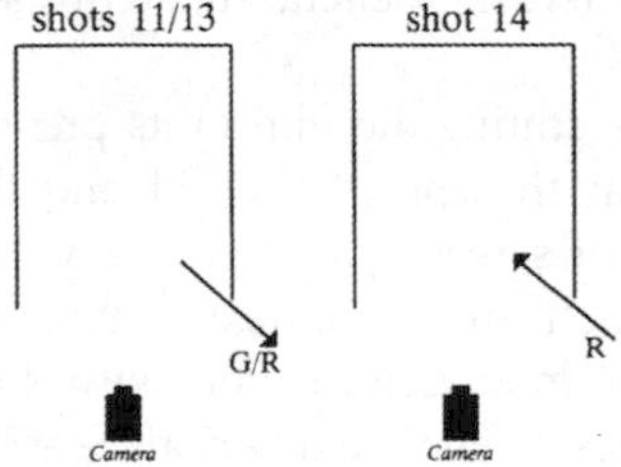

G = Direction of movement by General in shot 11

R = Direction of movement by Rose in shots 13 and 14

Figure 2. Relationship of exits and entry into shot within reverse and adjacent fields

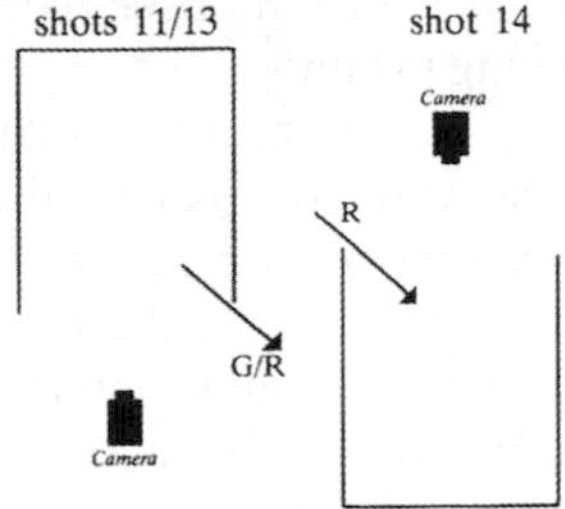

G = Direction of movement by General in shot 1

R = Direction of movement by Rose in shots 13 and 14

1

2

3

4

5

6

over two shots and inscribing continuity through gesture towards off-frame space, was intercut with the General sitting on the bench. In short, the preferred solution favoured action of some kind on the screen rather than the absence of action, even if this risked confusion in shot 12 where the General apparently sits talking to himself.

If one accepts this as the reason for editing the film in its present form, why do I assume that Rose's absence at the end of shot 11 and the beginning of shot 13 was deemed a violation of screen space? Primarily, her absence contradicted a dramatic principle which, in the context of fictional narratives, favoured anthropomorphic presence in any given shot. With Rose and the General leaving shot 11, the shot becomes, in effect, a descriptive shot, a scene without anthropomorphic or narrative interest. While the descriptive syntagm was used by film-makers in non-fiction genres in this period,[9] surviving Swedish fiction films do not use a single descriptive shot introducing a fictional narrative before 1916,[10] and a three-shot descriptive syntagm does not appear before 1917.[11] Rose's absence, therefore, transgressed what we may posit, on intertextual grounds, as an operational principle with regard to fictional narratives, and editing was adopted as a means of retaining human interest while achieving narrative progression.

Although further corroboration from other films would be needed to draw more general conclusions, one can, none the less, suggest that while narrational continuity could be achieved (principally through the relaying of action via gesture to off-frame space),[12] spatio-temporal continuity was not a fully determining operational principle of narration in *Trädgårdsmästaren*. Thus narrational disjunction not only constituted a viable and possible alternative mode of organising a given narrative, but at this point in the diachronic development of Swedish fictional narratives, had a status more or less equal to that of spatio-temporal continuity. As a working hypothesis this can be corroborated by looking at the deployment of intertitles.

Intertitle 9, which announces 'a noble patron', serves an obliquely informational function. It also has a structural function in that it inaugurates the development of narrative action. Intertitle 9 thus has a narrational status equal to that of gesture towards off-frame space. The intertitle binds, in other words, the image chain through language in a manner similar in degree, though not in kind, to action which binds, as we have seen, shots 8 to 9, 9 to 10, and shot 11/13 to shot 12/14. While, therefore, intertitles 7 and 9 define different types of coherence (respectively, a coherence of space and a coherence for upcoming action centred on the General), intertitle 8, placed after the first two shots in the extract, renders discontinuous what at the level of the action is continuous. Moreover, given that Rose's willingness to work is more than evident from the speed with which she sets about serving in the tea gardens, intertitle 8, in referential terms, verges on redundancy. Unless, that is, intertitles generally serve another, as yet unidentified, narrational function. A further extract will enable me to examine the issue of temporality more closely, and will raise a major narrational issue, before returning me to a reconsideration of the role of intertitles in the first extract.

The second extract is the opening of the film:

Title 1 'The Broken Spring Rose. Part 1.' *Cut to*

Title 2 'Chief Actress. Mrs Lilli Beck [sic] of Copenhagen.'[13] *Cut to*

Title 3 'The Playmates.' *Cut to*

Shot 1 Exterior, ELS, a woodland bank. Rose, visible to right of centre behind a tree, runs down woodland bank at right of centre pursued by Cedric. He tries to catch Rose as they dodge around the tree. As they run towards foreground left, the camera pans left to reframe the teenagers at left of centre foreground. They embrace, and, as Cedric draws Rose towards the extreme foreground, *cut to*

Title 4 'Three years later. A joyful message "Cedric arriving to-morrow from school."' *Cut to*

Shot 2 Interior, L.S., Rose's cottage framed towards right-hand corner of the living room. Rose stands at foreground left looking eagerly at her jacket as she prepares to go to meet Cedric. She puts jacket on table at centre foreground, and goes quickly towards rear right of centre to bring a mirror from on top of mantelpiece by stove to the table. She places mirror on the table, and looks at herself. She puts on jacket, turns away from camera to look at her rear view, then, turning back, begins to button up her jacket. *Cut to*

Title 5 'At home again(.) The young student.' *Cut to*

Shot 3 Exterior, L.S., ferry landing-stage. Rose and her father stand with backs to camera towards foreground left. Other people awaiting the ferry (also with backs to camera) stand, mid-field, on the landing-stage. A small steamboat draws up, people disembark and greet those on the landing-stage. Cedric, wearing a student cap, disembarks, greets his parents at mid-field, centre of shot. He kisses his mother, and, glancing over his right shoulder towards foreground of shot (see Plate 7), catches sight of Rose. Rose and her father turn towards Cedric (i.e. towards camera profile) as he approaches them. Cedric, at foreground centre, greets Rose. As Cedric's parents approach him and his mother moves towards foreground right, Cedric's father draws Cedric away from Rose (see Plate 8). Cedric and his parents exit front right past camera as Rose, approaching M.L.S. (see Plate 9), gazes past camera towards front right in the direction of the departing (now off-frame) figure of Cedric. She looks on spell-bound, then exits front right past camera. As her father begins to exit front right past camera, *cut to*

Shot 4 Interior, L.S., Rose's cottage, framed slightly to the left of the camera set-up for shot 2. The table, at foreground centre, has been moved slightly.[14]

First, a look at the intertitles with regard to their temporal denotation. Title 3, 'the playmates', primarily designates the couple whom we see in shot 1. It also denotes the relationship between the two protagonists, and determines our reading of the action, youthful play, rather than, say, a prelude to seduction. To what extent, however, does this shot denote a repeated state of affairs rather than a singulative action? In the context of the first part of the following intertitle which denotes the passing of three years, the action of the shot is not strictly iterative (we do not infer, for instance, that the couple are forever chasing one another round the tree), yet its temporal mode is, none the less, modified by the time given in the following intertitle. Thus, the opening of the film confirms the function intertitles perform in specifying the narrative focus of a scene. But it also is an example of the reading and viewing process typical of narrative film which requires the spectator to reappraise a given action through information supplied, as in this instance, by a subsequent intertitle.

A further instance of the dual nature of the reading process is the relationship of shot 3 to its preceding intertitle. Shot 3 marks the time of intertitle 5 as successive to shot 2. However, the intertitle, taken out of the context of the following shot, could be construed as indicating simultaneity and initiating an alternating syntagm. Such a reading, however, is quickly resolved in favour of a sequential and causal reading. Thus, there is in fact an ellipsis between shots 2 and 3 as Rose, now standing on the landing-stage, awaits Cedric's return. Unity of action in this instance determines the preferred reading of the narrative's temporality, so removing the ambiguity contained in the intertitle itself. In arguing that the first title-image conjunction allows for two temporal readings, and that the ambiguous time frame of intertitle 5 is resolved by action in the following shot, I want to question the notion that a temporally specific diegesis is only inscribed through shots or titles and point to the important relationship which obtains in pre-classical narration between intertitle and shot. This has obvious implications with regard to narrational address.

Title 4 informs us that a joyful message is received. Joyful for whom? Evidently for Rose, as shot 2 shortly confirms. However, if the message is joyful for Rose, from whom does it originate? Cedric? Hardly, for the intertitle shows no trace of the personal pronoun 'I'. Unless, therefore, authorship of the message is attributed to an as yet unidentified diegetic source, one must assume that the joy spoken of in the intertitle serves not only a referential function (designating, like title 3, a state of being), but implies a narrating instance which invites the spectator to share a position of omniscience by providing an intimation of Rose's (but, possibly, also Cedric's) psychological state. Interestingly, the action of the following shot at no point confirms the narrative purport of the intertitle: we see Rose neither receive nor read a message. Rather, the intertitle functions primarily to inscribe a narration that is focalised. Furthermore, so used are we to narrational omniscience from the novel that we do not doubt for a moment the authority of the narrating instance. Not only do we take on trust the authority of the extradiegetic narrator, we are also willing to ignore the temporal ellipsis designated in intertitle 4. While the ellipsis may be insignificant in diegetic terms, given that shot 3 institutes a hermeneutic, ellipsis may, in this instance, retrospectively acquire narrational significance. This becomes evident when we consider the action of shot 3 in relation to the ellipsis inscribed in title 4.

Shot 3 opens with Rose and her father standing towards foreground left. With their backs to camera, we cannot, during the first part of the shot, read Rose's face, although something of her emotional state may be inferred from the

7

8

9

manner in which, contrary to her animated presentation in the two previous shots, she stands rather statically looking towards mid-field space. Her emotional state in shot 3 is thus signalled as different to that earlier in the film. The position of her figure in the frame also means that we look past Rose towards the recessed space of the scene, so enabling us to see clearly the developing action. From this spatial arrangement, we infer that Rose is able to see what we see: what we deduce, she, too, is capable of deducing. The boat draws up, Cedric disembarks, he greets his parents, he greets Rose. No sooner does Cedric greet Rose, however, than his father draws him away from her. Why should the father act in this fashion? This question cannot be resolved at this point: it hinges, as the narrative later implies, on the issue of class, the threat which Rose is deemed to represent to Cedric's filial devotion, and rivalry between father and son for the attention of Rose. What alerts the spectator, however, is that neither Rose (as is evident from the manner in which she leaves the shot) nor Cedric detects anything untoward in the father's gesture. His action inaugurates what Ben Brewster, in considering other pre-classical films, has identified as a hierarchy of relative knowledge. This aspect of the narration involving action and intertextual address is further amplified through generic convention and what we may presume was Lili Bech's known screen persona.[15] It starts a series of narrative enigmas not fully articulated until Cedric is banished from home by his father. By constituting a hermeneutic, narration is rendered dynamic as the viewer mentally returns to the ellipsis in intertitle 4 in the hope of gaining explanation. However, given that explanation is not forthcoming in the narrative at this point, the ellipsis, in narrational terms, now becomes a paralipsis, propelling the viewer onward into the narrative. Narration, in other words, withholds motivation for the father's action until a later point in the narrative. Expositional material, therefore, when distributed along the syntagmatic axis of narration, may, in some instances, become narratively integrated, not at the level of spatio-temporal continuity, but as part of a process of supra-syntagmatic reading.

So far, I have argued that narrational coherence in *Trädgårdsmästaren* depends on a reading process that integrates, but at the same time moves backwards as well as forwards through, the syntagmatic chain, as in the opening of the film where, in strictly spatio-temporal terms, there is little evidence of continuity. Text and image, though interdependent, are relatively autonomous, and distil action in concentrated form in any one title or shot. This strategy seems largely typical of the film's narrational style, and suggests that narration regulates and paces the narrative by alternating between discontinuous passages and passages which, more continuous, can be characterised as being more expansive. The film's more general narrational principles allow one to identify one further function with regard to the deployment of intertitles, indicative of the manner in which pre-classical narration may have offered narrative pleasures different to those later instituted in the classical period.

I began by noting that intertitles functioned to secure coherence of space, action and, as in the instance of the title which introduced the General, narrative momentum. I have since noted their metadiegetic, discursive operation. The question arises whether issues of narrative momentum and discursivity are also appropriate to the intertitles in our first extract. When I initially discussed this extract, it seemed that intertitle 8 was in fact redundant. At the risk of pleonasm, one could say that intertitles mark an insistence on the part of the narrating instance to punctuate each stage of the narrative with an intertitle. In the context of the first extract, intertitle 8 not only singles out Rose (rather than Cedric's parents) as a central protagonist in the developing action, but, in so doing, focalises her activity. Shortly, intertitle 9 introduces the General, and, as mentioned earlier, secures narrative progression. In other words, intertitles focus more spectatorial attention on a particular protagonist, yet, as in the case of the General's introduction, they do so very obliquely: for, why *a noble patron* rather than, say, *the General*?

When I considered the narrational hermeneutics of the second extract, I noted that a particular hierarchy of relative knowledge was inscribed between the narrative and the spectator. It seems that in the way in which the General is introduced the intertitle encodes a hermeneutic which momentarily makes his introduction an enigma. Given a historically specific spectatorial competence familiar with generic encoding, i.e. a familiarity with the type of narrative constituted in a melodrama such as *Järnbäraren* (Gustaf Linden, Svenska Biografteatern (1911)) in which a lower-class, well-meaning *ingénue* falls foul of a wealthy, aristocratic male, the oblique introduction of the General inaugurates a narrative situation predicated on a class discourse. More specifically, 'A noble patron' does not so much serve as the oblique introduction of the General to the viewer as mobilise a discursive field associated with a given film genre. In this context, the sequencing of intertitles and action in the tea gardens episode – 'In the tea gardens', 'An energetic help', 'A noble patron', the action of shot 14 in conjunction with the following intertitle, 'Troubled idyll' (irrespective of what the following shot reveals) – activates a predictive narrative itinerary. Elsewhere in the film, such a narrational strategy is clear: 'Destroyed dreams of youth', 'Turned out' (i.e. dispossession), 'Seized by a stroke', 'Again without a home and bare of protection', all foreshadow narrative events, and, in so doing, forecast a narrative of pain, anguish and humiliation. In short, intertitles (singly or in concert) act as signifiers of anticipation, which, relayed through subsequent shots, work to confirm or postpone a predictive scenario itself established by intertitles. In so doing, they demonstrate that narration can activate an intertextual regime and vectorise a given narrative situation. Narration and action, text and image, work together in a process which, different to the phantasmal and synthetic conceptualisation of space associated with the later classical period, involves a predictive scenario.

Conceived thus, narration in pre-classical film offers a very different conception of readerly pleasure. As in the instance of this Swedish melodrama, it is a quasi-formulaic, aggregative process in which trauma is signalled ahead of its delivery, a well-posted route similar in kind to that which earlier constituted a major genre of film-making elsewhere in Europe, the Passion Play. In this context, we can perceive the hallmark of the discontinuous style: a foreshadowed chronicle of travail and humiliation ending, as in the instance of *Trädgårdsmästaren*, in death. Only then can the chronicle be concluded, only then can intertitles admit to the past tense.[16] Narrative closure, inscribing both the end of the story and its telling, signals the end of reading, but not its extinction for, although other stories remain to be told, similar anticipations await to be mobilised.

Intertitles thus play a central role in generating and regulating narrative momentum. To secure narrative progression, they may mark the invocation of an intertextual field, so evidencing a historically specific, readerly competence with regard to generic convention. They also instance an extradiegetic origin to whom, finally, responsibility for invoking a given diegesis may be delegated. The text-spectator relationship, then, requires readerly involvement, but finally absolves the viewer of culpability, a vicarious pleasure indeed. Whether this defines a more general or nationally specific pleasure with a consistent mode of address, only further work can identify. However, given that such a practice constituted a mode of address not confined to the cinema in the pre-classical period, we can reasonably adduce that it was increasingly threatened as Swedish films moved towards that type of narrational pleasure constituted in the classical period. In the light of this scenario, the diachronic history of narration in pre-classical film can no longer be characterised as a process in transition. Rather, it can only be characterised as one increasingly in crisis or, at the very least, dynamic contest. In charting that process and in characterising its conflicts, a new historiographic project can be identified.

Notes

An earlier version of this paper was first presented to a Graduate Studies Weekend School in the Film Department of the University of East Anglia, 2–3 December 1988. I would like to thank Thomas Elsaesser for his close reading of my manuscript and the helpful suggestions he made.

1. Tom Gunning, 'Non-continuity, Continuity, Discontinuity: A Theory of Genres in Early Film', pp. 86–94 of this volume.
2. Gunning has since indicated (in conversation, Pordenone, 4 October 1988) that he now regards the eyeline match and the shot/reverse-shot system as more typically constitutive of the development of the classical paradigm.
3. The title of the film, usually translated as 'The Head Gardener', may also be translated as 'The Master of the Garden'. The English-language title of the film (discovered in the collection of the Library of Congress in 1979) is 'The Broken Spring Rose'. In preparing this paper, I have viewed a 35 mm print of the film held at Svenska Filminstitutet, Stockholm. This print, restored from the Library of Congress print, is, from internal evidence, incomplete, and its intertitles almost certainly differ from those that would have been prepared for the film's Swedish release. Given that the original Swedish intertitles list has not survived, there is, at present, no means of checking the English-language intertitles against the original Swedish intertitles. It should also be noted that the film was banned in Sweden on 20 August 1912.
4. In *Ringvall på äventyr* (Georg af Klercker, Pathé Frères, Stockholm, premièred 3 September 1913.
5. In films such as *Thomas Graals bästa film* (Mauritz Stiller, Svenska Biografteatern, premièred 13 August 1917) and *Tösen från stormyrtorpet* (Victor Sjöström, Svenska Biografteatern, premièred 10 September 1917). It should also be noted that in 1917 Georg af Klercker, working for Hasselbladfilm, Göteborg, employed a rudimentary form of scene dissection involving an extended use of cut-ins and reverse shots in films

such as *Förstadsprästen* (premièred 3 September 1917), *Reveli* (premièred 26 December 1917) and *Fyrvaktarens dotter* (premièred 2 April 1918).

6. It should be noted that I do not use the term 'discontinuous' to denote that type of syntagmatic construction identified by Gunning. I use the term in its more general sense, to denote a narrational process which, in filmic terms, is other than continuous.
7. Given, however, that all pre-classical film deployed narrative intertitles on an increasingly regular basis before the development of dialogue intertitles, the example of Swedish film may have more general application.
8. For a general consideration of these and other issues, see David Bordwell, *Narration in the Fiction Film* (London: Methuen, 1985), and Edward Branigan, *Point of View in the Cinema: A Theory of Narration and Subjectivity in Classical Film* (New York: Mouton 1984). See also Edward Branigan, 'The spectator and film space – two theories', *Screen*, vol. 22 no. 1, Spring 1981, pp. 55–78, and Elena Dagrada, 'The diegetic look. Pragmatics of the point-of-view shot', *Iris*, vol. 4 no. 2, 1986, pp. 111–24.
9. Consider the use of the descriptive syntagm in, for example, panoramics and scenics, or in Swedish films such as *Badlif vid Mölle* (Viking, 1911, premièred 29 August 1911), the numerous scenics evidenced in Svenska Biografteatern company records with regard to *Veckorevy* (see *AB Nordiska Filmsfabriken* (unpublished company production ledger) for the period 2 March 1914–21 December 1914, pp. 154–73), or a film such as *Emigranten* (Robert Olsson, Svenska Biografteatern, 1910) where in one sequence thirteen shots out of a total narrative of forty shots include six shots of an emigrant steamer leaving port, five actuality shots of passengers on board the steamer during its voyage, and two shots taken from on deck during the voyage. While this last film is, ostensibly, a fictional narrative, there is a strong 'realist' interest which overdetermines the narrative interest at one point in the film. Of course, even though we lose sight of the protagonists in the narrative during the actuality syntagms, most of the shots retain some human interest.
10. In the opening shot of *Terje Vigen* (Victor Sjöström, Svenska Biografteatern, 1916, premièred 29 January 1917).
11. In the opening syntagm of *Tösen fran stormyrtorpet* (Victor Sjöström, Svenska Biografteatern, 1917, premièred 13 August 1917). In the context of our discussion, it is interesting to note that the second and third shots of this syntagm are constituted as pans across the natural landscape.
12. A procedure adopted as late as 1915 by Georg af Klercker in a film such as *I minnenas band* (Hasselbladfilm, premièred 3 January 1916).
13. Lili Bech (variously spelt, elsewhere, as Lili Beck, Lilli Bech, Lilly Bech and Lilly Beck) entered the Danish film industry from Folketeatret, Copenhagen in 1911 (see Marguerite Engberg, *Dansk Stumfilm* (Copenhagen: Rhodes, 1977), vol. 2, pp. 537, 631). She was contracted initially to Det Skandinavisk-Russiske Handelshus (see Engberg, *Dansk Stumfilm*, vol. 1, p. 328), and appeared in three films which received their premières in Copenhagen in 1911: *Morfinisten*, *Taifun* and *Den Utro Hustru* (see Marguerite Engberg, *Registrant over danske film 1896–1914* (Copenhagen: Institut for Filmvidenskab, 1977), vol. 2, pp. 302, 303, 306). In the following year, three further films made for Det Skandinavisk-Russiske Handelshus received their Danish premières: *Den Staerke Magt*, *Den Flyvende Cirkus* and *Biørnetaemmeren* (see Engberg, *Registrant*, vol. 2, pp. 503, 505, 507). Of these Danish productions, *Den Utro Hustru* (submitted to the Swedish censor on 13 October 1911 under the Swedish title of *Pengar*) was banned outright in Sweden (see Engberg, *Registrant*, vol. 2, p. 303), while *Taifun* (Swedish title, *Hämnden*), *Den Flyvende Cirkus* (Swedish title, *Den Flygande Cirkus*) and *Bjørnetaemmeren* (Swedish title, *Björntämmaren*) received certificates permitting their exhibition to adult audiences from the Swedish censor on, respectively, 13 October 1911, 30 March 1912, and 18 May 1912 (see Engberg, *Registrant*, vol. 2, p. 303). During 1912, when she was under contract to Svenska Biografteatern, Bech worked (in order of production) on *Vampyren* (Phoenix/Svenska Biografteatern (Phoenix was an affiliated distribution company), Mauritz Stiller, premièred Fenix and Röda Kvarn's Sveasalen, Stockholm, 17 February 1913) which was shot in the second half of May (see Lars Åhlander (ed.), *Svensk Filmografi* (Stockholm: Svenska Filminstitutet, 1986), vol. 1, p. 198). She then worked on *Trädgårdsmästaren* which was banned in Sweden (see

Åhlander, *Svensk Filmografi*, vol. 1, p. 198), and in the first half of June, worked on *Barnet* (Mauritz Stiller, premièred Röda Kvarn's Sveasalen, 13 May 1913, see Åhlander, *Svenska Filmografi*, vol. 1, p. 195). This production was followed, in the second half of July and early August, with the production of *De Svarta Maskerna* (Mauritz Stiller, premièred Röda Kvarn's Sveasalen, 21 October 1912, see Åhlander, *Svenska Filmografi*, vol. 1, p. 186). *De Svarta Maskerna* was thus Bech's first appearance in a Swedish film before a Swedish audience. The film was a spy drama set in a circus milieu (see Gösta Werner, *Mauritz Stiller och hans filmer, 1912–1916* (Stockholm: Norstedts, 1969), pp. 80–4). Although the film is no longer extant, given Bech's appearance in Danish material such as *Den Flyvande Cirkus* and *Bjørnetaemmeren*, it is likely that *De Svarta Maskerna* would have confirmed, if not her specific screen persona associated with Danish films, at least a social milieu encountered in previous Danish films exhibited in Sweden. In this regard, it is interesting to note that for the Russian market where, according to Engberg, Bech was particularly popular, *De Svarta Maskerna* was provided with an alternative, tragic ending (see Engberg, *Dansk Stumfilm*, vol. 1, p. 322, Bengt Idestam-Almquist, *När Filmen kom till Sverige* (Stockholm: Norstedts, 1959), p. 491, Åhlander, *Svensk Filmografi*, vol. 1, p. 186, and Gösta Werner, *Mauritz Stiller*, pp. 97, 100). For a brief, contemporary characterisation of the Russian market and its predilection for tragic endings, see 'Linsen', 'Svensk filminspelning just nu. Ett besök i Svenska Biografteaterns ateljé a Lidingön', *Filmbladet*, vol. 1 no. 14, 1 August 1915, p. 177.

14. For a consideration of the way in which furniture, placed in a different position, was used in the context of *Ingeborg Holm* (Victor Sjöström, Svenska Biografteatern, 1913, premièred 3 November 1913) to denote the passing of time, see Ben Brewster, 'Deep Staging in French Films, 1900–1914', pp. 45–55 of this volume.
15. See Noël Burch and Anita Fernandez (co-scriptwriters), *What Do Those Old Films Mean?*, programme 3, Eleventh Hour/Channel Four, first UK broadcast, July 1986. Lili Bech's participation in *Trädgårdsmästaren* would likely have inscribed a different screen persona to that constituted in Danish film or in a Swedish production such as *De Svarta Maskerna* (see Note 13 above). In a Danish film such as *Den Flyvende Cirkus* she was cast not only as a threat to male sexuality, but as the embodiment of female independence. Such a forceful screen persona should, however, be qualified by her appearance in other Danish films such as *Bjørnetaemmeren* (which I have not seen) where, according to Ron Mottram, she was presented as a much weaker character (see Ronald James Mottram, 'The Danish Cinema 1896–1917', Ph.D. Dissertation, New York University, October 1980, pp. 204–5). Until work on the intertextual address of Bech's screen persona can be conducted, the full meaning of her presence in this film can only be surmised. We may propose, however, that it was a complex if not contradictory *locus* of meaning derived, principally, from the Danish *sensationsfilm*. For a consideration of Bech's work in Denmark, see Engberg, *Dansk Stumfilm*, vol. 2, pp. 534, 544–6.
16. In full, the final intertitle reads: 'Broken spring rose(.) With the dawn of day they found her dead.'

The Student of Prague

LEON HUNT

The real creator of the film must be the camera. Getting the spectator to change his point of view, using special effects to double the actor on the divided screen, superimposing other images – all this, technique, form, gives the content its real meaning. (Paul Wegener[1])

A particular regime of textual repetition is, of course, specific to each individual system, contributing, with its multiple modes, to defining the system's status with regard to the fiction. (Raymond Bellour[2])

Eisner, Kracauer and Film History

The original version of *The Student of Prague* was made for Bioscope in 1913, written by Hanns Heinz Ewers and directed by Stellan Rye, with Paul Wegener as the student Baldwin. Seeing it today, one is aware of the way a similar teleological construction which used to inform histories of American film has also determined approaches to early German cinema, subsuming everything that precedes the pivotal film *The Cabinet of Dr Caligari* (1919) under the retrospective construction 'German Expressionism'.

In this respect *The Student of Prague* is in the position which Noël Burch ascribes to Porter's films, namely having one foot effectively in the past and one in the future,[3] and displaying the features of classical narrative alongside evidence of a more primitive mode of representation. The danger, however, is to see the film as simply falling between two stools; a primitive film which is almost, but not quite, classical. Where the film has been dealt with – and it has not been written about very much – it has occupied precisely this position, as in Lotte Eisner's comments that this film, coming six years before *Caligari*, already exhibits many of the properties which one finds in the so-called classical films of the 20s,[4] and Kracauer's complementary assertion that 'its significance undoubtedly rests less on the camera work than on the story proper.'[5]

It is worth drawing attention to the extent to which these historians of Expressionism have failed to come to terms with the formal properties of this fascinating film. Eisner's statement, for instance (that the film's images 'lack the quality and depth of focus to which the German cinema of the twenties has accustomed us: the real interiors . . . seem rather flat'[6]) is not only misleading but should be contrasted with the comments of the film's star, Paul Wegener, quoted at the beginning of this paper. What Wegener says is significant for three reasons:

1. Terms such as 'spectator' and 'point of view' imply a discursive (as opposed to a purely performative) text, making the film's 'primitivism' highly problematic.

2. The divided screen, identified by Wegener as a technique involving the doubling of the actor, is a central concern for any formal system not based on continuity editing. Such techniques become the film's codes, functioning, as he puts it, 'to give the content its real meaning'.
3. In so far as Wegener is speculating on the relationship between form/technique and narrative/content, one clearly needs to interrogate the interplay between the referential material and the filmic signifier. *The Student of Prague* involves two extra-filmic referents: the importance of social mobility, embodied in Baldwin's transformation from poverty to wealth (enabling a binary opposition of rich/poor), and the motif of the Alter Ego, which the film itself locates in terms of literary antecedents (the epigraph is by Alfred de Musset), but which points forward to film noir and horror films, where it is also articulated through an interplay of spatial codes.

The division of the frame and the distinction between foreground and background of an image composed in depth becomes the basis of a textual system of repeated and alternated spatial articulations. Two central oppositions, left/right and near/far, are amplified by a third, less powerful term, frontal/diagonal. What will be elaborated in the analysis is that the film's 'meaning' is determined by this complex organisation of space. As a result, the film is 'about' Baldwin and his mirror-image occupying the left or the right hand of the frame; it is 'about' movements from the background (far-space) to the foreground (near-space) and back; finally, it is 'about' Baldwin's room being framed either frontally or diagonally.

My use of certain terms – text, repetition, alternation – should indicate the importance of Raymond Bellour's work in my analysis, particularly with regard to finding the appropriate interplay of codes with which to reconstruct the filmic system. However, other work on the evolution of the cinematic codes – specifically that of Barry Salt and Noël Burch – needs to be taken into account when dealing with a film which occupies such a curious place in film history. If my position on the question of evolution appears somewhat ambivalent, it is only because I have subordinated the notion of a developing system of cinematic codes as crucial in situating an early silent film, to the necessity of locating an internally specific system of codes. Again, this choice stems largely from *The Student of Prague*'s reluctance to sit easily within a history of film form constructed, as it were, after the fact.

Primitive or Classical?

I want to address three formal areas of early cinema as a way of introducing the properties of this film: frontality, camera movement and cutting.

1. The frontality of many shots, particularly interiors, corresponds to Burch's discussion of a residually theatrical space. Burch rejects this idea, preferring instead to equate it with an audience as yet unable to piece together fragmented views of an object. This raises two fundamental problems. For one thing, it sits uneasily with his picture of an idealised non-bourgeois audience contrasted

with the new, middle-class audience unable to find its place within the primitive film's diegesis.[7] Second, *The Student of Prague*, whose characters more often move *through* rather than *across* the frame, contains sufficient frontality and non-centred images to suggest formal primitivism. Closer analysis, however, reveals that not only are frontality and non-centred image tied to neither theatricality nor primitivism, but the fact that they are codified in the text becomes vital to its reading.

The film's deceptive use of space is well represented by its second shot, an autonomous narrative segment. It is a centred, interior, frontal long shot, with the Countess and her father seated at a table in the middle of the frame. The segment's first entrance is striking not only because it avoids the screen right/screen left choice associated with theatrical primitive cinema – inscribing itself instead into the film's space by means of a door at the rear of the frame – but also because this door opens on to an exterior of trees and woodland which will be taken up in the next segment, the hunt leading to the Countess' first meeting with Baldwin. This autonomous shot is indicative of how the film will continue to open up a new space as it breaks free of what initially appear to be the restrictions of the frame. Equally, the film's non-centred images, best typified by the opening segment (to be discussed more fully), make complex demands on the spectator's ability to scan and read the frame, while providing spatial cues central to an understanding of the narrative's unfolding.

2. Camera movement in the film largely accommodates the 'classical German' paradigm, and what Salt has identified as a particular property of the early Western;[8] it is functional, barely noticeable and occurs largely to keep actors in shot or centred in the frame. Segment seventeen, however, contains an interesting camera movement, pertaining to something like Bellour's seeing/seen opposition,[9] in what can be considered an alternative to the American paradigm of shot/reverse shot. As Baldwin makes his way to the duel with the rival he has no intention of fighting, he meets his reflection in the woods. They face each other on either side of a tree, Baldwin screen left and his double screen right, wiping his sword ominously. The reflection leaves near right, and Baldwin moves towards the rear, frame right. In the next shot (51), he is reframed in medium long shot, still right, as he backs against a tree; the camera moves to the right, reframing Baldwin on the left and opening up background space, where we can see the Baron's corpse, attended by his seconds. In early viewings, the camera appears to follow the gaze of Baldwin – he looks/we wonder what he looks at/we see what he looks at (as in classical point-of-view editing) – but in fact we see the scene before he does. The film rarely privileges the characters' gaze; as they look themselves, they are constantly also the object of the spectator's look. Baldwin's look is thus anticipated by the camera rather than causing it to move. This narratively motivated camera movement, while it confirms the suspicions of the character and the audience concerning the double's actions, none the less privileges the spectator's look by identifying it with the camera's.

3. Strictly speaking, the film does not use the classical model of continuity

The duel.

editing; the 180 degree line does not quite seem to hold, but in such a way that the cutting around the figures (which occurs rarely but noticeably) raises important questions about spatial construction in non-American films.

Segment four, the fourteenth shot in the film, introduces the mirror image into the diegesis. Baldwin's room is framed diagonally (↗), in the first interior break with frontality, Baldwin screen left, profile largely obscured, the mirror frame right, inscribing the reflection of Baldwin into the frame. As Baldwin fences with his reflection, we see what it is very tempting to read as a shot/reverse-shot structure (there is certainly a reverse field view of the hero) within a single composition, initiating the 180 degree continuity line. It is not a fanciful whim which compels one to attempt to follow through this line of thinking, for on two occasions the film cuts around Baldwin and his released reflection in what appears to be 180 degree spatial/temporal continuity.

In shot 27 (segment eight), Baldwin and the Countess walk together on the battlements, framed diagonally (↗), observed by Lyduschka. The Baron, rival for the Countess' hand, enters right and leads the Countess away, leaving Baldwin alone. He finds the Countess' dropped handkerchief and moves *to the right of the frame*, writing a note. He then turns, moves to the back of the frame and leans against a pillar, looking off to the rear. So strong is the sense of contiguity with the subsequent shots that several viewings still create the impression of classical continuity or even a primitive point-of-view cut to shot 28, with Baldwin in long shot at the rear of the frame, but now facing the camera and *framed left*. His mirror image, foregrounded, is seated in profile on the wall, *framed right*. The angle is preserved (↗), but despite strong temporal cues, an analysis of the frozen frame reveals spatial disruption. While the supernatural content of the story allows one to ignore reading the absence of the reflection framed left at the extreme rear of shot 27 as a spatial cue, it is also clear that not only is Baldwin no longer leaning on the pillar in shot 28 as a marker for a match cut, but his position is extremely difficult to read in terms of how and when he moved there from the frame in shot 27. Since we cannot assume correct eyeline matching, the reading of the two shots in reverse field cutting, in the classical sense, becomes equally problematic and ahistorical. This dilemma is scarcely helped by the uncertain status of the print currently available. Neither its authenticity, nor the precise form in which the film was seen in 1913, has been ascertained.[10]

In shot 69 (segment twenty-one), Baldwin's horse-drawn carriage, fleeing from the double, approaches the camera, passing it in close proximity. Shot 70 would match contiguously as the camera is placed behind the carriage, slightly diagonal (↗), as it moves from close behind it to pull up in front. Shot 71 match-cuts on Baldwin climbing from the coach in the previous shot, now employing an approximately 90 degree cut to medium long shot. He looks to the *top left* of the frame and our gaze is directed towards the coach driver, now revealed to be the released mirror image. The fact that these three shots roughly employ classical continuity, even down to a match cut on action, leaves us with several choices. According to Salt's account of it, this film, in 1913, would be somewhat primitive if it did not have a general conception of reverse field cutting; one might therefore conclude either that it *is* primitive and has hit upon continuity editing by accident in isolated instances, or alternatively that it does have some conception of classical scene dissection but has yet to perfect it fully.

Both these conclusions commit us to a teleological model, but the film offers a third and altogether more provocative possibility, one arising precisely out of the discovery of its specific textual system. What is important about these two segments is the way that once the double has been introduced into the text, subsequent cutting systematically explores and sustains the divided screen (and the respective demarcation of its two halves), as a code that is spatially and narratively crucial to the trajectory of the hero.

The importance of such an observation is to redefine the notion of primitivism by focusing on the codification of space first suggested by Noël Burch. While I have taken issue with certain of his conclusions, this idea none

Fencing with the reflection.

the less seems to me to be one of the most exciting contributions to film analysis. The importance of Bellour's work, on the other hand, is a more global concern with discovering filmic systems; from Griffith (*The Lonedale Operator*) to Hitchcock (*North by Northwest*, *The Birds*), the bridge between the empirical and the conceptual is negotiated by a close attention to the specific formal properties of the individual film. Bellour – more than Burch – has pointed out that narrative consists in the connection and movement between the organisation of the referential, the extra-textual, and the organisation of a filmic signifier such as the articulation of space. To a large extent, the filmic text, the system to be accounted for, is precisely the result of the imbrication of several levels of operation, and the extent to which they either support or redefine each other.

Social and Narrative Space

Thomas Elsaesser, working towards a different construction of the specificity of certain narrative and social concerns in German cinema, has drawn attention to the central motif of economic success and social mobility, and its relation to questions of genre, notably the tales of the fantastic. He writes,

> What interests me is how it gets encoded in fantastic forms, and why – given that it is a theme not only common to a lot of quite dissimilar films in Germany, but one that the cinema of other countries has made use of, especially in America.[11]

Clearly, this engages broader issues than can be dealt with here, but it is not difficult to see its importance to *The Student of Prague*. Not only is the story of Baldwin's rise to wealth encoded in fantastic terms via the mystic Scapinelli and the release of the mirror-image to haunt the student's bourgeois existence, but the cinematic realisation of these fantastic elements also encodes social mobility in a way that makes spatial organisation the signifier of social organisation, and also vice versa – social divisions imply screen division.

For in so far as it can be isolated from the mirror-divided screen struggle, the theme of social mobility can be seen to work as a rich/poor opposition along three broad spatial articulations.

First, through an alternation in the first seven segments leading to the formation of the couple. These segments unfold as follows: A. the inn; Baldwin and students (poor); B. Countess and her father (rich); C. Baldwin and the Countess meet at the hunt (poor/rich). Once established, there is an acceleration in the system of repetition/alternation, marking the beginning of Baldwin's rise, taken up spatially in the frame, and developed through the eventual elimination of the opposition between the two characters; D. Baldwin in his room (poor); E. Baldwin at the Countess' home (poor/rich); F. Baldwin in his room, joined by Scapinelli (poor/rich); G. Baldwin and Countess at the ball (poor/rich).

Second, the opposition between Baldwin and his mirror-image. This operates at two levels. The straightforward opposition between figures is established in segment four as Baldwin playfully fences with his mirror-image. The same framing occurs in segment six, at the end of which the reflection leaves the mirror; in his subsequent appearances, during Baldwin's social rise, the dress of the double, reflecting the poverty of the hero's former existence, is juxtaposed with the more lavish clothes he now wears. But while the double reminds the viewer of the rich/poor opposition, the room with the mirror from which he escapes also encodes Baldwin's changed circumstances, by way of angle (↗), décor and *mise en scène*. In some respects, the exit of Baldwin's double is the exit of poverty from his lodgings, only to appear elsewhere. In segments four and six, both angle and composition of the master shot of the room are established, to be repeated subsequently; the room is bare, with simple wooden tables and chairs. But when Scapinelli pours money on to the table in segment six, the shot predicts segment fourteen where Baldwin's changed fortunes are reflected in the transformed setting; luxurious chairs and gold candelabras replace the former simplicity, Baldwin is better dressed and, through a change of shot scale along the diagonal axis, the mirror is excluded from the frame.

Third, the depth of the frame inscribes an opposition between near and far, so that the film operates a distinction between rich and poor space and between isolated and social space, again central to the trajectory of the hero. This last point needs further expansion, dealing as it does more broadly with the complexity of the film's space. Perhaps the best place to start is the opening segment of the film, a long autonomous shot which demonstrates the constant use of space to articulate narrative concerns. It initiates a number of the film's codes and leads into the division of the frame into near and far space.

The shot is structured by an intricate circular return to its opening state, through a series of entrances and exits, so that it begins and ends with an empty, foregrounded table and chairs.[12] But there is also a compositional movement from right to left, already alluding to the coded division of the screen. When the segment opens, the empty table and chairs are framed right, until occupied by Baldwin, at which point they are centred in the frame by a discreet camera movement; as Scapinelli and Baldwin leave at the end of the segment, there is a slight camera movement to the right, so that the table, too, completes a movement from the right to the left of the frame as if propelled by the entrances and exits of the two foreground figures.

As the shot begins, its frontal staging inscribes two depth cues and two dramatic areas, marking out the diegetic space and defining the spectator's place within a non-centred frame. The students are at the rear of the frame, but the spectator's gaze is also directed towards the empty table and chairs, foreground right, inscribing a marked, because foregrounded, absence. The camera moves to the right as Baldwin enters, and the table is centred in two ways: first by the movement to reframe it, and second by Baldwin's gaze which marks two spaces for both himself and the spectator; two choices, by looking first at the students from whom both socially and spatially he will isolate himself (the first employment of near/far) and then his look at the table, which he occupies, designating it as a space of immediate narrative interest.

This division of spatial depth initiates both the placement of Baldwin, marking the beginning of his trajectory as hero, and subsequently of Lyduschka, the rejected gypsy girl, whose placement in the rear of the frame exploits the near/far opposition to transfix her constantly as both spectator and object.[13] The spectator first sees her as exhibitionist/object, as she dances at the rear of the frame.[14] She both watches Baldwin and is observed by the spectator, but Baldwin's gaze is almost made equal in force to that of the spectator by the hero's ability to withhold his; Baldwin's and Lyduschka's gazes meet briefly when he turns, but as he faces outwards, refusing to participate, Lyduschka remains the object of the spectator's gaze and herself spectator, who fails to draw the privileged gaze of Baldwin; he in turn becomes the sight object of the Countess, her father and the Baron, in segment five through a similar interplay of coded gazes.[15]

The entrance of Scapinelli in scene one acts as a particularly striking example of sub-segmental punctuation, closing the opening near/far 'isolation' sub-segment. Scapinelli inserts himself into the narrative through the first of a series of entrances into Baldwin's solitude. Most significant, however, is the form of this entrance: his carriage enters from the left-hand side of the frame into the medium distance, not only consolidating Baldwin's isolation from his peers, but actually removing them from the frame. By the time the carriage moves offscreen via the right-hand side of the frame, the students have actually disappeared from the rear of the frame. Lyduschka reappears in the background, and a triangle of gazes develops, not represented in the form of the classical point-of-view structure. Instead, all three gazes face towards the camera, with Lyduschka again both spectator and object, placed at the rear of the frame. In a segment that is frontal and shot from a fixed position, with no use of scene dissection, space is thus split up between near and far, seeing/seen, while movement within the composition underlines the division between screen left and screen right.

The near/far opposition is fully taken up in segment two, consisting of an autonomous frontal shot, but this time an interior where the Countess and her father are in their home. The depth of the previous shot does not seem to

The scene on the battlements.

exist, until the door at the rear opens on to an exterior space and a deep background which has been masked, much as Scapinelli's carriage masked and demarcated spatial relationships in segment one. It is from this extreme rear that a servant enters to announce the riders, moving from far to near into a space which privileges the Countess and her father. But the full syntagmatic force of the inscription of these spaces only emerges in segment five, an identical composition to that of segment two – both are autonomous shots – when Baldwin repeats the movement of the servant from far to near. At this point, two oppositions – one cinematic, one referential – are operating in the text through a repetition of framing, depth and movement: near/far is directly paralleled by rich/poor.

This system is developed further in segment seven, shot 21, at the ball to which Baldwin is invited by the Countess, through the extension of space to a third level of depth, thus complicating the narrative. The Countess, flanked by her father and the Baron, is centred in the foreground of the shot. Behind them, a background is composed of dancers, echoing the students in segment one, but taken further by a staircase behind the dancers, down which Baldwin enters from the extreme rear of the frame, repeating his movement from far to near which now embodies his narrative movement. Set apart from his peers by self-imposed isolation, he is also set apart by his poverty. He moves not only into a new, bourgeois society but directly into the privileged space occupied by the Countess. Both these movements – from isolation to an already established social group, from poor to rich – reach their apogee in segment nineteen, which repeats the spatial codes from segments one and seven, marking the circularity of both the narrative trajectory and the hero's fate within it. In a composition so close to that of segment seven, shot 21, that one at first assumes the setting to be identical (a closer analysis reveals that it is not), Baldwin occupies the centred, foreground space in an interior frontal shot. This near space, set against a background of dancers soon joined by Lyduschka (who repeats her provocative dance from segment one) is the one Baldwin has entered in his move into rich society, but also the space he now occupies in isolation. Thus, coming as it does after Baldwin's disgrace in the duel, it signals the culmination of his rise to power, shortly before his fall. Yet it also constitutes a return to the isolated space of the film's opening. Significantly, this autonomous shot concludes with the bored, depressed Baldwin exiting past the dancers, *from near to far* at the rear left of the frame.

The Double and the Divided Screen

In so far as the element of the fantastic exists separately from the story of social advancement – which I would suggest it does, simply by virtue of its signifying force in the textual system – its key area of articulation is the divided screen. Its function as one of a number of codes supporting the rich/poor opposition and its centrality to the structural movement of the opening segment does not fully exhaust the formal permutations associated with it. In fact, the moment at which screen division starts to operate coincides with the first appearance of the mirror in segment four, at this point still containing Baldwin's image. For the first time, Baldwin faces his reflection, here in a mock duel, specifically as an opponent ('My opponent is my mirror-image'). More significantly, the two figures are placed in their respective halves of the frame, Baldwin on the left and his reflection on the right. When in segment six – an identical composition to segment four – the reflection disappears from the mirror its absence disrupts the spatial balance of the shot, but at the same time determines screen division as an articulated code. The divided screen henceforth signifies the double even before he makes his appearance, and the conflict between Baldwin and his *alter ego* surfaces whenever the double is placed in the space of the absent mirror, as in segments eight, twelve and seventeen. This is why, on the two occasions mentioned, where editing preserves the placement of the two figures in their respective screen space, on the battlements and by the coach, recognition of the double registers as such a shock.

If the presence of the double during Baldwin's rise to power acts as a reminder of his former life, then its presence during his decline signifies more accurately a change in power between the two. This is marked directly by a reversal of position within the frame, violating space once more so that the absence of the mirror and the crossing of the divided frame announce narrative complications in the opposition between Baldwin and his reflection. In segment twenty, Baldwin is *seated right* at a gambling table; when the seat *on the left hand side of the table* is vacated by one of the departing losers, it is occupied by the double. This new division is repeated throughout segment twenty-one (shots 61, 63, 71, 74), where Baldwin is always on the right side of the frame when he confronts his double, who is on the left. The one exception is segment eleven, shot 33, where the double appears in the Countess' room as Baldwin tries to protest his innocence in the murder of the Baron. Interestingly, the Countess' room contains a mirror (the first whose reflection can be seen since segment six), which has the effect of reinscribing the double briefly on the right-hand side of the frame. The codes so far established are not broken, but renegotiated by the presence of the mirror; the absence of the reflection in the mirror and its actual presence (as Double) in the room adequately preserve the system.[16]

The film's final shot, returning to Baldwin's room, the place where space was first violated, marks a return to interior frontality, while the disruption of space is resolved by the removal of man and image. The hero's shooting of the screen-left Baldwin is, in effect, a suicide, as opposed to simply a destruction of part of his 'soul'. He has, quite literally, destroyed his own screen-space, the occupation of and struggle for which constitute the narrative trajectory.

Text and History

Clearly, this aspect of *The Student of Prague* recalls the iconography of the cinema of the fantastic generally, most notably in the horror film (but also across a broader range of American genres, with the mirror inscribing an imaginary space of the *alter ego* in such different films as *The Big Heat* and *Psycho*). Here, then, is a film which looks both backwards, to a certain Gothic *literary* tradition, embodied by writers such as E. T. A. Hoffmann, and forwards, to a cinematic codification of space whose operation is fundamental to the creation of horror and the fantastic. This prompts some speculation about its historical position in the coding of filmic horror, particularly in the notion of the mirror-*doppelgänger*. While certain aspects of the film – specifically, its technical trickery, doubling and magical disappearances – belong to a recognisable tradition, stretching back to Méliès and other early cinema 'magic', the beginning of a visual code might profitably be sought in three versions of *Dr Jekyll and Mr Hyde*, one from Selig in 1908, one by Nordisk in 1910, employing a dream ending, and one from Thanhouser with James Cruze as Dr Jekyll in 1912 (and, apparently, Harry Benham, uncredited as Mr Hyde). More strikingly, Denis Gifford, having declared that the 'German nightmare would begin, in reality, in the Summer of 1914' (the release of *Der Golem*), mentions a film made by Dueskes in 1909, *The Haunted Man*: 'Wherever he goes the same ghostly figure (apparent to none but himself) rises up with horrid imitations of his own actions.'[17] But perhaps the most interesting is the Edison Company's 1910 *Frankenstein*, with Charles Ogle as the monster. The creation of the monster in a huge cauldron, in which it takes substance before the spectator's eyes, suggests the extent to which the fantastic takes precedence over the scientific background of the story. Two sequences in particular, however, are pertinent in this context. Sickened by what he has done, Frankenstein returns to his bride-to-be and her father – his experiments take place while he is a student, again producing a social mobility subtext – and prepares for his marriage. Alone in the library, he sees the monster's reflection in the mirror; the monster sees it and flees, horrified by his own image. In the final scene, writes Anthony Slide:

> The monster, so broken down by his attempts to be with his creator, stands before a large mirror and holds out his hands entreatingly. Gradually, the real monster fades away, leaving only his reflection in the mirror. Frankenstein enters the room, and in the mirror sees the monster's reflection and not his own. Only with his love for his bride does the monster's image fade, and does Frankenstein see his own image reflected in the mirror once again.[18]

The struggle around the mirror, the disruption of space, the horror of the reflection: the apparent similarity of this 'lost' film to *The Student of Prague* complicates the relationship between certain narrative motifs, specifically those that have been identified with a national cinema – and a particular cinematic style, here one that privileges spatial coherence (even as it violates it) over scene dissection.

Returning to Paul Wegener's statement, that the technique and form of a film 'give the content its real meaning', one could argue that investigation of the individual textual system remains central to any understanding of a narrative which is not a preconceived text (whether filmic or literary or national) but determined by an interplay of specifically cinematic and referential elements. Only by decoding them as a system, which in *The Student of Prague* is grounded in the division of space between near and far, between left and right, frontal and diagonal, can one begin to comprehend the 'meaning' of this particular film, and distinguish it from its antecedents and successors. *The Student of Prague* thus both belongs to a tradition (if not of German Expressionism, then of films that give priority to spatial codes) and is *sui generis* (by the way it deploys these codes through transgressions). Film history needs film analysis, but analysis needs history just as much.

Notes

1. Quoted by Lotte Eisner in *The Haunted Screen* (London: Secker & Warburg, 1973), p. 40.
2. 'Cine-repetitions', *Screen*, vol. 20 no. 2, Summer 1979, p. 69.
3. 'Porter or ambivalence', *Screen*, vol. 19 no. 4, Winter 1978/9, pp. 91–105.
4. Eisner, *Haunted Screen*, p. 41.
5. *From Caligari to Hitler* (Princeton: Princeton University Press, 1974), p. 30.
6. Eisner, *Haunted Screen*, p. 43.
7. Noël Burch, *Correction Please* (London: Arts Council of Great Britain, 1980), pp. 4 (The People's Eyespan), 5 (Up Front).
8. 'The Early Development of Film Form', *Film Form*, No. 1, Spring 1976, p. 97.

9. The binary opposition which Bellour uses in his analyses of *North by Northwest* and *The Birds*. See 'Le blocage symbolique', *Communications*, No. 23, 1975, and '*The Birds*: analysis of a sequence', British Film Institute Seminar Paper, 1972.
10. See, for instance, Helmut H. Diederichs (ed.), *Der Student von Prag: Einführung und Protokoll* (Stuttgart: Verlagsgemeinschaft Focus Film-Texte, 1985), p. 39.
11. Thomas Elsaesser, 'Social mobility and the fantastic: German silent cinema', *Wide Angle*, vol. 5 no. 2, 1982, p. 16.
12. Something very similar is observed by Marshall Deutelbaum in his 'Structural patterning in the Lumière films' (*Wide Angle*, vol. 3 no. 1, 1979, pp. 30, 31): '... the film [*Sortie d'usine*] is a complete process: the doors open, the workers begin to leave the factory, the doors close. The film begins with the beginning of a sequential process and concludes with that process having run to its inherent conclusion.' And about *Carmaux: Défournage du coke*, Deutelbaum writes: 'As the steps of the cooling of the coke and its breakup continue, the mass moves from the upper left of the frame to the lower right.'
13. This has been noted by Mary Ann Doane, who links Lyduschka with the Double, in 'both narrative and frame', as signifying the threat of castration. On several occasions, Lyduschka is placed in the same position as the Double, hiding in a doorway, appearing unseen on the battlements. Both Lyduschka and the Double represent something from which Baldwin averts his eyes, because they are a threat to the unified self ('The Student of Prague', unpublished paper, University of Iowa, 1978).
14. Elsaesser, 'Social mobility and the fantastic', p. 18: 'We, the spectators, are made to identify with two distinct points of view: we participate as spectator-voyeurs in the girl's self-display (and are thus part of the 'student scene'), but we also identify with Baldwin's refusal to participate: as spectators we are already split well before Baldwin's double appears.'
15. The gaze, inscribed without *découpage*, plays a part in creating Baldwin as object in segment five in particular. As Baldwin enters, he is the object of four gazes; the spectator, the Countess, her father and the Baron. As he approaches the Countess, the three onscreen gazes turn to her, but she remains privileged in space. As he leaves, the gazes are as follows: Baron: Baldwin (hostile; the Baron bends his stick like a sword); Countess: Baldwin (tender, but to some extent amused); Father: Baldwin and the Countess (shifting gaze).

    This, coming as Baldwin moves to his 'far' position, marks him as object of jealousy/contempt, class division and condescension, while codifying, through the father's look, the possibility of a diegetic couple and a change of position.
16. It might be objected that this segment makes the left/right division redundant as a code, but it should be clear that it merely adds to its complexity. I would argue that other narrative features in shot 59 can account for the momentary transgression of spatial organisation.
17. Denis Gifford, *A Pictorial History of Horror Movies* (London: Hamlyn, 1973), p. 46.
18. Anthony Slide, *Early American Cinema* (New York: A. S. Barnes, 1970), p. 17.

Afterword

Recasting Traditional Film Theory

For nearly a century the opposition Lumière vs. Méliès has set the terms for a historical approach to the quest for the so-called 'language of the cinema', and left film theory with seemingly ineluctable dualisms between the realist tendencies of the cinema and its formalist potential. Long take vs. montage, ontology of the image vs. linguistic theory of the sign, phenomenology vs. semiology, perceptual vs. enunciative system are the oppositions that still determine the disagreements over the cinema as a distinct mode of signification and of subject-effects, as against its mimetic function and reality-effects.

In the preceding pages, both explicitly and implicitly, it was argued that these concepts may not be as antagonistic as they appear, but merely present different perspectives of the same object. Many of the issues dividing both traditional and contemporary film theory, for instance, seem to revolve around either stressing the material *dis*continuity of the *filmic* process, or the perceptual *con*tinuity of the *viewing* process. But the discontinuity of the filmic process, rightly regarded as a necessary condition for film to be a signifying practice or 'textual system', is usually treated, under the name of 'montage', in the historical context of modernist and constructivist theories of art (such as Eisenstein's or Vertov's), while other ways of utilising discontinuity (such as Porter's or Griffith's), are discussed as 'editing', mainly from the vantage point of the inexorable logic of the ideal of continuity. However, the forms of non-continuity and discontinuity in the films of Méliès, G. A. Smith, Williamson, Hepworth, or Ralph Ince, Maurice Tourneur and Reginald Barker, of the early Pathé productions, or Vitagraph, in the use of the external commentator or of intertitles cannot and should not be subsumed under a polemical and political division dating from the late 1910s and early 20s. Neither can the very complex issue of spatial coherence and staging in depth be subsumed under Bazinian notions of deep focus and the long take. Rather, in the context of early cinema films from the first two or three decades are becoming the occasion for re-examining both the historical conditions and the ideological implications of the emblematic split between montage and realism, which such an investigation may well reveal as not having been a split after all.[1]

Likewise, the continuity-effect, though it has always been central to critical theories of realism, has until recently not been analysed in the light of the relation between film technology and spectatorial subjectivity (the cinematic apparatus and its psychic 'dispositif'). Though the fundamental role of narrative in producing coherence both as a 'reality effect' (a verisimilitude) and a 'subject effect' (a point of address) is better understood, narrative (in the form of the screenplay or the continuity script functioning as a technical blue-print) had until recently not been studied. Narrative now appears crucially determined not only by ideological or anthropological factors but by industrial and economic factors (degree of standardisation, division of labour, ownership of copyright and patents). Once these implications of the new film history are fully grasped, the schisms in film theory may come to be regarded as resulting from different methodological choices: whether priority is accorded to cinema as a specific form of production (aesthetic, technologic, semiologic) or as a specific form of experience (perceptual, psychic, cognitive), whether one is looking at a 'commodity' or a 'service'.

Such a formulation would point to the properly historical ground on which the traditional antinomies are built, because in one case it requires a detailed study of the interaction between technology, economics, style and signification: precisely, a given cinema's mode of representation. In the other case, an equally historical investigation is necessary into the conditions of reception, detailing the changing forms of presenting film to a public, the different exhibition contexts and commodities, the 'building' of audiences, but also the histories of pleasure and affect, of subjectivity and gender, of memory, perception and cognition, as they are taken in charge by the cinema. Thus, while the attempt to give film *theory* a historical grounding may not be the primary motive of current research into early cinema, its close study has acted as a powerful stimulus, certain to revise ideas about the 'language of cinema', if only by proposing a vocabulary that avoids the metaphoric and misleading associations of the term *grammar* which tended to dominate earlier discussions. It could also open out the linguistic models typical of recent, semiological analyses, towards more context-sensitive accounts of how meaning is constructed and coherence produced, making fruitful new work in narratology, pragmatics, and cognitive theory.

The Evolution of Film: A History of Forms or Pragmatics of Norms?

Film historians have often behaved as if cinema had evolved inexorably towards a goal or an ideal form, usually an ever greater approximation of reality and natural perception. This assumption takes for granted the transparency of the medium, for any realism argument ultimately gives the cinema the status of a natural language.[2] Yet as we know from literature or painting, the arts have always developed special modes of depiction and description (the application of the conventions of perspective in painting, or point-of-view technique in the novel), in order to convey realism to the beholder or reader.[3] Empirically the argument is also problematic: if the advent of sound could still be seen as 'adding realism', already the introduction of colour needed to be conventionalised before it was accepted as 'realistic'.[4] More recently, the extensive use of special effects and dolby sound has created not an impression of realism, but an ever greater illusionism, itself a complex and contradictory state of mind and perception. Early cinema is a very convincing case that film too, from its very beginnings, relied on convention to make images intelligible, while its pleasures became very complex, and thus, as a medium, it developed its own representational 'codes'. Ben Brewster has pointed to this other side of representation when he argued that one of the major pleasures of any system of representation consists precisely in the particular combination of contradictory exigencies, such as telling a story in beautifully composed pictures – exigencies potentially so contradictory that they will always give rise to alternative ways of recombining them.[5]

To the 'ideal form' argument, where progress is measured by recourse to a 'film grammar', from which a history of forms could be derived, the films of the first twenty years of the cinema also pose a challenge. Many are very nearly incomprehensible if viewed as faltering examples and tentative approximations of an optimally expressive or formally 'correct' film language. Similarly, their diversity seems a mere matter of chance or whim if one believes in forms generating a momentum of their own towards a manifest destiny. Evolutionary theories of the cinema, whether teleological as with André Bazin,[6] or Darwinian as with Barry Salt,[7] are problematic wherever a single objective is deemed to push in one direction, to the exclusion of others. Historically, the modalities of change are perhaps best understood as compromises arising out of contending options and priorities. These ultimately refer to forces operating outside the cinema – be they 'cultural' in the broadest sense, or economic and institutional, or having to do more narrowly with the pleasuress or experiences individuals are prepared to invest time in or pay for, on which in turn such economic priorities as profit maximisation depend. As far as the cinema is concerned, such larger systems would seem to have less to do with realism and more with narrative, less with micro-units of signification like phonemes, and more with macro-units like syntagms, less with perception and more with modes of conceptualisation and codes of representation. In this respect, the early cinema situates itself in a tension between presentation and representation,[8] performance and narrative,[9] showing and telling – with the proviso that one should not see such binary oppositions as mutually exclusive, but rather as polarities that imply each other or 'values' that regulate each other.

Primitive Cinema/Classical Cinema

The most influential work in cinema studies in recent years has centred on what has always been perceived as a pervasive though culturally distinct form of film-making, that associated with Hollywood. Without going into the different definitions and ramifications of classical cinema,[10] one can say that it was, paradoxically, the very normative force of this style or mode which revitalised the study of its historical antecedents and alternatives, in contrast to the search for the origins of film as language.

In analysing 'primitive', 'early' or 'pre-Griffith' cinema, there has thus been throughout a tendency to define it against what it was not, by using the classical paradigm as the implicit vantage point. This is where the 'old' history intersects with the 'new', and where one needs to be especially vigilant not to construct binary models around early cinema, but also not to posit total rupture between different modes. The most productive approach seems to be to elaborate internal criteria for each mode, leaving open the possibility of more points of transition (the American 1910s now appear much more contradictory and interesting), persistence of elements from earlier modes (the European cinema of both the 1910s and early 20s) and more subtle transformations (alternatives within the classical mode).

In deciding whether a given film belongs to one mode rather than another, three aspects seem to be of special significance. The first of these is *mise en scène* or staging, which includes the relation of the filmic to the pro-filmic, the construction of a distinct space, and the function of the frame. Secondly there is editing, which involves the relation between shots, and of shot to scene, and the creation of a distinct temporality and causality. And finally there is filmic narration – the relation between 'showing' and 'telling', the kinds of spectator-positioning and modes of address – which needs to be studied both at the micro-level, starting with the single scene film or tableau, and at the macro-level, in the multi-reel film and the full feature films of Griffith, with their very complex and yet often non-classical organisation of narrative.

For instance, if the benchmarks for the emergence of the classical style are, say, match-cutting and diegetic unity from scene to scene, then shot transitions not governed by the rules of continuity editing naturally become important markers of difference. Likewise, if frontal staging is generally agreed to be a typical feature of non-classical paradigms, then attention and the weight of differentiation will be concentrated on whether a film shows evidence of deep staging or is constructed in shallow space, what lighting it employs, and how its figures are placed in relation to the frame. If point-of-view shots are generally agreed as signs of the classical mode, it now seems that different kinds of point-of-view shots served as narrational links even during the 'primitive' or 'transitional' period. And if the state of film technique allows only for a fixed camera position, then shot-size or scale become decisive signifying elements. On the other hand, once certain technical constraints no longer operate, a different set of variables will make up the filmic system and provide a pertinent trait: this is the case of the cutting speed and shot length from the 1910s onwards – according to Barry Salt the most reliable indices for periodisation and for individual or national stylistic differences. All of this work on space, editing, narration – some presented in Part I of this Reader – points decisively to the fact that 'primitive' cinema can no longer be seen as the medium's infancy or latency period, nor as chaos and disorder. What it does not prove conclusively is whether one is dealing with a signifying system in its own right.

An Autonomous Mode of Representation?

In trying to get away from the notion of grammar or language, while none the less recognising the fundamentally 'semiotic' (constructed and signifying) character of filmic images, Burch gave currency to the term 'mode of representation' which set out to cover a broader field than just the filmic. Burch's mode of representation embraces: historically pertinent media and spectacle intertexts (optical toys, dioramas, vaudeville, variety theatre, operetta, stage melodrama); formal parameters (staging, shot relations, kinds of closure, editing, inserts); the social parameters (spectatorial foreknowledge of story material, ethnic appeal, class and respectability, gender and morality); and finally, the recognition that changes in film style and film technique are determined not by acts of God or individual genius, but by an interaction of several, often unevenly operating pressures or constraints.

Since questions of historically specific 'representations' have dominated the field of cultural studies generally, the term is useful because it wants to bridge certain divisions and recast the question of style in the context of both ideology and cultural history, indeed cultural epistemology. It is also indicative of the wider change from a civilisation of the word to a civilisation of the image alluded to at the outset. Burch has been most consistent in defending the position that early cinema is a distinct mode of representation, though conceding that it evolved over time (under complex and sometimes contradictory determinations) and that it contained, within its own specific terms, other systems, of which the classical is only one possible – albeit for more than half a century the dominant – mode.[11]

Burch's close reading of films by Porter,[12] and later those of the Lumières and Griffith, attempted to show that from their work other modes of representation – those of the different avant-gardes, but also of European art films – could draw their examples, and consequently, there was little that was inevitable about the turn film form had taken in the 1910s and 20s. Hence his interest in the filmic avant-gardes and in non-Hollywood national cinemas, such as that of Japan, or of Scandinavia, France, Germany and Russia in the 1920s. Burch also argued that in order to understand films historically, pre-cinematic and non-cinematic forms of spectacle, storytelling and imaging have to be taken into account: from still photography and picture postcards, panoramas and dioramas, to the influence of the legitimate stage and newspaper cartoons. But he also tried to rescue political and social history as determinants. In some of Burch's work, notably 'Porter or Ambivalence', there is the suggestion that the primitive mode defines a wholly autonomous system, which cannot only be described, but can also be explained in terms of distinct historical and ideological factors. Later, he tended to regard the different kinds of staging, editing and narrating up to 1907 'archaeologically': as a distinct mode, separated from subsequent developments of the cinema epistemologically, even if this was not strictly the case historically.[13]

Other writers have not followed him in this direction, not least because Burch's model of the dynamic of change and transformation seemed too obviously cast in ideological terms and to rely on historical generalisations which could not be sustained by the available evidence. For Burch, the motive force of change was the cinema's rapid appropriation by the ideological interests of the bourgeoisie: their conception of the individual, their need to 'centre' the spectator (rather than let him/her scan the image), to repress the apparatus for illusionist purposes (rather than display the devices of illusionism) and to engage the viewer in a voyeuristic relation with the representation (rather than letting the spectator judge a 'presentation'). Since these criteria are identical with the ideological characteristics identified by Comolli and Baudry not only for classical cinema, but for all bourgeois modes of representation, Burch's argument for explaining change tends to be tautological: the cinema became bourgeois because the bourgeoisie imposed its mode of representation on the cinema.

The Search for Formal Criteria and Stable Norms

It is possible to discover similar 'blind spots' or hidden tautologies in the models for change put forward by other writers. In much of Salt's work, for instance, correctness, smoothness, cutting speed and realism remain implicitly the motive forces of stylistic change. Conversely, positing internally generated norms or attempting to establish variables which operate as a system of functional equivalent means sooner or later going outside stylistic evidence in order to explain change historically. Thus, as some of the essays in Part II of this Reader have indicated, it may well be the case that the cinema's history has been more decisively determined by the industrial-institutional context than by the texts, and that within this context the dynamics of audience-gathering through exhibition practices and distribution control have been more decisive than the organisation of the production process, making it especially difficult to separate the 'history' of films from cinema history. Ben Brewster's (so far unpublished) work on multi-reel films seems to me exemplary in reading specific films across a very sophisticated approach to both industry and distribution data.

Stylistic and technical norms, established comparatively, are beginning to provide pertinent and stable criteria for basic historical research. Besides allowing historians to classify and attribute undated or newly discovered films, and establish the parameters available at a given time to a director or studio in a given country, they also serve to index more general changes in film form – though not, as claimed in traditional accounts of the cinema's evolution, in terms of any teleological progression towards some ideal, be it realism or technical correctness. On the contrary, it becomes clear that change is not linear, but occurs in leaps; not on a single front, but in more jagged lines and waves: the history of film form emerges as a complicated transformational process involving shifts in several dimensions.

The problem for the historian who has learnt to guard against viewing early cinema as infantile and incoherent, is to resist presenting it as static. David Bordwell, Janet Staiger and Kristin Thompson, in their *Classical Hollywood Cinema* have pointed to the paradox that, while during the first twenty years of the cinema, from 1896 to 1917, change seems to have been rapid, abrupt and momentous, from 1917 to 1967 the dominant film form (exemplified by mainstream American cinema) underwent only very slow and gradual change. By comparison, Gunning offers a more dialectical view of a film form in transition – rather like a system of constraints and possibilities, within which particular logics and ideologies of filmic representation manifest themselves, without adhering to any overall design or ideal type. On the other hand, the couplet 'cinema of attraction'/'cinema of narrative integration' is itself problematic. Whereas the first term has considerable descriptive power, because of the many levels of textual differentiation it allows, the second risks being used in a tautological way, with practices that are in fact heterogeneous becoming unified around a theoretical construct virtually indistinguishable from (definitions of) classical Hollywood cinema.

A way forward would be to regard stylistic norms determined by the interplay of several factors – generic, social, economic and technical – which would constitute a recognisable mode, only in a more restricted sense. Here two views are possible. On the one hand early cinema can be considered (as it is by Burch, Chanan, Musser) to be mimetic of certain social, instructional and entertainment forms predating the cinema – thus emphasising the historical specificity of the cinema experience as well as its continuity with other screen practices or spectacle attractions. Or on the other hand (in this case following Salt, Brewster, Staiger and Thompson) the emphasis would be more on questions of intelligibility, narrative efficacy and diegetic coherence – the cinema as the production of a distinct and unique economy of the visible. In this second model, changes, if not exactly linear, inscribe themselves in a continuum determined either by the imperatives of narrative (how best to tell a story), or the technological-economic developments of the cinema (how to organise the making of films as a mass-production industry). Gunning's division, in a sense, leans first to one side, then the other.

Showing and Telling: Institution and Text

André Gaudreault on the other hand, tries to understand the shifts and changes from one mode to another within a unitary conceptual framework: that of narration. His distinctions name a continuum of narrational stances and narrative instances, allowing for different types of narration, of which one class he calls monstration ('showing'). This is intended not only to overcome the difficulties of Burch's opposition between presentation and representation, but also to shift the debate away from form (as a static or structural principle) to process and structuring principles. For the term 'mode of representation', useful though it is for signalling the interrelation off quite different aspects of cinema and as a counterweight to the term 'mode of production', inherently raises a number of problems. For instance, in order to comprehend film as a system, one has to see the filmic coding of space and time not in isolation but in conjunction with narrative codes.

Gaudreault's work, while heavily theoretical at one level, and quite taxonomical at another, draws attention to precisely the forces that organise and unify the text, which in the early cinema can be 'monstrative', that is constituted and constructed from outside the text. Accounts which see magic lantern shows, dioramas, Hale's Tours or vaudeville as the 'precursors' of the cinema need to decide whether the subjects and genres which the first films adapted or copied from already popular sketches or story material were not significantly transformed by the manner in which the cinema's 'monstration' is a fundamentally different way of 'telling' than, say, the same 'story' as a comic book image sequence. By his very insistence on different modes of presentation and 'performance', Gaudreault reminds us that we need to look at the larger context of early cinema, if we want to understand its history, leaving open the possibility that monstration may be a mode of narration that has coexisted in different ways alongside 'classical' modes throughout the history of the cinema (for example, in comedy shorts, in performer oriented genres such as musicals). With this, attention is directed towards the institution cinema and its historical dynamics.

The second part of the Reader thus in some sense inverts the perspective of the first, and documents a different, though complementary, way of writing the history of early cinema. When films were first shown to a paying public in 1896, most of the technologies and inventions necessary – photography, moving images, projection techniques – already had a history. Similarly, the entertainment form the Lumière cinematographe helped to create – the cinema – was in important respects a continuation of what had gone before, developing out of existing show-businesses. As such, it inherited many of the 'screen practices'[14] of the 19th century. Equally important, the cinema could draw on already existing audiences – though quite diverse in class and taste – who were accustomed to magic lantern shows and vaudeville, the music hall and variety theatre, who bought optical toys for their children or attended illustrated lectures of popularised scientific experiments, who frequented department stores and undertook railway journeys.[15]

Parallel to the study of the formal properties of early film, the last decade has thus seen a new conception of the material history of cinema, both at the production level (as an industry) and in the way the cinema (as social and demographic fact) has occupied and transformed a number of public spheres. Several different strands in this history can be made out. A new assessment of the role of film technology, of patent wars, litigation and licensing agreements has sketched a picture of early cinema within the general history of the changes from artisanal manufacture, to entrepreneurial and then managerial capitalism. Focusing on the dynamics of standardisation, division of labour and product differentiation has generated useful paradigms for researching the first production companies, their various strategies for survival and dominance, culminating in the emergence of the studio system.

While in the United States the enormous demand from the public meant that the industry rapidly had to develop novel forms of industrial organisation and business methods to regulate the circulation of capital and product, in Europe (but not only there) the cinema as an emergent social institution found itself drawn into debates worrying about public order and demanding, in the name of morality, new social controls (often aimed at women and the lower classes) that expressed fear of the cinema's impact on consumption and consumer behaviour. Research on the Nickelodeon boom (in America the 'engine' of the cinema's change of social status), its definition of its basic commodity and transformation of its production methods) suggest that the history of the cinema might indeed have been exhibition-driven rather than production-driven, thus raising interesting questions about the film-text, its mode of closure and narrative coherence especially in the crucial years between the single-reel film and the multi-reel feature as the standard product. Since the economics of film distribution and film exhibition appear to have determined not only the organisation of production but also a reorientation of production towards narrative subjects over documentary films and vaudeville sketches, it seems likely that the question of formal and stylistic changes (and thus the shifts between the primitive mode, transitional mode and classical mode) can only be answered by studying the distribution and exhibition sectors with this new agenda in mind. In particular, their respective degree of control (financial, but also 'editorial') over the production sector at a given time has come under closer scrutiny.

These lines of research have also given a more symptomatic but also systematic importance to such apparently marginal aspects of early cinema as the lecturer, the use of sound-effects and musical accompaniment (which Gaudreault sees as part of a film's narrational processes), but also to the kinds of control exerted by the exhibitor in the sequencing of reels for a given performance (what today in television we would call the programme schedule, where a similar 'editorial control' is crucial to the whole institution as well as the viewing experience). Such a material history of the cinema's beginnings would provide a valid model for studying other periods in transition, when technological and economic factors push for change on an international scale.

Film History – A Dialectics of Transformations

Future work in early cinema might well fall into several categories: investigations inspired by nothing less than the reconstruction of the fabric of history itself as it pertains to the films both extant and lost, preferring descriptive accounts to any placing of cinema in a wider conceptual framework. By contrast work on the contexts (the cultural and demographic facts, the industrial and economic ones) reflects the fact that some historians are thinking about the cinema more and more against a background of television, which is so much more context- than text-defined, just as its production apparatus is distribution-, exhibition- and audience-oriented, rather than author-oriented. But to write film history from an engagement with the present means also being able to judge the distinctiveness of the past, and not foregrounding features which at a given point in history may not have had the same importance.

It is in problems of theory, then, and their implementation in a properly historical method that the most abstract and most concrete issues in early cinema converge. In historical explanation, which is a retrospective process, the object of analysis only emerges as a construction of a theoretical discourse. For Burch, this was a central concern and lay at the base of his efforts to define the relationship between the primitive and the institutional mode of representation. Although he tended to restrict this process to the period preceding the consolidation of the institutional mode, there is no reason why the historical or geographical parameters cannot be extended.[16] Gaudreault's categories around narration, Gunning's 'continuity, non-continuity, discontinuity', Bordwell, Staiger and Thompson's work on the classical cinema's mode of production, or Brewster's distinction between different forms of spatial organisation and his work on point of view are proving productive in that they allow an understanding of the development of other practices, such as the European ones in the 1910s and 20s, which fit awkwardly into either primitive or classical modes.[17]

Far from simply developing from the primitive to the classical mode, cinema throughout its history has retained and redeployed aspects of the primitive as well as the institutional mode, each responding to a certain set of problems. From this perspective, Gunning's cinema of narrative integration may take on an extended meaning, in that it could imply its opposite – narrative dis-integration – especially if one regards 'integration' not simply as a feature of narrative or visual style, but as the site of economic, technological and industrial struggles as well. The history of the cinema would then be that of its incessant, centrifugal and decentering transformations, driven by forces which are themselves caught in but not limited to, the revolutions undergone by capitalism as it seeks to integrate more and more aspects of material and immaterial culture, forcing these cultures into ever novel forms of differentiation as the source of both meaning and pleasure.

Thomas Elsaesser

Notes

1. For a similar argument, see Noël Burch, 'Charles Baudelaire vs. Dr Frankenstein', *Afterimage* no. 8/9, Winter 1980/81, pp. 4–21.
2. 'First there is the prevailing thesis concerning these beginnings, according to which a language gradually emerged out of a sort of primordial chaos generally described as 'theatrical': *the* language, the cinema's *natural language*. (Noël Burch, 'Porter or Ambivalence', *Screen*, vol. 19 no. 4, Winter 1978/9, p. 95.)
3. Noël Burch, as one of the major proponents of the 'return' to early cinema, has always had a particular interest in the nature of the cinematic signifier and film form. See, for instance, his *Theory of Film Practice* (London: Secker and Warburg, 1973).
4. This has been most cogently argued in Edward Branigan, 'Color and Cinema: Problems in the Writing of History', *Film Reader* 4, 1979, pp. 16–34.
5. Ben Brewster, 'Early Cinema, Editing, Subject Matter, Space', presentation at the 'Putting Narrative in Place' Conference, Derby, December 1982.
6. See André Bazin, 'Towards the Evolution of Filmic Language' in *What is Cinema?, vol. I*, trans. Hugh Grey, (Berkeley: University of California Press, 1971).
7. See Barry Salt, who speaks of 'evolutionary dead ends' in 'Film Form 1900–1906' (above, p. 31).
8. Noël Burch's terms in 'Porter or Ambivalence', p. 93.
9. This pair of terms might subsume both the distinction made by Mitry between theatricality and narrativity (*Histoire du cinéma*, Paris: Editions Universitaires, 1967, p. 200), and the critique of Mitry formulated by Gaudreault (' "Théâtralité" et "narrativité" dans l'oeuvre de Georges Méliès' in *Méliès et la naissance du spectacle cinématographique*, Paris: Klincksieck, 1984, p. 199–219) and Tom Gunning's reformulation in *Early Development of Film Narrative: D. W. Griffith's First Films at Biograph (1908–1909)*, doctoral thesis, New York University, 1985.
10. As a brief reminder, these comprise ideological readings, inspired by Louis Althusser and associated with Jean Louis Comolli; semiological analyses drawing on Saussure and Barthes, known mainly through Christian Metz and Peter Wollen; psychoanalytic readings by Raymond Bellour and Stephen Heath; feminist deconstructions by Laura

Mulvey, Teresa de Lauretis and Mary Ann Doane; formalist definitions proposed by David Bordwell and Kristin Thompson; statistical style analysis by Barry Salt; economic definitions by Douglas Gomery, Robert C. Allen and Janet Staiger.

11. Burch's writings on the subject have now been collected (and extensively revised) in his book *La Lucarne de l'infini* (published in English as *Life to those Shadows*, trans. and ed. Ben Brewster (London: British Film Institute and Berkeley: University of California, forthcoming)).
12. Burch called Porter the 'Janus' of early cinema. See 'Porter or Ambivalence', p. 99.
13. See Noël Burch, 'Un mode de representation primitive?', *Iris* vol. 2 no. 1, 1984, pp. 112–123 (in English, above, pp. 220–7).
14. The term comes from Charles Musser, 'Towards a History of Screen Practice' (*Quarterly Review of Film Studies*, vol. 3 no. 1, Winter 1984), pp. 59–69.
15. See Henry V. Hopwood, who writes in *Living Pictures* (1899): 'A film for projecting a living picture is nothing more, after all, than a multiple lantern slide' (quoted in Charles Musser, 'Towards a History of Screen Practice', p. 59).
16. In a subsequent article Burch is precisely trying to formulate the relation between primitive cinema and television, and to develop a notion of an ongoing transformational process. See Noël Burch, 'Narrative/Diegesis – Threshold, Limits', *Screen* vol. 23 no. 2, July/August 1982, pp. 16–33.
17. Even for the European cinemas of the 1920s the label 'avant garde' raises many problems, both textual and economic, since the so-called German Expressionist cinema, the Soviet cinema and even French surrealist cinema point to ongoing struggles within national film industries, and between national film industries and Hollywood: struggles which make these 'avantgardes' not only formally very different from each other.

Select Bibliography

This bibliography is not exhaustive. It lists original date and place of publication (where applicable) for the essays included in the Reader, as well as a selection of references cited in the introductions and elsewhere. Many of the entries come from reading lists, compiled by myself, but also by colleagues at the University of East Anglia, the University of Kent, and Derby College of Higher Education. The emphasis is on studies that have appeared since the 1970s. A number of earlier works are also included, be they standard texts, with which the 'new film history' is in dialogue and debate, or be they labours of love and scholarship which, whatever their shortcomings, are still the best reference works available.

Books

a. *General Reference Works and Early Cinema in the United States*

AFI Catalog of Feature Films, 1911–1920 (Berkeley: University of California Press, 1989).

Robert C. Allen and Douglas Gomery, *Film History: Theory and Practice* (New York: Alfred H. Knopf, 1985).

David Bordwell, Janet Staiger, Kristin Thompson, *The Classical Hollywood Cinema: Film Style and Mode of Production to 1960* (London: Routledge and Kegan Paul, 1985).

Kevin Brownlow, *The Parade's Gone By* (London: Paladin, 1968).

Kevin Brownlow, *Hollywood the Pioneers* (London: Collins, 1979).

Noël Burch, *Theory of Film Practice* (New York: Praeger, 1970).

—— *Life To Those Shadows* (London: British Film Institute and Berkeley: University of California Press, 1990).

Gary Carey, *Lost Films* (Greenwich, CT: New York Graphic Society, 1970).

C. W. Ceram, *Archaeology of the Cinema* (London: Thames and Hudson, 1965).

Paolo Cherchi Usai and Lorenzo Codelli (eds.), *Sulla Via di Hollywood/The Path to Hollywood* (Pordenone: Edizioni Biblioteca dell'Immagine, 1988).

David Cook, *A History of Narrative Film* (New York: W. W. Norton, 2nd ed., 1989).

Donald Crafton, *Before Mickey: The Animated Film 1898–1928* (Cambridge, MA: The MIT Press, 1982).

Richard deCordova, *Picture Personalities: The Emergence of the Star System in America, 1907–1922* (Champaign: University of Illinois Press, 1990).

Jacques Deslandes and Jacques Richard, *Histoire comparée du cinéma* vol. II Du cinématographe au cinéma 1896–1906 (Tournai: Casterman, 1968).

Marshall A. Deutelbaum (ed.), *'Image': On the Art and Evolution of the Film* (New York: Dover, 1979).

William K. Everson, *American Silent Film* (New York: Oxford University Press, 1978).

John L. Fell, *A History of Films* (New York: Holt, Rinehart and Winston, 1979).

John L. Fell (ed.), *Film Before Griffith* (Berkeley: University of California Press, 1983).

Raymond Fielding, *The American Newsreel, 1911–1967* (Norman, Oklahoma: University of Oklahoma Press, 1972).

André Gaudreault (ed.), *Ce que je vois de mon ciné* (Paris: Meridiens Klincksieck, 1988).

Robert Grau, *The Theatre of Science: A Volume of Progress and Achievement in the Motion Picture Industry* (New York: Broadway Publishing Co., 1914).
Gordon Hendricks, *Origins of the American Film* (New York: Arno Press, 1972).
Roger Holman (ed.), *Cinema 1900–1906: An Analytical Study* (Brussels: Fédération Internationale des Archives du Film, 1982) (second volume edited by André Gaudreault).
Lewis Jacobs, *The Rise of the American Film* (New York: Teachers College Press, 1968).
Kalton C. Lahue, *Continued Next Week: A History of the Moving Picture Serial* (Norman, Oklahoma: Oklahoma University Press, 1964).
Einar Lauritzen and Gunnar Lundquist, *American Film Index 1908–1915* (Stockholm, 1976).
Jay Leyda, Charles Musser (eds.), *Before Hollywood* (New York: American Federation of the Arts, 1987).
Gerald Mast (ed.), *The Movies in Our Midst* (Chicago: University of Chicago Press, 1982).
Lary May, *Screening out the Past: The Birth of Mass Culture and the Motion Picture Industry* (New York: Oxford University Press, 1980).
Kenneth McGowan, *Behind the Screen: The History and Technique of the Motion Picture* (New York: Delta, 1965).
Jean Mitry, *Histoire du cinéma: art et industrie*, vol. I (1895–1914) and II (1915–1925) (Paris: Editions Universitaires, 1967/69).
Hugo Munsterberg, *Film: A Psychological Study* (New York: Dover, 1970).
Charles Musser, *Thomas Edison Papers: A Guide to Motion Picture Catalogues by American Producers and Distributors 1894–1908* (Frederick, MD: University Publications of America, 1985).
—— *The Emergence of Cinema: The American Screen to 1907* (New York: Scribner/Macmillan, 1990).
Kemp R. Niver, *Motion Pictures from The Library of Congress Paper Print Collection 1894–1912* (Berkeley and Los Angeles: University of California Press, 1967).
—— *The First Twenty Years: A Segment of Film History* (Los Angeles: Locare Research Group, 1968).
Joseph H. North, *The Early Development of the Motion Picture 1887–1909* (New York: Arno Press, 1973).
George C. Pratt (ed.), *Spellbound in Darkness, A History of the Silent Film* (Greenwich, Conn.: New York Graphic Society, 1973).
Terry Ramsaye, *A Million and One Nights* (New York: Simon and Schuster, 1926).
Georges Sadoul, *Histoire générale du cinéma*, vol. 1–5 (Paris: Denoel, 1973ff).
Richard Sanderson, *A Historical Study of the Development of American Motion Picture Content and Technique Prior to 1904* (New York: Arno Press, 1977).
Wolfgang Schivelbusch, *The Railway Journey: Trains and Travel in the 19th Century* (New York: Urizen Books, 1980).
Robert Sklar, *Movie-Made America* (New York: Random House, 1975).
Anthony Slide, *Early American Cinema* (London, New York: A. S. Barnes and Co., 1970)
—— *Aspects of American Film History Prior to 1920* (Metuchen, NJ: The Scarecrow Press, 1978).
Paul Spehr, *The Movies Begin, Making Movies in New Jersey 1887–1920* (Newark: The Newark Museum/Morgan and Morgan, 1977).
Edward Wagenknecht, *The Movies in the Age of Innocence* (Norman, Oklahoma: University of Oklahoma Press, 1962).

b. *Cinema and Other Media*

Robert C. Allen, *Vaudeville and Film 1895–1915: A study in media interaction* (New York: Arno Press, 1980).
Eric Barnouw, *The Magician and the Cinema* (New York: Oxford University Press, 1981).
Olive Cook, *Movement in Two Dimensions* (London: Hutchinson, 1963).
Michael Chanan, *The Dream That Kicks* (London: Routledge and Kegan Paul, 1980).
Hassan El Nouty, *Théâtre et pré-cinéma. Essai sur la problématique du spectacle au 19è siècle* (Paris: 1978).

John L. Fell, *Film and the Narrative Tradition* (Norman, Oklahoma: University of Oklahoma Press, 1974).
G. A. Household, *To Catch a Sunbeam: Victorian Reality through the Magic Lantern* (London: Michael Joseph, 1979).
Steve Humphries, *Victorian Britain Through the Magic Lantern* (London: Sidgwick and Jackson, 1989).
The Magic Lantern Society of Great Britain, *The Ten Year Book* (London, 1986).
Stephan Oettermann, *Das Panorama: Geschichte eines Massenmediums* (Frankfurt/Main: Syndikat, 1980).
Nicholas Vardac, *Stage to Screen: Theatrical Method from Garrick to Griffith* (Cambridge, MA: Harvard University Press, 1949).

c. *The Film Industry*

Tino Balio (ed.), *The American Film Industry* (Madison: University of Wisconsin Press, 1976).
Fred Balshofer and Arthur C. Miller, *One Reel a Week* (Berkeley and Los Angeles: University of California Press, 1967).
Paolo Cherchi Usai (ed.), *Vitagraph Co of America: il cinema prima di Hollywood* (Pordenone: Edizioni Biblioteca dell'Immagine, 1987).
Benjamin D. Hampton, *History of the American Film Industry* (New York: Dover, 1970).
Kalton Lahue, *Motion Picture Pioneer: The Selig Polyscope* (New York: AS Barnes and Co., 1973).
Timothy James Lyons, *The Silent Partner, The History of the American Film Manufacturing Company 1910–1921* (New York: 1974).
Anthony Slide, *The Big V: A History of the Vitagraph Company* (Metuchen, NJ: Scarecrow Press, 1987).
Robert Stanley, *The Celluloid Empire* (New York: Hastings House, 1978).
Nancy Wood, *The Film Industry* (London: BFI Education Department, June 1985).

d. *Film Technology*

Brian Coe, *The History of Movie Photography* (London: Ash and Grant, 1981).
Raymond Fielding (ed.), *A Technological History of Motion Pictures and Television*: An anthology from the pages of the Journal of the Society of Motion Picture and Television Engineers (Los Angeles, Berkeley: University of California Press, 1967).
Reese Jenkins, *Images and Enterprise: Technology and the American Photographic Industry 1839–1925* (Baltimore: Johns Hopkins Press, 1975).
Barry Salt, *Film Style and Technology: History and Analysis* (London: Starword, 1983).

e. *Individual Studies of Film 'Pioneers'*

Karl Brown, *Adventures with D. W. Griffith* as told to Kevin Brownlow (New York: Farrar, Straus and Giroux, 1973).
Tom Gunning, *D. W. Griffith and the Origins of American Narrative Film* (Champaign: University of Illinois Press, 1990).
John Frazer, *Artificially Arranged Scenes, the Films of Georges Méliès* (Boston: G.K. Hall, 1979).
Harry M. Geduld (ed.), *Focus on D. W. Griffith* (Englewood Cliffs, NJ: Prentice-Hall, 1971).
Alice Guy, *Autobiographie d'une pionière du cinéma* (Paris: Denoel, 1976).
Paul Hammond, *Marvellous Méliès* (London: Gordon Frazer Gallery, 1974).
Robert M. Henderson, *D. W. Griffith, the Years at Biograph* (New York: Farrar, Straus and Giroux, 1970).
Gordon Hendricks, *The Edison Motion Picture Myth* Berkeley and Los Angeles: University of California Press, 1961).
Pierre Jenn, *Georges Méliès cinéaste* (Paris: Albatros, 1984).
Richard Koszarski (ed.), *The Rivals of D. W. Griffith: Alternate Auteurs 1913–1918* (Minneapolis: Walker Arts Centre, 1976).
Kalton Lahue, *World of laughter, the motion picture comedy short 1910–1930* (Norman, Oklahoma: University of Oklahoma Press, 1966).

David Levy, *Edwin S. Porter and the Origins of the American Narrative Film, 1894–1907* (PhD thesis, McGill University, 1983).
Madeleine Malthête-Méliès (ed.), *Méliès et la naissance du spectacle cinématographique* (Paris: Klincksieck, 1984).
Jean Mottet (ed.), *D. W. Griffith* (Paris: L'Harmattan, 1984).
Paul O'Dell, *Griffith and the Rise of Hollywood* (New York: A. S. Barnes, 1970).
Georges Sadoul, *Lumière et Méliès* (Paris: Lherminier, 1986).

f. *British Cinema*
John Barnes, *The Beginnings of the Cinema in England* (London: David and Charles, 1976).
—— *The Rise of the Cinema in Great Britain* (London: Bishopsgate Press, 1983).
Michael Chanan, *The Dream That Kicks* (London: Routledge and Kegan Paul, 1980).
Denis Gifford, *The British Film Catalogue 1895–1970* (London, New York: McGraw-Hill Book Company, 1973).
Rachael Low and Roger Manvell, *The History of the British Film 1896–1906* (London: George Allen and Unwin, 1948).

g. *French Cinema*
Richard Abel, *French Cinema: The First Wave* (Princeton: Princeton University Press, 1987).
Pierre Guibbert (ed.), *Les premiers ans du cinéma français* (Perpignan: Institut Jean Vigo, 1985).
Philippe d'Hugues and Michel Marmin, *Le cinéma français: le muet* (Paris: 1986).

h. *German Cinema*
Paolo Cherchi Usai, Lorenzo Codelli (eds.), *Before Caligari: German Cinema 1897–1920* (Pordenone, Edizioni Biblioteca del'Immagine and London: British Film Institute, 1990).
Fritz Güttinger, *Der Stummfilm im Zitat der Zeit* (Frankfurt/M: Deutsches Filmmuseum, 1984).
Joachim Paech, *Literatur und Film* (Stuttgart: J. B. Metzler, 1988).
Heide Schlüpmann, *Frühes Kino zwischen Emanzipation und Reform* (Frankfurt am Main: Roter Stern, 1990).
Friedrich von Zglinicki, *Der Weg des Films: Die Geschichte der Kinematographie und ihrer Vorläufer* (Hildesheim: Olms, 1979).

i. *Italian Cinema*
Aldo Bernardini, *Cinema muto italiano* (3 vols.: 1896–1904, 1905–1909, 1910–1914) (Bari: 1980–82).
Gian Piero Brunetta, *Storia del cinema italiano 1895–1945* (Rome: Riuniti, 1979).

j. *Russian Cinema*
Paolo Cherchi Usai and Yuri Tsivian (eds.), *Silent Witnesses, Russian Films 1908–1919* (Pordenone, Edizioni Biblioteca dell'Immagine and London: British Film Institute, 1989).
Jay Leyda, *Kino, A History of the Russian and Soviet Film* (London: George Allen and Unwin, 1960).

k. *Scandinavian Cinema*
Paolo Cherchi Usai (ed.), *Schiave bianche allo specchio. Le origini del cinema in Scandinavia* (Pordenone, Edizioni Studio Tesi, 1986).
Ron Mottram. *The Danish Cinema, 1896–1917* (Ann Arbor: University of Michigan Press, 1982).

Films and Television Programmes

Noël Burch, *Correction Please, or How We Got into Pictures* (Arts Council of Great Britain) GB 1979. 52 mins/col./16mm.

—— *What Do These Old Films Mean?* (Channel Four/FR3/PI Productions) UK/France 1985. 6 × 30 mins.

Helmut Herbst, *Der Film Pionier Guido Seeber* (Stiftung Deutsche Kinemathek Berlin) West Germany 1971. 59 mins/col./16mm.

Charles Musser, *Before the Nickelodeon* (Films for Thought) USA 1982. 60 mins/col./16mm.

Werner Nekes, *Film Before Film* (Werner Nekes Film) West Germany 1985/86. 83 mins/col./16mm.

Special Issues of Journals

Afterimage, no. 8/9, Spring 1981 ('Beginnings . . .').

L'Avant-Scène Cinéma, no. 334, November 1984 ('Les pionniers du cinéma français 1895–1910').

Cinema Journal, vol. 14, no. 2, Winter 1974/5 ('Symposium on the Methodology of Film History').

Les Cahiers de la Cinématèque, no. 17, 1975 ('David Wark Griffith').

—— no. 29, hiver 1979 ('Le cinéma des premiers temps 1900–1906').

—— no. 35/36, automne 1982 ('Spécial Méliès').

—— no. 41, hiver 1984.

Iris, vol. 2 no. 1, 1984 ('Archives, Document, Fiction: Film Before 1907').

—— vol. 2 no. 2, 1984 ('Pour une théorie de l'histoire du cinéma').

—— vol. 4 no. 1, 1986 ('The Kuleshov Effect').

Journal of Popular Film and Television, vol. 15 no. 3, Fall 1987 ('Special Issue: The "Silent" Cinema').

Quarterly Review of Film Studies, vol. 6, no. 1, Winter 1981 ('D. W. Griffith').

—— Winter 1984 ('Archaeology of the Cinema').

Screen, vol. 23, no. 2, July/August 1982 ('Early Cinema').

The Silent Picture.

Wide Angle, vol. 3, no. 1, 1979 ('Silent Film').

—— vol. 5, no. 2, 1982 ('Film History').

Articles in Journals and Multi-author Books

Richard Abel, 'Scenes from Domestic Life in Early French Cinema', *Screen*, vol. 30 no. 3, 1989, pp. 4–28.

Robert L. Adams, 'D. W. Griffith and the Use of Off-Screen Space', *Cinema Journal*, vol. 15 no. 2, Spring 1976, pp. 53–7.

Jeanne Allen, 'Copyright Protection in Theatre, Vaudeville and Early Cinema', *Screen*, vol. 21 no. 2, Summer 1980, pp. 79–91.

—— 'The Industrial Context of Film Technology: Standardization and Patents' in S. Heath and T. de Lauretis (eds.), *The Cinematic Apparatus*, London: Macmillan, 1980, pp. 26–36.

—— 'The Decay of the MPPC' in Tino Balio (ed.), *The American Film Industry*, pp. 119–134.

—— 'The Film Viewer as Consumer', *Quarterly Review of Film Studies*, vol. 5 no. 4, Fall 1980, pp. 481–99.

Richard Allen, 'Excavating Porter', *Framework*, no. 22/3, Autumn 1983, pp. 12–13 (review of Musser, *Before the Nickelodeon*).

Robert C. Allen, '*Traffic in Souls*', *Sight and Sound*, vol. 44 no. 1, Winter 1974/5, pp. 50–52.

—— 'Film History: The Narrow Discourse', *1977 Film Studies Annual* II, Purdue University, 1978, pp. 9–16.

—— 'Contra the "Chaser Theory"', *Wide Angle*, vol. 3 no. 1, 1979, pp. 4–11.

—— 'Motion Picture Exhibition in Manhattan 1906–1912: Beyond the Nickelodeon', *Cinema Journal*, vol. 19 no. 2, Spring 1979, pp. 2–15.

—— 'Vitascope/Cinematographe: Initial Patterns of American Film Industrial Practice', *Journal of the University Film and Video Association*, Spring 1979, pp. 13–18.

Rick Altman, 'Toward a Historiography of American Film', *Cinema Journal* vol. 16 no. 1, Spring 1977, pp. 1–25.
—— '*The Lonely Villa* and Griffith's Paradigmatic Style', *Quarterly Review of Film Studies*, vol. 6 no. 2, Spring 1981, pp. 123–34.
—— 'Dickens, Griffith, and Film Theory Today', *South Atlantic Quarterly*, vol. 88 no. 2, Spring 1989, pp. 321–59.
Barthélémy Amengual, '*The Life of an American Fireman* et la naissance du montage', *Cahiers de la Cinémathèque*, no. 17, 1975, pp. 23–7.
Jacques Aumont, 'Griffith, le cadre, la figure' in Raymond Bellour (ed.), *Le Cinéma américain*, vol. I (Paris: Flammarion, 1980), pp. 51–67.
Pierre Baudry, 'Les aventures de l'idée', *Cahiers du cinéma*, nos. 240 and 241, 1972, pp. 51–9 and 31–45.
Peter Baxter, 'On the History and Ideology of Film Lighting', *Screen*, vol. 16 no. 3, Autumn 1975, pp. 83–106 (see also Barry Salt's reply in *Screen*, vol. 16 no. 4, Winter 1975, pp. 119–23).
Ben Brewster, 'A Scene at the "Movies"', *Screen*, vol. 23, no. 2, July/August 1982, pp. 4–15.
—— 'Deep Staging in French Films 1900–1914' (in French in P. Guibbert (ed.), *Les premiers ans du cinéma français*, pp. 204–17.
Raymond Bellour, 'To Alternate/To Narrate', *Australian Journal of Screen Theory*, no. 15/16, 1983, pp. 35–56.
John Belton, 'The Art of Melodramatic Style: D. W. Griffith and *Orphans of the Storm*', *The Silent Picture*, no. 15, Summer 1972, pp. 28–32.
—— '*True Heart Susie*', *The Silent Picture*, no. 17, Spring 1978, pp. 25–9.
David Bordwell and Kristin Thompson, 'Linearity, Materialism and the Study of the Early American Cinema', *Wide Angle*, vol. 5 no. 3, 1983, pp. 4–15.
—— 'Toward a Scientific Film History?', *Quarterly Review of Film Studies*, Summer 1985, pp. 224–37 (review article of Salt, *Film Style and Technology*).
Stephen Bottomore, 'Shots in the Dark: The Real Origins of Film Editing', *Sight and Sound*, vol. 57, no. 3, Summer 1988, pp. 200–4.
—— 'Dreyfus and Documentary', *Sight and Sound*, vol. 53 no. 4, Autumn 1984, pp. 290–93.
Eileen Bowser, 'The Brighton Project: An Introduction', *Quarterly Review of Film Studies*, vol. 4 no. 4, Fall 79, pp. 509–38.
—— 'Griffith's Film Career before *The Adventures of Dollie*', *Quarterly Review of Film Studies*, vol. 6 no. 1, Winter 1981, pp. 1–9.
—— 'The Reconstitution of *A Corner in Wheat*', *Cinema Journal*, vol. 15 no. 2, Spring 1976, pp. 42–52.
—— 'Toward Narrative, 1907: *The Mill Girl*', in Fell, *Film Before Griffith*, pp. 330–38.
—— 'The Telephone and Early Cinema' (in French in P. Guibbert (ed.), *Les premiers ans du cinéma français*, pp. 218–24).
Nick Browne, 'Griffith and Freud: Griffith's Family discourse', *Quarterly Review of Film Studies*, vol. 6 no. 1, Winter 1981, pp. 67–80.
Kevin Brownlow, 'The Dark is Light Enough', *Films in Review*, January 1975, pp. 13–16.
—— 'Silent Film – What was the right Speed?', *Sight and Sound*, Summer 1980, pp. 164–7.
—— '*Traffic in Souls*' in Cherchi Usai (ed.), *Vitagraph Co. of America: il cinema prima di Hollywood* (Pordenone: Edizioni Biblioteca dell'Immagine, 1987), pp. 227–37.
Pascal Bonitzer, 'It's Only a Film/ou La Face du Néant', *Framework*, no. 14, Spring 1981, pp. 22–4.
Noël Burch, 'Porter or Ambivalence', *Screen*, vol. 19 no. 4, Winter 1978/9, pp. 91–105.
—— 'Notes on Fritz Lang's First Mabuse', *Cine-tracts*, no. 13, Spring 1981, pp. 1–13.
—— 'Charles Baudelaire versus Doctor Frankenstein', *Afterimage*, no. 8/9, Spring 1981, pp. 4–21.
—— 'Un mode de représentation primitif?', *Iris*, vol. 2 no. 1, 1984, pp. 112–123.
—— 'Passion, poursuite', *Communications*, no. 38, 1983, pp. 30–50.
—— 'How We Got into Pictures: Notes Accompanying *Correction Please*', *Afterimage*, no. 8/9, Spring 1981, pp. 24–38.
—— 'The IMR and the Soviet Response', *October*, no. 11, pp. 77–98.
—— 'A Parenthesis on Film History' in *To the Distant Observer* (London: Scolar Press, 1979), pp. 61–6.

Noël Burch, 'Primitivism and the Avant-Gardes: A Dialectical Approach', in P. Rosen (ed.), *Narrative, Apparatus, Ideology* (New York: Columbia University Press, 1986), pp. 483–505.
—— 'Narrative/Diegesis – Threshold, Limits', *Screen*, vol. 23 no. 2, July/August 1982, pp. 16–33.
—— 'Fritz Lang: The German Period' in R. Roud (ed.), *Cinema A Critical Dictionary* (London: Secker and Warburg, 1980), pp. 583–609.
Noël Burch and Jorge Dana, 'Propositions', *Afterimage*, no. 5, pp. 40–66.
Edward Buscombe, 'A New Approach to Film History', *1977 Film Studies Annual* II, Purdue University, 1978, pp. 1–8.
Ernest Callenbach, 'Film Style', *Film Quarterly*, Summer 85, pp. 45–50 (review of Salt, *Film Style and Technology*).
Ralph Cassady Jr, 'Monopoly in Motion Picture Production and Distribution 1908–1915', *Southern California Law Review*, vol.. 32, no. 4, Summer 1959, pp. 25–67.
Brad Chisholm 'Reading Intertitles', *Journal of Popular Film and Television*, vol. 15 no. 3, Fall 1987, pp. 137–43.
Keith Cohn, 'On the Spot, in the Raw: Impressionism and Cinema', *Film Reader*, no. 3, 1978, pp. 150–68.
Roland Cosandey, 'Revoir Lumière', *Iris*, vol. 2 no. 1, 1984, pp. 71–82.
Donald Crafton, 'Genre and Technology in 1909', *Journal of Popular Film and TV*, vol. 13 no. 4, Winter 1986, pp. 166–70.
—— 'Emile Cohl's Clair de Lune Espagnol' (in French in P. Guibbert (ed.), *Les Premiers ans du cinéma français*, pp. 242–7).
Jean Louis Comolli, 'Technique and Ideology: Camera, Perspective, Depth of Field', *Film Reader*, no. 2, 1977, pp. 128–40.
Richard de Cordova, 'The Emergence of the Star System in America', *Wide Angle*, vol. 6 no. 4, 1985, pp. 4–13.
—— 'From Lumière to Pathé: The Break-Up of Perspectival Space', *Cinetracts*, no. 15, Fall 1981, pp. 55–63.
Michael Chanan, 'Economic Conditions of Early Cinema' in R. Holman (ed.), *Cinema 1900–1906*, pp. 115–29.
Mary Ann Doane, 'The Moving Image', *Wide Angle*, vol. 7, nos. 1–2, 1985, pp. 42–58.
Marshall Deutelbaum, 'Structural Patterning in the Lumière Films', *Wide Angle*, vol. 3 no. 1, 1979, pp. 28–37.
—— 'D. W. Griffith and the Possibilities of *Enoch Arden*', *Quarterly Review of Film Studies*, vol. 6 no. 1, Winter 1981, pp. 27–44.
Mick Eaton, 'Putting Narrative in Place', *Screen*, vol. 24 no. 4/5, July/October 1983, pp. 142–4.
Thomas Elsaesser, '*Correction Please*', *Framework*, nos. 15/16/17, 1981, pp. 33–5 (review of Noël Burch's film).
—— 'Innocence Restored', *Monthly Film Bulletin*, December 1984, pp. 363–6.
—— 'The New Film History', *Sight and Sound*, Autumn 1986, pp. 246–51.
—— 'Secret Affinities: F. W. Murnau', *Sight and Sound*, vol. 58, no. 1, Winter 1988/89, pp. 33–42.
Elizabeth Ewen, 'City Light: Immigrant Women and the Rise of the Movies', *Signs*, vol. 4 no. 3 (supplem.), Spring 1980, pp. 45–65.
John Fell, 'Motive, Mischief and Melodrama: the state of film narrative in 1907', *Film Quarterly*, vol. 33 no. 3, Spring 1980, pp. 30–37.
—— 'The Evolution of Narrative', in *A History of Films*, pp. 28–53.
Lucy Fischer, 'The Lady Vanishes: women, magic and the movies', *Film Quarterly*, vol. 33 no. 1, Fall 1979, pp. 30–40.
Robert Fisher, 'Film Censorship and Progressive Reform: the National Board of Censorship of Motion Pictures, 1909–1922', *Journal of Popular Film*, vol. 4 no. 1, 1975, pp. 2–14.
Raymond Fielding, 'Hale's Tours: Ultra-realism in the Pre-1910 Motion Picture', *Cinema Journal*, vol. 10 no. 1, Fall 1970, pp. 34–47.
David Francis, 'The Trick Film 1896–1901' (in French in P. Guibbert (ed.), *Les premiers ans du cinéma français*, pp. 143–6).

Anne Friedberg, 'A Properly Adjusted Window' (unpublished paper, New York University).
John Fullerton, 'Spatial and Temporal Articulation in Pre-Classical Swedish Film' (unpublished paper, University of East Anglia).
—— 'AB Svenska Biografteatern: Aspects of Production 1912–20' (paper given at the 'Putting Narrative in Place' conference, Derby, December 1982).
—— 'Notes towards a history of Early Swedish Film as Institution' (unpublished paper).
Jon Gartenberg, 'The Brighton Project', *Iris*, vol. 2 no. 1, 1984, pp. 5–16.
—— 'Camera Movement in Edison and Biograph Films 1900–06', *Cinema Journal*, vol. 19 no. 1, Spring 1980, pp. 1–16.
—— 'From the D. W. Griffith Collection at the MOMA', *Films in Review*, February 1981, pp. 90–104.
—— 'Vitagraph before Griffith: Forging Ahead in the Nickelodeon Era', *Studies in Visual Communication*, vol. 10 no. 4, Fall 1984, pp. 7–23.
André Gaudreault, 'Temporality and Narrativity in Early Cinema' in R. Holman (ed.), *Cinema 1900–1906*, pp. 201–18.
—— 'The Infringement of Copyright Laws and its Effects (1900–1906)', *Framework*, no. 29, 1985, pp. 2–14.
—— 'Theatricality, Narrativity and 'Trickality': Re-evaluating the Cinema of George Méliès', *Journal of Popular Film and Television*, vol. 15 no. 3, Fall 1987, pp. 110–19.
—— 'Film, récit, narration: le cinéma des Frères Lumière', *Iris*, vol. 2 no. 1, 1984, pp. 61–70.
—— 'A Tale of Two Stories: *Scenes of Convict Life*' (in French in P. Guibbert (ed.), *Les premiers ans du cinéma français*, pp. 233–41).
—— 'Detours in Film Narrative: Cross-Cutting', *Cinema Journal*, vol. 19 no. 1, Fall 1979, pp. 39–59.
—— 'Un spectacle monstratif à narration assistée' in *Du littéraire au filmique* (Paris: Meridiens Klincksieck, 1988), pp. 159–70.
—— 'Narration et monstration au cinéma', *Hors-Cadre*, no. 2, April 1984, pp. 87–98.
—— 'Le cinéma des premiers temps: l'histoire et la théorie en question' (unpublished paper).
André Gaudreault and Tom Gunning, 'Le cinéma des premiers temps: un défi à l'histoire du cinéma?' (unpublished paper given at the Cérisy conference on Film History, August 1985).
André Gaudreault and David Levy, *Filmographie partielle de l'oeuvre d'Edwin S. Porter à la compagnie Edison entre 1903 et 1909*, Quebec: Université Laval, 1980.
Douglas Gomery, 'Move Audiences, Urban Geography, and the History of the American Film', *The Velvet Light Trap*, no. 19, 1982, pp. 23–9.
—— 'The Growth of Movie Monopolies: the Case of Balaban and Katz', *Wide Angle*, vol. 3 no. 1, 1979, pp. 54–63.
—— 'The Picture Palace: Economic Sense or Hollywood Nonsense?', *Quarterly Review of Film Studies*, vol. 3 no. 1, Winter 1978, pp. 23–36.
—— 'The Movies Become Big Business: Public Theatres and the Chain Store Strategy', *Cinema Journal*, vol. 18 no. 2, Spring 1979, pp. 26–40.
Roman Gubern, 'D. W. Griffith et l'articulation cinématographique', *Les Cahiers de la Cinémathèque*, no. 17, 1975, pp. 7–21.
Tom Gunning, 'Weaving a Narrative: Style and Economic Background in Griffith's Biograph Films', *Quarterly Review of Film Studies*, Winter 1981, pp. 11–25.
—— 'The Non-Continuous Style of Early Film 1900–1906' in R. Holman (ed.), *Cinema 1900–1906, An Analytical Study*, pp. 219–30.
—— 'Non-Continuity, Continuity, Discontinuity: a Theory of Genres in Early Film', *Iris*, vol. 2 no. 1, 1984, pp. 101–12.
—— 'The Cinema of Attraction: Early Film its Spectator and the Avant-Garde', *Wide Angle*, vol. 8 nos. 3/4, Fall 1986, pp. 63–70.
—— 'Vitagraph Film and the Cinema of Narrative Integration' in Cherchi Usai (ed.), *Vitagraph Co of America*, pp. 225–40.
—— 'An Unseen Energy Swallows Space: The Space in Early Film and its Relation to American Avant Garde Film' in J. Fell (ed.), *Film Before Griffith*, pp. 355–66.

Tom Gunning, 'Filmed Narrative and the Theatrical Ideal: Griffith and the film d'art' (in French in P. Guibbert (ed.), *Les premiers ans du cinéma français*, pp. 123–9).
—— 'Rebirth of a Movie: How the MOMA restored Griffith's *Way Down East*', *American Film*, October 1984, pp. 18–9.
—— 'What I Saw from the Rear Window of the Hôtel des Folies-Dramatiques, or the Story Point of View Films Told', in A. Gaudreault (ed.), *Ce que je vois de mon ciné*, pp. 33–44.
Paul Hammond, 'Georges, this is Charles', *Afterimage*, no. 8/9, Winter 80/81, pp. 39–49.
Miriam Hansen, 'Early Silent Cinema: Whose Public Sphere?', *New German Critique*, no. 29, Spring/Summer 1983, pp. 147–84.
—— 'Reinventing the Nickelodeon: Notes on Kluge and Early Cinema', *October*, no. 46, Fall 1988, pp. 179–98.
—— 'The Mother and the Whore', *South Atlantic Quarterly*, vol. 88 no. 2, Spring 1989, pp. 368–88.
Gordon Hendricks, 'A New Look at an "Old Sneeze"', *Film Culture*, no. 22/23, 1961, pp. 90–95.
—— 'The History of the Kinetoscope' in T. Balio (ed.), *The American Film Industry*, pp. 33–45.
Charlotte Herzog, 'Movie Palaces and Exhibition', *Film Reader*, no. 2, 1977, pp. 185–97.
—— 'The Movie Palace and the Theatrical Sources of its Architectural Style', *Cinema Journal*, vol. 20 no. 2, Spring 1981, pp. 15–37.
Leon Hunt, '*The Student of Prague*: Division and Codification of Space' (unpublished paper, University of East Anglia).
Lea Jacobs, 'Spatial Continuity in the work of Marey and Louis Lumière' (unpublished paper, University of California Paris Program).
Mikhail Jampolski, '"Les experiences de Kulechov" et la nouvelle anthropologie de l'acteur', *Iris*, vol. 4 no. 1, 1986, pp. 25–48.
—— '"Totaler" Film und "Montage" Film', *Kunst und Literatur* (Berlin/GDR), no. 5, September/October 1983, pp. 661–72.
William Johnson, 'Early Griffith: A Wider View', *Film Quarterly*, vol. 29 no. 3, Spring 1976, pp. 2–13.
Gorham Kindem, 'The Demise of Kinemacolor: Technological, Legal, Economic, and Aesthetic Problems in Early Color History', *Cinema Journal*, vol. 20 no. 2, Spring 1981, pp. 3–14.
Norman King, 'The Sound of Silents', *Screen*, vol. 25 no. 3, May-June 1984, pp. 2–15.
Vance Kepley, '*Intolerance* and the Soviets', *Wide Angle*, vol. 3 no. 1, 1979, pp. 22–7.
Katherine Singer Kovacs, 'Georges Méliès and the *Feérie*', *Cinema Journal*, vol. 16 no. 1, Fall 1976, pp. 2–13.
Paul Kerr, 'Re-inventing the Cinema', *Screen*, vol. 21 no. 4, 1980/81, pp. 80–84.
Annette Kuhn, 'History of Narrative Codes', in Pam Cook (ed.), *The Cinema Book* (London: BFI Publishing, 1985), pp. 208–11.
Yann Lardeau, 'King David', *Cahiers du Cinéma*, no. 346, April 1983, pp. 31–37.
Patrick G. Loughney, 'In the Beginning Was the Word: Six Pre-Griffith Motion Picture Scenarios', *Iris*, vol. 2 no. 1, 1984, pp. 17–32.
David Levy, 'Edison Sales Policy and the Continuous Action Film 1904–1906' in J. Fell (ed.), *Film Before Griffith*, pp. 207–22.
—— 'Re-constructed Newsreels, Re-enactments and the American Narrative Film' in R. Holman (ed.), *Cinema 1900–1906*, pp. 243–60.
S. Levine, 'Monet, Lumière and Cinematic time', *Journal of Aesthetics and Art Criticism*, vol. 36 no. 4, Summer 1978.
Jay Leyda, 'Toward a New Film History', *Cinema Journal* vol. 14 no. 2, Winter 1974/75, pp. 40–41.
Judith Mayne, 'Immigrants and Spectators', *Wide Angle*, vol. 5 no. 2, 1982, pp. 32–41.
—— 'Der primitive Erzähler', *Frauen und Film*, no. 41, 1986, pp. 4–16.
—— 'The Two Spheres of Early Cinema' in *Private Novels, Public Films* (Atlanta: University of Georgia Press, 1988), pp. 68–94.
Patrick McInroy, 'The American Méliès', *Sight and Sound*, Autumn 1979, pp. 250–54.
Helen McNeil, 'Building Blocks of the Dream Factory', *Quarto*, January/February 1982, pp. 8–9.

George Mitchell, 'The Consolidation of the American Film Industry 1915–29', *Cine-tracts*, nos. 6 and 7/8, Spring, Summer/Fall 1979, pp. 27–36 and pp. 63–70.
Russell Merritt, 'Nickelodeon Theatres 1905–1914: Building an Audience for the Movies', in T. Balio (ed.), *The American Film Industry*, pp. 59–70.
—— 'Dixon, Griffith and the Southern Legend', *Cinema Journal*, vol. 12 no. 1, Fall 1972, pp. 26–45.
—— 'Rescued from a Perilous Nest: D. W. Griffith's Escape from Theatre into Film', *Cinema Journal*, vol. 21 no. 1, Fall 1981, pp. 2–30.
—— 'On first looking into Griffith's Babylon', *Wide Angle*, vol. 3 no. 1, 1979, pp. 12–21.
Jean Mitry, 'Thomas H. Ince, His Aesthetics, His Films, His Legacy', *Cinema Journal*, vol. 22 no. 2, Winter 1983, pp. 2–25.
Charles Musser, 'The American Vitagraph 1897–1901' in J. Fell (ed.), *Film Before Griffith*, pp. 22–66.
—— 'Vitagraph 1901–1905: Gli anni dimenticati', in Cherchi Usai (ed.), *Vitagraph Co. of America* (Pordenone: Edizioni Biblioteca dell'Immagine, 1987), pp. 89–102.
—— 'The Travel Genre: Moving Towards Narrative', *Iris*, vol. 2 no. 1, 1984, pp. 47–60.
—— 'The Early Cinema of Edwin Porter', *Cinema Journal*, vol. 19 no. 1, Fall 1979, pp. 1–38.
—— 'The Eden Musée: Exhibitor as Creator', *Film and History*, vol. 11 no. 4, December 1981, pp. 73–83.
—— 'Towards a History of Screen Practice', *Quarterly Review of Film Studies*, vol. 3 no. 1, Winter 1984, pp. 59–69.
—— 'Another Look at the "Chaser Theory"', *Studies in Visual Communications*, vol. 10 no. 4, Fall 1984, pp. 24–44.
—— 'The Nickelodeon Era Begins: Establishing the Framework for Hollywood's Mode of Representation', *Framework*, 22/23, Autumn 1984, pp. 4–11.
Richard Alan Nelson, 'Movie Mecca of the South: Jacksonville as an early rival to Hollywood', *Journal of Popular Film and TV*, vol. 8 no. 3, 1980, pp. 38–51.
—— 'Stock Failures and Con Men: A Neglected Economic Aspect of America's Early Motion Picture Industry', *Journal of Popular Film and TV*, vol. 11 no. 1, Spring 1983, pp. 12–23.
Martin F. Nordon, 'Women in the Early Film Industry', *Wide Angle*, vol. 6 no. 3, 1984, pp. 58–67.
Geoffrey Nowell-Smith, 'Facts about Films and Facts of Films', *Quarterly Review of Film Studies* vol. 1 no. 3, 1976, pp. 272–5.
Vlada Petric, 'Griffith's *The Avenging Conscience*: An Early Dream Film', *Film Criticism*, vol. 6 no. 2, Winter 1982, pp. 5–27.
—— 'D. W. Griffith' in R. Roud (ed.), *Cinema A Critical Dictionary* (London: Secker and Warburg, 1980), pp. 449–62.
David Robinson, 'Hollywood', *Sight and Sound*, vol. 49 no. 3, Summer 1980, pp. 159–63.
Marie-Claire Ropars, 'The Ouverture of *October*', *Enclitic* vol. 2 no. 2, Fall 1978, pp. 50–72.
Barry Salt, 'Film Form 1900–1906', *Sight and Sound*, Summer 1978, pp. 148–53.
—— 'Fresh Eyes', *BFI News*, July 1976.
—— 'The Early Development of Film Form', *Film Form*, vol. 1 no. 1, Spring 1976, pp. 92–106 (also in J. Fell (ed.), *Film Before Griffith*, pp. 284–98).
—— 'What Can We Learn From The First Twenty Years of Cinema', *Iris*, vol. 2 no. 1, 1984, pp. 83–90.
—— 'The World Inside Ernst Lubitsch' (unpublished paper, given at the University of East Anglia 'Space Frame Narrative' conference, December 1984).
—— 'The Physician of the Castle', *Sight and Sound*, vol. 54 no. 4, Autumn 1985, pp. 284–5.
—— 'White Slaves and Circuses – The Pursuit of Sensation' (in Italian in P. Cherchi Usai (ed.), *Schiave bianche*, pp. 61–78).
—— 'The Space Next Door' (in French in P. Guibbert (ed.), *Les premiers ans du cinéma français*, pp. 198–203).
—— 'Vitagraph Films – A Touch of Class' (in Italian in P. Cherchi Usai (ed.), *Vitagraph Co of America*, pp. 171–202).
—— 'What's wrong with this picture?', *Sight and Sound*, vol. 57 no. 2, Spring 1988, pp. 131–3.

Barry Salt, 'The Unknown Ince', *Sight and Sound*, vol. 57 no. 4, Autumn 1988, pp. 268–72.
Thomas Schatz, 'Film Archives', *Critical Studies in Mass Communication*, March 1984, pp. 83–8.
Martin Sopocy, 'A Narrated Cinema: The Pioneer Story of James A. Williamson', *Cinema Journal*, vol. 18 no. 1, Fall 1978, pp. 1–28.
—— 'Crisis in the Nickelodeon – James A. Williamson's American Market' (unpublished paper).
—— 'The Theatrical Frame' (in French in P. Guibbert (ed.), *Les premiers ans du cinéma français*, pp. 190–7).
Pierre Sorlin, 'Promenade de Rome', *Iris*, vol. 2 no. 2, 1984, pp. 4–8.
Paul Spehr, 'Film Making at the American Mutoscope and Biograph 1900–1906', *Quarterly Journal of the Library of Congress*, Summer/Fall 1980, pp. 413–21.
Janet Staiger, 'The Eyes are Really the Focus: Photoplay Acting and Film Form and Style', *Wide Angle*, vol. 6 no. 4, pp. 14–23.
—— 'Dividing Labor for Production Control: Thomas Ince and the Rise of the Studio System', *Cinema Journal*, vol. 19 no. 2, Spring 1979, pp. 16–25.
—— 'Combination and Litigation: Structures of US Film Distribution, 1896–1917', *Cinema Journal*, vol. 23 no. 2, Winter 1983, pp. 41–71.
—— 'Mass-produced Photoplays: Economic and Signifying Practice in the First Years of Hollywood', *Wide Angle*, vol. 4 no. 3, Fall 1980, pp. 12–27.
—— 'Seeing Stars', *The Velvet Light Trap*, no. 20, 1983, pp. 10–14.
Janet Staiger and Douglas Gomery, 'History of World Cinema: A Model for Economic Analysis', *Film Reader* 4, 1979, pp. 35–44.
Rod Stoneman, 'Perspective Correction: Early Film to the Avant-Garde', *Afterimage*, no. 8/9, Spring 1981, pp. 50–63.
Kristin Thompson, 'The Formulation of the Classical Hollywood Style, 1909–1928' in David Bordwell, Janet Staiger, Kristin Thompson, *The Classical Hollywood Cinema*, pp. 157–240.
—— 'French Companies and the Formation of the MPPC (in French in P. Guibbert (ed.), *Les premiers ans du cinéma français*, pp. 116–22).
—— 'Cinema 1900/06: An Analytical Study', *Iris*, vol. 2 no. 1 (no. 3), 1984, pp. 139–143 (book review).
Jérome Tonnerre, 'Les Conquérants du nouveau monde', *Cinématographe*, no. 65, February 1981, pp. 2–6.
Yuri Tsivian, 'Notes historiques en marge de l'expérience de Koulechov', *Iris*, vol. 4 no. 1, 1986, pp. 49–59.
—— 'Eisenstein's *October* and Russian Symbolist Culture' (unpublished paper, 'Eisenstein at 90' conference, Oxford, 1988).
Maureen Turim, 'Designs of Motion: A Correlation between Early Serial Photography and the Avantgarde', *Enclitic*, vol. 7 no. 2, Fall 1983, pp. 44–54.
Dai Vaughan, 'Let There Be Lumière', *Sight and Sound*, vol. 50 no. 2, Spring 1981, pp. 126–7.
Janet Wasko, 'D.W. Griffith and the banks: a case study in film financing', *Journal of the University Film Association*, vol. 30 no. 1, Winter 1978.
Alan Williams, 'The Lumière Organization and "Documentary Realism"' in J. Fell (ed.), *Film Before Griffith*, pp. 153–61.
Linda Williams, 'Film Body: An Implantation of Perversions', *Cine-tracts*, no. 12, Winter 1981, pp. 19–35.
William F. Van Wert, 'Intertitles', *Sight and Sound*, Spring 1980, pp. 98–105.
Gosta Werner, 'How to reconstruct lost films', *Cinema Journal*, vol. 14 no. 2, Winter 1974/5, pp. 11–15.
Klaus Wyborny, 'Random Notes on the Conventional Narrative Film', *Afterimage*, no. 8/9, Spring 1981, pp. 112–32.